W9-BCJ-874

The Pirate Primer

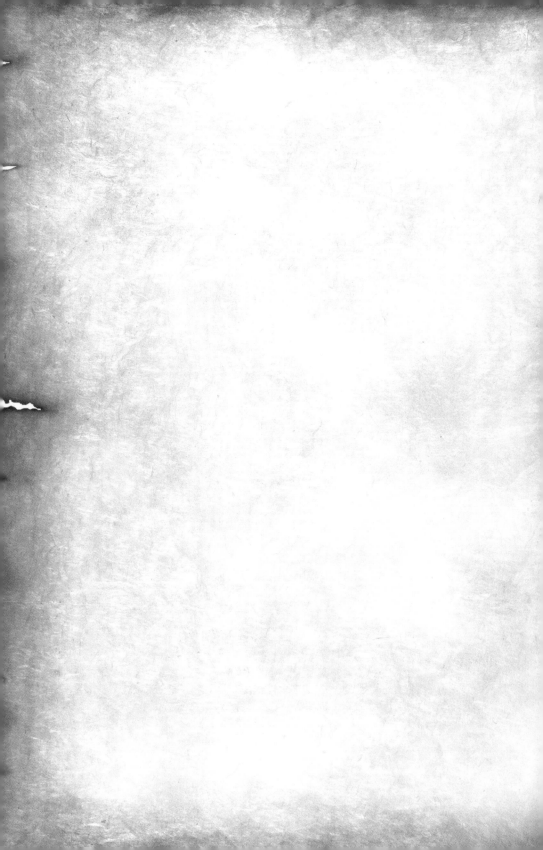

The Pirate Primer

Mastering the Language of Swashbucklers and Rogues

GEORGE CHOUNDAS

WRITER'S DIGEST BOOKS

writersdigestbooks.com
Cincinnati, Ohio

The Pirate Primer: Mastering the Language of Swashbucklers and Rogues. Copyright © 2007 by George Choundas. Manufactured in Canada. All rights reserved. No other part of this book may be reproduced in any form or by any electronic or mechanical means including information storage and retrieval systems without permission in writing from the publisher, except by a reviewer, who may quote brief passages in a review. Published by Writer's Digest Books, an imprint of F+W Publications, Inc., 4700 East Galbraith Road, Cincinnati, Ohio 45236. (800) 289-0963. First edition.

11 10 09 08 07   5 4 3 2 1

Distributed in Canada by Fraser Direct
100 Armstrong Avenue
Georgetown, ON, Canada L7G 5S4
Tel: (905) 877-4411

Distributed in the U.K. and Europe by David & Charles
Brunel House, Newton Abbot, Devon, TQ12 4PU, England
Tel: (+44) 1626 323200, Fax: (+44) 1626 323319
E-mail: postmaster@davidandcharles.co.uk

Distributed in Australia by Capricorn Link
P.O. Box 704, Windsor, NSW 2756 Australia
Tel: (02) 4577-3555

Library of Congress Cataloging-in-Publication Data
Choundas, George.
The pirate primer : mastering the language of swashbucklers and rogues / by George Choundas.--1st ed.

   p. cm.

 Includes bibliographical references.

ISBN-13: 978-1-58297-489-7 (alk. paper)

ISBN-10: 1-58297-489-6 (alk. paper)

 1. Pirates--Terminology. I. Title.
G535.C46 2007
910.4'5--dc22

                     2006028609

Editor: Lauren Mosko
Designer: Claudean Wheeler
Illustrator: J. Cobb/Instreme Interactive
Production Coordinator: Mark Griffin

F+W PUBLICATIONS INC

Excerpts from *The Guardship* by James L. Nelson. Copyright © 2000 by James L. Nelson. Reprinted by permission of HarperCollins Publishers.

Excerpts from *The Guardship* by James L. Nelson, published by Corgi. Reprinted by permission of The Random House Group Ltd.

Excerpts from *The Blackbirder* by James L. Nelson. Copyright © 2001 by James L. Nelson. Reprinted by permission of HarperCollins Publishers.

Excerpts from *The Blackbirder* by James L. Nelson, published by Corgi. Reprinted by permission of The Random House Group Ltd.

Excerpts from *The Pirate Round* by James L. Nelson. Copyright © 2002 by James L. Nelson. Reprinted by permission of HarperCollins Publishers.

Excerpts from *The Pirate Round* by James L. Nelson, published by Corgi. Reprinted by permission of The Random House Group Ltd.

Excerpts from *The Buccaneers of America* by Alexander O. Exquemelin, translation by Alexis Brown (A.E. Baumann), published by Dover Publications, Inc. Reprinted by permission of Dover Publications, Inc.

Excerpts from *Captain Blood Returns* by Rafael Sabatini. Copyright © 1930, 1931 by Rafael Sabatini, renewed in 1959 by Christine Sabatini. Reprinted by permission of Houghton Mifflin Company. All rights reserved.

Excerpts from *The Fortunes of Captain Blood* by Rafael Sabatini. Copyright © 1938 by Rafael Sabatini, renewed in 1966 by Christine Sabatini. Reprinted by permission of Houghton Mifflin Company. All rights reserved.

Excerpts from *Captain Blood: His Odyssey, Captain Blood Returns, The Fortunes of Captain Blood* by Rafael Sabatini. Reprinted by permission of A P Watt Ltd on behalf of Action Medical Research, Cancer Research UK and the Royal National Institute for the Blind.

Excerpts from *Dead Man's Chest: The Sequel to Treasure Island* by Roger L. Johnson. Copyright © 1992. Reprinted by permission of Commander Roger L. Johnson, U.S. Navy (retired).

Excerpts from *Black Bartlemy's Treasure, Winds of Chance (Winds of Fortune), Martin Conisby's Vengeance, Adam Penfeather: Buccaneer* by Jeffery Farnol. Reprinted by permission of Jane Farnol Curtis.

Excerpts from *Gasparilla, Pirate Genius* by James Kaserman. Reprinted by permission of James F. Kaserman.

Excerpts from *The Gun Ketch* by Dewey Lambdin. Copyright © 1993 by Dewey Lambdin by arrangement with Wieser & Elwell, Inc. Reprinted by permission of Wieser & Elwell, Inc.

Excerpts from *A High Wind in Jamaica* by Richard Hughes. Copyright © 1928, 1929 by Richard Hughes, renewed in 1956 by Richard Hughes. Reprinted by permission of Harold Ober Associates Incorporated.

Excerpts from *The Pirate Hunter: The True Story of Captain Kidd* by Richard Zacks. Copyright © 2002 by Richard Zacks. Reprinted by permission of Hyperion. All rights reserved. Available wherever books are sold.

Excerpts from *Pirates and Buccaneers of the Atlantic Coast* by Edward Rowe Snow. Reprinted by permission of Dorothy Snow Bicknell.

Excerpts from *The Queen's Corsair* by Alexander McKee. Reprinted by permission of Souvenir Press Ltd.

Excerpts from *Sir Francis Drake: The Queen's Pirate* by Harry Kelsey. Reprinted by permission of Yale University Press.

Excerpts from *Villains of All Nations* by Marcus Rediker. Copyright © 2004 by Marcus Rediker. Reprinted by permission of Beacon Press, Boston.

DEDICATION

To Adis Choundas, who taught me a love of language. To Panagiotis Choundas, who raised me on true-life accounts of mastering hurricane seas and irregular verbs. To Marina Choundas, who schooled me in the creative use of abusive epithets. And to Cathy Kane, who is my perfection.

ACKNOWLEDGMENTS

There are people I need to thank. Some never suspected they'd get caught up in a project like this one. That makes x-plus-me of us. But unpredictability makes the world go round.

Okay, fortunately the earth's steady rotation is utterly nonrandom and has nothing to do with unpredictability. Let's move on.

Earnest thanks to Gary Heidt at Imprint, and Lauren Mosko and Jane Friedman at Writer's Digest, for their perspicacity, their enthusiasm, and their hard work.

All respect and admiration for John "Ol' Chumbucket" Baur, Mark "Cap'n Slappy" Summers, and Dave Barry, respectively the founders and advocate of Talk Like a Pirate Day—every September 19, blow fair or blow foul. What they began is a very good thing. I stand on the shoulders of giants.

Thanks to Jane Farnol Curtis and to her father's excellent legacy. Jeffery Farnol's pirate novels are among the great narratives of the sweet trade, and their author was one of the finest—if not the finest—writer of pirate dialogue in history.

There are hundreds of impressive places and events in this country that celebrate pirates and the maritime tradition. I've had the privilege of experiencing a few—the Gasparilla Pirate Festival in Tampa, the New England Pirate Museum in Salem, the Pirate Soul Museum and the Mel Fisher Maritime Museum in Key West, the Pirate Walk in Newport, the Pirate Ring on the World Wide Web—and I applaud all the rest for helping preserve a very unique, powerfully American, implausibly fascinating strand of history.

The mother of the small fat man who lives in my house is a land angel. She wrote this book with her infinite patience and support. I'd marry her a third time if solemnly called upon.

Finally, one of the proofs of God's existence is the trolley pirate. May his supply of unsuspecting tourists be steady, his fake-boarding forever be fake-terrifying. May all good things come to the trolley pirate.

Table of Contents

PART II: HOW TO SAY IT

APPENDIXES

Preface

On vacation, my beautiful wife and I drive from Miami to Key West (my left forearm cooking down to jerky under driver-window sun), park the car in a municipal lot, and—leaving behind everything else, including a beach copy of *Treasure Island*—hop onto a sightseeing trolley around the island.

I remember pieces of the tour—pastel bungalows, a museum—but not much else. Except this: We turn a corner. Out of nowhere comes a giant pirate racing after our trolley on foot, swinging a cutlass, screaming pirate epithets like we're stealing his treasure and feeding it to his dying mother.

He hauls after us for a block or so. Then he stops, stares a moment, and walks away. Cutlass dragging after him. No explanations.

On our last day, we happen into a costume shop. The person behind the desk looks familiar. We've seen him before—his elaborate pirate regalia is a hint. It's the trolley pirate. He confesses: Several times a day, he charges out the door after tourists, harasses them nine different kinds of pirate-like, then calmly steps back into the shop and resumes his business.

I think to myself: That's got to be the best job in the world.

Then I think: If only there were some kind of manual.

Introduction

THE POINT OF THE *PRIMER*

You hold in your hands the world's only complete guide to the pirate language.

But this begs the question: Is there such a thing as a "pirate language"?

The short answer is yes. If one were to take the statements made by or attributed to English-speaking pirates in historical accounts, literature, film, and television and then distill and identify all those words and patterns that are distinctive from—or used with disproportionate frequency as compared with—modern English, the resulting compilation would be a freestanding pirate language. This is precisely what the *Primer* does.

The long answer is also yes, with stops along the way. The term "language" suggests a *uniform* way of talking. But not every pirate speaks in the same way. Not every pirate uses the same words or pronunciations. Not every pirate sounds like Long John Silver (played by Robert Newton) in Walt Disney's 1950 production of "Treasure Island" or hails from Bristol or the southwestern parts of England. Many or most of the pirates in film, television, and literature are obviously colorful stereotypes, not authentic representations of the diverse breed of criminals who actually sailed the seas. In his book *Under the Black Flag: The Romance and the Reality of Life Among the Pirates*, David Cordingly writes of the pirate we all know: "Over the years fact has merged with fiction. ... The picture [of pirates] which most of us have turns out to be a blend of historical facts overlaid with three centuries of ballads, melodramas, epic poems, romantic novels, adventure stories, comic strips, and films." (xiii-xiv)

The truth, however, is that heterogeneity is a feature of every language. A New Yorker's vowels are generally not the same as a San Franciscan's, and the vocabulary of a college graduate in either city will likely vary from that of the high-school drop-out living across the street. Pirates similarly hailed from different places, ethnicities, and educational backgrounds (see introduction to Chapter 17: Pronunciation), which makes the consequently diverse elements of their speech all the more interesting.

Pirate speech varies even among pirates in the same company: *Treasure Island*'s Israel Hands uses distinctive terms and patterns more frequently than Long John Silver; *The Pirate Round*'s Henry Nagel speaks more "piratically" than his pretentious boss Elephiant Yancy. And just as a stockbroker might speak differently with important clients at a meeting than with colleagues at a sports bar, oftentimes the same pirate speaks more piratically with certain people (*Treasure Island*'s Long John Silver with Israel Hands, *Winds of Chance*'s Japhet Bly with his messmates) than with others for whom he might consider standard English more appropriate (Long John Silver with Captain Smollett, Japhet Bly with Ursula Revell).

The term "language" also suggests a *communal* way of speaking. Frenchmen say "oui" to communicate with their compatriots because French is their common, official language. One might observe that pirates, on the other hand, often say things not because they are members of the pirate community, but because they are seamen ("fair winds and following seas") or eighteenth-century Englishmen ("alack now") or for any number of other reasons. The reality, however, is that, beyond (and sometimes even within) a very basic vocabulary of core terms, every language contains elements mirroring the non-ethnic, non-geographic identities of its speakers—their other affiliations, interests, beliefs, pursuits. French doctors and lawyers, for example, communicate in sub-vocabularies better attributable to their professions than to any shared geography or ancestry. And, conversely, the pirate language includes a certain core vocabulary of terms spoken by pirates *qua* pirates—"arrgh" (see Chapter 15: Arrgh), for example, or "gentleman adventurer" (see Chapter 16: Cultural Terms). Moreover, the simple truth is that pirate language *is* communal. Pirates may not all hail from the same political unit or ethnic group, but the existence of their identifiable community—with its discrete cultural patterns and unique speech elements—is more than adequate to render those patterns and elements a language.

Finally, the term "language" suggests a *general* way of speaking. Its elements are used by, or at least familiar to, a large population claiming knowledge of the language. The pirate language, however, includes terms and phrases that only a single pirate might have used—and invented. When Peter Blood announces in *Captain Blood: His Odyssey*, "It's the same reason that's been urging me to pick a quarrel with you so that I might have the satisfaction of **slipping a couple of feet of steel into your vitals**" (287), we can be relatively sure that this bold formulation—colorful, powerful, memorable—is Blood's own, and likely not being bandied about by pirates around globe and across centuries. But modern languages grow new words all the time—invented by teenagers, percolated through blogs and chat-rooms, synthesized in popular culture and mass media. Languages are living things, and additions are not the products of nationwide legislation. They are the bottom-up innovations of brain-fired tongues. Peter Blood's formulation is featured in the *Primer* for the same reason that a seventy-year-old English professor can still walk away from a dictionary having learned something new.

All the above analysis is really a way of explaining to ourselves a truth we already understand. We know that pirates do, in fact, speak distinctively—even if not uniformly or communally or generally—because our popular notion of what it is to be a pirate involves speech, as much as dress, action, and mission.

The *Primer* is the world's first compendium that captures, reveals, analyzes, and organizes that speech in a systematic manner. It adopts the universe of pirate speech written and acted over the last three centuries, catalogs its elements, lays bare its internal workings, and reveals it for the language it really is.

Split me sideways else.

THE METHOD OF THE *PRIMER*

The *Primer* is a comprehensive compilation of the words, pronunciations, and grammatical patterns that are either unique to or mostly used in pirate speech. Words and patterns that pirates share in common with modern speakers, and which are used by modern speakers as frequently as by pirates, are not included. Take, for example, the following excerpt from Jeffery Farnol's *Winds of Chance*, wherein pirate Jeremy Jervey prepares to tell Ursula Revell about his captain's quest for vengeance:

> "Why 'tis mighty black and foul yarn, **ma'm**, but if I must, well, stand by! Years agone, **lady**, this here Cap'n Ingleby was one o' three as wrought black shame on a sweet lady, poor soul, and she a noble lady o' Spain. ..." (229)

Jervey's use of the term "ma'm" to address Revell is typical of both pirate speakers and modern speakers, and so is not featured in the *Primer*. Jervey's use of the term "lady" as a form of address, on the other hand, is not typical in modern English. Because the usage of "lady" in that manner is distinctive to pirate speech and not modern English, the term is included in the *Primer*.

Note that pirates occasionally speak Elizabethan English and forms distinctive thereto. See, for example: "I've a message for **thee** to give to him. Do it, and when I'm skipper, **thou'lt** be first mate." (Humble Bellows, "The Crimson Pirate" 55:22) Pronouns like "thee" and "thou" and verbs like "wilt" are examples of speech distinctive to the English language during Queen Elizabeth I's reign (1558–1603) and more broadly during the era of Early Modern English from roughly 1450 through 1650. Elizabethan forms represent a very small proportion of pirate speech (though admittedly a larger proportion for the pirate characters in Jeffery Farnol's books), and, conversely, pirates represent a very small proportion of those who have, and are popularly understood to have, spoken it.

In light of that twice-weak association (and in view of the related fact that Elizabethan usages of the 1500s generally predate the pirate era of the late 1600s and early 1700s, and are more closely associated with the cant of the peasant's village than that of the seaman's tavern), the *Primer*, with only a few exceptions, does not cover Elizabethan forms. Works exploring Elizabethan usages include Alexander Schmidt's *Shakespeare Lexicon and Quotation Dictionary* (Dover Publications, 1971) and William Brohaugh's *English Through the Ages* (Writer's Digest Books, 1998).

A few of the entries are not necessarily parts of a general vocabulary, but because of their utility or memorable quality, should not be lost or excluded here. The earlier example of Peter Blood's "I might have the satisfaction of **slipping a couple of feet of steel into your vitals**" (*Captain Blood: His Odyssey*, 287) is a good one.

Nearly every entry in the *Primer*—whether a term of vocabulary, an item of pronunciation, or a form of grammar—is accompanied by one or more examples of pirate speech reflecting its use. The excerpts are exact quotations from historical accounts, works of literature, films, and television episodes, except in those instances in which seventeenth- and eighteenth-century spelling conventions (*e.g.*, capitalization of nouns, italicization of proper nouns, use of "f" for "s," obscure or confusing spellings that do not bear on pronunciation) have been disregarded in favor of a contemporary-English rendering for clearer reference and comprehension.

THE ELEMENTS OF THE *PRIMER*

Each entry in Part I: What to Say consists of (1) a term or phrase, (2) alternative pirate pronunciations of that term or phrase, (3) a definition, (4) often a supplemental explanation, and (5) almost always, an excerpt of actual pirate speech reflecting the usage of the featured term or phrase.

ENTRY TERMS AND PHRASES

Entry terms and phrases in the vocabulary chapters of Part I are listed in alphabetical order, without regard to initial articles, apostrophes, or placeholder elements (such as blanks or capitalized placeholder words like "EPITHET" or "VERB").

Where an entry term or phrase is used typically with one or more other words, it appears along with a blank (__) when followed by a single word or finite group of words, or with an ellipsis (...) when followed by an indeterminate number of words.

The term or phrase in each entry typically appears in its most basic form—for example, "greetings to you" and not "greetin's ter ye" or any number of other possible forms or pronunciations. However, a term or phrase sometimes appears in a form other than its most basic if that alternative form is more frequently used (*e.g.*, "body o' me" and not "body of me," "good luck to 'ee" and not "good luck to you").

Where some part of the entry term or phrase is optional—that is, used occasionally but not always—such part is set off in parentheses. Take the following entries, for instance:

h(e)earkee in your ear

I'll take my (affi)davy

look here (now)

The parentheses in these three entries are used to set off, respectively, an optional letter ("e" in "hearkee"), an optional part of a word ("affi" in "affidavy"), and an optional word ("now" in "look here now").

Entries and definitions for phrases that require the use of a pronoun generally feature the placeholder pronoun "one" ("dare Fortune on **one's** own account," "lose **one's** passage"). However, for phrases that are either closely associated with or more meaningfully explained by use of the first or second person, the phrase is set out and defined with the corresponding pronoun ("good fortune attend **you**," "**I** don't care a louse").

PRONUNCIATIONS

Because there is often more than one way of saying or spelling a term, an alternative formulation, or orthography, is found in brackets and italics following the main term or phrase in each entry. Different pronunciations of a single term (or of a single syllable within a term) are divided by forward slashes. For example:

blast your eyes [*blarrst/blass ya/yarr/ye/yer/yere/yore eye'ees*]

buccaneer [*barka/barker/buccarr/bucker-nee-arr*]

Where a term or syllable is subject to two or more pronunciations that consist of different numbers of words, the term "OR" is used to clearly separate those pronunciations. Take for instance:

let me be [*laaht me OR lemme be*]

The above orthography uses "OR" to separate "laaht me" from "lemme." Each of those pronunciations can then be combined with "be" to produce either "laaht me be" or "lemme be."

Different words that might be used in place of a particular term (for example, pirates often use "on" when a modern speaker might say "of") are divided by backward slashes:

in a manner of speaking [*i' a mayner o'\on speakin'*]

The following are examples of orthographies featuring both forward slashes and backward slashes, because they reflect both different pronunciations and different term equivalents:

better days ahead [*be'er\gooder dayees a'ead/ahayd/'head*]

I'll choke those words down your throat [*I'ee'ull chooke/cho'ooke dose/t'ose\dem/them\dey/ they warrds dowoon ya/yarr/ye/yer/yere/yore thro'oot*]

Apostrophes in orthographies signify (1) letter omissions, or (2) shifts or breaks between consecutive vowel sounds. In the orthography below—

the bones [*t' boones/bo'oones*]

—the first apostrophe signifies a letter omission (specifically of the letters "he" from the word "the"), while the second marks a shift between consecutive vowel sounds (the sound "oh" and the sound "oo"). An apostrophe between vowel sounds appears only where a shift or break between them is not otherwise apparent from the spelling alone. Thus, apostrophes appear in orthographies for the words "bone" and "eye"—[*bo'oone*], [*eye'ee*]—but not for the words "my" and "now"—[*myee*], [*nowoo*]—as the vowel progressions in the latter two pronunciations are readily discernible from the spellings alone.

Each orthography is disjunctive. That is, the alternative pronunciations need not be used all at once but should be viewed as a menu of possibilities, for use in various combinations. Thus, the entry for the term "delicate" in Chapter 10: Respectful Address reads:

delicate [*daahl-er-cayte/kert*]

The orthography for "delicate" offers several different possible pronunciation combinations—from "delercate" to "daahlerkert"—depending on which alternative syllable pronunciations the reader chooses to deploy. One might opt for an alternative pronunciation of only the first syllable, or only the last—or none at all.

Each orthography typically includes the most likely or obvious candidates, but does not purport to be an exhaustive inventory of all possible alternative pronunciations. Other credible pronunciations are conceivable in nearly every instance. Use of Appendix B: Sound List as a supplemental reference is encouraged. Note also that the orthographies in the *Primer* always include alternative pronunciations, sometimes include alternative terms (where they are especially equivalent or used with notable frequency), but never include alternative structures. Consequently, for alternative ways of structuring the insult "you've neither sense nor memory," for example, one must look beyond the orthography provided ("[ya've/ye've/yer've needer/nee'er/nyder/ny'er saahnse narr/noor mammary/membry/mem'ry]") and to Part II: How to Say It for suggestions on alternative formulations like "neither sense nor memory 'ave you" or "here's you wi' neither sense nor memory" or "you're no man for sense or memory."

Where no orthography is provided, the entry term or phrase is not readily associated with any obvious alternative pronunciations. However, a speaker's own phonetic tendencies or creative inclinations might nevertheless yield different pronunciations.

DEFINITIONS AND EXPLANATIONS

The meat of each entry consists of one or both of two elements: a definition (a term or phrase that is synonymous with or roughly comparable to, or briefly expository of, the entry term or phrase in most sentences) and an explanation (a discussion of the meaning of the entry term or phrase, which may include a description of how it is typically used, a comparison with other terms and phrases, or other commentary). Definitions are in fragment format and come first, while explanations follow in sentence format with capitalization and punctuation.

Take, for example, the following entry from Chapter 6: Oaths:

> **by my deathless soul** [*byee me/myee dath/deff-less sool/so'ool*] I swear; I swear on my soul
> The term "deathless" amplifies the speaker's oath, as he emphasizes with the use of that term the infinite consequences of any falsehood on his part (*i.e.*, not simply damnation, but eternal damnation).
>
> "Ha, **by my deathless soul**—what's doing yonder?" (Resolution Day, glimpsing out of the corner of his eye the pursued ship take on sudden speed and assume an offensive position, *Martin Conisby's Vengeance* 104)

The first element ("I swear; I swear on my soul") is a definition, and the prose underneath ("The term 'deathless' amplifies ...") is an explanation.

EXCERPTS

Finally, each entry contains one or more excerpts, chosen as the most efficient example(s) of the featured word or phrase. The *Primer*'s excerpts are taken from forty-two books, nineteen films, thirteen television episodes, and one amusement park attraction.

With rare exceptions, the *Primer*'s source excerpts were spoken by pirates—real or fictional. Long John Silver's parrot Cap'n Flint is technically not a pirate, but his pirate vocabulary was learned from pirates over decades. Tavernkeepers who associate with pirates—the Dutch proprietor of the pirate tavern in the film "Pirates," and Long John Silver's girlfriend Purity Pinker (in "Long John Silver's Return to Treasure Island" and "The Adventures of Long John Silver")—are included because their vocabularies reflect (and, indeed, perhaps exaggerate) the pirate usages of the clientele they try so hard to engage and control. Pinker's speech is moreover included because her boyfriend is a pirate; because much of her character is about besting customers and boyfriend in the use of abusive and authentically piratical language; and because she simply has too many memorable lines, and uses too many notable piratical elements, to be excluded from any comprehensive compilation.

Each excerpt consists of a quotation, as well as a parenthetical notation specifying (1) the person speaking the quoted material; (2) on occasion, a description of the context in which s/he speaks it; and (3) the page number in the book, or the time in hours, minutes, and seconds in the film or television episode, at which the quoted material is found.

Take the following excerpt, for instance:

> "Come, you are indeed **of right mettle**, and I like your spirit." (Abraham Dawling, laughing on seeing young Barnaby True brandish his pistol, *The Book of Pirates* "The Ghost of Captain Brand" 48)

The parenthetical notation indicates that the excerpted words were spoken by a pirate named Abraham Dawling in a story called "The Ghost of Captain Brand" in Howard Pyle's 1921 book titled *The Book of Pirates*. The number "48" indicates that the excerpted words can be found on page 48 of the edition specified in the list at the end of this introduction—in this case, the Dover Publications edition published in 2000.

Book citations specifying page numbers may correspond only to the particular editions listed beginning on page 10. Book citations specify chapters rather than, or in addition to, page numbers in those few instances where the book is in the public domain and either difficult to find (such that online versions may be most accessible) or extant in several page-variant editions.

No time marks are provided for excerpts from the "Pirates of the Caribbean" Disney attraction, as the ride-through nature of the attraction creates variation in times at which particular scenes are encountered, characters viewed, and dialogue heard. Where a given excerpt is specific to a particular version of the attraction (which has been modified over the years), an approximate year during which that excerpt might have been experienced is specified.

The notation "Compare:" appears before an excerpt when that excerpt reflects the use of a term or phrase different from, but similar or equivalent to, the entry term or phrase, such that the excerpt nevertheless helps illustrate the meaning and/or typical usage of the entry term or phrase.

Where cited throughout the *Primer*, book titles are italicized (*Treasure Island*), while film, television, and short story titles are set off in quotation marks ("The Adventures of Long John Silver").

Where an excerpt accompanying an entry is spoken by a single person or character, it is wrapped in quotes and the speaker is identified in the parentheses that follow:

"I'll stay here a bit." (Billy Bones, *Treasure Island* 4, Chap. 1)

Where an excerpt is an exchange between more than one person, it is wrapped in quotes and angle brackets and the speakers are identified, in speaking order, in parentheses:

< "Who was yon?" "Pedro the Portingale." > (Roger Snaith & Joe, *Winds of Chance* 301)

A few excerpts are wrapped in asterisks. These excerpts contain text that is not directly quoted speech—either because the entire excerpt consists of speech that is paraphrased or otherwise reflected, rather than directly quoted, or because the excerpt contains contextual text in addition to directly quoted speech:

[O]ne of the villains took hold of him, and said, G[o]d d[a]m[n] him, he would give him good quarters presently, and made the poor Spaniard kneel down on his knees, then taking his fusil, put the muzzle of it into his mouth, and fired down his throat. (attribution to pirate in Edward Low's company, *The General History of the Pyrates* 327)

"Take a cutlass, him that dares, and I'll see the colour of his inside, crutch and all, before that pipe's empty." Not a man stirred; not a man answered. "That's your sort, is it?" (Long John Silver, *Treasure Island* 159, Chap. 28)

INCONSISTENT USAGES

Part II: How To Say It presents ways in which pirates pronounce their words and structure their sentences. For example, Section 22.3.1 explains how pirates often switch their verbs, using singular verbs with plural nouns: "We **takes** our treasure serious, and our women seriouser."

However, pirates are not consistent about sentence structure, or anything else for that matter (except perhaps their capacity for greed). Pirates might say instead: "We **take** our treasure serious, and our women seriouser." Thus, for every guideline of pirate speech, the *Primer* also includes—where found—any excerpts that reflect its *non*-application. These "inconsistent" examples are noted as a reminder that no rule of pirate speech is absolute and that inconsistency is itself one of the cornerstones of pirate speech. Indeed, Section 18.5: Inconsistency is dedicated to exploring the role of inconsistency in pirate speech, and it lays out several examples.

THE SOURCES FOR THE *PRIMER*

The following is a list of the sources (forty-one books, twenty films, thirteen television episodes, and one amusement park attraction) from which the speech in the *Primer* is excerpted:

BOOKS

Ballantyne, R.M. *The Coral Island*. 1858. New York: Oxford University Press, 1990.

Barrie, J.M. *Peter Pan*. 1911. New York: Signet Classics, 1987.

Cooper, James Fenimore. *The Red Rover*. 1828. Lincoln, NE: University of Nebraska Press, 1963.

Cordingly, David. *Under the Black Flag: The Romance and the Reality of Life Among the Pirates*. New York: Harcourt Brace & Company, 1996.

Dampier, William. *A New Voyage Round the World*. 1697. London: Hummingbird Press, 1998.

Defoe, Daniel. *The King of Pirates*. 1719. London: Hesperus Press Limited, 2002.

Dow, George Francis and John Henry Edmonds. *The Pirates of the New England Coast, 1630–1730*. 1923. Mineola, NY: Dover Publications, Inc., 1996.

Doyle, Arthur Conan. *The Dealings of Captain Sharkey and Other Tales of Pirates*. 1922. Amsterdam, The Netherlands: Fredonia Books, 2001.

Ellms, Charles. *The Pirates Own Book*. 1837. New York: Book-of-the-Month Club, 2002.

Exquemelin, Alexander O. *The Buccaneers of America*. 1969 translation by Alexis Brown of 1678 Dutch edition. Mineola, NY: Dover Publications, Inc., 2000.

Exquemelin, Alexander O. *Bucaniers of America*. Vol. I, Part III, Ch. XII. Reproduction of 1924 George Routledge and Sons Ltd./Stallybrass modernized edition of 1684 Crooke edition. Annapolis, MD: Naval Institute Press, 1993.

Farnol, Jeffery. *Black Bartlemy's Treasure*. 1920. London: Pan Books Ltd., 1972.

Farnol, Jeffery. *Martin Conisby's Vengeance*. Boston: Little Brown & Co, 1921.

Farnol, Jeffery. *Winds of Chance*. Boston: Little Brown & Co, 1934.

Farnol, Jeffery. *Adam Penfeather: Buccaneer*. New York: Doubleday, Doran and Co., 1941.

Hayward, Arthur L., ed. *Lives of the Most Remarkable Criminals*. 1735. London: George Routledge & Sons, Ltd., 1927.

Hughes, Richard. *A High Wind in Jamaica*. 1929. New York: New York Review of Books Classics, 1999.

Johnson, Captain Charles. *The General History of the Pyrates*. 1724.

Johnson, Roger L. *Dead Man's Chest: The Sequel to Treasure Island*. New York: ibooks, inc., 2003.

Kaserman, James. *Gasparilla: Pirate Genius*. Fort Myers, FL: Pirate Publishing International, 2000.

Kelsey, Harry. *Sir Francis Drake: The Queen's Pirate*. New Haven, CT: Yale University Press, 1998.

Lambdin, Dewey. *The Gun Ketch*. New York: Ballantine Books, 1993.

Marryat, Captain Frederick. *The Pirate*. 1836. Whitefish, MT: Kessinger Publishing, reprint. www.kessinger.net

McKee, Alexander. *The Queen's Corsair: Drake's Journey of Circumnavigation 1577–1580*. New York: Stein and Day, 1978.

Nelson, James L. *The Guardship*. New York: Perennial, 2000.

Nelson, James L. *The Blackbirder*. New York: William Morrow, 2001.

Nelson, James L. *The Pirate Round*. New York: William Morrow, 2002.

Pyle, Howard. *The Book of Pirates*. 1921. Mineola, NY: Dover Publications, Inc., 2000.

Rediker, Marcus. *Villains of All Nations: Atlantic Pirates in the Golden Age*. Boston: Beacon Press, 2004.

Ringrose, Basil. *Bucaniers of America*. Vol. 2, Part 4. 1685 (Crooke edition).

Ringrose, Basil. *The South Sea Waggoner*. 1682. Berkeley: University of California Press, 1992.

Rogers, Woodes. *A Cruising Voyage Round the World*. 1712. Crabtree, OR: The Narrative Press, 2004.

Sabatini, Rafael. *Captain Blood: His Odyssey*. 1922. Washington, DC: Regnery Publishing, 1998.

Sabatini, Rafael. *Captain Blood Returns*. New York: P.F. Collier & Son Company, 1931.

Sabatini, Rafael. *The Fortunes of Captain Blood*. 1936. New York: Popular Library, 1962.

Smith, A.D. Howden. *Porto Bello Gold*. 1924. Ithaca, NY: McBooks Press, 1999.

Snow, Edward Rowe. *Pirates and Buccaneers of the Atlantic Coast*. 1944. Beverly, MA: Commonwealth Editions 2004.

Stevenson, Robert Louis. *Treasure Island*. 1883. New York: Bantam Classic reissue, 1992.

Stevenson, Robert Louis. *The Master of Ballantrae*. 1889. New York: Random House Modern Library, 2002.

Wafer, Lionel. *A New Voyage and Description of the Isthmus of America*. 1699. New York: Burt Franklin, 1970.

Zacks, Richard. *The Pirate Hunter: The True Story of Captain Kidd*. New York: Hyperion, 2002.

FILMS

"The Black Pirate" (Elton Corporation 1926) (Douglas Fairbanks).

"Blackbeard the Pirate" (RKO Radio Pictures 1952) (Robert Newton, Linda Darnell).

"Blackbeard's Ghost" (Walt Disney Pictures 1968) (Peter Ustinov, Dean Jones).

"Captain Blood" (Warner Bros. Pictures 1935) (Errol Flynn, Olivia de Havilland).

"Captain Kidd" (Miracle Productions 1945) (Charles Laughton, Randolph Scott, Barbara Britton).

"The Crimson Pirate" (Warner Bros. Pictures 1952) (Burt Lancaster, Nick Cravat, Eva Bartok).

"Cutthroat Island" (Carolco Pictures Inc. 1995) (Geena Davis, Matthew Modine).

"Hook" (Amblin Entertainment/TriStar Pictures 1991) (Dustin Hoffman, Robin Williams, Julia Roberts, Bob Hoskins).

"Long John Silver's Return to Treasure Island" (Treasure Island Pictures Pty. Ltd. 1954) (Robert Newton, Connie Gilchrist).

"Pirates" (Accent Films/Carthago Coop. Cinematografica/Cominco 1986) (Walter Matthau).

"Pirates of the Caribbean: The Curse of the Black Pearl" (Walt Disney Pictures 2003) (Johnny Depp, Geoffrey Rush, Orlando Bloom, Keira Knightley).

"Pirates of the Caribbean 2: Dead Man's Chest" (Walt Disney Pictures 2006) (Johnny Depp, Orlando Bloom, Keira Knightley, Bill Nighy).

"Pirates of Tortuga" (Clover Productions 1961) (Ken Scott, Leticia Roman, Dave King, John Richardson).

"Swashbuckler" (Universal Pictures 1976) (Robert Shaw, James Earl Jones, Peter Boyle, Beau Bridges).

"Treasure Island" (Metro-Goldwyn-Mayer 1934) (Wallace Beery, Jackie Cooper, Lionel Barrymore).

"Treasure Island" (Walt Disney Pictures 1950) (Robert Newton, Bobby Driscoll).

"Treasure Island" (The DuPont Show of the Month 1960) (Hugh Griffith, Boris Karloff).

"Treasure Island" (Massfilms 1972) (Orson Welles, Kim Burfield).

"Treasure Island" (Turner Network Television 1990) (Charlton Heston, Christian Bale, Oliver Reed).

"Treasure Island" (Fries Film Group/Isle of Man Film Commission/Kingsborough Greenlight Pictures 1998) (Jack Palance, Kevin Zegers, Patrick Bergin).

TELEVISION

"The Adventures of Long John Silver" (Treasure Island Productions 1955) (Robert Newton, Connie Gilchrist):
  "The Necklace" (Episode 1)
  "Pieces of Eight" (Episode 2)
  "The Orphans' Christmas" (Episode 3)
  "Execution Dock" (Episode 4)
  "The Eviction" (Episode 5)
  "The Pink Pearl" (Episode 6)
  "The Tale of a Tooth" (Episode 7)
  "Ship o' the Dead" (Episode 8)
  "Sword of Vengeance" (Episode 9)
  "Turnabout" (Episode 10)
  "Miss Purity's Birthday" (Episode 11)
  "Dead Reckoning" (Episode 12)
  "Devil's Stew" (Episode 13)

OTHER

Pirates of the Caribbean attraction, Disneyland/Walt Disney World.

Other sources cited, but not excerpted, include:

Ritchie, Robert C. *Captain Kidd and the War Against the Pirates*. Cambridge, MA: Harvard University Press, 1986.

Sugden, John. *Sir Francis Drake*. New York: Henry Holt and Company, 1990.

Thomson, George Malcolm. *Sir Francis Drake*. New York: William Morrow & Co., 1972.

CHAPTER 1

Greetings & Partings

When pirates meet, they may or may not kill each other. They might exchange pleasantries before changing their minds and proceeding with full-blown slaughter.

Words of parting should be offered without expectation of reciprocity. Corpses cannot talk. Dead men bid no farewells.

The following are terms and phrases used as first greetings, in introductory exchanges, and as parting comments. Definitions are provided only where meaning is not otherwise apparent.

ahoy [*ahooy/ahoyee*]
  (1) hello; hi
  Often combined with "there" [*tharr/theyarr/theyerr*].

  "**Ahoy**, mates! We've come for tradin'." (Long John Silver, on encountering the island's natives for the first time, "The Adventures of Long John Silver: The Pink Pearl" 9:22) "**Ahoy there**, mates!" (Long John Silver, greeting the patrons of the Cask & Anchor as he enters, "The Adventures of Long John Silver: The Necklace" 7:42)
  (2) good-bye; farewell

  "When your boat stops, please be steppin' out on your right. **Ahoy**, maties. Have a safe voyage." (pirate voice bidding farewell at disembarkation point, "Pirates of the Caribbean" Disney attraction)

all my duty to you [*awrl me/myee dooty t'/ta/ter 'ee/ya/ye/yer*] I give you my respects; I give you my best
  A polite, respectful greeting.

  "Good-day to you, sir, and **all our dooties to** the squire and Cap'n Smollett." (Long John Silver, *Treasure Island* 170, Chap. 30)

__ **am I** [__ *arrm/em\be I'ee*] I am __; my name is __

Used to introduce oneself.

"Absalom Troy **am I**." (Absalom Troy, *Adam Penfeather, Buccaneer* 5)

are you come? [*ahrr 'ee/ya/ye/yer cahm/carrm/coohm?*]

Used not so much as a literal question but as an acknowledgment of another's presence, comparable to modern equivalents such as "is that really you?" The question form suggests suprise or pleasure at seeing the addressee.

"Lads, **are ye come?** I'm glad to see ye; I have been looking out for ye for a great while." (John Upton, greeting his fellow company mates, *Lives of the Most Remarkable Criminals* 476)

at your service [*a'/hat ya/yarr/ye/yer/yere/yore sarrvice*]

A very respectful and, depending on context, possibly deferential greeting.

"Captain Silver, **at your service**, Master Hawkins." (Long John Silver, greeting Jim Hawkins at the stockade, "Treasure Island" [1960] 1:01:44)

be that you? [*be tharrt ya/ye/yer?*] is that you?

< "**Be that you**, the Reverend Monaster?" "No, it'd be Ironhand." > (Purity Pinker & Ironhand, speaking through a locked bedroom door, "Long John Silver's Return to Treasure Island" 53:21)

be (right) welcome [*be (rawt/righeet) wahhlcahm/carrm/coohm*] welcome

A greeting.

"Captain Penfeather **be welcome** aboard my *Lady's Delight*." (Black Bartlemy, *Adam Penfeather, Buccaneer* 276) "So come ashore, my good sir; come ashore and **be right welcome**." (Roger Snaith, *Winds of Chance* 321)

best respects [*baahst/barrst respecks*] I give you my respects; I give you my best

A polite, respectful greeting.

"**Best respects**, ma'm!" (Jeremy Jervey, upon meeting Ursula Revell, *Winds of Chance* 210)

better days ahead [*be'er\gooder dayees a'ead/ahayd/'head*] things will get better; tomorrow's another day

Words of consolation and encouragement for the sad or defeated, especially on parting.

"Good luck, Major Folly. **Better days ahead**." (Ned Lynch, "Swashbuckler" 24:26)

(I) bid you good day [*(I'ee) bed 'ee/ya/ye/yer g' dayee*]

A parting that can be modified to suit the time of day. Alternatives to "day" include "morning" [*marn-in'*], "evening" [*evenin'/ev'n'n*], and "night" [*nawt/nigheet*].

"**Bid you good night**,/Good night,/Good night./Yes, **I bid you good night**,/Good night,/Good night." (from song sung by Nick Debrett and two female companions, "Swashbuckler" 56:48) "I now take pleasure to **bid you Good-day!**" (Adam Penfeather, *Adam Penfeather, Buccaneer* 324)

by your leave [*byee ya/yarr/ye/yer/yere/yore leef*] excuse me; beg your pardon

Often used as a very respectful and, depending on context, possibly deferential greeting that suggests the interaction proceeds at the other's will.

"Well, sir, **by your leave**, sir, John Silver's come back to do his dooty." (Long John Silver, "Treasure Island" [1950] 1:30:02) "**By your leave**, sweet lady!" (Japhet Bly, upon entering Ursula Revell's cabin, *Winds of Chance* 51)

come aboard [*cahm/carrm/coohm abarrd*]

Used to invite persons aboard a vessel, but also more generally to receive or welcome persons to any place or event.

"[I]f you want to speak to Captain Merry, then **come aboard**." (George Merry, inviting Squire Trelawney into his company's encampment, "Treasure Island" [1998] 1:18:11) **"Come aboard,** Jim lad!" (Long John Silver, opening the door to the dentist's office and calling Jim Hawkins inside, "The Adventures of Long John Silver: The Tale of a Tooth" 3:39)

come you in [*cahm/carrm/coohm 'ee/ya/ye/yer in*] come in; enter

"**Come you in**, Smy, and sit likewise." (Absalom Troy, *Adam Penfeather, Buccaneer* 17)

evening (to you) [*evenin'/ev'n'n (t'/ta/er 'ee/ya/ye/yer)*] good evening

< "**Evenin'**, Ben Gunn." "**Evenin'**, Barbecue." > (Long John Silver & Ben Gunn, "Treasure Island" [1990] 2:05:48) "**Evenin' to 'ee**, maties. Had too much, he has." (Patch, greeting soldiers on patrol and diverting their attention away from drugged Slygo, "The Adventures of Long John Silver: The Necklace" 23:37)

fair dreams attend you [*farr/fayarr/fayerr dreams arrt-aahnd 'ee/ya/ye/yer*]
A parting at bedtime.

"Good night, Joanna—**fair dreams attend thee**." (Resolution Day, *Martin Conisby's Vengeance* 160)

a fair good morrow [*a farr/fayarr/fayerr g' mahrr-owoo*]

"Morrow" means both "tomorrow" and "morning." "A fair good morrow" is accordingly used either as a parting at nighttime or bedtime to wish another a good tomorrow or next morning, or as a greeting at the start of the day to wish another a good morning.

"Sleep like a babe, sweet lass, ay, a pretty buxom babe, and wake thus all vivid with abundant life to revile the poor, meek fellow that now bids thee **a fair good morrow** ..." (Japhet Bly, *Winds of Chance* 311)

a fair good night to you [*a farr/fayarr/fayerr g' nawt/nigheet t'/ta/ter 'ee/ya/ye/yer*]

"And now to slumber. **A fair good night to thee**, Madam Bly." (Japhet Bly, *Winds of Chance* 179)

a fair morning to you [*a farr/fayarr/fayerr marnin' t'/ta/ter 'ee/ya/ye/yer*]

"**A fair morning t' your honour!**" (Ned Bowser, *Adam Penfeather, Buccaneer* 94)

fair winds and following seas [*farr/fayarr/fayerr win's/wints an'/'n' fol-ler/lowoo-in' seas*]

A parting used to wish another well. Though the phrase refers literally only to ideal sailing conditions (a steady wind to propel a vessel in the intended direction, a sea that swells behind a vessel but does not overtake her), it is understood to propose more broadly a good journey, good fortune, and well-being.

"May the Lord grant ya **fair winds and followin' seas!**" (Long John Silver, *Dead Man's Chest* 42)

fare you well (until we meet again) [*farr/fayarr/fayerr 'ee/ya/ye/yer waahl ('til we meet agayn/agin/'gain/'gayn)*]
A parting.

"And so, gentlemen, kind friends, God be with you and **fare ye well**." (Japhet Bly, *Winds of Chance* 291) "Now **fare thee well until we meet again**, as we surely must—here, or in the Infinite God Knoweth Where." (Japhet Bly, in a letter to Ursula Revell, *Winds of Chance* 284)

fortune with you and yours [*farr-chern/toon weth/wi'/wiff/witt 'ee/ya/ye/yer an'/'n' yarrs/yer'n/yourn\theys*]

A parting. "Fortune" is sometimes capitalized to anthropomorphize, or give human form to, the notion of fortune, appropriate for a speaker's wish that Fortune be the addressee's companion.

"Good lad. Bide where you are, Jo, and **Fortune with you and yours**." (Adam Penfeather, saying farewell to Joel Bym, *Black Bartlemy's Treasure* 107)

from whence came you? [*ferm waahnce cayeeme 'ee/ya/ye/yer?*] where are you from?

"Damn you for Villains, who are you? And, **from whence came you?**" (Blackbeard, *General History of the Pyrates* 80 & *The Pirates Own Book* 342)

give my service to __ [*gi'/giff me/myee sarrvice t'/ta/ter __*] give my regards to __; tell __ I said hello

A greeting or parting to a third party communicated to and entrusted for delivery with the addressee.

*[T]hey gave them a boat to row themselves ashore, ordering them to **give their service to** Haman, and to tell him, they would send him his sloop again when they had done with it.* (attribution to Calico Jack Rackham's company, *General History of the Pyrates* 625)

give you good day [*gi'/giff 'ee/ya/ye/yer g' dayee*] wish you a good day

"I give you good day" or "Give you good day" is used at any time of day before evening as both a greeting and a parting.

"[W]e've walked across to stretch our legs, and to **give you good-day**." (Peter Blood, *Captain Blood: His Odyssey* 168)

give you good morning [*gi'/giff 'ee/ya/ye/yer g' marn-in'*] good morning

"We've walked across to **give you good morning** but, faith, it seems we've interrupted some business of yours." (Peter Blood, "Captain Blood" 1:20:56)

give you good night [*gi'/giff 'ee/ya/ye/yer g' nawt/nigheet*] good night

Used at nighttime as both a greeting and a parting, though more frequently as a parting.

"**Give you good-night**, sir." (Peter Blood, *The Fortunes of Captain Blood* 158)

God be with you [*Garrd/Gott/Gud be weth/wi'/wiff/witt 'ee/ya/ye/yer*]

A parting.

"And so, gentlemen, kind friends, **God be with you** and fare ye well." (Japhet Bly, *Winds of Chance* 291)

God speed you [*Garrd/Gott/Gud speed 'ee/ya/ye/yer*]

A parting.

"Good luck, captain! **God speed you** on your honeymoon!" (crew of the *Happy Delivery*, bidding a mocking farewell to their marooned captain and the leprous female prisoner with whom they have sent him off, *The Dealings of Captain Sharkey* "The Blighting of Sharkey" 59)

good fortune attend you [*g' farr-chern/toon arrt-aahnd 'ee/ya/ye/yer*]

A parting. "Fortune" is sometimes capitalized to anthropomorphize, or give human form to, the notion of fortune, appropriate for a speaker's wish that Fortune be the addressee's companion.

"So now, Martin, **good Fortune attend you**." (farewell in letter from Adam Penfeather to Martin Conisby, *Black Bartlemy's Treasure* 164)

good luck to 'ee [*g' loohk t'/ta/ter ya/ye/yer/you*]

A parting.

"Good-bye, matey! **Good luck to 'ee!**" (Long John Silver, "Treasure Island" [1950] 1:34:44)

good luck to 'ee and a fair wind [*g' loohk t'/ta/ter ya/ye/yer/you an'/'n' a farr/fayarr/fayerr win'/wint*]

A parting used to wish another well. Though the phrase refers literally to ideal sailing conditions (a steady wind to propel a vessel in the intended direction), it is understood to propose more broadly a good journey, good fortune, and well-being.

"But **good luck t'ye and a fair wind**, say I!" (Roger Tressady, *Black Bartlemy's Treasure* 302)

good morrow [*g' mahrr-owoo*] good morning

"Morrow" means both "tomorrow" and "morning." Though "good morrow" can be used as a parting at nighttime or bedtime to wish someone a good tomorrow or next morning, it is almost always used as a greeting at the start of the day to wish another a good morning.

> "**Good morrow**, child!" (Ezekiel Penryn, *Winds of Chance* 124)

greeting(s) (to you) [*greetin'(s) (t'/ta/ter 'ee/ ya/ye/yer)*]

> "**Greeting**, Don Federigo! The ship's afire and 'tis an ill thing to burn, so do I bring you kinder death!" (Captain Jo, *Martin Conisby's Vengeance* 116) < "John Silver?! Is that you?" "**Greetings**, Charley. Glad to see me?" > (Charles Noble & Long John Silver, *Dead Man's Chest* 14) "Harr, ah, **greetin's to 'ee**." (Long John Silver, upon first meeting the chief of the island natives, "The Adventures of Long John Silver: The Pink Pearl" 10:57)

heave ahead [*'eave/heeff a'ead/ahayd/'head*] come in; come on in

Though the phrase "heave ahead" is used literally to command another to move forward, it is used figuratively to receive or welcome persons and invite them to enter.

> < "Who knocks?" "The Faithful Friend!" "And who d'ye seek, Faithful Friend?" "Master Adam Penfeather." "Why then, Faithful Friend, **heave ahead**!" > (Joel Bym & Martin Conisby, *Black Bartlemy's Treasure* 78)

here our ways divide [*'ee'arr/'ee'err/'ere/ hee'arr/hee'err arr/owarr wayees dee/der-vyeede*] we go our separate ways

> "Ursula, 'twould seem ... I am to bid thee farewell. **Here our ways divide** ... my course is run, thank God. ..." (Japhet Bly, hopeless in his sick bed, *Winds of Chance* 95)

here's a friend for you [*'ee'arr/'ee'err/'ere/ hee'arr/hee'err is\be a fraynd/frien' farr/fer 'ee/ ya/ye/yer*]

A sincere greeting from one friend to another, and an ironic one otherwise.

> "**Here's a friend for ye**, Bill." (Blind Pew, on entering the Admiral Benbow and meeting Billy Bones for the first time in years, "Treasure Island" [1950] 6:06)

here's luck and a fair wind to you [*'ee'arr/ 'ee'err/'ere/hee'arr/hee'err is\be loohk an'/'n' a farr/ fayarr/fayerr win'/wint t'/ta/ter 'ee/ya/ye/yer*]

Used as both a greeting and a parting.

> "**Here's luck and a fair wind t'ye**, Marty!" (Roger Tressady, upon recognizing Martin Conisby after years of not having seen him, *Martin Conisby's Vengeance* 155)

ho (there) [*ho'oo (tharr/theyarr/theyerr)*] hello (there)

> "**Ho there**, Jeremy!" (Peter Blood, *Captain Blood: His Odyssey* 354)

holloa [*hollo'oo'a*] hello

> "**Holloa**! Mr. Brownlaw, is that you?" (Johnson, *The Pirate Round* 313)

how are 'ee? [*howoo/'ow/'owoo be you/ya/ ye/yer?*] how are you?

> "**How are 'ee**, me bucko?" (Long John Silver, greeting Patch upon entering the Cask & Anchor, "The Adventures of Long John Silver: The Necklace" 7:45)

how are you called? [*howoo/'ow/'owoo be 'ee/ya/ye/yer cawrled?*] what's your name?

> "And **how are ye called**, lad?" (Long John Silver, *Dead Man's Chest* 11)

how are you named? [*howoo/'ow/'owoo is\be 'ee/ya/ye/yer nayeemed?*] what's your name?

> "And such proud madam, such luscious piece, —a voluptuous creature. **How is she named**, my lord?" (Roger Snaith, *Winds of Chance* 316)

how be my matey? [*howoo/'ow/'owoo be me/myee ma'/mayeet-ey?*] how's my buddy?; how are you?

> "And there's Jim. **How be my** little **matey**?" (Long John Silver, "Treasure Island" [1950] 58:34)

how (d'ye) do? [*howoo/'ow/'owoo (do/does 'ee/ya/ye/yer) do?*] how are you?

> "**How do**, Mister Silver?" (Ben Gunn, "Treasure Island" [1950] 1:29:12) "How is't with ye, lad, **how d'ye do** now, I wonder?" (Absalom Troy, greeting Adam Penfeather as Penfeather rises from a drunken slumber, *Adam Penfeather, Buccaneer* 7)

how fares your day? [*howoo/'ow/'owoo farrs/fayarrs/fayerrs ya/yarr/ye/yer/yere/yore dayee?*] Used at any time of day before evening as a greeting.

> "**How fares your day** today, ey?" (Blackbeard, "Blackbeard's Ghost" 44:15)

how goes it? [*howoo/'ow/'owoo gooes/go'ooes ett/'n/'t?*] how's everything going?; how are things coming along?

> < "**How goes it**, Ned?" "All ready and ship-shape, sir." > (Adam Penfeather & Ned Bowser, *Adam Penfeather, Buccaneer* 229)

how is't with you? [*howoo/'ow/'owoo is\be ett/'n/'t weth/wi'/wiff/witt 'ee/ya/ye/yer?*] how are you?; how are you doing?

> "**How is't with ye**, lad, how d'ye do now, I wonder?" (Absalom Troy, greeting Adam Penfeather as Penfeather rises from a drunken slumber, *Adam Penfeather, Buccaneer* 7)

how now [*howoo/'ow/'owoo narr/nowoo*] hello; hey there

> "**How now**, messmate! Won't you come and drink a dram of rum with us?" (Abraham Dawling, urging Barnaby True to join him and his men for a drink, *The Book of Pirates* "The Ghost of Captain Brand" 45)

how's the wind? [*howoo/'ow/'owoo be\is t' win'/wint?*] how are you?; how are things going?

> "And **how's the wind**, shipmate?" (Adam Penfeather, *Black Bartlemy's Treasure* 45)

__ I am [__ *I'ee arrm/em\be*] I am __; my name is __

Used to introduce oneself.

> "Oh, poor **Ben Gunn, I am**." (Ben Gunn, "Treasure Island" [1950] 49:15)

I am called __ [*I'ee arrm/em\be cawrled __*] I am __; my name is __

Used to introduce oneself.

> "**I am called Blood**, sir. Captain Blood." (Peter Blood, *The Fortunes of Captain Blood* 124)

I am the pirate __ [*I'ee arrm/em\be t' py-eeret/errt/raaht __*] I am __; my name is __

Used to introduce oneself. See Section 16.1 for discussion of the pirate's typical reluctance to identify himself as such, and of the circumstances in which he may prove more willing to do so.

> "**I am the pirate Cain**, and was the captain of the *Avenger*!" (Cain, announcing himself to the judge in a court of law in order to testify on his stepson's behalf, *The Pirate* 137, Chap. XVII)

I be __ [*I'ee be __*] I am __; my name is __

Used to introduce oneself.

> "**I be Long John Silver**, lad." (Long John Silver, "Treasure Island" [1998] 33:53)

I be so [*I'ee be so'oo*]

Used to reply affirmatively to the question, "Are you __?" or "You're __, aren't you?"

> < "Are you the Ben that gave a gold cross to my maid Deborah?" "Ay, **I be so**, lady." > (Ursula Revell & Ben, *Winds of Chance* 75)

I bid you farewell for the nonce [*I'ee bed 'ee/ya/ye/yer farr/fayarr/fayerr-waahl farr/fer t' narrnce*] goodbye for now

A parting given in hope or expectation of seeing the addressee again.

> "Howbeit I trust you, Martin, and in **bidding you farewell for the nonce**, subscribe myself [y]our faithful friend and comrade to serve. ..." (letter from Adam Penfeather to Martin Conisby, *Black Bartlemy's Treasure* 164)

I bid you good-day [I'ee bed 'ee/ya/ye/yer g' dayee] I wish you a good day

Used at any time of day before evening as both a greeting and a parting, though the term "bid" is generally associated more closely with partings.

> "I now take pleasure to **bid you Goodday!**" (Adam Penfeather, *Adam Penfeather, Buccaneer* 324)

I come from hell and I'll carry you there presently [I'ee cahm/carrm/coohm ferm 'ell an'/'n' I'ee'ull kerry 'ee/ya/ye/yer tharr/theyarr/theyerr per/praah/pree-sently]

A surly response to any question regarding the speaker's identity, background, or place of origin.

> *When William Bell happened upon the tall, intimidating pirate on the Carolina coast and asked who he was and whence he came, Blackbeard replied that "**he came from Hell and he would carry him [there] presently.**"* (*Villains of All Nations* 153)

I give you best [I'ee gi'/giff 'ee/ya/ye/yer baahst/barrst] congratulations; my compliments

> < "[C]asks of gold—there's six or seven hundred-weight of it at the least. We've brought it with us." "**I give you best.**" > (Yberville & Peter Blood, *Captain Blood Returns* 184–85)

I give you (hearty) greeting [I'ee gi'/giff 'ee/ya/ye/yer ('ahrrt/'eart/hahrrt-y) greetin']

A greeting.

> "Aha, messmates, be welcome to this place o' tribulation; **a martyr gives ye**

right hearty greeting." (Absalom Troy, greeting Adam Penfeather and Joel Bym to the locked cell where he lies prisoner, *Adam Penfeather, Buccaneer* 65)

I have been looking out for you [I'ee 'aff/'ave/ha'/haff been a-lookin' arrt/ou'/owoot farr/fer 'ee/ya/ye/yer]

A milder, more matter-of-fact version of the modern equivalents "I've been looking forward to seeing you" and "I've missed you."

> "Lads, are ye come? I'm glad to see ye; **I have been looking out for ye** for a great while." (John Upton, greeting his fellow company mates, *Lives of the Most Remarkable Criminals* 476)

I hope I see you well [I'ee ho'oope/hoope/'o'oope/'ope I'ee see 'ee/ya/ye/yer waahl] I hope you're well; I hope you're doing well

> "My duty to ye, Master Ormerod. **I hopes I sees you** and your friend **well.**" (Long John Silver, *Porto Bello Gold* 123)

I hope the Lord prospers your handy works [I'ee ho'oope/hoope/'o'oope/'ope t' Larrd prarrspers ya/yarr/ye/yer/yere/yore 'andy/hendy warrks]

A parting.

> *Roberts ... spent two or three merry nights with them, and at parting, said, **he hoped the L[ord] would prosper their handy works.*** (account of Bartholomew Roberts' encounter with two aspiring pirates off Hispaniola's north coast, *General History of the Pyrates* 221)

I joy (heartily) to see you [I'ee joyee/j'y ('ahrrt/'eart/hahrrt-ily) t'/ta/ter see 'ee/ya/ye/yer] very nice to see you

> "Adam lad! Ha, messmate, now **I joy heartily to see thee** or I'm a soused gurnet!" (Absalom Troy, *Adam Penfeather, Buccaneer* 55)

I make you my duty [I'ee mayeeke 'ee/ya/ye/yer me/myee dooty]

A polite, respectful greeting.

"**I makes you my duty**, and says as how, seeing I was one of them vouchsafed a miraculous salvation, I hopes you'll permit me to offer my most humble thanks." (Long John Silver, *Porto Bello Gold* 20)

I pray God preserve you from __ [*I'ee prayee Garrd/Gott/Gud pee/per/pree-sarrve 'ee/ya/ye/yer ferm __*]

A parting used to convey words of care and concern to the addressee. Note a close friend or ally might finish the parting with "yourself" for a good-natured jibe: "I pray God preserve you from yourself."

"Till then, Black Bartlemy, ay, and thereafter, **I pray God preserve you from—Black Bartlemy.**" (Adam Penfeather, *Adam Penfeather, Buccaneer* 282)

I recommend him to your politeness [*I'ee rec'/recker-men' 'im t'/ta/ter ya/yarr/ye/yer/yere/ yore per-lawt/lyeete-ness*]

Spoken on introducing one to a third person.

"And this, ladies, is a young gentleman who has embarked with me to learn the trade of piracy. **I recommend him to your politeness.**" (Henry Morgan, introducing two young ladies to Harry Mostyn, *The Book of Pirates* "With the Buccaneers" 89)

I take my leave of you [*I'ee tayeeke me/myee leef o'\on 'ee/ya/ye/yer*]

A matter-of-fact parting.

"And, now returning to her, **I take my leave of you.**" (Adam Penfeather, *Adam Penfeather, Buccaneer* 280)

I wish you a fair wind ever and always [*I'ee wersh/wesh 'ee/ya/ye/yer a farr/fayarr/fayerr win'/wint ebber/e'er an'/'n' al-way/wayees*]

A parting used to wish another well. Though the phrase refers literally only to ideal sailing conditions, it is understood to propose more broadly a good journey, good fortune, and well-being.

"Howsoever, come life or death, here's Abnegation doth **wish ye a fair wind ever and always**, master." (Abnegation Mings, *Black Bartlemy's Treasure* 319)

if it aren't __ [*eff/eff'n/if'n ett/'n/'t ain't/bain't/ ben't/hain't/i'n't __*] if it isn't __

Used on suddenly recognizing or unexpectedly encountering another. The speaker finishes with the name of the addressee. Note the switched verb "aren't"; see Section 22.3.1 for more on switched verbs.

"Why, why—bleed me! If—**if it aren't**— aye 'tis—**Martin!**" (Roger Tressady, upon recognizing Martin Conisby, *Black Bartlemy's Treasure* 302)

I'll be wishing you a very good day [*I'ee'ull be a-wersh/wesh-in' 'ee/ya/ye/yer a vaah/vay-ry g' dayee*]

The preface "I'll be wishing you" and its air of finality make the usage more appropriate for a parting than a greeting.

"If that's your last word, **I'll be wishing you a very good day.**" (Peter Blood, *Captain Blood Returns* 105)

I'll miss 'ee [*I'ee'ull mess ya/ye/yer/you*] I'll miss you

"**We'll miss 'ee**, Thorpe. And I 'ope I'm forgiven for clappin' you in irons." (Long John Silver, "The Adventures of Long John Silver: The Pink Pearl" 23:04)

I'm all seized over with joy at seeing your friendly physiognomy again [*I'eem awrl seest ober/o'er weth/wi'/wiff/witt joyee/j'y a'/hat a-seein' ya/yarr/ye/yer/yere/yore fraynd/ frien'-ly physio'-nermy\phiz agayn/agin/'gain/ 'gayn*] it's very good to see you again

"**I'm all seized over with joy at seein' your frien'ly physio'nomies again.**" (Thomas Bartholomew Red, greeting his old company mates for the first time in years, "Pirates" 59:17)

I'm glad for to clap eyes on you [*I'eem glarrd farr/fer t'/ta/ter clarrp eye'ees arrn/o' 'ee/ya/ye/ yer*] I'm glad to see you

> "Sir, by cock but **I'm glad for to clap eyes on ee** again, ay, that I am, sir—and my lady too!" (Joel Bym, *Adam Penfeather, Buccaneer* 284)

I'm __, I am [*I'eem __ I'ee arrm/em\be*] I am __; my name is __

Used to introduce oneself.

> "**I'm Mings, I am**, mate!" (Abnegation Mings, introducing himself to Adam Penfeather, *Adam Penfeather, Buccaneer* 16)

I'm pleased to make your acquaintance [*I'eem pleast t'/ta/ter mayeeke ya/yarr/ye/yer/ yere/yore acquayeen/akayn/'kayn/'quayeen- ternce*] pleased to meet you

> "**I'm pleased to make your acquaintance.**" (Ben Gunn, "Treasure Island" [1990] 59:15)

is it you? [*be ett/'n/'t 'ee/ya/ye/yer?*]
is it yourself? [*be ett/'n/'t 'ee/ya/yarr/ye/yer/ yere/yore-seff?*]

Used on suddenly recognizing or unexpectedly encountering another.

> "Ha, **is it you**, shipmate!" (Adam Penfeather, *Black Bartlemy's Treasure* 119) "**Is't yourself**, ma'm Ursula? Here's vasty honour! ... Had I known, they should ha' shaved me." (Japhet Bly, greeting Ursula Revell from his sickbed, *Winds of Chance* 85)

__ is me [*__ 's\be me*] I am __; my name is __

Used to introduce oneself.

> "The bo'sun's mate **Samuel Spraggons is me**, friend—Sam for short, called likewise Smiling Sam—come, come, never scowl on Sam—nobody ever quarrels with the Smiler, I'm friends wi' everyone, I am, friend." (Sam Spraggons, *Black Bartlemy's Treasure* 128)

__ is the name [*__ 's\be t' nayeeme*] I am __; my name is __

Used to introduce oneself.

> "**Captain Sharkey is the name**, gentlemen, and this is Roaring Ned Galloway, the quartermaster of the *Happy Delivery*." (John Sharkey, revealing his identity to the shocked captain and mate of the *Morning Star*, *The Dealings of Captain Sharkey and Other Tales of Pirates* "How the Governor of Saint Kitt's Came Home" 21–22)

it be me [*ett is/'s OR 'tes/'tis me*] it's me

Used on encountering another after a long time, or in circumstances that prevent the other from recognizing the speaker.

> "Sir Henry! **It be me**, Sir Henry! Long John, what saved your little daughter Elizabeth's life." (Long John Silver, "The Adventures of Long John Silver: Execution Dock" 14:53)

it be none other than __ [*ett 's\be OR 'tes/'tis narrn/noohn o'er/udder 'n/thayn\nor __*]

Used on encountering another unexpectedly or after a long time, typically to express joy, surprise, or warm regard.

> "Well, scuttle me if **it be none other'n** me old ship mate, Jimmy Hawkins!" (Long John Silver, *Dead Man's Chest* 293)

it were a pleasure meeting you [*ett/'t warr\ warss/was a plaah/play-zharr a-meetin' 'ee/ya/ ye/yer*] it was a pleasure to meet you

> "**It were a pleasure meetin' ya**, Govn'r." (Henry Morgan, *Dead Man's Chest* 129)

it's a (very) good day\night I'll be wishing you [*ett be\is OR 'tes/'tis a (vaah/vay-ry) g' dayee\nawt/nigheet I'ee'ull be a-wersh/wesh-in' 'ee/ya/ye/yer*]

The suffix "I'll be wishing you" and its air of finality make the usage more appropriate for a parting than a greeting.

> "**It's a very good day we'll be wishing you**, Captain." (Peter Blood, *Captain Blood Returns* 35) "**It's a very good**

night I'll be wishing you, Major, darling." (Peter Blood, *Captain Blood Returns* 265)

a joy [*a joyee/j'y*] a pleasure (to meet you); delighted (to meet you)

   "'S blood, sir, **a joy!**" (Benjamin Trigg, on meeting Luiz Alphonso y Valdez, *Adam Penfeather, Buccaneer* 192)

joy go with you [*joyee/j'y go'oo weth/wi'/ wiff/witt 'ee/ya/ye/yer*]
   A parting.

   "When I am dead, take what ye may and **joy go with thee**, Brother." (Will to his former company mate Japhet Bly, *Winds of Chance* 246)

know me for __ [*knowoo me farr/fer __*] I am __; my name is __
   Used to introduce oneself.

   "Now speak me o' thyself—nay, first **know me for Lovepeace Farrance the gunner**, once cornet of Oliver's horse, and one that helped to slay a wicked king." (Lovepeace Farrance, introducing himself to Ursula Revell, *Winds of Chance* 47)

luck, matey [*loohk, ma'/mayeet-ey*] good luck, friend
   A parting.

   "**Luck, matey**." (William Bones, waving goodbye to Jim Hawkins, "Treasure Island" [1950] 9:17)

luck with you [*loohk weth/wi'/wiff/witt 'ee/ ya/ye/yer*] good luck
   A parting.

   < "I'll to my cabin." "Wouldst be better i' the clean air, Adam. Howbeit go thy ways and **luck with thee** brother." > (Adam Penfeather & Absalom Troy, *Adam Penfeather, Buccaneer* 61)

my compliments to you [*me/myee carrm-plee/pler-mants t'/ta/ter 'ee/ya/ye/yer*]
   A warm, polite greeting.

"My compliments to 'ee, El Toro." (Long John Silver, greeting fellow pirate El Toro Mendoza, "Long John Silver's Return to Treasure Island" 17:00)

my duty (to you) [*me/myee dooty (t'/ta/ter 'ee/ya/ye/yer)*]
   A polite, respectful greeting.

   "**My duty**, Master Ormerod, and I hopes we'll know each other better soon." (Long John Silver, *Porto Bello Gold* 44)
   "**My duty to ye** both, sirs, and always pleased to serve." (Long John Silver, *Porto Bello Gold* 30)

my handle be __ [*me/myee 'and/hend-le be __*] I am __; my name is __
   Used to introduce oneself. "Handle" is another term for "name," as in: "Me handle be Redhands, an' it bain't 'cause they been out in the sun."

   Compare: < "Name." "Adam Mercy, sir." "Oh, so it's you. 'Mercy,' that's a comical **handle** for a blade of fortune, 'Mercy'." > (William Kidd & Adam Mercy, *Captain Kidd* 18:44)

my respects [*me/myee respecks*]
   A polite, respectful greeting.

   "**My respects**, ma'am." (Blackbeard, "Blackbeard's Ghost" 1:41:28)

my service (to you) [*me/myee sarrvice (t'/ta/ ter 'ee/ya/ye/yer)*]
   Used as both a greeting and a parting.

   "Doctor, **my service**." (Long John Silver, greeting Doctor Livesey on entering the stockade, "Treasure Island" [1990] 1:14:46) "**My sarvice to ee** sirs, and which of ee be Master Adam Penfeather, if ye please?" (Joel Bym, *Adam Penfeather, Buccaneer* 63)

name o' __ [*nayeeme o'\on __*] I am __; my name is __
   Used to introduce oneself.

"Name o' Silver, sir—John, says my sponsors in baptism." (Long John Silver, *Porto Bello Gold* 20)

__'s the name [__'s t' *nayeeme*] I am __; my name is __
    Used to introduce oneself.

    < "And how are ye called, lad?" "Morgan! Henry Morgan's the name, Govn'r!" > (Long John Silver & Henry Morgan, *Dead Man's Chest* 11)

nobody more welcome than yourself [*no'oo-bahee/barrdy marr/moor waahl-cahm/carrm/coohm 'n/thayn\nor 'ee/ya/yarr/ye/yer/yere/yore-seff*] welcome; you are most welcome

    "Come away, Hawkins, come and have a yarn with John. **Nobody more welcome than yourself**, my son." (Long John Silver, *Treasure Island* 54, Chap. 10)

our courses'll cross again sometime [*arr carr/coor-ses'll crarss/crost agayn/agin/'gain/'gayn sahm/sarrm/soohm-tawm/tyeeme*]
    A parting given in hope or expectation of seeing the addressee again.

    "**Our courses'll cross again sometime**." (Long John Silver, "Treasure Island" [1934] 1:40:53)

our wakes'll cross again some day [*arr wayeekes'll crarss/crost agayn/agin/'gain/'gayn sahm/sarrm/soohm dayee*]
    A parting given in hope or expectation of seeing the addressee again.

    "Farewell, Ben Gunn. **Our wakes'll cross again some day**, you can lay to *that*." (Long John Silver, *Dead Man's Chest* 7)

pleased I am to meet you [*pleast I'ee arrm/em\be t'/ta/ter meet 'ee/ya/ye/yer*] glad to meet you

    "**Pleased I am to meet you**." (Long John Silver, "Treasure Island" [1990] 33:11)

quite a time since I clapped eyes on you [*quawt/quieete a tawm/tyeeme sence I'ee clarrped eye'ees arrn/o' 'ee/ya/ye/yer*] it's been a long time since I last saw you

"**Quite a time since I've clapped eyes on ya**, matey." (Captain Flint, "The Adventures of Long John Silver: Execution Dock" 11:33)

__'s respects [__'s *respecks*]
    A signal by the speaker to the addressee that he carries word from a third person.

    < "**Mister Blair's respects**, Captain." "Yes, Mister Bowen?" "The *Reaper*'s five miles off and closing." > (Bowen & Morgan Adams, "Cutthroat Island" 53:38)

right pleased to meet you [*rawt/righeet pleast t'/ta/ter meet 'ee/ya/ye/yer*]

    "**Right pleased ta meet ya**, Mister Forrestal." (Ben Gunn, *Dead Man's Chest* 146)

soft repose and pleasant dreams [*sarff/sarrft/soff re-poose/po'oose an'/'n playsant dreams*]
    A parting at bedtime.

    "[S]**oft repose and pleasant dreams** ..." (The Red Rover, wishing a good night to his female prisoners, *The Red Rover* 378)

speak me of yourself [*speak me o'\on 'ee/ya/yarr/ye/yer/yere/yore-seff*] tell me about yourself; tell me what you've been up to; tell me what's been happening

    "Now **speak me o' thyself**. ..." (Lovepeace Farrance, inviting Ursula Revell to tell him about herself, *Winds of Chance* 47)

speak me your tidings [*speak me ya/yarr/ye/yer/yere/yore tawd/tyeed-in's*] tell me what you've been up to; tell me what's been happening

    "Now **speak me your tidings**, Joel." (Adam Penfeather, *Adam Penfeather, Buccaneer* 289)

still alive and kicking [*stell '/er-lawv/lyeeve an'/'n a-keck-in'*] you're still around; I can't believe you're still around
    Often spoken as a question—"Still alive and kickin', Donald Holt, ya pie-lovin' brigand?"

    "Diddler, **still alive an' kickin'**, you old skulk, you." (Thomas Bartholomew Red, seeing a company mate for the first time, "Pirates" 59:27)

stop aboard [*starrp abarrd*]

Used to invite persons aboard a vessel, but also more generally to receive or welcome persons to any place or event, especially for a short time or for a specific purpose. A pirate standing at the threshold of his favorite tavern and recognizing an old friend walking down the street might call out, "Stop abarrd, Tom, you're showin' as you could like a drench."

> Compare: "Why else did ye ever consent to **stop aboard** when we weighed anchor?" (Tim, *The Fortunes of Captain Blood* 168)

such is my name, to be sure [*sarrch/sich/soohch be me/myee nayeeme, t'/ta/ter be sharr/shorr*] that is indeed my name

Used on being addressed by name without proper introduction.

> "**Such is my name, to be sure.**" (Long John Silver, on first hearing Jim Hawkins address him by name, "Treasure Island" [1990] 32:50)

tell what's chanced you [*taahl wharrt's/whorrt's charrnced 'ee/ya/ye/yer*] tell me what you've been up to; tell me what's been happening

> "Come, wet your whistle, Joel, then pipe up and **tell what's chanced you** all this time." (Adam Penfeather, *Adam Penfeather, Buccaneer* 284)

that same [*tharrt sayeeme*]

Used to reply affirmatively to the question, "Are you __?" or "You're __, aren't you?"

> < "You are Samuel Morris, I think?" "**That same**, your honour." > (Adam Penfeather & Sam Morris, *Adam Penfeather, Buccaneer* 215)

__, that's me [__, *tharrt's me*] I am __; my name is __

Used to introduce oneself.

> "Ben Gunn, that's me." (Ben Gunn, introducing himself to Jim Hawkins, "Treasure Island" [1972] 52:08)

__ they calls me [*__ dey/theyee\dem/t'em/them cawrls me*]

__ they names me [*__ dey/theyee\dem/t'em/them nayeemes me*] I am __; my name is __

Used to introduce oneself.

> "**Long John Silver, they calls me.**" (Long John Silver, "Treasure Island" [1934] 25:34)
> "**Billy 'Bones,' they names me.** Capt'n Billy Bones, o' the Ancient Brotherhood, like." (Billy Doyle, introducing himself to Alan Lewrie, *The Gun Ketch* 159)

'tis I [*ett 's\be OR 'tes I'ee*]

A way of presenting oneself to one or more persons one has met previously.

> "Aye, me hearties, **'tis I.**" (Thomas Bartholomew Red, greeting his old company mates for the first time in years, "Pirates" 58:51)

'tis joy to see you again [*ett 's\be OR 'tes joyee/j'y t'/ta/ter see 'ee/ya/ye/yer agayn/agin/'gain/'gayn*] nice to see you again; it's a pleasure to see you again

> "Japhet, old messmate, **'tis joy to see thee again!** Come alongside ..." (Will, *Winds of Chance* 207)

(so) 'tis yourself [*(so'oo) ett/it/'n/'t 's\be OR 'tes 'ee/ya/yarr/ye/yer/yere/yore-seff*] it's you

Used on suddenly recognizing or unexpectedly encountering another.

> "So, **'tis yourself** again, Madam Mischief! What do ye here?" (Japhet Bly, encountering Ursula Revell on deck of the *Joyful Deliverance*, *Winds of Chance* 64)

to you [*t'/ta/ter 'ee/ya/ye/yer*]

An element of many a greeting and parting, and a pair of suffix words that can be added to almost any expression of goodwill to form a greeting or parting.

"Good morning to ye, ma'am." (Peter Blood, *Captain Blood: His Odyssey* 271)
"A safe voyage home to you, Colonel, darling." (Peter Blood, *Captain Blood: His Odyssey* 290)

top of the day to you [*tarrp o'\on t' dayee t'/ta/ter 'ee/ya/ye/yer*] good day to you
   Used as both a greeting and a parting.

   "Top o' the day to ya, Captain Silver." (Ben Gunn, *Dead Man's Chest* 277)

we will meet again [*we well meet agayn/ agin/'gain/'gayn*]
   A parting that might be delivered amiably or threateningly.

   "We will meet again." (Davy Jones, bidding farewell at completion of ride, "Pirates of the Caribbean" Disney attraction [2006])

welcome aboard [*waahl-cahm/carrm/coohm abarrd*]
   Used to invite persons aboard a vessel, but also more generally to receive or welcome persons to any place or event.

   "Welcome aboard!" (Long John Silver, greeting Trip Fenner as Fenner rides up to Purity Pinker's tavern on a horse, "The Adventures of Long John Silver: The Eviction" 25:30)

what EPITHET be you? [*wharrt/whorrt ... be 'ee/ya/ye/yer?*]
   A rude, nasty way of greeting another. See Chapter 9 for a comprehensive list of epithets.

   "Eh, what cursed younker be you, and what doing, eh, kid, eh?" (Abner, kicking Adam Penfeather's sleeping body, *Adam Penfeather, Buccaneer* 8)

what be your name? [*wharrt/whorrt be ya/yarr/ ye/yer/yere/yore nayeeme?*] what's your name?

   "What be your name, gal?" (Blackbeard, "Blackbeard the Pirate" 6:38)

what do you here? [*wharrt/whorrt d'/does 'ee/ya/ye/yer 'ee'arr/'ee'err/'ere/hee'arr/hee'err?*] what are you doing here?

"So, 'tis yourself again, Madam Mischief! **What do ye here?**" (Japhet Bly, encountering Ursula Revell on deck of the *Joyful Deliverance*, *Winds of Chance* 64)

what do you seek (here)? [*wharrt/whorrt d'/does 'ee/ya/ye/yer seek ('ee'arr/'ee'err/'ere/ hee'arr/hee'err)?*]

what do you want here? [*wharrt/whorrt d'/does 'ee/ya/ye/yer warrnt 'ee'arr/'ee'err/'ere/ hee'arr/hee'err?*]
   A brusque way of greeting another.

   "What d'ye seek, Murray? Come to look us over?" (John Flint, *Porto Bello Gold* 129) "What do you seek here?" (Blackbeard, shouting over to an approaching privateer vessel sent to destroy him, *The Book of Pirates* "Jack Ballister's Fortunes" 144) "Boy, what do you want here, boy?" (Captain Kidd's comrade, confronting Tom Chist as Chist stumbles upon Kidd and his comrades burying treasure, *The Book of Pirates* "Tom Chist and the Treasure Box" 104)

what doing? [*wharrt/whorrt a-doin'?*] (1) what are you doing?; what are you up to? (2) what's up?; what's going on?

   "Eh, what cursed younker be you, and **what doing**, eh, kid, eh?" (Abner, kicking Adam Penfeather's sleeping body, *Adam Penfeather, Buccaneer* 8)

what ho? [*wharrt/whorrt ho'oo?*] what's up?; what's going on?

   "What ho, gentlemen?" (Elizabeth Marlowe, *The Pirate Round* 234)

what might you call yourself? [*wharrt/whorrt mawt/migheet 'ee/ya/ye/yer cawrl 'ee/ya/yarr/ye/ yer/yere/yore-seff?*] what's your name?

   "What might ya call yourself, mate?" (Ben Gunn, "Treasure Island" [1950] 50:43)

what might your name be? [*wharrt/whorrt mawt/migheet ya/yarr/ye/yer/yere/yore nayeeme be?*] what's your name?

"And now, **what might your name be?**" (Absalom Troy, on meeting Adam Penfeather, *Adam Penfeather, Buccaneer* 5)

what was you wanting? [*wharrt/whorrt warss\warr/were 'ee/ya/ye/yer a-warrnt-in'?*] what do you want?

A brusque way of greeting another.

> Compare: "**What was you wanting**, in the article of guns?" (Henry Nagel, *The Pirate Round* 179)

what would you (have)? [*wharrt/whorrt wood 'ee/ya/ye/yer ('aff/'ave/ha'/haff)?*] what do you want?

A brusque way of greeting another.

> "Well, who the devil are you and **what would you?**" (Japhet Bly, upon first setting eyes on Matthew Swayne, *Winds of Chance* 266) "Why then, in the Fiend's name **what would ye have?**" (Adam Penfeather, *Black Bartlemy's Treasure* 48)

what's acting? [*wharrt/whorrt is\be hactin'?*] what's happening?; what's going on?; what's up?

> "**What's acting?**" (battery captain on Quail Island, demanding an update from a newly arrived reinforcement, *The Pirate Round* 350)

what's doing? [*wharrt/whorrt is\be a-doin'?*] what's going on?; what's happening?

> "Ha, by my deathless soul—**what's doing** yonder?" (Resolution Day, glimpsing out of the corner of his eye the pursued ship take on sudden speed and assume an offensive position, *Martin Conisby's Vengeance* 104) "Ods wounds, **what's doing?**" (Benjamin Trigg, seeing his friend Adam Penfeather pummeled to the ground, *Adam Penfeather, Buccaneer* 72)

what's the word? [*wharrt/whorrt is\be t' warrd?*] what's up?; what's going on?

"Well, **what's the word?**" (Abnegation Mings, sitting down across a campfire from Martin Conisby, *Black Bartlemy's Treasure* 30)

what's to do (here)? [*wharrt/whorrt is\be t'/ta/ter do ('ee'arr/'ee'err/'ere/hee'arr/hee'err)?*] what's going on?; what's happening? what's up?

> "Why, smite me stiff in gore if y' aren't all of a quake and pallid as a shark's belly! What's amiss, man, **what's to do?**" (Benjamin Trigg, seeing inexplicable anxiety and agitation in Adam Penfeather's face, *Adam Penfeather, Buccaneer* 245) "How now, my hearty! **What's to do here?**" (Benny Willitts, *The Book of Pirates* "The Ruby of Kishmoor" 235)

what's your trouble? [*wharrt/whorrt is\be ya/yarr/ye/yer/yere troohble?*] what's your problem?; what's your story?

A gruff challenge to another to speak up and explain himself.

> "**What's your trouble**, Murray?" (John Flint, *Porto Bello Gold* 123)

who be you? [*'oo be 'ee/ya/ye/yer?*] who are you?

> "Aha! And **who be you?**" (Abnegation Mings, *Black Bartlemy's Treasure* 30) < "Hi, Captain, won't you dance with me?" "**Who be you?**" > (bride at wedding celebration & an uninvited Blackbeard, *The Book of Pirates* "Jack Ballister's Fortunes" 136)

who be you, who and what? [*'oo be 'ee/ya/ye/yer, 'oo an'/'n' wharrt/whorrt?*] who are you?

> "**Who be you**, bully, **who and what?**" (Roger Tressady, *Martin Conisby's Vengeance* 155)

who might you be? [*'oo mawt/migheet 'ee/ya/ye/yer be?*] who are you?

> "An' **who might ye be**, I'm askin'?" (Billy Doyle, on first encountering Alan Lewrie, *The Gun Ketch* 159)

you be? [*ya/ye/yer be?*] who are you?

< "You be?" "Jim Hawkins, sir, new cabin boy of the *Hispaniola*." > (Long John Silver & Jim Hawkins, "Treasure Island" [1998] 34:06)

you come in a fair breeze [ya/ye/yer cahm/carrm/coohm i'/'n a farr/fayarr/fayerr breeze] it's fortunate that you've come; it's good to see you

"You come in a fair breeze, Master Hawkins." (Israel Hands, "Treasure Island" [1934] 31:30)

you might call me __ [ya/ye/yer mawt/migheet cawrl me __] I am __; my name is __
Used to introduce oneself.

"What you mought call me? **You mought call me captain**." (Billy Bones, *Treasure Island* 4, Chap. 1)

you need not fear meeting with a friend, whenever you meet with me again [ya/ye/yer need narrt fee-arr/err a-meetin' weth/wi'/wiff/witt' a fraynd/frien', waahn-effer/'ver 'ee/ya/ye/yer meet weth/wi'/wiff/witt me agayn/agin/'gain/'gayn]

A parting especially appropriate between two persons who until recently were enemies, strangers, or remote acquaintances; or when one might appreciate a warm, explicit assurance of friendship from the other.

"[You] need not fear meeting with a friend, whenever [you] me[e]t with [us] again." (members of Edward Low's company, bidding farewell to a well-liked prisoner, *Pirates of the New England Coast* 193)

you see before you __ [ya/ye/yer see afarr/afore/befarr/'farr/'fore 'ee/ya/ye/yer __] I am __; my name is __
A slightly dramatic or disarmingly facetious way of introducing oneself.

< "Why, yes, —but first tell me your story and how you come to know Captain Japhet." "Well, ma'm, **you see afore you Jeremy Jervey**, as sailed out o' Falmouth twenty odd year ago as gunner's mate aboard the *Falcon*, with Captain Amos Trevoe and seventy-odd stout lads and all of 'em dead." > (Ursula Revell & Jeremy Jervey, *Winds of Chance* 210)

your humble servant [ya/yarr/ye/yer/yere/yore hoohm/'um-ble sarrvint]
A polite, respectful greeting, used often in conjunction with an introduction.

"**Your humble servant**, madam!" (Barnabas Rokeby, upon meeting Ursula Revell for the first time, *Winds of Chance* 12)

CHAPTER 2

Calls

The seafaring life is one of sprawling distances, and ships are big places. As a result, pirates often speak to each other across wide spaces: A look-out in a crow's nest might call out to the main deck on sighting a black-sailed ship. A gunner might call up from the lower deck to report she's finally sailed within range. And a first mate, after nervously clearing his throat, might call to his captain on realizing that the foreboding ship is somehow identical—except for the color of her canvas and the absence of anyone on board—to the ship they mercilessly burned and sank the day before.

This chapter introduces "calls"—words and phrases called out to alert another that he is being addressed. "Ahoy" is a familiar example.

Note that many calls are also used as greetings. In modern English, someone trying to get a passerby's attention might call out "hey" or "hello," then—realizing the passerby is an old friend—might repeat the same word (albeit likely with a warmer tone and sharper inflection) as a greeting. Similarly, calls like "ahoy," "hallo," and "ho there" do double duty in pirate speech as both calls and greetings, depending on context. See Chapter 1 for a full discussion and list of greetings and partings.

☠

---

aft there [*arrft/haft tharr/theyarr/they-err*] you, back there; hey there, in the aft part of the vessel

Used to call back toward the rear of a vessel, and often to the helmsman.

> "**Aft there!** Pass the word for Absalom Troy and his mates!" (Japhet Bly, *Winds of Chance* 113)
> "**Aft there**. Ahoy, Abnegation!"

(Absalom Troy, *Adam Penfeather, Buccaneer* 76)

ahoy (there) [*ahooy/ahoyee (tharr/theyarr/theyerr)*] hey; hello (there)

> < "**Ahoy**, doctor! We have Jim Hawkins. **Ahoy**, doctor!" "**Ahoy!**" > (Long John Silver & Doctor Livesey, calling out to each other from opposite sides

of the stockade fence, "Treasure Island" [1950] 1:18:27) **"Ahoy there.** I say, lad! Ye wouldn't be of a mind to be helpin' an old seafarin' man ashore, would ya?" (Long John Silver, *Dead Man's Chest* 11)

all hands [*awrl 'ands/'an's/han's*] everyone
Used by a captain, quartermaster, or other senior member of a company to address the entire crew.

> "**All hands** to the boats!" (Jack Sparrow, "Pirates of the Caribbean: The Curse of the Black Pearl" 1:47:46)

aloft there [*err-larrft tharr/theyarr/theyerr*] you, up there; hey, up there
Used to call out to someplace above a speaker's position, especially to a vessel's rigging from its deck, or to a ship's deck from a boat alongside.

> "Oho, Cap'n, **aloft there**! Us be thy lads o' the old *Deliverance*! Cap'n ahoy!" (crew of the *Deliverance*, calling out for Japhet Bly from a path below him, *Winds of Chance* 366)

at the windlass [*a'/hat t' win'/wint-lass*]
Used to call out to any crewman manning a vessel's anchor. A windlass, like a capstan, is a drum or winch around which the anchor line or cable is wrapped. Those manning an anchor can lift it by turning the windlass, which has the effect of pulling in the anchor line. A windlass is typically positioned horizontally and turned by cranking or pumping one or more levers, while a capstan is positioned vertically and turned by being pushed by a ship's hands walking around it in a circle.

> "**At the windlass**, stand by! Man the braces and square away!" (Ezekiel Penryn, *Winds of Chance* 108)

below there [*b'lowoo tharr/theyarr/theyerr*] down there; hey, down there
Used to call out to a person somewhere physically below the speaker's position, especially from an upper deck to a lower, from

the main deck to below decks, or from a larger vessel to a boat alongside, and especially by an officer or person of authority within a company to one or more hands.

> "**Below there**! Belvedere, ahoy—go about, or she'll rake us ..." (Resolution Day, *Martin Conisby's Vengeance* 104)

between decks [*'tween\betwixt/'twixt dacks*]
Used to call out to someone in the space between a vessel's decks.

> "Silence there, **between decks**!" (Billy Bones, "Treasure Island" [1934] 10:41)

bold adventurers all [*bol'/boold/bo'oold a'van/a'ven/arrdvan/arrdven/'van/'ven-charr/ terr-arrs awrl*]
Used especially by a captain or other leading figure to address members of a company, particularly to preface words of inspiration or encouragement.

> "Shipmates and **Bold Adventurers all**, yonder come pirate rogues to destroy us—if they can." (Absalom Troy, *Adam Penfeather, Buccaneer* 119)

comrades all [*carrmrades awrl*]
Used especially by a captain or other leading figure to address members of a company, particularly to preface words of inspiration or encouragement.

> "So fight it is, **comrades all**, and a cheer for Captain Jo—ha, Joanna!" (Resolution Day, *Martin Conisby's Vengeance* 112)

fore and aft [*farr an'/'n' arrft/haft*] everybody
The phrase literally means "front and back" or "from front to back," but is used to call the attention of everyone who hears.

> "Silence, **fore an' aft**!" (Long John Silver, "Treasure Island" [1990] 1:39:09)

forward there [*farr/forr-ad/ard/edd/erd tharr/ theyarr/theyerr*] you there, in the forward part of the vessel
The phrase can be used to call out to anyone forward of the speaker—that is, anyone

standing closer to the front of a vessel. However, the phrase is better known as a captain's call to officers or hands aboard a vessel in anticipation of issuing instructions to them, as a captain typically commands a vessel from an aft position (usually while standing on or pacing the poop deck or the quarterdeck).

> "Forrard there! Stand by, my lads, I'm with ye!" (Absalom Troy, shouting words of encouragement during a wreck-threatening storm, *Adam Penfeather, Buccaneer* 160)

hallo (there) [*hallo'oo (tharr/theyarr/theyerr)*] hello (there); hey (there)

> "Hallo, Ralph! that chap seems to have taken a sudden fancy to you, or he must be an old acquaintance." (Bloody Bill, on observing one of the native chiefs suddenly recognize Ralph Rover and greet him by rubbing noses, *The Coral Island* 237–38) "Hallo there! one o' you tumble up and light the cabin lamp, and send that boy aft to the captain—sharp!" (pirate, *The Coral Island* 203–04)

hands [*'ands/'an's/han's*]
Used to call out to members of a company or crew.

> "Hands, stand ready to come about!" (Thomas Marlowe, *The Guardship* 278)

here (you) [*'ee'arr/'ee'err/'ere/hee'arr/hee'err ('ee/ya/ye/yer)*] hey (you)

> "Here, you great sons of whores, listen here!" (Henry Nagel, *The Pirate Round* 212) "Here, you, here's the captain. Show some sodding respect." (seaman aboard Plymouth Prize, upbraiding Ezekiel Ripley for keeping his back turned on the approaching captain, *The Guardship* 243)

hey (there) [*heyee/'eyee (tharr/theyarr/theyerr)*]

> "Hey! Hey there! Avast!" (Long John Silver, yelling after the fleeing Jim Hawkins, "Treasure Island" [1950] 1:33:05)

hillo [*hillo'oo/'illo/'illo'oo*] hello; hey

> "Why, hillo! look here now: this ain't lucky! You've gone and cut this out of a Bible." (Long John Silver, *Treasure Island* 163, Chap. 29)

ho (there) [*ho'oo (tharr/theyarr/theyerr)*] hey; hello

> "What Ezekiel—ho, Zeke! Aft here, Zeke!" (Lovepeace Farrance, calling Ezekiel Penryn over to speak with Ursula Revell, *Winds of Chance* 47) "Ho there, shipmate." (Long John Silver, *Porto Bello Gold* 48)

hoa [*ho'oo'a*] hey; hello

> "Hoa! On deck! Deck there! You've sprung a bloody plank! Hoa!" (Thomas Marlowe, *The Pirate Round* 276)

holloa [*hollo'oo'a*] hey; hello

> "Holloa! Mr. Brownlaw, is that you?" (Johnson, *The Pirate Round* 313)

in the waist [*i'/'n t' waisht/wayeest/wayeesht*]
Used to call out to the common members of a crew, who—when working—are generally positioned either in the waist (the middle part of a vessel's upper deck, forward of the quarterdeck and to the rear of the forecastle) or up in the rigging.

> "In the waist! Mr. Rakestraw, we shall be falling off a bit, make ready at the braces. Gunners, you know your duty!" (Thomas Marlowe, *The Guardship* 348)

men and messmates all [*men an'/'n' mass/mesh-mayeetes awrl*]
Used especially by a captain or other leading figure to address members of a company, particularly to preface words of inspiration or encouragement.

> "Men and messmates all, in especial such as be new among us, hearkee: This ship is the *Joyful Deliverance*, pledged to fight all slaveships, no matter what flag they fly, and free all slaves." (Japhet Bly, *Winds of Chance* 68)

oho [*oho'oo*] hey; hello

"Having beached their boat, they fell to letting off their calivers and pistols and hallooing: 'Oho, Captain!' they roared, 'Bartlemy, ahoy!'" (Adam Penfeather, *Black Bartlemy's Treasure* 90)

on deck [*arrn/o' dack*] you there, on deck; attention, those on deck; those on deck, be advised

"**On deck!** Sail, ho! One point abaft the starboard beam!" (lookout aboard *Elizabeth Galley*, *The Pirate Round* 256)

shipmates (all) [*shep/shi'-mayeetes (awrl)*] Used especially by a captain or other leading figure to address members of a company.

"**Shipmates**, Divine Providence has seen fit to deliver this here vessel from the tyranny of your degenerate and Dago masters." (Thomas Bartholomew Red, addressing the newly liberated crew of the Spanish galleon *Neptune*, "Pirates" 50:43) "**Shipmates** and Bold Adventurers **all**, yonder come pirate rogues to destroy

us—if they can." (Absalom Troy, *Adam Penfeather, Buccaneer* 119)

stand by [*stan'/starrn'/starrnd byee*] give me your attention; listen up

"Stand by" is used most often to mean "stand ready" or "be prepared," typically shouted to one's crew or comrades in anticipation of some action. However, the phrase is also a call used to secure the attention of a group of persons, usually before a speech or some other lengthy or particularly meaningful statement.

"Comrades all, **stand by**!" (Japhet Bly, addressing for the first time the newly freed slaves aboard a galley taken by his company, *Winds of Chance* 77)

what [*wharrt/whorrt*] hey; hello

"**What**, Purdy man, stand by with that water lest the lady swoon." (Japhet Bly, *Winds of Chance* 79) "Japhet, ahoy! **What** Japhet man!" (crew of the *Deliverance*, calling out for Japhet Bly, *Winds of Chance* 366)

CHAPTER 3

Flourishes

Pirate talk is strong talk. Pirates make statements in life-and-death situations and for high stakes. They exhort each other to action—typically based on little more than strength of character and sword-arm. As a result, statements of fact are rarely made without smaller statements—interjected at the starts, middles, and/or ends of sentences—that add emphasis or commentary. These smaller statements we'll call "flourishes."

For example, one might say, "Tharr's the treasure map," and leave it at that. Or one might instead say, "**Shiver me timbers**, tharr's the treasure map." By adding the flourish, the speaker communicates not simply his observation, but also (a) its significance, (b) its effect on him, (c) the certainty with which he made the observation, and (d) the conviction with which he's now communicating it. That's a lot of meaning from only a couple of words.

Pirates also put flourishes in the middles of sentences ("There's the treasure map, **look'ee**, an' the treasure too") and at the ends ("Tharr's the treasure map, **no mistake**"). And, of course, they can combine more than one flourish in a given sentence: "**Shiver me timbers**, there's the treasure map, **look'ee**, an' the treasure too, **no mistake**."

Flourishes are ways for pirates to modify, qualify, draw attention to, reinforce, or otherwise supplement what they're saying. There are various types:

- appeals for the listener's attention ("hark'ee now")
- appeals for the listener's belief ("I dare swear")
- exclamations ("hillo!")
- requests for affirmation ("all right?" "savvy?")
- catch-alls ("and all," "and belike")
- categoricals ("first and last")

- conditioners ("if you ask me," "I take it")
- diminishers ("like")
- meta-commentaries ("as it were")

Below is a comprehensive list of flourishes, set out in alphabetical order. For other auxiliary-type words often used to amplify a speaker's meaning, see Chapter 6: Oaths and Chapter 7: Curses.

For a list of flourishes, oaths, and curses organized by the position in the sentence in which they actually have been used by pirates in history, fiction, and film—*i.e.* start, middle, end—see Appendix A: Openers, Middlers, & Closers.

☠

add to this [*add t'/ta/ter dis/t'is*] moreover, furthermore; in addition

> "Capt. Harris ... had routed the Spaniards away from the town and gold mines of Santa Maria, so that they had never attempted to settle there since. **Add to this**, that the Indian neighborhood ... were fast friends and ready to receive and assist us." (William Dampier, explaining why his company would have prospered had they stayed to establish a gold-mining operation at Santa Maria, *A New Voyage Round the World* 85)

ah [*arrgh*]

Used to draw attention to what is about to be said, particularly before statements expressing conviction, surprise, discovery, pleasure, or contentment.

> "**Ah**, Bill, Bill, we have seen a sight of times, us two, since I lost them two talons." (Black Dog, holding up his mutilated hand, *Treasure Island* 11, Chap. 2)

ah-harr [*arr-hahrr*]

Used to preface any statement, especially a firm assertion, similar to "you know what" or "I'll tell you what," or to preface a command, instruction, exclamation, or any sharp or definitive statement, similar to "hey" or "now."

> "**Ah-harr**, Mistress Alvina, have a little gulp." (Blackbeard, giving Alvina another drink, "Blackbeard the Pirate" 31:41)

aha [*aharr*]

Used to express surprise, pleasure, or sudden discovery or understanding.

> < "Blowpipe?" "Aye—this! The Indians use 'em longer than this—aye, six foot I've seen 'em, but then, Lord! they'll blow ye a dart from eighty to a hundred paces sometimes, whereas I never risk shot farther away than ten or twenty at most; the nearer the surer, **aha**!" > (Martin Conisby & John, discussing John's poison-dart blowpipe, *Martin Conisby's Vengeance* 183)

ain't it? [*aren't/bain't/ben't/hain't/i'n't ett/'n?*] isn't it?

> "See here, now, Hawkins, here's a blessed hard thing on a man like me, now, **ain't it**?" (Long John Silver, *Treasure Island* 45, Chap. 8)

airr you know what; I'll tell you what

Used to preface any statement, especially a firm assertion.

> "**Airr**, medallion there be, but medallion I ain't got nor knows who has." (Long John Silver, "Long John Silver's Return to Treasure Island" 8:20)

alack (now) [*aleck (narr/nowoo)*] alas; unfortunately

"Free? **Alack**, ma'm, you forget how a moment's folly hath clamped on me the shackles matrimonial ..." (Japhet Bly, *Winds of Chance* 218) < "Be dumb, sir! I have sent for you to demand that you turn back this ship and instantly restore me to ... to my friends." "And your woman, gracious lady?" "And my woman, of course." "**Alack now!** I fear this is out o' the question." > (Ursula Revell & Japhet Bly, *Winds of Chance* 38)

alas [*alarss*] unfortunately; regrettably

"Ma'm, according to the rules of our fellowship and my sworn oath as Captain, whatsoever falleth prey to us of the *Deliverance* must be shared, and these fellows, rum-beguiled, do look on you as plunder, as indeed you are, **alas**!" (Japhet Bly, *Winds of Chance* 81)

all right [*awrl rawt/righeet*] indeed; that's for sure

"It was Flint's idea to run off, **all right**." (Ben Gunn, *Dead Man's Chest* 137)

all right? [*awrl rawt/righeet?*] understand?; are we clear?

"Listen, son, we don't expect ya to have that chart in your pocket, but I'll wager you've got the spot where that gold's buried burned into that little noggin of yours like a cow brand, **all right?**" (George Merry, "Treasure Island" [1998] 51:16)

all told [*awrl tol'/toold/to'oold/tolt*] ultimately; in the end

"You're a good boy, or I'm mistook; but you're on'y a boy, **all told**." (Ben Gunn, *Treasure Island* 100, Chap. 19)

amen, so be it [*arr/ayee-man, so'oo be ett/'n/'t*] Used after an assertive or forthright statement, especially of one's views, beliefs, or desires.

"Well, now I tell you, I never seen good come o' goodness yet. Him as strikes first is my fancy; dead men don't bite; them's my views—**amen, so be it**." (Israel Hands, *Treasure Island* 141, Chap. 26)

and a pity it is [*an'/'n' a petty/pi'y ett/'n/'t be* OR *'tes/'tis*] unfortunately; regrettably

"I'll finish with 'em at the island, as soon's the blunt's on board, **and a pity it is**." (Long John Silver, *Treasure Island* 60, Chap. 11)

and all [*an'/'n' awrl*] and everything; and stuff
Used to make a preceding statement more expansive or emphatic. The phrase signals the speaker's intention to convey the sense of his statement rather than the precise meaning of its terms, or to include things comparable to and not limited to that which she has specifically identified or described.

"It was a master surgeon, him that ampytated me—out of college **and all**—Latin by the bucket, and what not." (Long John Silver, *Treasure Island* 57, Chap. 11)

and be done (with it) [*an'/'n' be doohn (weth/ wi'/wiff/witt ett/'n/'t)*] and get it over with; and get it done already
Used in urging another to do something that renders unnecessary something else more involved or demanding, or that is the optimal or appropriate thing to do despite the addressee's refusal or reluctance to do it.

"Hang 'em **and be done** ... Let's do 't forthright ... Up, ye mutinous lubbers!" (crew aboard the *Joyful Deliverance*, *Winds of Chance* 56) "You just take my orders, Cap'n Hawkins, and we'll sail slap in **and be done with it**." (Israel Hands, *Treasure Island* 142, Chap. 26)

and belike [*an'/'n' b'-lawk/lyeeke*]
This phrase literally means "and probably" or "and in all likelihood" but is used as a closer to convey that the preceding statement is mere suggestion, understatement, deliberate imprecision, or figurative meaning. A modern speaker might use "or something" or "and all" in the same context.

"Why not a woman's love, comrade, why not good works, rank **and belike**—children to honour your memory?" (Adam Penfeather, *Black Bartlemy's Treasure* 329)

and bloody end to them as shall gainsay me [*an'/'n' bloohd/bluh'/blutt-y aynd t'/ta/ter dem/'em/ t'em\dey/they as shawrl gayeen-sayee me*] and anyone who says different can go to hell

To gainsay someone is to challenge, contradict, or doubt him. The phrase "bloody end to them" is a curse (listed as "bloody end to you" in Chapter 7: Curses), but "bloody end to them as shall gainsay me" is a flourish, as it is used to convey the speaker's conviction rather than to wish harm on another.

> "I'm telling ye she's our ship, **and bloody end to them as shall gainsay us!**" (Toby Drew, *Adam Penfeather, Buccaneer* 212)

and fair enough [*an'/'n' farr/fayarr/fayerr enarrff/enow/'nough*]

Used to endorse a preceding statement (or its subject) as fair, equitable, or acceptable.

> "I got eight hundred pounds for my leg— **and fair enough**, if you asks me." (Long John Silver, *Porto Bello Gold* 65)

and glad of it [*an'/'n' glayd o'\on ett/'n/'t*]

Used to characterize the speaker or some specified person as pleased with, or as a result of, the subject of a preceding statement.

> "Will ye dare preach me forgiveness, you of 'em all? You, Zeke, that I've seen ere now all spattered wi' blood o' your foes **and glad of it**; you that is ever foremost in fight and readiest with steel or shot or hangman's noose." (Japhet Bly, *Winds of Chance* 110)

and I know it [*an'/'n' I'ee knowoo ett/'n/'t*]

Used to emphasize the truth or certainty of a preceding statement, or to make clear the speaker's knowledge or awareness thereof.

> "I'm as good as pork, **and I knows it**." (Ben Gunn, "Treasure Island" [1950] 49:55)

and more [*an'/'n' marr/moor*] moreover; furthermore; in addition

> < "So you've slaved at an oar, then?" "Aye, shipmate!" "Endured the shame of stripes and nakedness and filth?" "Aye, shipmate. **And more**, I've fought for my life on the Inca Death-stone ere now, as you may see by my ears if you know aught of the Maya Indians. > (Martin Conisby & Adam Penfeather, *Black Bartlemy's Treasure* 47)

and more's the pity [*an'/'n' marr's/moor's t' petty/pi'y*] I'm sorry to say; unfortunately

> < "You ... you will dare abduct me?" "Ay, ay, ma'm, abduct it is **and more's the pity**." > (Ursula Revell & Japhet Bly, *Winds of Chance* 19)

and no bones about it [*an'/'n' no'oo boones/ bo'oones abarrt/abowoot/'barrt/'bout/'bowoot ett/'n*] no doubt about it; that's for sure

> "We're willing to submit, if we can come to terms, **and no bones about it**." (Long John Silver, *Treasure Island* 106, Chap. 20)

and no mistake [*an'/'n' no-oo mee/meh-stayeeke*] that's a fact; that's for sure; definitely

> "Cut me a quid, as 'll likely be the last, lad; for I'm for my long home, **and no mistake**." (Israel Hands, *Treasure Island* 141, Chap. 26)

and nothing more [*an'/'n' nuff/nutt-in' marr/ moor*] and nothing else; and that's all

> "She's a swivel gun on 'er poop, **and nothin' more**." (Alacan the Turk, *Dead Man's Chest* 52)

and now you see [*an'/'n' narr/nowoo 'ee/ya/ ye/yer see*]

Used to proceed logically or for purposes of persuasion from one or more statements to a summary or concluding statement.

> "I've been always good to you. Never a month but I've given you a silver fourpenny for yourself. **And now you see**, mate, I'm pretty low, and deserted by

all; and, Jim, you'll bring me one noggin of rum, now, won't you, matey?" (Billy Bones, *Treasure Island* 14, Chap. 3)

and quite right [*an'/'n' quawt/quieet rawt/ righeet*] and that's right

> "All he thinks of, says you, is a lot of villains as has likely slaughtered his messmates and looted his ship, **and quite right**." (Long John Silver, *Porto Bello Gold* 66)

and small blame either [*an'/'n' smawrl blayeeme eeder/ee'er/iyder/iy'er\needer/nee'er/ neither/nyder/ny'er*]

> "I know it and the lads forrad know it, and Belvedere he knows it and is mighty feared of her **and small blame either**— aye, and mayhap you'll be afeard of her when you know her better." (Diccon, *Martin Conisby's Vengeance* 69)

and small wonder [*an'/'n' smawrl woohnd/wunner*] and with good reason; and no wonder

> < "Rogues and villains all! Ay, and villainous as their looks!" "Their looks? Ay, **and small wonder**, for, most dainty ma'm, these be men, like those you may read of in the Scriptures, that have come out of great tribulation ..." > (Ursula Revell & Japhet Bly, *Winds of Chance* 40)

and so be done [*an'/'n' so'oo be doohn*] and get it over with; and get it done already

Used in urging another to do something that renders unnecessary something else more involved or demanding, or that is the optimal or appropriate thing to do despite the addressee's refusal, reluctance, or disinclination to do it.

> "I am here to say that since you are so desperate earnest to be wed eftsoons,— wed you I will, **and so be done**." (Japhet Bly, *Winds of Chance* 51)

and such [*an'/'n' sarrch/sich/soohch*]
and that [*an'/'n' tharrt*] and so on; etcetera

> "He asked to be carried away, to his secret place, where he can pray **and such**." (Henry Nagel, *The Pirate Round* 209) "I want to go into that cabin, I do. I want their pickles and wines, **and that**." (Israel Hands, *Treasure Island* 59)

and that's all there is of it [*an'/'n tharrt's awrl tharr/theyarr/theyerr 's\be o'\on ett/'n/'t*] and that's that; and there's nothing more to say

> "The divil knows where I've hid my money, and I know where I've hid it; and the longest liver of the twain will git it all. **And that's all there is of it**." (Blackbeard, *The Book of Pirates* "Jack Ballister's Fortunes" 138)

and that's fair [*an'/'n' tharrt's farr/fayarr/fayerr*] and that's a fair statement; and that's not an unreasonable statement

Used by a speaker to endorse what he has just said as accurate, balanced, reasonable, or true, especially when making an extreme, provocative, or potentially controversial or objectionable statement.

> "Look ye, Captain Atkinson, it is not that we care a t[ur]d for your company, G[o]d d[am]n ye; G[o]d d[am]n my soul, not a t[ur]d by G[o]d, **and that's fair**; but G[o]d d[am]n ye, and G[o]d's b[loo]d and w[oun]ds, if you don't act like an honest man G[o]d d[am]n ye, and offer to play us any rogues'y tricks by G[o]d, and G[o]d sink me, but I'll blow your brains out; G[o]d d[am]n me, if I don't." (William Fly, *General History of the Pyrates* 610–11)

and that's flat [*an'/'n' tharrt's flat*] and that's for sure; and that's the truth

> "I'll not trust you, Murray, **and that's flat**." (John Flint, *Porto Bello Gold* 92)

and the like [*an'/'n' t' lawk/lyeeke*] and so on; etcetera

> "[I]f the needful number of officers and of particular occupations should not happen to be lotted out, the sloop might be obliged to go out to sea without a sur-

geon, or without a carpenter, or without a cook, **and the like**." (Captain Avery, *The King of Pirates* 38)

and there's an end on it [*an'/'n tharr/theyarr/ theyerr is\be a aynd o'/of ett/'n/'t*] and that's that; and there it is; and there's nothing more to say

> "Many's the time I regretted not learnin' it meself. Still, too late now, **and there's an end on it**." (Thomas Bartholomew Red, of his failure to learn the carpentry trade, "Pirates" 22:56)

and there's for you (now) [*an'/'n' tharr/ theyarr/theyerr is\be farr/fer 'ee/ya/ye/yer (narr/nowoo)*] and there you go

Used especially after any unusual or extraordinary statement as a way to let the addressee know that the speaker is aware of its unusual nature or content but is nevertheless confident of its truth or propriety.

> "Japhet, you're a stout captain, a prime sailorman, a good friend, but a fond and feckless fool, **and there's for ye**, Captain and sir!" (Crabtree, *Winds of Chance* 89)

> "'Tis song as was made for dead men, of dead men, by a dead man, **and there's for ye now**!" (Abnegation Mings, *Black Bartlemy's Treasure* 31)

and welcome [*an'/'n' waahl-cahm/carrm/ coohm*]

Used to convey defiant invitation when responding to a threat, a report of bad news, or an otherwise unpleasant statement. Also used to grant a request. Modern equivalents include "please do," "go right ahead," "go for it," and "be my guest." The excerpt below reflects the second usage.

> < "I want to speak with the boy alone." "Speak **an' welcome**, an' make a note of that, too." > (Doctor Livesey & Long John Silver, "Treasure Island" [1950] 1:23:33)

and what not [*an'/'n' wharrt/whorrt narrt*] and so on; etcetera, etcetera

> "For thirty years, I've sailed the seas, and seen good and bad, better and worse, fair weather and foul, provisions running out, knives going, **and what not**." (Israel Hands, *Treasure Island* 141, Chap. 26)

and what's worse [*an'/'n' wharrt/whorrt is\be warrse/warrser/woorse/woorser/worser*] and even worse

> "Here's been murder done, and, look'ee, this coxcombly captain hath got it into his skull that you're the murderer—aye, **and what's worse**, every soul aboard likewise save only Godby and myself." (Adam Penfeather, *Black Bartlemy's Treasure* 142)

and willing [*an'/'n' a-well-in'*]

Used to convey defiant invitation when responding to a threat, a report of bad news, or an otherwise unpleasant statement.

> < "Belvedere be our Cap'n—we want Belvedere!" "Why then, take him, bullies, take him **and willing**!" > (pirates aboard the *Happy Despatch* & Resolution Day, with Resolution heaving Captain Belvedere's corpse onto the lower deck, *Martin Conisby's Vengeance* 111)

and you know it [*an'/'n' 'ee/ya/ye/yer know-oo ett/'n/'t*]

Used to accuse the addressee of knowledge he either disclaims or pretends not to have.

> "You do talk rank folly, Adam, folly, **and ye know it**!" (Roger Tressady, *Black Bartlemy's Treasure* 316)

answer I [*ansarr I'ee*]

Used to preface a statement made in answer to another's question, after repeating another's question, or after having posed a question.

> "And there be many worse things than a mere pirate, brother. And what? You'll go for to ask. **Answer I**—Spanishers, Papishers, the Pope o' Rome and his bloody Inquisition, of which I have lasting experi-

ence, *camarado*—aye, I have I!" (Resolution Day, *Martin Conisby's Vengeance* 72)

arrgh aye; yes indeed

See Chapter 15 for other uses of "arrgh," and for definitions of thirteen other noise terms.

"But I can say one thing for ye, lad. I admire your honesty. **Arrgh.**" (Long John Silver, "Long John Silver's Return to Treasure Island" 1:04:47)

as ever [*as ebber/e'er*] as always

"But see here, you have come to the right place, **as ever.**" (Billy Bird, *The Blackbirder* 142)

as ever was [*as ebber/e'er warss\warr/were*] for sure; indeed

"[A]nd you all know, if that had been done, that we'd 'a' been aboard the *Hispaniola* this night **as ever was** ..." (Long John Silver, *Treasure Island* 164, Chap. 29)

as I do know [*as I'ee do knowoo*] I know; as I happen to know; as I have reason to know

"A man must be hale and strong to suffer apt and properly, **as I do know.**" (Japhet Bly, *Winds of Chance* 151)

as I guess [*as I'ee gayss*] I suppose; I suspect

< "Oh, Mr. Barnabas, doth the poor wretch suffer pain that he so waileth?" "Chiefly in his temper, madam, **as I guess.** For I've brought him hither against his orders." > (Ursula Revell & Barnabas Rokeby, *Winds of Chance* 86–87)

as I hear [*as I'ee 'ear/'ee'arr/'ee'err/hee'arr/hee'err*] I hear; I understand

"We came on a burned village, the work of their damned Spanish allies—ay, and English, **as I hear,** with a curse!" (Japhet Bly, *Winds of Chance* 207)

as I say [*as I'ee sayee*] as I said; as I mentioned

< "Where do we make for, Resolution?" "To a little island well beknown to the Fraternity, comrade—that is three islands

close-set and called Foremast, Main and Mizzen islands, *amigo*, where we are apt to meet friends, **as I say,** and sure to find good store of food and the like, brother." > (Martin Conisby & Resolution Day, *Martin Conisby's Vengeance* 146)

as I (do) think [*as I'ee (do) fink/thenk/t'ink*] I think; I understand

"Ursula, 'twas very salt tear yon, and, **as I think,** the most unselfish those eyes ever shed." (Japhet Bly, *Winds of Chance* 230) < "Know you this place and all the wonder of it?" "Somewhat, Ursula, for I have visited it but once to wood and water. 'Tis an island, **as I do think,** and never a human soul on it, though a man might live there all his days and lack for naught, so rich and bounteous is kind Nature in these latitudes." > (Ursula Revell & Ezekiel Penryn, *Winds of Chance* 133)

as it chances [*as ett/'n/'t charrnces*] as it happens; as it turns out

"But **as it chances,** our crew find confronting them a task of difficulty ..." (Andrew Murray, *Porto Bello Gold* 112)

as it were [*as ett/'n/'t warr OR 'twarr/'twere*] (1) you might say; in a sense

< "Well, I don't see your ship, Captain." "I'm in the market, **as it were.**" > (Commodore Norrington & Jack Sparrow, "Pirates of the Caribbean: The Curse of the Black Pearl" 17:47)

(2) as it turns out; as it happens

"He said it wasn't right with the code. That's why he sent off a piece of the treasure to you, **as it were.**" (Pintel, "Pirates of the Caribbean: The Curse of the Black Pearl" 1:41:52)

as I've reason to know [*as I'eev reasern/reas'n t'/ta/ter knowoo*]

"What I'm thinking is that in this engagement with the fort M. de Rivarol, who's a lubberly fellow, **as I've reason to know,** will be taking some damage that may make the odds a trifle more even." (Peter Blood, *Captain Blood: His Odyssey* 354)

as like as not [*as lawk/lyeeke as narrt*] in all likelihood; probably

Though literally meaning "as likely as not" the phrase is almost always used to assert an affirmative probability.

"Well, my mate Bill would be called the captain, **as like as not.**" (Black Dog, *Treasure Island* 9, Chap. 2)

as sure as God sees me [*as sharr/shorr as Gard/ Gott/Gud sees me*] without a doubt; certainly

"**As sure as God sees me,** I'd sooner lose my hand." (Tom, *Treasure Island* 75, Chap. 14)

as the case were [*as t' cayeess warr*] as the case may be

"Like enough, I would set no limits to what gentlemen might consider shipshape, or might not, **as the case were.**" (Long John Silver, *Treasure Island* 108, Chap. 20)

as you might say [*as 'ee/ya/ye/yer mawt/ migheet sayee*] you might say; if you will

"I don't know no bloody villains like that. I ha' seen 'em, yes—a sight too many of 'em **as ye might say.**" (Long John Silver, *Porto Bello Gold* 21)

as you'll agree [*as ye'll arrgree*]

Used by a speaker to suggest a preceding statement is either uncontroversial or inevitably persuasive.

"Now when they were gone I took counsel with myself, for here were two desperate, bloody rogues, very well armed, and here was I, a solitary man with nought to my defence save for Nick's knife and the silver-hilted dagger, which was heavy odds, Martin, **as you'll agree.**" (Adam Penfeather, *Black Bartlemy's Treasure* 92)

assure yourself [*asharr/ashorr 'ee/ya/yarr/ye/ yer/yere/yore-seff*] believe me; you can be sure

"I should have been put to death for killing a prisoner in cold blood; but **assure your self** my friends would have brought me off on such an occasion." (Walter Kennedy, *Villains of All Nations* 40)

aye [*aheee/arrgh*] yes

"**Aye,** here be your scuttler, without a doubt. Arrgh, a scuttler he is." (Blackbeard, "Blackbeard the Pirate" 42:17)

aye? [*aheee/arrgh?*] yes?; right?

"There's nothing like a sea-voyage to stir up the imagination, excepting of course the chink of gold doubloons a-trickling through your fingers, **aye?**" (Long John Silver, "Treasure Island" [1960] 36:12)

aye faith [*aheee/arrgh fayeeth*] yes indeed

"**Ay, faith,** a slave ship and such like is a something hard school that kills or cures ... cruelty begets ferocity." (Japhet Bly, *Winds of Chance* 220)

aye so [*aheee/arrgh so'oo*] yes; indeed so

"I changed me from dreaming young fool, sighing and puling for the impossible, into sober man and right cheery soul content to take whatsoever comes and make the best o't, a fellow bold in adversity and jibing at woe, **ay so,** or may I rot!" (Absalom Troy, *Adam Penfeather, Buccaneer* 7)

aye verily [*aheee/arrgh vaahrrily/vay-rily*] yes, indeed; yes, absolutely

"**Ay verily,** I've smote and been smitten right heartily ere now to the chastening o' poor, erring humanity, —in especial cursed Spanishers, Portugales, Papists and Pirates, rot 'em!" (Smy Peters, *Adam Penfeather, Buccaneer* 18–19)

be sure (of that) [*be sharr/shorr (o'\on tharrt*)] for sure; you can believe it

"'Stead of biding in safety, whiles Caripuna and I took toll o' yon rogues, playing 'em Hell's delight, you must run yourself into Snaith's foul clutches, whereupon I, **be sure**, must get myself rapped o' the sconce and tied up like so much dunnage that Johnny may leap in and play Providence to the helpless pair of us!" (Japhet Bly, *Winds of Chance* 332) "Oh, he wants her, naturally enough; but he wants not us, nor would he keep us long, **be sure of that**." (Peter Blood, *Captain Blood Returns* 24)

belike [*b'-lawk/lyeeke*] in all likelihood

"And, comrade, henceforth the steel that smiteth me shall smite you also, **belike**." (Adam Penfeather, *Black Bartlemy's Treasure* 82)

besides which [*b'-sawds/syeedes whech*] moreover; furthermore; in addition

"The west end of Golfo Dulce is very high land, and a high rock lies close off it. **Besides which**, two other rocks lie farther out; the outermost of which is a mile distant from the shore." (Basil Ringrose, *Bucaniers of America* Part IV, Ch. XIX)

beyond doubt [*b'-yarrn'/yarrnd/yon'/yont darrt/dowoot*] without a doubt; undoubtedly

"Yon's blowing weather, **beyond doubt**." (Ezekiel Penryn, observing a storm-threatening cloud, *Winds of Chance* 124)

but [*barrt*]

Used for emphasis at or near the beginning of a simple declarative statement.

"Ay, by thunder, **but** I wanted some o' that!" (Israel Hands, after a long drink of rum, *Treasure Island* 136, Chap. 25)

by all accounts [*byee awrl accarrnts/accowoonts/ 'carrnts/'cowoonts*] according to all; based on all reports

"Davis was a man, too, **by all accounts**." (Long John Silver, *Treasure Island* 57, Chap. 11)

by my reckoning [*byee me/myee a-rack-onin'*] as I see it; I figure; my thinking is that

"Well, **by my reckoning**, if Caripuna ever reached the coast, our friends should have been in sight or hereabouts—yesterday morning." (Japhet Bly, *Winds of Chance* 357–58)

by the looks of it [*byee t' looks o'\on ett/'n/'t*] by all appearances; it seems; it appears

"Slow and cranky **by the looks of it**." (Montbars' mate aboard the *Chepillo*, "Pirates of Tortuga" 37:45)

certes [*sartees*] certainly; truly

"'Tis said that Kidd discovered it, and **certes**, others of the old-time buccaneers were wont to maintain themselves there." (Andrew Murray, *Porto Bello Gold* 104)

come (now) [*cahm/carrm/coohm (narr/nowoo)*]

Used when attempting to persuade another of something. The usage serves as an invitation or plea to understand the speaker's circumstance or point of view, to shed a hollow or implausible claim or belief, or to be reasonable. Often combined with the name of the addressee.

"**Come**, Bill, you know me; you know an old shipmate, Bill, surely." (Black Dog, *Treasure Island* 11, Chap. 2) "Well, no more o' this! **Come now**, so soon as the supper things be washed and stowed, I'll seize you up fast to yonder tree, Johnny ..." (Japhet Bly, tiring of Ursula Revell's efforts to reconcile him and John Barrasdale, *Winds of Chance* 256)

content you [*cahn/carrn/coohn/kern-tant 'ee/ ya/ye/yer*] don't worry; relax; take it easy

"A man o' lies and blood, to be rooted out, child! Yet **content ye**, for by the Lord's grace, thou shalt see me slit his treacherous weasand anon." (Lovepeace Farrance, promising violence to Don Luiz da Ramirez, *Winds of Chance* 46)

darr [*dahrr*]

Used to preface any statement, especially a firm assertion, as you would use "you know what" or "I'll tell you what," or to preface a command, instruction, exclamation, or any especially sharp or definitive statement, as you would use "hey" or "now."

> "**Darr**, you'd be slaughtered like hogs in springtime." (Long John Silver, "Long John Silver's Return to Treasure Island" 1:19:38)

depend on\upon it [*der-pen' arrn\'parrn/'pon/ uparrn ett/'n/'t*] take it from me; believe me; you'd better believe it

> "**Depend on it**, if we accept this tenth, he'll find a pretext to cheat us of all." (Trenam, *Captain Blood Returns* 284) "I have made allowance for that, and, **depend upon it**, as she makes the eastern passage, we must soon fall in with her. ..." (Cain, *The Pirate* 47, Chap. VIII)

devil a doubt (but) [*daahv/dayv/debb/div-il a darrt/dowoot (barrt)*] there's no question that; there can be no doubt that

> "Sure, now, it's the very work that ye're fitted for, **devil a doubt**." (Peter Blood, *Captain Blood Returns* 141) "Meanwhile, Jerry, if ye're prudent, ye'll be keeping the ship. **Devil a doubt but** Tondeur will be looking for you." (Peter Blood, *Captain Blood Returns* 197)

devil doubt it but [*daahv/dayv/debb/div-il dowoot ett/'n barrt*]

Used to preface a bold or firm statement. The speaker suggests thereby that, though even the devil may doubt what she's about to say, she'll say it anyway.

> "**Devil doubt it, but** whether I'm changed or no, I'll take my affidavy that you are the same old half-witted Hi that you used to be." (Blueskin, *The Book of Pirates* "Blueskin, the Pirate" 161)

do you hear? [*d'/does 'ee/ya/ye/yer 'ear/'ee'arr/ 'ee'err/hee'arr/hee'err?*] do you hear me?

Used after a command or other especially assertive statement.

> "I tell you things when I am ready, **do you hear**?" (Elephiant Yancy, *The Pirate Round* 317) "I'm Captain here ... ay, Captain o' this ship to be obeyed, **d'ye hear**?" (Adam Penfeather, *Adam Penfeather, Buccaneer* 189)

(you) don't make no doubt of that [(*ya/ye/ yer) don'/doon't/dorrn't mayeeke no'oo darrt/ dowoot o'\on tharrt*] you can be sure of that

> "Why, in a place like this, where nobody puts in but gen'lemen of fortune, Silver would fly the Jolly Roger, **you don't make no doubt of that**." (Ben Gunn, *Treasure Island* 100, Chap. 19)

d'ye see [*do/does 'ee/ya/yer/you see*]

Used before a statement of explanation or exposition to invite the speaker to comprehend or accept what follows.

> "By the blood! **d'ye see** 'tis a strange accident, indeed, that lays two men by the heels and lets the third go without a scratch!" (Benny Willitts, *The Book of Pirates* "The Ruby of Kishmoor" 236)

d'ye think? [*do/does 'ee/ya/yer/you fink/thenk/ t'ink?*] don't you think?; don't you agree?

Used after a suggestion or other statement with which the speaker hopes to secure the addressee's agreement.

> "Bit dowdy, now, **d'ye think**?" (Billy Doyle, of a woman prisoner he's mistreated, *The Gun Ketch* 161)

d'ye understand? [*do/does 'ee/ya/ye/yer arrn/hun/oohn-darr/'ner-starrnd?*]

> "You can go out somewhere, **d'ye understand**?" (Blueskin, urging his stepbrother to leave the house in anticipation of meeting his pirate comrades there, *The Book of Pirates* "Blueskin, the Pirate" 165–66)

err

(1) you know what; I'll tell you what: Used to preface any statement, especially a firm assertion.

< "Fortunate I be that you fell in my hands when you did." "I don't understand." "**Err**, you will. You will." > (Blackbeard & Edward Maynard, "Blackbeard the Pirate" 21:15)

(2) hey; now: Used to preface a command, instruction, exclamation, or any especially sharp or definitive statement.

"**Err**, you swabs, I ain't buried yet!" (Long John Silver, yelling down in frustration his company mates' expressions of concern that his illness may be fatal, "The Adventures of Long John Silver: Execution Dock" 2:58)

See Chapter 15 for more definitions of "err."

every one [*ebber'/ebbry/e'ery/ever'/ev'ry 'un/ woohn*]

Used where the speaker intends his statement to apply to the entire set of people or things referenced earlier in the sentence.

"They liked a bit o' fun, they did. They wasn't so high and dry, nohow, but took their fling, like jolly companions **every one**." (Israel Hands, *Treasure Island* 60, Chap. 11)

faith (now) [*fayeeth (narr/nowoo)*] indeed

< "Yet look to it, sir, dare so much as lay your wicked hands on me, and, so soon as chance serve, I vow to kill you. You believe me sir?" "**Faith**, I believe ye might try." > (Ursula Revell & Japhet Bly, *Winds of Chance* 29) "**Faith, now**, it glitters, to be sure. But it isn't gold." (Peter Blood, *Captain Blood Returns* 23)

favor [*faah/fayee-varr*]

The term projects generous or goodhearted intention on the part of either speaker or addressee. It is used to preface a tip, suggestion, or other statement intended for the addressee's benefit (as in, "I'll do you a favor"); a request put to the addressee (as in, "Do me a favor"); or any statement the speaker wishes to make as pleasantly or hospitably as possible.

"**Favor**, keep a weather eye open, maties." (libidinous pirate, "Pirates of the Caribbean" Disney attraction [2000])

first and last [*farrst/firsht/firs'/fust an'/'n' las'/lasht*] from start to finish; throughout; for the entire time

"[I]t was this same boy that faked the chart from Billy Bones. **First and last**, we've split upon Jim Hawkins." (Long John Silver, *Treasure Island* 158, Chap. 28)

for all o' me [*farr/fer awrl o'\on me*] for all I care; as far as I'm concerned

"And what are you? You that wed me for no reason but love of yourself ... the saving of that so precious body! Well, you may keep it **for all o' me**. I'll none of it, husband or no ..." (Japhet Bly, *Winds of Chance* 92)

for certain [*farr/fer sarrten*] without a doubt; definitely

< "Why, 'tis the cabin boy." "Arrgh, someone's pinked him **for certain**." > (George Merry & Long John Silver, seeing Jim Hawkins on the ground with a wounded shoulder, "Treasure Island" [1950] 1:15:28)

for my part [*farr/fer me/myee pahrrt*] as far as I'm concerned

"**For my part**, I don't know and I don't care what the Gospel does to them, but I know that when any o' the islands chance to get it, trade goes all smooth and easy; but where they ha'nt got it, Beezelbub himself could hardly desire better company." (pirate, *The Coral Island* 213–14)

for sure [*farr/fer sharr/shorr*] without a doubt

"Why **for sure** 'tis my bonnet Marty as saved my skin time and again aboard the *Faithful Friend*!" (Roger Tressady, *Black Bartlemy's Treasure* 302)

forsooth [*farr/fer-soof/soot*] in truth; indeed

"They villify us, the scoundrels do, when there is only this difference, they rob the poor under the cover of law, **forsooth**, and we plunder the rich under the protection of our own courage ..." (Captain Bellamy to the captain of a captured Boston sloop, *General History of the Pyrates* 587)

from hence [*ferm 'ence*] as a result; consequently; accordingly

"[T]heir eye-lids bend and open in an oblong figure, pointing downward at the corners, and forming an arch or figure of a crescent with the points downwards. **From hence**, and from their seeing so clear as they do in a moon-shiny night, we us'd to call them moon-ey'd." (Lionel Wafer, *Isthmus of America* 134)

give me leave to say [*gi'/giff me leef t'/ta/ter sayee*] let me say

"Gentlemen, **give me leave to say**, that tho' we are pirates, yet we are men ..." (Edward Low, *Pirates of the New England Coast* 191)

ha [*harr*]

A sharp, laughlike utterance used to convey a judgmental, smug, or supercilious attitude; to preface a crisp, knowing, or overbearing pronouncement; or to express surprise or sudden pleasure.

"**Ha**, will ye kill the wench, y' black spawn!" (Ned, castigating Pompey for hurting Ursula Revell, *Winds of Chance* 322)

ha-harr [*har-hahrr*]

(1) well; you know: Used to preface a suggestion, impression, or other soft statement—any statement the speaker wishes to express gently, tenatively, or unpresumptuously.

< "If it hadn't been for you, we'd have been taken and sacked." "**Ha-harr**, well, sometimes it takes a man o' my ilk to catch them kind o' rattlesnakes." >

(Governor Strong & Long John Silver, "The Adventures of Long John Silver: The Eviction" 23:58)

(2) you know what; I'll tell you what: Used to preface any statement, especially a firm assertion.

< "We'll be here a week. Morgan will be on us long afore." "**Ha-harr**, let 'im." > (Ben Worley & Blackbeard, "Blackbeard the Pirate" 43:38)

(3) hey; now: Used to preface a command, instruction, exclamation, or any especially sharp or definitive statement.

"**Ha-harr**, sawbones, you'll pay for that. That were your last load." (Blackbeard, mocking Edward Maynard for squandering his pistol's last shot on the wrong man, "Blackbeard the Pirate" 1:15:00)

(4) that's right; that's it: Used to lend emphasis or express conviction.

"Fetch Mainyard up here. We'll tie him to the riggin' and flog 'im. **Ha-harr**. Maybe that'll keep ya pretty head up." (Blackbeard, threatening Edwina Mansfield with the whipping of her lover, "Blackbeard the Pirate" 1:18:03)

See Chapter 15 for more definitions of "ha-harr."

h(e)ark you [*'ark/hahrrk 'ee/ya/ye/yer*]
h(e)arkee [*'ark'ee/hahrrkee*] listen; listen up; listen to me

"**Heark ye**, you Cocklyn and la Bouche, I find by strengthening you, I have put a rod into your hands to whip my self, but I am still able to deal with you both ..." (Howel Davis, *General History of the Pyrates* 175) "Now, go, make a fire on that point; and **hark'ee**, youngster, if you try to run away, I'll send a quick and sure messenger after you." (pirate, brandishing his gun, *The Coral Island* 196)

h(e)arkee in your ear [*'arkee/hahrrkee i'/'n ya/yarr/ye/yer/yere/yore ee-arr/err*] listen; listen to this

> "[T]alk we o' life and the joy of it for, — **hearkee in thine ear**, —at my last and most secret computation, we are grown rich beyond even mine own expectation ..." (Benjamin Trigg, *Adam Penfeather, Buccaneer* 246)

h(e)arkee me [*'arkee/hahrrkee me*] listen; listen to me; listen to what I'm saying

> "**Hearkee me**, sirrah, you lousy, pittiful, ill-look'd dog; what have you to say why you should not be tuck'd up immediately, and set a sun-drying like a scare-crow?" (George Bradley, *General History of the Pyrates* 293)

h(e)arkee now [*'arkee/hahrrkee narr/nowoo*] now listen; listen up now

> < "Captain Jo commands here—" "Say ye so, Resolution, say ye so, lad? Now **mark me**—and keep both hands afore ye—so, my bully—**hark'ee now**—there's none commands where I am save Roger Tressady!" > (Resolution Day & Roger Tressady, *Martin Conisby's Vengeance* 156)

harr [*hahrr*]

(1) you know what; I'll tell you what: Used to preface any statement, especially a firm assertion.

> < "Ironhand!" "Yes, sir!" "**Harr**. Ah, I've got a little job for 'ee." > (Long John Silver & Ironhand, "The Adventures of Long John Silver: Devil's Stew" 12:23)

(2) hey; now: Used to preface a command, instruction, exclamation, or any especially sharp or definitive statement.

> "**Harr**, listen to this, ha-harr, 'tis a cackle." (Blackbeard, "Blackbeard the Pirate" 28:58)

See Chapter 15 for more definitions of "harr."

hear you [*'ear/ee'arr/ee'err/hee'arr/hee'err 'ee/ya/ye/yer*] listen; listen up

> "**Hear ye**, you Cochlyn and La Boise, I find, by strengthening you, I have put a rod into your hands to whip myself ..." (Captain Davis, *The Pirates Own Book* 210)

hear (you) me [*'ear/ee'arr/ee'err/hee'arr/hee'err ('ee/ya/ye/yer) me*] listen; listen to me

> "**Hear me**, Yancy, when I am king here, we shall have a regular army, see? Drills, uniforms, the whole thing." (Obadiah Spelt, *The Pirate Round* 146) < "I say once for all I'll not be caged here to be clucked over as I were some roupy chicken or plaguey fowl, d'ye hear?" "Ay, I hear, and now **hear you me**, sir—except you have air and light and proper nursing, we shall be heaving ye overboard in shotted hammock pretty soon, ay so, demme!" > (Japhet Bly & Crabtree, *Winds of Chance* 89)

hear me? [*'ear/ee'arr/ee'err/hee'arr/hee'err me?*] do you hear me?; do you understand?

Used after a command or other especially assertive statement.

> < "We need a harbor, we're leaking like an unstanched wench. D'ya not hear our pumps going?" "Very well, then, but keep your goddamned distance, **hear me?**" > (Thomas Marlowe & watchman aboard pirate ship at Smith Island, *The Guardship* 89)

heigho [*heighee ho'oo*]

Used to express joy, mirth, enthusiasm, or sudden or intense determination.

> "As for me, shipmate, I shall scarce close an eye till we be clear o' the Downs, so 'tis a care-full man I shall be this next two days, **heigho!**" (Adam Penfeather, *Black Bartlemy's Treasure* 113)

here (now\you) [*'ee'arr/'ee'err/'ere/hee'arr/hee'err (narr/nowoo\'ee/ya/ye/yer)*] hey

Used to call another's attention or to focus it on what is about to be said.

< "Water!" "**Here**, you fool, that water will sear your insides." > (pirate in Long John Silver's company & Patch, as the first pirate stops to drink muddy water from a jungle pond, "The Adventures of Long John Silver: Pieces of Eight" 12:08) "**Here now**, he clings to you like pitch, he does." (Long John Silver, "Long John Silver's Return to Treasure Island" 50:27) "**Here, you**, here's the captain. Show some sodding respect." (seaman aboard *Plymouth Prize*, *The Guardship* 243)

here and now [*'ee'arr/'ee'err/'ere/hee'arr/ hee'err an'/'n' narr/nowoo*]
Used in delivering a command, threat, or other forceful declaration.

"I should take off yer hand **here an' now**!" (Joshua Smoot, *Dead Man's Chest* 157)

hillo [*'illo*] hello; wow; what's this
Used for emphasis, especially to express surprise, astonishment, or intense pleasure.

"Why, **hillo**! look here now: this ain't lucky! You've gone and cut this out of a Bible." (Long John Silver, *Treasure Island* 163, Chap. 29)

huzza [*huzzer/'uzza/'uzzer*] hurrah; hooray
Shouted, especially by more than one person, to express joy, celebration, encouragement, or optimistic determination.

"**Huzza**, mates, altogether!" (George Merry, on first seeing the place marked by the treasure map and urging his comrades to rush toward it, *Treasure Island* 184, Chap. 33)

I am much mistaken if [*I'ee arrm/em\be mar-rch/moohch mee/meh-stayeekern\stook an'\eff/ eff'n/if'n*]

"**I am much mistaken if** you do not find him to your taste on the quarter-deck." (The Red Rover, endorsing his choice of Harry Wilder as his second-in-command, *The Red Rover* 110)

I can tell you [*I'ee cayn/kin taahl 'ee/ya/ye/yer*]

"And thorough-goin' blackguards some o' them traders are; no better than pirates, **I can tell you**." (Bloody Bill, *The Coral Island* 220)

I cannot question but [*I'ee cayn/kin-arrt quarrs-chun barrt*]

"[W]e knew not how to get any shipping to convey us unto Jamaica; for **we could not question but** our own ships were either departed long before that time or at least taken up and carried away by our companions and deserters ... " (William Dick, *Bucaniers of America* 352)

I dare prophesy [*I'ee darr/dayarr/dayerr pruh-phesy*] I suspect that; I have a hunch that; I predict that

"**I dare prophesy** you shall come to think o' Japhet daily, hourly and by the min-ute." (Japhet Bly, *Winds of Chance* 15)

I dare say [*I'ee darr/dayarr/dayerr sayee*] I suppose; I think it probable that
Often used to make modest-sounding a state-ment that might otherwise be misconstrued as presumptuous, challenging, or offensive.

"And we know you want money in England: **I dare say** our General, Captain Avery, and his particular gang who have the main riches, would not grudge to advance five or six million ducats to the government to give them leave to return in peace to Eng-land, and sit down quietly with the rest." (Captain Avery, *The King of Pirates* 70)

I dare to think [*I'ee darr/dayarr/dayerr t'/ta/ter fink/thenk/t'ink*] I suppose; I think
Often used to make modest-sounding a state-ment that might otherwise be misconstrued aspresumptuous, challenging, or offensive.

"I have wines and cordials which, **I dare to think**, you may pronounce worthy and precious as your own." (Adam Penfeather, *Adam Penfeather, Buccaneer* 322)

I do protest [I'ee do pro-tes'/tesht] I state with certainty that; I insist that

> "For all the world, sleeping like two babes and your two arms fast about him, my dear mem, as you had plucked him to your heart from the very claws o 'death, as **I do protest** ye did in very truth, or demme!" (Crabtree, *Winds of Chance* 96)

I don't reckon [I'ee don'/doon't/dorrn't rackon] Used after stating a negative proposition.

> "We thought he was dead, with ... the cancer ... you know. But he wasn't, just overcome. But he ain't long for us, **I don't reckon.**" (Henry Nagel, *The Pirate Round* 209)

I doubt [I'ee darrt/dowoot] I fear; I suspect
The word "doubt" here is used in its archaic sense to mean "believe" or "suspect" in an affirmative way—the opposite of its typical meaning "disbelieve."

> "'Tis her soul, **I doubt!**" (Diccon, speculating on the cause of Captain Jo's sickness, *Martin Conisby's Vengeance* 100)

I doubt not [I'ee darrt/dowoot narrt] I don't doubt that; I have no doubt that

> "And **I doubt not** we shall, one way or other, find our way with our merchandise and money to come into France, if not quite home to my own country." (Captain Avery, *The King of Pirates* 76)

I fancy [I'ee fancy] I believe; I guess

> "John, **I fancy** we shall require triple bonds on this prisoner." (Andrew Murray, *Porto Bello Gold* 45)

I fear [I'ee fee-arr/err] I'm afraid that
The phrase "I fear" is used not to express actual fear, but rather to acknowledge that what is being described or conveyed is unfortunate or suboptimal in some way.

> < "Be dumb, sir! I have sent for you to demand that you turn back this ship and instantly restore me to ... to my friends." "And your woman, gracious lady?" "And my woman, of course." "Alack now! **I fear** this is out o' the question." > (Ursula Revell & Japhet Bly, *Winds of Chance* 38)

I give you my Bible oath [I'ee gi'/giff 'ee/ya/ ye/yer me/myee baah/baw/byee-bul oaf/o'oof/ o'ooth] I swear

> "I give ye me Bible-oath no harm 'll come t' these young tits, an' I'll leave 'em safe an' sound on French Cay'r West Caicos." (Billy Doyle, offering Alan Lewrie the lives of his women prisoners in exchange for a clean getaway, *The Gun Ketch* 160)

I grant it [I'ee grant ett/'n] I admit it; that much is true; granted

> "In my mood I struck your mother; **I grant it.**" (Cain, *The Pirate* 101)

I have pleasure in saying [I'ee 'aff/'ave/ha'/ haff plaah/play-zharr i'/'n a-sayin']

> "**I have pleasure in saying**, that the humour of my people is already expended ..." (The Red Rover, *The Red Rover* 367)

I hold that [I'ee hol'/hoold/ho'oold/'old tharrt] I firmly believe that; it's my view that

> "For **I hold that** we're in no case to fight against such odds." (Peter Blood, *Captain Blood: His Odyssey* 250)

(as) I judge [(as) I'ee joohdge] I figure; I believe; I think; as far as I can tell

> "I judged about the middle of the day, we were at the distance of twenty leagues S.S.W. from the said islands." (Basil Ringrose, describing his company's voyage between the islands of Cayboa and Gorgona, *Bucaniers of America* Part IV Chap. IX) "In about half-an-hour, **as I judge**, they will be letting fly with their fore-chase guns ..." (Absalom Troy, *Adam Penfeather, Buccaneer* 121)

I lay [I'ee layee] I bet

> "An' **I lay** it wouldn't go too good for you neither, Ben Gunn, to be discovered with

yer prisoner at the water line ..." (Long John Silver, *Dead Man's Chest* 7)

I may tell you plainly [*I'ee mayee taahl 'ee/ya/ye/yer playeenly*] I'll be straight with you; I'll say it clearly; I'll tell you the honest truth

"**I may tell you plainly** that I am no poor hand at the reading of faces." (Benny Willitts, *The Book of Pirates* "The Ruby of Kishmoor" 237)

I must needs say [*I'ee marrst/moohst needs sayee*] I have to say

"Gentlemen, the master, **I must needs say**, has spoke nothing but what is very reasonable, and I think he ought to have his sloop." (Edward Low, *Pirates of the New England Coast* 177)

I protest [*I'ee pro-tes'/tesht*]

Used to preface any assertive or insistent statement, especially when expressing consternation, displeasure, offense, or any sharp or intense sentiment.

< "[T]herefore I must be his death—or he mine." "How then, you'll fight him, messmate?" "Indeed!" "Nay, lad, **I protest** 'tis fool's way to deal with a murderer." > (Adam Penfeather & Absalom Troy, *Adam Penfeather, Buccaneer* 13)

I reckon [*I'ee rackon*]

The term "reckon" has different shades of meaning, but they all have one thing in common: uncertainty. Below are five definitions, set out in increasing order of uncertainty—belief, expectation, prediction, assumption, and speculation.

(1) I believe; I think

"But now **I rackon** the dons has their bellyful, see how thick they lie afore our rampire!" (Ned Bowser, *Adam Penfeather, Buccaneer* 340) "Put a name on what you're at; you ain't dumb, **I reckon**." (Long John Silver, *Treasure Island* 159, Chap. 28)

(2) I expect

"**I reckon** he ain't gonna get away if he's sailing up a fucking river, Captain. Gotta run out of water sometime." (William Darnall, *The Guardship* 281) "But Caripuna should be at Bartlemy's Bay by now, **I reckon**." (Japhet Bly, *Winds of Chance* 333)

(3) I predict; I bet

"Guardship's coming about. **I reckon** he misses stays and we'll be right aboard him." (William Darnall, *The Guardship* 283) "Johnny, our powder is nigh spent ... enough to withstand every assault for—another hour or thereabouts, **I reckon** and then, John ... a bullet apiece." (Japhet Bly, *Winds of Chance* 362)

(4) I suppose; I assume

"**I reckon**, **I reckon**, Cap'n Hawkins, you'll kind of want to get ashore, now." (Israel Hands, *Treasure Island* 137, Chap. 25) "You'd just as soon save your lives, **I reckon**. That's yours." (Long John Silver, "Treasure Island" [1990] 1:15:25)

(5) I guess; I imagine

"**I reckon** we could try." (Long John Silver, "Treasure Island" [1998] 1:28:40) "Have her to the Cap'n, **I reckon**, messmate." (Tom, on discovering Ursula Revell hidden in the brush, *Winds of Chance* 313)

I say(s) [*I'ee sayee(s OR sayz)*]

Used to preface or follow any assertive or insistent statement, especially a command or instruction or an expression of one's point of view.

"He ain't fit to be captain, fucking lunatic! He ain't fit, **I say**!" (LeRois' boatswain, *The Guardship* 210) "If he dies, it ain't goin' to be from drinkin' witch juice, and **I says** he ain't goin' to die." (Long John Silver, "The Adventures of Long John Silver: Sword of Vengeance" 8:15)

I say again [*I'ee sayee agayn/agin/'gain/'gayn*]

Used when a speaker repeats or para-phrases something he has already said, typi-cally for emphasis or out of some surfeit of feeling.

> "You and me'll just go back into the par-lour, sonny, and get behind the door, and we'll give Bill a little surprise—bless his 'art, **I say again**." (Black Dog, *Treasure Island* 10, Chap. 2)

I should say so [*I shoood sayee so'oo*]
Used to affirm emphatically what the speaker has just said.

> < "And pray, why must he trouble you; why could not his lordly godship come for me himself?" "Why now, lady, lookee, he do be that full o' business, —love my eyes, **I should say so!**" > (Ur-sula Revell & Jeremy Jervey, *Winds of Chance* 248)

I shouldn't doubt [*I'ee shoont darrt/dowoot*]
I'm sure; in all likelihood

> "Blood poisonin', **I shouldn't doubt**." (George Merry, "Treasure Island" [1950] 1:15:31)

(and) I shouldn't wonder [*(an'/'n') I'ee shoont woohnd/wunn-er*] I'm sure; in all likelihood; I wouldn't be surprised

> "You'm gettin' quite a leadin' hand in this here crew. You'll be cap'n next, **I shouldn't wonder**." (Long John Silver, "Treasure Island" [1950] 1:19:52) "Dig away, boys, you'll find some pig-nuts **and I shouldn't wonder**." (Long John Silver, goading his company mates with the knowledge that the sought-for treasure has already been dug up, *Treasure Island* 185, Chap. 33)

I take it [*I'ee tayeeke ett/'n/'t*] I think; I believe; I understand; I assume

> "Now, look here, you give me food and drink and an old scarf or ankecher to tie my wound up, you do; and I'll tell you how to sail here; and that's about

square all round, **I take it**." (Israel Hands, *Treasure Island* 137, Chap. 25)

I tell you [*I'ee taahl 'ee/ya/ye/yer*]
Used to preface or follow any assertive or insistent statement, especially when ex-pressing one's point of view or taking issue with another's.

> "You boat would have leaked and swamped with you, Martino! **I tell you** the cursed thing would ha' gone to pieces at the first gust of wind!" (Captain Jo, *Martin Conisby's Vengeance* 35) "That doctor's a fool, **I tell you**." (Billy Bones, *Treasure Island* 14, Chap. 3)

I tell you true [*I'ee taahl 'ee/ya/ye/yer troo*] I'm telling you the truth; this is the truth

> "**I tell you true**, I never rightly liked to hear it since." (unnamed pirate, *Treasure Island* 178, Chap. 31)

I tell you what it is [*I'ee taahl 'ee/ya/ye/yer wharrt/whorrt ett/'n be OR 'tes/'tis*] I tell you what; I'll tell you what

> "As for a pilot, **I tell ye what 'tis**—if any man hereabouts goes out there to pilot that villain in 'twill be the worst day's work he ever did in all of his life." (Blackbeard, warning North Carolina locals against ren-dering assistance to his enemy, *The Book of Pirates* "Jack Ballister's Fortunes" 137)

I think it but reason [*I'ee fink/thenk/t'ink ett/'n/'t barrt reasern/reas'n*] I think it only makes sense; I think it's only logical

> "**I think it but reason**, to use such methods as may prevent your passionate design ... " (gunner in Edward Low's company, *Pirates of the New England Coast* 182)

I verily believe [*I'ee vaah/vay-rily b'/ber-leef*] I indeed believe; I certainly believe

> "Gentlemen, you all know ... how Capt. Russel, and some more, were angry with the master of the sloop, and, **I verily be-lieve**, without any cause by him given to

any of you designedly ..." (John Russell, *Pirates of the New England Coast* 191)

I wager [*I'ee waah/wayee-jarr/jerr*]
I'd wager [*I'eed waah/wayee-jarr/jerr*]
I'll wager [*I'ee'ull waah/wayee-jarr/jerr*] I'll bet; I'd bet; I'm willing to bet

"Ain't they a handsome pair o' young pieces, squire's son? Pretty'z yer sister, **I wager**." (Billy Doyle, bringing out two women prisoners for Alan Lewrie to see, *The Gun Ketch* 159) "**I'd wager** he killed a man for it ..." (Long John Silver, *Dead Man's Chest* 281) "If Cap'n Smollet lays 'is 'ands on old Long John, I'll be swingin' from that same yard what me goods been hoisted from, an' before week's end, **I'll wager**." (Long John Silver, *Dead Man's Chest* 7)

I warrant me\you [*I'ee waah/weh-runt me\'ee/ ya/ye/yer*] I declare; I assure you

A guarantee by the speaker of the truth or certainty of a preceding statement.

< "You warned 'em to stand by for my word?" "Ay, I did, sir, and they'm both a tip-toe wi' years on the stretch at this moment, **I warrant me**." > (Adam Penfeather & Ned Bowser, *Adam Penfeather, Buccaneer* 235) "A wholesome-looking craft that! and one well found, **I warrant you**." (officer aboard the *Dolphin*, *The Red Rover* 87)

I will so [*I'ee well so'oo*]

Used to emphasize the speaker's commitment to do what he has stated.

"Should he prove anyways obstreperous, send for me and I'll tie him abed or post two stout fellows to hold him,—ay, **I will so**, Japhet, or demme!" (Crabtree, *Winds of Chance* 90)

I won't say as __ [*I'ee woont sayee as __*]

If one wants to say "x," one might instead put it, more colorfully and perhaps more humbly or modestly, "I won't say not x." Thus, instead of "I'd like something to drink," one might say, "I won't say I ain't minded

to take a drain." This usage is particularly appropriate when used in connection with attitudes, intentions, preferences, and other similarly subjective states of mind.

< "Don't you ever yearn for our dear, sweet England, Jeremy? To be walking its shady lanes, or standing atop of some wind-kissed hill—don't you?" "Why, no, but there's a little back alley in Deptford nigh to Mill Lane, wi' a little tavern o' one corner and at the end a cottage, littlest of all, and a front room so narrer and strait a man can scarce turn, —**I won't say as I ha'n't** wished myself there mighty often, along o' my old mother ..." > (Ursula Revell & Jeremy Jervey, *Winds of Chance* 213)

I won't say no [*I'ee woont sayee no'oo*] (1) I'll not deny it (2) it's not out of the question (3) I could be persuaded

"Well, maybe we'd been taking a glass, and a song to help it round. **I won't say no**." (Long John Silver, *Treasure Island* 157, Chap. 28)

I would wager a handsome venture [*I'ee woood waah/wayee-jarr/jer a 'an'/'and/han'- sahm/sarrm/soohm ven-charr/churr/terr*] I would bet a lot of money; I would bet something big

"**I would wager a handsome venture** that the sail in sight is, by some mysterious process, magnified to six in his fertile fancy." (The Red Rover, *The Red Rover* 417)

I wouldn't doubt [*I'ee woont darrt/dowoot*] there's a good chance; it wouldn't surprise me

"Bloody stupid Yancy, run it right into the ground, **I wouldn't** fucking **doubt**." (Roger Press, *The Pirate Round* 220)

if ADJECTIVE'er can be said by mortal seaman OATH\CURSE [*eff/eff'n/if'n __'er cayn/kin be sayd byee marrt/mor'-al seaman ...*] if anyone ever said anything more __, then OATH\CURSE

Used to call attention to the speaker's preceding statement as remarkable in some way. The speaker thereby defies the addressee to find another seaman who has said anything as true, fair, generous, outlandish, or whatever other quality the speaker initially specifies.

"If you like the service, well, you'll jine; and if you don't, Jim, why, you're free to answer no—free and welcome, shipmate; and if fairer **can be said by mortal seaman**, shiver my sides!" (Long John Silver, *Treasure Island* 156, Chap. 28)

if God be kind [*eff/eff'n/if'n Garrd/Gott/Gud be kin'/kyeen'/kyeend*] God willing

< "Ha, you know Nombre de Dios?" "I ha' lived and suffered there, master, and 'tis there I be a-going for to make an end o' Bloody Valdez, **if God be kind**." > (Martin Conisby & John, *Martin Conisby's Vengeance* 182)

if I may make so bold [*eff/eff'n/if'n I'ee mayee mayeeke so'oo bol'/boold/bo'oold*]

Used before a statement that might be understood as challenging, presumptuous, or excessive in order to persuade the addressee that the statement is intended more modestly or unoffensively.

"**If I may make so bold**, sir, I'll borry your boat, I ain't takin' you to Jamaiker." (Long John Silver, "Treasure Island" [1950] 1:32:09)

if I mistake not [*eff/eff'n/if'n I'ee mee/meh-stayeeke narrt*] if I'm not mistaken

"**If I mistake not**, fellow, you overacted your own part to-day, and were a little too forward in leading on the trouble." (The Red Rover, *The Red Rover* 352)

if I recollect [*eff/eff'n/if'n I'ee rec'/recker-leck*] if I recall correctly; if memory serves

"You've a burden to carry inside, **if I recollect**!" (Long John Silver, *Dead Man's Chest* 13)

if what I hear be right [*eff/eff'n/if'n wharrt/whorrt I'ee 'ear/'ee'arr/'ee'err/hee'arr/hee'err be rawt/righeet*] if my information is correct

"[F]orty thousand louis, spent by fives and tens, a good bit of it going to feed gillies in the heather or gambled away in some *clachan* of the Cameron country, **if what I hear be right**." (Andrew Murray, *Porto Bello Gold* 100)

if you asks me [*eff/eff'n/if'n 'ee/ya/ye/yer aks/arrsks me*] in my view; as far as I'm concerned

"I got eight hundred pounds for my leg—and fair enough, **if you asks me**." (Long John Silver, *Porto Bello Gold* 65)

if you kindly will [*eff/eff'n/if'n 'ee/ya/ye/yer kine/kyeen'/kyeend-ly well*] if you would

Used following an invitation or request, usually in a spirit of graciousness or generosity.

"Sit'ee down at table t' starboard, **if ye kindly will**." (Long John Silver, "Treasure Island" [1950] 16:49)

if you please [*eff/eff'n/if'n 'ee/ya/ye/yer please*] please

< "Well, well ... Jack Sparrow, isn't it?" "Captain Jack Sparrow. **If you please**." > (Commodore Norrington & Jack Sparrow, "Pirates of the Caribbean: The Curse of the Black Pearl" 17:45)

I'll gamble [*I'ee'ull gemble*] I'll bet

"And that eight hundred pounds **I'll gamble** you ha' stowed away in a safe hole, John." (Ezra Pew, *Porto Bello Gold* 65)

I'll lay my head [*I'ee'ull layee me/myee 'ead/hayd*] I'll bet my life

"Some swam in rum to kingdom come,/Full many a lusty fellow./And since they're dead **I'll lay my head**/They're flaming now in hell O." (from song sung by Abnegation Mings, *Black Bartlemy's Treasure* 29)

I'll lay to that [*I'ee'ull layee t'/ta/ter tharrt*]
I'll bet on that

> "You'll be back, **I'll lay to that!**" (Long John Silver, *Dead Man's Chest* 9)

I'll lay you a __ [*I'ee'ull layee 'ee/ya/ye/yer a __*]
I'll bet you a __

The speaker names, after saying "I'll lay you a," a kind of coin or unit of currency. The more valuable the unit named, the more certain the speaker purports to be. See Section 16.7 for names of various types of currency.

> "**I'll lay ye a castellano** there was a whole watch awake on her the night long." (Jemmy, *Porto Bello Gold* 139)

I'll not omit to tell you [*I'ee well narrt hom-ett t'/ta/ter taahl 'ee/ya/ye/yer*]

Used to preface a statement the speaker wishes to suggest contains essential or important information.

> "But here, that he may be known, **I will not omit to tell you** that the chief occasion of his grudge against us was because we reproached him for his ill-behaviour in the engagement we had with the Armadilla of Panama ..." (William Dick, *Bucaniers of America* 337)

I'll tell you plain [*I'ee'ull taahl 'ee/ya/ye/yer playeen*]

> "[I]f we don't get it, why, **I'll tell you plain**, we'll burn them bloody crafts of yours that we've took over yonder, and cut the weasand of every clodpoll aboard of 'em." (Captain Richards, threatening the governor of South Carolina into giving him a supply of medicines, *The Book of Pirates* "Buccaneers and Marooners of the Spanish Main" 30)

I'll warrant (me) [*I'ee'ull waah/weh-runt (me)*]
I'll declare; I'll assure you

A guarantee by the speaker of the truth or certainty of the statement that follows.

> "**I'll warrant** he has not had half the adventures that I have." (Billy Bird, *The Blackbirder*

91) "Lord love you, sir, we'll ha' no lack o' men, **I'll warrant me**, for the old *Santy* is known ashore as the *Golden Fortune*." (Martin Frant, *Adam Penfeather, Buccaneer* 293)

I'm a dog if [*I'eem a dahg/darrg/dorrg an'\ eff/eff'n/if'n*]

Used to negate emphatically whatever statement follows, in a way comparable to the modern English phrase "I'll be damned if." The term "dog" is a much more potent epithet among pirates than among modern speakers; the negating phrase "I'm a dog if" is correspondingly more emphatic.

> "Adam, **I'm a dog**, —I say I'm a lewdly-yapping cur if ye don't work us plaguey hard and beyond all reason!" (Benjamin Trigg, *Adam Penfeather, Buccaneer* 224)

I'm free to say [*I'eem free t'/ta/ter sayee*] I can safely say; I'm not going out on a limb when I say

> "I volunteered for blind curiosity, hopin' for to discover what he was up to, and **I'm free to say** I've had my trouble for my pains." (Long John Silver, *Porto Bello Gold* 50)

I'm sure [*I'eem sharr/shorr*]

> "So if 'tis all the same to ee, ma'm, I'd rayther be tied up again all reg'lar and shipshape and take my half-dozen according to orders, thanking you kindly, ma'm, **I'm sure**." (Ben, *Winds of Chance* 103)

I'm telling you [*I'eem a-taahlin' 'ee/ya/ye/yer*]
Used to preface any assertive or insistent statement, especially when expressing one's point of view or taking issue with another's.

> "Mates, **I'm telling you**, that man knew it all along." (George Merry, "Treasure Island" [1972] 1:26:38) "**I'm telling you** things is changed since we signed them articles." (Captain Easterling, *Captain Blood Returns* 283)

I'm thinking [*I'eem a-fink/thenk/t'ink-in'*] I think; I believe

"But look'ee now, Marty, here's me wishing ye well and you wi' a barker in your fist, 'tis no fashion to greet a shipmate, **I'm thinking.**" (Roger Tressady, *Black Bartlemy's Treasure* 302)

in a manner of speaking [*i'/'n a mayner o'\on a-speakin'*] you might say; as it were

> < "Can it be entered at low-time?" "Arrgh. There's a kind of a passage being dug there, **in a manner of speakin'**, by nature." > (Captain Smollett & Long John Silver, "Treasure Island" [1950] 43:47)

in faith [*i'/'n fayeeth*] indeed; truly

> "**I' faith!** Here's fine stuff for the gallows!" (Adam Penfeather, *Black Bartlemy's Treasure* 111)

in fine [*i'/'n fyeene*] in sum; in conclusion; finally

> "His sport is rape and slaughter of the defenceless, he is, **in fine**, a very bloody, vile rogue and damned rascal, —eh, Smy?" (Absalom Troy, *Adam Penfeather, Buccaneer* 19-20)

in the meanwhile [*i' t' mean-wyell/wyool*] in the meantime; meanwhile

> "[W]e immediately sent away another canoe with more men, to supply them in their attempts. But **in the meanwhile** the first canoe, which had departed the evening before this day, came aboard ..." (Basil Ringrose, *Bucaniers of America* Part IV, Chap. XVI)

in very truth [*i'/'n vaah/vay-ry troof*] truly; certainly

> "For all the world, sleeping like two babes and your two arms fast about him, my dear mem, as you had plucked him to your heart from the very claws o 'death, as I do protest ye did **in very truth**, or demme!" (Crabtree, *Winds of Chance* 96)

incredible fact [*en-creder/cre'i/cre'-ble fack*] incredibly; unbelievably

"You have, sir, **incredible fact**, —affronted me, and this is so new in my experience that it becomes my pleasure to inflict you upon myself to our mutual exacerbation." (Black Bartlemy, *Adam Penfeather, Buccaneer* 255)

is my notion [*be me/myee noo/no'oo-shern/shoohn*] that's what I think

> "We wants that treasure, and the means to have it. The question is how. Without a drop of bloodshed, **is my notion**." (Long John Silver, "Treasure Island" [1960] 55:07)

it is plain beyond disputing [*ett 's\be playeen b'-yarrn'/yarrnd/yon'/yont deh/der-spoo-tin'*] it is absolutely clear; it is undoubtedly the case

> "**It is plain, beyond disputing**, that you can be no way partaker with us in any capture, while you are only a constrain'd prisoner ..." (John Russell, *Pirates of the New England Coast* 174)

it seems [*ett/i' seems*]

> "I arrive a trifle late, **it seems**." (Peter Blood, *Captain Blood Returns* 287) "[B]y God, my lord, you are a true Conisby, **it seemeth!**" (Adam Penfeather, *Black Bartlemy's Treasure* 80)

it's in my mind [*ett 's\be OR 'tes/'tis i'/'n me/myee mawnd/min'/myeen'/myeend*] I'm thinking; I'm of the opinion, supposition, belief, or understanding that

> "And is that all now! Faith, **it was in my mind** ye might be asking us to recover the value of your slaves from this Captain-General of Havana ..." (Peter Blood, *The Fortunes of Captain Blood* 117)

it's odds [*ett 's\be OR 'tes/'tis arrds*] it's likely that; it's probable that

> < "I can trust you?" "Ye're not obliged to. And **it's odds** ye'll waste your time in any case." > (Captain Easterling & Peter Blood, *Captain Blood Returns* 20)

I've taken a notion into my old numbskull
[*I'eev tayee-kern a noo/no'oo-shern/shoohn inta/ interr me/myee ol'/oold/o'oold narrm/noohm-skoohl*] I have a hunch; I suspect

> "I've taken a notion into my old numb-skull." (Long John Silver, on realizing that Allardyce's skeleton is itself a mark-er pointing the way to Flint's treasure, *Treasure Island* 177, Chap. 31)

let me perish [*laaht/le' me parrish/parsh/ persh*] let me die; a milder alternative to an oath like "damn me" or "I'll be damned"

"Me" oaths are generally used to convey intense surprise, frustration, disgust, or dis-appointment, often (but not always) directed at or as a result of oneself, one's own ac-tions, or the matter at hand, rather than at the addressee, and often (but not always) spoken in a modest or good-natured way that makes clear to the addressee that he is not the cause of the negative sentiment being expressed.

> "Go to't, lass, drink hearty—here's you and me agin world and damn all, says I. **Let me perish**!" (Roger Tressady, *Martin Conisby's Vengeance* 158)

let that rest there [*laaht/le' tharrt rest tharr/ theyarr/theyerr*] enough said; I won't say any more

> "I as your quarter-master, as my office requires, will see it executed, and, per-haps, in a more favourable manner than at first I design'd, or he really deserves at mine or your hands either; but **let that rest there**." (John Russell, *Pirates of the New England Coast* 192)

like [*lawk/lyeeke*]

Used generically after a statement to convey suggestion, understatement, deliberate impreci-sion, or figurative meaning. A modern speaker might use "or something," "and all," or "a bit" in the same context.

> "Dick! you just jump up, like a sweet lad, and get me an apple, to wet my pipe **like**." (Long John Silver, *Treasure Island* 61, Chap. 11)

like as not [*lawk/lyeeke as narrt*] in all likeli-hood; probably

Though literally meaning "as likely as not," the phrase is almost always used to assert an affirmative probability.

> < "They are fouled with the blood of nine men." "Ay, lass, and many others, **like as not**." > (Ursula Revell & Japhet Bly, *Winds of Chance* 339)

like enough [*lawk/lyeeke enarrff/enow/'nough*] in all likelihood; probably

> "**Like enough**, I would set no limits to what gentlemen might consider shipshape, or might not, as the case were." (Long John Silver, *Treasure Island* 108, Chap. 20)

listen here [*lessen 'ee'arr/'ee'err/'ere/hee'arr/ hee'err*]

Used before making any assertive state-ment, especially when the speaker is attempt-ing or purporting to exercise his will over the addressee in some way, or to persuade the addressee of something.

> "Now, **listen here**, Patch. We'll need ex-tra anchor overboard." (Long John Silver, "The Adventures of Long John Silver: Miss Purity's Birthday" 8:55)

little wonder [*lil' woohnd/wunn-er*] no won-der; it stands to reason

> "It's there she learned 'Pieces of Eight,' and **little wonder**; three hundred and fifty thousand of 'em, Hawkins!" (Long John Silver, *Treasure Island* 55, Chap. 10)

(you) look here (now) [*(ya/ye/yer) look 'ee'arr/ 'ee'err/'ere/hee'arr/hee'err (narr/nowoo)*]

Used before making any assertive state-ment, especially when the speaker is attempt-ing or purporting to exercise his will over the addressee in some way, or to persuade the addressee of something.

"Now, **look here**, you've run me down; here I am; well, then, speak up: what is it?" (Billy Bones, *Treasure Island* 11, Chap. 2) "And now, **you look here**, we've had about enough of this foolery." (Israel Hands, *Treasure Island* 141, Chap. 26) "Why, hillo! **look here now**: this ain't lucky! You've gone and cut this out of a Bible." (Long John Silver, *Treasure Island* 163, Chap. 29)

look now [*look narr/nowoo*]

"Here shall be no need for fight, for **look now**, Tressady, though you are fool, you are one I have yearned to meet ..." (Captain Jo, fooling Roger Tressady into a friendly exchange just before slaughtering him, *Martin Conisby's Vengeance* 157–58)

look you (now) [*look 'ee/ya/ye/yer (narr/nowoo)*]

Used in conjunction with any assertive statement. Note that "now" may be used at the beginning or end of the phrase.

"And I did it—**look'ee**, because he failed me once, d'ye see!" (Roger Tressady, explaining his reasons for killing Tom Purdy, *Black Bartlemy's Treasure* 312) "**Lookee now**, when I goes for to kiss a woman, she ain't agoin' for to deny me, no nor nobody else ain't neither ..." (Abner, raving in a drunken fit, *Adam Penfeather, Buccaneer* 14) "**Now, look'ee**, you have named me rogue and good as called me liar, which is great folly seeing you do lie in my power." (Adam Penfeather, *Black Bartlemy's Treasure* 325)

look you here (now) [*look 'ee/ya/ye/yer 'ee'arr/ 'ee'err/'ere/hee'arr/hee'err (narr/nowoo)*]

Used before making any assertive statement, especially when the speaker is attempting or purporting to exercise his will over the addressee in some way, or to persuade the addressee of something.

"Now, **look you here**, Jim Hawkins, you're within half a plank of death, and, what's a long sight worse, of torture." (Long John

Silver, *Treasure Island* 160, Chap. 28) "**Lookee here, now**, squire's son. I wanna deal with ye." (Billy Doyle, *The Gun Ketch* 159) "**Now look here**, if you leave this inn right away, we'll stop bringin' charges against you for ill behavior." (Long John Silver, "The Adventures of Long John Silver: The Eviction" 6:40)

looks like [*looks lawk/lyeeke*] it appears; it seems; from what I can tell

"Slipped him a potion, **looks like**." (Trip Fenner, "The Adventures of Long John Silver: The Necklace" 23:21)

mark [*mahrrk*] listen; remember

"Monkeys, cease your chattering and list to Joanna. And **mark**—my prisoners go aboard this very hour, yes." (Captain Jo, *Martin Conisby's Vengeance* 62)

(you) mark me [*(ya/ye/yer) mahrrk me*] listen to me; remember this

"**Mark me**, 'twould be perfectly feasible for me to give you the slip any dark night. ..." (Andrew Murray, *Porto Bello Gold* 91) "But **you mark me**, cap'n, it won't do twice, by thunder!" (Long John Silver, *Treasure Island* 107, Chap. 20)

mark (well) my word(s) [*mahrrk (waahl) me/ myee warrd(s)*] listen to what I'm saying; remember my words

< "I'm sorry, Miss Pinker, but I'm acting under orders." "Under orders, indeed. Well, **mark my word**, Long John Silver's having council with Governor Strong this very moment, and you and your soldiers will be obliged to cart every last thing inside when he returns." > (guard sergeant & Purity Pinker, "The Adventures of Long John Silver: The Eviction" 11:10) "If we don't do something soon, **mark my words**, we'll be knitting doilies." (Patch, "The Adventures of Long John Silver: The Eviction" 15:17) "And **mark well me words**, maties: Dead

men tell no tales." (talking skull, "Pirates of the Caribbean" Disney attraction)

mark that [*mahrrk tharrt*] listen to what I just said; remember that

> < "[T]he Lord hath set you here i' this flowery garden like Adam and her like Eve—" "And yourself like the serpent!" "Ha' done, Martin, ha' done! 'The Lord shall root out deceitful lips and the tongue that speaks proud things!' **mark that!**" > (Resolution Day & Martin Conisby, *Martin Conisby's Vengeance* 168)

mark this [*mahrrk dis/t'is*] listen to this; remember this

> "But **mark this!** Let any man fail of his duty to me but once and I shoot that man or hang him out o' hand—is't understood?" (Adam Penfeather, *Black Bartlemy's Treasure* 317)

mark you [*mahrrk 'ee/ya/ye/yer*]
you mark [*ya/ye/yer mahrrk*] listen; remember

> "Faith, now, I'll not say that it might not be worth a trifle of sacrilege—just a trifle, **mark you**—to squeeze his plunder out of this rogue of a Captain-General." (Peter Blood, *The Fortunes of Captain Blood* 119) "Then **mark ye.** Our ship is foul with long voyaging and needeth cleansing out and in." (Japhet Bly, to the crew of the *Joyful Deliverance*, *Winds of Chance* 152) "They're going to throw me off. But, **you mark,** I stand by you through thick and thin." (Long John Silver, *Treasure Island* 160, Chap. 28)

mark you here [*mahrrk 'ee/ya/ye/yer 'ee'arr/ 'ee'err/'ere/hee'arr/hee'err*] listen to me; remember this

> "But **mark you here:** I'm an easy man— I'm quite the gentleman, says you; but this time it's serious." (Long John Silver, *Treasure Island* 61, Chap. 11)

(and) mark you this [(*an'/'n'*) *mahrrk 'ee/ya/ ye/yer dis/t'is*] listen to this; remember this

"Well now, these be predatory tribes very warlike, that for the present have cast in their lot with the Spaniards, though— **and mark you this**—at one time they and these Aztecs were one great race." (Japhet Bly, *Winds of Chance* 197)

may I be damned, eyes and liver, if [*mayee I'ee be damt, eye'ees an'/'n levv/libb/li'-er, an'\ eff/eff'n/if'n*]

Used to negate emphatically whatever statement follows, in a way comparable to the modern phrase "I'll be damned if."

> "If I catch you pryin' around **may I be [damned], eyes and liver, if** I don't cut your heart out." (Blueskin, *The Book of Pirates* "Blueskin, the Pirate" 166)

may I drink a bowl of brimstone and fire with the devil if [*mayee I'ee drenk a bowool o'\on bremstoone/sto'oone an'/'n' farr/fyarr weth/wi'/wiff/witt t' daahv/dayv/debb/div-il an'\eff/eff'n/if'n*]

Used to negate emphatically whatever statement follows, in a way comparable to the modern phrase "I'll be damned if."

> "[B]ut if you will be a villain and betray your trust, may G[o]d strike me dead, and **may I drink a bowl of brimstone and fire with the D[evi]l, if** I don't send you head-long to H[e]ll, G[o]d d[am]n me ..." (William Fly, *General History of the Pyrates* 611)

may I perish [*mayee I'ee parrish/parsh/persh*] may I die

Used to swear on pain of death to the truth or certainty of the statement being made. The speaker is essentially saying "kill me otherwise" or "kill me if it isn't true."

> "I've been in somebody's debt ever since I can remember. But this—**may I perish!**— is a debt of another kind." (George Fairfax, *The Fortunes of Captain Blood* 154)

maybe [*mayee-bee*]

Used often to preface or follow an ironic, mocking, or cutting comment.

"Ha-harr, **maybe** you thought you was cap'n 'ere? Fetch the water bucket." (Long John Silver, "Treasure Island" [1950] 1:15:49)

methinks [*me-finks/thenks/t'inks*] I think; I believe; I suspect

"And **methinks** the secret cast a shadow betwixt us that grew ever deeper, for as the days passed and no sail appeared, there came a strangeness, an unlove betwixt us that grew ..." (Adam Penfeather, *Black Bartlemy's Treasure* 89)

mind (you) [*mawnd/min'/myeen'/myeend ('ee/ ya/ye/yer)*] remember; note; keep in mind

"I'm still your cap'n, **mind**—till you outs with your grievances, and I reply ..." (Long John Silver, *Treasure Island* 164, Chap. 29) "I'll put on my old cocked hat, and step along of you to Cap'n Trelawney, and report this here affair. For, **mind you**, it's serious, young Hawkins ..." (Long John Silver, *Treasure Island* 45, Chap. 8)

mind this [*mawnd/min'/myeen'/myeend dis/t'is*] remember this; note this; keep this in mind

"Ay, do as ye will, but—**mind this**, —when you are with your friends o' the lower deck you shall infallibly sink to their level soon or late!" (Absalom Troy, *Adam Penfeather, Buccaneer* 99)

more's the pity [*marr/moor is\be t' petty/pi'y*] unfortunately; regrettably; sadly enough

"Aye, there won't be much left when Sam is done wi' you, **more's the pity**." (Roger Tressady, *Black Bartlemy's Treasure* 305)

neither [*needer/nee'er/nyder/ny'er*]

Used at the end of compound statements instead of terms and phrases like "too," "also" or "as well," where the statement includes some negative aspect or element. Thus, "He's a rogue an' a right sorry seaman, **neither**."

"They kin use some 'blunt' in the pocket, 'cause they ain't no prize money to share out over pirates, an' damn' little head money per foe, **neither**." (Billy Doyle, attempting to bribe Alan Lewrie by offering his men loot, *The Gun Ketch* 159)

never a doubt [*nebber/ne'er a darrt/dowoot*] no doubt; without a doubt

"'Tis they, **never a doubt**." (Long John Silver, watching two other ships of Andrew Murray's company approach, *Porto Bello Gold* 73)

never doubt it [*nebber/ne'er darrt/dowoot ett/'n*] don't doubt it; be sure of it

"'Sblood! That will we, Smy, **never doubt it!**" (Benjamin Trigg, *Adam Penfeather, Buccaneer* 332)

never you fear [*nebber/ne'er 'ee/ya/ye/yer fee-arr/err*] don't worry

"I'll see to 'Lord' Dinwiddie, **never you fear**." (Roger Press, *The Pirate Round* 223)

no doubt [*no'oo darrt/dowoot*]
not a doubt [*narrt a darrt/dowoot*] without a doubt

"And Don Miguel, **no doubt**, 'll intend to hang you from the yardarm." (Cahusac, *Captain Blood Returns* 140) < "An account—a strict account would have been asked of Spain." "And it would have been rendered, **not a doubt**." > (Chevalier de Saintonges & Peter Blood, *The Fortunes of Captain Blood* 77)

no less [*no'oo lass*] indeed

Used following an assertive statement to emphasize that the speaker intends its meaning to the fullest extent and without qualification.

"Rot me, child, it's a duty, **no less**." (George Fairfax, *The Fortunes of Captain Blood* 160)

none denying [*narrn/noohn a-denyin'*] absent any disagreement; given no view to the contrary

< "So now, since I command here, **none denying**—" "And what o' Captain Jo?" >

(Roger Tressady & Resolution Day, *Martin Conisby's Vengeance* 157)

not but what [*narrt barrt wharrt/whorrt*] however; that notwithstanding

> < "You think them in a better temper than they were?" "I know it, sir. **Not but what** the will to work mischief is to be found in two or three of the men; but they dare not trust each other." > (The Red Rover & Davis, *The Red Rover* 351)

now [*narr/nowoo*]

Used before or after any assertive statement.

> "**Now**, a friend o' mine be sailin' tonight to a French island, Martinique. We'll get 'ee aboard." (Long John Silver, "The Adventures of Long John Silver: Turnabout" 22:11) "A remark spoke slighting like that could raise a man's blood **now**, could it not?" (Blackbeard, "Blackbeard's Ghost" 22:46)

now I tell you [*narr/nowoo I'ee taahl 'ee/ya/ye/yer*]

Used to preface any assertive or insistent statement, especially when expressing one's point of view or taking issue with another's.

> "Well, **now I tell you**, I never seen good come o' goodness yet. Him as strikes first is my fancy; dead men don't bite; them's my views—amen, so be it." (Israel Hands, *Treasure Island* 141, Chap. 26)

now then [*narr/nowoo thayn*]

Used before making any assertive statement, especially when it follows from or is made in connection with some earlier speech or conduct.

> "**Now then**, matey, don't ye take it so hard." (Long John Silver, "Treasure Island" [1950] 47:30)

o(h) [*o'oo*]
oho [*oho'oo*]

Used for emphasis, especially to express surprise, disbelief, displeasure, or conviction, or in conveying a sudden reaction or sharply felt sentiment.

> "**O** a right cunning, fierce rogue was Adam, and none to match him but me." (Roger Tressady, *Black Bartlemy's Treasure* 304) "**Oh**, I've run aground." (Blackbeard, on discovering his rum bottle empty, "Blackbeard's Ghost" 41:29) "**Oho**, Cap'n Penfeather, 'tis the Smiler hath saved ye the labour, look'ee!" (Sam Spraggons, gleefully congratulating himself on assaulting Roger Tressady, *Black Bartlemy's Treasure* 316)

or burn me [*arr barrn me*]

Used to affirm on pain of burning to the truth or certainty of a preceding statement. The term "burn" arguably has double significance, referring principally to damnation (to the extent a person damned is thought to suffer the fires of hell) but also to profound misfortune (as fire is easily the thing most dreaded among pirates, most of whom cannot swim and who rely on the integrity of the wood underneath their feet for survival).

> < "Yet this shall not let or stay the hand o' Justice." "No whit, old lad, **or burn me**!" > (Smy Peters & Absalom Troy, *Adam Penfeather, Buccaneer* 22)

or I be not NAME [*arr I'ee be narrt ___*]

Used following a statement for the purpose of declaring that such is as true or certain as the fact that the speaker bears his own name.

> "By all what's holy and unholy, I'll have that treasure some day **or I be not Long John Silver**!" (Long John Silver, *Dead Man's Chest* 9)

or I'm mistook [*arr I'eem mee/meh-stook*] or I'm mistaken

> "You're a good boy, **or I'm mistook**; but you're on'y a boy, all told. Now, Ben Gunn is fly." (Ben Gunn, *Treasure Island* 100, Chap. 19)

or I've got a dead man's dinghy [*arr I'eev garrt a dayd man's denghy*]

Used after a statement to express the conviction with which it is made. The speaker suggests he believes his statement to be as true as the proposition that he has "a dead man's dinghy" is absurd and implausible.

"Fairy footprints, Captain. He's Peter Pan **or I've got a dead man's dinghy**." (Smee, "Hook" 44:18)

or let me drown [*arr laaht/le' me drowoond*]
Used to affirm on pain of death by drowning to the truth or certainty of a preceding statement. As most pirates (and seamen of the seventeenth and eighteenth centuries) cannot swim, the reference is to a circumstance that many of them fear profoundly.

"Twas woundy miracle **or let me drownd!**" (Abnegation Mings, *Adam Penfeather, Buccaneer* 16)

or so [*arr so'oo*]
Used generically after a statement to convey suggestion, understatement, deliberate imprecision, or figurative meaning. A modern speaker might use "or something" or "maybe" in the same context.

"Hows'ever, us can give 'em a broadside **or so** afore they run us aboard—eh, John?" (Ned Bowser, *Adam Penfeather, Buccaneer* 118)

perceive me now [*parr/pre-ceive me narr/nowoo*] listen to what I'm saying; make a note of what I'm telling you; pay attention

< "'Twas cruel and bloody murder!" "Why, **perceive me now**, *amigo*, let us reason together, *camarado*—thus now it all dependeth upon the point o' view ..." > (Martin Conisby & Resolution Day, *Martin Conisby's Vengeance* 99)

regard now [*regahrrd narr/nowoo*] listen; pay attention

"**Regard now**, Master Innocence. You have crossed me once. You have beat me once. You have refused me honourable fight. You have hurt me with vile club." (Captain Jo, *Martin Conisby's Vengeance* 21)

right enough [*rawt/righeet enarrff/enow/'nough*] all right; sure enough; as one might have expected; certainly

"It's the *Chepillo* **right enough**. Sneaking home with her tail between her legs." (unnamed pirate on Tortuga, "Pirates of Tortuga" 46:41)

savvy? understand?

"Name me captain, I'll sail under your colors, I'll give you ten percent of me plunder, and you get to introduce yourself as Commodore Barbossa, **savvy?**" (Jack Sparrow, "Pirates of the Caribbean: The Curse of the Black Pearl" 1:46:31)

say(s) I [*sayee(s OR sayz) I'ee*]
Used when making an assertive or insistent statement, especially a command or instruction or an expression of one's point of view.

"But good luck t'ye and a fair wind, **say I!**" (Roger Tressady, *Black Bartlemy's Treasure* 302) "And God's will be done, **says I**, though here be we as must go solitary awhile and Joanna sick to death, comrade." (Resolution Day, *Martin Conisby's Vengeance* 164) < "Where's Finney!" "Woy, 'iz lordship's aft, Admiral. An' bad cess t'the brainless bugger, **sez oy!**" > (Alan Lewrie & pirate aboard the *Caroline, The Gun Ketch* 311)

say now [*sayee narr/nowoo*] well, now; say
Used to preface a suggestion, impression, or other soft statement—that is, any statement the speaker wishes to express gently, tenatively, or unpresumptuously.

"But **say now**, I had always heard there was a fellow, name of Yancy, who run things on St. Mary's." (Elephiant Yancy, *The Pirate Round* 246)

says you [*sayees/sayz 'ee/ya/ye/yer*]
Used after characterizing, conveying, describing, or summarizing a position,

view, belief, inclination, or thought of the addressee. Used especially when the speaker is projecting or guessing at what the addressee might or would say about something, rather than repeating back what has actually been said.

> "And neither you nor me's come out of it with what I should make so bold as to call credit. Nor you, neither, **says you**." (Long John Silver, *Treasure Island* 45, Chap. 8)

see here [*see 'ee'arr/'ee'err/'ere/hee'arr/hee'err*]
Used especially before a statement of explanation or exposition.

> "**See here**, my bright lads, learn this— when you come aboard my ship and I say to one o' ye do this or do that, he does it, d'ye see, or—up to the yard-arm he swings by his thumbs or his neck as occasion warrants." (Adam Penfeather, *Black Bartlemy's Treasure* 111)

see now [*see narr/nowoo*]
Used especially before a statement of explanation or exposition.

> "**See now**, here's you and Merrilees and Godby, here's Farnaby and Toby Hudd the bo'sun, Treliving the carpenter, and McLean his mate, here's Robins and Perks and Taffery the armourer—good mariners all." (Adam Penfeather, *Black Bartlemy's Treasure* 124)

see (you) [*see ('ee/ya/ye/yer)*]
Used before or after any statement of explanation or exposition to invite the speaker to comprehend or accept what was stated.

> "Hear me, Yancy, when I am king here, we shall have a regular army, **see**? Drills, uniforms, the whole thing." (Obadiah Spelt, *The Pirate Round* 146) "Japhet is wily fellow, for **see you** while he held Ramirez in parley, we were stealing up outboard to take 'em suddenly from above." (Barnabas Rokeby, *Winds of Chance* 57)

so d'ye see [*so'oo do/does 'ee/ya/yer/you see*]
Used to proceed logically or for purposes of persuasion from one or more statements to a summary or concluding statement.

> < "Have you so many children, Jeremy?" "Ninety and four, ma'm, and others on the road; **so, d'ye see**, here I must abide." > (Ursula Revell & Jeremy Jervey, *Winds of Chance* 249)

so ho [*so'oo ho'oo*] well, now; well, well; hello

> "**So-ho**, then, labour and sweat, my pretty man: it shall be all vain, aha—vain and to no purpose." (Captain Jo, *Martin Conisby's Vengeance* 27)

so it is that [*so'oo ett/'n/'t be OR 'tes/'tis tharrt*]
Used to proceed logically or for purposes of persuasion from one or more statements to a summary or concluding statement.

> < "This man o' blood hath burned Tuyayani village yonder, slaying many o' the folk, and is now marching 'gainst Pazaquil that is a fair town, to slay more innocents, and all this for base gold!" "And **so it is that** I am for Pazaquil also, to do my endeavour in defence o' these same innocents ..." > (Matthew Swayne & Japhet Bly, *Winds of Chance* 275)

so so [*so'oo so'oo*]
Used to express surprise or disbelief, to convey a reaction to new information, or to set out an assessment, a considered observation, or some other summary or conclusory statement.

> "**So, so**! That means, then, that he will be returning by way of the Tortuga Channel?" (Peter Blood, *The Fortunes of Captain Blood* 67)

stand by to go about [*stan'/starrn'/starrnd byee t'/ta/ter go'oo abarrt/abowoot/'barrt/'bout/'bowoot*] hold everything; wait just a minute
Used before proposing something radical or contrary to expectation, on asserting

something at odds with existing views or understandings, or to rivet another's attention suddenly and urgently. The phrase is actually a sailing command meaning to prepare to turn around and head in the opposite direction by turning a vessel's bow through the wind—that is, "get ready to turn right around."

> "Come, this won't do. **Stand by to go about**. This is a rum start, and I can't name the voice: but it's someone skylarking—someone that's flesh and blood, and you may lay to that." (Long John Silver, announcing his suspicion that someone is masquerading as John Flint's ghost, *Treasure Island* 180, Chap. 32)

sure [*sharr/shorr*]

(1) indeed; truly; certainly; definitely

> "O Lord love me! **Sure** there's not your like i' the whole world, Martin!" (Adam Penfeather, *Black Bartlemy's Treasure* 328) "I have been in worse places, **sure**." (Thomas Marlowe, *The Pirate Round* 316)

(2) obviously; of course

> < "Whence came his fetters?" "Out of the satchel, **sure**." > (Ursula Revell & Japhet Bly, *Winds of Chance* 159)

sure and certain [*sharr/shorr an'/'n' sarrten*] for sure; absolute(ly) and definite(ly)

A nice example of stylistic redundancy; see Section 18.2.2.

> "Not much to look at, master—no, but 'tis death **sure and sarten**, howsomever." (John, showing Martin Conisby one of his poisoned thorns, *Martin Conisby's Vengeance* 181)

sure enough [*sharr/shorr enarrff/enow/'nough*] as one might have expected; certainly

> "And **sure enough** in a while comes the big man Tressady a-stealing furtive-fashion and falls to hunting both in the open grave and round about it but, finding nothing, steals him off again." (Adam

Penfeather, describing Roger Tressady's attempts to find Black Bartlemy's dagger around Bartlemy's grave, *Black Bartlemy's Treasure* 92)

sure now [*sharr/shorr narr/nowoo*]

Used in conjunction with a confident or assertive statement, especially when disagreeing with, qualifying or correcting something said by, or expressing a viewpoint different from that of the addressee.

> "**Sure, now**, he was a gallant fellow, Spaniard or no Spaniard." (Peter Blood, *Captain Blood Returns* 182) "For every thousand pieces that the Spaniard offers, **sure, now**, I'll offer two." (Peter Blood, *Captain Blood Returns* 143)

surely [*sharrly/shorrly*] undoubtedly; certainly

> "**Surely** nought is there in all this wretched world so desolate as a loveless woman!" (Captain Jo, *Martin Conisby's Vengeance* 95) "Ye've the fever, Captain, **surely**." (Tim, *The Fortunes of Captain Blood* 159)

that's a true word [*tharrt is\be a troo warrd*] that's the truth

> "That was how the rum took him. Blue! well, I reckon he was blue. **That's a true word**." (George Merry, *Treasure Island* 180, Chap. 32)

that's clear [*tharrt is\be clee-arr/err*] that much is clear; I know

> "Ye don't know Colonel Bishop, **that's clear**." (Wolverstone, *Captain Blood: His Odyssey* 251)

then [*thayn*]

Used following an assertive statement, especially when the statement follows from or is made in connection with some earlier speech or conduct.

> "So ho—he knoweth my name **then**!" (Roger Tressady, reacting to Martin Conisby's addressing him by name, *Black Bartlemy's Treasure* 301)

there is this much to say, and of that you may believe me [*tharr/theyarr/theyerr 's\be dis/t'is marrch/moohch t'/ta/ter sayee, an'/'n o'\on tharrt 'ee/ya/ye/yer mayee b'/ber-leef me*]

A twofold expression, combining the modern equivalents "I'll say this much" and "you can believe me when I say."

> "Well, I am sorry for the way you were handled, but **there is this much to say, and of that you may believe me**, that nothing was meant to you but kindness ..." (Abraham Dawling, *The Book of Pirates* "The Ghost of Captain Brand" 66)

thing of it is [*fing/theng/thin'/t'in'/t'ing o'\on ett/'n/'t be*] the thing is; here's the thing

> "**Thing of it is**, sir, the men thought they was signing on aboard a merchantman, and maybe for the Red Sea." (Duncan Honeyman, *The Pirate Round* 74)

think ye? [*fink/thenk/t'ink 'ee/ya/ye/yer?*] do you think?

> "And how many fighting men shall Guatamoxin muster, **think ye**, 'twixt Tuyayani yonder and Pazaquil?" (Japhet Bly, *Winds of Chance* 276)

'tis beyond doubt [*ett/it 's\be* OR *'tes b'-yarrn'/yarrnd/yon'/yont darrt/dowoot*] without a doubt; undoubtedly

> "None the less someone aboard this ship signalled yon black craft by means of a lanthorn, **'tis beyond doubt!**" (Adam Penfeather, *Black Bartlemy's Treasure* 123)

'tis in my mind [*ett/it 's\be* OR *'tes i'/'n me/myee mawnd/min'/myeen'/myeend*] I think; I suspect; I believe; I have a hunch; I'm of the view that; it occurs to me that

> "These jewels were thine, Ma'm Bly, and what's thine is mine, and **'tis in my mind** we shall sorely need such fortune one day." (Japhet Bly, *Winds of Chance* 334)

to be sure [*t'/ta/ter be sharr/shorr*] indeed; certainly

> "Though **to be sure** this boat is right well equipped, both for victuals and weapons." (Resolution Day, *Martin Conisby's Vengeance* 146) "Merry, standin' for cap'n again? You're a pushy lad, **to be sure**." (Long John Silver, "Treasure Island" [1972] 1:26:49)

to my sorrow [*t'/ta/ter me/myee sahrr-owoo*] regretfully; unfortunately

> < "And you—a woman!" "Aye, **to my sorrow!**" > (Martin Conisby & Captain Jo, *Martin Conisby's Vengeance* 9)

to own the truth [*t'/ta/ter owoon t' troof*] to tell the truth; truthfully

> < "And is it usual for ships in the trade to carry so heavy an armament?" "Perhaps it is—perhaps not. **To own the truth**, there is not much law on the coast, and the strong arm often does as much as the right." > (Harry Wilder & officer aboard the *Dolphin*, *The Red Rover* 87)

to speak it all in a word [*t'/ta/ter speak ett/'n awrl i'/'n a warrd*] in a word; to sum it up

> "[I]n that dangerous action, **to speak it all in a word**, he shewed himself more like a coward than one of our profession, that is to say a true Buccaneer." (William Dick, *Bucaniers of America* 337)

true as true [*troo as troo*] that's absolutely true

> "[T]here's precious few landsmen as stop to figger out the chances a poor sailor must take and never a thankee from his owners nor aught but curses from his skipper, like as not. **True as true**, young gentleman." (Long John Silver, *Porto Bello Gold* 20)

true enough [*troo enarrff/enow/'nough*] certainly; definitely

> "Here's Bartlemy's dagger **true enough**, Martin." (Adam Penfeather, *Black Bartlemy's Treasure* 100)

truly [*troolee*] indeed; certainly

"Why, **truly**, Thomas Ford, remember Pompey, but forget not Job as died so sudden—in the midst o' life he were in death, were Job!" (Resolution Day, *Martin Conisby's Vengeance* 90)

'twould seem ['*twoood seem*] it would seem; it would appear

"Here's you now, you that was so mighty and fierce—aye, a very hell-fire roarer— here's that same you a-hanging here a very helpless, pitiful fool, shipmate, and thirsty **'twould seem** ..." (Adam Penfeather, *Black Bartlemy's Treasure* 58)

unless I am mistook [*arrn/hun/oohn-lass* OR *less'n I'ee arrm/em\be mee/meh-stook*] unless I'm mistaken; if I'm correct

"I think you will come and drink with us; for, **unless I am mistook**, you are Mr. Barnaby True, and I am come here to tell you that the *Royal Sovereign is come in*." (Abraham Dawling, urging Barnaby True to join him and his men for a drink, *The Book of Pirates* "The Ghost of Captain Brand" 45–46)

upon my honour ['*parrn/'pon/uparrn me/myee arrn-arr*] on my word

Used after making a promise or representation.

"But you keep your weather-eye open, Jim, and I'll share with you equals, **upon my honour**." (Billy Bones, *Treasure Island* 16, Chap. 3)

verily [*vaah/vay-rily*] indeed; truly; certainly

"Oh, **verily** there is more life, more fire and passion in a small, dead fish than in all thy great, slow body!" (Captain Jo, *Martin Conisby's Vengeance* 48)

well and good [*waahl an'/'n' good*] that's okay; that's all right; that's fine

Used to preface a statement conveyed as true or certain notwithstanding the truth or existence of some other fact or statement, or used to suggest that what has been said is

plain or uncontroversial, and to point greater attention to what the speaker is about to say next. The ultimate effect is to acknowledge one thing but divert attention toward another, like "that may be true but," "setting that aside," and "in any event." Spoken often about something unpleasant or unsatisfactory in order to communicate the speaker's indifference thereto.

< "Heaven's mercy! What would you have me eat?" "Beef, lass, flesh of an ox, ma'm, bouccaned that it may keep—what, no? **Well and good**, shalt devour it with sweet avidity anon." > (Ursula Revell & Japhet Bly, *Winds of Chance* 158) "Yonder in our lee four miles and coming up handily be Moorish pirates and lusty fighters, perchance worth the looting—**well and good**. But aboard these floating hells, slaving 'neath the lash to serve their oars, be men the like of us ..." (Japhet Bly, *Winds of Chance* 68)

well now [*waahl narr/nowoo*]

A prefatory interjection comparable to "well," but a bit more emphatic.

"**Well now**, let me burn if I ever heard or met the like of you, Captain Adam." (Black Bartlemy, *Adam Penfeather, Buccaneer* 280)

well so [*waahl so'oo*] well; in that case

A prefatory interjection used before a statement that follows from or relates to an earlier statement.

< "Stop! If you will to murder each other, spare me the horror if it." "**Well so**, Johnny, since madam hath put an end to our gentlemanly diversion, we'll see thee safe abed,—come!" > (Ursula Revell & Japhet Bly, *Winds of Chance* 141-42)

what [*wharrt/whorrt*] hey; say; you know what

Used to call another's attention to what the speaker is about to say without communicating any particular substantive meaning.

"**What**, messmate, here cometh one to lay alongside you awhile, old Resolution

63

Day, friend, mate o' this here noble ship *Happy Despatch*, comrade, and that same myself, look'ee!" (Resolution Day, *Martin Conisby's Vengeance* 72)

what I says (to you) is [*wharrt/whorrt I'ee sayees/sayz (t'/ta/ter 'ee/ya/ye/yer) be*]

Used to preface any assertive or insistent statement, especially when expressing one's point of view or taking issue with another's.

"God or no, we'm Englishmen to take rough along o' smooth and make the best o' both, so **what I says is**, —let's do 't." (Ned Bowser, *Adam Penfeather, Buccaneer* 180) "**What I says to you is**, get to wind'ard o' vengeance—nay, heave it overboard, shipmate, and you'll ride the easier, aye and sweeter, and seek something more useful—gold, for instance, 'tis a handy thing, I've heard say—so ha' done wi' vengeance!" (Adam Penfeather, *Black Bartlemy's Treasure* 61)

what would you say but [*wharrt/whorrt woood 'ee/ya/ye/yer sayee barrt*]

Used before a statement to suggest it is indisputably true or undeniably persuasive.

"And if them pirates camp ashore, Jim, **what would you say but** there'd be widders in the morning?" (Ben Gunn, *Treasure Island* 101, Chap. 19)

(and) what's better [*(an'/'n') wharrt/whorrt is\be be'er\gooder*] even better; still better

"Whatever ship she's aboard of has all the luck, wind, weather, and—**what's better**, rich prizes, Job." (Diccon, describing Captain Jo as the company's luck, *Martin Conisby's Vengeance* 69) < "I saw the Spaniards on the cliff when we sailed." "Aye, **and what's better**, they saw us." > (Jim Hawkins & Patch, "The Adventures of Long John Silver: The Pink Pearl" 20:25)

(and) what's more (to me) [*(an'/'n') wharrt/whorrt is\be marr/moor (t'/ta/ter me)*] moreover; furthermore

And what is more, they've succeeded." (Peter Blood, *Captain Blood: His Odyssey* 187) "There's for you, lass, and right proper bed you'll find it, yet first—this!" "Well, what now?" "A device shall save ye walking in your sleep or, **what's more**, walking in mine—" (Japhet Bly, showing Ursula Revell a piece of rope with which he intends to tie her up, *Winds of Chance* 147) "... I am here with some thought of enlisting your powers with mine 'gainst Santo Domingo, a place of much wealth, sacked years agone by Frankie Drake, but far richer booty to-day, and—**what's more to me**, famous for the warm beauty of its women." (Black Bartlemy, *Adam Penfeather, Buccaneer* 253)

when all is said [*waahn awrl 's\be sayd*] when all is said and done; ultimately; at the end of the day

"Ye're a white-livered cur **when all is said**." (Peter Blood, *Captain Blood: His Odyssey* 194)

(the) which God forbid\forfend [*(t') whech Garrd/Gott/Gud farr/fer-bed\fen'*] God forbid; heaven forbid

"So I'll away to prepare me, therefore, and do thou set by that rapier and take stout broad-sword instead, for 'twill be close and bloody work should the wind drop, **the which God forbid**!" (Smy Peters, *Adam Penfeather, Buccaneer* 116–17) "Spanish troops are marching from the South; so, ma'm, beside this wilderness its cruelty, you are very like to see what Spanish soldiery can do in that way—**which God forfend**!" (Japhet Bly, *Winds of Chance* 168)

which is better [*whech be be'er\gooder*] even better; still better

"Sit down, Martin, and let us eat and, **which is better**, drink together!" (Abengation Mings, *Martin Conisby's Vengeance* 156)

which is worse [*whech be warrse/warrser/ woorse/woorser/worser*] even worse

> "So the rascal lives and, **which is worse**, lives but to win 'em back, for he knoweth their value and such lure shall certainly bring him to his own death—or ours." (Japhet Bly, *Winds of Chance* 339)

while this was doing [*wy-ell/ool dis/t'is warss\warr/were a-doin'*] in the meantime; meanwhile

> "But now we wanted canoes to land our men, and we had no other way but **to** cut down trees and make as many as we had occasion for, these islands affording plenty of large trees fit for our purpose. **While this was doing**, we sent 150 men to take Puebla Nova, a town upon the main near the innermost of these islands, to get provision." (William Dampier, *A New Voyage Round the World* 113)

why [*whyee*] well; well then

> < "Bill, why is it that you are so gloomy? Why do you never speak to any one?" **"Why**, I s'pose it's because I hain't got nothin' to say!" > (Ralph Rover & Bloody Bill, *The Coral Island* 208) "[S]hould a captain be so saucy as to exceed prescription at any time, **why**, down with him!" (Henry Dennis, *General History of the Pyrates* 194–95 & *The Pirates Own Book* 83)

why now [*whyee narr/nowoo*]

An interjection comparable to "why," but a bit more emphatic.

> < "Ah, Master Troy, I perceive you are considering what small, puny wretch I am, eh, sir?" **"Why now**, Adam, let me die but there a'n't a vasty deal o' thee, —now is there?" > (Adam Penfeather & Absalom Troy, *Adam Penfeather, Buccaneer* 10)

why then [*whyee thayn*]

Used when something said earlier gives the speaker some reason or context for saying what he is about to say.

> < "Belvedere be our Cap'n—we want Belvedere!" **"Why then**, take him, bullies, take him and willing!" > (pirates aboard the *Happy Despatch* & Resolution Day, with Resolution then heaving Captain Belvedere's corpse down onto the lower deck, *Martin Conisby's Vengeance* 111)

with a curse [*weth/wi'/wiff/witt a carrse/carrst/ coorse/cursh/curst*]

(1) Used to curse in an inspecific way the addressee or another person or thing referenced.

> "There never was such a murderer born into this wicked world as Adam Penfeather, **with a curse!**" (Roger Tressady, *Black Bartlemy's Treasure* 302)

(2) Used not to curse, but rather to convey a dark, aggressive, spiteful, or otherwise malicious mood, sense, or attitude consistent with that of someone inclined to curse.

> "I am Japhet ... Japhet o' the *Deliverance* ... to sail and fight, an outcast to the end, for my witness is dead ... no proof **with a curse!**" (Japhet Bly, bemoaning his bleak prospects, *Winds of Chance* 92)

(3) Used for emphasis, especially to **express** surprise, disbelief, displeasure, or conviction.

> < "Didst try to find thy wife and family, Zeke?" "No, messmate, no! The children will be grown by now ... well, let 'em think me dead ... as I should be, but for you and Japhet, **with a curse!**" > (Barnabas Rokeby & Ezekiel Penryn, *Winds of Chance* 32)

without (a) doubt [*weth/wi'/wiff/witt-arrt/ou'/ owoot (a) darrt/dowoot*] undoubtedly

> "I suppose I need not tell you, for, **without doubt**, you know it already, that all these islands to windward are in great scarcity of victuals ..." (John Russell, *Pirates of the New England Coast* 166) < "We just saw torches inside!" "Thieves!" "Desperate cutthroats, **without a doubt**." > (Purity

Pinker & Jim Hawkins, reporting suspicious activity to passing soldiers, "The Adventures of Long John Silver: Miss Purity's Birthday" 24:21)

word is [*warrd be*] it's said that; reportedly or supposedly

"I've heard tell of that treasure, Dutch, but **word is** nobody's alive what knows where it's buried." (Henry Morgan, *Dead Man's Chest* 131)

yea [*yayee*] yes; indeed

"[E]ach canoe had six, eight, or ten men on board, **yea** some had fourteen and more." (William Dick, *Bucaniers of America* 333)

you can have my balls for breakfast if [*ya/ ye/yer cayn/kin 'aff/'ave/ha'/haff me/myee bawrls farr/fer brayk/breff-farrst/fess an'\eff/eff'n/if'n*]

Used to affirm, on pain of having one's testicles eaten, the truth or certainty of a preceding statement.

"It was good sport, though, by thunder, 'twas indeed, **you can have me balls for breakfast it wasn't.**" (Thomas Bartholomew Red, on seeing his lieutenant outswim a shark, "Pirates" 7:46)

you don't make no doubt of that [*ya/ye/yer don'/doon't/dorrn't mayeeke no'oo darrt/dowoot o'\on tharrt*] you can be sure of that

"Why, in a place like this, where nobody puts in but gen'lemen of fortune, Silver would fly the Jolly Roger, **you don't make no doubt of that.**" (Ben Gunn, *Treasure Island* 100, Chap. 19)

(and) you (can\may) lay to it\that [*(an'/'n') 'ee/ya/ye/yer (cayn/kin\mayee) layee t'/ta/ter ett/'n/'t\tharrt*] you can bet on it; you can be sure of it

This phrase is an extremely popular one among pirates, and consequently there are several well-worn variations.

"**You can lay to it** I'm a-goin' to give myself a chance to hop up from below."

(Long John Silver, *Porto Bello Gold* 76)

"When you sees Black Dog, **you lay to it**, the man with the one leg ain't far off." (William Bones, "Treasure Island" [1950] 4:14) "There's never a man yet looks me between the eyes and lives to see a good day afterwards, Tommy, **you may lay to that.**" (Long John Silver, drawing a bloody knife out of Tom's body, "Treasure Island" [1972] 46:44) "You won't fight as gentlemen of fortune should; then, by thunder, you'll obey, **and you may lay to it!**" (Long John Silver, *Treasure Island* 159, Chap. 28) "Farewell, Ben Gunn. Our wakes'll cross again some day, **you can lay to that.**" (Long John Silver, *Dead Man's Chest* 7) "... by the horns of Nick there be none of all the coastwise Brotherhood quicker or readier when there's aught i' the wind than Abnegation, **and you can lay to that**, my delicate cove!" (Abnegation Mings, *Black Bartlemy's Treasure* 31)

you may be sure [*ya/ye/yer mayee be sharr/ shorr*] you can be certain

"And though it was a great while after this that I took a like run, yet **you may be sure** I formed a resolution from that time to do the like." (Captain Avery, *The King of Pirates* 73)

you may depend upon it [*ya/ye/yer mayee der-pen' 'parrn/'pon/uparrn 'n/'t*]

"[Y]ou must be sure to say you are married, and have five or six children; for it is only that, that will prevent your being forced; tho', **you may depend upon it**, Russel will do what he can to perswade the company to break the article ..." (members of Edward Low's company, urging a well-liked prisoner to invoke a company article forbidding the forced enlistment of married men, *Pirates of the New England Coast* 163)

you may take it [*ya/ye/yer mayee tayeeke ett/'n/'t*] you can believe; it's safe to say

Often used ironically to preface something so true, obvious, or well known that the cautious phrase "you may take it" becomes playful understatement. For example, "**You may take it** he did not like havin' my cutlass in his belly."

> "**You may take it** they were chagrined at Roseau, when they heard St. Eustatius had got him!" (Otto, *A High Wind in Jamaica* 128)

you mind [*ya/ye/yer mawnd/min'/myeen'/myeend*] remember; note; keep in mind

> "But there he was, **you mind**, and the six all dead—dead and buried." (Ben Gunn, *Treasure Island* 82, Chap. 15)

you must believe [*ya/ye/yer marrst/moohst b'/ber-leef*] you better believe; believe me

> "[H]ow will you do to make your cargo of salt, having no hands, and having nothing wherewith to hire the natives to help you to make it, or to pay for their bringing it down on their asses; for **you must believe** I understand trade." (John Russell, *Pirates of the New England Coast* 166)

you see [*ya/ye/yer see*]

Used following a statement of explanation or exposition.

> "So him they burned, her they buried alive and me they tormented into the wrack **ye see**." (Resolution Day, *Martin Conisby's Vengeance* 73)

you'll allow [*ye'll allowoo*] you must admit

> "But you can ransom her with the doubloons you hide. **You'll allow** that's generous, now." (unnamed pirate impersonator of Peter Blood, *The Fortunes of Captain Blood* 48)

you'll be a bold man\one to say no to that [*ye'll be a bol'/boold/bo'oold man\'un/woohn t'/ta/ter sayee no'oo t'/ta/ter tharrt*] you can't deny that; that much you have to agree with

> "First, you've made a hash of this cruise— **you'll be a bold man to say no to that**." (George Merry, *Treasure Island* 164, Chap. 29)

you'll not deny [*ye'll narrt denyee*] you can't deny; you have to agree

> "Yet you've seen what you've seen, and **you'll not deny** that in ships and guns we are returning stronger than we went." (Peter Blood, *Captain Blood: His Odyssey* 194)

CHAPTER 4

Commands

Commands are essential in pirate talk. The activities that constitute pirate life—sailing, boarding, fighting, defending, capturing, looting, hoarding, safekeeping, reprovisioning—require central direction, coordination, and cooperation. Pirate crews are floating democracies, but their elected officials—especially captain and quartermaster—rule, and are expected to rule, strictly and confidently. They do so through commands.

Pirates in authority use top-down commands for companywide governance. But run-of-the-mill pirates also use commands in everyday conversation. (There's no better way to convey a surly, aggressive attitude.) Threats, oaths, and curses are well and good, but they only serve as means to get the listener to do what the speaker wants. The command, therefore, is the heart of pirate communication.

Remember, you can use commands—especially ship commands—metaphorically. Thus, you can use the command "clap on sail!" to mean "hurry up!" or "let's get going!" and not just to convey its strictly literal meaning, "expose more sail to the wind so that we can sail faster!"

Section 4.1: Command Elements sets out the various types of commands along with the ways of forming and replying to commands. Specifically, this section covers:

- "You" Commands ("**come you here!**")
- "Me" Commands ("**take me that there pistol!**")
- Friendly Commands ("**starb'ard it is!**")
- Epithet Commands ("**stint yer clack fer a lubber!**")
- Negative Commands ("**don't let's lag be'ind!**")
- Command Openers ("**up and** fetch me more rum!**")
- Command Closers ("fetch me more rum **an' lively!**"
- Compliant Replies ("**ay so**")

Section 4.2: General Commands is a list of commands for every situation. Finally, Section 4.3: Special Commands covers four types of special commands:

- Battle Commands ("**fire as you bear!**")
- Boarding Commands ("**grappling hooks away!**")
- Boat Commands ("**break your backs!**")
- Ship Commands ("**crowd on sail!**")

4.1 COMMAND ELEMENTS

4.1.1 "YOU" COMMANDS
The word "you" is often added after a command to make it more emphatic.

- "**Sit'ee** down at table t' starboard, if ye kindly will." (Long John Silver, "Treasure Island" [1950] 16:49)
- < "What is it?" "Death! So **walk you** where I walk." > (Ursula Revell & Japhet Bly, with Bly warning Ursula of patches of quicksand nearby, *Winds of Chance* 174)
- "**Go you** back with that answer, Captain." (pirates aboard the *Valiant*, *Captain Blood Returns* 284)

Note that the same speaker might use a "You" Command in one place but a simple verb command in another—even in a single sentence:

- "**Lie you** and rest, Johnny, **sleep** if you can against what's to do this night, with a curse!" (Japhet Bly, *Winds of Chance* 357)
- "Well, **dig you** a pit about the boat as deep as may be, **bank** the sand about your pit as high as may be. Then **cut you** a channel to high-water mark and beyond. ..." (Captain Jo, *Martin Conisby's Vengeance* 27)

4.1.2 "ME" COMMANDS
The word "me" is often added after a command involving a transitive verb—that is, a verb that takes an object.

The exclamatory sentence, "Kill and run!" contains intransitive verbs, and therefore cannot be used with a "Me" Command. On the other hand, "**Kill me** the doctor and **run me down** 'is wife!" contains transitive verbs, and therefore can be used with "Me" Commands.

The effect of a "Me" Command is to make a command more imperious.

- "**Fetch me** my map!" (Long John Silver, "The Adventures of Long John Silver: The Tale of a Tooth" 16:35)
- "So be done wi' your babble; **loose me** the woman and go." (Roger Snaith, *Winds of Chance* 323)
- "**Bind me** his arms, for I will be safe of my life!" (Francis Drake, instructing that Thomas Doughty be restrained, *The Queen's Corsair* 85)

Again, notice the choice of constructions is often inconsistent. The pirate's tongue is an erratic thing, wagged by whim and dripping caprice.

- "**Run me** the flag of Spain aloft, and **bid** Ogle empty his chasers at the Bonaventure as we go about." (Peter Blood, *Captain Blood Returns* 54)

4.1.3 FRIENDLY COMMANDS
There are ways of speaking commands that are a bit more gracious or a bit less gruff than the standard command. Friendly Commands are formed by adding the phrases below. Some go before the command, some

are combined with the present participle form of the command, and some go after the command.

Before Commands

Add the following phrases before commands.

be so good to [*be so'oo good t'/ta/ter*]

"And now, ma'm, **be so good to** get you to bed." (Japhet Bly, *Winds of Chance* 41)

come now and [*cahm/carrm/coohm narr/no-woo an'/'n'*]

"Say no more, Zeke! **Come now and** watch old Lovepeace at work." (Japhet Bly, urging Ezekiel Penryn to join him in watching gunner Lovepeace Farrance fire at a pursuing ship, *Winds of Chance* 111)

do you [*d'/does 'ee/ya/ye/yer*]

"That blackguard Romata is in the dumps, and nothing will mollify him but a gift; so **do you** go up to his house and give him these whale's teeth, with my compliments." (pirate captain, *The Coral Island* 245)

I'll thank you to [*I'ee'ull t'ank/thenk 'ee/ya/ye/yer t'/ta/ter*]

"And **I'll thank ya to** keep your voice down or I'll tear your tongue out." (Purity Pinker, "The Adventures of Long John Silver: The Eviction" 6:29)

it will be [*ett well* OR *'twell/'twill be*]

Used before the command, with "for you" afterwards.

"**It'll be** place and rank **for you**, messmate, or a chance to swim wi' the sharks." (Long John Silver, *Porto Bello Gold* 51)

pray [*prayee*]

"So, Ned, **pray** overhaul the ship, her every rope, spar and timber." (Adam Penfeather, *Adam Penfeather, Buccaneer* 293)

prithee [*per/preh-thee*]

< "Then let us turn north or south—anywhere but in yon hateful man's neighbor-

hood." "Nay, **prithee** ha' patience and hear me out." > (Ursula Revell & Japhet Bly, *Winds of Chance* 303)

see

"**See** a boat be prepared, Smy, and then we'll heave-to and be quit o' this lubberly Sharp and his fellows forthright." (Absalom Troy, *Adam Penfeather, Buccaneer* 77)

see that [*see tharrt*]

"Get 'im out of 'ere. Vittle and clothe him. And **see that** he works for it. Jump to it, now." (Long John Silver, "The Adventures of Long John Silver: The Tale of a Tooth" 12:19)

there's a good lad [*tharr/theyarr/theyerr is\be a good lad*]

"Dick, **there's a good lad**, jump up and fetch me an apple from the barrel there." (Long John Silver, "Treasure Island" [1990] 47:28)

wilt [*welt*]

"Love my eyes! Smy, **wilt** look now at my young Adam." (Absalom Troy, *Adam Penfeather, Buccaneer* 31)

you\we best [*ya/ye/yer\we baahst/barrst*]

"Captain Walker, if ye've a mind to come with us on this venture and seek to recover what ye've lost, **ye'd best** be scuttling that *guarda-costa* and fetching your hands aboard the *Arabella*." (Peter Blood, *The Fortunes of Captain Blood* 119) < "Where to, Morgan?" "I told you. Madagascar." "But that's in Africa." "Then **we best** get busy." > (William Shaw & Morgan Adams, "Cutthroat Island" 1:56:58)

you will [*ya/ye/yer well*]

< "I've been goin' ashore for thirty years in my shirtsleeves." "Not while I be about. Now **you'll** put your coat on." "Arrgh." > (Long John Silver & Purity Pinker, "The

Adventures of Long John Silver: The Eviction" 14:09)

you'll maybe [*ye'll mayee-be*]

"You're a funny man, by your account; but you're over now, and **you'll maybe** step down off that barrel, and help vote." (George Merry, *Treasure Island* 163, Chap. 29)

Combine With Present Participle

Combine the following phrases with the present participle forms of commands.

just be [*jast/jarrst/jarrs'/joohst/jus' be*]

"There's a knife yonder. **Just be** slipping it through these plaguey thongs." (Peter Blood, *Captain Blood Returns* 156)

let's be [*laaht's/less be*]

"**Let's be** going, my lad." (Peter Blood, *Captain Blood Returns* 209)

you best be [*ya/ye/yer baahst/barrst be*]

"Now, **you best be** servin' the good cap'n and his mate." (Long John Silver, "Long John Silver's Return to Treasure Island" 57:33)

you'll be [*ye'll be*]

"So **you'll** just **be** stepping to the poop-rail with me, and bidding them put the helm over." (Peter Blood, *The Fortunes of Captain Blood* 167)

After Commands

Add the following phrases after commands.

and welcome [*an'/'n' waahl-cahm/carrm/coohm*]

< "And what I ask is, how a sailor-man comes to know the patter o' the flash coves!" "'Tis no matter, but since you're o' the Brotherhood sit ye **and welcome**, 'tis dry enough here in this cave." > (Martin Conisby & Abnegation Mings, *Black Bartlemy's Treasure* 30)

I bid you [*I'ee bed 'ee/ya/ye/yer*]

"Stand off, **I bid you**, and let the chaplain approach!" (The Red Rover, *The Red Rover* 499)

if you please [*an\eff/eff'n/if'n 'ee/ya/ye/yer pleass*]

"You may trip, and we will make all sail, **if you please**." (Andrew Murray, *Porto Bello Gold* 57)

is the word [*'s\be t' warrd*]

"Forrard'**s the word**, messmates." (Japhet Bly, directing Barnabas Rokeby and Ezekiel Penryn to move ahead, *Winds of Chance* 14)

it is [*ett be* OR *'tes/'tis*]

"We beat off yon Englishman once and so we will again. So fight **it is**, comrades all, and a cheer for Captain Jo—ha, Jo-anna!" (Resolution Day, *Martin Conisby's Vengeance* 112)

will you [*well 'ee/ya/ye/yer*]

"Just take a bearing, **will you**, along the line of them bones." (Long John Silver, guessing that Allardyce's skeleton points the way to the treasure, *Treasure Island* 177, Chap. 31)

with you [*weth/wi'/wiff/witt 'ee/ya/ye/yer*]

< "[D]amn you, let me rest!" "Nary respite till noon—up **with ye**, I say!" > (John Barrasdale & Japhet Bly, *Winds of Chance* 155)

you go [*'ee/ya/ye/yer go'oo*]

"Up **you go**, Frogger, but keep low." (Long John Silver, "Long John Silver's Return to Treasure Island" 1:17:06)

4.1.4 EPITHET COMMANDS

The opposite of a Friendly Command is an Epithet Command, which permits one to instruct and demean in the space of a single statement. The speaker combines a command ("Shut your gob!") and an epithet ("shallow-pated lubber") with the word "for," as in "Shut your gob fer a shallow-pated lubber!"

Any of the commands listed in Section 4.2 can be combined with any of the epithets listed in Chapter 9 to form an Epithet Command. The possibilities are functionally infinite. A couple of ready-made examples:

- "Get back to your place for a lubber, Tom." (Long John Silver, *Treasure Island* 44, Chap. 8)

- "Belay for a — lackey, ye slab-faced chunk o' rotted seahorse!" (John Flint, *Porto Bello Gold* 83, omission in original)

4.1.5 NEGATIVE COMMANDS

A command *not* to do something can be formed in several different ways.

don't be __ing [*don'/doon't/dorrn't be a-__in'*]

"Well, **don't be callin'** me no stranger." (Purity Pinker, "The Adventures of Long John Silver: The Pink Pearl" 7:05)

don't go __ing [*don'/doon't/dorrn't go'oo a-__in'*]

"But **don't go wavin'** it in the face of every man who asks for a glass of stout." (Long John Silver, giving Jim Hawkins an impressive-keeping pistol and a few words of caution, "Treasure Island" [1950] 25:00)

don't let's [*don'/doon't/dorrn't laaht's/less*]

"**Don't let's** have any more of this talk about doin' away wi' yourself." (Smee, "Hook" 1:03:43)

he that __ makes an enemy of me [*'e tharrt __ mayeekes a ann-ermy o'\on me*]

"Our work is done! **He that** strikes another blow **makes an enemy of me.**" (The Red Rover, calling off his men's onslaught aboard an enemy ship, *The Red Rover* 493)

heed not to [*'eed narrt t'/ta/ter*]

"And talking o' tempest, I like not the look o' the sky—take you the tiller whiles I shorten sail and **heed not to** disturb Joanna." (Resolution Day, *Martin Conisby's Vengeance* 145)

never [*nebber/ne'er*]

"**Never** heed his jealous bellowing, little one." (unnamed pirate impersonator of Peter Blood, *The Fortunes of Captain Blood* 48)

(we'll have) none of your [(*we'll 'aff/'ave/ha'/haff*) *narrn/noohn o'\on ya/yarr/ye/yer/yere/yore*]

"Get out of it, boy. And **none o' yer** keyholin', neither." (Black Dog, "Treasure Island" [1998] 13:11) "Here, **we'll 'ave none o' yore** snivellin' 'ere." (Long John Silver, "The Adventures of Long John Silver: The Eviction" 23:07)

none of your __ for me [*narrn/noohn o'\on ya/yarr/ye/yer/yere/yore __ farr/fer me*]

"**None of your** keyholes **for me,** sonny." (Black Dog, warning Jim Hawkins against eavesdropping on his conversation with Billy Bones, *Treasure Island* 11, Chap. 2)

__ not [*__ narrt*]

"I'll fire two guns to warn you aboard, and tarry **not,** for the ship lieth within a sunken reef and we must catch the flood." (Adam Penfeather, *Black Bartlemy's Treasure* 330)

there will be no [*tharr/theyarr/theyerr well be no'oo*]

"It is certain that after alarming the coast **there will be no** staying here, and the shortness of provision and water make voyages dangerous ..." (John Smith, *General History of the Pyrates* 364)

there's no [*tharr/theyarr/theyerr is\be no'oo*]

"**There's no** packing off a treasure there when we come within saker-shot." (Wolverstone, *Captain Blood Returns* 182)

we'll have no more (of your) [*we'll 'aff/'ave/ ha'/haff no'oo marr/moor (o'\on ya/yarr/ye/ yerr/yore)*]

"Now **we'll have no more** grumblin'. And up anchor." (Long John Silver, "The Adventures of Long John Silver: The Pink Pearl" 24:22)

__ you shan't [*__ 'ee/ya/ye/yer shen't*]

"[S]o either discharge your trust like an honest man; for go **you shan't**, by G[o]d, or I'll send you with my service to the D[evi]l; so no more words, G[o]d d[am]n ye." (William Fly, *General History of the Pyrates* 611)

you'll not be __ing [*ye'll narrt be a-__in'*]

"I am Captain Blood. So **you'll not be supposing** that a little peril more or less will daunt me." (Peter Blood, *The Fortunes of Captain Blood* 94)

4.1.6 COMMAND OPENERS

Certain words are used regularly just before or just after commands. These Command Openers and Command Closers add urgency or emphasis to the commands they accompany. One might shout at a lazy pirate, "Get movin!" Or one might instead shout: "**Now** get movin'! Get movin', **I say**! Arrgh!" (Long John Silver, forcing at gunpoint a reluctant Salamander the Greek to walk alone into a Spanish ambush, "The Adventures of Long John Silver: Pieces of Eight" 18:34)

The Command Opener "now" and the Command Closer "I say" make the command sharper and stronger than the command on its own.

Note that a single command can have both an opener and a closer.

- "**Here**, catch hold **there**." (Blackbeard, "Blackbeard the Pirate" 49:00)

What's more, the opener and the closer for a single command can even be the same word.

- "**Now** look sharp **now**! (Long John Silver, urging Jim Hawkins to get dressed and packed to leave for school in Bermuda, "The Adventures of Long John Silver: Dead Reckoning" 7:03)

Below is a comprehensive list of Command Openers.

ah [*arrgh*]

"**Ah**, ya idiot, come 'ere." (George Merry, "Treasure Island" [1998] 51:55)

come [*cahm/carrm/coohm*]

"If the woman's here, t'others should be skulking about—**come**, bouse about and stand away, and lively, ye scratchings!" (Ned, ordering Tom and Tony to find Ursula Revell's companions, *Winds of Chance* 314)

come now [*cahm/carrm/coohm narr/nowoo*]

"But, **come now**, stand by to go about. This won't do." (Long John Silver, *Treasure Island* 45, Chap. 8)

ha [*harr*]

"**Ha**, stand by! Yonder sounds the rally, and this means me." (Ned Bowser, *Adam Penfeather, Buccaneer* 119)

here [*'ee'arr/'ee'err/'ere/hee'arr/hee'err*]

"**Here**, lads, take him by the legs and heave him in—quick!" (pirate captain, *The Coral Island* 198)

here now [*'ee'arr/'ee'err/'ere/hee'arr/hee'err narr/nowoo*]

"And when you comes back aboard, I'll have a nice goat stew waitin' for 'ee to warm your honest bellies. **Here now**, get goin'." (Long John Silver, "The Adventures of Long John Silver: Devil's Stew" 15:15)

here you [*'ee'arr/'ee'err/'ere/hee'arr/hee'err 'ee/ya/ye/yer*]

"**Here you**, matey, bring up alongside and help up my chest." (Billy Bones, *Treasure Island* 4, Chap. 1)

a mercy's sake [*a marrcy's sayeeke*]

< "Think on't, sir, —her tender-sweet body to fry ... to shrink and shrivel in the scorching fire—" "Hold, —**a mercy's sake**—hold!" > (Black Bartlemy & Adam Penfeather, *Adam Penfeather, Buccaneer* 258)

mind you [*mawnd/min'/myeen'/myeend 'ee/ ya/ye/yer*]

"Would you do me a kindness and sing a little while I nod off? And **mind you**, sing, and don't bray like a donkey." (Thomas Bartholomew Red, "Pirates" 1:55:36)

now [*narr/nowoo*]

"**Now** go below, and stay there till I call you." (pirate captain, *The Coral Island* 201)

now come [*narr/nowoo cahm/carrm/coohm*]

"**Now come**, sweet comrade, let us march." (Japhet Bly, *Winds of Chance* 307)

now then [*narr/nowoo thayn*]

"**Now then**, boy, take me to Captain Billy Bones or I'll break your arm." (Blind Pew, "Treasure Island" [1950] 5:47)

up and [*arrp an'/'n'*]

< "What, then, have I angered thee?" "No! But I'm a man little used to such womanish caresses, d'ye see; so belay, lass, belay ... **up and** get thee to bed, or sink me, but you'll be kissing my lips next, and then—ha, get thee to roost!" (Ursula Revell & Japhet Bly, *Winds of Chance* 261)

you there [*ye/yer tharr/theyarr/theyerr*]

"**You there**! Reeve off a new tackle, quickly!" (Duncan Honeyman, *The Pirate Round* 237)

4.1.7 COMMAND CLOSERS

This section lists Command Closers, or words used immediately after commands for additional emphasis.

ahoy [*ahooy/ahoyee*]

Used especially when issuing a command to a large number of people or to someone at a distance.

"All hands make sail, **ahoy**!" (Nightingale, *The Red Rover* 420)

and cheerily [*an'/'n' cheerily*]

"Heave now ... heave all **and cheerily**—yo—ho—ho!" (Martin Frant, *Adam Penfeather, Buccaneer* 127)

and lively [*an'/'n' lawv/lyeeve-ly*]

"So come and bring away Tressady first—march it is for Roger, **and lively**, lads!" (Resolution Day, *Martin Conisby's Vengeance* 162)

and lively ho [*an'/'n' lawv/lyeeve-ly ho'oo*]

"Three tankards! **And lively ho**!" (Absalom Troy, ordering a round of ale, *Adam Penfeather, Buccaneer* 17)

and look sharp about it [*an'/'n' look shahrrp abarrt/abowoot/'barrt/'bout/'bowoot ett/'n*]

"Clap on sail **and look sharp about it**." (Long John Silver, "Long John Silver's Return to Treasure Island" 15:56)

and sharp too [*an'/'n' shahrrp too*]

"And our wisest move be ta put to sea. **And sharp, too**." (Long John Silver, "Long John Silver's Return to Treasure Island" 55:04)

and with a will [*an'/'n' weth/wi'/wiff/witt a well*]

< "I save my breath!" "Ay, you'll need it, John Christopher; this current fetcheth past the island, so get to your oars now and row." "And if I refuse?" "This! So up and pull, man; pull **and with a will**!" > (John Barrasdale & Japhet Bly, with Bly brandishing a rope's end and threatening to whip John Barrasdale should he refuse to row, *Winds of Chance* 139)

come now [*cahm/carrm/coohm narr/nowoo*]

"So, Adam, like most wise and sapient commander, you'll turn and run at first sight of any sail, **come now!**" (Benjamin Trigg, *Adam Penfeather, Buccaneer* 226)

d'ye hear? [*do/does 'ee/ya/yer/you 'ear/'ee'arr/ 'ee'err/hee'arr/hee'err?*]

"Come, tumble to 't, my lass; no standing off and on; here's no place for fine lady megrims; you'll do your trick along o' me and yon lubberly Johnnyman—so jump, ma'm, bustle to 't, **d'ye hear?**" (Japhet Bly, gruffly urging a resistant Ursula Revell to action, *Winds of Chance* 145)

hearkee [*'arkee/hahrrkee*]

"Row, John man, row and rowing, **hearkee!**" (Japhet Bly, *Winds of Chance* 139)

here [*'ee'arr/'ee'err/'ere/hee'arr/hee'err*]

"Now you get down in the hole and I'll pass 'n down to 'ee. Here, lend a hand **here.**" (Blackbeard, "Blackbeard the Pirate" 52:21)

I say(s) [*I'ee sayee(s OR sayz)*]

"Stand off, there! Stand off, **I say!**" (anchor watch aboard *Bloody Revenge*, *The Pirate Round* 310) "Make ya play, **I says!**" (Israel Hands, "Treasure Island" [1934] 1:11:09)

in mercy's name [*i'/'n marrcy's nayeeme*]

< "A renegade and coward ... a traitor to Heaven." "Hush, Antonia, **in mercy's name!**" > (Antonia Chievely & Adam Penfeather, *Adam Penfeather, Buccaneer* 291)

like you're being paid for it [*lawk/lyeeke ya're/ yer/ye're/yore bein' payeed farr/fer ett/'n/'t*]

"Heave! Heave **like you're being paid for it!**" (Joshamee Gibbs, "Pirates of the Caribbean 2: Dead Man's Chest" 2:06:51)

mind (you) [*mawnd/min'/myeen'/myeend ('ee/ya/ye/yer)*]

"Dowse a bucket o' water over him, then let him be ironed and take him forward to the fo'castle; he shall serve you all for sport—but no killing, **mind.**" (Captain Jo, *Martin Conisby's Vengeance* 85) "You give me a good half-hour to get up to windward, **mind ye.**" (Long John Silver, "Treasure Island" [1990] 2:06:16)

now [*narr/nowoo*]

"Stand by to wear ship, **now.**" (Blackbeard, "Blackbeard's Ghost" 32:04) "Answer me, **now**, and mind you tell no lies." (pirate captain, *The Coral Island* 204)

quick [*queck*]

"Here, lads, take him by the legs and heave him in—**quick!**" (pirate captain, *The Coral Island* 198)

say I [*sayee I'ee*]

"Rum for all hands, **say I.**" (Billy Bones, "Treasure Island" [1934] 7:09)

sharp (now) [*shahrrp (narr/nowoo)*]

"Hallo there! one o' you tumble up and light the cabin lamp, and send that boy aft to the captain—**sharp!**" (pirate, *The Coral Island* 203–4) "Here, you go back aboard now, and send Patch and Fenner here. **Sharp, now.**" (Long John Silver, "The Adventures of Long John Silver: The Eviction" 17:00)

so [*so'oo*] there you go; that's it

"Thy starboard oar, pull, man—and again,—**so**—as she is!" (Japhet Bly, *Winds of Chance* 140)

there [*tharr/theyarr/theyerr*]

The term "there" is often added to many commands. Familiar examples include "Avast there!" and "Belay there!" As commands aboard vessels are often given at a distance, the use of the word "there" in conjunction is accordingly quite natural.

< "Make speed **there**, Wolverstone." "Speed it is, Peter." > (Peter Blood, "Captain Blood" 1:31:04)

will you [*well 'ee/ya/ye/yer*]

"Follow that swab and bring 'im back here, **will ya?**" (Long John Silver, ordering his men to chase after Black Dog, "Treasure Island" [1960] 23:09)

with a will [*weth/wi'/wiff/witt a well*] with grit or determination; like you mean it

"Pull **with a will**, my men, pull; in an hour, you shall rummage the store-rooms of that fool for your reward!" (The Red Rover, urging his men to row quickly away from a King's ship back to the Dolphin, *The Red Rover* 447)

you hear? [*ya/ye/yer 'ear/'ee'arr/'ee'err/ hee'arr/hee'err?*]

"Give me rum, **ya hear?**" (Billy Bones, "Treasure Island" [1990] 6:03)

4.1.8 COMMAND RESPONSES

The following are typical responses spoken to express acknowledgement of, assent to, or compliance with a command.

REPEAT COMMAND

< "Steady at the helm!" "**Steady at the helm!**" > (Cahusac and helmsman aboard Levasseur's ship, "Captain Blood" 1:18:31)

arrgh, that I will [*arrgh, tharrt I'ee well*]

< "Then come down after me." "**Arrgh, that I will.**" > (Edward Maynard & Blackbeard, "Blackbeard the Pirate" 1:14:43)

as you say(s) [*as 'ee/ya/ye/yer sayee(s OR sayz)*]

< "Fire when ready." "Aye, **as you say**, Jim." > (Jim Hawkins & Long John Silver, preparing to pull a sore tooth out of Jim's mouth with a string tied to a door, "The Adventures of Long John Silver: The Tale

of a Tooth" 6:46) < "And you, Tressady, I would not hear, so—be dumb!" "**As you says**, Captain, **as you says!**" > (Black Bartlemy & Roger Tressady, *Adam Penfeather, Buccaneer* 253)

REPEAT COMMAND aye [*... aheee/arrgh*]

< "Steady as she goes!" "**Steady as she goes, aye!**" > (Long John Silver and member of Long John Silver's company, "The Adventures of Long John Silver: Sword of Vengeance" 3:18)

aye aye(s) [*aheee/arrgh aheee(s)/arrgh(s)*]

< "Away with you." "**Ay, ay.**" > (George Fairfax & Tim, *The Fortunes of Captain Blood* 160) < "You get to your galley. The hands will want their dinner." "**Aye ayes**, Cap'n." > (Captain Smollett & Long John Silver, "Treasure Island" [1934] 38:38)

aye aye, sir [*aheee/arrgh aheee/arrgh, sarr*]

Note the interesting suggestion in James L. Nelson's *The Guardship* that pirates, as distinguished from naval or merchant seamen, typically omit the word "sir" when acceding aloud to shipboard commands: *Lieutenant Rakestraw, just visible by the cathead, called back "Aye!," leaving out the "sir" as Marlowe had instructed.* (account of the efforts of Thomas Marlowe's guardship crew to pass as pirates, *The Guardship* 89)

< "Take in top-sails." "**Ay, ay, sir-r-r.**" > (pirate first mate & pirate crew, *The Coral Island* 210) < "[M]an our stern-chase guns, for we're pursued." "**Ay, ay, sir!**" > (Adam Penfeather & John Fenn, *Adam Penfeather, Buccaneer* 186)

aye, cap'n [*aheee/arrgh, cap'n*]

< "As for you, Bo'sun, have up a flask o' the Spanish wine—the black seal!" "**Aye, cap'n!**" > (Adam Penfeather & Joel Bym, *Black Bartlemy's Treasure* 78–79)

aye so [*aheee/arrgh so'oo*]

> < "Stand by to grapple by the larboard." "Ay so, Japhet." > (Japhet Bly & Ezekiel Penryn, *Winds of Chance* 76)

aye, that I will [*aheee/arrgh, tharrt I'ee well*]

> < "Stand here and take care of him if he tries to come back." "Aye, that I will, that I will." > (Blackbeard & Ben Worley, "Blackbeard the Pirate" 18:07)

heartily [*'ahrrt/'eart/hahrrt-ily*]

> < "Open the door!" "Heartily—heart-ily!" > (Martin Conisby & one-eared pirate, *Black Bartlemy's Treasure* 22)

REPEAT COMMAND it is [*... ett/'n be* OR *'tes/'tis*]

> < "Prepare to come on the starboard tack!" "Starboard tack it is!" > (members of Levasseur's company, "Captain Blood" 1:18:27)

(why,) very well [(*whyee,*) *vaah/vay-ry waahl*]

> < "Sirs, by your leaves, the Cap'n wants ye alow in 's cabin." "Why, very well, Absalom." > (Absalom Troy & Ezekiel Penryn, *Winds of Chance* 49)

with joy [*weth/wi'/wiff/witt joyee/j'y*]

> < "And now be so good to leave me." "With joy, ma'm, tempered with woe, for to talk with women is rare experience these days and you, though termagant and something shrewish, are very woman." > (Ursula Revell & Japhet Bly, *Winds of Chance* 52)

4.2 GENERAL COMMANDS

about it [*abarrt/abowoot/'barrt/'bout/'bowoot ett/'n*] get to it; get on it; go about it

> "So about it, Don Francisco. You shall have what mules you need." (Peter Blood, *Captain Blood: His Odyssey* 181)

about ship [*abarrt/abowoot/'barrt/'bout/'bowoot shep*] about face; turn around; go back

Literally a nautical command meaning "reverse course," the phrase is used more broadly to order any kind of change in direction or course of action, whether physical or abstract.

> "'Bout ship, mates! This here crew is on a wrong tack, I do believe." (George Merry, *Treasure Island* 182, Chap. 32)

aft here [*arrft/haft 'ee'arr/'ee'err/'ere/hee'arr/ hee'err*] come back here

A command to move toward the rear part of the vessel. The command is also used where the speaker is not in the rear part of a vessel, or on a vessel at all, to convey a tone of authority, as pirate captains and other persons of authority within a company—who typically work and live in the aft part of a vessel—use "aft here" as an authoritative way of beckoning to others.

> "What Ezekiel—ho, Zeke! Aft here, Zeke!" (Lovepeace Farrance, calling Ezekiel Penryn over to speak with Ursula Revell, *Winds of Chance* 47)

aft with __ [*arrft/haft weth/wi'/wiff/witt __*] take __ toward the rear part of the vessel

> "Lord love me! Aft with him—to the coach ..." (Captain Belvedere, ordering that his prisoner Martin Conisby be moved to cabin quarters, *Martin Conisby's Vengeance* 66)

aft with me [*arrft/haft weth/wi'/wiff/witt me*] come with me toward the rear part of the vessel

The command is also used to mean simply "come with me" even where the speaker is not in the rear part of a vessel, or on a vessel at all, when the speaker wishes to convey a tone of authority, as pirate captains and other persons of authority within a company—who typically work and live in the aft part of a vessel—use "aft with me" as an authoritative way of urging others to accompany them.

> < "Ply 'em with our stern chase, Master Gunner." "Ay so! Aft wi' me, lads!" >

(Japhet Bly & Lovepeace Farrance, *Winds of Chance* 109)

all hands on deck [*awrl 'ands/'an's/han's arrn/o' dack*] everyone on deck

"**All hands on deck!**" (John Wolverstone, "Captain Blood" 1:30:28)

arrest [*arrast*] (1) stop (2) wait; hold on

"**Arrest**, ye fools—stand by! Yon man be the property o' Captain Jo—'tis Joanna's man and whoso harms him swings ..." (Diccon, *Martin Conisby's Vengeance* 84)

avast [*avarrst/'varrst/'vast*]

(1) stop

"**Avast**, sons o' dogs, stand off or I'll bowel ye." (Ned, brandishing a long knife, *Winds of Chance* 313)

(2) wait; hold on

"[T]o-morrow—we sail, all on us, aboard my ship *Vengeance*, as lieth 'twixt Fore and Main islands yonder, ready to slip her moorings!" "**Avast**, friend! The captain o' the Coast Brotherhood is Joanna here ..." (Roger Tressady & Resolution Day, *Martin Conisby's Vengeance* 156)

(3) shut up

"**Avast**! Belay that, Abny, you'll be having all the lubbers about the place aboard of us!" (Roger Tressady, quieting Abnegation Mings and his singing, *Black Bartlemy's Treasure* 96)

(4) stop __ ; put an end to __

"**Avast** heavin'! Belay! Steady as she goes!" (Long John Silver, "The Adventures of Long John Silver: Sword of Vengeance" 3:13)

avast and likewise belay [*avarrst/'varrst/'vast an'/'n' lawk/lyeeke-wawse/wyeese belayee*] stop, stop!

"Avast" and "belay" both mean "stop." The redundancy adds urgency. See Section 18.2.2 for more on stylistic redundancy.

< "I say there is no God, no—" "Lord, sir, **avast now and likewise belay!**" (Benjamin Trigg & Ned Bowser, *Adam Penfeather, Buccaneer* 180)

avast there [*avarrst/'varrst/'vast tharr/theyarr/theyerr*] stop

"**Avast there!** Who are you, Tom Morgan? Maybe you thought you was cap'n here, perhaps." (Long John Silver, *Treasure Island* 159, Chap. 28)

away (with you) [*awayee/'way/'wayee (weth/wi'/wiff/witt 'ee/ya/ye/yer)*] go away; get out of here; leave

< "At least, sir, at the least, tell me whither you carry me?" "Not I, ma'm, suffice it that yourself and myself upon wide ocean are being wafted by winds o' fortune to such fortune, good or ill, as Fortune shall decree. Now peace, ma'm, **away** nor cheat a weary mariner of his sleep." > (Ursula Revell & Japhet Bly, *Winds of Chance* 43) "Now **away with ya** and divvy up his belongin's." (Ben Worley, "Blackbeard the Pirate" 24:26)

away with __ [*awayee/'way/'wayee weth/wi'/wiff/witt __*] take __ away

"**Away with him** into the boat. Look alive! the breeze is freshening." (pirate captain, *The Coral Island* 198) "Heave him overboard if dead, if not—tie him up till I can tend him—**away with him**." (Adam Penfeather, *Adam Penfeather, Buccaneer* 189)

back to your post [*back t'/ta/ter ya/yarr/ye/yer/yere/yore po'oost*]

Used to instruct a hand to return to his assigned position or to summarily dismiss him after a brisk exchange.

"The first swab ta make a move I'll blast to Kingdom Come. **Back to yer posts**, you mutinous dogs!" (Long John Silver,

"The Adventures of Long John Silver: The Tale of a Tooth" 15:16)

batten down your hatches [*batten dowoon ya/yarr/ye/yer/yere/yore 'atch-ers*] shut up; be quiet

Hatches are watertight covers that, when closed, block hatchways or other means of access to spaces below deck. To "batten down one's hatches," literally, is to fasten or secure a vessel's hatches or material covering them with one or more "battens" or pieces of wood. The figurative use of the phrase, therefore, compares the shutting a hole in a vessel's deck to the shutting of one's mouth.

"No one else may know of me presence here. So **batten down your hatches**." (Thomas Bartholomew Red, *Pirates* 1:19:03)

be comforted [*be cahm/carrm/coohm-farrted/f'ted*] cheer up; don't worry; relax; take it easy

"**Be comforted**, lass. He lives." (MacTavish, consoling Michel's unnecessarily mournful lover, "The Black Pirate" 1:11:42)

be cool [*be coo-ell*] calm down; take it easy

"**Be cool!** The schooner is fixed hard enough, and will not go down; we shall save everything by-and-by." (Cain, *The Pirate* 122, Chap. XVI)

be done with your babble [*be doohn weth/wi'/wiff/witt ya/yarr/ye/yer/yere/yore babble*] shut up; be quiet

"So **be done wi' your babble**; loose me the woman and go." (Roger Snaith, *Winds of Chance* 323)

be dumb [*be doohmb*] shut up; be quiet

< "So ho now, ye hear him, Captain? This paltry skipjack, —ye hear him?" "And you, Tressady, I would not hear, so—**be dumb!**" > (Roger Tressady & Black Bartlemy, *Adam Penfeather, Buccaneer* 253)

be easy calm down; relax; don't worry

"Madam, **be easy**, we are rude rough-hewn fellows, but none of our men should hurt you, or touch you ..." (Captain Avery, *The King of Pirates* 58–59)

be gone (you) [*be garrn ('ee/ya/ye/yer)*] go away; get out of here; leave

< "As only me know the way, you live or die with me." "**Be gone**." > (Salamander the Greek & Long John Silver, "The Adventures of Long John Silver: Pieces of Eight" 8:23) "Come, Doctor, **begone you** to your surgery and leave this luscious armful to me ..." (Roger Snaith, *Winds of Chance* 323)

be off [*be arrf*] go away; get out of here; leave

"Gather your hands and **be off**, and God be with you, my friend." (Peter Blood, *The Fortunes of Captain Blood* 131)

be off __ [*be arrf __*] get off __; leave __

"**Be off** this ship at once, and tell your blackguards that if the Valiant is still there by noon I'll blow her out of the water." (Captain Easterling, *Captain Blood Returns* 286)

be quick about it [*be queck abarrt/abowoot/'barrt/'bout/'bowoot ett/'n*] quickly; hurry up

"Sing out an order instantly for my mate and my bos'n to come here to the cabin, and **be quick about it**, for my finger's on the trigger, and it's only a pull to shut your mouth forever." (John Scarfield, *The Book of Pirates* "Captain Scarfield" 203)

be seen and not heard [*be seen an'/'n' narrt 'arrd/'eard/harrd*] shut up; be quiet

< "Japhet, you rush upon destruction." "This is as may be, ma'm, but for the nonce, sweet poppet, **be seen and not heard**." > (Ursula Revell & Japhet Bly, *Winds of Chance* 334)

be smart [*be smahrrt*] get to it; get moving
  A command used to rouse or urge one or more persons to action.

> "**Be smart**, lads!, that's her: furl the awnings, and run the anchor up to the bows ..." (Cain, calling the crew to action after spotting a Portuguese ship, *The Pirate* 48, Chap. VIII)

be speedy [*be spee'y*] hurry up

> "The rope ... pay it about the sapling yonder and ... comrade, **be speedy**." (Japhet Bly, explaining to Ursula Revell how to go about rescuing Bly from a patch of quicksand, *Winds of Chance* 175)

be tranquil [*be trankil*] calm down; relax; take it easy; don't worry

> < "Wild beasts, Japhet?" "Ay, but only four-legged ones, that shall not shoot us from ambush nor dare our fire: it's the beast o' two legs is the greater menace, so **be tranquil**." > (Ursula Revell & Japhet Bly, *Winds of Chance* 160)

be warned [*be wahrrned/wahrrnt*] beware; be careful

> "**Be warned**! The moments are speeding. The ten minutes have all but fled, and either I and my friends depart, or we all sink together in this bottom." (Peter Blood, *Captain Blood Returns* 37)

bear away along o' me [*barr/bayarr/bayerr awayee/'way/'wayee alarrng/'larrng/'long o'\on me*] come with me; come along

> "Rouse up, messmate, and **bear away along o' me**." (Absalom Troy, *Adam Penfeather, Buccaneer* 4)

belay [*b'-layee*]
  (1) stop

> < "I should take off yer hand here an' now!" "**Belay**! I be needin' that hand fer diggin' up the treasure!" (Joshua Smoot & Henry Morgan, *Dead Man's Chest* 157)

  (2) shut up; be quiet

> "Why, the smell of you alone is enough to wrinkle the noses of pigs." "Arrgh, **belay**, Purity." (Purity Pinker & Long John Silver, "Long John Silver's Return to Treasure Island" 34:21)

  (3) attention; listen up; stop what you're doing and listen

> < "**Belay**!" "What's this?" "This here be a special recipe known only to me and Lieutenant Leon." > (Long John Silver & Patch, with Silver bringing to the dinner table a specially made dessert of Crepes Suzette, "The Adventures of Long John Silver: Turnabout" 25:18)

  (4) stop __; put an end to __

> "**Belay** the hammers!" (Purity Pinker, calling out to the guards boarding up her inn, "The Adventures of Long John Silver: The Eviction" 11:49) "Flanders, **belay** that for now!" (Thomas Marlowe, *The Pirate Round* 328)

belay and veer [*b'-layee an'/'n' vee-arr/err*] stop and go away; stop and get out of here

> "Avast! **Belay and veer**, my bully boys; veer and stand away, lest we run ye aboard." (Japhet Bly, confronting the four gentlemen who have asked Ursula Revell to leave Bly and come with them, *Winds of Chance* 14)

belay now [*b'-layee narr/nowoo*] stop now

> "Here, **belay now**. The cap'n be served before the crew in this here galley." (Long John Silver, "Long John Silver's Return to Treasure Island" 57:53)

belay that [*b'-layee tharrt*]
  (1) stop; stop that

> < "An' now there's no reason ta keep this one alive no more, is there?" "**Belay that**! You can kill him, but not before we hear what our visitor has to say about the *Silver Cloud*'s departure." > (Henry Morgan & Joshua Smoot, *Dead Man's Chest* 197)

(2) shut up; be quiet

> < "What, great heavens, what's this? Captain! You're short of a leg! Ohh, an active man like yourself, what a tragedy." "**Belay that**. Me doubloons." > (Dutch & Thomas Bartholomew Red, "Pirates" 55:17)

belay that __ [*b'layee tharrt __*] stop that talk; shut up; be quiet

> "**Belay that guff**, and get these carcasses aboardship." (Billy Bones, *Porto Bello Gold* 50) "**Belay that talk**, John Silver. This crew has tipped you the black spot in full council, as in dooty bound. ..." (George Merry, *Treasure Island* 163, Chap. 29) "**Belay that tongue**! One thing ol' Blackbeard don't take kindly to it's them sort of insinuendos." (Blackbeard, "Blackbeard's Ghost" 26:16)

belay there [*b'-layee tharr/theyarr/theyerr*]
(1) stop

> "**Belay there**, you shirking lubbers!" (Blind Pew, "Treasure Island" [1990] 21:19) "**Belay there**!" (bosun aboard the *Arabella*, *The Fortunes of Captain Blood* 111)

(2) shut up; be quiet

> < "Great guns, if Flint were livin' now, this'd be a hard spot for you and me." "**Belay there**, stow this talk—Flint's dead." > (Tom Morgan & Long John Silver, "Treasure Island" [1990] 1:52:41)

belay your __ [*b'-layee ya/yarr/ye/yer/yere/yore __*] shut up; be quiet

> "**Belay yer cackle**." (Long John Silver, to his laughing parrot Cap'n Flint, "Long John Silver's Return to Treasure Island" 44:05) "Lubber, **belay your chaffer**!" (Ned Bowser, *Adam Penfeather, Buccaneer* 165) "**Belay your cursed jaw-tackle**!" (Adam Penfeather, silencing Smiling Sam while deliberately imitating pirate Absalom Troy's style of speech, *Adam Penfeather, Buccaneer* 73) "**Belay yer swivel tongue**, Purity." (Long

John Silver, "Long John Silver's Return to Treasure Island" 2:47)

bend your back (to it) [*baynd/ben'/bent ya/yarr/ye/yer/yere/yore back (t'/ta/ter ett/'n/'t)*] work at it; put your back into it

An exhortation to work hard at some laborious task or physical exertion.

> "Here, **bend your back**!" (Blackbeard, "Blackbeard the Pirate" 48:36) "Faster, you lazy dogs! **Bend your backs to it**, you louts!" (George Fairfax, *The Fortunes of Captain Blood* 150)

bend your ear to this [*baynd/ben'/bent ya/yarr/ye/yer/yere/yore ee-arr/err t'/ta/ter dis/t'is*] listen to this

> "Now **bend your ear to this**. I got your niece here and I'll trade her for the throne of Kapetec Anhuac." (Thomas Bartholomew Red, "Pirates" 1:21:53)

bestir (yourself) [*bestarr ('ee/ya/ye/yer/yere/yore-seff)*] move; get to it; let's go; come on

> "Send aloft every man you can spare, to loose sail once we're out of the channel. **Bestir**, Trenam! **Bestir**!" (Peter Blood, *Captain Blood Returns* 288) "You and your men go first. And **bestir yourselves**! We've no mind to drown like rats." (pirate aboard the Bonaventure, *Captain Blood Returns* 37)

bide a moment [*bawd/byeede a momernt/mo'nt/mo'ooment*] wait a moment

> < "Ursula, Ursula, by heaven, here's your miracle!" "Where? Oh, where?" "**Bide a moment** and you shall see." > (Japhet Bly & Ursula Revell, *Winds of Chance* 345)

bide where you are [*bawd/byeede wayarr/wayerr/wharr 'ee/ya/ye/yer be*] stay where you are

> "Bo'sun, **bide where you are**." (James Danvers, *Adam Penfeather, Buccaneer* 90)

bouse about [*bowoose abarrt/abowoot/'barrt/'bout/'bowoot*] move; get a move on

To bouse means to hoist or lift; the term is used here to instruct the addressee to raise himself up from a state of relative inactivity and move himself about to useful purpose.

> "Haul off, cast about, stand off and on. If the woman's here, t'others should be skulking about—come, **bouse about** and stand away, and lively, ye scratchings!" (Ned, ordering Tom and Tony to find Ursula Revell's companions, *Winds of Chance* 314)

bowse up [*bowoose arrp*] (1) get up; wake up (2) move; get to it; let's go; come on

"Bowse" is an alternate spelling for "bouse."

> "So **bowse up**, lad, stand away wi' me and rum it shall be." (Absalom Troy, *Adam Penfeather, Buccaneer* 4)

break your back [*brayeek ya/yarr/ye/yer/yere/yore back*] work at it; put your back into it

An exhortation to work hard at some laborious task or physical exertion.

> "Come on, you swabs, **break your backs**!" (Long John Silver, "Treasure Island" [1990] 1:17:36)

bring to [*breng ter*] stop; halt

Used to halt a ship's movement or, metaphorically, a person's movement or activity.

> "**Bring to**! **Bring to** for a queen's officer, or you shall all hang!" (Roger Press, *The Pirate Round* 84)

bring up alongside [*breng arrp alarrng/'larrng/'long-sawd/syeede*] come here; get over here

> "Here you, matey, **bring up alongside** and help up my chest." (Billy Bones, *Treasure Island* 4, Chap. 1)

bring yourself to [*breng 'ee/ya/ye/yer/yere/yore-seff ter*] stop; hold on; wait a minute

Used to stop a person's movement or activity.

> "[Y]ou gentlemen, **bring yourselves to**!—you needn't stand up for Mr. Hawkins; *he'll* excuse you, you may lay to that." (Long John Silver, *Treasure Island* 156, Chap. 28)

budge [*boohdge*] go away; get out of here

> "**Budge**, you skulk! Dirk was a fool and a coward from the first—you wouldn't mind him." (Pew, *Treasure Island* 26, Chap. 5)

bustle [*barr/booh-sle*] hurry up; get busy; get going

> "Stand forward the new men—show a leg and **bustle**, ye dogs!" (Adam Penfeather, *Black Bartlemy's Treasure* 110–11)

bustle to it [*barr/booh-sle t'/ta/ter ett/'n/'t*] get to it; let's go; snap to it

> "Come, tumble to 't, my lass; no standing off and on; here's no place for fine lady megrims; you'll do your trick along o' me and yon lubberly Johnnyman—so jump, ma'm, **bustle to 't**, d'ye hear?" (Japhet Bly, gruffly urging a resistant Ursula Revell to action, *Winds of Chance* 145)

cast about [*carrst abarrt/abowoot/'barrt/'bout/'bowoot*] look around; search all over

> "Haul off, **cast about**, stand off and on. If the woman's here, t'others should be skulking about—come, bouse about and stand away, and lively, ye scratchings!" (Ned, ordering Tom and Tony to find Ursula Revell's companions, *Winds of Chance* 314)

catch hold [*ketch hol'/hoold/ho'oold/'ol'/'old*] take hold; grab that

> "Here, **catch hold** there." (Blackbeard, "Blackbeard the Pirate" 49:00)

catch your wind [*ketch ya/yarr/ye/yer/yere/yore win'/wint*] shut up; quiet

> "Nay, hush thee, my Benjamin, **catch thy wind**. ..." (Adam Penfeather, *Adam Penfeather, Buccaneer* 310–11)

cease shut up; be quiet

> < "It is the language of truth; and ears like yours cannot be deaf to the sounds. If—" "Lady, **cease**." > (Mrs. Wyllys & The Red Rover, *The Red Rover* 452)

cease your chattering [*cease ya/yarr/ye/yer/ yere/yore a-charrter-in'*] shut up; be quiet

> "Apes! Monkeys, **cease your chattering** and list to Joanna." (Captain Jo, *Martin Conisby's Vengeance* 62)

cinch up [*cench arrp*] (1) get ready (2) come on; let's go

"Cinch up" means literally to pull tight or tighten, as with a belt.

> "**Cinch up**, Polonski. There's work to be done." (Moonbeam, "Swashbuckler" 7:07)

clap a stopper on your eyes [*clarrp a star-rper arrn/o' ya/yarr/ye/yer/yere/yore eye'ees*] stop crying

> "So you're blubbering, are you, you obstinate whelp? I don't allow any such weakness aboard o' this ship. So **clap a stopper on your eyes**, or I'll give you something to cry for." (pirate captain, *The Coral Island* 201)

clear the turn and run him up [*clee-arr/err t' tarrn an'/'n' roohn 'im arrp*] hang him; string him up

> "**Clear the turn and run him up!** a clear whip, and a swift run to heaven!" (members of The Red Rover's company, *The Red Rover* 498–99)

close that mouth\yawp [*cloose/clo'oose tharrt mowooth\yarrp*] shut up; be quiet

> "Tressady, **close that** vile **mouth** and remove your viler carcase!" (Black Bartlemy, *Adam Penfeather, Buccaneer* 276) "**Close your yawp** or I'll close it for ya!" (Ben Worley, "Blackbeard the Pirate" 4:32)

cock your piece [*carrk ya/yarr/ye/yer/yere/ yore peesh*]

A command to cock a firearm—that is, to ready it for imminent use by pulling its hammer all the way back.

> "**Cock your pieces,** —they'll ha' discovered our trick by now ..." (Absalom

Troy, preparing for a rush of angry men from belowdecks, *Adam Penfeather, Buccaneer* 76)

come aboard [*cahm/carrm/coohm abarrd*]

Used metaphorically when not aboard a ship as an invitation to enter.

> "[I]f you want to speak to Captain Merry, then **come aboard**." (George Merry, inviting Squire Trelawney into his company's encampment, "Treasure Island" [1998] 1:18:11)

come along [*cahm/carrm/coohm alarrng/ 'larrng/'long*] come on

> "**Come along**, you men! Push the wounded ones aside, them that can't pull an oar!" (Thomas Marlowe, *The Pirate Round* 342)

come alongside [*cahm/carrm/coohm alarrng/ 'larrng/'long-sawd/syeede*] come here

> "Japhet, old messmate, 'tis joy to see thee again! **Come alongside** ..." (Will, *Winds of Chance* 207)

come away [*cahm/carrm/coohm awayee/'way/ 'wayee*] come over here; leave what you're doing and come here

> "**Come away**, Hawkins, come and have a yarn with John." (Long John Silver, *Treasure Island* 54, Chap. 10)

come (you) hither [*cahm/carrm/coohm ('ee/ ya/ye/yer) heh/'i-ther*] come here

> "**Come hither**, lad, **come hither**; tell me what you make of the sail in the south-western board." (The Red Rover, handing a telescope to Scipio, *The Red Rover* 402) "Ho, Ned, **come you hither**!" (Adam Penfeather, *Adam Penfeather, Buccaneer* 197)

come now [*cahm/carrm/coohm narr/nowoo*] come on; let's go

"**Come now**, Jim, lad, time be wastin'." (Long John Silver, "Treasure Island" [1950] 21:02)

come on if you're coming [*cahm/carrm/coohm arrn an'\eff/eff'n/if'n ya're/yer/ye're/yore a-cahm/carrm/coohm-in'*] come on

> "**Come on if you're comin'.**" (Long John Silver, "Treasure Island" [1934] 1:28:10)

come you [*cahm/carrm/coohm 'ee/ya/ye/yer*] come here; come over here

> "Ahoy, Ben! Ben, **come you** and bear this lady aloft." (Lovepeace Farrance, *Winds of Chance* 75)

come you in [*cahm/carrm/coohm 'ee/ya/ye/yer 'n*] come in; enter

> "**Come you in**, Smy, and sit likewise." (Absalom Troy, *Adam Penfeather, Buccaneer* 17)

come your ways [*cahm/carrm/coohm ya/yarr/ ye/yer/yere/yore wayees*] come here; come over here; come forward

> "If I kill thee, John, it shall be foot to foot in fight. Meantime, I'll tie thee up, Johnny man, lest you steal on me in my sleep and brain me with your fetters, —so **come your ways**, Johnny, come!" (Japhet Bly, *Winds of Chance* 260)

content you [*cahn/carrn/coohn/kern-tant 'ee/ya/ye/yer*]

(1) relax; don't worry

> "A man o' lies and blood, to be rooted out, child! Yet **content ye**, for by the Lord's grace, thou shalt see me slit his treacherous weasand anon." (Lovepeace Farrance, promising violence to Don Luiz da Ramirez, *Winds of Chance* 46)

(2) be happy; be grateful: Said often to one who complains without reason, or who too hastily overlooks the good to protest the bad.

"And if the reek o' bilge offends thy delicacy,—well, 'tis better than searing bullet or to be crushed 'neath falling spar. So **content you**, madam." (Japhet Bly, *Winds of Chance* 72)

cough up your tale [*carrf arrp ya/yarr/ye/yer/ yere/yore tayell*] speak up; start talking; out with it; spit it out; say what you have to say

> "Well, **cough up your tale**, lad." (Long John Silver, urging Richard Thorpe to tell more about his search for his missing brother, "The Adventures of Long John Silver: The Pink Pearl" 5:05)

cutlasses [*carrt/cooht-lerss/lish-es*]
A battle cry commanding one's fellows to use their swords (a cutlass is a thick, heavy, slightly curving sword with a flat, single-edged blade) against the enemy.

> "Truce be over! **Cutlasses**, you swabs!" (Long John Silver, "Treasure Island" [1950] 1:00:46)

despatch [*ders-patch*] (1) go; get out of here (2) go to it; do it

> "Go! And bid Vardon and Morris here to me. Come now, **despatch**!" (Adam Penfeather, *Adam Penfeather, Buccaneer* 214)

discourse [*des-carrse/coorse*] speak up; start talking; out with it; spit it out; say what you have to say

> "Who be you, bully, who and what? Speak, my hearty, **discourse**, or kiss this Silver Woman o' mine!" (Roger Tressady, gripping a silver dagger, *Martin Conisby's Vengeance* 155)

don't speak a\one (single) word [*don'/doon't/ dorrn't speak a\'un/woohn (sengle) warrd*]

Compare: *He ... went up to one Morrice Cundon, then at the helm, ... and swore damn him, if he **spoke one word**, or stirr'd either hand or foot, he would blow his brains out ...* (attribution to William Fly, *General History of the Pyrates* 606)

don't stir either hand or foot [*don'/doon't/ dorrn't starr eeder/ee'er/iyder/iy'er\needer/nee'er/ neither/nyder/ny'er 'an'/'and/han' arr foot*] don't move a muscle; don't move an inch

> *He ... went up to one Morrice Cundon, then at the helm, ... and swore damn him, if he spoke one word, or **stirr'd either hand or foot**, he would blow his brains out ...* (attribution to William Fly, *General History of the Pyrates* 606)

don't you breathe a word to a soul [*don'/ doon't/dorrn't 'ee/ya/ye/yer breeve a warrd t'/ ta/ter a sool/so'ool*] don't tell anybody

> "Now **don't you breathe a word to a soul** that we're here." (Long John Silver, "The Adventures of Long John Silver: The Pink Pearl" 20:16)

don't you worry yourself [*don'/doon't/dorrn't 'ee/ya/ye/yer warry/woory 'ee/ya/yarr/ye/yer/ yere/yore-seff*] don't worry

> "Don't ye **worry yourself**, captain." (Long John Silver, *Porto Bello Gold* 47)

drop anchor [*drarrp han-karr*]
drop your hook [*drarrp ya/yarr/ye/yer/yere/ yore 'ook*] (1) stay a while (2) wait a minute; hold on (3) stay where you are

> "**Drop anchor**, matey. We'll fill the cask where you lie." (Billy Bones, stopping Jim Hawkins so that he can immediately drink the rum Jim's carrying, "Treasure Island" [1934] 7:00) "Oh, well then, welcome aboard and **drop your hook**." (Blackbeard, "Blackbeard's Ghost" 27:37)

ease off [*eass arrf*] calm down; don't worry
> < "But he told us we were bound for Treasure Island." "**Ease off**! I've a feeling Cap'n Silver'll change MacDougal's course." > (Trip Fenner & Patch, "Long John Silver's Return to Treasure Island" 57:19)

easy calm down; relax; don't worry
> < "I being a quiet soul—" "And a pirate, like as not!" "**Easy**, shipmate, **easy**. Passion is an ill word to steer by." > (Adam Penfeather & Martin Conisby, *Black Bartlemy's Treasure* 48)

easy all [*easy awrl*] calm down; relax
Used to address more than one person.

> "Hold your fire, lads—no shooting; we want 'em all alive! **Easy all**, bullies—nary a gun, mates—we'll lay 'em 'longside and board ..." (pirates aboard the *Happy Despatch*, eager not to harm the women they believe are on the ship they're about to board, *Martin Conisby's Vengeance* 103)

Used to address one person emphatically.

> < "Damned spy!" "**Easy all**, shipmate! Use me kindly, for I'm a timid soul with a good heart, meaning no offence." > (Martin Conisby & Adam Penfeather, *Black Bartlemy's Treasure* 46)

easy now\there [*easy narr/nowoo\theyerr*] take it easy; calm down; relax

> "Doff his bandage, Smidge, and **easy now**!" (Adam Penfeather, *Adam Penfeather, Buccaneer* 202) "**Easy there**!" (Long John Silver regarding Ben Gunn's poor handling of a rope load, *Dead Man's Chest* 6)

enough of words [*enarrff/enow/'nough o'\on warrds*] shut up; be quiet

> "Howbeit I am no murderer, woman." "Ah—bah! **Enough of words**, Master Innocent." (Martin Conisby & Captain Jo, *Martin Conisby's Vengeance* 9)

fall back [*fawrl back*] get back; move back
Often, though not always, used to order a retreat from a battle or confrontation.

> "All right, mates, **fall back! Fall back!**" (pirate in Long John Silver's company, ordering a retreat after a failed attack on the stockade, "Treasure Island" [1960] 57:10) "**Fall back, fall back**, I say; you

taint the quarter-deck." (The Red Rover, commanding his mutinous men to step away, *The Red Rover* 337)

fetch aft __ [*fatch arrft/haft* __] bring __ over here; bring __ to me

Literally, this phrase means "bring back," but it is used more generally to mean "bring over here" or "bring to me." As the captain and other senior members of a company generally live in and command from the rear part of a vessel, the phrase is closely associated with persons of authority.

"**Fetch aft** the brandy, Charles Noble, an' a dry towel what ta wipe off me transom." (Long John Silver, *Dead Man's Chest* 29)

fetch ahead [*fatch a'ead/ahayd/'head*] move ahead; onward; go on; let's go; keep going

"**Fetch ahead** for the doubloons." (Long John Silver, *Treasure Island* 178, Chap. 31)

fetch up __ [*fatch arrp* __] get ahold of __; grab and bring __; bring up __

"**Fetch up** the powder and ball!" (Blackbeard, "Blackbeard the Pirate" 45:00)

forward [*farr-ad/ard/edd/erd*]

(1) move to or toward the front part of the ship

"Now **forrard** two o' ye and take me up this two-legged beast." (Adam Penfeather, *Adam Penfeather, Buccaneer* 189)

(2) move ahead; go on; let's go; keep going

"Scatter as you advance, and keep low. God speed you, Ned! **Forward!**" (Peter Blood, *Captain Blood Returns* 167)

get along lively [*ge'/git alarrng/'larrng/'long lawv/lyeeve-ly*] move; let's go; hurry up now

"**Get along lively!**" (Blair, "Cutthroat Island" 48:53)

get\go below [*ge'/git\go'oo b'-lowoo*] go belowdecks

A command typically given (1) out of protective concern, in order to direct another to

a place of relative safety, (2) out of annoyance or expediency, in order to direct another out of the way of those sailing or doing battle on a vessel's main deck, or (3) out of aggressive caution, in order to direct another where he may be guarded or secured easily and with minimal resistance.

"Now **get below** to my cabin and prepare to—. **Get below!**" (Long John Silver, ordering dentist Angus MacAllister belowdecks, "The Adventures of Long John Silver: The Tale of a Tooth" 23:10) "**Get** you **below**, sir. I'll come to you as soon as we are under way and the course is set." (Tim, *The Fortunes of Captain Blood* 152) "Now **go below**, and stay there till I call you." (pirate captain, *The Coral Island* 201)

get out of it [*ge'/git arrt/ou'/owoot o'\on ett/'n/'t*] get out of the way; get out of here

"**Get out of it**, boy. And none o' yer keyholin', neither." (Black Dog, "Treasure Island" [1998] 13:11)

get to windward of __ [*ge'/git t'/ta/ter win'-'ard/erd/wahrrd o'\on* __] be careful of __; be wary of __; stay away from __; keep your distance from __

Though the phrase means literally to keep oneself between the wind and the object to be avoided or cautiously dealt with (to allow the seafarer maximum maneuverability), its everyday sense is an equivalent of common cautions like "be careful of" or "stay away from."

"What I says to you is, **get to wind'ard o'** vengeance—nay, heave it overboard, shipmate, and you'll ride the easier, aye and sweeter, and seek something more useful—gold, for instance, 'tis a handy thing, I've heard say—so ha' done wi' vengeance!" (Adam Penfeather, *Black Bartlemy's Treasure* 61)

get under way [*ge'/git arrn/hun/oohn-der/ner wayee*] (1) sail away: A command to sail away, especially after some time at anchor. (2) prepare to sail away: A command to undertake or complete preparations necessary for sailing away. (3) go away; get out of here; leave

"Get under way, at once, Tim!" (George Fairfax, *The Fortunes of Captain Blood* 151)

get you gone [*ge'/git 'ee/ya/ye/yer garrn*] go away; get out of here; leave

"The boat lieth yonder; take her and what you will—only—get you gone!" (Captain Jo, *Martin Conisby's Vengeance* 172)

get you to __ [*ge'/git 'ee/ya/ye/yer t'/ta/ter __*]

"D'ye hear me? Get you to bed, rot you!" (George Fairfax, *The Fortunes of Captain Blood* 162)

give away [*gi'/giff awayee/'way/'wayee*] get to it; let's go

< "And you are armed, I see!" "Ay, I am, John, a brace o' barkers and two swords,— so set to work, John, and lay your rogue's back into it—give away!" > (John Barrasdale & Japhet Bly, *Winds of Chance* 139)

give me some sweat [*gi'/giff me sahm/sarrm/soohm swaaht*]

An exhortation to work hard at some laborious task or physical exertion.

"Give me some sweat there, you swabs!" (Long John Silver, "Treasure Island" [1990] 53:20)

give us room [*gi'/giff arrss roohm*] get out of the way

"Now, my pretty lads, d'ye give us room or do I make ye—which?" (Japhet Bly, *Winds of Chance* 14)

give way [*gi'/giff wayee*]
(1) get out of the way

"Give way, you land lubber!" (Blackbeard, "Blackbeard's Ghost" 35:29)

(2) go on; get going; move

"Forward there, Johnny; give way and with a will." (Japhet Bly, *Winds of Chance* 276)

give yourself no uneasiness [*gi'/giff 'ee/ya/ye/yer/yere-seff no'oo arrn/hun/oohn-eas'ness*] don't worry; relax; take it easy

"Give yourself no uneasiness on account of the personal animosity which a few of the fellows saw fit to manifest against yourself." (The Red Rover, *The Red Rover* 347)

give yourself peace [*gi'/giff 'ee/ya/ye/yer/yere/yore-seff peesh*] calm down; don't worry

"Give yourself peace. This is no great matter." (Peter Blood, *The Fortunes of Captain Blood* 150)

go about [*go'oo abarrt/abowoot/'barrt/'bout/'bowoot*] about face; turn around; go back

Literally a nautical command meaning "reverse course," the phrase is used broadly to order any kind of change in direction or course of action, whether physical or abstract.

"Below there! Belvedere, ahoy—go about, or she'll rake us ..." (Resolution Day, *Martin Conisby's Vengeance* 104)

go to your several duties [*go'oo t'/ta/ter ya/yarr/ye/yer/yere/yore sebber/seb'r/sev'r-al dooties*]

Used to direct members of a crew to their assigned tasks or stations, especially after a time of rest or inactivity.

"Go then, gentlemen, to your several duties." (The Red Rover, commanding his crew to undertake preparations for battle while waiting for a prize ship to approach, *The Red Rover* 408)

go to't [*go'oo t'/ta/ter ett/'n*] go for it; go at it

"Go to't, lass, drink hearty—here's you and me agin world and damn all, says I. Let me perish!" (Roger Tressady, *Martin Conisby's Vengeance* 158)

go you back [*go'oo 'ee/ya/ye/yer back*]

"Go you back with that answer, Captain." (pirates aboard the *Valiant*, *Captain Blood Returns* 284) "Remind him of that, Captain. **Go you back** and tell him." (Trenam, *Captain Blood Returns* 285)

go your ways [*go'oo ya/yarr/ye/yer/yere/yore wayees*] go on; go where you're headed

"Go your ways" is a milder usage than "away with you" or "off with you." All of these direct the addressee to leave, but the first is a gentler direction to proceed where he will, rather than a sharp rebuke.

> "**Go your ways**, brother, and leave old Resolution to pray a little, aye—and, mayhap weep a little, if God be kind." (Resolution Day, *Martin Conisby's Vengeance* 175)

handle your piece [*'andle ya/yarr/ye/yer/yere/yore peesh*] have your gun at the ready

> "Ho, musketeers, stand by! **Handle your pieces**—" (Captain Sharp, reacting immediately to Benjamin Trigg's cocking of his pistol, *Adam Penfeather, Buccaneer* 75)

hands aloft [*'ands/'an's/han's err-larrft*] put your hands up

Note in Section 4.3.4 the very different meaning of this command when uttered in a nautical context.

> "**Hands aloft**, please." (Captain Vallo, "The Crimson Pirate" 7:12)

handsomely [*'an'/'and/han'-sahm/sarrm/soohm-ly*] quickly but neatly

> "All slack! Ease away, **handsomely**, **handsomely**!" (pirate overseeing the hoisting of a large chest into the *Elizabeth Galley*'s hold, *The Pirate Round* 329)

hark (to __) [*'ark/hahrrk (t'/ta/ter __)*] listen (to __)

> < "But thee, Joanna, I grieved thee surely dead—" "Nay, I screamed and dropped in time, but—**hark**, the Englishman's fire is ceasing and see, Resolution—look yonder!" > (Resolution Day & Captain Jo, *Martin Conisby's Vengeance* 109) "I've set 'em a trail they shall not miss—aha,

yonder they give tongue, baying to it like very dogs—**hark to** 'em!" (Japhet Bly, *Winds of Chance* 301–02)

h(e)arkee [*'ark/hahrrk-ee*] listen; listen up

> "**Harkee**, lad. You're right. That be de Vegas." (Long John Silver, "The Adventures of Long John Silver: Sword of Vengeance" 9:14) "How, are ye dumb? Then **hearkee**! I ha' brought you to sea, my fine lady, for divers reasons, and one of 'em this; to show you that you, in your proud selfishness, know so little o' life, how desperate real life is." (Japhet Bly, *Winds of Chance* 39–40)

h(e)arken [*'ar/hahrr-ken*] listen

> "**Hearken**! You may hear the dogs like bees in a hive and be cursed to 'em!" (John, *Martin Conisby's Vengeance* 187)

haste (to ...) [*'aste/'ayeeste/hayeeste (t'/ta/ter ...)*] hurry; hurry up (and ...)

> "If you have aught to smooth the dying moment to fellow-mortal, **haste to** impart it!" (The Red Rover, *The Red Rover* 499)

hasten [*'asten/hayeesen*] hurry; hurry up

> "Why then, Lord love you, Martin—**hasten**!" (Adam Penfeather, *Black Bartlemy's Treasure* 333)

haul away [*'aul/'awrl/hawrl awayee/'way/'wayee*] pull

A command to pull hard—and almost always to pull on a line (rope) or to pull at something attached to the line being handled.

> "Hands to the halyards, **haul away**!" (Thomas Marlowe, *The Pirate Round* 82)

haul off [*'aul/'awrl/hawrl arrf*] let's go; move; get a move on

To haul off means literally to move away or to shift oneself or one's activities to a new location.

> "**Haul off**, cast about, stand off and on. If the woman's here, t'others should be skulking

about—come, bouse about and stand away, and lively, ye scratchings!" (Ned, ordering Tom and Tony to find Ursula Revell's companions, *Winds of Chance* 314)

haul your wind [*'aul/'awrl/hawrl ya/yarr/ye/yer/yere/yore win'/wint*] stop; wait; hold on

"I'm no fine gentleman for ye to bruise, so **haul your wind** and listen!" (Adam Penfeather, *Black Bartlemy's Treasure* 326)

have at __ [*'aff/'ave/ha'/haff a'/hat __*] take care of __; direct your attention or effort to __

"**Have at** the dishes whiles I go prepare a couch for thee." (Japhet Bly, *Winds of Chance* 146)

have done [*'aff/'ave/ha'/haff doohn*] enough; that's enough; stop that

< "[T]he Lord hath set you here i' this flowery garden like Adam and her like Eve—" "And yourself like the serpent!" "**Ha' done**, Martin, **ha' done**! 'The Lord shall root out deceitful lips and the tongue that speaks proud things!' mark that!" > (Resolution Day & Martin Conisby, *Martin Conisby's Vengeance* 168)

have forth __ [*'aff/'ave/ha'/haff farrth*] hand over __; give me __; give __ up; turn over __

"The women! **Have forth** the women! Us wants the women!" (crew aboard the *Joyful Deliverance*, pounding on Ursula Revell's cabin door, *Winds of Chance* 80)

heave ahead [*'eave/heeff a'ead/ahayd/'head*] move ahead; onward; let's go; keep going

"So up wi' you, lass! **Heave ahead**, Carrion!" (Japhet Bly, ordering his two companions forward, *Winds of Chance* 155)

heave ho [*'eave/heeff ho'oo*] work at it

An exhortation to work hard at some laborious task or physical exertion.

"**Heave-ho**, there! That don't weigh nothin'!" (Blackbeard, "Blackbeard the Pirate" 44:49)

heave to [*'eave/heeff ter*]

To "heave to" is to bring a vessel to a stop, specifically by pointing its bow into the wind so that it remains motionless except for drifting. The phrase is often used figuratively in reference to a person rather than a vessel, with various meanings incorporating some version of the concept of slowing, stopping, or yielding.

(1) stop; hold on

"Well, **heave to**, Roger, bring up in shade o' this rock. Ahoy, bosun, pipe down." (Rogerson, *Winds of Chance* 353)

(2) stay a while

"Here, **heave to**, maties." (libidinous pirate, engaging his visitors in friendly conversation, "Pirates of the Caribbean" Disney attraction [2000])

(3) come in; enter

"That you, Jim? **Heave to**." (Billy Bones, responding to a knock on his door, "Treasure Island" [1960] 3:23)

(4) go along with me; do what I ask

"**Heave to**, matey, for pity's sake, **heave to**. **Heave to** for Cap'n Billy." (Billy Bones, begging Jim Hawkins to give him a drink of rum, "Treasure Island" [1960] 11:48)

heed how you come [*'eed howoo/'ow/'owoo 'ee/ya/ye/yer cahm/carrm/coohm*] watch where you're going

"Easy all! Have your pistols ready and **heed how you come**." (Adam Penfeather, *Black Bartlemy's Treasure* 107)

here a hand [*'ee'arr/'ee'err/'ere/hee'arr/hee'err a 'an'/'and/han'*] give me a hand here; help me out here

"**Here a hand**." (pirate unloading rowboat, "Treasure Island" [1998] 2:41)

hist [*hest*] hush; shut up; be quiet

"But, **hist**! Heard you nothing?" (The Red Rover, hearing something fall into the water, *The Red Rover* 350)

hold [*hol'/hoold/ho'oold/'ol'/'old*] stop; wait

> "**Hold!** Don Domingo is my prisoner, and I have pledged my word that he shall suffer no violence!' (Peter Blood, *Captain Blood Returns* 171)

hold a minute\moment [*hol'/hoold/ho'oold/ 'ol'/'old a min't/minnert\momernt/mon't/ mo'ooment*]

> < "You are in command of the ships until I return. We may need to do a bit of disciplining up there." "Aye, sir." "**Hold a minute** ..." > (Roger Press & Josiah Brownlaw, with Press stopping Brownlaw for a moment to rethink his orders, *The Pirate Round* 282) "**Hold a moment**, Captain!" (Duncan Honeyman, *The Pirate Round* 110)

hold fast [*hol'/hoold/ho'oold/'ol'/'old farrst/ fass*] stop right there; wait just a moment

> < "Come along." "**Hold fast!** You'll obey orders from your cap'n or you'll walk the plank! You mutinous maggot!" > (Trip Fenner & Long John Silver, "The Adventures of Long John Silver: Execution Dock" 13:01)

hold hard [*hol'/hoold/ho'oold/'ol'/'old 'ard/ 'ahrrd/hahrrd*] hold on; wait

> The term "hard" lends urgency and emphasis to the command.

> < "Cast her off!" "Nay, **hold hard** a moment, Master Sweetlocks!" > (Birthmark Sweetlocks & one of his comrades, *The Dealings of Captain Sharkey and Other Tales of Pirates* "The Blighting of Sharkey" 59)

hold off [*hol'/hoold/ho'oold/'ol'/'old arrf*] stop; lay off; get away

> "**Hold off** or I'll mischief ye!" (Benjamin Trigg, seeing his friend Adam Penfeather pummeled to the ground, *Adam Penfeather, Buccaneer* 72)

hold (on) there [*hol'/hoold/ho'oold/'ol'/'old (arrn) tharr/theyarr/theyerr*] stop; stop right there; stop where you are

> < "I'll die first! So do as you will but I fear neither you nor any of your villainous company, these base rogues that do your bidding—" "**Hold there!** You ha' seen but six of us and these friends and comrades endeared to me by bitter adversity ..." > (Ursula Revell & Japhet Bly, *Winds of Chance* 40)
> < "A big, ugly, booze-soaked rummy!" "**Hold on there!** There be no call to put the fuddler's name on your newfound shipmate." (Steve Walker & Blackbeard, "Blackbeard's Ghost" 30:18)

hold your clack [*hol'/hoold/ho'oold/'ol'/'old ya/ yarr/ye/yer/yere/yore clack*] shut up; be quiet

> "What now? Are ye dumb? Then stow thy whids, **hold thy clack** and, since ye talk o' savagery, of savages I'll tell thee, though of another sort." (Japhet Bly, *Winds of Chance* 178)

hold your fire [*hol'/hoold/ho'oold/'ol'/'old ya/yarr/ye/yer/yere/yore farr/fyarr*] do not fire; no shooting

> "**Hold your fire**, lads—no shooting; we want 'em all alive!" (pirates aboard the *Happy Despatch*, *Martin Conisby's Vengeance* 103)

hold your gab [*hol'/hoold/ho'old/'ol'/'old ya/yarr/ye/yer/yere/yore garrb*] shut up; be quiet

> "But **hold your gab**. I'll do the talking." (Long John Silver, *Porto Bello Gold* 48)

hold your peace [*hol'/hoold/ho'old/'ol'/'old ya/ yarr/ye/yer/yere/yore peesh*] shut up; be quiet

> *[T]he rest of the pirates laugh[ed] heartily, desiring Roberts to sit down and **hold his peace**, for he had no share in the pallaver with Plunkett at all.* (*Villains of All Nations* 97)

hold your tongue [*hol'/hoold/ho'oold/'ol'/'old ya/yarr/ye/yer/yere/yore toohngue*] shut up; be quiet

Used especially when the addressee had just said something annoying, offensive, or otherwise objectionable.

> < "We've been scuttled." "**Hold yer tongue!**" > (pirate aboard the *Thistle* & Long John Silver, "Long John Silver's Return to Treasure Island" 1:03:37)

hold your whining [*hol'/hoold/ho'oold/'ol'/ 'old ya/yarr/ye/yer/yere/yore a-wawn/wyeen-in'*] quit your whining; shut up

> "Now you **hold** your tongue and **your whin-in'** for them that's at your beck and call, because I ain't." (Purity Pinker, replying hotly to the supercilious Lady Harwood's abusive comments, "The Adventures of Long John Silver: Dead Reckoning" 20:57)

hop to it [*harrp t'/ta/ter ett/'n/'t*] get on it; get to it; get started

> "**Hop to it!**" (Captain Vallo, "The Crimson Pirate" 37:01)

hush you [*harrsh/hoohsh 'ee/ya/ye/yer*] shut up; quiet

> "Nay, **hush thee**, my Benjamin, catch thy wind ..." (Adam Penfeather, *Adam Penfeather, Buccaneer* 310-11)

I want movement [*I'ee warrnt moobment*] get moving; let's go

> "Scurry! Scurry, **I want movement! I want movement!**" (Jack Sparrow, "Pirates of the Caribbean 2: Dead Man's Chest" 16:57)

it'll be place and rank for you [*ett'll/'n'll OR 'twell/'twill be playeece an'/'n' renk farr/fer 'ee/ ya/ye/yer*] fall into line; get with the program; work and obey like everybody else

> "**It'll be place and rank for you**, messmate, or a chance to swim wi' the sharks." (Long John Silver, *Porto Bello Gold* 51)

it's loose moorings and stand away [*ett/'n is\be OR 'tes/'tis loose moorin's an'/'n' stan'/ starrn'/starrnd awayee/'way/'wayee*] let's go; let's get out of here

> "Then, brother, **it's loose moorings and stand away.**" (Smy Peters, *Adam Penfeather, Buccaneer* 27)

jump (lively) [*joohmp (lawv/lyeeve-ly)*] move quickly; get to it; snap to it; let's go; come on

> "Let go weather braces, **jump**, ye dogs, **jump!**" (Captain Belvedere, *Martin Conisby's Vengeance* 104) "You lazy scum! Back to yer duties! **Jump lively** now!" (Long John Silver, "The Adventures of Long John Silver: The Tale of a Tooth" 10:40)

jump to (it) [*joohmp to (OR t'/ta/ter ett/'n/'t)*] move quickly; get to it; let's go; come on

> "**Jump to** and weigh!" (Blackbeard, "Blackbeard the Pirate" 1:15:18) "Get 'im out of 'ere. Vittle and clothe him. And see that he works for it. **Jump to it**, now." (Long John Silver, "The Adventures of Long John Silver: The Tale of a Tooth" 12:19)

keep a weather eye open [*keep a waahther eye'ee ho/hoo/oo-perrn*] be on the lookout; keep a close watch

> "But **keep a weather eye open**, mates, and hold on tight." (talking pirate skull, "Pirates of the Caribbean" Disney attraction)

keep an eye lifting [*keep a eye'ee a-left-in'*] be on the lookout; keep a close watch

> "Well, **keep an eye lifting** and if you find out aught worth the telling, let one o' your lads ride post to Deptford, Jo." (Adam Penfeather, *Black Bartlemy's Treasure* 107)

keep both hands afore you [*keep bofe 'ands/ 'an's/han's afarr/befarr/before/'farr/'fore 'ee/ya/ ye/yer*] keep your hands in front of you

Used when confronting someone the speaker suspects is armed or intends violence.

> < "Captain Jo commands here—" "Say ye so, Resolution, say ye so, lad? Now mark me—and **keep both hands afore ye**—so,

my bully—hark'ee now—there's none commands where I am save Roger Tressady!" > (Resolution Day & Roger Tressady, *Martin Conisby's Vengeance* 156)

keep your eyes peeled (for __) [*keep ya/yarr/ye/yer/yere/yore eye'ees peelt (farr/fer __)*] be on the lookout (for __); keep a close watch (for __)

"And not that I'm sayin' anythin' agin Bartholemew, oh, no, but you might run into a bit o' trouble, so **keep your eyes peeled**." (Long John Silver, "The Adventures of Long John Silver: Devil's Stew" 14:54) "Patch, you and the rest of 'em stay here and **keep your eyes peeled for** treachery." (Long John Silver, "The Adventures of Long John Silver: The Pink Pearl" 10:41)

keep your tongue behind your teeth [*keep ya/yarr/ye/yer/yere/yore toohngue b'-hawnd/hin'/hyeend/'ind ya/yarr/ye/yer/yere/yore teef*] keep your mouth shut; shut up; be quiet

"**Keep your tongue behind your teeth!** Hold still, the two o' ye, or I'll give ye a bellyful o' pickling brine." (John Flint, *Porto Bello Gold* 132)

lay aft (here) [*layee arrft/haft ('ee'arr/'ee'err/'ere/hee'arr/hee'err)*] come back here
A command to move toward the rear part of the vessel.

"'Here, Griffin, **lay aft**!' Marlowe shouted, and with a suspicious look Griffin left off his bravado and ambled back to the quarterdeck." (Thomas Marlowe, *The Blackbirder* 159) "Belay that, **lay aft here**!" (Roger Press, *The Pirate Round* 282)

lay ahold of __ [*layee er-hol'/hoold/ho'oold/'ol'/'old o'\on __*] grab __; take hold of __

"**Lay ahold of** them sheets!" (Ben Worley, "Blackbeard the Pirate" 6:00)

lay down __ [*layee dowoon __*] put down __; drop __

"**Lay down** your swords, lads." (Ned Lynch, "Swashbuckler" 1:08:28)

lay 'em aboard [*layee 'em abarrd*] go get 'em; go after 'em; attack 'em

"At him, Pompey! Now's ye time, boy! **Lay 'im aboard**, lad, 'e be a-swounding!" (pirates aboard the *Happy Despatch*, urging Pompey to finish off an injured Martin Conisby, *Martin Conisby's Vengeance* 83)

lay to [*layee ter*] stop; hold off; don't move; don't do anything
To "lay to" is to bring a vessel to a stop, specifically by pointing its bow into the wind so that it remains motionless except for drifting.

"You'll get plenty o' cut-and-rip when the time comes, but until I gives the signal, **lay to**." (Long John Silver, "Treasure Island" [1950] 40:51)

lay your back in(to) it [*layee ya/yarr/ye/yer/yere/yore back i'/'n\(in-ta/terr) ett/'n/'t*] work at it; put your back into it
An exhortation to work hard at some laborious task or physical exertion.

< "And you are armed, I see!" "Ay, I am, John, a brace o' barkers and two swords,—so set to work, John, and **lay your** rogue's **back into it**—give away!" > (John Barrasdale & Japhet Bly, *Winds of Chance* 139)

lead on [*lead arrn*] lead the way

< "Here, you, be you certain this is the way?" "On the soul of my mother." "It had better be, or I'll slit your throat. **Lead on**." > (Long John Silver & Salamander the Greek, "The Adventures of Long John Silver: Pieces of Eight" 11:49)

lean into it [*lean in-ta/terr ett/'n/'t*] work at it; put your back into it
An exhortation to work hard at some laborious task or physical exertion.

"Lean into 'n!" (Blackbeard, "Blackbeard the Pirate" 44:58)

leave it\that [*leaf ett/'n/'t\tharrt*]

A command either (1) to drop the subject under discussion or (2) to stop **talking** altogether.

> "**Leave that. Leave it,** I say, or we'll waste the day in talk." (Chard, *Captain Blood Returns* 30)

leave me [*leaf me*] go away; get out of here

> "Go then! Keep your chains—aye, I will give ye to the mercy of this rabble crew ... **leave me!**" (Captain Jo, *Martin Conisby's Vengeance* 88)

let be [*laaht be OR lebbe*] leave it alone

A command to abandon some view, concern, or intention, often for the addressee's own good.

> "Nay, **let be,** Resolution, I'm a-dying—yes!" (Captain Jo, *Martin Conisby's Vengeance* 173)

let him away [*laaht/le' 'im awayee/'way/ 'wayee*] let him go

> "Ay, **let her away,** messmate, 'twill be best for her and us." (Absalom Troy, *Adam Penfeather, Buccaneer* 32)

let me be [*laaht me OR lemme be*] leave me alone

> < "Water!" "Here, you fool, that water will sear your insides." "**Let me be!**" "Get up! Up, I say! Get up!" > (pirate in Long John Silver's company & Patch, as the first pirate stops to drink muddy water from a jungle pond, "The Adventures of Long John Silver: Pieces of Eight" 12:12)

let no man stir [*laaht/le' no'oo man starr*] no one move

> "Bide still all and **let no man stir** till I give word." (Roger Tressady, *Black Bartlemy's Treasure* 314)

let's (get) away [*laaht's/less (ge'/git) awayee/ 'way/'wayee*] let's go; let's get out of here

> "And don't stay to take up anchor. Cut the cable. Hoist sail and **let's away.**" (George Fairfax, *The Fortunes of Captain Blood* 151)
>
> "So come, and **let us get away.**" (Abraham Dawling, urging Barnaby True away to a waiting boat, *The Book of Pirates* "The Ghost of Captain Brand" 48)

let's get moving [*laaht's/less ge'/git a-movin'*] let's go; let's get going

> "Ha-harr, me bucko, **let's get movin'.**" (Long John Silver, "The Adventures of Long John Silver: The Necklace" 21:37)

let's have at it [*laaht's/less 'aff/'ave/ha'/haff a'/hat ett/'n/'t*] let's get to it; let's do it

> < "Where be the treasure?" "Aye, let's get our hands on it and begin counting." "**Let's have at it,** I say." > (Old Stingley, Ned Shill, & Patch, "Long John Silver's Return to Treasure Island" 1:13:24)

let's sheer off [*laaht's/less shee-arr/err arrf*] let's go; let's get out of here

> "Come, cover that white head o' thine and **let's sheer off** ..." (Absalom Troy, leading Adam Penfeather away from his uncle's burning house, *Adam Penfeather, Buccaneer* 25)

let's to breakfast\supper\dinner [*laaht's/ less t'/ta/ter brayk/breff-farrst/fess\soohpper\ di'er*] let's eat

> "And now, **let us to supper.**" (Japhet Bly, *Winds of Chance* 219)

let's to it [*laaht's/less t'/ta/ter ett/'n/'t*] let's do it; let's get on it; let's go for it

> "Od's my life, but I love thee, Adam, **let's to 't.**" (Benjamin Trigg, on hearing Adam Penfeather's decision to pay Absalom Troy a visit and fight him, *Adam Penfeather, Buccaneer* 112)

list to __ [*lest t'/ta/ter __*] listen to __

"Apes! Monkeys, cease your chattering and list to Joanna." (Captain Jo, *Martin Conisby's Vengeance* 62) "List ye to this, now!" (Resolution Day, *Martin Conisby's Vengeance* 74)

listen here [*lessen 'ee'arr/'ee'err/'ere/hee'arr/hee'err*] listen; listen up

"All right, all right, listen here." (William Darnall, calling together the *Vengeance*'s crew to decide their next destination, *The Guardship* 210)

lively (it is) [*lawv/lyeeve-ly (ett/'n/'t be OR 'tes/'tis)*]

lively (now) [*lawv/lyeeve-ly (narr/nowoo)*] move quickly; get to it; let's go; come on

"Now we're for it! Cast out the lines and pull for the shore. Lively!" (Long John Silver, "Treasure Island" [1950] 46:38) "Now, you lazy swabs, stir yourselves! Lift anchor. Shake out the main! Lively now! Or I'll carve your gizzard and fry it for me supper!" (Blackbeard, "Blackbeard's Ghost" 1:45:41)

look alive [*look '/er-lawv/lyeeve*] move; get a move on; get to it; snap to it; let's go; come on

"Look alive, boy! Clew up the fore-sail. Drop the main-sail peak. Them squalls come quick sometimes." (Bloody Bill, *The Coral Island* 263)

look at the cut of you [*look a'/hat t' carrt/cooht o'/on 'ee/ya/ye/yer*] take a look at yourself

"Look at the cut of ya. Look at the cut of ya. Dirt stains on your clothes as though you've been fightin' like an ordinary gamecock and rollin' in the alleys." (Purity Pinker, "Long John Silver's Return to Treasure Island" 34:09)

look lively [*look lawv/lyeeve-ly*] move; quickly; get to it; snap to it; let's go; come on

"Hoist anchor. Man all canvas. Look lively." (Humble Bellows, "The Crimson Pirate" 32:24)

look sharp [*look shahrrp*]

(1) get ready; watch out; be alert

"He's gone! Look sharp, now!" (Long John Silver, hurrying his wanted companion off the floor and urging him to safety, "The Adventures of Long John Silver: Turnabout" 24:40)

(2) move quickly; get to it; let's go

"Now look sharp now!" (Long John Silver, urging Jim Hawkins to finish preparations for the trip to Bermuda, "The Adventures of Long John Silver: Dead Reckoning" 7:03)

look there [*look tharr/theyarr/theyerr*] look over there; look at that

"Now, look there; there's a pet bit for to beach a ship in." (Israel Hands, *Treasure Island* 142, Chap. 26)

look to __ [*look t'/ta/ter __*] look after __; keep an eye on __; take care of __

"Lookee, friend Matt, this lady, this spouse of mine, this right buxom Madam Bly, I set in charge o' thee awhile; look to her, Matt, look to her, for she indeed is all the wife I have, so shield her well." (Japhet Bly, *Winds of Chance* 278–79)

look to it [*look t'/ta/ter ett/'n/'t*] do it; see to it; get it done

"You keep your ship very foul ... But I am aboard and this shall be amended—look to it." (Captain Jo, *Martin Conisby's Vengeance* 68)

look to your priming [*look t'/ta/ter ya/yarr/ye/yer/yere/yore praw/pryee-min'*]

A command literally to have one's musket or pistol in firing condition and, more broadly, to have one's firearm ready for imminent use. Priming can refer either to priming powder (a fine powder loaded into a firearm's priming pan) or to the priming pan itself.

> "To cover, lads, and **look to your primings** and wait my word." (Roger Tressady, *Black Bartlemy's Treasure* 312–13)

lookee (here) [*lookee ('ee'arr/'ee'err/'ere/ hee'arr/hee'err)*] look at this; look over here

> "Toby Ingleby shall murder and ravish no more and here's proof—**lookee.**" (Japhet Bly, pointing to Ingleby's severed head on the point of a warrior's spear, *Winds of Chance* 226) "Oh, Tony! Oh, Tony, come and **lookee here.**" (Tom, on discovering Ursula Revell hidden in the brush, *Winds of Chance* 313)

loose __ [*loosh __*] release __; let __ go; get your hands off __

> "**Loose me**, accursed renegade, loose me, I say!" (Smy Peters, *Adam Penfeather, Buccaneer* 335) "**Loose him!**" (Adam Penfeather, *Adam Penfeather, Buccaneer* 189)

make an effort [*mayeeke a aff-art*] get to it; let's go; come on

> "Come on down, lad. **Make an effort.**" (Thomas Bartholomew Red, urging his lieutenant to climb down off a raft's mast, "Pirates" 5:58)

make haste [*mayeeke 'aste/'ayeeste/hayeeste*] hurry; hurry up

> "Captain Drake, if you fortune to come to this port, **make haste** away, for the Spaniards which you had with you here last year have bewrayed this place, and taken away all that you left here." (John Garret, in a note left for Francis Drake on a tree in Port Pheasant, *The Queen's Pirate* 51)

make (you) ready [*mayeeke ('ee/ya/ye/yer) rea'-eee*] get ready

> "Here they come. **Make ready**, lads." (William Kidd, "Captain Kidd" 17:33) < "Give me knife or pistol and I will prove my words." "Why, so you shall, yet not now, for now we

ride; so **make you ready.**" > (Ursula Revell & Japhet Bly, *Winds of Chance* 29)

make ready at the __ [*mayeeke rea'-eee a'/hat t' __*] get ready to work the __; be prepared to handle the __

> "In the waist! Mr. Rakestraw, we shall be falling off a bit, **make ready at the** braces. Gunners, you know your duty!" (Thomas Marlowe, *The Guardship* 348)

make ready the __ [*mayeeke rea'-eee t' __*] prepare the __; get the __ ready

> "**Make ready the** guns. Run out the sweeps." (Barbossa, "Pirates of the Caribbean: The Curse of the Black Pearl" 1:22:25) "**Make ready the** longboat." (El Toro Mendoza, "Long John Silver's Return to Treasure Island" 23:02)

make smart with it [*mayeeke smahrrt weth/ wi'/wiff/witt ett/'n/'t*] move it; snap to it; let's go; come on

> "Come alongside with me chest. **Make smart with it.**" (Billy Bones, urging along a porter carrying his sea-chest, "Treasure Island" [1960] 1:53)

march [*mahrrch*] move; let's go

> < "Vive la France!" "**March!**" > (Lieutenant Leon & Long John Silver, with Silver urging the Lieutenant on with a pistol, "The Adventures of Long John Silver: Turnabout" 21:15)

mew not [*mew narrt*] shut up; be quiet

> "Peace, Abnegation, peace! **Mew not** and hark to the words o' Davy: 'The Lord is known to execute judgment, the ungodly is trapped in the work of his own hands' ..." (Resolution Day, *Martin Conisby's Vengeance* 161)

mind your noise [*mawnd/min'/myeen'/myeend ya/yarr/ye/yer/yere/yore no'eese*] quiet down; pipe down

< "Ned! Ned!" "Arrgh, **mind your noise!**" > (Ben Worley & Blackbeard, with Worley waking up Blackbeard with urgent news of missing men, "Blackbeard the Pirate" 56:25)

mind your tongue [*mawnd/min'/myeen'/myeend ya/yarr/ye/yer/yere/yore toohngue*] watch your mouth; watch what you say

< "So, you're from that tavern woman, that common—" "Uh, ah-arrgh, now, **mind your tongue.**" > (Miss Willoughby & Long John Silver, "The Adventures of Long John Silver: The Orphans' Christmas" 15:42)

mind yourself [*mawnd/min'/myeen'/myeend 'ee/ya/yarr/ye/yer/yere/yore-seff*] watch yourself; quit it; stop what you're doing

< "Step aside!" "Hey, **mind yourself!**" > (Will Turner and Bootstrap Bill Turner, fighting over a rope line, "Pirates of the Caribbean 2: Dead Man's Chest" 1:12:55)

move fast [*move farrst/fass*]
move lively now [*move lawv/lyeeve-ly narr/nowoo*]
move sharply [*move shahrrply*] move; quickly; get to it; snap to it; let's go; come on

"Now, you have your orders. **Move fast.**" (Long John Silver, "The Adventures of Long John Silver: Turnabout" 16:20) "**Move lively now!**" (mate of the *Cordoba*, "Long John Silver's Return to Treasure Island" 56:40) "**Move sharply, move sharply!**" (Israel Hands, "Treasure Island" [1934] 1:01:00)

mum [*moohm*] shut up; quiet

"Why, here's a leading question—but **mum!** Here's a hand that knoweth not what doth its fellow—**mum**, boy, **mum!**" (Abnegation Mings, *Black Bartlemy's Treasure* 32)

never say it [*nebber/ne'er sayee ett/'n'/'t*] don't say it; hold your tongue; watch your mouth

Used to castigate another for referring to something dreadful, inconceivable, or implausible.

< "Oh, Japhet, it were strangely terrible if, despite all your cunning stratagems and care of me, I should end by killing myself, as did your poor Spanish lady and for the same ... shameful reason—" "God's death! **Never say it** ... never think such vile thing ..." > (Ursula Revell & Japhet Bly, *Winds of Chance* 304)

never you mind [*nebber/ne'er 'ee/ya/ye/yer mawnd/min'/myeen'/myeend*] don't worry

"Ah, but **never you mind**, Master Hawkins, they'll take care of 'im." (Long John Silver, "Treasure Island" [1960] 23:52)

no more of that [*no'oo marr/moor o'\on tharrt*]

A command either (1) to drop the subject under discussion or (2) to stop talking altogether.

< "So this is your special way with muchachoes, huh?" "Argh, shifty in the eye, he be. But **no more o' that.**" > (El Toro Mendoza & Long John Silver, "Long John Silver's Return to Treasure Island" 22:58)

no more words [*no'oo marr/moor warrds*] enough; silence; shut up; quiet

"[S]o either discharge your trust like an honest man; for go you shan't, by G[o]d, or I'll send you with my service to the D[evi]l; so **no more words**, G[o]d d[am]n ye." (William Fly, *General History of the Pyrates* 611)

no standing off and on [*no'oo a-starrnd-in' arrf an'/'n' arrn*] no wasting time; no lying around; no fooling around

"Come, tumble to 't, my lass; **no standing off and on**; here's no place for fine lady megrims ..." (Japhet Bly, gruffly urging a resistant Ursula Revell to action, *Winds of Chance* 145)

not a word [*narrt a warrd*] shut up; quiet

"Well, John Christopher, in a month or less you shall be no more than mere chattel, a much poorer, very naked knave to sweat and cower 'neath driver's whip, as many a better man hath done ... **not a word**, sir!" (Japhet Bly, *Winds of Chance* 113)

off [*arrf*] keep away; lay off

"**Off** ... ye dogs!" (Adam Penfeather, *Adam Penfeather, Buccaneer* 189)

off with you [*arrf weth/wi'/wiff/witt 'ee/ya/ye/yer*] go away; get out of here; leave

"[S]ee to it we are nowise interrupted, Ben, **off with ye!**" (Absalom Troy, *Adam Penfeather, Buccaneer* 6)

open within [*ho/hoo/oo-perrn weth/wi'/wiff/witt-in*] open up; open this door; let me in

"**Open within!**" (Captain Keitt's sailing master, knocking on Jonathan Rugg's door and demanding it be opened, *The Book of Pirates* "The Ruby of Kishmoor" 229)

open your lugholes [*ho/hoo/oo-perrn ya/yarr/ye/yer/yere/yore larrg/loohg-ho'ooles/'oles/'o'ooles*] listen; listen up

"Lughole" means "ear."

"Come over 'ere and **open your lug'oles**. If they should question us, remember this: 'enceforth, I'm Benjamin Parr of London." (Thomas Bartholomew Red, "Pirates" 15:39)

out of your crib [*arrt/ou'/owoot o'\on ya/yarr/ye/yer/yere/yore creb*] get out of bed; wake up

"**Out of your crib!**" (Thomas Bartholomew Red, ordering the bumbling Governor of Maracaibo out of bed, "Pirates" 1:23:56)

out with you [*arrt/ou'/owoot weth/wi'/wiff/witt 'ee/ya/ye/yer*] get out; get out of here; leave

"**Out with 'ee!** Don't ye know enough to bathe when you're in the shadow of ya betters?" (Long John Silver, "Long John Silver's Return to Treasure Island" 10:30)

pass the word for ... [*parss t' warrd farr/fer ...*] make it known that ...; spread the word that ...

"**Pass the word for** not a man to go below, Hawkhurst." (Cain, *The Pirate* 54, Chap. IX)

pass the word for __ [*parss t' warrd farr/fer __*] bring __ here; tell __ I want to talk to him

*"**Pass the word for** Tasker," he said to the man who stood sentry near the veranda door, and he heard the name echoing around the house. A minute later Tasker was there.* (Roger Press, *The Pirate Round* 226)

pause a moment [*pawrrse a momernt/mon't/mo'ooment*] wait a moment; hold on a moment

"**Pause a moment**, what agent will you use?" (The Red Rover, stopping the General to ask how he plans to go about kidnapping Harry Wilder's companions, *The Red Rover* 110)

peace [*peesh*] shut up; quiet

< "They tell me you are but half lost to feeling for your kind ..." "**Peace!** You speak in vain." > (priest aboard the *Dart* & The Red Rover, *The Red Rover* 500)

pipe down [*pawp/pyeepe dowoon*]

A command given at the end of the day and meaning "lights out" or "time to turn in" or "silence about the deck." The command is used to direct the company's boatswain (or bosun) to pipe certain tones or cadences on his whistle that mean that the workday has come to an end and that quiet should prevail.

"Well, heave to, Roger, bring up in shade o' this rock. Ahoy, bosun, **pipe down**." (Rogerson, *Winds of Chance* 353)

pour it on [*parr ett/'n/'t arrn*] go for it; go to it; give it your all

An all-purpose instruction to do something—especially fight—intensely and unyieldingly.

"**Pour it on**, mates! Show no quarter!" (Long John Silver, "Long John Silver's Return to Treasure Island" 9:37)

pronounce [*per/pree-nowoonce*] speak up; start talking; out with it; say what you have to say

> "Come now, what's your reason, in a word? **Pronounce!**" (Benjamin Trigg, *Adam Penfeather, Buccaneer* 224)

push on [*push arrn*] keep pushing; keep going; don't stop

A command to continue doing something—especially march, row, or otherwise make progress by some physical exertion—with determination or persistence.

> "**Push on**, ye swabs; **push on!**" (Long John Silver, *Porto Bello Gold* 48)

put a name on what you're at [*put a nayeeme arrn/o' wharrt/whorrt ya're/yer/ye're/yore a'/hat*] spit it out; tell me what you're getting at; say what you have to say

> "**Put a name on what you're at**; you ain't dumb, I reckon." (Long John Silver, *Treasure Island* 159, Chap. 28)

put about [*put abarrt/abowoot/'barrt/'bout/'bowoot*] turn around; go back

> "Be off now, and **put about**." (George Fairfax, *The Fortunes of Captain Blood* 160)

put up [*put arrp*] put it away; put it down

Used especially with reference to a weapon being held threateningly.

> "**Put up**, Belvedere, **put up!** No shooting, stabbing nor maiming till *she* gives the word, Captain. ..." (Resolution Day, stepping between Captain Belvedere's drawn pistol and Martin Conisby, *Martin Conisby's Vengeance* 100)

put your back in(to) it [*put ya/yarr/ye/yer/yere/yore back i'/'n\(in-ta/terr) ett/'n/'t*] work at it

An exhortation to work hard at some laborious task.

> "Come on, **put your backs in it!**" (Thomas Bartholomew Red, urging his company mates along as they lift a golden Aztec throne out of a galleon's hold, "Pirates"

1:48:59) < "Take me away from this hateful place this moment, ere I grow sick." "Ay, ay, ma'm! What, Johnny man, you hear? Take paddle and **put your back into 't**." > (Ursula Revell & Japhet Bly, *Winds of Chance* 254)

quick (now) [*queck (narr/nowoo)*] quickly

> "[W]ave your hat to them. **Quick**, or your brains will be over your coat." (John Sharkey, *The Dealings of Captain Sharkey and Other Tales of Pirates* "The Dealings of Captain Sharkey with Stephen Craddock" 42) "Here, fetch a sheet, lad, and lower me away. **Quick, now**." (Long John Silver, "Long John Silver's Return to Treasure Island" 39:27)

quick on __ [*queck arrn/o' __*]

A command to complete a specified task quickly.

> "**Quick on** all canvas!" (Captain Vallo, "The Crimson Pirate" 00:19)

quick's the word [*queck's t' warrd*] quickly

> "His throat, cully—**quick's the word!**" (black-eyed pirate, *Black Bartlemy's Treasure* 127)

quiet you [*quierrt 'ee/ya/ye/yer*] quiet; shut up

> < "God of Heaven!" "**Quiet you**." > (Madame de Coulevain & Peter Blood, *Captain Blood Returns* 237)

ready to __ [*rea'-eee t'/ta/ter __*] be prepared to __; get set to __

> "All right, lads, **ready to** board!" (Long John Silver, ordering his men to get set for an attack on the stockade [but note they immediately charge toward the stockade on hearing this command, rather than waiting—as they should—for further instruction], "Treasure Island" [1990] 1:20:00)

remove your carcass [*rer-moof ya/yarr/ye/yer/yere/yore cahrr-cahss/cush/kerss*]
remove yourself [*rer-moof 'ee/ya/yarr/ye/yer/yere/yore-seff*] go away; get out of here; leave

"Tressady, close that vile mouth and **remove your** viler **carcase!**" (Black Bartlemy, *Adam Penfeather, Buccaneer* 276) < "Sir, you may now **remove yourself**." "Anon, sir, anon. I hurry myself for no man, few women, and take orders from neither." > (Adam Penfeather & Black Bartlemy, *Adam Penfeather, Buccaneer* 254)

rest you [*rast/resht 'ee/ya/ye/yer*] have a rest; take a break; relax

"**Rest thee** ... lie down—so, whiles I try a shot at them." (Japhet Bly, encouraging Ursula Revell to lie down in the canoe while he fires a musket at their pursuers, *Winds of Chance* 296)

rip 'em up [*rep 'em arrp*]

An exhortation to do something—especially battle or some laborious task—intensely or vigorously.

"Dig! **Rip 'em up**, you swabs!" (Long John Silver, "Treasure Island" [1950] 1:28:02)

roll out [*rowell arrt/ou'/owoot*] wake up; get up; get out of bed

"**Roll out! Roll out!**" (pirate voice in Neverland, "Hook" 36:14)

rouse out\up [*rowoose arrt/ou'/owoot\ arrp*] wake up; get up; get out of bed

"Up, slugabed! **Rouse out**, messmate, and stand by for breakfast!" (Japhet Bly, *Winds of Chance* 148) "Hallo, Ralph boy! **rouse up**, lad; we're safe now." (Bloody Bill, waking Ralph Rover up from his feverish swoon, *The Coral Island* 256)

run and twist [*roohn an'/'n'twest/twiss*] suffer; struggle all you want

A command that is more of a goad than an instruction, mocking an enemy or victim for his helplessness to prevent the violence the speaker intends to do to him.

"**Run an' twist**, me little harem girl!" (Alacan the Turk, referring to a seaman on

an enemy ship during an attack, *Dead Man's Chest* 55)

scupper this [*scarr/skooh-per dis/t'is*] get rid of that

"Blast ye, woman! Where's your hide? Rum! And **scupper** all **this!**" (pirate from El Toro Mendoza's company at the *Cask and Anchor*, "Long John Silver's Return to Treasure Island" 1:38)

scupper your hide out of here [*scarr/skooh-per ya/yarr/ye/yer/yere/yore hawd/hyeede/'ide arrt/ou'/owoot o'\on 'ee'arr/'ee'err/'ere/hee'arr/hee'err*] go away; get out of here; leave

"**Scupper yer hide outta here** before I lose me temper." (Purity Pinker, "Long John Silver's Return to Treasure Island" 3:05)

scurry [*skoohry*] get moving; let's go

"On deck! **Scurry! Scurry**, I want movement!" (Jack Sparrow, "Pirates of the Caribbean 2: Dead Man's Chest" 16:54)

see to __ [*see t'/ta/ter __*] take care of __

"Hawkhurst! down at once into the spiritroom, and **see to** the money ..." (Cain, *The Pirate* 56, Chap. IX)

see to it [*see t'/ta/ter ett/'n/'t*] do it; see that it gets done

"I'll have a hammock slung for him in the cuddy. **See to it**, Alcatrace." (Tim, *The Fortunes of Captain Blood* 155)

seek look around; look for it

< "Here's no dagger. Here's empty sheath but no steel in't." "'Tis fallen out! **Seek**, Ben, **seek!**" > (Ben and Roger Tressady, searching the body of Black Bartlemy for a dagger containing the secret to hidden treasure, *Black Bartlemy's Treasure* 91)

serve up your piece [*sarrve arrp ya/yarr/ye/yer/yere/yore peesh*] speak up; start talking; out with it; say what you have to say

"Now **serve up your piece**." (Long John Silver, "Long John Silver's Return to Treasure Island" 4:28)

set to work [*sat t'/ta/ter warrk*] get to work

< "And you are armed, I see!" "Ay, I am, John, a brace o' barkers and two swords,—so **set to work**, John, and lay your rogue's back into it—give away!" > (John Barrasdale & Japhet Bly, *Winds of Chance* 139)

set yourself down [*sat 'ee/ya/ye/yer/yere/yore-seff dowoon*] sit down; take a seat

"Come, **set yourself down**." (Long John Silver, "Treasure Island" [1990] 34:10)

shake a leg [*shayeeke a layg*] move; quickly; get to it; snap to it; let's go; come on

"So cheerly O and cheerly O,/Come **shake a leg**, lads, all O." (from song sung by Abnegation Mings, *Black Bartlemy's Treasure* 29)

shake up your timbers [*shayeeke arrp ya/yarr/ye/yer/yere/yore tem-barrs*] move; get moving; snap to it; wake up

"George, **shake up your timbers**, son, and help Dr. Livesey over the ship's side." (Long John Silver, *Treasure Island* 168, Chap. 30)

sheer off [*shee-arr/err arrf*] go away; get out of here; leave

"Why then, **sheer off**, afore I rip out your livers, —both o' ye!" (Absalom Troy, *Adam Penfeather, Buccaneer* 27)

shiver your timbers (for a span) [*shevv/shibb/shi'-er ya/yarr/ye/yer/yere/yore tem-barrs (farr/fer a span)*] wait a minute; hold on

< "Well, then, if *that's* none of my business, get to what is! Why this important meeting?" "If ye'll **shiver yer timbers fer a span**, I will." > (Charles Noble & Long John Silver, *Dead Man's Chest* 29)

shove off [*shoohve/shub arrf*] go away; get out of here; leave

"Here, you **shove off**." (Long John Silver, shooing Ironhand away from his private conversation with Patch, "The Adventures of Long John Silver: Miss Purity's Birthday" 9:00)

show a glim [*showoo a glem*] move; quickly; get to it; snap to it; let's go; come on

A glim is a source or point of light, such as the flame of a match or candle. "Show a glim," therefore, is an appeal to the addressee to display some energy or to "show some fire."

"**Show a glim**, ye drunken dogs!" (pirate outside hedge-tavern, *Black Bartlemy's Treasure* 23)

show a leg [*showoo a layg*] move; quickly; get to it; snap to it; let's go; come on

"Stand forward the new men—**show a leg** and bustle, ye dogs!" (Adam Penfeather, *Black Bartlemy's Treasure* 110–11)

show no quarter [*showoo no'oo quahrr/quahtter*] show no mercy; take no prisoners

"Pour it on, mates! **Show no quarter!**" (Long John Silver, "Long John Silver's Return to Treasure Island" 9:37)

shut it [*sharrt/shooht ett/'n*] shut up; quiet

< "No. That's a tree." "Oh, **shut it**." > (Hadras & Jack Sparrow, "Pirates of the Caribbean 2: Dead Man's Chest" 1:55:23)

shut your ___ [*sharrt/shooht ya/yarr/ye/yer/yere/yore ___*] shut up; quiet

< "Lord, what a dumb arse." "**Shut your fucking gob**." > (Thomas Marlowe & Roger Press, *The Pirate Round* 288) "So **shut your trap** before I ram this down your throat." (Israel Hands, "Treasure Island" [1960] 46:50)

silence (there) [*saw/syee-lence (tharr/theyarr/theyerr)*] shut up; quiet

"**Silence!** the plate! the money for the troops—where are they?" (Cain, interrogating a Portuguese ship's supercargo about the plunder aboard, *The Pirate* 56, Chap. IX) "Silence, **there**, between decks!" (Billy Bones, quieting Doctor Livesey from across the room, *Treasure Island* 7, Chap. 1)

silence all [*saw/syee-lence awrl*] shut up, all of you; quiet, everybody

"**Silence all**, for a mother's last words to her children." (James Hook, *Peter Pan* 150)

sit you (down) [*set 'ee/ya/ye/yer (dowoon)*] sit down; take a seat

"**Sit ye**, Martin!" (Adam Penfeather, *Black Bartlemy's Treasure* 123) "**Sit ye down** here on my throne o' straw." (Absalom Troy, welcoming Adam Penfeather and Joel Bym to his locked cell, *Adam Penfeather, Buccaneer* 65)

skip [*skep*] go; get out of here; leave

"**Skip** now." (William Bones, after stuffing Flint's treasure map down Jim Hawkins' shirt, "Treasure Island" [1950] 9:12)

slash 'em down [*slarrsh 'em dowoon*] kill 'em

"**Slash 'em down**!" (Long John Silver, "Treasure Island" [1950] 1:00:55)

snap to [*snap t'/ta/ter*] get moving; get to it; let's go

"Come on, **snap to** and make sail, you know how this works." (Jack Sparrow, "Pirates of the Caribbean 2: Dead Man's Chest" 9:27)

speak of it later [*speak o'\on ett/'n/'t lay'er*] we'll talk about this later; we'll finish this another time

"**Speak of it later**." (Thomas Bartholomew Red, incensed at Dutch's refusal to purchase Red's hostages, "Pirates" 58:32)

speak on [*speak arrn*] continue; keep going

Used to direct an addressee who has paused or been interrupted in the course of some statement or narrative to continue.

"Pray **speak on**, sir." (Black Bartlemy, *Adam Penfeather, Buccaneer* 323)

speak up plain [*speak arrp playeen*] speak up; be clear

"So now **speak up plain**, young gentleman, and tell us what is your mind in this business, and whether you will adventure any farther or not." (Abraham Dawling, urging Barnaby True to embark on a mysterious boating trip with him and his men, *The Book of Pirates* "The Ghost of Captain Brand" 47)

speed hurry; hurry up

"**Speed** there, lads!" (Peter Blood, "Captain Blood" 1:39:26)

spread your sails [*sprayd ya/yarr/ye/yer/yere/yore sayells*] (1) sail away (2) go away; get out of here; leave

"[P]ut your men aboard that brigantine, **spread your sails**, and be off whilst I am still here to make your departure safe." (Peter Blood, *The Fortunes of Captain Blood* 130)

square away [*squarr/squayarr/squayerr/squerr awayee/'way/'wayee*] let's go

Among seamen, to "square away" means literally to square the yards of a vessel directly before the wind so as to make maximum speed, and more loosely to put things in order or get things ready. "Square away" as a general command is said just before some undertaking to express an enthusiasm for, or to urge a determined and fully prepared approach to, its attempt and completion.

"Zounds—no! Here fevers shall creep o' night; no, we must on to the highlands, so sheet home and **square away**, shipmate." (Japhet Bly, rejecting Ursula Revell's suggestion to set up camp near patches of quicksand, *Winds of Chance* 176)

stand away [*stan'/starrn'/starrnd awayee/'way/'wayee*] go away; get out of here; leave

"Sink me—but here would be no murder, lass; it should be no more than act of plain common sense, very reasonable—**stand away** now!" (Japhet Bly, urging Ursula Revell to get out from between his pointed pistols and John Barrasdale, *Winds of Chance* 259)

stand away with me [*stan'/starrn'/starrnd awayee/'way/'wayee weth/wi'/wiff/witt me*] come away with me; come along

"So bowse up, lad, **stand away wi' me** and rum it shall be." (Absalom Troy, *Adam Penfeather, Buccaneer* 4)

stand by [*stan'/starrn'/starrnd byee*]
(1) wait

"Clear the guns, bawcocky boys; 'tis our turn next—but **stand by** till she comes about ..." (Resolution Day, rallying the pirates of the *Happy Despatch* after a devastating surprise broadside from Adam Penfeather's ship, *Martin Conisby's Vengeance* 105)

(2) get ready for action; stand ready

"**Stand by**, messmates; I snuff foul weather down wind yonder." (Japhet Bly, *Winds of Chance* 13)

(3) listen; listen up

"Why, 'tis mighty black and foul yarn, ma'm, but if I must, well, **stand by**!" (Jeremy Jervey, on being asked to explain Bly's quest for vengeance, *Winds of Chance* 229)

(4) stand firm

"Forrard there! **Stand by**, my lads, I'm with ye!" (Absalom Troy, shouting words of encouragement during a wreck-threatening storm, *Adam Penfeather, Buccaneer* 160)

stand by for __ [*stan'/starrn'/starrnd byee farr/ fer* __] get ready for __; prepare for __

"**Stand by for** trouble." (Long John Silver, "Treasure Island" [1950] 1:28:14) "Up, slugabed! Rouse out, messmate, and **stand by for** breakfast!" (Japhet Bly, *Winds of Chance* 148)

stand by there [*stan'/starrn'/starrnd byee tharr/theyarr/theyerr*] (1) wait (2) get ready for action; stand ready

"**Stand by, there!** Prepare to board!" (Peter Blood, *Captain Blood: His Odyssey* 355)

stand by to ... [*stan'/starrn'/starrnd byee t'/ta/ ter ...*] get ready to ...; prepare to ...

"**Stand by to** put a shot across her bows, Mister Mercy." (William Kidd, "Captain Kidd" 43:03) "As to you, Farnaby, muster the hands, and **stand by to** go aboard in half an hour—every unhung rascal." (Adam Penfeather, *Black Bartlemy's Treasure* 111)

stand by to go about [*stan'/starrn'/starrnd byee t'/ta/ter go'oo abarrt/abowoot/'barrt/'bout/ 'bowoot*] hold everything; wait just a minute

Often used before proposing something radical or contrary to expectation, or asserting something at odds with an existing view or understanding.

"Come, this won't do. **Stand by to go about**. This is a rum start, and I can't name the voice: but it's someone skylarking—someone that's flesh and blood, and you may lay to that." (Long John Silver, announcing his suspicion that someone is masquerading as John Flint's ghost, *Treasure Island* 180, Chap. 32)

stand clear (of __) [*stan'/starrn'/starrnd cleearr/err (o'\on __)*] keep away (from __); move away (from __)

"Ahoy! **Stand clear**, or I'll send you down!" (member of Blackbeard's company to a fishing fleet passing close by, "Blackbeard the Pirate" 39:55) "**Stand clear of** that rum." (Haggott, "Treasure Island" [1950] 1:06:55

stand fast [*stan'/starrn'/starrnd farrst/fass*] stand your ground; stick tight

"**Stand fast** at your guns, lads!" (Thomas Tew, *The Pirate Round* 5)

stand forward [*stan'/starrn'/starrnd farr-ad/ard/edd/erd*] come forward; step forward

"**Stand forward** the new men—show a leg and bustle, ye dogs!" (Adam Penfeather, *Black Bartlemy's Treasure* 110–11)

stand off [*stan'/starrn'/starrnd arrf*] keep away; get back; stay back

Often called to an approaching ship or boat to stop its approach or keep it away.

"**Stand off! Stand off**, ya rutting bastards, the ship is ours!" (Duncan Honeyman, *The Pirate Round* 263)

stand off and on [*stan'/starrn'/starrnd arrf an'/'n' arrn*]

To stand off and on means literally to sail near a coast for some period of time by repeatedly sailing toward land and then away from it. The phrase can be used figuratively to mean "go back and forth," "look everywhere," or "go over every inch of this place."

"Haul off, cast about, **stand off and on**. If the woman's here, t'others should be skulking about—come, bouse about and stand away, and lively, ye scratchings!" (Ned, ordering Tom and Tony to find Ursula Revell's companions, *Winds of Chance* 314)

stand out [*stan'/starrn'/starrnd arrt/ou'/owoot*]

Used to direct another to step forward, especially from a group or crowd.

"**Stand out**, Sweetlocks, and I will lay you open!" (John Sharkey, calling out to the leader of his mutinous crew to kill him, *The Dealings of Captain Sharkey and Other Tales of Pirates* "The Blighting of Sharkey" 58)

stand ready (to __) [*stan'/starrn'/starrnd rea'-eee (t'/ta/ter __)*] be prepared (to __); get ready (to __)

"Rig the messenger! Nippers, **stand ready**!" (William Darnall, barking in-

structions to get the *Vengeance* under way, *The Guardship* 37) "Hands, **stand ready** to come about!" (Thomas Marlowe, *The Guardship* 278)

stand to it [*stan'/starrn'/starrnd t'/ta/ter ett/'n/'t*] let's do it; go to it

An exhortation to confront a situation or circumstance with strength, determination, and intensity.

"**Stand to't**, my bullies! Clear the guns, bawcocky boys; 'tis our turn next—but stand by till she comes about ..." (Resolution Day, rallying the pirates of the *Happy Despatch* after a devastating surprise broadside from Adam Penfeather's ship, *Martin Conisby's Vengeance* 105)

stay [*stayee*]

(1) relax; calm down; take it easy

< "Ha' ye come on the chart, Ben, ha' ye found the luck in't Ben?" "**Stay**, Roger, I've but just picked it up ..." > (Roger Tressady & Ben, just after Ben's discovery of Black Bartlemy's hollow-hilted dagger in which Bartlemy's treasure map is secreted, *Black Bartlemy's Treasure* 92)

(2) hold on; wait a minute; stop

< "D'ye know the secret o' this thing, Roger?" "Not I, Ben!" "Why then must I break it asunder. Hand me yon piece o' rock." "**Stay**, Ben lad, 'twere pity to crush the silver woman, but if you will, you will Ben—take hold!" > (Ben & Roger Tressady, discussing how to open Black Bartlemy's silver-hilted dagger in order to find the map inside, *Black Bartlemy's Treasure* 93)

stay your claws [*stayee ya/yarr/ye/yer/yere/yore clawers*] keep your hands to yourself; take your hands away; get your hands off me

"**Stay yer claws** afore ya tear the parchment." (Patch, "Long John Silver's Return to Treasure Island" 8:04)

stay your tears [*stayee ya/yarr/ye/yer/yere/ yore tee-arrs/errs*] don't cry; stop crying

> "Now, now, **stay your tears**. You'll only swell up your eyes." (Long John Silver, to a despondent Purity Pinker, "The Adventures of Long John Silver: The Eviction" 12:40)

steady [*stea'-eee*]

(1) hold on: An exhortation to persist firmly in a given course of action, typically despite good reasons not to.

> "**Steady**, lads, they're coming right to us!" (Thomas Marlowe, *The Pirate Round* 57)

(2) relax; take it easy

> "**Steady**, lad. It be your ol' shipmate, Long John." (Long John Silver, quieting Jim Hawkins after awakening him, "Long John Silver's Return to Treasure Island" 38:09)

steady as she goes [*stea'-eee as she go'ooes*] easy; nice and easy

Words of encouragement spoken to someone faced with a difficult or demanding task or challenge.

> "**Steady as she goes**, my friend. **Steady as she goes**!" (Ned Lynch, "Swashbuckler" 9:40)

steady it is [*stea'-eee ett/'n/'t be OR 'tes/'tis*] relax; take it easy

> "[S]teady, Martin, **steady it is**! Your sudden ways be apt to startle a timid man and my finger's on the trigger." (Adam Penfeather, *Black Bartlemy's Treasure* 160)

steady there [*stea'-eee tharr/theyarr/theyerr*]

A command to do something steadily and smoothly, and to avoid any sudden interruption or variation.

> "**Steady there**, mate, an' give me some slack!" (Long John Silver, overseeing Ben Gunn's lowering of Silver's heavy sea chest from the *Hispaniola* into a boat alongside, *Dead Man's Chest* 7)

step forward [*stap farr-ad/ard/edd/erd*]

> "Rogue, **step forrard**." (John Fenn, *Adam Penfeather, Buccaneer* 200)

step to (it) [*stap ter (ett/'n/'t)*] get moving; get to it; let's go

> "Come on, Will, **step to**!" (Joshamee Gibbs, urging Will Turner to descend quickly into the waiting longboat, "Pirates of the Caribbean 2: Dead Man's Chest" 2:11:39)
> "Secure the mast tackle, Mister Turner! **Step to it**!" (bosun aboard the *Flying Dutchman*, "Pirates of the Caribbean 2: Dead Man's Chest" 1:12:46)

step up (here) [*stap arrp ('ee'arr/'ee'err/'ere/ hee'arr/hee'err)*] come here; get over here; come forward

Hands in a vessel's waist—the lower part of a vessel's deck where much of the rough labor is performed—would have to "step up" to the quarterdeck or poop deck (higher rear portions of a ship's deck), or at least step toward the quarterdeck and look up, if the captain, mate, or other officer wished to speak with them. Thus, "step up" is a natural equivalent of "come here" for seamen accustomed to command, even where no step or raised deck might be involved.

> "**Step up**, lad. I won't eat you." (Long John Silver, *Treasure Island* 163, Chap. 29) "Was that you drinking with him, Morgan? **Step up here**." (Long John Silver, *Treasure Island* 43, Chap. 8)

still and patient [*stell an'/'n' paah/payee- shoohnt*] nice and calm; nice and easy

> "Now lift his barkers, Abny—in his pockets. **Still and patient**, lad, **still and patient**!" (Roger Tressady, directing Resolution Day to keep still while Abnegation Mings takes away his weapons, *Martin Conisby's Vengeance* 156)

still the guns [*stell t' garrns/goohns*] cease fire

> "**Still the guns**, and stow 'em!" (bosun aboard *Black Pearl*, "Pirates of the Caribbean: The Curse of the Black Pearl" 40:33)

stint this foolery [*stent dis/t'is foo'ell/fool'-ry*] stop this nonsense; enough of this foolishness

"Ha, damnation! **Stint this foolery**, Adam ..." (Absalom Troy, *Adam Penfeather, Buccaneer* 114)

stint your clack [*stent ya/yarr/ye/yer/yere/yore clack*] shut up; quiet

< "'Tis wicked, hateful lie, as well you know, and so are you hateful liar, a wantonly wicked, hateful, odious, beastly fellow—" "Avast, lass, avast! **Stint thy clack**, a mercy's sake, for I'm plaguey weary and must sleep." > (Ursula Revell & Japhet Bly, *Winds of Chance* 290)

stir not [*starr narrt*] don't move

"**Stir not**, nor so much as cock musket, Johnny, till needs must." (Japhet Bly, *Winds of Chance* 352)

stir your bones\stumps [*starr ya/yarr/ye/yer/yere/yore boones/bo'oones\stoohmps*]

stir yourselves [*starr 'ee/ya/ye/yer/yere/yore-seffs*] move; get moving; get to it; snap to it; let's go; come on

"We shall have the Alcalde and all the *alguaziles* of La Hacha aboard if we delay. So **stir your** damned **bones**." (George Fairfax, *The Fortunes of Captain Blood* 151) "**Stir your stumps**, you lousy swabs." (Billy Bones, *Porto Bello Gold* 59) "Now, you lazy swabs, **stir yourselves**!" (Blackbeard, "Blackbeard's Ghost" 1:45:35)

stop aboard [*starrp abarrd*] come aboard; welcome

Used especially when he who comes aboard does so only for a short time, or for a specific purpose. Also used metaphorically when not aboard a ship as an invitation to enter.

Compare: "Why else did ye ever consent to **stop aboard** when we weighed anchor?" (Tim, *The Fortunes of Captain Blood* 168)

stop (your) gabbing [*starrp (ya/yarr/ye/yer/yere/yore) a-gabbin'*] shut your mouth; shut up; quiet

< "What's to be done?" "Number one, **stop gabbin'**. Number two, do as you're told." > (galleon hand & Thomas Bartholomew Red, "Pirates" 40:49) "Aah, **stop your gabbin'**!" (Tom Morgan, annoyed with Jim Hawkins' impudent questioning, "Treasure Island" [1960] 1:02:25)

stop your clapper [*starrp ya/yarr/ye/yer/yere/yore clapper*] shut your mouth; shut up; quiet

"**Stop your clapper**, Jack. Give the boy a junk o' meat. Don't you see he's a'most going to kick the bucket?" (pirate, *The Coral Island* 201–02)

stop your sniveling [*starrp ya/yarr/ye/yer/yere/yore a-snev-erlin'/erling//'lin'/'ling*] quit your whining; shut up; be quiet

"**Stop yer snivelin'**! Die game, damne ye!" (John Laidlaw, rebuking a younger pirate for pleading pathetically for his life, *The Gun Ketch* 279)

stow that [*stowoo tharrt*] (1) forget that; never mind that (2) shut your mouth; shut up; quiet

"**Stow that**, John. I'll do the talkin'." (John Flint, *Porto Bello Gold* 123)

stow that\this __ [*stowoo tharrt\dis/t'is* __] shut up; quiet

"**Stow that** drunken **guff** and make your play!" (Israel Hands, "Treasure Island" [1934] 1:11:19) "**Stow this gab**." (James Hook, *Peter Pan* 149) < "Great guns, if Flint were livin' now, this'd be a hard spot for you and me." "Belay there, **stow this talk**—Flint's dead." > (Tom Morgan & Long John Silver, "Treasure Island" [1990] 1:52:41)

stow your __ [*stowoo ya/yarr/ye/yer/yere/yore* __] shut up; quiet

"[B]elay [your] jaw-tackle, **stow [your] clack** and avast." (Japhet Bly, quieting John Barrasdale during their journey into mountainous country, *Winds of Chance* 343) "So **stow your gab**, and come wi' me willingly, and no blows struck or feelings injured." (John Flint, *Porto Bello Gold* 133) "Oh, **stow your squealing**, you French rat." (Captain Easterling, *Captain Blood Returns* 36) "**Stow your tongue** or I'll broil 'ee for dinner!" (Long John Silver, quieting his parrot Cap'n Flint, "The Adventures of Long John Silver: Turnabout" 2:11) "What now? Are ye dumb? Then **stow thy whids**, hold thy clack and, since ye talk o' savagery, of savages I'll tell thee, though of another sort." (Japhet Bly, *Winds of Chance* 178)

strike (sail) [*strawk/stryeeke (sayell)*] surrender

The command literally is to lower the topsails of one's vessel as a sign or acknowledgment of defeat or concession, but is fundamentally a demand for surrender regardless of the state of an enemy's topsails.

> "**Strike**, you dogs!" (Robert Culliford, demanding the surrender of a merchant vessel, *The Pirate Hunter* 173) "**Strike sail!**" (pirate aboard the *Golden Hind*, demanding the surrender of the Spanish treasure ship *Cacafuego*, *The Queen's Corsair* 183)

strike your colors [*strawk/stryeeke ya/yarr/ye/yer/yere/yore cahlerrs*] (1) surrender (2) that's enough; stop what you're doing; don't do that

While the phrase is used literally to command another to lower his flag in a sign of surrender, it is also used figuratively to order another to abandon a course of action. The notion of giving up is common to both usages.

> "**Strike your colors**, ya bloomin' cockroaches!" (Barbossa, "Pirates of the Caribbean: The Curse of the Black Pearl" 1:26:47) "**Strike your colors**, you brazen wench. No need to expose your superstructure." (pirate auctioneer, cautioning his female prisoner against disrobing for the auction crowd, "Pirates of the Caribbean" Disney attraction)

strong and sure [*strahhng/strarrng an'/'n' sharr/shorr*]

An exhortation, especially appropriate during or in anticipation of battle, to engage a task or challenge with strength, determination, and intensity.

> "**Strong and sure!**" (Peter Blood, boarding a French ship with his company mates, "Captain Blood" 1:51:30)

sway away [*swayee awayee*] hang him; string him up

> "**Sway away!**" (Nightingale, urging the hanging of Harry Wilder, *The Red Rover* 506)

take\to cover [*tayeeke\t'/ta/ter coohv/cubb-er*]

A command to seek protection behind some object from gunfire or some other type of deadly projectile (arrows, knives, etc.).

> "**Take cover**, all of 'ee." (Long John Silver, "Long John Silver's Return to Treasure Island" 1:14:33) "**To cover**, lads, and look to your primings and wait my word." (Roger Tressady, *Black Bartlemy's Treasure* 312–13)

take 'em [*tayeeke 'em*] at 'em; go get 'em

An exhortation to attack or fight.

> "**Take 'em**, lads! Them or us!" (pirate urging his colleagues to fight Alan Lewrie's men rather than surrender, *The Gun Ketch* 156)

take hold [*tayeeke hol'/hoold/ho'oold/'ol'/'old*] take this; here you go; here you are

> < "D'ye know the secret o' this thing, Roger?" "Not I, Ben!" "Why then must I break it asunder. Hand me yon piece o' rock." "Stay, Ben lad, 'twere pity to crush the silver woman, but if you will, you will Ben—**take hold!**" > (Ben & Roger Tressady, intent on opening Black Bartlemy's silver-hilted dagger in order to find the map inside, *Black Bartlemy's Treasure* 93)

take up __ [*tayeeke arrp __*] pick up __

> "**Take up** that carrion. Hang it from the yardarm. Let it serve as a warning to

those swine on the *Valiant* of what happens to them as gets pert with Captain Easterling." (Captain Easterling, *Captain Blood Returns* 287)

take your ease [*tayeeke ya/yarr/ye/yer/yere/ yore eass*] relax; take it easy

< "Sir, I am humbly grateful for this respite." "Why then, Johnny, lie there and **take your ease**, ay and you too, ma'm ..." > (John Barrasdale & Japhet Bly, *Winds of Chance* 165)

tell me true [*taahl me troo*] tell me the truth

"Henry, how loyal are the men of this island to me?" "My lord." "**Tell me true**." (Elephiant Yancy & Henry Nagel, *The Pirate Round* 97)

think on it [*fink/thenk/t'ink arrn/o' ett/'n/'t*] think about it

"**Think on it**, lads. Seven hundred thousand pound." (Long John Silver, "Treasure Island" [1990] 1:56:35)

to arms [*t'/ta/ter ahrrms*]

A command to engage in fight or battle, particularly where the need to do so is sudden and unanticipated.

"Turn out! **To arms! To arms**!" (anchor watch aboard *Bloody Revenge*, *The Pirate Round* 310)

to it [*t'/ta/ter ett/'n/'t*] go to it; do it; get on it

"**To it**, lads, sa-ha—at him then, good bullies!" (Captain Jo, urging her pirates to beat Martin Conisby, *Martin Conisby's Vengeance* 63)

trifle not [*traw/tryee-fle narrt*] don't play around; don't mess with me

< "Now, in one word, sir, where is the treasure? **Trifle not**, or, by Heaven—!" "Name not Heaven, you have had my answer." > (Cain & Portuguese bishop, *The Pirate* 59, Chap. IX)

tumble to it [*toohmble t'/ta/ter ett/'n/'t*] move; get moving; get to it; snap to it; let's go

"Come, **tumble to 't**, my lass; no standing off and on; here's no place for fine lady megrims ..." (Japhet Bly, gruffly urging a resistant Ursula Revell to action, *Winds of Chance* 145)

tumble up [*toohmble arrp*] get up; get moving

"Hallo there! one o' you **tumble up** and light the cabin lamp, and sent that boy aft to the captain—sharp!" (pirate, *The Coral Island* 203–4)

turn out [*tarrn arrt/ou'/owoot*] get to your stations; time for action

A command to report to one's assigned position or task, or to rise to a state of general readiness.

"**Turn out**! To arms! To arms!" (anchor watch aboard *Bloody Revenge*, *The Pirate Round* 310)

turn to [*tarrn ter*] get on it; snap to it

"We've an hour to get what we can, so **turn to**!" (Billy Bird, *The Pirate Round* 324)

tush [*tarrsh/toohsh*]

(1) quiet; shut up

< "Here's death! Death, wench!" "**Tush**! I fear death no more than I fear you, and as for your claw—go scratch where you will!" > (Roger Tressady & Captain Jo, with Roger Tressady brandishing his iron hook at Captain Jo, *Martin Conisby's Vengeance* 157)

(2) enough; nonsense

< "I were a-saying to Job that here was a fellow to match Pompey at last." "**Tush**! Pompey would quarter him wi' naked hands." > (Diccon & Captain Belvedere, *Martin Conisby's Vengeance* 67)

tut [*tarrt/tooht*] (1) quiet; shut up (2) enough; nonsense

"**Tut**! We'll turn no hair gray for that." (Blackbeard, dismissing as easily resolved the scarcity of medicines aboard,

The Book of Pirates "Buccaneers and Marooners of the Spanish Main" 29)

unloose him [*arrn/hun/oohn-loose 'im*] let him go

"Ben, **unloose him**." (Japhet Bly, directing Ben to untie John Barrasdale's bonds, *Winds of Chance* 21)

up anchor [*arrp han-karr*] let's go

A nautical phrase literally meaning "raise the anchor" and uttered in anticipation of getting a vessel under way. The phrase is also used figuratively to order a departure of any kind.

"Here, lad, would you like to step ashore?" "Aye, Captain." "Then **up anchor**. We're on our way." (Long John Silver & Jim Hawkins, with Silver using "up anchor" metaphorically as he and Jim are on an anchored ship and are planning to go ashore in a boat, "The Adventures of Long John Silver: The Eviction" 15:30)

up with you [*arrp weth/wi'/wiff/witt 'ee/ya/ye/yer*] get up

"Get up, Jim. Get up, ya weak-kneed sniveller or, by thunder, we'll leave you behind! **Up with 'ee**!" (Long John Silver, rousing Jim Hawkins to his feet, "The Adventures of Long John Silver: Pieces of Eight" 16:49)

up you get [*arrp 'ee/ya/ye/yer git*] get up

"Come on, on your feet. **Up you get**. Come on, you men. Look alive." (Patch, waking the members of Long John Silver's company before another trek through the Panamian jungle, "The Adventures of Long John Silver: Pieces of Eight" 16:04)

'vast [*avarrst/'varrst*] avast

A frequently used abridgment of "avast," "'vast" can be used variously to mean "stop," "wait," or "shut up." The excerpt below reflects the first of these meanings.

"**'Vast** fighting! **'Vast** fighting!" (Thomas Marlowe and Hesiod, *The Pirate Round* 322)

veer and stand away [*vee-arr/err an'/'n' stan'/starrn'/starrnd awayee/'way/'wayee*] go away; get out of here; leave

"Avast! Belay and veer, my bully boys; **veer and stand away**, lest we run ye aboard." (Japhet Bly, confronting the four gentlemen who have asked Ursula Revell to leave Bly and come with them, *Winds of Chance* 14)

wait a shake [*wayeet a shayeeke*] wait a moment

"Just you **wait** here **a shake**, Master Ormerod, and I'll see what I can do." (Long John Silver, *Porto Bello Gold* 29)

wait for it [*wayeet farr/fer ett/'n/'t*] let me finish

Used to deflect another's interruption, or to convey that the speaker has more to say.

"No, **wait for it**. This is what you don't know." (Roger Press, *The Pirate Round* 306)

wait my word [*wayeet me/myee warrd*] listen for instruction

A command to be attentive to anything further the speaker might say, especially given when the need for some sudden action is anticipated.

"To cover, lads, and look to your primings and **wait my word**." (Roger Tressady, *Black Bartlemy's Treasure* 312–13)

'ware __ ['*warr/'wayarr/'wayerr __*] beware __

"The window! Shutters! **'Ware** bullets!" (Adam Penfeather, reacting just after Roger Tressady's escape to the danger of the open window and the risk of incoming bullets, *Black Bartlemy's Treasure* 102) "And **'ware** the starboard scuttle!" (Resolution Day, alerting Martin Conisby to the possibility of danger coming from a hatchway overhead, *Martin Conisby's Vengeance* 79)

weigh anchor [*wayee han-karr*] come on; let's go

Literally a command to lift or raise a vessel's anchor in order to sail away, the phrase is used figuratively to urge another to action.

> "**Weigh anchor** now, ya swabbies. What be I offered for this winsome wench?" (pirate auctioneer, prodding a crowd of reluctant bidders, "Pirates of the Caribbean" Disney attraction)

we're for it [werr farr/fer ett/'n/'t] let's go; let's do it

> "Now **we're for it**! Cast out the lines and pull for the shore. Lively!" (Long John Silver, "Treasure Island" [1950] 46:38)

what you will [wharrt/whorrt 'ee/ya/ye/yer well] do whatever you want

> "The boat lieth yonder; take her and **what you will**—only—get you gone!" (Captain Jo, *Martin Conisby's Vengeance* 172)

whisht now [whesht narr/nowoo] hush now; quiet now

> "**Whisht now**! Don't be committing suicide by telling me another falsehood; and there's no need." (Peter Blood, *The Fortunes of Captain Blood* 166)

will you ascend? [well 'ee/ya/ye/yer arr-saynd?] come up here

A polite command by a captain or other senior member of a company, spoken in the form of a question, directing a crew member aboard a vessel to ascend to the quarterdeck or poop (where captain and officers typically station themselves) to speak privately or at length.

> "Mr. Wilder, the air is fresher on this poop, and more free from the impurities of the vessel. **Will you ascend?**" (The Red Rover, *The Red Rover* 346)

witness your eye [wet-nerss ya/yarr/ye/yer/yere/yore eye'ee] see for yourself; take a look for yourself

> "'Tis a fine, bull-bodied boy, Job, all brawn and beef—**witness your eye**, Lord love me!" (Diccon, *Martin Conisby's Vengeance* 65)

yap not [yarrp narrt] shut up; quiet

> "**Yap not**, cur." (Japhet Bly, *Winds of Chance* 165)

yarely [yarrly] quickly

> "Come along, Black Dog. **Yarely**, my hearties!" (Long John Silver, *Porto Bello Gold* 48)

__ you shan't [__ 'ee/ya/ye/yer shen't] you will not __

> "[S]o either discharge your trust like an honest man; for go **you shan't**, by G[o]d, or I'll send you with my service to the D[evi]l; so no more words, G[o]d d[am]n ye." (William Fly, *General History of the Pyrates* 611)

you won't snap your tongue [ya/ye/yer won't/woon't/worrn't snarrp ya/yarr/ye/yer/yere/yore toohngue] shut up; quiet

> "While I stand on the deck of my ship, **you won't snap your tongue** like that." (El Toro Mendoza, "Long John Silver's Return to Treasure Island" 18:51)

4.3 SPECIAL COMMANDS

4.3.1 BATTLE COMMANDS

The following is a list of Battle Commands—that is, commands shouted in the course of a sea battle while trading gunfire or engaged in hand-to-hand fighting with the crew of an opposing ship. These commands are almost always given by the captain, who has supreme and unfettered authority during battle, and otherwise by the first mate or other senior company member on the captain's behalf.

Different Battle Commands are appropriate at different stages of a sea battle. "To your stations," for example, is a command properly issued just before or at the start of a fight. Instructions to open gun ports or fire cannon, on the other hand, will typically come later.

The Battle Commands below have been extracted from various narratives in which pirates were waging sea battle. (All-purpose fighting commands that might be given outside the sea-battle context, on the other hand—*e.g.* "cock your piece," "to arms"—appear above in Section 4.2: General Commands.) Battle Commands are listed below, montage-style, in roughly the same order in which they would be employed were they all uttered in the course of a single battle. As a result, this section provides not only an inventory of possible Battle Commands but also a rough chronology in which they might be given.

"Beat to quarters—drummer boy." (Blackbeard, "Blackbeard's Ghost" 1:24:53)

< "Have the bosun pipe to quarters!" "Pipe to quarters!" > (William Kidd & Jose Lorenzo, "Captain Kidd" 42:14)

"Forward, men, to your stations." (Peter Blood, "Captain Blood" 1:43:58)

"Jump to and weigh!" (Blackbeard, "Blackbeard the Pirate" 1:15:18)

"[R]un the anchor up to the bows ..." (Cain, *The Pirate* 48, Chap. VIII)

"[F]url the awnings ..." (Cain, *The Pirate* 48, Chap. VIII)

"Cut out the sails!" (Montbars, "Pirates of Tortuga" 38:13)

"Run out the sweeps." (Barbossa, "Pirates of the Caribbean: The Curse of the Black Pearl" 1:22:26)

"Clear decks for action!" (John Wolverstone, "Captain Blood" 1:44:13)

"Clear the decks, lads." (pirate captain, "Pirates of the Caribbean" Disney attraction)

"Make ready the guns." (Barbossa, "Pirates of the Caribbean: The Curse of the Black Pearl" 1:22:25)

"Keep the ports closed, but clear away the port guns ..." (John Sharkey, *The Dealings of Captain Sharkey and Other Tales of Pirates* "The Dealings of Captain Sharkey with Stephen Craddock" 42)

"Clear them lashings from the guns and prepare for battle!" (Long John Silver,

"The Adventures of Long John Silver: Sword of Vengeance" 2:36)

"Man the guns!" (Blackbeard, "Blackbeard the Pirate" 1:15:16)

"[M]an the larboard guns." (Peter Blood, *Captain Blood Returns* 291)

"Man your port guns!" (John Wolverstone, "Captain Blood" 1:49:12)

"[M]an the long gun, and see that every shot is pitched into her ..." (Cain, referring to the *Avenger*'s rotating brass cannon firing 32-pound shot, *The Pirate* 49, Chap. VIII)

"Number four gun crew, stand by for action!" (Adam Mercy, "Captain Kidd" 43:05)

"[U]nship the starboard ports." (Cain, *The Pirate* 105, Chap. XIV)

"Load the guns!" (Joshamee Gibbs, preparing to battle Davy Jones' kraken, "Pirates of the Caribbean 2: Dead Man's Chest" 2:03:36)

"Load but do not run out the great guns." (Roger Press, *The Pirate Round* 218)

"Load the great guns and run them out ..." (LeRois, *The Guardship* 213)

"Gun two, load!" (Ben Worley, "Blackbeard the Pirate" 1:15:20)

"Stand by your guns!" (Cahusac, "Captain Blood" 1:18:35)

"Stand to't, my bullies! Clear the guns, bawcocky boys; 'tis our turn next—but stand by till she comes about ..." (Resolution Day, *Martin Conisby's Vengeance* 105)

"Stand by ready to fire as soon as we come amidships." (Peter Blood, "Captain Blood" 1:46:21)

"[S]tand by for a broadside." (John Sharkey, *The Dealings of Captain Sharkey and Other Tales of Pirates* "The Dealings of Captain Sharkey with Stephen Craddock" 42)

"Open your ports!" (Henry Hagthorpe, "Captain Blood" 1:46:29)

"Run out your gun!" (Israel Hands, "Treasure Island" [1990] 1:03:45)

"Stand by as your guns bear!" (pirate captain, "Pirates of the Caribbean" Disney attraction)

"Musketeers, to your stations!" (John Wolverstone, "Captain Blood" 1:45:18)

"Hoist up the Jolly Roger!" (Montbars, "Pirates of Tortuga" 38:15)

"The flag, raise the flag!" (LeRois, *The Guardship* 214)

"Hoist our colors!" (Morgan Adams, "Cutthroat Island" 1:35:26)

"Run up the colours. Show the —s the Jolly Roger!" (Teach, *The Master of Ballantrae* 40, omission in original)

"See that the ensign blows out clear." (Cain, *The Pirate* 105, Chap. XIV)

"Shout, lads—shout for Roger, give tongue to Jolly Roger!" (Diccon, *Martin Conisby's Vengeance* 96)

"Give them a gun, one gun!" (LeRois, *The Guardship* 214)

"Give it to 'em again, lads!" (pirate captain, "Pirates of the Caribbean" Disney attraction)

"Give 'em a broadside!" (pirate captain, "Pirates of the Caribbean" Disney attraction)

"[L]et us have a few broadsides here!" (Thomas Marlowe, *The Pirate Round* 260)

"On command!" "All ports!" "Cannons ready!" "Guns forward!" "Fire!" (Dawg Brown, Bishop, & Morgan Adams, "Cutthroat Island" 1:35:01)

"Ready?! Fire!" (Adam Mercy, "Captain Kidd" 43:33)

"Two and three cannon, load!" (Patch, "The Adventures of Long John Silver: Turnabout" 3:07)

"Fire four! Fire three!" (pirate gunnery mate aboard the *Blarney Cock*, "Swashbuckler" 8:45)

"On the up-roll! Fire!" (Thomas Marlowe, *The Pirate Round* 260)

"Stand by, we'll fire together! Fire!" (Blackbeard, "Blackbeard the Pirate" 1:19:34)

"Rapid fire, men!" (Peter Blood, "Captain Blood" 1:50:41)

"Fire as you bear!" (Ezra Pritchard, *Dead Man's Chest* 183)

"Fire all!" (Marcus, ordering a broadside against the *Black Pearl*, "Pirates of the Caribbean 2: Dead Man's Chest" 2:01:14)

"Fire at will!" (pirate captain, "Pirates of the Caribbean" Disney attraction; Patch, "The Adventures of Long John Silver: Turnabout" 3:08; pirate gunnery mate aboard the *Blarney Cock*, "Swashbuckler" 10:20)

"[D]ouble them up!" (Peter Blood, ordering that the ship's guns be double-shotted, or loaded with two shots each rather than one, "Captain Blood" 1:50:43)

"[G]ive them the hot galley broadside!" (Peter Blood, ordering the firing of guns loaded with hot coals so as to set the enemy ships on fire, "Captain Blood" 1:47:36)

"Grape now! Grape and langrage ... !" (Thomas Marlowe, ordering the firing of guns loaded with, respectively, small iron balls packed in canvas bags and pieces of jagged scrap iron, *The Pirate Round* 260)

"High it is, my lads—aim high." (Lovepeace Farrance, directing his gunners to incline their gun barrels before firing in order to mow down enemy crew gathered on a close-approaching ship's poop and forecastle, *Winds of Chance* 75)

"Maximum elevation ... !" (Thomas Marlowe, directing his gunners to incline their gun barrels before firing in order to inflict maximum damage on enemy crew gathered at a close-approaching ship's rails, *The Pirate Round* 260)

"Sweep their fo'castle and poop; so shall the Lord make 'em as corn to the sickle. ..." (Lovepeace Farrance, *Winds of Chance* 75)

"Aim for her rails, lads, sweep her deck!" (Thomas Tew, *The Pirate Round* 6)

"So aim true, Johnny, and aim low. ..." (Japhet Bly, *Winds of Chance* 354)

"Keep hammering that waterline, Hagthorpe!" (Peter Blood, "Captain Blood" 1:49:58)

"[T]ake yer time strippin' off her plankin'!" (Ezra Pritchard, *Dead Man's Chest* 182)

"Pound 'em lads, pound 'em!" (pirate captain, "Pirates of the Caribbean" Disney attraction)

"Blast 'em from the sea!" (Dawg Brown, "Cutthroat Island" 1:37:11)

"Hold your fire!" (Long John Silver, "The Adventures of Long John Silver: Turnabout" 3:19)

"Still the guns, and stow 'em!" (bosun aboard the *Black Pearl*, "Pirates of the Caribbean: The Curse of the Black Pearl" 40:33)

"Stow the fuse! Belay the cannon!" (Patch, executing Long John Silver's instructions to hold fire, "The Adventures of Long John Silver: Turnabout" 3:27)

"[R]epel boarders!" (Long John Silver, "Treasure Island" [1950] 25:05)

"[P]ikes and cutlasses! Aloft to repel boarders. Follow me!" (John Fenn, *Adam Penfeather, Buccaneer* 128)

"Strike, you dogs!" (Robert Culliford, demanding the surrender of a merchant vessel, The Pirate Hunter 173) "Strike sail!" (pirate aboard the Golden Hind, demanding the surrender of the Spanish treasure ship Cacafuego, *The Queen's Corsair* 183) "Strike your colors, ya bloomin' cockroaches!" (Barbossa, "Pirates of the Caribbean: The Curse of the Black Pearl" 1:26:47)

4.3.2 BOARDING COMMANDS

Boarding other ships is the defining activity of piracy. One cannot plunder without first boarding, and nearly everything a pirate does—putting to sea, trickery, pursuit, intrigue, battle—leads up to the boarding of another ship.

Below is a list of commands given in the course of boarding. They are almost always given by the captain, who traditionally joins and often leads boarding parties. The commands appear below, montage-style, in roughly the same order in which they would be uttered during a single boarding attempt.

"We'll close for the kill and then board 'er!" (Blackbeard, "Blackbeard the Pirate" 1:20:32)

"Get your men forrard!" (Peter Blood, to mate John Wolverstone, "Captain Blood" 1:50:18)

"Aft boarders!" (Thomas Marlowe, *The Pirate Round* 261)

"Hard over! Prepare to ram!" (Long John Silver, "The Adventures of Long John Silver: Sword of Vengeance" 4:14)

"Straight into 'em!" (Peter Blood, ordering Jeremy Pitt to take the helm and sail straight into the enemy ship in preparation for boarding, "Captain Blood" 1:50:25)

"Musketeers to the prow!" (Peter Blood, "Captain Blood" 1:50:31)

"Tell those forward gunners to fire as hard as they can load!" (Peter Blood, "Captain Blood" 1:50:34)

"Cutlasses, you swabs!" (Long John Silver, "Treasure Island" [1950] 1:00:46)

"Pistols and cutlasses, men!" (Barbossa, "Pirates of the Caribbean: The Curse of the Black Pearl" 1:27:29)

"Men, firearms and powder." (Long John Silver, "Long John Silver's Return to Treasure Island" 1:23:25)

"Out hooks!" (Blackbeard, "Blackbeard the Pirate" 1:20:48)

"[T]he grapnels!" (Peter Blood, *Captain Blood: His Odyssey* 355)

"Out, grapplin' hooks! Prepare to board!" (Long John Silver, "The Adventures of Long John Silver: Sword of Vengeance" 4:26)

"Hands, grapnels at the ready! Prepare to board!" (Barbossa, "Pirates of the Caribbean: The Curse of the Black Pearl" 1:26:51)

"Grappling hooks to larboard!" (Peter Blood, "Captain Blood" 1:50:33)

"Stand by to grapple by the larboard." (Japhet Bly, *Winds of Chance* 76)

"Pass Farrance [the gunner] the word to cease fire." (Japhet Bly, *Winds of Chance* 76)

"Gunners, stand by! In guns all! Close and bar all ports!" (John Fenn, *Adam Penfeather, Buccaneer* 128)

"Up into the shrouds, men!" (Peter Blood, "Captain Blood" 1:50:57)

"Grapnels over!" (Peter Blood, "Captain Blood" 1:51:31)

"[P]ipe the boarders!" (Japhet Bly, *Winds of Chance* 76)

"Stand by, there! Prepare to board!" (Peter Blood, *Captain Blood: His Odyssey* 355)

"All right, my hearties, follow me!" (Peter Blood, "Captain Blood" 1:52:12)

"To me!" (Thomas Marlowe, leaping into his own ship's mizzen shrouds before leading his men onto the Moorish ship alongside, *The Pirate Round* 261)

"Follow on, men!" (John Wolverstone, "Captain Blood" 1:52:38)

"Board 'em, boys, board 'em! Board 'em, you swabs!" (Long John Silver, "Treasure Island" [1950] 1:01:08) "Now, by the powers, board 'em!" (Long John Silver, "Treasure Island" [1934] 1:06:20)

"Boarders away!" (Blackbeard, "Blackbeard the Pirate" 1:20:49; Resolution Day, *Martin Conisby's Vengeance* 97; Japhet Bly, *Winds of Chance* 76)

"Strong and sure!" (Peter Blood, "Captain Blood" 1:51:30)

"To it, lads ... at 'em, old seadogs, point and edge ... sa-ha!" (Absalom Troy, *Adam Penfeather, Buccaneer* 129)

"At 'em, you dogfish, at 'em!" (Long John Silver, "Treasure Island" [1934] 1:07:26)

"Slash 'em down!" (Long John Silver, "Treasure Island" [1950] 1:00:55)

"Cut the cap'n down!" (Long John Silver, "Treasure Island" [1950] 1:02:00)

"By God ... we have 'em!" (Absalom Troy, *Adam Penfeather, Buccaneer* 129)

"She is ours!" (Thomas Marlowe, announcing victory after boarding a Moorish ship and defeating the men aboard, *The Pirate Round* 262)

4.3.3 BOAT COMMANDS

In order to spend their plunder, terrorize landsmen, or bury treasure, pirates need boats. Boat Commands are critical to everyday pirate life, as pirates need to move between ship and land. Below is a list of boat commands, appearing roughly in the same order as they would be given in the course of any given boat trip.

Note the tendency of pirates to arm themselves before deploying in a boat. Boat expeditions strip pirates away from the sheltered decks of their cannon-studded vessels, making them more vulnerable to attack, and almost always take them to a point of possible encounter—a populated shore, for example, or an enemy vessel. Hence the close association for pirates between boats and weapons.

"Out boats, men! as fast as you can ..." (Cain, *The Pirate* 122, Chap. XVI)

"[L]et every man provide himself with arms and ammunition." (Cain, ordering all hands to arm themselves before taking to three boats, *The Pirate* 122, Chap. XVI)

"Muskets and cutlasses." (Roger Press, ordering all hands to arm themselves before forming shore parties and getting into their boats, *The Pirate Round* 223)

"Issue pistols and powder, and lower a longboat." (Long John Silver, "The Adventures of Long John Silver: The Pink Pearl" 8:57)

"So stand by to let go the halyard and ship oars when I give word, *amigo*." (Resolution Day, *Martin Conisby's Vengeance* 151)

"Away the longboat!" (Tom Scully, "Cut-throat Island" 59:20)

"Out oars! Pull away!" (Ben Worley, "Blackbeard the Pirate" 3:17)

"Shove off, lads." (Long John Silver, "Treasure Island" [1934] 53:30)

"Cast off, forrard!" (Long John Silver, "Treasure Island" [1990] 53:03)

"Now we're for it. Cast out the lines and pull for the shore. Lively!" (Long John Silver, "Treasure Island" [1950] 46:38)

"Give way, my lads!" (Hawkhurst, directing his men to resume rowing toward a better landing place further upcreek, *The Pirate* 93, Chap. XIII) "Give way, lads! Give way!" (Adam Penfeather, urging his boatmen to row speedily to their ship so as to make the turning tide, *Black Bartlemy's Treasure* 334)

"Pull, you lazy, worthless bastards!" (Elephiant Yancy, *The Pirate Round* 333) "Pull, dog's leavings, —arms and legs and backs to it—pull, ye lubbers!" (Benjamin Trigg, *Adam Penfeather, Buccaneer* 310)

"Faster, you lazy dogs! Bend your backs to it, you louts!" (George Fairfax, *The Fortunes of Captain Blood* 150)

"Break your backs, you lubbers!" (Long John Silver, "Treasure Island" [1990] 53:11)

"Give me some sweat there, you swabs!" (Long John Silver, "Treasure Island" [1990] 53:20)

"Up the stroke." (Long John Silver, "The Adventures of Long John Silver: Pieces of Eight" 6:00)

"Easy all—so!" (Joel Bym, ordering a quiet approach upriver to his comrades pulling muffled oars, *Adam Penfeather, Buccaneer* 327)

"Backwater!" (Roger Press, instructing his men to reverse-row in order to stop the boat's forward movement and propel it backwards, *The Pirate Round* 81)

"Oars, my lads! —oars! (Hawkhurst, directing his men and two other boats to stop rowing so that he and Cain might select a better landing place, *The Pirate* 93, Chap. XIII)

"Stand by to beach her!" (Long John Silver, "Treasure Island" [1990] 53:30)

4.3.4 SHIP COMMANDS

Below are commands used by pirates in sailing a vessel from one point to another. Most are nautical instructions used by sailors in general, and not exclusively by pirates, but the fact they appear in pirate narratives highlights their importance to the sweet trade.

Note: The use of the term "port" to mean "left" is occasional, but not typical, among pirates, as the term was not widely used aboard sailing vessels until the 1800s, long after the golden age of piracy. Pirates generally used the term "larboard" to mean "left." The term "port" is accordingly accompanied by an asterisk (*) wherever it appears below, to remind the reader of its limited use in pirate speech.

all hands make sail [*awrl 'ands/'an's/han's mayeeke sayell*]

Used to direct all members of a crew to loosen and spread more sail in order to get a vessel under way or increase its speed.

"**All hands make sail**, ahoy!" (Nightingale, *The Red Rover* 420)

all slack [*awrl slarrk*]

A command to remove all slack from—that is, to make taut—one or more lines (ropes), typically given just before an instruction to haul or pull on such lines.

"**All slack!** Ease away, handsomely, handsomely!" (pirate directing the hoisting of a large chest into the *Elizabeth Galley's* hold, *The Pirate Round* 329)

(away) aloft [(*awayee/'way/'wayee*) *err-larrft*] upward; up above; up into the rigging

Used especially to direct members of the crew into the rigging to adjust sails, to make repairs or other adjustments, or to prepare to board another vessel by jumping down on its deck from above.

"**Aloft! Stand by all!** Volunteers to go aloft wi' me to cut away the t'gallant—Follow me, shipmates!" (Japhet Bly, calling for men to follow him up into the rigging to cut away a fallen mast and sail, *Winds of Chance* 127) "Furl it! **away aloft**, and furl it!" (The Red Rover, aghast at seeing one of his hands unfurl a sail despite the crew's careful efforts to remain unseen by an approaching ship, *The Red Rover* 411)

back to your stations [*back t'/ta/ter ya/yarr/ ye/yer/yere/yore stayee-sherns/shoohns*]

Used to direct hands of a crew to return to their assigned positions.

"**Back to your stations!** The lot o' ya!" (Joshamee Gibbs, rescinding his order that the ship be turned about after Jack Sparrow's countermanding instruction that the ship proceed on its heading, "Pirates of the Caribbean 2: Dead Man's Chest" 17:37)

bear up [*barr/bayarr/bayerr arrp*]

Used to direct a helmsman to change a vessel's direction so that it sails with the wind, rather than across or into it. One might think it odd to use the word "up" to refer to the sailing of a vessel with the wind, rather than into it. However, a helmsman on a vessel sailing across the wind turns to sail with the wind by lifting up that side of the wheel closest to the wind, or pushing up on the whipstaff (large pole connected to the rudder) so that it inclines away from the wind—that is, "bearing up" on it.

"**Bear up! Bear up!** He still hath the weather gage of us." (Andrew Murray, *Porto Bello Gold* 154)

beat to quarters [*bea' t' quahrr/quaht-ters*]

A command given to a vessel's drummer to make certain drumbeats understood by the crew to mean that all hands should re-

port immediately to assigned battle stations. Drummers were found less frequently aboard pirate ships than aboard naval vessels.

"**Beat to quarters**—drummer boy." (Blackbeard, "Blackbeard's Ghost" 1:24:53)

bring her about [*breng 'er abarrt/abowoot/ 'barrt/'bout/'bowoot*] turn the vessel around

"Jack's hat! **Bring 'er about!**" (Joshamee Gibbs, ordering that the ship be turned about so that Jack Sparrow's hat might be retrieved from the ocean surface, "Pirates of the Caribbean 2: Dead Man's Chest" 17:29)

bring to\up [*breng ter\arrp*]

A command to stop a vessel's movement, typically by turning into the wind and arranging the vessel's sails in such a manner that they counteract each other and yield no forward or backward progress.

"**Bring to! Bring to** for a queen's officer, or you shall all hang!" (Roger Press, *The Pirate Round* 84) "Well, heave to, Roger, **bring up** in shade o' this rock. Ahoy, bosun, pipe down." (Rogerson, *Winds of Chance* 353)

capstan—heave [*carrpstan—'eave/heeff*]

A command given just before sailing in order to direct members of a crew to raise a vessel's anchor. The capstan is a drum or winch around which the anchor line or cable is wrapped. Those manning the capstan can lift the anchor by turning the capstan, which has the effect of pulling in the anchor line.

"**Capstan—heave!**" (Ezekiel Penryn, calling out just after getting Japhet Bly's shore party aboard under cannon fire from a pursuing ship, *Winds of Chance* 109)

cast off __ [*carrst arrf __*]

A command given just before sailing that one or more lines (ropes) securing a ship or boat to a dock or piling be loosed.

"**Cast off** helm!" (Captain Vallo, "The Crimson Pirate" 13:59) "**Cast off** stern!" (Captain Vallo, "The Crimson Pirate" 14:03)

clap on sail [*clarrp arrn sayell*]

A command to loosen and spread more sail in order to get a vessel under way or increase its speed.

> "**Clap on** all the **sail** we have!" (Long John Silver, "The Adventures of Long John Silver: Ship o' the Dead" 20:21)

clear __ [*clee-arr/err __*] clear away any obstacles from __

> "**Clear** the port tops'l!" (pirate aboard the *Blarney Cock*, "Swashbuckler" 9:06)

clear the braces [*clee-arr/err t' brayeeces*]

Braces are lines (ropes) connected to the yards (wood poles supporting a sail and set perpendicular to and extending horizontally across a mast) of a square-rigged vessel and used to adjust the angle or position at which a sail is set relative to the wind. "Clear the braces" is a command to remove any obstruction, including other lines, near a vessel's braces that might prevent necessary adjustment. The command is typically given when an adjustment in the position of a vessel's sails is being contemplated.

> "Aloft, topmen! **Clear the braces**, John, you'd better take the helm." (Billy Bones, *Porto Bello Gold* 53)

clew up __ [*cloo arrp __*]

A command to raise the lower corners of a sail.

> "Look alive, boy! **Clew up** the fore-sail. Drop the main-sail peak. Them squalls come quick sometimes." (Bloody Bill, *The Coral Island* 263)

close-haul __ [*cloose/clo'oose-'aul/'awrl/hawrl __*]

A command to draw down the lower corners of one or more sails to windward, such that a vessel might sail into the wind—*i.e.*, sail "close-hauled."

> "**Close-haul** that jib." (Captain Vallo, "The Crimson Pirate" 1:34:36)

crowd on sail [*crowood arrn sayell*]
crowd that canvas [*crowood tharrt canverss*]

A command to loosen and spread large amounts of sail so as to get a vessel under way or increase its speed.

> "**Crowd on sail**, and let her run before the wind." (Peter Blood, *Captain Blood Returns* 290) < "We have our heading." "Finally! Cast off those lines, weigh anchor, and **crowd that canvas!**" > (Jack Sparrow & Joshamee Gibbs, "Pirates of the Caribbean 2: Dead Man's Chest" 1:20:21)

cut out the sails [*carrt/cooht arrt/ou'/owoot t' sayells*]

A command to quickly or suddenly diminish or eliminate completely the amount of sail exposed to the wind.

> "**Cut out the sails!** Hoist up the Jolly Roger!" (Montbars, "Pirates of Tortuga" 38:13)

cut the cable [*carrt/cooht t' caah/cayee-bul*]

A command to cut a vessel's anchor cable, either to counteract some lodging of the anchor or other malfunction preventing the anchor from being lifted or, more typically, to permit the vessel to sail away hastily or quietly (that is, without the delay or noise that comes with heaving in the anchor).

> "And don't stay to take up anchor. **Cut the cable.** Hoist sail and let's away." (George Fairfax, *The Fortunes of Captain Blood* 151)

douse __ [*dowoose __*]

A command to lower or slacken something, often a sail or part of a sail.

> "Now, let fly your halyard, **douse** your sail—so!" (Resolution Day, *Martin Conisby's Vengeance* 152)

down (with your) helm [*dowoon (weth/wi'/wiff/witt ya/yarr/ye/yer/yere/yore) 'elm*]

Used to direct a helmsman to change a vessel's direction so that it sails into the wind, rather than across or with it. One might think it odd to use the word "down" to refer to the sailing of a vessel into the wind, rather than with it. However, a helmsman on a vessel sailing across the wind turns to sail into it by pushing down on that side of the wheel closest to the wind, or on the whipstaff (large pole connected to the rudder) so that it inclines into the wind.

> "**Down helm!**" (Adam Penfeather, *Adam Penfeather, Buccaneer* 236) "**Down wi' your helm**—down!" (Captain Belvedere, *Martin Conisby's Vengeance* 104)

draw on every rag of canvas the yards will hold [*drawrr arrn ebber'/ebbry/e'ery/ever'/ev'ry rarrg o'\on canverss t' yahrrds well hol'/hoold/ho'oold/'ol'/'old*]

A command to loosen and spread every bit of sail aboard a vessel, so as to get it under way or increase its speed to maximum velocity.

> "We're changing course. **Draw on every rag of canvas the yards will hold**." (Peter Blood, "Captain Blood" 1:30:20)

drop __ [*drarrp __*]

A command to lower something, especially a sail or part of a sail.

> "Look alive, boy! Clew up the fore-sail. **Drop** the main-sail peak. Them squalls come quick sometimes." (Bloody Bill, *The Coral Island* 263)

ease away [*eass awayee/'way/'wayee*]

A command to slacken a line (rope) or set of lines.

> "All slack! **Ease away**, handsomely, handsomely!" (pirate overseeing the hoisting of a large chest into the *Elizabeth Galley*'s hold, *The Pirate Round* 329)

ease off __ [*eass arrf __*]

A command to slacken a line (rope) or set of lines.

> "That will do, my lads: starboard; **ease off** the boom-sheet; let her go right round, Hawkhurst ..." (Cain, *The Pirate* 49, Chap. VIII)

ease off to __ [*eass arrf t'/ta/ter*]
ease your helm to __ [*eass ya/yarr/ye/yer/yere/yore 'elm t'/ta/ter __*]

Used to direct a helmsman to adjust a vessel's direction slowly or smoothly.

> "**Ease off** a p'int to starboard." (Patch, "The Adventures of Long John Silver: The Pink Pearl" 20:20) "**Ease your 'elm to** starboard." (Long John Silver, "The Adventures of Long John Silver: The Tale of a Tooth" 11:21)

easy as she goes [*easy as she go'ooes*]

Used to advise a helmsman that a vessel's present heading is an acceptable one, and to instruct him to maintain it.

> "**Easy ... as she goes!**" (Adam Penfeather, *Adam Penfeather, Buccaneer* 185)

fall off [*fawrl arrf*]

A command to a helmsman to steer a vessel down wind—that is, to turn the vessel so that it is sailing with the wind.

> "**Fall off**, helmsmen, **fall off**, damn your eyes!" (Thomas Marlowe, *The Guardship* 277)

fetch up your hook [*fatch arrp ya/yarr/ye/yer/yere/yore 'ook*]

A command to raise a vessel's anchor.

> "**Fetch up your hook!**" (Ben Worley, "Blackbeard the Pirate" 5:08)

full and by [*full an'/'n' byee*]

A command given to a helmsman when sailing close to the wind (that is, headed into the wind) to be careful to keep an optimal heading. It instructs the helmsman not to steer so sharply into the wind that it slaps at the sails ineffectually, rather than filling them (hence the instruction "full," as in "keep the sails full"), and not to steer away from the wind so much that the vessel wanders too far off her intended course (hence the instruction "by," as in "keep by the wind").

> "Haul up, **full and by**." (Captain Vallo, "The Crimson Pirate" 14:36)

get sail on her [ge'/git sayell arrn/o' 'er]

A command to loosen and spread the sail aboard a vessel in order to get it under way or increase its speed.

> "Captain's orders. Said to cat the anchor, Bill, and **get sail on her**." (unnamed pirate aboard Andrew Murray's brig, *Porto Bello Gold* 53)

get (her) under water\way [ge'/git ('er) arrn/hun/oohn-der/ner wahh/warr-ter\way-ee]

(1) A command to sail away, especially after some time at anchor. (2) A command to undertake or complete preparations necessary for sailing away. (3) A command to leave or depart, generally.

> "Now, hearties, **get her under water**, and out to our luck once more." (John Sharkey, *The Dealings of Captain Sharkey and Other Tales of Pirates*: "The Blighting of Sharkey" 54) "**Get under way**, at once, Tim!" (George Fairfax, *The Fortunes of Captain Blood* 151)

go about [go'oo abarrt/abowoot/'barrt/'bout/'bowoot] turn around

A command to change a vessel's direction to an opposite course by bringing its bow through the wind.

> "**Go about** and lay a course for Cartagena." (George Fairfax, *The Fortunes of Captain Blood* 159) "Below there! Belvedere, ahoy— **go about**, or she'll rake us ..." (Resolution Day, *Martin Conisby's Vengeance* 104)

hands aloft to loosen sail ['ands/'an's/han's alarrft t'/ta/ter loosen sayell]

Used to direct members of the crew into the rigging to loosen and spread sail so as to get a vessel under way or increase its speed.

> "Mr. Dinwiddie, **hands aloft to loosen tops'ls**, and then let us haul up to the best bower." (Thomas Marlowe, *The Pirate Round* 75)

hands to braces ['ands/'an's/han's t'/ta/ter brayeeces]

A command to members of a crew to man a vessel's braces (lines or ropes used to turn a yard or sail horizontally), typically given just before an order to adjust the position of its sails.

> "On deck, you scabrous dogs! **Hands to braces!**" (Jack Sparrow, "Pirates of the Caribbean: The Curse of the Black Pearl" 2:12:37)

hands to halyards ['ands/'an's/han's t'/ta/ter 'al-yerds]

"Halyards" are lines (ropes) used to hoist or lower sails. "Hands to halyards" is a command to members of a crew to man a vessel's halyards, typically in preparation for hoisting sail in order to increase the vessel's speed.

> "**Hands to the halyards**, haul away! Sheet home!" (Thomas Marlowe, *The Pirate Round* 82)

hard a-larboard ['ahrrd/'ard/hahrrd a-la'b'd/larbarrd/larberrd]
hard a-port* ['ahrrd/'ard/hahrrd a-parrt]
hard to larboard ['ahrrd/'ard/hahrrd t'/ta/ter la'b'd/larbarrd/larberrd]
hard to port* ['ahrrd/'ard/hahrrd t'/ta/ter parrt] turn hard to the left

A command given to a vessel's helmsman.

> "Larboard, **hard a-larboard!**" (Joel Bym, *Adam Penfeather, Buccaneer* 327) "**Hard to larboard!**" (Long John Silver, "The Adventures of Long John Silver: Sword of Vengeance" 2:33)

hard alee ['ahrrd/'ard/hahrrd alee]

Used to direct a helmsman to turn a vessel sharply to leeward (that is, away from the wind), especially to avoid some obstacle or perceived threat, to speed the vessel onto a new course as quickly as possible, or to counteract a vessel's tendency to pitch violently down into valleys between waves when sailing close-hauled (that is, into the wind).

> "Ready about! **Hard alee, hard alee!**" (Blackbeard, "Blackbeard's Ghost" 32:10)

hard a-starboard ['*ahrrd*/'*ard*/*hahrrd a-sta'b'd/starbarrd/starberrd*]

hard to starboard ['*ahrrd*/'*ard*/*hahrrd t'/ta/ter sta'b'd/starbarrd/starberrd*] turn hard to the right

A command given to a vessel's helmsman.

*[I]n a moment Captain Morgan roared out of a sudden to the man at the helm to put it **hard a starboard**.* (account of Henry Morgan's escape out of Porto Bello harbor, *The Book of Pirates* "With the Buccaneers" 94) < "**Hard to starboard**." "Starboard she is, sir." > (William Kidd & unnamed helmsman, "Captain Kidd" 43:42)

hard over ['*ahrrd*/'*ard*/*hahrrd ober/o'er*] turn hard

Used to direct a helmsman to turn the helm, and thereby the vessel itself, sharply in a given direction.

"Larboard your helm! **Hard over!**" (Thomas Marlowe, *The Pirate Round* 83)

haul ['*aul*/'*awrl*/*hawrl*] pull

The term "haul" refers specifically to the pulling of a line (rope) without the assistance of blocks, tackles, pulleys, rollers, or other mechanical means. Any noun used as an object immediately after "haul" will typically be the name of a specific kind of line.

"[H]aul the bloody mainsheet, you damned buggers, I'll thank you to mind your work, the mainsail looks like bloody washing hung out to dry." (Peleg Dinwiddie, *The Pirate Round* 45)

haul away ['*aul*/'*awrl*/*hawrl awayee*/'*way*/'*wayee*] pull away; go ahead and pull; pull hard

"Hands to the halyards, **haul away!** Sheet home!" (Thomas Marlowe, *The Pirate Round* 82)

haul away all ['*aul*/'*awrl*/*hawrl awayee*/'*way*/'*wayee awrl*]

A command given to two or more members of a crew to pull.

"Come along, you bloody laggards, **haul away all!**" (William Darnall, *The Guardship* 37)

heave away\'round ['*eave*/*heeff awayee*/'*way*/'*wayee\arowoon*/'*arowoond*/*arowoont*/'*roun*'/'*round*/'*rowoon*'/'*rowoond*/'*rowoont*]

A command given to members of a crew working a vessel's capstan (that is, a drum or winch around which the anchor line is wrapped) to turn it so as to haul up the anchor line. Typically given just before sailing.

"**Heave away!**" (William Darnall, ordering the hands aboard the *Vengeance* to work the capstan and raise the ship's anchor, *The Guardship* 37) "Very well, Mr. Honeyman, **heave 'round!**" (Thomas Marlowe, *The Pirate Round* 76)

heave up the\your anchor ['*eave*/*heeff arrp t'\ya/yarr/ye/yer/yore han-karr*]

A command to raise a vessel's anchor.

"It wouldn't surprise me none to hear you say, '**Heave up the anchor**. We sails on the hour.'" (Long John Silver, "Treasure Island" [1950] 18:25) "**Heave up your anchor** and set sail. Other boats may follow." (pirate mate, "The Black Pirate" 1:24:12)

helm a-starboard ['*elm a sta'b'd/starbarrd/starberrd*] turn to the right

A command given to a helmsman to steer the vessel to the right. A command to steer to the left would use "larboard" or "port" in place of "starboard."

"**Helm a-starboard!** Keep her north-westerly." (Adam Penfeather, *Adam Penfeather, Buccaneer* 237)

helm quarter to larboard ['*elm quahrr/quahter t'/ta/ter la'b'd/larbarrd/larberrd*]

helm quarter to port* ['*elm quahrr/quahter t'/ta/ter parrt*] turn one quarter of a point to the left

A command given to a helmsman to steer the vessel one quarter of a point to the left. A point is equal to 1/32 of a compass circle, or

11.25 degrees. A quarter of a point, therefore, equals 2.8125 degrees. To steer a quarter of a point to the right, the command would use "starboard" in place of "larboard" or "port."

> "Jeremy, **helm quarter to port.**" (Peter Blood, "Captain Blood" 1:49:01)

helms alee ['*elms alee*] turn to leeward; turn away from the wind

A command given to a vessel's helmsman.

> "Ready ... **helms alee!**" (Thomas Marlowe, turning the *Plymouth Prize* onto a new tack, *The Guardship* 278)

hoist anchor [*hoyeest/'oist han-karr*]

A command to raise a vessel's anchor.

> "**Hoist anchor.** Man all canvas. Look lively." (Humble Bellows, "The Crimson Pirate" 32:24)

hoist sail [*hoyeest/'oist sayell*]
hoist the sails [*hoyeest/'oist t' sayells*]

A command to lift a vessel's sails and spread them against the wind so as to get a vessel under way or increase its speed.

> "And don't stay to take up anchor. Cut the cable. **Hoist sail** and let's away." (George Fairfax, *The Fortunes of Captain Blood* 151) "Weigh anchor! **Hoist the sails!** Spread quick, you ninnies!" (Anamaria, "Pirates of the Caribbean: The Curse of the Black Pearl" 1:16:30)

hoist up the Jolly Roger [*hoyeest/'oist arrp t' Jarrly Raah/Rarr-ger*]

A command to raise a pirate flag—typically a white skull and crossbones on a black field—over a vessel in order to intimidate an enemy or intended prize, or to inspire the crew of the attacking pirate vessel.

> "Cut out the sails! **Hoist up the Jolly Roger!**" (Montbars, "Pirates of Tortuga" 38:15)

hold\keep her so [*hol'/hoold/ho'oold/'ol'/'old\keep 'er so'oo*]

A command given to a helmsman to maintain a vessel's present heading.

> "How's she lie now, Penryn?" "... West and by south, sir!" "**Hold her so,** sir." > (Japhet Bly & Ezekiel Penryn, *Winds of Chance* 62) "She rides sweet to 't! **Keep her so,** Ben." (Japhet Bly, *Winds of Chance* 63)

keep her __ [*keep 'er __*]

Used to direct a helmsman to maintain a particular course.

> "Helm a-starboard! **Keep her** north-westerly." (Adam Penfeather, *Adam Penfeather, Buccaneer* 237)

keep her steady [*keep 'er stea'-eee*]

A command given to a helmsman to keep a vessel from deviating from its present heading.

> "Two points to starboard. And **keep her steady.**" (Blair, "Cutthroat Island" 1:31:13)

keep her trimmed by the head [*keep 'er tremmed/trimt byee t' 'ead/hayd*]

A command to weigh down the forward part of a vessel with cargo and/or ballast so that it rides lower and draws more water than the after part. A vessel may be trimmed by the head for various reasons—to keep aft-stowed cargo dry from drainage leaking out of forward-stowed cargo or from water leaking in through a broken bulkhead forward; to incline and therefore eke out more range from cannon positioned aft; to shrink the area of hull bottom exposed to shallow, rocky sea bottom—though trimming by the head tends to compromise a vessel's speed and responsiveness to the helm. Vessels that are neither trimmed by the head nor trimmed by the stern are said to be even-keeled or to sail on an even keel.

> "**Keep her trimmed by the head,** Wolf." (Peter Blood, "Captain Blood" 1:43:55)

larboard a little [*la'b'd/larbarrd/larberrd a lil'*]
port* a little [*parrt a lil'*] turn slightly left; steer a bit to the left

> "Starboard a little. **Larboard a little.**" (Israel Hands, "Treasure Island" [1990] 1:31:32) "Starboard a little—starboard

yet—steady, so—there's the true passage my lads; **port a little**—steady." (Hawkhurst, guiding the *Avenger* through a maze of island coral reefs, *The Pirate* 122, Chap. XVI)

larboard yet [*la'b'd/larbarrd/larberrd yat*]
port* yet [*parrt yat*] keep turning left; turn more to the left

> Compare: "Starboard a little—**starboard yet**—steady, so—there's the true passage my lads; port a little—steady." (Hawkhurst, guiding the *Avenger* through a maze of island coral reefs, *The Pirate* 122, Chap. XVI)

larboard your helm [*la'b'd/larbarrd/larberrd ya/yarr/ye/yer/yere 'elm*]
port* your helm [*parrt ya/yarr/ye/yer/yere/ yore 'elm*] turn left; steer to the left

> *"**Larboard your helm!** Hard over!" Marlowe shouted to the helmsmen, who shoved the tiller hard to the larboard side.* (Thomas Marlowe, *The Pirate Round* 83)

lay a course for__ [*layee a carrse farr/fer __*] prepare to sail toward __ ; chart a route to the destination of __

> "Go about and **lay a course for** Cartagena." (George Fairfax, *The Fortunes of Captain Blood* 159)

let fly __ [*laaht/le' flyee __*] let go of __
A command given to release something that, when no longer secured, moves quickly or readily as a result of gravity or the action of some countervailing weight.

> "Now, **let fly** your halyard, douse your sail—so!" (Resolution Day, *Martin Conisby's Vengeance* 152)

let go __ [*laaht/le' go'oo __*] release the __

> "**Let go** weather braces, jump, ye dogs, jump!" (Captain Belvedere, *Martin Conisby's Vengeance* 104)

let go and haul [*laaht/le' go'oo an'/'n' 'aul/ 'awrl/hawrl*]

A command given aboard a tacking vessel as its bow is turned through the wind to indicate that the vessel is in line with the wind.

> "**Let go, and haul!**" (Tim, *The Fortunes of Captain Blood* 167)

let her run before the wind [*laaht/le' 'er roohn afarr/afore/befarr/'farr/'fore t' win'/wint*]

A command to sail a vessel directly downwind—that is, in line with and in the same direction as the wind.

> "Crowd on sail, and **let her run before the wind**." (Peter Blood, *Captain Blood Returns* 290)

lift anchor [*left/liff han-karr*]

> "Now, you lazy swabs, stir yourselves! **Lift anchor**. Shake out the main!" (Blackbeard, "Blackbeard's Ghost" 1:45:38)

luff [*larrff/loohff*]

A command given to a helmsman to steer a vessel further into the wind.

> "Now, my hearty, **luff**!" (Israel Hands, *Treasure Island* 142, Chap. 26) "**Luff**, you lubber, here's the rock." (Smee, *Peter Pan* 90–91)

make all sail [*mayeeke awrl sayell*]

A command to members of a crew to loosen and spread every bit of a vessel's sail in order to get it under way at, or to increase its speed to, maximum velocity.

> "Cast loose from the prize, Master Martin, and **make all sail**." (Andrew Murray, *Porto Bello Gold* 177)

make fast [*mayeeke farrst/fass*]

A command to secure or firmly fasten something.

> "**Make fast** there!" (Blackbeard, overseeing the battening down of hatches over the prisoners below, "Blackbeard the Pirate" 1:30:13)

make sail [*mayeeke sayell*]

A command to loosen and spread the sail aboard a vessel in order to get it under way or increase its speed.

"Mister Bellows, **make sail**! (Captain Vallo, "The Crimson Pirate" 14:07)

make speed [*mayeeke speed*]

A command to increase a vessel's velocity by loosening and spreading more of its sail.

"**Make speed** there! To your halyards! Tacks and braces! We head for Port Royal." (John Wolverstone, "Captain Blood" 1:31:19)

make your course __ [*mayeeke ya/yarr/ye/yer/yere/yore carrse* __] head in the direction of __; steer the vessel __

"**Make your course** north-northwest, a quarter west." (LeRois, *The Guardship* 40)

make your head to __ [*mayeeke ya/yarr/ye/yer/yere/yore 'ead/hayd t'/ta/ter* __] fix a course in order to __; steer in order to __

"**Make your head** to pass Hog Island!" (Thomas Marlowe, *The Guardship* 274)

man all canvas [*man awrl canverss*]

A command to loosen and spread all of a vessel's sail in order to get under way at, or increase the vessel's speed to, maximum velocity.

"Hoist anchor. **Man all canvas**. Look lively." (Humble Bellows, "The Crimson Pirate" 32:24)

man the braces [*man t' brayeeces*]

A command given to members of a crew to take hold of a vessel's braces in anticipation of some adjustment in the position of the vessel's sails, or in execution of some such adjustment already ordered.

"Stingley! Fenner! **Man the braces**! Clear for action! Come on, look alive, lads!" (Patch, "The Adventures of Long John Silver: Sword of Vengeance" 2:41) "At the windlass, stand by! **Man the braces** and square away!" (Ezekiel Penryn, *Winds of Chance* 108)

man the capstan [*man t' carrpstan*]

A command given just before sailing in order to direct members of a crew to raise a vessel's anchor. The capstan is a drum or winch around which the anchor line or cable is wrapped.

"**Man the capstan**!" (Captain Vallo, "The Crimson Pirate" 00:50)

man the guns [*man t' garrns/goohns*]

A command to those members of a crew responsible for loading and firing a vessel's cannons to report to their assigned positions and prepare to operate the cannons.

"Avast! **Man the guns**!" (Captain Vallo, "The Crimson Pirate" 1:01:43)

man the yards [*man t' yahrrds*]

Yards are wood poles that are set perpendicular to and extend horizontally across a mast and support a sail. "Man the yards" is a command to effect some already or soon-to-be specified task relating to the yards, typically involving the adjustment of the sail supported on them.

"**Man the yards**!" (Captain Vallo, "The Crimson Pirate" 00:17)

midships [*med-sheps*]

A command given to a helmsman to turn the helm to the center position—that is, tending neither to larboard nor to starboard.

*"**Midships**!" he called to the helmsmen, and they moved the tiller to the center-line ...* (Thomas Marlowe, *The Pirate Round* 83)

more sails [*marr/moor sayells*]

A command to loosen and spread more of a vessel's sail in order to get it under way or to increase its speed.

"Ship ahoy!" "It bears Silver's crew. **More sails**." (lookout aboard the *Thistle* & El Toro Mendoza, "Long John Silver's Return to Treasure Island" 56:02)

pack on all canvas [*pack arrn awrl canverss*]

A command to loosen and spread all of a vessel's sail in order to get under way at, or increase the vessel's speed to, maximum velocity.

"**Pack on all canvas**, you fairy-tale sea snakes! (Captain Vallo, "The Crimson Pirate" 1:33:31)

pipe __ [*pawp/pyeepe __*]

A command given to a vessel's bosun to use his pipe or whistle to issue a specified instruction to the crew.

"**Pipe** the crew aft, Absalom!" (Japhet Bly, *Winds of Chance* 68)

pipe all hands [*pawp/pyeepe awrl 'ands/'an's/han's*]

A command given to a vessel's bosun to use his pipe or whistle to order the entire crew to report and gather abovedecks (typically in the vessel's waist), usually so that the captain or other senior company member may address them from the quarterdeck.

"Well, then, you get on a horse, and go to—well, yes, I will!—to that eternal doctor swab, and tell him to **pipe all hands**." (Billy Bones, *Treasure Island* 15–16, Chap. 3)

pipe to quarters [*pawp/pyeepe t'/ta/ter quahrr/quaht-ters*]

A command given to a vessel's bosun to use his pipe or whistle to order the crew to move immediately to battle stations.

"**Pipe to quarters**!" (Jose Lorenzo, "Captain Kidd" 42:18) "**Pipe** the hands **to quarters**, Jake. We weigh at once." (Peter Blood, *The Fortunes of Captain Blood* 107)

put on that line [*put arrn tharrt lawn/lyeene*]

A command to secure or attach a line (rope) to something else, such as a mast, a yard, or another line.

"**Put on that line**." (pirate aboard the *Blarney Cock*, "Swashbuckler" 4:35)

put up the helm [*put arrp t' 'elm*]

A command to a helmsman to turn a vessel into a different heading by bringing its bow through the wind.

"**Put up the helm**. We go about." (Peter Blood, *Captain Blood Returns* 291)

reef __

A command to reduce the area of a sail by rolling up or lowering a portion of it, then tying off that portion with short lines (ropes).

"**Reef** the fore topsail!" (John Wolverstone, "Captain Blood" 1:39:28)

reeve off __ [*reeve arrf __*]

A command to pass a line (rope) through something, typically in order to fasten or secure it or to connect it to something else.

"You there! **Reeve off** a new tackle, quickly!" (Duncan Honeyman, *The Pirate Round* 237)

round up [*roun'/rount/rowoon'/rowoond/rowoont arrp*]

A command to pull on a line (rope) passing perpendicularly through one or more blocks (devices containing one or more rollers or pulleys).

"Stand by with your anchor, there! **Round up**, right over there." (Patrick Quigley, *The Pirate Round* 364)

rouse away [*rowoose awayee/'way/'wayee*] pull away; go ahead and pull; pull hard

The term "rouse" refers specifically to the pulling of a line (rope) without the assistance of blocks, tackles, pulleys, rollers, or other mechanical means.

"**Rouse away**!" (Adam Penfeather, ordering his company to sail off with the galleon they've just boarded, *Adam Penfeather, Buccaneer* 185)

run away with __ [*roohn awayee/'way/'wayee weth/wi'/wiff/witt __*]

A command given to take hold of one or more lines (ropes)—typically a line that passes through one or more blocks, tackles, pulleys, or rollers—and to pull on it while running along or across the deck with it.

"**Run away with** your halyards!" (Billy Bird, getting the *Elizabeth Galley* under way as fast as possible in an attempt to sail clear of a nearby sinking ship, *The Pirate Round* 347)

run out the sweeps [*roohn arrt/ou'/owoot t' sweeps*]

A command to deploy a vessel's oars, typically given when speed is required but the wind is too weak to furnish it.

> "Make ready the guns. **Run out the sweeps.**" (Barbossa, "Pirates of the Caribbean: The Curse of the Black Pearl" 1:22:25)

run up more sail [*roohn arrp marr/moor sayell*]

A command to loosen and spread more of a vessel's sail in order to get it under way or to increase its speed.

> "**Run up more sail**, Patch." (Long John Silver, "The Adventures of Long John Silver: Pieces of Eight" 23:49)

run up the signals [*roohn arrp t' segnals*]

A command to raise one or more flags as a means of communication with other vessels or persons on shore.

> "**Run up the signals!**" (Montbars, "Pirates of Tortuga" 1:04:05)

set sail [*sat sayell*]

A command to loosen and spread a vessel's sail in order to get it under way.

> "Heave up your anchor and **set sail**. Other boats may follow." (pirate mate, "The Black Pirate" 1:24:12)

set the course for __ [*sat t' carrse farr/fer __*] prepare to sail toward __; chart a route to the destination of __

> "Sweet, merciful heaven, haven't you ears? **Set the course for** Port Royal!" (Peter Blood, "Captain Blood" 1:30:54)

shake out a reef [*shayeeke arrt/ou'/owoot a reef*]

A reef is a portion of a sail rolled up and tied off so as to reduce the sail's total area and exposure to the wind. "Shake out a reef" is a command to loosen and spread such a portion of sail in order to increase a vessel's speed incrementally.

> "**Shake out a reef** or we'm pooped!" (Ned Bowser, *Adam Penfeather, Buccaneer* 165)

shake out the main [*shayeeke arrt/ou'/owoot t' mayeen*]

A command to loosen and spread a vessel's mainsail—that is, the lowest, largest sail on its mainmast.

> "Now, you lazy swabs, stir yourselves! Lift anchor. **Shake out the main!**" (Blackbeard, "Blackbeard's Ghost" 1:45:38)

sheet home [*sheet ho'oome/'ome/'o'oome*]

A command to haul on a vessel's sheets (lines or ropes connected to the lower aft corners of a square sail) until the foot (bottom edge) of the attached sail is as straight and taut as possible.

> "Hands to the halyards, haul away! **Sheet home!**" (Thomas Marlowe, *The Pirate Round* 82)

sheets and tacks [*sheets an'/'n' tacks*]

A command to adjust or attend to a vessel's sheets (lines or ropes connected to the lower aft corners of square sails) and tacks (lines or ropes connected to the lower forward corners of square sails) in order to change course or speed or adapt to shifting wind conditions.

> "Ho, **sheets and tacks!**" (Ned Bowser, shouting his first instruction after Adam Penfeather's order to sail away with the galleon they've just boarded, *Adam Penfeather, Buccaneer* 185)

shift your helm [*sheft/shiff ya/yarr/ye/yer/yere/yore 'elm*]

A command given to a helmsman to turn the helm sharply into the opposite direction—that is, from larboard to starboard or from starboard to larboard.

> *"**Shift your helm!**" The helmsmen swung the tiller in an arc across the deck, all the

way to starboard.* (Thomas Marlowe, *The Pirate Round* 83)

shorten sail [*sharrten sayell*]

A command to reduce the area of a sail.

"**Shorten sail** there, Wolf." (Peter Blood, "Captain Blood" 1:39:16)

so [*so'oo*] that's it; just like that

Used to communicate approval, and often to suggest that the addressee maintain or continue whatever it is he is doing.

"Starboard a little—starboard yet—steady, **so**—there's the true passage my lads; port a little—steady." (Hawkhurst, guiding the *Avenger* through a maze of island coral reefs, *The Pirate* 122, Chap. XVI)

spread quick [*sprayd queck*]

An urgent command to loosen and spread a vessel's sail immediately in order to get it under way or increase its speed.

"Weigh anchor! Hoist the sails! **Spread quick**, you ninnies!" (Anamaria, "Pirates of the Caribbean: The Curse of the Black Pearl" 1:16:30)

square away [*squarr/squayarr/squayerr/squerr awayee/'way/'wayee*]

A command to set a square-rigged vessel's yards (wood poles, set perpendicular to a mast, supporting a square sail) at right angles to the vessel's keel.

"At the windlass, stand by! Man the braces and **square away**!" (Ezekiel Penryn, *Winds of Chance* 108)

stand on [*stan'/starrn'/starrnd arrn*] keep going; proceed

A command to continue along a vessel's present heading.

"And if you'd beach her, then just **stand on**, there be a bar of but one fathom deep just ahead." (unnamed pirate on Smith Island, *The Guardship* 89)

starboard a little [*sta'b'd/starbarrd/starberrd a lil'*] turn slightly right; steer a bit to the right

"**Starboard a little**. Larboard a little." (Israel Hands, "Treasure Island" [1990] 1:31:32)

starboard yet [*sta'b'd/starbarrd/starberrd yat*] keep turning right; turn more to the right

A command given to a vessel's helmsman.

"Starboard a little—**starboard yet**—steady, so—there's the true passage my lads; port a little—steady." (Hawkhurst, guiding the *Avenger* through a maze of island coral reefs, *The Pirate* 122, Chap. XVI)

starboard your helm [*sta'b'd/starbarrd/starberrd ya/yarr/ye/yer/yere/yore 'elm*] turn right; steer to the right

A command given to a vessel's helmsman.

"Starboard, Master Martin! **Starboard your helm**, if you please." (Andrew Murray, *Porto Bello Gold* 114)

steady [*stea'-eee*]

A command given generally to members of a crew to take a smooth and deliberate approach with respect to any given task, and specifically to a vessel's helmsman to discourage him from oversteering or from turning the helm too sharply or suddenly.

"[S]**teady**, so—there's the true passage my lads; port a little—**steady**." (Hawkhurst, guiding the *Avenger* through a maze of island coral reefs, *The Pirate* 122, Chap. XVI)

steady as she goes [*stea'-eee as she go'ooes*]
steady as you go [*stea'-eee as 'ee/ya/ye/yer go'oo*]

A command given to a helmsman to maintain a vessel's present heading. The verb "is" or "be" is often substituted for "goes" in "steady as she goes."

< "We don't tack, we just run right into that fucking *cochon*." "**Steady as she goes**!" > (LeRois & William Darnall, aiming the bow of the *Vengeance* straight into the ship they hope to destroy, *The Guardship* 283) "**Steady as she is**!" (Adam Penfeather, *Adam Penfeather, Buccaneer*

185) "Steady as you go!" (Ben Worley, directing the helmsman to maintain a course straight for a Spanish galleon, "Blackbeard the Pirate" 1:15:47)

steady at the helm [*stea'-eee a'/hat t' 'elm*]
A command given to a helmsman to maintain a vessel's present heading.

> < "Steady at the helm!" > (Cahusac to helmsman aboard Levasseur's ship, "Captain Blood" 1:18:31)

tacks and braces [*tacks an'/'n' brayeeces*]
A command to adjust or attend to a vessel's tacks (lines or ropes connected to the lower forward corners of square sails) and braces (lines or ropes connected to the ends of a vessel's yards—wood poles set perpendicular to a vessel's masts and supporting its sails) in order to change course or speed or to adapt to shifting wind conditions.

> "Make speed there! To your halyards! **Tacks and braces!** We head for Port Royal." (John Wolverstone, "Captain Blood" 1:31:19)

take in __ [*tayeeke i'/'n* __]
A command to reduce the area of one or more of a vessel's sails.

> "Take in the t'ga'nt s'l [topgallant sail]." (John Wolverstone, "Captain Blood" 1:39:31)

take up anchor [*tayeeke arrp han-karr*]

> Compare: "And don't stay to **take up anchor.** Cut the cable. Hoist sail and let's away." (George Fairfax, *The Fortunes of Captain Blood* 151)

to your __ [*t'/ta/ter ya/yarr/ye/yer/yere/ yore* __]
A command given to members of a crew to move toward, attend to, and perform tasks concerning a specified part or feature of a vessel.

> "Make speed there! **To your** halyards! Tacks and braces! We head for Port Royal." (John Wolverstone, "Captain Blood" 1:31:19)

topside [*tarrp-sawd/syeede*] get up on deck
Used to direct someone belowdecks to come out onto a vessel's main deck.

> "**Topside,** you swabs!" (Captain Vallo, "The Crimson Pirate" 1:01:52)

trim your sails [*trem ya/yarr/ye/yer/yere/yore sayells*]
A command to tighten the lines (ropes) attached to a vessel's sails, typically given when a weakening or shifting wind causes the sails to flap rather than fill.

> "**Trim yer sails** for more speed and begin firing at the *Walrus!*" (Joshua Smoot, *Dead Man's Chest* 183)

turn the hands up [*tarrn t' 'ands/'an's/han's arrp*] call the crew to the deck

> < "The ship's company wish to know where we are going, sir." "Have they deputed you to ask the question?" "Not exactly, sir; but I wish to know myself." "**Turn the hands up:** as one of the ship's company under my orders, you will, with the others, receive the information you require." > (Hawkhurst & Cain, *The Pirate* 110, Chap. XV)

unmoor [*arrn/hun/oohn-moo-arr/err*]
A command given to free a vessel for sailing by releasing a line (rope) securing it to a fixed object or by raising an anchor.

> "All hands, **unmoor! unmoor!**" (The Red Rover, *The Red Rover* 377)

up anchor [*arrp han-karr*]

> "Move fast. Clap on sail. **Up anchor.**" (Long John Silver, "Long John Silver's Return to Treasure Island" 1:07:25)

upon deck [*arrp arrn/o' dack*] get up on deck
Used to direct someone belowdecks to come out onto a vessel's main deck.

> "**Upon deck,** you dog, for we shall lose no more time about you." (mutinous Alexander Mitchel, just before taking Captain John Green abovedecks and tossing

him over the side, *General History of the Pyrates* 607)

up that rigging [*arrp tharrt reggin'*]

A vessel's rigging is the network of lines (ropes) connected to its sails, yards, and masts. "Up that rigging" is a command to members of a crew to climb up into the rigging, especially to adjust sails, to make repairs or other adjustments, or to prepare to board another ship by jumping down on its deck from above.

> "**Up that rigging**, you monkeys! Aloft!" (Peter Blood, making preparations to sail out of Port Royal aboard the *Cinco Llagas*, "Captain Blood" 1:01:40)

up there [*arrp tharr/theyarr/theyerr*]

A command to members of a crew to climb up into a vessel's rigging, especially to adjust sails, to make repairs or other adjustments, or to prepare to board another ship by jumping down on its deck from above.

> "**Up there** and furl top-gallant sails; we'll likely have a breeze, and it's well to be ready." (pirate captain, *The Coral Island* 222)

warp her head to __ [*wahrrp 'er 'ead/hayd t'/ta/ter __*]

A command to turn a vessel by hauling on the line attached to a dropped anchor.

"I want to shift our anchorage somewhat ... **warp her head** round to starboard. ..." (Adam Penfeather, *Adam Penfeather, Buccaneer* 275)

wear ship [*warr/wayarr/wayerr/werr shep*]

A command to turn a vessel in an opposite direction by bringing the wind behind and across the ship's stern.

> "Veer, Resolution, **wear ship** and man the larboard guns ... they are cool ... I must go tend my hurt—a curst on't!" (Captain Jo, *Martin Conisby's Vengeance* 110)

weather quarters [*waath/wayth/wedd-er quahrr/quaht-ters*]

A command to members of a crew to prepare a vessel's deck, sails, and rigging for imminent stormy weather.

> "**Weather quarters!**" (pirate aboard the *Joyful Deliverance*, in anticipation of a quickly rising storm, *Winds of Chance* 126)

weigh (anchor) [*weighee (han-karr)*]

A command to lift a vessel's anchor.

> "Jump to and **weigh!**" (Blackbeard, "Blackbeard the Pirate" 1:15:18) "**Weigh anchor!** Hoist the sails! Spread quick, you ninnies!" (Anamaria, "Pirates of the Caribbean: The Curse of the Black Pearl" 1:16:30)

CHAPTER 5

Threats

In May 1680, Captain Sawkins and his ships lay at anchor off the Spanish island town of Tavoga, near Panama. This was no secret mission. The Spanish knew these buccaneers were in their midst. Sawkins had already taken a Spanish ship headed for Panama—and the 51,000 pieces of eight (over $1 million in today's money) aboard meant as payroll for the soldiers garrisoned there.

It came as no surprise, therefore, when a few merchants came aboard Sawkins' ship with a message from the Governor of Panama: "From whom do you have your commission, and to whom ought I to complain for the damages you have already done us?"

Sawkins sent back a message. It began politely, almost apologetically: "As yet, all my company has not come together." Then came the rest:

> "But when they come up we will come and visit you at Panama, and bring our commissions on the muzzles of our guns, at which time you should read them as plain as the flame of gunpowder can make them." (*Bucaniers of America* [account of Basil Ringrose] Chap. VIII)

Sawkins, of course, had no commission, and the moral of the story is plain: Who needs a privateer's commission, or anything else for that matter, when a powerful threat will do?

5.1 TYPES OF THREATS

Threats are the spoken currency of pirates. The more specific and vivid the threat and, of course, the more credible in light of the speaker's history of making good on threats in similar circumstances, the higher the speaker's resulting station in any exchange.

There are primarily four kinds of threats:

1. The **will-do threat** is a simple state-ment of the speaker's intent to harm the addressee: "I'll bend a marlinspike 'round yer loaf." Notice other ways of forming the will-do threat: "You'll see me bend a marlinspike 'round yer loaf." "I've a mind to bend a marlinspike 'round yer loaf."

2. The **I'll-do-or-be-damned threat** is an oath by the speaker inviting misfortune on himself if he does not harm the addressee: "May God strike me dead if I don't bend a marlinspike 'round yer loaf."

3. The **if-then threat** lays out a condi-tion, then the harmful consequence for the addressee if that condition is satisifed: "Pick up that cutlass and I'll bend a marlinspike 'round yer loaf." If-then threats can include the addi-tional phrase "would you": "Pick up that cutlass, would you, and I'll bend a marlinspike 'round yer loaf."

4. The **or-else threat** lays out a command, then the harmful consequence for the addressee if that command is disobeyed: "Leave that cutlass alone or I'll bend a marlinspike 'round yer loaf." "Leave that cutlass alone less'n you want a marlin-spike 'round yer loaf."

5.2 RETORTS TO THREATS

There are at least four ways of replying defiantly or indignantly to another's threat. The first three suggest doubt that the addressee will follow through with his threat; the last one conveys indifference to the consequences if he does.

1. **Is it:** Repeat the threat made, then add the challenging question, "is it?" "Cut my throat, is it?"

   < "Aye, you'll be blind enough soon—" "Blind **is it**, Cap'n—ha, good!" > (Captain Belvedere & pirate in Captain Jo's com-pany, *Martin Conisby's Vengeance* 60)

2. **Say you:** Reply with the doubting or mocking question "say you?" "Cut my throat, say you?"

   < "So, damned gaoler, be wary! Watch ever and sleep light—" "**Sayst thou**, Johnny, **sayst thou**? Lookee now! When we see a noxious insect, we step on it, or loathly reptile, we kill it, Johnny. ..." > (John Barrasdale & Japhet Bly, *Winds of Chance* 259)

3. **Will ya:** Repeat the threat made, then add the doubting question "will ya?" "Cut my throat, will ya?"

   < "And if you don't keep off it I'll fire the cannon and get a proper watch aboard." "Oh, **will ya**?" > (Israel Hands & Haggott, "Treasure Island" [1950] 1:07:00)

4. **OATH + you'd try that:** Reply with an oath, any oath (see Chapter 6 for a list of oaths), then the phrase "you'd try that." "Cut my throat? Blood and wounds you'd try that."

   "[B]y G[o]d **he'd try that**." (drunk gunner aboard the *Whidaw*, after mistaking the lines of a pirate play being performed on deck for a threat to a crewmate, and just before throwing a lit grenade among the actors, *General History of the Pyrates* 588)

See Chapter 11: Retorts for a complete list of retorts to threats and other kinds of statements.

5.3 CATALOG OF THREATS

Below is a list of threats. Definitions are pro-vided only where meaning is not otherwise apparent. Threats listed as entries are not always identical to the pertinent terms or phrases appearing in accompanying excerpts, but in every instance are based on them. See also Section 16.4, which lists methods of tor-ture and punishment—colorful material for composing your own threats.

are you tired of your life? [are 'ee/ya/ye/yer tarrd/tyarrd/tyerrd o'\on ya/yarr/ye/yer/yore lawf/lyeefe?]

> "Mutiny!, open, violent, and blood-seeking mutiny! Are ye tired of your lives, men?" (The Red Rover, facing down a riot among his men, *The Red Rover* 336)

blame your own self for your death [blayeeme ya/yarr/ye/yer/yere/yore arrn/owoon seff farr/fer ya/yarr/ye/yer/yere/yore dath/deff]

> "Blame your own self for your death!" (Hunt, *The Book of Pirates* "The Ruby of Kishmoor" 227)

bones is what you'll be [boones/bo'oones be wharrt/whorrt ye'll be]

> "Bones is what they are now." (Long John Silver, *Treasure Island* 178, Chap. 31)

death and damnation shall be yours [dath/deff an'/'n' dam-may/mayee/nayee-shern/ shoohn shawrl be yarrs/yer'n/yourn\theys]

> "'Tis my assured hope this **death and damnation shall be theirs** and we the instruments o' Grace by means o' steel and round-shot to plunge 'em forthwith to the very deeps of hell." (Amos Perrin, *Adam Penfeather, Buccaneer* 117)

death is but your due [dath/deff be barrt ya/yarr/ye/yer/yere/yore doo]

> "I mean not to shoot you, and as for Don Federigo, since **death is but his due**, a bullet were kinder—so charge now these my pistols." (Captain Jo, *Martin Conisby's Vengeance* 48–49)

the death you face will make men's blood run cold for a hundred years [t' dath/deff 'ee/ya/ye/yer fayeece well mayeeke men's bloohd/ blut roohn col'/coold/co'oold/colt farr/fer a hoohn/ oohn/'un-derd yarrs/yee'arrs/yee'errs]

> "I pledge on the soul of my madre to catch you, Silver, and when I do **the death you face will make men's blood run cold for a hundred years**." (El Toro Mendoza,

"Long John Silver's Return to Treasure Island" 1:08:54)

death's got his grapples aboard you [dath's/ deff's garrt 'is grarpples abarrd 'ee/ya/ye/yer]

A grapple, known also as a grapnel or grappling hook, is an iron shaft with hooks or claws at one end, typically thrown with a rope tied to the other end and used to grasp, hold, or pull on the object it catches.

> "**Death's got his grapples aboard me** now." (Humphrey, *Black Bartlemy's Treasure* 272)

do you fancy a swim with Davy Jones? [d'/does 'ee/ya/ye/yer fancy a swem weth/wi'/ wiff/witt Daah/Dayee-vy Joones/Jo'oones?]

"Davy Jones" (or "Davy Jones' locker") is the seaman's traditional personification of, and way of referring to, the bottom of the ocean, especially as a graveyard for those killed at sea.

> "Where be Cap'n Jack Sparrow? Speak up, or **do you fancy a swim with Davy Jones?**" (pirate dunking magistrate in well, "Pirates of the Caribbean" Disney attraction [2006])

don't be committing suicide [don'/doon't/ dorrn't be a-commet-tin' su'-cyeede/sawd]

> "**Don't be committing suicide** by telling me another falsehood; and there's no need." (Peter Blood, *The Fortunes of Captain Blood* 166)

don't make me hafta cut you [don'/doon't/ dorrn't mayeeke me 'afta/hafter carrt/cooht 'ee/ya/ye/yer]

> "**Don't make me hafta cut ya**, Morley." (Dick Walpole, *Dead Man's Chest* 249)

d'ye ... or do I make ye—which? [do/does 'ee/ya/yer/you ... arr d'/does I'ee mayeeke 'ee/ ya/ye/yer—whech?]

> "Now, my pretty lads, **d'ye give us room or do I make ye—which?**" (Japhet Bly, *Winds of Chance* 14)

here's death ['ee'arr/'ee'err/'ere/hee'arr/hee'err is\be dath/deff]

< "Tush! Here is one that talketh very loud and fool-like and flourisheth iron claw to no purpose, since I heed one no more than t'other—" **"Here's death!** Death, wench!" > (Captain Jo & Roger Tressady, with Roger Tressady brandishing his iron hook, *Martin Conisby's Vengeance* 157)

I charge you on pain of death [*I'ee chahrrge 'ee/ya/ye/yer arrn/o' payeen o'\on dath/deff*]

Used to preface and combine a command or enjoiner with a threat.

"**I charge you on pain of death** not once to come before the mast, for if you do, I swear I shall have you hanged!" (Francis Drake, excoriating his shipboard minister Francis Fletcher, *The Queen's Corsair* 283)

I have a pistol and a brace of balls ready for you [*I'ee 'aff/'ave/ha'/haff a peh-shtol an'/'n' a brayeece o'\on bawrls rea'-eee farr/fer 'ee/ya/ye/yer*]

"**I have a pistol and a brace of balls ready for** any one, who dare oppose me herein." (John Russell, *Pirates of the New England Coast* 185–86)

I should do God and my country good service, by ridding the world of such a EPITHET [*I'ee shoood do Garrd/Gott/Gud an'/'n' me/myee cahn/carrn/coohn/kern-try good sarrvice, byee a-redd-in' t' warrld o'\on sarrch/sich/soohch a ...*]

"[I'm] sure [I] **should do God and** [my] **country good service, by ridding the world of such a** traiterous villain." (John Russell, furious at George Roberts for toasting King George rather than his Roman Catholic rival James Edward Stuart, *Pirates of the New England Coast* 179)

if you enjoy living [*an'\eff/eff'n/if'n 'ee/ya/ye/yer ann-joyee/j'y a-levv/liff-in'*]

"And **if you** all **enjoy living**, you will remember that." (William Kidd, "Captain Kidd" 31:18)

I'll bash your skull in [*I'ee'ull barrsh ya/yart/ye/yer/yere skoohl 'n*]

"Hell and corruption, get out of here before **I bash your skull in!**" (Billy Bones, "Treasure Island" [1960] 8:49)

I'll be death for you [*I'ee'ull be dath/deff farr/fer 'ee/ya/ye/yer*]

"Now, I am Captain Adam Penfeather, your captain, and one ye shall obey or, by the God above us, **I'll be death for** some o' ye afore I die." (Adam Penfeather, *Adam Penfeather, Buccaneer* 189)

I'll bend a marlinspike around your loaf [*I'ee'ull baynd/ben'/bent a mahrrlen/mahrrlin/mar'n-spawk/spyeeke aroun'/arount/arowoon'/arowoond/arowoont/'roun'/'round/'rount/'rowoon'/'rowoond/'rowoont ya/yarr/ye/yer/yere/yore loof/lo'oof*]

A marlinspike is a pointed metal spike used in working with rope and cable, and especially in prying apart strands of rope. "Loaf" means "head" or "skull."

"Take your hands off this mo'n't or **I'll bend a marlinspike 'round your loaf**." (Blackbeard, "Blackbeard's Ghost" 31:35)

I'll blast you from the sea [*I'ee'ull blarrst/blass 'ee/ya/ye/yer ferm t' sea*]

"**Blast 'em from the sea!**" (Dawg Brown, "Cutthroat Island" 1:37:11)

I'll blast you over the horizon [*I'ee'ull blarrst/blass 'ee/ya/ye/yer ober/o'er t' hoo/'o-rizon*]

"With this information, ya gives chase with ya men-o'-war and **blast 'im over the 'orizon**." (Long John Silver, "Long John Silver's Return to Treasure Island" 12:59)

I'll blast you to Davy Jones [*I'ee'ull blarrst/blass 'ee/ya/ye/yer t'/ta/ter Daah/Dayee-vy Joones/Jo'oones*]

"Davy Jones" (or "Davy Jones' locker") is the seaman's traditional personification of, and way of referring to, the bottom of the ocean, especially as a graveyard for those killed at sea.

< "We must sail at once for Isla de Oro, my father's home." "Hold fast there. Us face land guns?" "**They'd blast us to Davy Jones!**" > (Sean O'Flaherty, Big Eric, & Trip Fenner, "The Adventures of Long John Silver: Sword of Vengeance" 11:53)

I'll blast you to Kingdom Come [*I'ee'ull blarrst/blass 'ee/ya/ye/yer t'/ta/ter Ken'/Keng/Kin'-derm/'om Cahm/Carrm/Coohm*]

Taken from the line "thy kingdom come, thy will be done" in the Lord's Prayer, "Kingdom Come" refers literally to the reign of heaven on earth and is used more loosely to mean the next world or the end of time.

"The first swab ta make a move **I'll blast to Kingdom Come**. Back to yer posts, you mutinous dogs!" (Long John Silver, "The Adventures of Long John Silver: The Tale of a Tooth" 15:16)

I'll blast you to perdition [*I'ee'ull blarrst/blass 'ee/ya/ye/yer t'/ta/ter parr/peer/pree-deh-shern/shoohn*]

"Perdition" means "eternal damnation."

"Follow me, rogue, or by my blood, Master Fenn's gun yonder **shall blast** some o' **ye to perdition**—come!" (Adam Penfeather, *Adam Penfeather, Buccaneer* 200)

I'll blast you where you stand [*I'ee'ull blarrst/blass 'ee/ya/ye/yer wayarr/wayerr/wharr 'ee/ya/ye/yer stan'/starrn'/starrnd*]

"Come outta there, or **I'll blast ye where you stand**." (Long John Silver, hearing a suspicious noise nearby and calling out in its direction, "The Adventures of Long John Silver: The Pink Pearl" 19:41)

I'll bleed you [*I'ee'ull bleed 'ee/ya/ye/yer*]

To "bleed" is to wound, and especially to kill by wounding.

< "Run him through." "Slit his throat." "**Bleed him.**" > (Old Stingley, Big Eric, & Trip Fenner, proposing various fates for Salamander the Greek, "The Adventures of Long John Silver: Pieces of Eight" 2:27)

I'll blood you [*I'ee'ull bloohd/blut 'ee/ya/ye/yer*]

"Man, I'm telling ye o' this same tall, great, ugly rascal, this scoundrelly, very lewd rogue provoked you lately to **blooding him** and very handsomely ye did it!" (Benjamin Trigg, *Adam Penfeather, Buccaneer* 208)

I'll blow out your brains [*I'ee'ull blowoo arrt/ou'/owoot ya/yarr/ye/yer/yere/yore brayeens*]
I'll blow your brains out [*I'ee'ull blowoo ya/yarr/ye/yer/yere/yore brayeens arrt/ou'/owoot*]

Captain Charles Johnson reports in *General History of the Pyrates* that "blow his brains out" was "a favourite phrase" among the pirates in Bartholomew Roberts' company. "Blow out your brains" is the same usage, though with the preposition "out" coming a bit early.

*Anne Bonny, having a drawn sword in one hand and a pistol in the other, attended by one of the men, went strait **to** the cabin where the two fellows lay who belonged to the sloop; the noise waked them, which she observing, swore, that if they pretended to resist, or make a noise, **she would blow out their brains** (that was the term she used).* (attribution to Anne Bonny, *General History of the Pyrates* 625) "If you don't tell me all you know, **I'll blow your brains out!**" (pirate captain, threatening fifteen-year old Ralph Rover with a cocked pistol, *The Coral Island* 198)

I'll blow you clear off the sea [*I'ee'ull blowoo 'ee/ya/ye/yer clea-arr/err arrf t' sea*]

"They'll sink us like rats in a trap. **They'll blow us clear off the sea.**" (Ben Worley, "Blackbeard the Pirate" 13:50)

I'll blow you out of the water [*I'ee'ull blowoo 'ee/ya/ye/yer arrt/ou'/owoot o'\on t' wahh/warr-ter*]

"Be off this ship at once, and tell your blackguards that if the *Valiant* is still there **by** noon **I'll blow her out of the water**." (Captain Easterling, *Captain Blood Returns* 286)

I'll blow you over the moon [*I'ee'ull blowoo 'ee/ya/ye/yer ober/o'er t' moon*]

"After that, I, **I'll blow him over the moon**." (Blackbeard, "Blackbeard the Pirate" 45:46)

I'll blow you to hell [*I'ee'ull blowoo 'ee/ya/ye/yer t'/ta/ter 'ell*]

"Get aboard that ransom ship. When night lowers, **blow her to Hell!**" (pirate mate, "The Black Pirate" 45:12)

I'll blow you to smithereens [*I'ee'ull blowoo 'ee/ya/ye/yer t'/ta/ter sme'er/smether/smi'er-eens*]

"Smithereens" are tiny fragments.

"**We'll blow Sir Henry to smithereens.**" (Blackbeard, "Blackbeard the Pirate" 43:58)

I'll bowel you [*I'ee'ull bowoo-ell 'ee/ya/ye/yer*]

To "bowel" someone is to cut into his abdomen and remove his intestines. "Disembowel" and "eviscerate" are modern terms referring to the same action.

"Avast, sons o' dogs, stand off or **I'll bowel ye.**" (Ned, brandishing a long knife, *Winds of Chance* 313)

I'll brain you [*I'ee'ull brayeen 'ee/ya/ye/yer*]

To "brain" someone is to hit him hard on the head or, more specifically, to smash his skull in so that his brain is exposed.

"There's dog of a lord for ye! A lewd cur to yap afore lady. Bark again and **I'll brain ye.**" (Japhet Bly, *Winds of Chance* 14)

I'll break you of these ADJECTIVE ways [*I'ee'ull brayeek 'ee/ya/ye/yer o'\on dese/t'ese ___ wayees*]

The speaker inserts an adjective describing or characterizing the "ways" of which he is complaining. Although there is no overt threat here, the promise "I'll break you" without further explanation of how the speaker intends to proceed is an ominous one.

"You young varmint. Why, **I'll break you of these** insolent **ways.**" (Long John Sil-

ver, "Long John Silver's Return to Treasure Island" 22:16)

I'll bring bloody death on you [*I'ee'ull breng bloohd/bluh'/blutt-y dath/deff arrn/o' 'ee/ya/ye/yer*]

"Back, ye vile scum or **I'll bring bloody death on ye.**" (Adam Penfeather, *Adam Penfeather, Buccaneer* 189)

I'll bring my boot to you [*I'ee'ull breng me/myee boot t'/ta/ter 'ee/ya/ye/yer*]

To "bring one's boot" to someone is to kick him hard.

"**I'll bring my boot to ya**, and I'll grind your mealy-mouthed jib into the dirt, I will!" (Blackbeard, "Blackbeard's Ghost" 1:03:25)

I'll carve your gizzard and fry it for my supper [*I'ee'ull cahrrve ya/yarr/ye/yer/yere/yore gezzard an'/'n' fryee ett/'n/'t farr/fer me/myee soohpper*]

The gizzard is a digestive organ found in birds and invertebrates that aids in the crushing and grinding of food. As humans do not have gizzards, the reference to "gizzard" here relates to one's stomach or, more generally, an internal organ of any kind.

"Shake out the main! Lively now! Or **I'll carve your gizzard and fry it for me supper!**" (Blackbeard, "Blackbeard's Ghost" 1:45:41)

I'll cast anchor in you [*I'ee'ull carrst han-karr i'/'n 'ee/ya/ye/yer*]

"Quiet, you scugs, or **I'll cast anchor in you.**" (James Hook, *Peter Pan* 148)

I'll chain you to the keel [*I'ee'ull chayeen 'ee/ya/ye/yer t'/ta/ter t' kee'ell*]

The keel is a large beam forming the spine of a vessel and running its full length underneath the centerline. Chaining someone to the keel of a vessel would mean certain drowning.

"**I'll have you chained to the keel!**" (El Toro Mendoza, "Long John Silver's Return to Treasure Island" 19:43)

I'll choke the life out of your pitiful carcass with my bare hands [*I'ee'ull chooke/cho'ooke t' lawf/lyeefe arrt/ou'/owoot o'\on ya/yarr/ye/yer/yere/yore petti/pi'i-ful cahrr-cahss/cush/kerss weth/wi'/wiff/witt me/myee barr/bayarr/bayerr 'ands/'an's/han's*]

> "I could snap ye across my knee, ay— choke the life out o' your pitiful carcass with my bare hands!" (Giles Tregenza, *Adam Penfeather, Buccaneer* 203)

I'll choke those words down your throat [*I'ee'ull chooke/cho'ooke dose/t'ose\dem/them\ dey/they warrds dowoon ya/yarr/ye/yer/yere/yore thro'oot*]

A threat that doubles as a concise retort to any unpleasantry.

> < "You're a wily bird, Silver. But this time you've overreached yourself. ..." "If you weren't the Governor of Porto Bello, I'd choke those words down your throat." > (Governor Strong & Long John Silver, "The Adventures of Long John Silver: Ship o' the Dead" 8:09)

I'll cleave you to the brisket [*I'ee'ull cleave 'ee/ya/ye/yer t'/ta/ter t' bres/brish-kert*]

"Brisket" is ribmeat taken from the chest of an animal.

> **"Cleave him to the brisket."** (James Hook, *Peter Pan* 160)

I'll cleave your skull asunder [*I'ee'ull cleave ya/yarr/ye/yer/yere/yore skoohl er-soohnder*]

> "I give you this caution; never to dispute the will of a pirate. For, supposing **I had cleft your scull asunder** for your impudence, what would you have got by it but destruction?" (Walter Kennedy, upbraiding captured captain William Snelgrave for resisting Kennedy's attempt to take Snelgrave's wig, *Villains of All Nations* 40)

I'll come aboard of you and gut you upon your own poop [*I'ee'ull cahm/carrm/coohm abarrd o'\on 'ee/ya/ye/yer an'/'n' garrt/gooht 'ee/ya/ye/yer 'parrn/'pon/uparrn 'ee/ya/ye/yer arrn/owoon poop*]

"Poop" is a reference to "poop deck," the rearmost deck of a vessel.

> "But if you play me false, then **I will come aboard of you and gut you upon your own poop.**" (John Sharkey, making Copley Banks his consort but threatening him with death for any betrayal, *The Dealings of Captain Sharkey and Other Tales of Pirates* "How Copley Banks Slew Captain Sharkey" 69)

I'll come back from hell to settle with you [*I'ee'ull cahm/carrm/coohm back ferm 'ell t'/ta/ter seh'le weth/wi'/wiff/witt 'ee/ya/ye/yer*]

> "[I]t shall be our turn, even if William Brand must **come back from hell to settle with you.**" (Abraham Dawling, promising vengeance from the ghost of William Brand, *The Book of Pirates* "The Ghost of Captain Brand" 50)

I'll crack you like a flea [*I'ee'ull crarrk/creck 'ee/ya/ye/yer lawk/lyeeke a OR liker flea*]

> "It is not in your power to do me harm. You are not even in my way. If you were, **I should crack you like a flea.**" (Captain Tondeur, *Captain Blood Returns* 199)

I'll cut off your ears [*I'ee'ull carrt/cooht arrf ya/yarr/ye/yer/yere/yore ee-arrs/errs*]

> "By God's life if he were my man **I would cut off his ears**; yea, by God's wounds I would hang him." (Francis Drake, *The Queen's Corsair* 104)

I'll cut out that tongue of yours and watch you eat it [*I'ee'ull carrt/cooht arrt/ou'/owoot tharrt toohngue o'\on yarrs/yer'n/yourn\theys an'/'n' warrtch 'ee/ya/ye/yer eat ett/'n*]

A threat that doubles as a concise retort to any unpleasantry.

> "Some day, Abny, some day, **I shall cut out that tongue o' yourn and watch ye eat it,** lad, eat it—hist, here cometh Gregory

at last—easy all." (Roger Tressady, *Black Bartlemy's Treasure* 96)

I'll cut out your liver [*I'ee'ull carrt/cooht arrt/ou'/owoot ya/yarr/ye/yer/yere/yore levv/libb/li'-er*]

"You old son of a bitch, I know you and you shall go along with us or **I'll cut out your liver.**" (pirate from the *Night Rambler* threatening a prisoner with a cutlass, *Lives of the Most Remarkable Criminals* 475)

I'll cut you down like so much bark [*I'ee'ull carrt/cooht 'ee/ya/ye/yer dowoon lawk/lyeeke so'oo marrch/moohch bahrrk*]

"Or **cuts 'em down like so much bark.** Flint's way, that'd be." (Long John Silver, "Treasure Island" [1972] 40:57)

I'll cut you down to the deck [*I'ee'ull carrt/cooht 'ee/ya/ye/yer dowoon t'/ta/ter t' dack*]

"**Cut 'im down to the deck.**" (Billy Bowlegs, "Long John Silver's Return to Treasure Island" 16:48)

I'll cut you in pound pieces [*I'ee'ull carrt/cooht 'ee/ya/ye/yer i'/'n poun'/pount/powoon'/powoond/powoont peeshes*]

*[T]hey ... ordered one of the prisoners, who had been an officer with Captain Mackra, to tell them the private signals between the [East India] Company's ships, the captain swearing **he would cut him in pound pieces**, if he did not do it immediately ...* (Edward England's successor, *General History of the Pyrates* 123)

I'll cut you in sunder [*I'ee'ull carrt/cooht 'ee/ya/ye/yer i'/'n soohnder*] I'll cut you in two; I'll cut you apart

"[I'll] **cut [you] in sunder** if [you] d[o]n't make haste to go on board the pirate with [your] books and instruments." (William White, forcing navigator Henry Gyles to join John Phillips' company, *Pirates of the New England Coast* 320)

I'll cut you into ounces [*I'ee'ull carrt/cooht 'ee/ya/ye/yer in-ta/terr owoonces*]

"**I will cut the man into ounces** who comes betwixt us!" (John Sharkey, claiming a female prisoner for himself, *The Dealings of Captain Sharkey and Other Tales of Pirates* "The Blighting of Sharkey" 55)

I'll cut you open [*I'ee'ull carrt/cooht 'ee/ya/ye/yer ho/hoo/oo-perrn*]

"Tell me, lad. Have ye the kidney fer **cuttin' a man open** fer 'is purse?" (Long John Silver, *Dead Man's Chest* 11)

I'll cut you to pieces [*I'ee'ull carrt/cooht 'ee/ya/ye/yer t'/ta/ter peeshes*]

*The first orders they issued ... chiefly forbade any man to set a foot abaft the main mast, except they were called to the helm, upon pain of **being immediately cut to pieces** ...* (account of John Gow and his fellow seven mutineers' instructions to the remaining crew after taking over a merchant vessel, *Lives of the Most Remarkable Criminals* 579)

I'll cut your heart out [*I'ee'ull carrt/cooht ya/yarr/ye/yer/yere/yore 'ahrrt/'eart/hahrrt arrt/ou'/owoot*]

"I am determined to possess myself of that ivory ball, and have it I shall, even though **I am obliged to cut out your heart** to get it!" (Hunt, *The Book of Pirates* "The Ruby of Kishmoor" 226)

I'll cut your heart out and eat it before you [*I'ee'ull carrt/cooht ya/yarr/ye/yer/yere/yore 'ahrrt/'eart/hahrrt arrt/ou'/owoot an'/'n' eat ett/'n afarr/afore/befarr/'farr/'fore 'ee/ya/ye/yer*]

"Get back there or **I'll cut your heart out and eat it afore ye.**" (Billy Bones, *Porto Bello Gold* 67)

I'll cut your throat ear to ear [*I'ee'ull carrt/cooht ya/yarr/ye/yer/yere/yore thro'oot ee-arr/err t'/ta/ter ee-arr/err*]

"Not a word to nobody sayin' where you took me to. That is, unless you wants your throat cut ear to ear." (Billy Bones, "Treasure Island" [1960] 2:27)

I'll cut your throat to the neckbone [*I'ee'ull carrt/cooht ya/yarr/ye/yer/yere/yore thro'oot t'/ta/ter t' nack-boone/bo'oone*]

> "It'd be a mortal shame if you was to cry out now—**I might** jus' let this here knife slip and **cut ya throat to the neck-bone**." (Long John Silver, "Treasure Island" [1990] 2:05:53)

I'll cut your weasand [*I'ee'ull carrt/cooht ya/yarr/ye/yer/yere/yore weasan'*]

A weasand is a throat.

> "[I]f we don't get it, why, I'll tell you plain, **we'll burn them** bloody crafts of yours that we've took over yonder, and **cut the weasand** of every clodpoll aboard of 'em." (Captain Richards, threatening the governor of South Carolina into giving him a supply of medicines, *The Book of Pirates* "Buccaneers and Marooners of the Spanish Main" 30)

I'll damn you and your vessel also [*I'ee'ull damn 'ee/ya/ye/yer an'/'n' ya/yarr/ye/yer/yere/ yore vassel awrl-so'oo*]

The term "damn" here is used figuratively to mean "destroy" rather than "condemn to hell."

> *Pirates told one captain ... if we catch you in "one lye, **we'll damn you and your vessel also**."* (*Villains of All Nations* 15)

I'll dangle you from the foreyard [*I'ee'ull dengle 'ee/ya/ye/yer ferm t' farr-yahrrd/yerd*]

A yard is a spar, or wood pole, that is set perpendicular to and extends horizontally across a mast, supporting a square sail. The foreyard is the lowest yard on a vessel's fore-mast (mast closest to the bow of a vessel with two or more masts).

> "And **I'll dangle Uncle Harry from the foreyard**." (Blackbeard, "Blackbeard the Pirate" 1:20:34)

I'll despatch you hot-foot to your mas-ter Sathanas [*I'ee'ull ders-patch 'ee/ya/ye/yer harrt-foot t'/ta/ter ya/yarr/ye/yer/yere/yore marrster Sathanas*]

An elaborate way of threatening to send the addressee to hell.

> "Aha, messmate, there's many such as **I've despatched hot-foot to their master Sathanas**, 'twixt then and now." (Resolution Day, *Martin Conisby's Vengeance* 73)

I'll devour you at a gulp [*I'ee'ull der-varr/ vowarr 'ee/ya/ye/yer a'/hat a goolp*]

> "[M]y ship is off the harbour. She carries two hundred of the toughest fighting-men, who **would devour your** spineless militia **at a gulp**." (Peter Blood, *Captain Blood Returns* 125)

I'll drown you in a puddle [*I'ee'ull drownd/ drowoon/drowoond 'ee/ya/ye/yer i'/'n a pooh-dle/pu'l*]

The puddle envisioned, in this case, is one consisting of the addressee's own blood.

> "Disobey me again and **I'll drown ye in a puddle**." (Roger Tressady, *Black Bartlemy's Treasure* 308)

I'll drub you within an inch of your life, and that inch also [*I'ee'ull droohb 'ee/ya/ye/yer weth/ wi'/wiff/witt-in a ench o'\on ya/yarr/ye/yer/yere/ yore lawf/lyeefe, an'/'n' tharrt ench awrl-so'oo*]

> "[S]peak out, or **I will drub you within an inch of your life, and that inch also!**" (John Sharkey, *The Dealings of Captain Sharkey and Other Tales of Pirates* "The Blighting of Sharkey" 57)

I'll eat your liver for breakfast [*I'ee'ull eat ya/yarr/ye/yer/yere/yore levv/libb/li'-er farr/fer brayk/breff-farrst/fess*]

> "One more word of your sauce, and **I'll eat your liver for breakfast!**" (Long John Sil-ver, "Treasure Island" [1990] 1:44:34)

I'll essay a sword trick or so on that car-case o' yours [*I'ee'ull ass-ayee a sarrd/swarrd* *treck arr so'oo o'\on tharrt cahrr-cahss/cush/ kerss o'\on yarrs/yer'n/yourn\theys]*

"And now, when you're ready, come to me in the coach and there **I'll essay a sword trick or so on that little carcase o' thine!**" (Absalom Troy, *Adam Penfeather, Buccaneer* 111)

I'll feed you piecemeal to __ [*I'ee'ull feed 'ee/ya/ye/yer peesh-mee'ell t'/ta/ter __*]

"Now clear up them there shambles, or **I'll feed you piecemeal to** the rats in the cellar." (Long John Silver, "Long John Silver's Return to Treasure Island" 2:17)

I'll feed you to the sharks [*I'ee'ull feed 'ee/ ya/ye/yer t'/ta/ter t' shahrrks/shairks*]

"And what did they do? Genteel, like me, you thinks? No. They slices them dons like bread loaves and **feeds them to the sharks.**" (Billy Bones, "Treasure Island" [1934] 8:18)

I'll fillet you like a herring [*I'ee'ull fillet 'ee/ ya/ye/yer lawk/lyeeke a OR liker 'err-in'*]

"So you get the 'ell out of 'ere before I **fillet you like a herring.**" (George Merry, "Treasure Island" [1998] 1:19:00)

I'll fly your bloody head as my banner [*I'ee'ull flyee ya/yarr/ye/yer/yere/yore bloohd/ bluh'/blutt-y 'ead/hayd as me/myee benner*]

"**I will fly his bloody head as my banner.**" (Morgan Adams, "Cutthroat Island" 7:25)

I'll get the heart of you [*I'ee'ull ge'/git t' 'ahrrt/'eart/hahrrt o'\on 'ee/ya/ye/yer*]

"The other's that young cub **I'm gonna get the heart of.**" (George Merry, "Treasure Island" [1972] 1:27:02)

I'll give you a bellyful of pickling brine [*I'ee'ull gi'/giff 'ee/ya/ye/yer a bellyful o'\on peck-lin' brawn/bryeene*]

The implication here is that the speaker intends to split the addressee's abdomen open, then dump him into the ocean.

"Keep your tongue behind your teeth! Hold still, the two o' ye, or **I'll give ye a bellyful o' pickling brine.**" (John Flint, *Porto Bello Gold* 132)

I'll give you the Spanish torture [*I'ee'ull gi'/giff 'ee/ya/ye/yer t' Sparrn-ersh/esh tarrture*]

The phrase "Spanish torture" can be used to refer to any number of seventeenth- and eighteenth-century torture methods and devices closely associated with or distinctive to the Spanish, in particular: the rack, whereupon a victim's back and limbs were slowly stretched to breaking; the mouth pear, a device consisting of a metal bulb on one end and a screw and shaft on the other, the bulb end of which was inserted into a victim's mouth and the screw turned so as to cause the bulb to unfold slowly but powerfully (thus destroying the lower part of the victim's face); "hoisting," in which a victim's hands were bound and looped over a rope that was then raised such that the victim's body was suspended in the air (with excruciating pain to wrists, shoulders, and back, and constriction of chest); and the whipping of the soles of one's feet.

"**Give 'im the Spanish torture!**" (member of Long John Silver's company, "Treasure Island" [1990] 1:39:50)

I'll grind your mealy-mouthed jib into the dirt [*I'ee'ull grawnd/grin'/gryeen'/gryeend ya/yarr/ye/yer/yere/yore mealy-mowoothed jeb in-ta/terr t'/ta/ter darrt*]

A jib is a triangular sail at the head of a vessel set on lines extending from the foremast and the bowsprit. Here "jib" is likely used as nautical slang for "face," probably in recognition of the jib's prominence as a vessel's forward-most feature.

"I'll bring my boot to ya, and **I'll grind your mealy-mouthed jib into the dirt,** I will!" (Blackbeard, "Blackbeard's Ghost" 1:03:25)

I'll gut you [*I'ee'ull garrt/gooht 'ee/ya/ye/yer*]
I'll disembowel you; I'll cut open your abdomen and remove your intestines

> "When I have **gutted** one or two of them
> they may hear reason." (John Sharkey,
> learning of his men's planned mutiny,
> *The Dealings of Captain Sharkey and Other
> Tales of Pirates* "The Blighting of Sharkey" 48)

**I'll hang you from a\the yardarm (by your
thumbs)** [*I'ee'ull 'ang 'ee/ya/ye/yer ferm a\t'
yahrrd-ahrrm/erm (byee ya/yarr/ye/yer/yere/
yore thoohmbs/t'umbs)*]
A yardarm is the end of a yard on a square-
rigged ship. A yard, in turn, is a wood pole
supporting a square sail.

> **I might** with justice **hang you from the
> yard-arm** with your ruffian, as pirates
> both." (Adam Penfeather, *Adam Penfeather,
> Buccaneer* 255) "Now you call me Cap'n
> or, by thunder, **I'm gonna** pin you to the
> wall with this cutlass and **hang you from
> a yardarm by your thumbs** and use
> you for musket practice." (Billy Bones,
> "Treasure Island" [1990] 6:51)

**I'll hang you over the end of a gun and
scatter your innards all over the sugar
cane fields** [*I'ee'ull 'ang 'ee/ya/ye/yer ober/
o'er t' aynd o'\on a garrn/goohn an'/'n' scarrter
ya/yarr/ye/yer/yere/yore ennards awrl ober/o'er
t' shu'ar cayeene fiel's*]
A threat appropriate for any pirate in the Caribbean, where sugar cane fields are prevalent.

> "Lads, lads, lads, we shouldn't hang this
> man. **Hang him over the end of a gun
> and I'll scatter his innards all over the
> sugar cane fields**." (Henry Hagthorpe,
> "Captain Blood" 1:00:02)

I'll hang you up [*I'ee'ull 'ang 'ee/ya/ye/yer
arrp*]

> "Deal with them as Magellan did. **Hang
> them up** to be an example to the rest!"
> (John Saracold, *The Queen's Corsair* 56)

I'll hang you up at the yard's arm [*I'ee'ull 'ang
'ee/ya/ye/yer arrp at t' yahrrds-ahrrm/erm*]

> "You d[o]g, Ashton, deserve to **be hang'd
> up at the yards arm**, for designing to
> cut us off." (Francis Farrington Spriggs,
> threatening a prisoner's life after discov-
> ering his plot to take over the ship, *Pirates
> of the New England Coast* 241)

**I'll have you first hanged and then behead-
ed** [*I'ee'ull 'aff/'ave/ha'/haff 'ee/ya/ye/yer farrst/
firss 'anged an'/'n' thayn b'-'ead/hayd-ered*]

> *Drake then appeared angry and said that
> if Pascual didn't shut up and do what
> he was told, **he would have him first
> hanged and then beheaded**.* (account of
> Francis Drake's interrogation of a Portu-
> guese pilot, *The Queen's Corsair* 226)

I'll have you for my prize [*I'ee'ull 'aff/'ave/
ha'/haff 'ee/ya/ye/yer farr/fer me/myee prawz/
pryeeze*]
A "prize" is any item plundered by pirates
by force or threat of force. It is used especially
to refer to a vessel taken by pirates, but here
the reference is to the addressee himself.

> "**Alacan'll have you fer his prize**, or send
> you to Davey Jones' locker." (Alacan the
> Turk, *Dead Man's Chest* 55)

I'll have you hanged [*I'ee'ull 'aff/'ave/ha'/haff
'ee/ya/ye/yer 'anged*]

> "I charge you on pain of death not once to
> come before the mast, for if you do, I swear
> **I shall have you hanged!**" (Francis Drake,
> excoriating his shipboard minister Francis
> Fletcher, *The Queen's Corsair* 283)

**I'll have you roved to a gun and flayed
with whips** [*I'ee'ull 'aff/'ave/ha'/haff 'ee/ya/
ye/yer rooved/ro'ooved t'/ta/ter a garrn/goohn
an'/'n' flayeed weth/wi'/wiff/witt wheps*]
"Rove" is the past tense of "reeve," which
means to pass (as in a rope) through a hole,
block, groove, or other opening. Used loosely,
to "reeve" someone to something is to tie him
to it. This threat is an implicit reference to an

eighteenth-century punishment administered in the Royal Navy known as the "gunner's daughter" or "kissing the gunner's daughter," wherein the disciplined sailor was tied to a cannon known by that name and prescribed a certain number of lashes.

> "You shall be rove to a gun and flayed with whips ..." (Captain Jo, *Martin Conisby's Vengeance* 94)

I'll have your eye out [*I'ee'ull 'aff/'ave/ha'/haff ya/yarr/ye/yer/yere/yore eye'ee arrt/ou'/owoot*]

> "Let's **have his eye out**." (The Frog, "Pirates" 1:23:07)

I'll have your (cowardly) heart for (my) supper [*I'ee'ull 'aff/'ave/ha'/haff ya/yarr/ye/yer/yere/yore (carrd/cowahrrd/cowar'/cowart-ly) 'ahrrt/'eart/hahrrt farr/fer (me/myee) soohpper*]

> "She be my prize this time, or by the powers, **I'll have yer cowardly heart fer me supper!**" (Alacan the Turk, *Dead Man's Chest* 52) "But if we set sail and this turns out to be another of yer lies, **I'll have yer heart fer supper!**" (Joshua Smoot, *Dead Man's Chest* 158)

I'll have your heart's blood [*I'ee'ull 'aff/'ave/ha'/haff ya/yarr/ye/yer/yere/yore 'ahrrt's/'eart's/hahrrt's bloohd/blut*]

> "Then a parcel of bloodhound rogues clashed their cutlasses and said **they would have** it or **our heart's blood** ..." (Solomon Lloyd's account of threats made by Robert Culliford's pirate company, *The Pirate Hunter* 173)

I'll have your life [*I'ee'ull 'aff/'ave/ha'/haff ya/yarr/ye/yer/yere/yore lawf/lyeefe*]

> "Ye bloody, murthering Quaker, I'll have that ivory ball, or **I'll have your life!**" (Benny Willitts, *The Book of Pirates* "The Ruby of Kishmoor" 239)

I'll heave you to the shore [*I'ee'ull 'eave/heef 'ee/ya/ye/yer t'/ta/ter t' sharr/shoor*]

> "Devil burn ya, you one-legged squid. **I'll heave ya to the shore.**" (Billy Bowlegs, "Long John Silver's Return to Treasure Island" 15:48)

I'll introduce you to the sharks [*I'ee'ull en-ter/tro'oo-duce 'ee/ya/ye/yer t'/ta/ter t' shahrrks/shairks*]

> "But **I'll cure you, lad, or introduce you to the sharks** before long." (pirate captain, *The Coral Island* 201)

I'll keel-haul you [*I'ee'ull kee'ell 'aul/'awrl/hawrl 'ee/ya/ye/yer*]

"Keel-hauling" is a punishment popular among pirates wherein the victim is hauled on a rope under a vessel's hull from one side to another or (less typically) from one end to another—quickly enough so that he does not die from drowning, but slowly enough that his body scrapes hard against the barnacles and other rough detritus accumlated on the hull surface.

> < "Oh, I very much doubt if Miss Willoughby will let the children accept your gifts." "She'd better, or else **I'll keel-'aul the ol' witch.**" > (Reverend Monaster & Long John Silver, "The Adventures of Long John Silver: The Orphans' Christmas" 6:03)

I'll kick you into the scuppers [*I'ee'ull keck 'ee/ya/ye/yer in-ta/terr t' scarr/skooh-pers*]

A "scupper" is a drain leading water from a gutter, or from a low point on a deck or in the floor of an enclosed space, over a vessel's side and into the sea. This threat is the seaman's equivalent to the street tough's menace, "I'll kick you into the gutter."

> < "But why is Absalom so prisoned?" "For saving the ship and **kicking lubberly Captain into the scuppers**, Adam." > (Adam Penfeather & Smy Peters, *Adam Penfeather, Buccaneer* 64)

I'll kick your figurehead clean adrift [*I'ee'ull keck ya/yarr/ye/yer/yere/yore fegger/figger-'ead/hayd clean a-dreff/dreft/driff*]

A vessel's figurehead is an ornamental carved-wood figure on the top part of a vessel's bow, below the bowsprit and facing forward. "Figurehead" here is used to refer to the addressee's skull.

> "Ay, sir, but looked like as you'd **kicked his figure'ead clean adrift**, Cap'n." (Thomas Ash, *Adam Penfeather, Buccaneer* 204)

I'll knock out your brains [*I'ee'ull knarrk arrt/ ou'/owoot ya/yarr/ye/yer/yere/yore brayeens*]

> "Kidd [is] a very lusty man, fighting with his own men on any little occasion, often calling for his pistols and threatening anyone that durst speak of anything contrary to his mind to **knock out their brains**—causes them to dread him." (William Mason, recalling the menacing words and shipboard behavior of Captain William Kidd, *The Pirate Hunter* 137)

I'll lash the hide off your back [*I'ee'ull larrsh t' hawd/hyeede/'ide/'ieede arrf ya/yarr/ye/yer/ yere/yore back*]

> "And keep your eyes off Captain Paxton or **I'll lash the hide off your back**." (Henry Morgan, "Pirates of Tortuga" 1:10:55)

I'll lay you open [*I'ee'ull layee 'ee/ya/ye/yer ho/hoo/oo-perrn*]

> "Stand out, Sweetlocks, and **I will lay you open**!" (John Sharkey, wishing his enemy to step forward in order to kill him, *The Dealings of Captain Sharkey and Other Tales of Pirates* "The Blighting of Sharkey" 58)

I'll let out your evil soul by incision of steel [*I'ee'ull laaht/le' arrt/ou'/owoot ya/yarr/ ye/yer/yere/yore ayvil sool/so'ool byee 'cision/ encision o'\on stee'ell*]

> "It is my constant prayer that I may be so blest to **let out his evil soul by incision of steel** beneath his fifth rib, or—watch him hang, for 'tis very son o' Belial." (Smy Peters, *Adam Penfeather, Buccaneer* 21)

I'll let you know which of us two is __ and which is __ [*I'ee'ull laaht/le' 'ee/ya/ye/yer knowoo whech o'\on arrs two be __ an'/'n' whech be __*]

Used to threaten someone while demeaning him. The speaker fills in the blanks with a pair of descriptions (of himself and of the addressee) that yield a comparatively unfavorable characterization of the addressee.

> "None of your rover tricks, Ned Galloway, unless they are called for, or **I'll let you know which of us two is** captain **and which is** quartermaster." (John Sharkey, annoyed by Galloway's over-eagerness to kill their prisoner, *The Dealings of Captain Sharkey and Other Tales of Pirates* "How the Governor of Saint Kitt's Came Home" 23)

I'll let you some of your sluggish blood [*I'ee'ull laaht/le' 'ee/ya/ye/yer sahm/sarrm/soohm o'\on ya/yarr/ye/yer/yere/yore sloohggish bloohd/blut*]

> "You have a sword, I mind—go fetch it and I will teach ye punto riverso, the stoccato, the imbrocato, and **let you some o' your sluggish**, English **blood**." (Captain Jo, *Martin Conisby's Vengeance* 18)

I'll make you refund [*I'ee'ull mayeeke 'ee/ya/ ye/yer refoohnd*] I'll make you pay

> *Lewis told his men, they were a parcel of rogues, and **he would make 'em refund**; accordingly run along side, his guns being all loaded and new primed, and ordered him to cut away his mast, or he would sink him.* (attribution to Captain Lewis, *General History of the Pyrates* 598–99)

I'll maroon you for a lifetime [*I'ee'ull mahrroon 'ee/ya/ye/yer farr/fer a lawf/lyeefe-tawm/tyeeme*]

> "I, by God's help, rebuked them, though many times [they had] their pistols to my breast telling me that if I would not, **they would maroon me for my lifetime**." (William Willock, describing the threatening words and conduct of Robert Culliford's company, *The Pirate Hunter* 170)

I'll mischief you [*I'ee'ull mes-cheff/cheef 'ee/ya/ye/yer*]

To "mischief" someone is to cause him serious harm in an inspecific way. Close modern equivalents to "I'll mischief you"—matching both the severity and the ambiguity of the threatened harm—include "I'll kick your ass" and "I'll fuck you up."

> "Hold off or **I'll mischief ye!**" (Benjamin Trigg, seeing his friend Adam Penfeather pummeled to the ground, *Adam Penfeather, Buccaneer* 72)

I'll peel your skin like a mango [*I'ee'ull pee'ell ya/yarr/ye/yer/yere/yore sken lawk/lyeeke a OR liker mango'oo*]

> "I promise you, Long John Silver, should you ever venture beyond the breakwater, **I will peel your skin like a mango.**" (El Toro Mendoza, "Long John Silver's Return to Treasure Island" 28:15)

I'll pin you to the wall with this cutlass [*I'ee'ull pen/pinnt 'ee/ya/ye/yer t'/ta/ter t' wawrl weth/wi'/wiff/witt dis/t'is carrt/cooht-lerss/lish*]

A cutlass is a thick, heavy, slightly curving sword with a flat, single-edged blade.

> "Now you call me Cap'n or, by thunder, **I'm gonna pin you to the wall with this cutlass** and hang you from a yardarm by your thumbs and use you for musket practice." (Billy Bones, "Treasure Island" [1990] 6:51)

I'll pipeclay you [*I'ee'ull pawp/pyeepe-clayee 'ee/ya/ye/yer*]

"Pipeclay" is a verb meaning "to clear away or get rid of" but is also a noun meaning a very fine white clay used in making tobacco pipes and pottery. This threat likely borrows on the first meaning (e.g., "I'll get rid of you," "I'll wipe you clean") rather than the second, though the threat "I'll turn you to pipeclay" admittedly finds a counterpart in the modern expression "I'll pulverize you."

> "**I'll pipeclay the** — who misses the — dago." (Martin, *Porto Bello Gold* 149, omissions in original)

I'll plunge you forthwith to the very deeps of hell [*I'ee'ull ploohnge 'ee/ya/ye/yer farrf/farrt/farrth/forf/fort-weth/wi'/wiff/witt t'/ta/ter t' vaah/vay-ry deeps o'\on 'ell*]

> "'Tis my assured hope this death and damnation shall be theirs and we the instruments o' Grace by means o' steel and round-shot to **plunge 'em forthwith to the very deeps of hell.**" (Amos Perrin, *Adam Penfeather, Buccaneer* 117)

I'll put a ball between your eyes [*I'ee'ull put a bawrl 'tween\betwixt/twixt ya/yarr/ye/yer/yere/yore eye'ees*] I'll shoot you dead

The "ball" referenced is the ball shot from a pistol or musket.

> "**Put a ball between his eyes.**" (Dawg Brown, "Cutthroat Island" 1:19:57)

I'll put a bullet through you [*I'ee'ull put a bullert t'roo 'ee/ya/ye/yer*]

> "Do but give me the word, Your Honor, and **I'll put another bullet through** the son of a sea cook." (John Malyoe's sailing master, *The Book of Pirates* "The Ghost of Captain Brand" 51)

I'll put an inch of my knife into you [*I'ee'ull put a ench o'\on me/myee knawf/knyeefe in-ta/terr 'ee/ya/ye/yer*]

The hyperspecificity of this threat makes it all the more real, imminent, and unsettling.

> "**Put an inch of your knife into him**, Ned. Now, will you wave your hat?" (John Sharkey, *The Dealings of Captain Sharkey and Other Tales of Pirates* "The Dealings of Captain Sharkey with Stephen Craddock" 42)

I'll rip out your liver [*I'ee'ull rep arrt/ou'/owoot ya/yarr/ye/yer/yere/yore levv/libb/li'-er*]

> "Why then, sheer off, afore **I rip out your livers,** —both o' ye!" (Absalom Troy, *Adam Penfeather, Buccaneer* 27)

I'll rip you from belly to chine [*I'ee'ull rep 'ee/ ya/ye/yer ferm belly t'/ta/ter chawn/chyeene*]

The chine is one's spine or backbone.

> "Question me honor again, would you, and I'll rip you from belly to chine." (William Kidd, "Captain Kidd" 5:31)

I'll rip you the length of your vest [*I'ee'ull rep 'ee/ya/ye/yer t' lenf o'\on ya/yarr/ye/yer/ yere/yore vast*]

The speaker threatens to slice the address-ee's abdomen from collar to waist. The refer-ence to a vest evokes implicitly the graphic possibility that the resulting wound might hang open or flap back and forth like the two halves of an unbuttoned garment.

> "I may live to rip you the length of your vest for this night's work." (John Shar-key, *The Dealings of Captain Sharkey and Other Tales of Pirates* "The Blighting of Sharkey" 49)

I'll run you through [*I'ee'ull roohn 'ee/ya/ ye/yer t'roo*]

To "run someone through" is to impale him with a sword, such that the end protrudes out his back.

> "The map! Tell me where it is or I'll run you through!" (Dawg Brown, "Cutthroat Island" 39:03)

I'll sacrifice you [*I'ee'ull sarrcri/sarrki-fawce/ fyeece 'ee/ya/ye/yer*]

> "Damn you I know you and will sacri-fice you." (Walter Kennedy, just before punching captured merchant captain Thomas Grant in the mouth, likely to avenge cruelties he had suffered as a merchant seaman under other captains, *Villains of All Nations* 40)

I'll scuttle you [*I'ee'ull scu'le 'ee/ya/ye/yer*]

To "scuttle" someone is to destroy or get rid of him.

> "Surrender your ship or we'll scuttle ya." (Montbars, "Pirates of Tortuga" 40:48)

I'll see the colour of your inside [*I'ee'ull see t' cahlerr o'\on ya/yarr/ye/yer/yere/yore en-sawd/syeede*]

> "Take a cutlass, him that dares, and I'll see the colour of his inside, crutch and all, before that pipe's empty." (Long John Silver, *Treasure Island* 159)

I'll see you bleed [*I'ee'ull see 'ee/ya/ye/yer bleed*]

> "Or I shall see you bleed ..." (Adam Pen-feather, *Adam Penfeather, Buccaneer* 280)

I'll see you in hell [*I'ee'ull see 'ee/ya/ye/yer i'/'n 'ell*]

The speaker apprises the addressee that he is about to die, while acknowledging that he himself is sufficiently villainous that he is also bound for hell.

> "I'll see you in hell." (Black Harry, "Cut-throat Island" 5:35)

I'll see you skewered on the end of a pike [*I'ee'ull see 'ee/ya/ye/yer skooered arrn/o' t' aynd o'\on a pawk/pyeeke*]

A pike is a long spear or spiked pole.

> "And I'd 'ate to see the likes o' you skew-ered on the end of a pike." (Long John Silver, "Treasure Island" [1950] 59:10)

I'll see you to Davy Jones [*I'ee'ull see 'ee/ya/ye/ yer t'/ta/ter Daah/Dayee-vy Joones/Jo'oones*]

"Davy Jones" (or "Davy Jones' locker") is the seaman's traditional personification of, and way of referring to, the bottom of the ocean, especially as a graveyard for those killed at sea.

> "By thunder, we'll see ya to Davy Jones!" (pirate captain, "Pirates of the Caribbean" Disney attraction)

I'll send a ball through your brisket [*I'ee'ull sen' a bawrl t'roo ya/yarr/ye/yer/yere/yore bres/ brish-kert*]

The ball referenced is the ball shot from a pistol or musket. Brisket is ribmeat taken from an animal's chest.

"Let one so much as level at me, Captain, and **I send a ball through your brisket,** forthwith." (Benjamin Trigg, *Adam Penfeather, Buccaneer* 75)

I'll send a quick and sure messenger after you [*I'ee'ull sen' a queck an'/'n' sharr/shorr massen-jarr arrf/ar/haf-ter 'ee/ya/ye/yer*]

The speaker's sly reference to "a quick and sure messenger" is to a pistol or musket ball.

"Now, go, make a fire on that point; and hark'ee, youngster, if you try to run away, **I'll send a quick and sure messenger after you.**" (pirate, brandishing his gun, *The Coral Island* 196)

I'll send you down [*I'ee'ull sen' 'ee/ya/ye/yer dowoon*]

A threat to sink or drown the addressee—to send him to the bottom of the ocean.

"Ahoy! Stand clear, or **I'll send you down!**" (member of Blackbeard's company to a fishing fleet passing close by, "Blackbeard the Pirate" 39:55)

I'll send you headlong to hell [*I'ee'ull sen' 'ee/ya/ye/yer 'ead/hayd-larrng t'/ta/ter 'ell*]

"[B]ut if you will be a villain and betray your trust, may G[o]d strike me dead, and may I drink a bowl of brimstone and fire with the D[evi]l, **if I don't send you head-long to H[e]ll,** G[o]d d[am]n me ..." (William Fly, *General History of the Pyrates* 611)

I'll send you to Davy Jones(') (locker) [*I'ee'ull sen' 'ee/ya/ye/yer t'/ta/ter Daah/Dayee-vy Joones/Jo'oones (larrker)*]

"Davy Jones" (or "Davy Jones' locker") is the seaman's traditional personification of, and way of referring to, the bottom of the ocean, especially as a graveyard for those killed at sea.

"And bring me Cap'n Sparrow, or **I'll be sendin' ya ta Davy Jones.**" (Barbossa, "Pirates of the Caribbean" Disney attraction [2006]) "Alacan'll have you fer his prize, or **send you to Davey Jones' locker.**" (Alacan the Turk, *Dead Man's Chest* 55)

I'll send you to feed the bleedin' catfish [*I'ee'ull sen' 'ee/ya/ye/yer t'/ta/ter feed t' bleedin' carrt-fesh*]

"You lay another hand on that lad, **I'll send you** where I sent many others these thirty years—**to feed the bleedin' catfish.**" (Long John Silver, "Treasure Island" [1960] 1:03:55)

I'll send you to hell-fire [*I'ee'ull sen' 'ee/ya/ye/yer t'/ta/ter 'ell-farr/fyarr*]

"Look'ee my hearty boys, the first man as setteth foot atwhart this line **I send to hell-fire** along o' Tom Purdy yonder!" (Roger Tressady, *Black Bartlemy's Treasure* 313)

I'll send you to the bottom [*I'ee'ull sen' 'ee/ya/ye/yer t'/ta/ter t' barrtom*]

A threat to sink or drown the addressee—to send him to the bottom of the ocean.

"Strike sail yourself, Master Juan de Anton, in the name of the Queen of England! Or **we'll send you to the bottom!**" (pirate aboard the *Golden Hind*, demanding the surrender of the Spanish treasure ship *Cacafuego*, *The Queen's Corsair* 183)

I'll send you to torment your father, the devil [*I'ee'ull sen' 'ee/ya/ye/yer t'/ta/ter tarrmant ya/yarr/ye/yer/yere/yore faahth/farrth/fodd-er, t' daahv/dayv/debb/div-il*]

"I'll split ya starboard from larboard with me cutlass and **send ya to torment yer father, the devil!**" (Henry Morgan, *Dead Man's Chest* 10)

I'll send you with my service to the devil [*I'ee'ull sen' 'ee/ya/ye/yer weth/wi'/wiff/witt me/myee sarrvice t'/ta/ter t' daahv/dayv/debb/div-il*]

"[S]o either discharge your trust like an honest man; for go you shan't, by G[o]d, or **I'll send you with my service to the D[evi]l**; so no more words, G[o]d d[am]n ye." (William Fly, *General History of the Pyrates* 611)

I'll sever your gullet [*I'ee'ull sebber ya/yarr/ ye/yer/yere/yore goohlet*]

> "You barnacle! Next time **I'll sever your gullet!**" (Billy Bones, "Treasure Island" [1934] 14:23)

I'll shoot into you [*I'ee'ull shoot in-ta/terr 'ee/ya/ye/yer*]

> "If you undertake to come aboard of me, **I'll shoot into you.**" (Blackbeard, warning off an approaching privateer vessel, *The Book of Pirates* "Jack Ballister's Fortunes" 145)

I'll shoot you dead upon the deck [*I'ee'ull shoot 'ee/ya/ye/yer dayd 'parrn/'pon/uparrn t' dack*]

> *Captain Morgan ... threatened them that the first man among them who touched a drop of rum without his permission **he would shoot him dead upon the deck.*** (account of Henry Morgan's efforts to keep his crew sober until reaching Port Royal, *The Book of Pirates* "With the Buccaneers" 97)

I'll shoot you down [*I'ee'ull shoot 'ee/ya/ ye/yer dowoon*]

> "If either of you offer to stir, **I'll shoot you down.**" (Edward Low, refusing the pleas of two prisoners to be released, *Pirates of the New England Coast* 229)

I'll shoot you through the head [*I'ee'ull shoot 'ee/ya/ye/yer t'roo t' 'ead/hayd*]

> "You dog you! if you will not sign our articles, and go along with me, **I'll shoot you thro' the head.**" (Edward Low, threatening Philip Ashton into joining his company, *Pirates of the New England Coast* 228)

I'll show you a liver yet [*I'ee'ull showoo 'ee/ ya/ye/yer a levv/libb/li'-er yat*]

> "Off wi' you, ye dogs, or **I'll show ye a liver yet** ..." (Roger Tressady, *Black Bartlemy's Treasure* 309)

I'll show you the color of your insides [*I'ee'ull showoo 'ee/ya/ye/yer t' cahlerr o'\on ya/yarr/ye/yer/yere/yore en-sawds/syeedes*]

> "Draw a cutlass, him that dares, and **I'll show you the color of his insides.**" (Long John Silver, "Treasure Island" [1990] 1:40:24)

I'll skewer your guts [*I'ee'ull skoo-arr/err ya/yarr/ye/yer/yere/yore garrts/goohts*]

> "If only you had **skewered for me the guts** of that pimp who got away, I'ld be still more grateful to you." (George Fairfax, *The Fortunes of Captain Blood* 154)

I'll skin you alive [*I'ee'ull sken 'ee/ya/ye/yer '/er-lawv/lyeeve*]

> "I'll hunt you down! **I'll skin you alive!**" (The Frog, "Pirates" 1:53:28)

I'll skin you from the neck [*I'ee'ull sken 'ee/ ya/ye/yer ferm t' nack*]

> "**Skin 'im from the neck,** mate." (Tom Morgan, "Treasure Island" [1990] 1:39:48)

I'll slaughter you like a hog in springtime [*I'ee'ull slarrter 'ee/ya/ye/yer lawk/lyeeke a OR liker harrg/'og i'/'n spren'/spreng/sprin'-tawm/ tyeeme*]

> "Darr, **you'd be slaughtered like hogs in springtime.**" (Long John Silver, "Long John Silver's Return to Treasure Island" 1:19:38)

I'll slice you like a bread loaf [*I'ee'ull slawce/slyeece 'ee/ya/ye/yer lawk/lyeeke a OR liker brayd loof/lo'oof*]

> "And what did they do? Genteel, like me, you thinks? No. **They slices them dons like bread loaves** and feeds them to the sharks." (Billy Bones, "Treasure Island" [1934] 8:18)

I'll slice you through from ear to ear [*I'ee'ull slawce/slyeece 'ee/ya/ye/yer t'roo ferm ee-arr/err t'/ta/ter ee-arr/err*]

"Cut-an'-rip, I say. **Slice 'im through from ear to ear**." (pirate aboard the *Thistle*, "Long John Silver's Return to Treasure Island" 58:46)

I'll slice your liver [*I'ee'ull slawce/slyeece ya/yarr/ye/yer/yere/yore levv/libb/li'-er*]

"Sink me, but **I will slice your liver**, Captain Hardy, if you do not make good your words!" (John Sharkey, *The Dealings of Captain Sharkey and Other Tales of Pirates* "The Blighting of Sharkey" 52)

I'll slip a couple of feet of steel into your vitals [*I'ee'ull slep a couple o'\on feet o'\on stee'ell in-ta/terr ya/yarr/ye/yer/yere/yore vawt/vy'/vyeet-als*]

The steel is the speaker's sword.

"It's the same reason that's been urging me to pick a quarrel with you so that **I might have the satisfaction of slipping a couple of feet of steel into your vitals**." (Peter Blood, *Captain Blood: His Odyssey* 287)

I'll slit the veins of your arms and use your blood to warm my rum [*I'ee'ull slett t' vay-eens o'\on ya/yarr/ye/yer/yere/yore ahrrms an'/'n' yooss ya/yarr/ye/yer/yere/yore bloohd/blut t'/ta/ter wahrrm me/myee roohm*]

"And what did they do to the beauteous ladies? Why after courtin' of their favor, as it were, savin' your presence matey, **they slits the veins of their pearly-white arms and uses their blue blood to warm their rum**." (Billy Bones, "Treasure Island" [1934] 8:33)

I'll slit your ears [*I'ee'ull slett ya/yarr/ye/yer/yere/yore ee-arrs/errs*]

"I've a mind to **slit your** pimpish **ears** so that they may see what happens to them as gets pert with Captain Easterling." (Captain Easterling, *Captain Blood Returns* 283)

I'll slit your gullet [*I'ee'ull slett ya/yarr/ye/yer/yere/yore goohlet*]

< "I'll be bound. It's John Perch." "Him as took the King's pardon for piracy. **Slit the rest of his gullet**, I says." > (Patch & Old Stingley, "Long John Silver's Return to Treasure Island" 3:46)

I'll slit your throat [*I'ee'ull slett ya/yarr/ye/yer/yere/yore thro'oot*]

< "Here, you, be you certain this is the way?" "On the soul of my mother." "It had better be, or **I'll slit your throat**. Lead on." > (Long John Silver & Salamander the Greek, "The Adventures of Long John Silver: Pieces of Eight" 11:49)

I'll slit your weasand [*I'ee'ull slett ya/yarr/ye/yer/yere/yore weasan'*]

A weasand is a throat.

"A man o' lies and blood, to be rooted out, child! Yet content ye, for by the Lord's grace, **thou shalt see me slit his** treacherous **weasand** anon." (Lovepeace Farrance, promising violence to Don Luiz da Ramirez, *Winds of Chance* 46)

I'll snap you across my knee [*I'ee'ull snarrp 'ee/ya/ye/yer acrost/'cross/'crost\athwart me/myee knee*]

"**I could snap ye across my knee**, ay—choke the life out o' your pitiful carcass with my bare hands!" (Giles Tregenza, *Adam Penfeather, Buccaneer* 203)

I'll spear you like a shark [*I'ee'ull spee-arr/err 'ee/ya/ye/yer lawk/lyeeke a OR liker shahrrk/shairk*]

"**He coulda speared me like a shark** if he'd struck today." (Blackbeard, "Blackbeard the Pirate" 45:32)

I'll spit you clean and sweet [*I'ee'ull spett 'ee/ya/ye/yer clean an'/'n' sweet*]

"I captured it from a Portugee trader at the sack of Cartagena! **I spitted him, clean and sweet**, against the headboard." (Blackbeard, "Blackbeard's Ghost" 27:20)

I'll spit you like I would a dog [*I'ee'ull spett 'ee/ya/ye/yer lawk/lyeeke I'ee woood a darrg*]

> "**Spit** the spy **as you would a dog!**" (Nightingale, *The Red Rover* 492)

I'll split you double [*I'ee'ull splett 'ee/ya/ye/yer darrble/doohble*]

A threat to split the addressee in two.

> "**I'll split ya double**, you ..." (Billy Bones, running at Doctor Livesey with a drawn cutlass, "Treasure Island" [1934] 11:00)

I'll split you starboard from larboard [*I'ee'ull splett 'ee/ya/ye/yer sta'b'd/starbarrd/starberrd ferm la'b'd/larrbarrd/larberrd*]

A threat to split the addressee in two.

> "**I'll split ya starboard from larboard** with me cutlass and send ya to torment yer father, the devil!" (Henry Morgan, *Dead Man's Chest* 10)

I'll split you wide open [*I'ee'ull splett 'ee/ya/ye/yer wawd/wyeede ho/hoo/oo-perrn*]

> "I'm going to **split you wide open**." (Dawg Brown, "Cutthroat Island" 5:28)

I'll squeeze your squeezy cheese-head off your body [*I'ee'ull squeess ya/yarr/ye/yer/yere/yore squeessy cheese-'ead/hayd arrf ya/yarr/ye/yer/yere/yore bahee/barrdy*]

> "Shiver me timbers, **I'd like to squeeze** Mendoza's **squeezy cheese-head off his body**." (Patch, "Long John Silver's Return to Treasure Island" 6:44)

I'll stove in your __ like a rum puncheon [*I'ee'ull stoove/sto'oove i'/'n ya/yarr/ye/yer/yere/yore __ lawk/lyeeke a OR liker roohm poohn-chern*]

The speaker fills in the blank with some body part (*e.g.* skull) or thing (*e.g.* idle hopes) associated with the addressee. "Stove in" in modern English is the past-tense form of "stave in," meaning to break in, dent, or crush, but is used here as the main (or infinitive form of the) verb itself. (See generally Chapter 18: Wrong Talk.) A rum puncheon is a large wooden cask used to hold rum.

> "Before this hour's out, you mark my words, Captain Smollett, **I'll stove in this blockhouse like a rum puncheon**." (Long John Silver, "Treasure Island" [1990] 1:17:02)

I'll stuff you with straw and hang you for a figurehead [*I'ee'ull starff/stoohff 'ee/ya/ye/yer weth/wi'/wiff/witt strawrr an'/'n' 'ang 'ee/ya/ye/yer farr/fer a fegger/figger-'ead/hayd*]

> "[I]f he had laid hands upon any one of them **he would have stuffed him with straw and hung him for a figurehead**." (John Sharkey, impersonating the governor of St. Kitt's and hypothesizing what Sharkey might do to the jurors who convicted him of piracy, *The Dealings of Captain Sharkey and Other Tales of Pirates* "How the Governor of Saint Kitt's Came Home" 18)

I'll sweep you into the sea [*I'ee'ull sweep 'ee/ya/ye/yer in-ta/terr t' sea*]

> "**We'll sweep them** Spanish scum **into the sea!**" (Long John Silver, "The Adventures of Long John Silver: Sword of Vengeance" 4:30)

I'll swing you aloft [*I'ee'ull sweng 'ee/ya/ye/yer er-larrft*]

To "swing someone aloft" is to execute him by hanging.

> "There be thirty and eight **shall swing ye aloft** so soon as I give 'em the word, Tressady." (Adam Penfeather, *Black Bartlemy's Treasure* 316)

I'll swing you up to the mainyard [*I'ee'ull sweng 'ee/ya/ye/yer arrp t'/ta/ter t' mayeen-yahrrd/yerd*]

The speaker threatens to hang the addressee from the lowest yard (horizontal pole) on a vessel's mainmast.

> "In a few short hours, Martin, here will be ninety odd souls earnestly seeking to **swing you up to the main-yard** and you a-slumbering sweet as any innocent babe, and burn me, shipmate, I love you

the better for't!" (Adam Penfeather, *Black Bartlemy's Treasure* 157)

I'll take a peek at your brain [*I'ee'ull tayeeke a peek a'/hat ya/yarr/ye/yer/yere/yore brayeen*]

> < "Let's pluck his eye out." "Aye, there's a pretty notion. **Let's take a peek at his brain!**" > (The Frog & Thomas Bartholomew Red, "Pirates" 1:23:12)

I'll teach you the meaning of pain [*I'ee'ull teach 'ee/ya/ye/yer t' meanin' o'\on payeen*]

> "**I'm goin' to teach you the meanin' of pain.**" (unnamed pirate, "Pirates of the Caribbean: The Curse of the Black Pearl" 1:59:44)

I'll tear out your tongue and let it flap in the sun [*I'ee'ull tarr/tayarr/tayerr arrt/ou'/owoot ya/yarr/ye/yer/yere/yore toohngue an'/'n' laaht/le' ett/'n/'t flarrp i'/'n t' soohn*]

> "We'll take this slaver away from Cap'n MacDougal, **tear out his pious tongue, and let it flap a sermon in the sun.**" (Old Stingley, "Long John Silver's Return to Treasure Island" 58:55)

I'll tear you in pieces [*I'ee'ull tarr/tayarr/tayerr 'ee/ya/ye/yer i'/'n peeshes*]

> "Ye know I dursn't accept your offer. Ye know my men would **tear me in pieces** if I did so without consulting them." (Crosby Pike, *Captain Blood Returns* 283)

I'll tear your tongue out [*I'ee'ull tarr/tayarr/tayerr ya/yarr/ye/yer/yere/yore toohngue arrt/ou'/owoot*]

> "And I'll thank ya to keep your voice down or **I'll tear your tongue out.**" (Purity Pinker, "The Adventures of Long John Silver: The Eviction" 6:29)

I'll throttle you with my bare hands [*I'ee'ull thrarrt/throh'-le 'ee/ya/ye/yer weth/wi'/wiff/witt me/myee barr/bayarr/bayerr 'ands/'an's/han's*]

> "Is this another one of your tricks, Long John? **I'll throttle you with my bare**

hands." (Tom Morgan, furious on finding Flint's treasure spot but no treasure, "Treasure Island" [1960] 1:10:43)

I'll throw you overboard with a double-headed shot about your neck [*I'ee'ull throwoo 'ee/ya/ye/yer ober/o'er-barrd weth/wi'/wiff/witt a darrble/doohble-'ead/hayd-ered sharrt abarrt/abowoot/'barrt/'bout/'bowoot ya/yarr/ye/yer/yere/yore nack*]

> *Pirates told one captain that they would "**throw him over board with a double headed shot about his neck**" if he concealed any money.* (*Villains of All Nations* 15)

I'll throw you to the fish\sharks [*I'ee'ull throwoo 'ee/ya/ye/yer t'/ta/ter t' fesh\shahrrks/shairks*]

> "I think **I will throw him to the fish.**" (El Toro Mendoza, "Long John Silver's Return to Treasure Island" 20:07) "[N]othing but the remembrance of your mother has prevented me, long before this, from **throwing your body to the sharks.**" (Cain, *The Pirate* 44, Chap. VII)

I'll trounce the devilment out of you [*I'ee'ull trowoonce t' daahv/dayv/debb/div-il-mant arrt/ou'/owoot o'\on 'ee/ya/ye/yer*]

> *[W]hen there was some grumbling and talk of a mutiny over the state of the provisions, he was of opinion that they should not wait for the dogs to rise, but that they should march forward and set upon them until **they had trounced the devilment out of them.*** (John Sharkey, impersonating the governor of St. Kitt's but freely expressing what he'd like to do to the mutinous hands among the crew, *The Dealings of Captain Sharkey and Other Tales of Pirates* "How the Governor of Saint Kitt's Came Home" 20)

I'll use you for musket practice [*I'ee'ull yooss 'ee/ya/ye/yer farr/fer moohs/mush-kert prattice*]

> "Now you call me Cap'n or, by thunder, **I'm gonna** pin you to the wall with this cutlass and hang you from a yardarm by

your thumbs and use you for musket practice." (Billy Bones, "Treasure Island" [1990] 6:51)

I'll watch you dance the Tyburn hornpipe [*I'ee'ull warrtch 'ee/ya/ye/yer darrnce t' Taw/Tyee-barrn/borrn 'arrn/harrn/'orn-pawp/pyeepe*] I'll watch you hang

Tyburn was London's traditional place of public execution, where inmates at Newgate Prison under death sentence were hanged. "Dance" is used here to refer cynically to the involuntary kicks and jerks that someone being hanged typically performs as he dies.

> "By God! **I'll watch you dance the Tyburn hornpipe** yet, the yardarm jig!" (Black Bartlemy, *Adam Penfeather, Buccaneer* 279–80)

I'll watch you dance the yardarm jig [*I'ee'ull warrtch 'ee/ya/ye/yer darrnce t' yahrrd-ahrrm/erm jeg*] I'll watch you hang

"Dance" and "jig" are used here to refer cynically to the involuntary kicks and jerks that someone being hanged typically performs as he dies.

> "By God! **I'll watch you dance** the Tyburn hornpipe yet, **the yardarm jig!**" (Black Bartlemy, *Adam Penfeather, Buccaneer* 279–80)

I'll watch you hang [*I'ee'ull warrtch 'ee/ya/ye/yer 'ang*]

> "It is my constant prayer that I may be so blest to let out his evil soul by incision of steel beneath his fifth rib, or—**watch him hang**, for 'tis very son o' Belial." (Smy Peters, *Adam Penfeather, Buccaneer* 21)

I'll wing you [*I'ee'ull weng 'ee/ya/ye/yer*]

To "wing" is to injure severely. A winged bird is one whose injury prevents it from flying. The speaker implies he will hurt the addressee seriously enough to cause more than pain—that is, to impair or incapacitate.

"Devil take the sot! **I'll go wing him** ..." (Absalom Troy, hearing of Abner's fit of drunken violence, *Adam Penfeather, Buccaneer* 14)

I'll wring your fat cow's head off your body [*I'ee'ull wreng ya/yarr/ye/yer/yere/yore fat cowoo's 'ead/hayd arrf ya/yarr/ye/yer/yere/yore bahee/barrdy*]

> "I claims Trelawney. And **I'll wring his fat cow's head off his body**." (Long John Silver, "Treasure Island" [1972] 1:00:00)

it may be well for you to keep from my path [*ett mayee be waahl farr/fer 'ee/ya/ye/yer t'/ta/ter keep ferm me/myee paff*]

> "**It may be well for him to keep from my path**, or he may get a lesson that shall prick his honesty." (The Red Rover, *The Red Rover* 104)

it'll be the worse for you [*ett'll be t' warrse/warrser/woorse/wooorser/worser farr/fer 'ee/ya/ye/yer*]

> < "**It'll be the worse for you**, Captain, if they go." "D'ye threaten, by God!" > (Crosby Pike & Captain Easterling, *Captain Blood Returns* 285)

it'll be your last [*ett'll/'twell/'twill be ya/yarr/ye/yer/yere/yore larrst*]

The speaker counsels the addressee against some act or undertaking by suggesting it will be her last—that is, she will die if she chooses nevertheless to proceed.

> "Raise that ugly claw to me once more and **it'll be yer last**. ..." (Henry Morgan, *Dead Man's Chest* 10)

it's the gallows for you [*ett be OR 'tes/'tis t' gallowoos farr/fer 'ee/ya/ye/yer*] you'll be hanged; you're as good as dead

> "I have sailed with many black men, you know, and they are as fierce as any. More so, in fact, because if they are caught there is no chance of pardon. **It's the gallows for them**, between the flux and flood of tides." (Billy Bird, *The Blackbirder* 92)

it's the locker for you [*ett be OR 'tes/'tis t' la-hrrker farr/fer 'ee/ya/ye/yer*] you're dead meat

"Locker" here is a reference to Davy Jones' locker, the seaman's traditional personification of, and way of referring to, the bottom of the ocean, especially as a graveyard for those killed at sea. Though the phrase refers literally to death by drowning, it may be used more broadly to refer to an imminent death of any kind.

> < "Yes, but the *Flying Dutchman* already has a captain, so there's really—" "Then **it's the locker for you!**" > (Jack Sparrow & Bootstrap Bill Turner, with Turner rebuffing Sparrow's attempt to talk his way out of his deal with Davy Jones, "Pirates of the Caribbean 2: Dead Man's Chest" 16:10)

my finger's on the trigger, and it's only a pull to shut your mouth forever [*me/myee feng/finn-er's arrn/o' t' tregger, an'/'n ett's/'n's/ 't's on'y a pull t'/ta/ter sharrt/shooht ya/yarr/ye/ yer/yere/yore mowooth farr/foor-ebber/e'er*]

> "[M]y finger's on the trigger, and it's only a pull to shut your mouth forever." (John Scarfield, *The Book of Pirates* "Captain Scarfield" 203)

my thumbs are itching to scrape your eyeballs out of your sockets [*me/myee thoohmbs/ t'umbs be etchin' t'/ta/ter scrayeepe ya/yarr/ye/ yer/yere/yore eye'ee-bawrls arrt/ou'/owoot o'\on ya/yarr/ye/yer/yere/yore sarrkets*]

> "My thumbs are itching to scrape Smollett's eyeballs out of their sockets." (Tom Morgan, "Treasure Island" [1960] 37:55)

one more for the sailmaker's palm and needle [*woohn marr/moor farr/fer t' sayell-mayeeker's parrm an'/'n' needler*]

When a pirate died at sea (assuming his corpse were sufficiently intact), he was often wrapped in sail cloth, bound in rope, and dropped over the vessel's rail into the sea.

> < "How many for the sailmaker's palm and needle?" "Three, captain." > (Andrew Murray & Long John Silver, *Porto Bello Gold* 123)

them that die'll be the lucky ones [*dem/ t'em tharrt daw/dyee-'ll be t' larr/looh-ky 'un's/ woohns*]

A threat promising such an intensely horrible fate that death would be preferable.

> Note the various permutations of this classic: "**Them of you that's dies'll be lucky.**" (Long John Silver, "Treasure Island" [1934] 1:05:58) "**Them that dies will be the lucky ones.**" (Long John Silver, "Treasure Island" [1972] 1:00:12) "You'll get what Flint gave to hands what went agin 'im. **Them that died were the lucky ones.**" (Long John Silver, "Long John Silver's Return to Treasure Island" 40:01)

there will be a yardarm for you [*tharr/ theyarr/theyerr well be a yahrrd-ahrrm/erm farr/fer 'ee/ya/ye/yer*] you'll hang

A yardarm is the end of a yard on a square-rigged ship. (A yard is a wood pole supporting a square sail.) Yardarms were used for shipboard hangings so frequently that they came to be associated with that form of execution.

> < "[W]hatever I do to Hagthorpe, you will do to my cousin." "That is the issue exactly." "Then, if I were to hang Hagthorpe." "**There would be a yardarm for your cousin.**" > (James Court & Peter Blood, *The Fortunes of Captain Blood* 105)

there'll be a widow [*tharr/theyarr/theyerr 'll be a wedowoo*]

> "Tell the Squire that if those pirates stay ashore this night, **there'll be widows in the mornin'.**" (Ben Gunn, "Treasure Island" [1990] 1:10:54)

there's never a man yet looks me between the eyes and lives to see a good day afterwards [*tharr/theyarr/theyerr is\be nebber/ ne'er a man yat looks me 'tween\betwixt/'twixt t'*] *eye'ees an'/'n' levvs/liffs t'/ta/ter see a g' dayee arrf/ar/haf-ter-wahrrds]*

> "There's never a man yet looks me be-tween the eyes and lives to see a good day afterwards, Tommy, you may lay to that." (Long John Silver, drawing a bloody knife out of Tom's body, "Trea-sure Island" [1972] 46:44)

'tis a sin to suffer such a EPITHET as you to live *[ett/it 's\be OR 'tes a sin t'/ta/ter soohffer soohch a ... as 'ee/ya/ye/yer t'/ta/ter levv/liff]*

> "'T[i]s a sin to suffer such a false traiter-ous dog as [you] to live." (John Russell, threatening George Roberts for toast-ing King George rather than his Roman Catholic rival James Edward Stuart, *Pi-rates of the New England Coast* 179)

'twon't be fit for him to live where I'm liv-ing *['two'oont be fett farr/fer 'im t'/ta/ter levv/liff wayarr/wayerr/wharr I'eem a-levv/liff-in']*

> "'Twon't be fit for him to live in these parts of America if I am living here at the same time." (Blackbeard, warning North Carolina locals against rendering assistance to his enemy, *The Book of Pi-rates* "Jack Ballister's Fortunes" 137)

up to the yardarm you'll swing by your thumbs\neck *[arrp t'/ta/ter t' yahrrd-ahrrm/erm ye'll sweng byee ya/yarr/ye/yer/yere/yore thoohmbs/t'umbs\nack]*

A yardarm is the end of a yard on a square-rigged ship. (A yard is a wood pole support-ing a square sail.) Yardarms were used for shipboard hangings so frequently that they came to be associated with that form of ex-ecution.

> "See here, my bright lads, learn this—when you come aboard my ship and I say to one o' ye do this or do that, he does it, d'ye see, or—up to the yard-arm he swings by his thumbs or his neck as occasion warrants." (Adam Penfeather, *Black Bartlemy's Treasure* 111)

you are a dead man *[ya/ye/yer be a dayd man]*

> "Listen to what I say or **you are a dead man**." (John Scarfield, *The Book of Pirates* "Captain Scarfield" 203)

you be dead men all *[ya/ye/yer be dayd men awrl]*

> < "We ha' come back out of hell to find we are dead and forgot—eh, Japhet?" "Ay, **we be dead men all**." > (Barnabas Rokeby & Japhet Bly, *Winds of Chance* 32)

you can keep your life *[ya/ye/yer cayn/kin keep ya/yarr/ye/yer/yere/yore lawf/lyeefe]*

The speaker offers to trade the address-ee's life for something he wants from the addressee.

> "You give us that there map, and **you can stay here and keep your lives**." (Long John Silver, "Treasure Island" [1950] 59:19)

you can say your prayers *[ya/ye/yer cayn/kin sayee ya/yarr/ye/yer/yere/yore prayee-arrs/errs]* you're a dead man

> "Now **Job can say his prayers**. He's had his slice o' luck, Job has." (Long John Sil-ver, "Treasure Island" [1950] 1:19:22)

you may expect not to have quarters *[ya/ye/yer mayee especk/espect/expeck/ 'speck/'spect narrt t'/ta/ter 'aff/'ave/ha'/haff quahrr/quaht-ters]* you can expect no mercy

> "[P]ray make conscience for once let me begg you and use th[a]t man as an hon-est man and not as a c[riminal] if we hear any otherwise **you may expect not to have quarters** to any of your island." (Bartholomew Roberts, in a threaten-ing letter to Lieutenant General William Mathew about a recently imprisoned pi-rate, *Villains of All Nations* 102)

you shall yearn for sweet easement of death *[ya/ye/yer shawrl yarrn farr/fer sweet eass-mant o'\on dath/ deff]*

"No, no, thou'rt destined to such living hereafter shall make thee **yearn for such sweet easement** as a pistol ball." (Japhet Bly, *Winds of Chance* 141)

EPITHET you were, EPITHET you are, EPITHET you die [...'ee/ya/ye/yer warr, ... 'ee/ya/ye/yer be, ... 'ee/ya/ye/yer dyee]

"Arrgh, yer haven't changed, Silver. A **one-legged serpent ya were, a one-legged serpent ye are, a one-legged serpent you die**." (Israel Hands, "Long John Silver's Return to Treasure Island" 1:17:29)

you were born for no common death [ya/ye/yer warr barrn farr/fer no'oo carr-man dath/deff] you're fated to die in an especially cruel or gruesome manner

"**You must be born for no common death**, Scarrow, since you have lain at my mercy and lived to tell the story. Tie him up, Ned." (John Sharkey, *The Dealings of Captain Sharkey and Other Tales of Pirates* "How the Governor of Saint Kitt's Came Home" 23)

you'd be the better for a bleeding [ya'd/ye'd/yer'd be t' be'er\gooder farr/fer a bleedin']

"His blood is getting too rich for him. **He'd be the better for a bleeding**." (William Kidd, *Captain Kidd* 59:11)

you'll answer to me [ye'll ansarr t'/ta/ter me]

"Hark'ee. There be rum in them there casks, but they're for sellin', not drinkin', and the first man who touches one drop **answers ta me**." (Long John Silver, "Long John Silver's Return to Treasure Island" 29:14)

you'll be dead as the pig I ate of last night [ye'll be dayd as t' peg I'ee ayeete o'\on larrst nawt/nigheet]

< "Are they dead?' "Nay, not yet, master; give 'em six minutes or say ten and **they'll be as dead as the pig you ate of last [night**.]" > (Martin Conisby & John, *Martin Conisby's Vengeance* 181)

you'll be good as pork [ye'll be good as parrk]

"If you was sent by Long John, **I'm as good as pork**, and I know it." (Ben Gunn, *Treasure Island* 81, Chap. 15)

you'll be meat for the sharks [ye'll be meat farr/fer t' shahrrks/shairks]

"**He's meat for the sharks** now, Mister Povy." (William Kidd, "Captain Kidd" 1:08:18)

you'll be overside with your guts full of shot [ye'll be ober/o'er-sawd/syeede weth/wi'/wiff/wit ya/yarr/ye/yer/yere/yore garrts/goohts full o'\on sharrt]

The speaker threatens both to shoot the addressee and to toss him overboard.

"Rot him! **He should be overside wi' his guts full o' shot** for this same heye of mine if 'twas my say ..." (Job, *Martin Conisby's Vengeance* 65)

you'll count amongst your treasure a ball from this pistol [ye'll coun'/cowoon/cowoont amarrngst ya/yarr/ye/yer/yere/yore tresherr a bawrl ferm dis/t'is peh-shtol]

Appropriate, of course, only when the speaker is actually brandishing a pistol. Otherwise the speaker might do well to substitute "a pistol" for "this pistol."

"The first man what makes a move can **count amongst his treasure a ball from this pistol**." (Long John Silver, "Long John Silver's Return to Treasure Island" 1:34:40)

you'll die like a dog [ye'll dyee lawk/lyeeke a OR liker dahg/darrg/dorrg]

"Villain! doubly d[amne]d villain! **thou'lt die like a dog**, and unrevenged!" (Cain, *The Pirate* 138, Chap. XVII)

you'll do a fine dance at rope's end [ye'll/yer'll do a fawn/fyeene dance a'/hat ro'oope's/roope's aynd] you'll be hanged; you'll die at the end of a noose

"By gum, you'll talk! Or **do a fine dance at rope's end**!" (pirate overseeing well-dunking of Spanish magistrate, "Pirates of the Caribbean" Disney attraction)

you'll find what you don't want [ye'll fawnd/ fin'/fyeen'/fyeend wharrt/whorrt 'ee/ya/ye/yer don'/doon't/dorrn't warrnt]

"[A]nd don't you come back, or **you'll find what you don't want** waiting for you." (Captain Kidd's comrade, confronting Tom Chist as Chist stumbles upon Kidd and his comrades burying treasure, *The Book of Pirates* "Tom Chist and the Treasure Box" 105)

you'll find yourself sliced in two [ye'll fawnd/fin'/fyeen'/fyeend 'ee/ya/yarr/ye/yer/ yere/yore-seff slawced/slyeeced i'/'n two]

"There be the sharpest knife in the galley sticking in your gizzard. One pipe out o' you and **you'll find yourself sliced in two**." (Long John Silver, "The Adventures of Long John Silver: Turnabout" 14:34)

you'll get what NAME gave to hands what went against him [ye'll ge'/git wharrt/whorrt ... gafe/gayeeve t'/ta/ter 'ands/'an's/han's wharrt/ whorrt wen' agaynst/agin/'gainst/'gaynst 'im]

The speaker inserts a reference to a pirate whose name or memory inspires fear or trepidation.

"**You'll get what Flint gave to hands what went agin 'im**." (Long John Silver, "Long John Silver's Return to Treasure Island" 39:57)

you'll go down with the tide [ye'll/yer'll go'oo dowoon weth/wi'/wiff/witt t' tawd/tyeede]

Especially appropriate as a threat to sink another's vessel. The speaker suggests that the addressee's destruction is as imminent and inevitable as the tide's ebb.

"Another broadside and **ya goes down with the tide**!" (pirate captain, "Pirates of the Caribbean" Disney attraction)

you'll join NAME [ye'll jine/joyeen ...] you're going to die

The speaker names an infamous dead pirate or, more broadly, any dead person.

"**They've all joined Cap'n Flint** for sure." (Big Eric, "The Adventures of Long John Silver: Sword of Vengeance" 5:55)

you'll lose your ears [ye'll lose ya/yarr/ye/ yer/yere/yore ee-arrs/errs]

"Move, or **you'll lose your ears**!" (Thomas Bartholomew Red, urging Hendricks to fetch his lieutenant, "Pirates" 56:30)

you'll make a pretty death of it [ye'll may-eeke a preh'y dath/deff o'\on ett/'n/'t] you're going to die

"There's a man of spirit, and one of my own kidney, and **he's going to make a very pretty death of it**!" (John Sharkey, *The Dealings of Captain Sharkey and Other Tales of Pirates* "How the Governor of Saint Kitt's Came Home" 22)

you'll rue the day your mother ever spawned you [ye'll roo t' dayee ya/yarr/ye/ yer/yere/yore maahth/mo'/mudd-er ebber/e'er spawrrned 'ee/ya/ye/yer] you'll be sorry you were ever born

"**You'll rue the day ya mother ever spawned ya**." (Purity Pinker, "Long John Silver's Return to Treasure Island" 55:38)

you'll taste my steel [ye'll tayeeste me/myee stee'ell]

The speaker refers to his sword, and specifically to his sword cutting into the addressee's flesh.

"Step forward, lad, and be the first to **taste my steel**." (Joshua Smoot, *Dead Man's Chest* 254)

you'll walk the plank [ye'll warrk t' plank]

< "Come along." "Hold fast! You'll obey orders from your cap'n or **you'll walk the plank**! You mutinous maggot!" > (Trip Fenner & Long John Silver, "The Adventures of Long John Silver: Execution Dock" 13:01)

you'll wish you died at birth [ye'll wersh/wesh 'ee/ya/ye/yer dawd/dyeed a'/hat barrth/birff]

"And if you've any mind o' treachery, so help me, **you'll wish you died at birth.**" (Long John Silver, "The Adventures of Long John Silver: Pieces of Eight" 4:33)

your blood or mine [ya/yarr/ye/yer/yere/yore bloohd/blut arr mawn/myeene]

"'Twas **his blood or mine**; dearly did he pay the forfeit of his brutality!" (The Red Rover, recounting how he killed an English commander who he heard belittle the American colonies, *The Red Rover* 355)

your blood shall run on this floor [ya/yarr/ ye/yer/yere/yore bloohd/blut shawrl roohn arrn/ o' dis/t'is flarr]

"**Your blood shall run on this floor** with that of the Governor's pigeon, and his." (El Toro Mendoza, referring to Governor Strong's daughter and Jim Hawkins, "Long John Silver's Return to Treasure Island" 26:38)

your brains will be over your coat [ya/ yarr/ye/yer/yere/yore brayeens well be ober/o'er ya/yarr/ye/yer/yere/yore co'oot]

The suggestion here is that the speaker will shoot the addressee in the head, such that his brain will spill or splatter onto his coat.

"[W]ave your hat to them. Quick, or **your brains will be over your coat.**" (John Sharkey, *The Dealings of Captain Sharkey and Other Tales of Pirates* "The Dealings of Captain Sharkey with Stephen Craddock" 42)

your course is run [ya/yarr/ye/yer/yere/yore carrse/coorse be roohn]

A nautical rendition of "your life is over."

"I, borne aloft on that mighty, hissing sea, strove no more, doubting not **my course was run.**" (Adam Penfeather, *Black Bartlemy's Treasure* 85)

your end will be the halter [ya/yarr/ye/ yer/yere/yore aynd well be t' 'alter] you'll be hanged

A halter is a rope with a noose used for hanging.

"Those who ha[ve] taken me [a]re no better than pirates, and **their end would be the halter** ..." (Nickola, *The Pirates Own Book* 368)

VERB your fill now, 'tis little you'll be VERB-ing presently [... ya/yarr/ye/yer/yere/ yore fell narr/nowoo, ett/it/'n/'t 's\be OR 'tes lil' ye'll be a-...-in' per/pree-sently]

Used to defy the addressee to undertake or continue some action objectionable to the speaker, who is claiming that his knowledge of the addressee's certain death (presumably at the speaker's hand) renders the speaker indifferent to it.

"**Stare your fill, now, 'tis little enough you'll be seeing presently.**" (Captain Belvedere, mocking Don Federigo's stunned gaze after telling him of the torture and death of his son, *Martin Conisby's Vengeance* 60)

your hide shall pay [ya/yarr/ye/yer/yere/yore hawd/hyeede/'ide/'ieede shawrl payee] you'll pay for it with your flesh

An oblique reference to lashing or whipping, and more generally a threat to make another's flesh or body suffer.

"Damn ye, you lye you dog, but d[am]n my b[loo]d, **your hide shall pay** for your roguery, and if I can't bring her off I'll burn her where she lyes." (William Fly, *General History of the Pyrates* 610–11)

your life shall pay the forfeit [ya/yarr/ye/ yer/yere/yore lawf/lyeefe shawrl payee t' farr/fer-fett] you'll pay for it with your life

"If you do not tell us the truth, **your life shall pay the forfeit.**" (Captain Jonsen, *A High Wind in Jamaica* 76)

your sands are run [*ya/yarr/ye/yer/yere/yore san's be roohn*] your life is over

> "On my soul's salvation, Peter, there was a moment when I thought **our sands were run.**" (Nathaniel Hagthorpe, *Captain Blood Returns* 37)

you're a dead man unless you can outrun a bullet [*ya're/yer/ye're/yo're a dayd man arrn/hun/oohn-lass OR less'n 'ee/ya/ye/yer cayn/kin arrt/ou'/owoot-roohn a bullert*]

> "[A]s they were entering a little thicket of trees, we appeared and, calling to them in English, told them they were our prisoners .... One of them looking behind ... I called to him and told him if he attempted to run for it **he was a dead man, unless he could outrun a musket bullet ...**" (Captain Avery, *The King of Pirates* 67)

you're a dead one [*ya're/yer/ye're/yo're a dayd 'un/woohn*]

> "**Captain's a dead one.** You just look to your own neck." (Thomas Marlowe, *The Pirate Round* 289)

you're a man to __ and __ you will (be) [*ya're/yer/ye're/yo're a man t'/ta/ter __ an'/'n' __ 'ee/ya/ye/yer well (OR ye'll be)*]

The speaker twice pronounces the addressee's fate, inserting two references to a single form of torture, punishment, mistreatment, murder, or death.

> "But **you're a man to hang and hanged you'll be** and you can lay to that, d'ye see?" (Adam Penfeather, *Black Bartlemy's Treasure* 145)

you're dead\good as pork [*ya're/yer/ye're/yo're dayd\good as parrk*]

> "We're sunk, you and me. **Dead as pork.** Might as well face up to it." (Blackbeard, "Blackbeard's Ghost" 38:14) "If you was sent by Long John, **I'm as good as pork**, and I know it." (Ben Gunn, *Treasure Island* 81, Chap. 15)

you're to die [*ya're/yer/ye're/yore t'/ta/ter dyee*]

> < "All because of him." "Belay." "Belay, says he. You may hold us out for a spell, Long John, but **he's to die**." > (Old Stingley & Long John Silver, "Long John Silver's Return to Treasure Island" 1:05:26)

you've had\seen your slice of luck [*ya've/ye've/yer've 'ad\seen ya/yarr/ye/yer/yere/yore slawce/slyeece o'\on loohk*]

A murky threat that can be used to mean either that the addressee will see nothing but misfortune for the rest of his life, or that the addressee will have little opportunity for any kind of fortune for the rest of his life because his death is imminent.

> "Now Job can say his prayers. **He's had his slice o' luck**, Job has." (Long John Silver, "Treasure Island" [1950] 1:19:22)
> "**He's seen his slice of luck**, has Dick, and you may lay to that." (Long John Silver, *Treasure Island* 163, Chap. 29)

you've seen the last of me but musket balls [*ya've/ye've/yer've seen t' larrst o'\on me barrt moohs/mush-kert bawrls*]

The speaker simultaneously communicates that he is (1) finished dealing with the addressee, presumably for having his patience or tolerance exhausted, and (2) intent on killing the addressee.

> "Refuse that, **you've seen the last o' me but musket balls**." (Long John Silver, "Treasure Island" [1990] 1:16:13)

CHAPTER 6

Oaths

Philip Ashton, the captain of a fishing schooner captured by Edward Low on June 15, 1722, spent eleven months living in captivity with Low's company. Buffeted by the pirates' constant profanity, Ashton was moved to record:

> I soon found that any death was preferable to being link'd with such a vile crew of miscreants, to whom it was a sport to do mischief; where prodigious drinking, monstrous cursing and swearing, hideous blasphemies, and open defiance of heaven, and contempt of hell it self, was the constant employment unless when sleep something abated the noise and revellings. (*Pirates of the New England Coast* 231)

In short, pirates have filthy mouths. Chapters 6: Oaths and 7: Curses are comprehensive guides to that filth, and how to put it in your own mouth.

What's the difference between an oath and a curse? Both are means by which a pirate can swear, but in very different ways.

A speaker utters an oath for two reasons: to add emphasis to what he says and to swear that it's true. Oaths are most often used to convey something sharply or deeply felt, such as joy, surprise, disbelief, anger, displeasure, frustration, or conviction. An oath says to the listener, "You should believe me."

A speaker utters a curse, on the other hand, to wish harm on someone or something—typically from either God ("damn your gizzard") or the Devil ("fiend take you"). A curse says to the listener (or to some third person or thing), "you'll suffer."

The only difference in wording between certain oaths and curses may be the word "me" or "you." A pirate captain might upbraid his company after a failed venture by saying, "**Damn my blood**, yer the saddest lot o' lubbers ever did sail the seas, **damn yer blood**." The first phrase "damn my blood" is an oath: The captain is swearing on pain of damnation to

---

Choosing Their Words Carefully

Pirate-speak may be harsh, but it's not careless.

"Me" and "my" oaths (*e.g.* "rot me," "blast my eyes") are generally used to convey intense surprise, frustration, disgust, or disappointment, often (but not always) directed at or as a result of oneself, one's own actions or the matter at hand, rather than the addressee, and often (but not always) spoken in a modest or good-natured way that makes clear to the addressee that he is not the cause of the negative sentiment being expressed.

Oaths featuring the word "love" or "bless" (*e.g.* "bless my guts," "Lord love you") tend to radiate an attitude of earnest modesty and good will, and are generally used to comment rather than condemn—that is, to convey surprise, fear, or disappointment as a result of someone or something other than the addressee, or to express mild surprise at or displeasure with the addressee in the lightest of terms.

Swearing by the powers of evil (*e.g.* "by Satan," "hell and the devil") is arguably either a very pious act (reflecting a conscientious effort to avoid swearing by something holy) or a very despicable one (reflecting a readiness to ally oneself with, and concede by the act of invocation a certain authority or respect to, the devil and his influence).

Abridgements and minced oaths (*e.g.* "bedad," "odso") allow the speaker to impart the same meaning without violating the traditional Judeo-Christian prohibition against speaking God's name for unworthy purposes. Similar proxy expletives in modern English include "by George" (for "by God"), "darn" (for "damn"), and "heck" (for "hell").

---

the truth of what follows. The latter phrase "damn yer blood," on the other hand, is a curse: The captain is wishing damnation on his sorry crew.

Every oath has a number of standard variations:

- **OATH:** "Death and damnation, I'm spent." "Stap me, I'm spent."
- **by + OATH:** "By death and damnation, I'm spent."
- **or + OATH:** "I'm spent, or stap me." (Used by the speaker to swear to the truth or certainty of what he has just said by inviting upon himself otherwise the fate or consequence his oath describes.
- **OATH + but:** "Death and damnation, but I'm spent." "Stap me, but I'm spent." (Used for emphasis, especially to express surprise, disbelief, displeasure, or conviction.)
- **OATH + else:** "I'm spent, stap me else." (Used by the speaker to swear to the truth or certainty of what he has just said by inviting upon himself otherwise the fate or consequence his oath describes.)
- **OATH + if:** "I'm spent, stap me if I bain't." "Stap me if I ben't spent." (Used to negate emphatically whatever statement precedes or follows.)

The following is a comprehensive list of pirate oaths.

---

all hell [*awrl 'ell*]

"What in **all hell** are these arseholes about?" (Flanders, *The Pirate Round* 263)

and be damned [*an'/'n' be damt*]

Used for emphasis and to convey a tough, devil-may-care attitude. The speaker implies that the accompanying statement is every-thing that is or should be important, and that all else can go to hell.

"'Tis like a happy family, rot me, all love and good-fellowship **and be damned!**" (Roger Tressady, *Martin Conisby's Ven-geance* 156)

as I'm a soul [*as I'eem a sool/so'ool*] as I live and breathe; as sure as I'm standing here

"Here's luck! Bad luck, **as I'm a soul.**" (Rog-er Tressady, *Black Bartlemy's Treasure* 97)

as sure as God sees me [*as sharr/shorr as Gard/Gott/Gud sees me*] without a doubt; certainly

"**As sure as God sees me**, I'd sooner lose my hand." (Tom, *Treasure Island* 75, Chap. 14)

bedad [*b'-darrd/dat/ded*]

A milder, sound-alike substitute for "by God."

< "What's amusing you now, Captain?" "Your rashness, **bedad!**" > (Sam & Peter Blood, *Captain Blood Returns* 150)

b'ged [*b'-garrd/gerrd*]

A milder, sound-alike substitute for "by God." Alternately spelled "b'gad."

< "Should he not be bled, sir?" "Step me vitals—no, mem! 'Tis blood we lack! There's more fine lads killed by the dem'd lancet than all y'r rapiers and small swords, **b'ged!**" > (Ursula Revell & Crabtree, *Winds of Chance* 89)

Bible oath [*baah/baw/byee-bul oaf/o'oof/o'ooth*] I swear; I swear to God

"Though wishful for to take the ship, I was agin killing you. **Bible Oath**, sir!" (Sam

Morris, insisting to Adam Penfeather he was mutinous but not murderous, *Adam Penfeather, Buccaneer* 215)

blast my eyes [*blarrst/blass me/myee eye'ees*]

A milder alternative to "damn me" or "damn my eyes."

"But, Cap'n, **blast my eyes**, sir, and axing your pardin, but you ... you hain't been and gone and ... killed pore Giles, 'ave ye, sir?" (Thomas Ash, *Adam Penfeather, Buccaneer* 204)

blasted [*blarrsted*]

Short for "I'll be blasted" and a milder al-ternative to "I'll be damned."

"**Blasted** if I see any sense in it. But what-ever he says, captain." (Billy Bones, *Porto Bello Gold* 58)

(the) blazes [*(t') blayeezes*] (the) hell

< "It was Ben that found the treasure." "By God, how in **blazes** did he do that without the map?" > (Doctor Livesey & Long John Silver, "Treasure Island" [1990] 1:58:57) "How **the blazes** did you get off that island?" (Barbossa, "Pirates of the Caribbean: The Curse of the Black Pearl" 1:16:41)

bleed me

A milder alternative to "damn me" or "I'll be damned." "Bleed" is a synonym for "kill," though its meaning has blurred into a more generic expletive given its sound-alike simi-larity to "blast."

"Why, why—**bleed me!** If—if it aren't—aye 'tis—Martin!" (Roger Tressady, upon recognizing Martin Conisby, *Black Bartle-my's Treasure* 302)

bless my guts [*blayss/blest me/myee garrts/goohts*]

< "Ha, d'ye mean fight, Smiler? Fall on 'em by surprise and recapture the ship—ha?" "O **bless my guts**—no!" > (pirate in Roger Tressady's company & Sam Spraggons, *Black Bartlemy's Treasure* 311)

bless your heart [*blayss/blest ya/yarr/ye/yer/yere/yore 'ahrrt/'eart/hahrrt*]

Used to express mild pity for, bemusement with, or sincere affection for or good will toward another.

> "You and me'll just go back into the parlour, sonny, and get behind the door, and we'll give Bill a little surprise—**bless his 'art**, I say again." (Black Dog, *Treasure Island* 10, Chap. 2)

bless your old\rusty heart [*blayss/blest ya/yarr/ye/yer/yere/yore ol'\rarrsty/roohsty 'ahrrt/'eart/hahhrt*]

Used in reference to one whose heart might appropriately or jokingly be said to be "old" or "rusty"—that is, a much older person, or a person who works with iron or other metal so much his heart might be said to be made of it (*e.g.*, a gunner, an armourer, a blacksmith).

> "And here, sure enough, is my mate Bill, with a spyglass under his arm, **bless his old 'art** to be sure." (Black Dog, *Treasure Island* 10, Chap. 2) "**Bless your rusty heart**, it's a gunner you are!" (Peter Blood, "Captain Blood" 56:50)

blimey [*blaw/blyee-mey*]

A sound-alike substitute for "blind me."

> "Can't dance the hornpipe, huh? **Blimey**." (Tom Morgan, "Treasure Island" [1960] 24:46)

blind me [*blawnd/blin'/blyeen'/blyeend/blyeent/blynt me*]

> "Split me! O **blind me** if I thought ye such a lubberly fool!" (Roger Tressady, *Black Bartlemy's Treasure* 303)

blister me [*blester me*]

A milder alternative to "damn me " or "I'll be damned." To "blister" is to subject to harsh physical treatment—to whip or beat severely, for example.

> "**Blister me**, young gentleman, but that's dreadful news." (Long John Silver, *Porto Bello Gold* 22)

blood and wound(s) [*bloohd/blut an'/'n' woun('s)/wount(s)*]

An abridgement of "God's blood and wounds" or "Christ's blood and wounds"—a reference to Jesus' crucifixion.

> < "We're taking him to the Roset School for Gentlemen." "Well, **blood and wound**, our Jim be goin' to Roset, too." > (Sir Percival Harwood & Long John Silver, "The Adventures of Long John Silver: Dead Reckoning" 8:11)

bloody hell [*bloohd/bluh'/blutt-y 'ell*]

Usually part of an exclamatory question beginning with an interrogative such as "what," "how," "when," "who," or "why," but can also stand alone.

> "What **the bloody hell** are you doing?" (Roger Press, *The Pirate Round* 223)

blow me down [*blowoo me dowoon*] I'll be darned

A milder alternative to "I'll be damned."

> < "I'm sure I could." "**Blow me down**, so 'ee could." > (Jim Hawkins & Long John Silver, "Treasure Island" [1950] 34:58) "Well, **blow me down** for an ol' sea calf." (Long John Silver, "Treasure Island" [1950] 22:11)

blow my scuttle-butt [*blowoo me/myee scu'le-barrt/booht*] I'll be darned

A milder alternative to "I'll be damned." A "scuttle-butt" is a cask aboard a vessel used to store the day's supply of drinking water.

> "I'd hate to be a nefarious fellow in your town. **Blow my scuttle-butt**, I would!" (Long John Silver, *Porto Bello Gold* 48)

body o' me [*bahee/barrdy o'\on me*] I swear; I swear on my soul

An abridgement of "by the body of me." The speaker swears on the health or integrity of his own body to the truth or certainty of his statement.

> "Ay, **body o' me**, that's the verity on't, sirs!" (Benjamin Trigg, *Adam Penfeather, Buccaneer* 115)

the bones [*t' boones/bo'oones*]

An oath referring to human mortality. Used for emphasis, especially to express surprise, disbelief, displeasure, or conviction.

> "I shut myself up with Lord Perrow, my brother, George D'Arcy and the Devil, losing my all at cards, sir, **the bones**—and by each am cursed, for my luck is out, sir." (Benjamin Trigg, *Adam Penfeather, Buccaneer* 112)

brimstone and gall [*brem-stoone/sto'oone an'/'n' gawrl*]

An oath comparable to "hell and the devil." "Brimstone" means sulfur, and "gall" means bile. Both substances are unpleasant in odor and appearance. The two words also have profound metaphorical implications: Brimstone is closely associated with hell (the phrase "fire and brimstone" traditionally stands in for the torments suffered by the eternally condemned), and bile with human bitterness and rancor. Consequently, the phrase "brimstone and gall" packs into four syllables the worst of both this world and the next.

> "**Brimstone and gall**, what cozening is here?" (James Hook, *Peter Pan* 94)

brush my barnacles [*broohsh me/myee bahrrn'cles/nerkles*]

Though ostensibly a nonsense phrase, "brush my barnacles" may be a fanciful reference to the sailing-era practice of periodically scraping and burning the seaweed and barnacles off a vessel's hull in order to maximize velocity or, more generally, to the process of "careening"—in which a crew so cleaned a vessel's bottom and effected any necessary repairs to the planking after hauling the vessel onto shore and turning her onto her side.

> "Oh, **brush me barnacles**! Now where be that little ol' fish dinner I been a-cravin'?" (gluttonous pirate, "Pirates of the Caribbean" Disney attraction [2005])

bugger [*boohger*] damn; screw it

Used to express anger, displeasure, frustration, or some other negative, sharply felt sentiment.

> "Oh, **bugger**." (Jack Sparrow, on being discovered by the cannibals from whom he thought himself to have escaped, "Pirates of the Caribbean 2: Dead Man's Chest" 35:14)

burn and sink me [*barrn an'/'n' senk me*]

Pirates often burned the ships they plundered, but burning a ship did not necessarily sink it: A ship's hull in a humid and windless clime might survive a fire, and floating hulls were sometimes encountered on the open sea. Thus, to burn *and* sink something is to take pains to assure its complete obliteration. "Burn and sink me" might therefore amount to something like "destroy me utterly."

> "Burn me, **burn and sink me** but Friendship is right good thing, Adam ..." (Absalom Troy, *Adam Penfeather, Buccaneer* 121)

burn me [*barrn me*]

A milder alternative to "damn me" or "I'll be damned." The term "burn" arguably has double significance, referring principally to damnation (to the extent a person damned is thought to suffer the fires of hell) but also to profound misfortune (as fire is easily the thing most dreaded among pirates, most of whom cannot swim and who rely on the integrity of the wood underneath their feet for survival).

> < "He sank the *Happy Despatch*!" "**Burn me**! And there's a stout ship lost to us." > (Captain Jo & Roger Tressady, *Martin Conisby's Vengeance* 158)

by all that is great and good [*byee awrl tharrt 's\be grayeet/grea'/grett an'/'n' good*]

An oath very indirectly invoking God, heaven, and the powers of good, and thereby avoiding what might be considered the blasphemous use of God's name for trivial purposes.

"I swear **by all that is great and good**, that if I know any thing whatsoever carry'd, or left on board the sloop against my order, or without my knowledge, that very instant I will set her on fire, and you in her." (John Russell, *Pirates of the New England Coast* 186)

by all what's holy and unholy [*byee awrl wharrt/whorrt is\be hoo'oo/'o-ly an'/'n' arrn/hun/oohn-hoo/ho'oo/'o-ly*]

An oath technically more comprehensive than either "by God" or "by Satan," as the speaker calls on the powers of both good and evil.

"**By all what's holy and unholy**, I'll have that treasure some day or I be not Long John Silver!" (Long John Silver, *Dead Man's Chest* 9)

by Christ [*byee Chrawst/Chryeest*]

"And you're near the mark there, **by Christ!**" (Long John Silver, "Treasure Island" [1990] 1:43:28)

by cock [*byee carrk*]

An oath comparable to "by George." "Cock" is often used as an admiring reference or a mild epithet for someone strong-willed or arrogant. Here, however, "cock" is used as a sound-alike substitute for "God."

"Aye, **by cock!** 'Tis 'witched he be!" (Joel Bym, *Black Bartlemy's Treasure* 104)

by cock's body [*byee carrk's bahee/barrdy*]

An oath comparable to "by George," and a milder alternative to "by God's body."

"Aye, Cap'n, by cock, them was the days, a fair wind, a quick eye an' no favour, aye, them was the days, **by cock's-body!**" (Joel Bym, *Black Bartlemy's Treasure* 80)

by fire and flame [*byee farr/fyarr an'/'n' flayeeme*] by the powers of hell; by Satan

"Fire" and "flame" are references to hell's torments, such that the speaker swears by the powers of hell to the truth or certainty of the statement that precedes or follows.

"You stand up and drink to His Majesty's health as a King's officer should or, **by fire and flame**, I'll have you shipped back to Newgate on the first vessel we speak." (William Kidd, "Captain Kidd" 26:18)

by Flint's (body and) bones [*byee Flent's (bahee/barrdy an'/'n') boones/bo'oones*]

An oath comparable to "by George." Captain John Flint, first featured in Robert Louis Stevenson's *Treasure Island*, was the powerful and deeply feared captain of the *Walrus*, under whom Long John Silver and Billy Bones served respectively as quartermaster and first mate.

"It's not the first time, Silver, but **by Flint's body and bones**, it'll be the last." (Purity Pinker, "The Adventures of Long John Silver: Miss Purity's Birthday" 10:36) "**By Flint's bones** I got 'n from Slygo." (Long John Silver, "The Adventures of Long John Silver: The Necklace" 10:55)

by gad [*byee ged*]

An oath comparable to "by George," and a sound-alike substitute for "by God."

< "I go to der *Walrus* or you go oudt der window." "**By gad**, you would! And after become captain in my place, no doubt." > (Peter Corlaer & Long John Silver, *Porto Bello Gold* 127)

by God [*byee Gard/Gott/Gud*]

While pirates often use bland proxies for "by God" like "by cock," "by gad," and "by gum," they frequently use the more profane "by God" precisely for its potential offensiveness.

"We are not children, **by God!** And we're not here to play, but to agree terms. And, **by God**, we'll agree them before you leave." (Captain Easterling, *Captain Blood Returns* 31–32)

by God's faith [*byee Garrd's/Gott's/Gud's fayeeth*]

*Pascual was prepared to testify that Drake's favourite oath was: "**By God's faith.**"* (account of the reports of a Portuguese pilot on Francis Drake's speech habits, *The Queen's Corsair* 233)

by God's life [*byee Garrd's/Gott's/Gud's lawf/lyeefe*]

An oath referring to Jesus' crucifixion, but arguably also a particularly bold oath sworn on God's very existence.

> "**By God's life** if he were my man I would cut off his ears; yea, by God's wounds I would hang him." (Francis Drake, *The Queen's Corsair* 104 & *The Queen's Pirate* 113)

by God's wounds [*byee Garrd's/Gott's/Gud's woun's/wounts*]

An oath referring to Jesus' crucifixion.

> "By God's life if he were my man I would cut off his ears; yea, **by God's wounds** I would hang him." (Francis Drake, *The Queen's Corsair* 104 & *The Queen's Pirate* 113)

by gum [*byee garrm/goohm*]

An oath comparable to "by George," and a sound-alike substitute for "by God."

> "You say this cruise is bungled. Ah! **by gum**, if you could understand how bad it's bungled, you would see!" (Long John Silver, *Treasure Island* 165, Chap. 29)

by Heaven(s) [*byee 'eaven(s)/'eav'n(s)/heav'n(s)*]

> < "Now, in one word, sir, where is the treasure? Trifle not, or, **by Heaven**—!" "Name not Heaven, you have had my answer." > (Cain & Portuguese bishop, *The Pirate* 59, Chap. IX) "Yes! **by heavens**! you are right, pretty lady, I do care ..." (Cain's mate, *The Pirate* 113, Chap. XV)

by Hell [*byee 'ell*]

> "**By Hell**, what do you mean?" (Captain Easterling, *Captain Blood Returns* 35)

by hook(e)y [*byee 'ooky*]

"Hookey" or "hooky" is a nineteenth-century word most often used together with "crooky" (a combination evolving into the more recent "by hook or by crook," meaning "by fair means or foul") to refer to questionable conduct or dishonest dealings of any kind. "By hookey," therefore, is a mild reference to mischief or darkness of character.

> "Ha! Tricked, **by hookey**! She's been towing a sea anchor!" (Resolution Day, *Martin Conisby's Vengeance* 104)

by my blood [*byee me/myee bloohd/blut*] I swear; I swear on my soul

The speaker swears on his own life—literally, his own blood—to the truth or certainty of the statement that precedes or follows.

> "Follow me, rogue, or **by my blood**, Master Fenn's gun yonder shall blast some o' ye to perdition—come!" (Adam Penfeather, *Adam Penfeather, Buccaneer* 200)

by my deathless soul [*byee me/myee dath/deffless sool/so'ool*] I swear; I swear on my soul

The term "deathless" amplifies the speaker's oath, as he emphasizes with the use of that term the infinite consequences of any falsehood on his part (*i.e.*, not simply damnation, but eternal damnation).

> "Ha, **by my deathless soul**—what's doing yonder?" (Resolution Day, glimpsing out of the corner of his eye the pursued ship take on sudden speed and assume an offensive position, *Martin Conisby's Vengeance* 104)

by my soul [*byee me/myee sool/so'ool*] I swear; I swear on my soul

> "And, anyway, easy or difficult, **by my soul**, I'm not leaving Nevis without you." (Peter Blood, *The Fortunes of Captain Blood* 100)

by Satan [*byee Sayee/Seh/Sy-tan*]

> "I say a curse o' this plaguey land travel, Roger! I say we'm out of our natural element, **by Satan**!" (Rogerson, *Winds of Chance* 353)

by the blood [*byee t' bloohd/blut*]

An ambiguous oath—as the speaker fails to specify whether he is swearing (vituperatively) by the blood of some saint or martyr, for example, or (less offensively and more earnestly) by his own blood—though the former is more strongly implied by the use of the article "the" rather than the personal pronoun "my."

> "**By the blood!** to be sure it is murder that has happened here." (Benny Willitts, *The Book of Pirates* "The Ruby of Kishmoor" 235)

by the blood in my heart [*byee t' bloohd/blut i'/'n me/myee 'ahrrt/'eart/hahrrt*]

The speaker swears on his own life—literally, his own lifeblood—to the truth or certainty of the statement that precedes or follows.

> "Patch, you an' I've sailed many a sea together. And I swear **by the blood in my heart** that if anything 'appens to this lad, I—I'd as soon give myself to the sharks." (Long John Silver, at the side of Jim Hawkins' sickbed, "The Adventures of Long John Silver: Pieces of Eight" 22:02)

by the blood of Henry Morgan [*byee t' bloohd/blut o'\on 'enry Margan*]

An oath comparable to "by George." Henry Morgan (1653–1696), was England's most accomplished privateer, best known for his daring attacks in 1668–1671 on the Spanish at Porto Bello, Maracaibo, and Panama and for his subsequent deputy governorship of the young colony of Jamaica.

> "**By the blood of Henry Morgan**, you'll draw that lad's tooth, or by thunder you'll be carried aboard your ship feet first to be buried in your bonnie Scotland!" (Long John Silver, persuading dentist Angus MacAllister to minister to Jim Hawkins' tooth, "The Adventures of Long John Silver: The Tale of a Tooth" 3:01)

by the devil's hoof [*byee t' daahv/dayv/debb/div-il's 'oof*]

by the devil's teeth [*byee t' daahv/dayv/debb/div-il's teef*]

by the devil's twisted tail [*byee t' daahv/dayv/debb/div-il's twerst/twest-ed tayell*]

> "Here, the lights! **By the devil's hoof**, what's happened to our lights?" (Long John Silver, "The Adventures of Long John Silver: The Eviction" 6:08) "**By the devil's teeth**, what's this?" (Henry Morgan, "Pirates of Tortuga" 1:09:38) "Ha-har. **By the devil's twisted tail**, they're safe. (Long John Silver, "Long John Silver's Return to Treasure Island" 29:48)

by the eternal holy [*byee t' ay/iy-tarnal hoo/ho'oo/'o-ly*]

by the holy eternal [*byee t' hoo/ho'oo/'o-ly ay/iy-tarnal*]

Meaning the same thing as "by God," these phrases are good examples of how pirates sometimes referred obliquely to things associated with God in order to convey the same forcefulness as, but without the offensiveness of, a blunt invocation of God's name.

> < "Thought you was dead." "Nay, nay, not dead—not dead by odds. But **by the Eternal Holy**, Hi, I played many a close game with old Davy Jones, for all that." > (Hiram White & Blueskin, *The Book of Pirates* "Blueskin, the Pirate" 160) "Well, **by the Holy Eternal**, Hi, if that isn't a piece of your tarnal luck." (Blueskin, *The Book of Pirates* "Blueskin, the Pirate" 161–62)

by the eternal Jesus [*byee t' ay/iy-tarnal Jaah/Jay-sus*]

> "[B]ut, **by the eternal J[esu]s**, you shan't live to see us hang'd." (William Fly, *General History of the Pyrates* 611)

by the God above us [*byee t' Gard/Gott/Gud 'bove arrss*]

> "Now, I am Captain Adam Penfeather, your captain, and one ye shall obey or, **by the God above us**, I'll be death for

some o' ye afore I die." (Adam Penfeather, *Adam Penfeather, Buccaneer* 189)

by the gods [*byee t' garrds/gotts/guds*] by God

"This time, **by the gods**, yer gonna stand an' fight!" (Henry Morgan, *Dead Man's Chest* 10)

by the holy poker [*byee t' hoo/ho'oo/'o-ly poo/po'oo-ker*]

A "holy poker" is a ceremonial scepter, mace, or staff associated with a university, carried at the head of academic processions and displayed at other formal university-related events, and typically wielded by and associated most closely with the bedel, a high-ranking university official common to British and European universities. The phrase "holy poker" also came to be used in the urban slang of nineteenth-century England to refer to a man's penis.

"Well done! John Portuguese, **by the holy poker**! I never gave you credit for so much pluck." (Hawkhurst, remarking an enemy Portuguese ship's deadly broadside, *The Pirate* 48, Chap. VIII)

by the horns of Nick [*byee t' 'arns/'orns/'oorns/ harns/hoorns o'\on Neck*] by Satan's horns

"Nick" and especially "Old Nick" are names long used to refer to the devil.

"First, there's Abnegation Mings as you shall hear tell of on the Main from Panama to St Catherine's, aye, **by the horns of Nick** there be none of all the coastwise Brotherhood quicker or readier when there's aught i' the wind than Abnegation, and you can lay to that, my delicate cove!" (Abnegation Mings, *Black Bartlemy's Treasure* 31)

by the living thunder [*byee t' levv/liff-in' t'und/tunn-er*] by God; by heaven

"Living thunder" is a phrase associated in Protestant Christian theology and verse with the Holy Spirit, or more generally with a powerful God-sent force animating its recipients with spiritual clarity and vigor.

"You stand by Hawkins, John, and Hawkins'll stand by you. You're his last card, and, **by the living thunder**, John, he's yours!" (Long John Silver, *Treasure Island* 160, Chap. 28)

by the powers [*byee t' parrs/powarrs*]

An oath comparable to "by God" or "by heaven."

"He begged, and he stole, and he cut throats, and starved at that, **by the powers**!" (Long John Silver, *Treasure Island* 58, Chap. 11)

by the saints [*byee t' sayeents*]

An oath comparable to "by heaven."

"**By the Saints**! Ye're a bold man, Don Francisco, to come to me with such a tale—to tell me that ye know where the ransom's to be raised, and yet to refuse to say." (Peter Blood, *Captain Blood: His Odyssey* 199)

by thunder [*byee t'und/tunn-er*]

An oath comparable to "by heaven," and an abridgement of "by the living thunder"

"You stood by me at the stockade and, **by thunder**, I'll stand by you." (Long John Silver, "Treasure Island" [1998] 1:16:51)

Caesar's ghost [*Ceezarr's ghoost/gho'oost*]

"It's been overhauled already, **Caesar's ghost**." (Black Dog, disgusted on discovering that someone else has already rifled the contents of Billy Bones' seachest, "Treasure Island" [1960] 17:46)

call me dogsbody [*cawrl me dahgs/darrgs/ dorrgs-bahee/barrdy*]

Used to affirm on pain of being considered and called a "dogsbody" to the truth or certainty of a preceding statement. "Dogsbody" is a slang term used to refer to a junior midshipman aboard a vessel of the British Royal Navy and connotes unimportance, utter subservience, and fitness to do only the basest of tasks.

"'[T]will touch me very sensibly, or **call me dogsbody**!" (Benjamin Trigg, *Adam Penfeather, Buccaneer* 263)

cherish my guts [charrish/charsh/chersh me/myee garrts/goohts]

A fanciful minced oath comparable to "God love me."

> "O love my limbs! O **cherish my guts**— leave him to me, Cap'n!" (Sam Spraggons, urging Roger Tressady to allow him to torture Martin Conisby, *Black Bartlemy's Treasure* 306–07)

Christ [Chrawst/Chryeest]

> "**Christ**, I wuz just aboard a year, sir, I don't know much, please don't shoot me when I tells ya I don't know somethin', please!" (hand aboard pirate schooner, *The Gun Ketch* 279)

confound it [cahn/carrn/coohn/kern-foun'/fount/fowoon'/fowoond/fowoont ett/'n]

"Confound" means to throw into confusion or disorder, but also to destroy or ruin. The term reflects the speaker's impulse that something be destroyed or ruined; the phrase "confound it" accordingly is a somewhat, though not substantially, milder one than "damn it."

> "**Confound it**, Druscilla, glove me." (James Hook, "Hook" 1:27:10)

crikey [craw/cryee-key]

A sound-alike substitute for "Christ."

> < "Can you dance the hornpipe yet?" "No, I can't." "Not dance the hornpipe?! **Crikey!**" > (Long John Silver & Jim Hawkins, "Treasure Island" [1960] 24:37)

curse it [carrse/carrst/coorse/cursh/curst 'n/'t]

Used for emphasis, especially to express anger, displeasure, frustration, or other negative, sharply felt sentiment.

> "'Sblood! You grow mighty uneasy and suddenly too! **Curse it**, man, why this quick alarm?" (Roger Snaith, *Winds of Chance* 319)

curse me [carrse/carrst/coorse/cursh/curst me]

> "There be nary one shall recognize such bloody cutthroat for what you was when you rode out wi' us for the holy Protestant cause, God prosper it! Would your own mother know ye? **Curse me**—no!" (Ezekiel Penryn, *Winds of Chance* 32)

curse me for a canting mugger [carrse/carrst/coorse/cursh/curst me farr/fer a cantin' moohgger]

To cant is to speak in a whining voice. A mugger is a crocodile native to India and the East Indies. The phrase is used to suggest that something—the subject of conversation, a statement just made by the addressee, a statement about to be made by the speaker himself—is as surprising or bizarrely implausible as the possibility that the speaker is a "canting mugger."

> "**Curse me for a canting mugger**, then, if I'll trade on it." (John Flint, *Porto Bello Gold* 92)

curse me for a lubber [carrse/carrst/coorse/cursh/curst me farr/fer a loohbber]

Used for emphasis. The term "lubber" refers to a person who is not a seaman, to a young or inexperienced sailor, or to any person who is incompetent or unreliable.

> "**Curse me for a lubber** if I wouldn't be slittin' their throats one by one if I be left onboard fer 'alf a fortnight." (Long John Silver, *Dead Man's Chest* 7)

curse me for papistical Spaniard [carrse/carrst/coorse/cursh/curst me farr/fer parr/per-pes/pish-tercal Span-iahrrd/isher/nerd]

Used to affirm on pain of being considered and cursed as a "papistical Spaniard" to the truth or certainty of a preceding statement. English-speaking pirates despised the Spanish for their claimed monopoly over the New World and its waters, as well as for their notoriously harsh treatment of prisoners.

> "Well, I watch for that which is not yet and yet shall be, or **curse me for papistical Spaniard**!" (Smy Peters, *Adam Penfeather, Buccaneer* 158)

curse me with everlasting torments [carrse/ carrst/coorse/cursh/curst me weth/wi'/wiff/witt ebber/ebbry/e'er/ev'ry-lastin' tarrments]

A milder alternative to "damn me" or "I'll be damned."

> "I say **curse me with everlasting torments** but 'twill never do, Adam!" (Benjamin Trigg, Adam Penfeather, Buccaneer 248)

cursed if [carrst/coorsed/cursed an'\eff/eff'n/ if'n]

Used to negate emphatically whatever statement precedes or follows, in a way comparable to the modern phrase "I'll be damned if."

> < "[I]f you will look up you will see that I have those at my back who will not see me mishandled." "**Cursed if** we do!" > (Birthmark Sweetlocks & one of his allies, The Dealings of Captain Sharkey and Other Tales of Pirates "The Blighting of Sharkey" 49)

damme damn

Used for emphasis, especially to express anger, displeasure, or consternation.

> "**Damme**, but I'd sail with the devil to deliver a friend from such hell o' suffering ..." (Adam Penfeather, Adam Penfeather, Buccaneer 294)

damn all [damn awrl]

Used for emphasis and to convey a tough, devil-may-care attitude. The speaker implies that the accompanying statement is everything that is or should be important, and that all else can go to hell.

> "Go to't, lass, drink hearty—here's you and me agin world and **damn all**, says I. Let me perish!" (Roger Tressady, Martin Conisby's Vengeance 158)

damn me

An expression of surprise, disbelief, displeasure, or self-reproach.

> "By G[od], Glasby shall not die; d[am]n me if he shall." (Valentine Ashplant, General History of the Pyrates 222)

damn me for a EPITHET [damn me farr/fer a ...] damn me, I'm such a EPITHET

An expression of surprise, disbelief, or displeasure, often spoken when the speaker herself is at fault somehow. The speaker inserts after "damn me for" either (1) an epithet or other negative characterization consistent with her feelings of self-condemnation ("He got away wi' the treasure whiles I were sleepin', damn me for **a brainless lubber**"), or (2) an absurd characterization meant to reflect the extent of one's surprise or disbelief ("Well, damn me for **a buttered parsnip**, you kilt the Black Pirate 'imself."). See Chapter 9 for a comprehensive list of epithets.

> "She reached around with the stiletto, pressed the razor-sharp blade against his throat, and stopped. ... 'Oh, **damn me for** a weak fool,' she whispered, letting Yancy's head drop." (Elizabeth Marlowe, The Pirate Round 297–98)

damn my blood [damn me/myee bloohd/blut]

> "Running away, too, are you? **Damn my blood**!" (George Fairfax, The Fortunes of Captain Blood 152)

damn my buttons [damn me/myee barrt/ booht/buh'-uns]

"Damn my buttons" is very likely a milder, less offensive substitute for "damn my blood."

> "**Damn me buttons**. There's a thin slice o' luck. See 'er colors?" (Thomas Bartholomew Red, on spotting a rescuing ship hoist the Spanish flag, "Pirates" 8:07)

damn my eyes [damn me/myee eye'ees]

> "**Damn my eyes**! I have not seen you since Port Royal was swallowed up by the sea!" (Billy Bird, The Pirate Round 237)

damn my gizzard(s) [damn me/myee gezzards]

A playful variation on "damn me." The reference to "gizzard" or "gizzards" here relates to one's stomach or, more generally, an internal organ of any kind.

"[Damn] my gizzards for a —, but we ha' done a clean job this morning." (Martin, *Porto Bello Gold* 161, omission in original)

damn my lights and gizzard [*damn me/myee lawts/ligheets an'/'n' gezzard*]

A playful variation on "damn me." Lights are eyes. The reference to "gizzard" here relates to one's stomach or, more generally, an internal organ of any kind.

"[Damn] my lights and gizzard if I ever see such a monstrous heap o' human flesh!" (Billy Bones, *Porto Bello Gold* 59)

damn my soul [*damn me/myee sool/so'ool*]
I'll be damned

"[Dam]n my s[ou]l if ever I turned my back to any man in my life, or ever will, by G[od] ..." (Valentine Ashplant, *General History of the Pyrates* 223)

damnation [*dam-may/mayee/nayee-shern/shoohn*]

Used for emphasis, especially by a speaker who is shocked or surprised or, more typically, angry, displeased, frustrated, or otherwise negatively affected.

"That was your day, son, was it not? Well, tweren't mine. **Damnation**, cannon ball tore my leg to shreds." (Thomas Bartholomew Red, "Pirates" 1:01:29)

damnation seize my soul [*dam-may/mayee/nayee-shern/shoohn seize me/myee sool/so'ool*]
I'll be damned

"**Damnation seize my soul** if I give you Quarters, or take any from you." (Blackbeard, *General History of the Pyrates* 80)

dash my buttons [*dash me/myee barrt/booht/buh'-ons*]

A sound-alike substitute for "damn my blood."

"**Dash my buttons** what a night!" (Long John Silver, *Porto Bello Gold* 48)

dear heart [*dee-arr/err 'ahrrt/'eart/hahrrt*]
Used for emphasis.

"**Dear heart**, but he died bad, did Flint!" (bandaged John, *Treasure Island* 178, Chap. 31)

death and damnation [*dath/deff an'/'n' dammay/mayee/nayee-shern/shoohn*]

Used for emphasis, especially by a speaker who is shocked or surprised or, more typically, angry, displeased, frustrated, or otherwise negatively affected.

"Od's body, this shall not achieve! **Death and damnation**—no!" (Benjamin Trigg, stopping Captain Sharp from doling out Adam Penfeather's punishment, *Adam Penfeather, Buccaneer* 74)

death and wounds [*dath/deff an'/'n' woun's/wounts*]

An abridgement of "God's death and wounds" or "Christ's death and wounds"—a reference to Jesus' crucifixion.

"**Death and wounds**—yonder he comes for all of us—O mates look!" (Humphrey, spotting a wild Martin Conisby on an otherwise deserted island, *Black Bartlemy's Treasure* 272)

demme [*damn*] damn

"On the contrary, ma'm, you'll obey and instantly, or **demme**, I'll bundle ye over my shoulder and carry ye." (Japhet Bly, *Winds of Chance* 62)

the devil [*t' daahv/dayv/debb/div-il*]

Used where a modern speaker might instead say "the hell," in phrases like "what the devil is this" or "we sailed the devil out of that place."

< "No matter, when you have decided, ay or no, you may send me word." "Ha, **the devil** I may!" > (Adam Penfeather & Black Bartlemy, *Adam Penfeather, Buccaneer* 279)

INTERROGATIVE a\the devil [___ *a\t' daahv/dayv/debb/div-il*]

Used with an interrogative like "how" and "why" for emphasis, especially to express surprise, disbelief, displeasure, or conviction.

"**What a devil**, is he a conjurer?" ... "[I]f he be such a mighty conjurer, **how the devil** was it that he did not conjure himself clear of us?" (members of Edward Low's company, questioning a prisoner's ability to sail away on a sloop without a sail, *Pirates of the New England Coast* 196) "**Where the devil** have you been?" (Wolverstone, *Captain Blood Returns* 157)

devil burn me [*daahv/dayv/debb/div-il barrn me*] I'll be damned

An oath typically used to register any sharp reaction or emotion, especially surprise, astonishment, anger, or disappointment. "Burn" here is a reference to the fires of hell and eternal damnation.

"[D]evil burn me but I'd fain spare thee any further pain, Smy." (Absalom Troy, *Adam Penfeather, Buccaneer* 336)

devil damn me [*daahv/dayv/debb/div-il damn me*] I'll be damned

"Glasby is an honest fellow, notwithstanding this misfortune, and I love him, **Devil damn me** if I don't." (Valentine Ashplant, *General History of the Pyrates* 223)

dog bite me [*dahg/darrg/dorrg bawt/byeete me*] A mild substitute for "God damn me."

"Why, **dog-bite me**—she crawls!" (Benjamin Trigg, bemoaning the slowness of the *Santissima Trinidad, Adam Penfeather, Buccaneer* 232)

drowned (and sink) me [*drowoond (an'/'n' senk) me*]

As most pirates (and seamen of the seventeenth and eighteenth centuries) cannot swim, the reference is to a circumstance that many of them fear profoundly.

"Lord love me, your fine lady, for all her pride, sings out for quarters mighty quick, and now **drowned me** if they bean't a billing like two turtle doves ... warms me very 'eart it do, lass, and minds me how

you and me might do likewise." (Ben, *Winds of Chance* 101) "Why sink and **drowned me**! I say **drowned and sink me** if it a'n't the little, crowing captain, the game-cock whiffler ..." (Roger Tressady, *Adam Penfeather, Buccaneer* 276)

ecod [*ecarrd*]
egad [*e-garrd/ged*]
Sound-alike substitutes for "oh, God."

"No, his best men were we and **ecod**, Deb, 'twas me as roared and bellered and sang out loudest." (Ben, *Winds of Chance* 101)

"**Egad**, if I am to live clean, I believe the only thing is to go and offer my sword to the King of Spain." (Peter Blood, *Captain Blood: His Odyssey* 345)

fetch me up daft [*fatch me arrp daff/darrft/deft*] call me crazy
"Daft" means insane or idiotic.

"Blasphemy or not, you can **fetch me up daft**, Charles, if we weren't cut from the same sailcloth ..." (Long John Silver, *Dead Man's Chest* 14)

fire and death [*farr/fyarr an'/'n' dath/deff*]
Used for emphasis, especially by a speaker who is shocked or surprised or, more typically, angry, displeased, frustrated, or otherwise negatively affected.

"**Fire and death**, a philosopher! You speak cultured." (William Kidd, "Captain Kidd" 18:49)

fire and thunder [*farr/fyarr an'/'n' t'und/tunn-er*]
Used for emphasis, especially to express surprise, disbelief, or displeasure. The phrase is a combined reference to both Satan or hell ("fire," as in the flames of hell) and God or heaven ("thunder" is an abridgement of "living thunder," a phrase associated in Protestant Christian theology with the Holy Spirit).

"Everyone wants to bargain with me, you and Mercy. **Fire and thunder**, what do you think I am, a stinking sausage merchant?" (William Kidd, "Captain Kidd" 55:23)

for all love [*farr/fer awrl loohve/lub*]
An abridgement of "for the love of God."

"Hoisted by his own petard, and by choice, **for all love!**" (Billy Bird, *The Pirate Round* 346)

for all the world [*farr/fer awrl t' warrld*]
A mild but exaggerative oath. The speaker would stake "all the world" on the truth or accuracy of his statement.

< "You look as if you'd eat a body." "Why, to be sure, you're a brazen one, **for all the world.**" > (bride at wedding celebration & an uninvited Blackbeard, *The Book of Pirates* "Jack Ballister's Fortunes" 136)

for the love of mother and child [*farr/fer t' loohve/lub o'\on maahth/mo'/mudd-er an'/'n' chyee'eld*] for the love of God
"Mother and child" is a reference to Jesus and the Virgin Mary, though the phrase "love of mother and child" serves as a broader, more generically emphatic reference to something as extreme, powerful, or significant as the bond between any mother and child.

"**For the love of mother and child**, Jack, what's coming after us?" (Joshamee Gibbs, pressing Jack Sparrow to explain his alarmingly sudden and terror-stricken haste, "Pirates of the Caribbean 2: Dead Man's Chest" 17:51)

'fore God [*afarr/afore/befarr/before/'farr Garrd/Gott/Gud*] before God
An oath, used either to warrant the truth of the statement that precedes or follows (the speaker suggests he is swearing "before God" to his statement's truth), or to express emphasis (especially to convey surprise, disbelief, or displeasure).

"**'Fore God!** this is a lass of spirit." (John Sharkey, pleased and surprised at his female prisoner's contrived friendliness, *The*

Dealings of Captain Sharkey and Other Tales of Pirates "The Blighting of Sharkey" 55)

gadso; gad so [*garrd/ged-so'oo*]
A sound-alike abridgement of "God's own" or "God's only son."

< "Permit me to remark that had you died but once I should be content." "**Gad so**, Johnny man, I know it." > (John Barrasdale & Japhet Bly, *Winds of Chance* 166)

glory be [*glar/gloo-ry be*]
Used for emphasis, especially to express surprise, astonishment, disbelief, pleasure, or excitement.

"And so 'tis Japhet took solemn oath to kill 'em all three and come nigh a-doing of it more than once ... and to-day he's made an end o' Toby Ingleby, **glory be!**" (Jeremy Jervey, *Winds of Chance* 229)

God damn me [*Garrd/Gott/Gud damn me*]

"[I]f you don't act like an honest man G[o]d d[am]n ye, and offer to play us any rogues'y tricks by G[o]d, and G[o]d sink me, but I'll blow your brains out; G[o]d d[am]n me, if I don't." (William Fly, *General History of the Pyrates* 610–11)

God damn my soul [*Garrd/Gott/Gud damn me/myee sool/so'ool*]

"Look ye, Captain Atkinson, it is not that we care a t[url]d for your company, G[o]d d[am]n ye; G[o]d d[am]n my soul, not a t[url]d by G[o]d, and that's fair. ..." (William Fly, *General History of the Pyrates* 610–11)

God love us [*Garrd/Gott/Gud loohve/lub arrss*]

< "Aye, Joel—Tressady's alive again." "**God love us!**" > (Adam Penfeather & Joel Bym, *Black Bartlemy's Treasure* 103)

God love you [*Garrd/Gott/Gud loohve/lub 'ee/ya/ye/yer*]

< "Yonder belike is death!" "Then I pray you hold fast my hand, never loose me whiles we live, Japhet." "**God love thee**,

comrade; come, then!" > (Japhet Bly & Ursula Revell, boldly confronting together the enemy natives arrayed before them, *Winds of Chance* 201)

God sink me [*Garrd/Gott/Gud senk me*]
A milder alternative to "God damn me." Used for emphasis.

> "[I]f you don't act like an honest man G[o]d d[am]n ye, and offer to play us any rogues'y tricks by G[o]d, and **G[o]d sink me**, but I'll blow your brains out; G[o]d d[am]n me, if I don't." (William Fly, *General History of the Pyrates* 610–11)

God's blood (and wounds) [*Garrd's/Gott's/Gud's bloohd/blut (an'/'n' woun's/wounts)*]
God's body [*Garrd's/Gott's/Gud's bahee/barrdy*]
God's death [*Garrd's/Gott's/Gud's dath/deff*]
God's wounds [*Garrd's/Gott's/Gud's woun's/wounts*]

Oaths referring to Jesus' crucifixion. Used for emphasis, especially to express surprise, disbelief, displeasure, or conviction.

> "I don't love many words, G[o]d d[am]n ye, if you have a mind to be well used you shall, **G[o]d's b[loo]d** ..." (William Fly, *General History of the Pyrates* 611) "[B]ut G[o]d d[am]n ye, and **G[o]d's b[loo]d and w[oun]ds**, if you don't act like an honest man G[o]d d[am]n ye, and offer to play us any rogues'y tricks by G[o]d, and G[o]d sink me, but I'll blow your brains out; G[o]d d[am]n me, if I don't." (William Fly, *General History of the Pyrates* 610–11) "**God's body**, I don't know what is happening these days. Is no one to be trusted?" (Billy Bird, *The Blackbirder* 201) < "Oh, Japhet, it were strangely terrible if, despite all your cunning stratagems and care of me, I should end by killing myself, as did your poor Spanish lady and for the same ... shameful reason—" "**God's death**! Never say it ... never think such vile thing ..." > (Ursula Revell & Japhet Bly, *Winds of Chance* 304)

"**God's wounds**, Doughty, what dost thou mean to use this familiarity with me, considering thou art not the General's friend?" (John Brewer, *The Queen's Corsair* 52 & *The Queen's Pirate* 99)

God's light [*Garrd's/Gott's/Gud's lawt/ligheet*]
An oath referring to God's power to enlighten and inspire. Used for emphasis, especially to express surprise, disbelief, displeasure, or conviction.

> < "Why, then, being two to one, we must force her to drink." "Force her to drink, comrade? Force Joanna—**God's light**—!" > (Martin Conisby & Resolution Day, discussing Captain Jo's refusal to take medicine, *Martin Conisby's Vengeance* 166)

God's my life [*Garrd's/Gott's/Gud's me/myee lawf/lyeefe*]
An oath used for emphasis, especially to express surprise, disbelief, displeasure, or conviction.

> "Yet, **God's my life**, it's more than a scratch. I'm bleeding like a Christian martyr." (George Fairfax, *The Fortunes of Captain Blood* 150)

a God's name [*a Gard's/Gott's/Gud's nayeeme*]
in God's name

> "**A God's name** what use is the ship to those poor ragamuffins?" (Captain Easterling, *Captain Blood Returns* 13)

good lack [*good leck*] good grief
A sound-alike substitute for "good Lord."

> < "Oh, Master Lovepeace, show me how to get up into the daylight." "How now! **Good lack**, is't thee, child?" > (Ursula Revell & Lovepeace Farrance, encountering each other on Farrance's gun deck, *Winds of Chance* 75)

great guns [*grayeet/grea'/grett garrns/goohns*]
A milder alternative to "good God." Used for emphasis, especially to express surprise, disbelief, displeasure, or conviction.

"Great guns! messmates, but if Flint was living, this would be a hot spot for you and me." (Long John Silver, *Treasure Island* 178, Chap. 31)

gut me [*garrt/gooht me*]

A milder alternative to "damn me" or "I'll be damned." Used for emphasis, especially to express surprise, disbelief, displeasure, or conviction. To "gut" is to disembowel or, more generally, to kill.

"Well, he's no good to me; **gut me** if he is!" (John Flint, *Porto Bello Gold* 129

gut me for a preacher [*garrt/gooht me farr/fer a preh-cher*]

An oath that sets out both a gruesome fate (implying that the speaker is willing to be disemboweled if his statement proves false) and an absurd proposition (implying that the notion that the speaker might be a preacher is as absurd or shocking or noteworthy as the subject of his current comment).

"I like it not. Here's trickery or ye may **gut me for a preacher**." (John Flint, *Porto Bello Gold* 190)

hang it [*'ang ett/'n/'t*]

A milder alternative to "damn it." Used for emphasis, especially to express surprise, disbelief, displeasure, or conviction.

"**Hang it**, Pew, we've got the doubloons!" (comrade of Pew's, *Treasure Island* 26, Chap. 5)

hang me for lewd cur [*'ang me farr/fer lood carr/coor*]

A cur is a base or worthless dog or person.

"I say, **hang me for lewd cur** if this isn't right cursed manner to treat thine old and valued friend and trusty messmate, Adam or may I sink and perish in blood!" (Benjamin Trigg, *Adam Penfeather, Buccaneer* 310)

hell [*'ell*]

"I just don't understand how or why you'd want'a put a joint in a peg leg. **Hell**, the

thing'd never hold me up." (Long John Silver, *Dead Man's Chest* 16)

hell and corruption [*'ell an'/'n' carr'p/carrup/corr'p-shern/shoohn*]

The term "corruption" here refers to evil or villainy.

"**Hell and corruption**, get out of here before I bash your skull in!" (Billy Bones, "Treasure Island" (1960) 8:48)

hell and furies [*'ell an'/'n' fee'oo/foo-rees*]

An expansive reference to hell, "furies" being popularly understood as the demons or evil spirits that inhabit it or seek to establish hell's dominion on earth.

"[B]ut—**hell and furies**, man, —what say you?" (Benjamin Trigg, *Adam Penfeather, Buccaneer* 225)

hell and the devil [*'ell an'/'n' t' daahv/dayv/debb/div-il*]

"**Hell and the Devil**, girl! If that don't matter, tell me what does." (George Fairfax, *The Fortunes of Captain Blood* 156)

hell-fire (and brimstone) [*'ell-farr/fyarr (an'/'n' brem-stoone/sto'oone)*]

Most often an abridgement of "damn you to hell-fire" (or "damn you to hell-fire and brimstone").

"**Hell-fire**! Do you burn me, damn you?" (George Fairfax, upon having his wound cauterized by Peter Blood, *The Fortunes of Captain Blood* 153) "**Hellfire and brimstone**!" (Long John Silver's parrot Cap'n Flint, "Treasure Island" [1960] 22:27)

hell's bells [*'ell's bells*]

A colorful phrase evoking the ominous sound of a dark and inevitable doom. Used to express surprise, disbelief, displeasure, or conviction.

"**Hell's bells**!" (Thomas Bartholomew Red, falling down and betraying his Spanish padre disguise by inadvertently revealing his wooden leg, "Pirates" 1:19:59)

hell's fury\furies ['ell's fee'oo\foo-rees]

An expansive reference to hell and, more specifically, eternal damnation.

> "**Hell's fury**, am I to be served?" (Benjamin Trigg, waiting with his horse in an empty stable yard, *Adam Penfeather, Buccaneer* 43) "I say **Hell's furies**, man." (Benjamin Trigg, castigating Adam Penfeather for nearly leaving him behind, *Adam Penfeather, Buccaneer* 310)

holy poker [hoo/ho'oo/'o-ly poo/po'oo/ker]

A ceremonial scepter, mace, or staff associated with a university, carried at the head of academic processions and displayed at other formal university-related events, and typically wielded by and associated most closely with the bedel, a high-ranking university official common to British and European universities. The phrase "holy poker" also came to be used in the urban slang of nineteenth-century England to refer to a man's penis.

> "**Holy poker**, that would have been too good to be true." (Thomas Bartholomew Red, frustrated to find a stolen key does not fit the locked door of a Spanish galleon's armoury, "Pirates" 32:10)

holy Saviour [hoo/ho'oo/'o-ly Saah/Sayee-viarr]

> < "[I]f one of you doesn't start talking this very instant, then God save you!" "Oh God, sweet Jesus, **holy Saviour**! Don't, sir, please!" > (Arthur Ballard & hand aboard pirate schooner, *The Gun Ketch* 279)

holy Virgin [hoo/ho'oo/'o-ly Varrgin]

> "**Holy Virgin**! Harry's blessed head!" (Mordachai Fingers, "Cutthroat Island" 34:56)

I dare swear [I'ee darr/dayarr/dayerr swarr/swayarr/swayerr] I'm sure; I'll state with certainty; I'll go so far as to swear

> "He was after me till darkness and sheered off more in fear o' the sands than for aught else, **I dare swear**." (Long John Silver, *Porto Bello Gold* 22)

I lay my oath (SUBJECT+VERB) [I'ee layee me/myee oaf/o'oof/o'ooth (...)]

The speaker precedes or follows her statement with "I lay my oath." The effect is one of real emphasis, as the speaker purports to both bet and swear to the truth or certainty of the matter he asserts. If "I lay my oath" comes after the main statement, the speaker may repeat the subject of the main statement (or the corresponding pronoun) and the appropriate form of "do." See generally Section 19.2.7: Oath Echo.

> "[S]ink and burn me but ye look all the better for 't, more manly, my lad, **I lay my oath ye do**!" (Absalom Troy, *Adam Penfeather, Buccaneer* 7)

I swear [I'ee swarr/swayarr/swayerr]

> "Very pretty wrote to be sure; like print, **I swear**." (Long John Silver, "Treasure Island" 163, Chap. 29)

I swear to Christ [I'ee swarr/swayarr/swayerr t'/ta/ter Chrawst/Chryeest]
I swear to Jesus God [I'ee swarr/swayarr/swayerr t'/ta/ter Jaah/Jay-sus Garrd/Gott/Gud]

Particularly severe versions of "I swear" or "I swear to God."

> "Jesus and Mary, ye ...! **I swear t' Christ**, this bitch is dead!" (Billy Doyle, furiously cutting his woman hostage's throat on seeing Alan Lewrie shoot one of Doyle's men in the head, *The Gun Ketch* 162) "It's a lie, what he said, Lord Yancy, **I swear to Jesus God** it is." (unnamed pirate claimant before Elephiant Yancy, *The Pirate Round* 93)

I vow (SUBJECT+VERB) [I'ee vowoo (...)]

The speaker precedes or follows her statement with "I vow," thereby swearing to the truth or certainty of the matter she asserts. If "I vow" comes after the main statement, the speaker may repeat the subject of the main statement (or the corresponding pronoun) and the appropriate form of "do." See generally Section 19.2.7: Oath Echo.

"Messmate, I protest you become my astonishment, **I vow you do**, or damme!" (Absalom Troy, *Adam Penfeather, Buccaneer* 17)

I vow and protest [*I'ee vowoo an'/'n' protes'/protesht*]

Used preceding or following any especially assertive or insistent statement, especially to express consternation, displeasure, offense, or any sharp or intense sentiment.

< "My name is Ursula." "Well, I like thee, Ursula, and shall doubtless like thee better anon, for thou'rt a lovesome thing, **I vow and protest**." > (Roger Snaith, *Winds of Chance* 316)

I would have my soul fry in hell-fire [*I'ee woood 'aff/'ave/ha'/haff me/myee sool/so'ool fryee i'/'n 'ell-farr/fyarr*]

The speaker swears to some belief, statement, or action on pain of damnation.

"Before I would do you any harm, **I would have my soul fry in hell-fire**." (William Kidd, reassuring his fellow pirate Robert Culliford, *The Pirate Hunter* 371)

I'll be blown [*I'ee'ull be blowoon*]

Used for emphasis, especially to express surprise, disbelief, displeasure, or conviction.

"Billy Bowlegs, **I'll be blown**." (Long John Silver, "Long John Silver's Return to Treasure Island" 15:16)

I'll be bound [*I'ee'ull be bowoond*] (1) I swear; I declare (2) I'm sure that; I'm certain that

"**I'll be bound**. It's John Perch." (Patch, "Long John Silver's Return to Treasure Island" 3:45)

I'll be damned [*I'ee'ull be damt*]

"**I'll be damned** if I account it our duty to protect folk whose hands are against us." (Wolverstone, *Captain Blood Returns* 100)

I'll be hanged [*I'ee'ull be 'anged*] I'll be damned

"**I'll be hanged** if I'll take any more from you." (Tom Morgan, "Treasure Island" [1960] 1:03:02)

I'll be sworn [*I'ee'ull be swarrn*] I'll swear

"Sir Rupert hath 'listed thirty new men, I hear, and rogues every one **I'll be sworn**." (Adam Penfeather, *Black Bartlemy's Treasure* 106)

I'll swear to it [*I'ee'ull swarr/swayarr/swayerr t'/ta/ter ett/'n/'t*]

"But where are the other cubs? **I'll swear to it** there were three, at least, if not more." (pirate, having spotted eighteen-year-old Jack and thirteen-year-old Peterkin along with fifteen-year-old Ralph, *The Coral Island* 197)

I'll take my (affi)davy [*I'ee'ull tayeeke me/myee (arrf-eh/er-)daah/dayee-vy*] I'll swear; I'll give you my word

"Affidavy" is a modified form of the word "affidavit." "Davy," in turn, is short for "affidavy." The speaker expresses a willingness to swear to the truth of what he's about to say.

"Devil doubt it, but whether I'm changed or no, **I'll take my affidavy** that you are the same old half-witted Hi that you used to be." (Blueskin, *The Book of Pirates* "Blueskin, the Pirate" 161) "You and me should get on well, Hawkins, for **I'll take my davy** I should be rated ship's boy." (Long John Silver, *Treasure Island* 45, Chap. 8)

if my name's __ [*eff/eff'n/if'n me/myee nayeeme's __*] as sure as my name's __

"Well, ye fooled me that time, Murray, but ye never will again, by thunder—not if **my name's John Flint**!" (John Flint, *Porto Bello Gold* 189)

if the God of my good mother sits aloft indeed [*eff/eff'n/if'n t' Garrd/Gott/Gud o'\on me/myee good maahth/mo'/mudd-er sets alarrft endeed*]

Used to affirm that the speaker's preceding statement is as true or certain as God's place in heaven.

"Ay, lad, but by death, agony may be transmuted into abiding joy—**if the God of my good mother sits aloft indeed**, so comfort thee, Adam." (Absalom Troy, *Adam Penfeather, Buccaneer* 8)

I'm bound [*I'eem bowoond*] (1) I swear; I declare (2) I'm sure; I'm certain

"You don't catch me tasting rum so much; but just a thimbleful for luck, of course, the first chance I have. **I'm bound** I'll be good, and I see the way to." (Ben Gunn, *Treasure Island* 81, Chap. 15)

in the devil's name [*i'/'n t' daahv/dayv/debb/div-il's nayeeme*]

Used for emphasis, especially to express surprise, disbelief, displeasure, or conviction.

"Faugh! Come away, Roger, ere I stifle—come, **i' the devil's name**!" (Roger Tressady, *Black Bartlemy's Treasure* 92)

in the fiend's name [*i'/'n t' fien's nayeeme*]

"Why then, **in the Fiend's name** what would ye have?" (Adam Penfeather, *Black Bartlemy's Treasure* 48)

INTERROGATIVE in the (foul) fiend's name [__ *i'/'n t' (fowool) fien's nayeeme*]

Used with an interrogative like "how" or "why" for emphasis, especially to express surprise, disbelief, displeasure, or conviction.

"**How, i' the fiend's name**, shall we achieve that we would except we come up with Japhet?" (Roger Snaith, *Winds of Chance* 353) "Adam, fool, **what i' the Fiend's name**—? Damme, but you've done it now!" (Absalom Troy, questioning Adam Penfeather's apparent blunder, *Adam Penfeather, Buccaneer* 33) "But, if you must have carpenter, **why** ... **why i' the foul fiend's name**, choose this fellow?" (Benjamin Trigg, *Adam Penfeather, Buccaneer* 208)

Jesus [*Jaah/Jay-sus*]

< "One ... two ..." "**Jesus**, no, don't do it, I'll tell ya, I'll tell ya!" > (Arthur Ballard & hand aboard pirate schooner, *The Gun Ketch* 279)

Jesus and Mary [*Jaah/Jay-sus an'/'n' Mahr/May-ry*]

"**Jesus an' Mary**, wot kind o' King's officer they givin' commissions t'now, damn ye?" (Billy Doyle, shocked at Alan Lewrie's unconventional tactics, *The Gun Ketch* 163)

lay me bleeding [*layee me a-bleedin'*]

To "lay one bleeding" is to wound someone and leave him bleeding, thus arguably subjecting him to an indignity worse than death (as well as to prolonged suffering) by abandoning him without thinking him worth vanquishing.

"Now **lay me bleeding** if I ever heard the like o' this!" (Benjamin Trigg, *Adam Penfeather, Buccaneer* 226)

let me burn [*laaht/le' me barrn*]

The term "burn" refers principally to damnation (to the extent a person damned is thought to suffer the fires of hell) but also to profound misfortune (as fire is easily the thing most dreaded among pirates, most of whom cannot swim and who rely on the integrity of the wood underneath their feet for survival).

"Well now, **let me burn** if I ever heard or met the like of you, Captain Adam." (Black Bartlemy, *Adam Penfeather, Buccaneer* 280)

let me die [*laaht/le' me dyee*]

"**Let me die** if I don't wish I'd left her on the island to end him her own way—wi' steel or kindness ..." (Captain Belvedere, *Martin Conisby's Vengeance* 67)

let me drownd [*laaht/le' me drowoond*]

"'Twas woundy miracle or **let me drownd**!" (Abnegation Mings, *Adam Penfeather, Buccaneer* 16)

let me perish [*laaht/le' me parrish/parsh/persh*]

> "**Let me perish**, I say sink me in blood if I can get a word in edgewise!" (Benjamin Trigg, *Adam Penfeather, Buccaneer* 312)

let me rot and perish [*laaht/le' me rarrt an'/'n' parrish/parsh/persh*]

> "**Let me rot and perish**, sir, if 'tisn't purest joy ... to play hosts to grandee o' Spain ..." (Benjamin Trigg, *Adam Penfeather, Buccaneer* 192)

Lord [*Lawrrd/Loord*]

> < "Alligators?" "Ay, lady, you'll see plenty o' they. But, **Lord**, they won't nowise trouble you, if you don't go a-troubling o' they." > (Ursula Revell & Jeremy Jervey, *Winds of Chance* 248-49)

Lord love __ [*Lawrrd/Loord loohve/lub __*]

Used to express wry affection for, bemusement with, perplexity at, or light derision of a specified person or thing.

> "**Lord love** thy lubberly pins!" (Absalom Troy, *Adam Penfeather, Buccaneer* 55)

Lord love me [*Lawrrd/Loord loohve/lub me*]
Lord love my eyes [*Lawrrd/Loord loohve/lub me/myee eye'ees*]
Lord love us [*Lawrrd/Loord loohve/lub arrss*]

Used often to preface a question, explanation, statement in one own's defense, apology, or request for mercy or consideration of some kind.

> "Mercy, Cap'n—mercy! Not the hook, Cap'n—O **Lord love me**—not the hook!" (Sam Spraggons, *Black Bartlemy's Treasure* 307) "**Lord love my eyes**! Now what's she, ay, and him, adoing here along?" (Ned Bowser, *Adam Penfeather, Buccaneer* 275) "Oh **Lord love us**, Cap'n Adam, —how can we be sure as our rogues shall fight?" (Ned Bowser, *Adam Penfeather, Buccaneer* 228)

Lord love you (now) [*Lawrrd/Loord loohve/lub 'ee/ya/ye/yer (narr/nowoo)*]

Used to convey a sincere but unspecific sense of modesty and goodwill toward the addressee, and consequently spoken often before correcting, contradicting, criticizing, disagreeing with, or otherwise saying something conceivably offensive or off-putting to the addressee.

> "Easy, shipmate, easy! **Lord love you**, Martin, what would you now?" (Adam Penfeather, upon being surprised by a delusional and knife-wielding Martin Conisby, *Black Bartlemy's Treasure* 130) "**Lord love you now**! You've a heart, lass, a very stout sailorly heart, to stand there a-singing so joyous!" (Lovepeace Farrance, *Winds of Chance* 60)

love me [*loohve/lub me*]
love my BODY PART [*loohve/lub me/myee __*]

Used often to preface a question, explanation, statement in one own's defense, apology, or request for mercy or consideration of some kind. Where the speaker refers to a part of his body, such part may or may not have anything to do with the tone or content of the related question, request, or statement.

> "And as for a-drugging of ye, Marty, true again! But **love me**! What was I to do?" (Roger Tressady, *Black Bartlemy's Treasure* 302) "**Love my eyes**! Smy, wilt look now at my young Adam." (Absalom Troy, *Adam Penfeather, Buccaneer* 31) "**Love my innards**—I thought no man aboard could do as much, Andy." (Sam Spraggons, *Black Bartlemy's Treasure* 128) "We'm done, lads, I tell ye. O **love my lights**—we'm done!" (Sam Spraggons, *Black Bartlemy's Treasure* 311)

Madre de Dios [*Marr/May-dray dee Dios*]
Spanish for "Mother of God."

> < "I go to kill my uncle." "**Madre de Dios**!" > (Adam Penfeather & Absalom Troy, *Adam Penfeather, Buccaneer* 13)

malediction [*malerdik-shern/shoohn*]

The word "malediction" means "curse." However, the term serves both as an oath—used for emphasis, especially to express anger, displeasure, frustration, or some other negative, sharply felt sentiment—and as a curse—used to wish harm on another (see Chapter 7: Curses). The excerpt below possibly reflects both uses.

"Desertion? Ha—**malediction**! What's the meaning o' this?" (Benjamin Trigg, on hearing news of the company's desertion, *Adam Penfeather, Buccaneer* 263)

may God strike me dead [*mayee Garrd/Gott/ Gud strawk/stryeeke me dayd*] may I die

"[B]ut if you will be a villain and betray your trust, **may G[o]d strike me dead**, and may I drink a bowl of brimstone and fire with the D[evi]l, if I don't send you head-long to H[e]ll, G[o]d d[am]n me ..." (William Fly, *General History of the Pyrates* 611)

may I burn(, choke, and perish) [*mayee I'ee barrn(, chooke/cho'ooke, an'/'n' parrish/parsh/ persh)*] may I be damned; I'll be damned

The term "burn" arguably has double significance, referring principally to damnation but also to profound misfortune (as fire is easily the thing most dreaded among pirates).

< "Ye've been lucky, so you have." "Lucky? **May I burn!**" > (Peter Blood & George Fairfax, *The Fortunes of Captain Blood* 154) "I say, sir, you are and shall be our right honoured guest or **may I burn, choke and perish!**" (Benjamin Trigg, *Adam Penfeather, Buccaneer* 192)

may I drink a bowl of brimstone and fire with the devil [*mayee I'ee drenk a bowool o'\on brem-stoone/sto'oone an'/'n' farr/fyarr weth/wi'/ wiff/witt t' daahv/dayv/debb/div-il*] may I be damned; I'll be damned; may I go to hell

"[B]ut if you will be a villain and betray your trust, may G[o]d strike me dead, and **may I drink a bowl of brimstone and fire with**

the D[evi]l, if I don't send you head-long to H[e]ll, G[o]d d[am]n me ..." (William Fly, *General History of the Pyrates* 611)

may I perish [*mayee I'ee parrish/parsh/persh*] may I die

"I've been in somebody's debt ever since I can remember. But this—**may I perish!**— is a debt of another kind." (George Fairfax, *The Fortunes of Captain Blood* 154)

may I rot [*mayee I'ee rarrt*] may I die; I'll be damned

"I changed me from dreaming young fool, sighing and puling for the impossible, into sober man and right cheery soul content to take whatsoever comes and make the best o't, a fellow bold in adversity and jibing at woe, ay so, or **may I rot!**" (Absalom Troy, *Adam Penfeather, Buccaneer* 7)

may I sink and perish in blood [*mayee I'ee senk an'/'n' parrish/parsh/persh i'/'n bloohd/ blut*] may I die

A reference to a desperately violent death.

"I say, hang me for lewd cur if this isn't right cursed manner to treat thine old and valued friend and trusty messmate, Adam or **may I sink and perish in blood!**" (Benjamin Trigg, *Adam Penfeather, Buccaneer* 310)

may the devil seize me [*mayee t' daahv/ dayv/debb/div-il seize me*] may I be damned; I'll be damned

"**May the devil seize me** if I do not choose you as a consort!" (John Sharkey, *The Dealings of Captain Sharkey and Other Tales of Pirates* "How Copley Banks Slew Captain Sharkey" 69)

mercy of God [*marrcy o'\on Garrd/Gott/Gud*]

"Ah, **mercy of God**—how the ship rolls!" (Captain Jo, *Martin Conisby's Vengeance* 92)

a mercy's sake [*a marrcy's sayeeke*]

An expression merging the terms and meanings of "God have mercy" and "for God's sake" while omitting the references to God.

> < "'Tis wicked, hateful lie, as well you know, and so are you hateful liar, a wantonly wicked, hateful, odious, beastly fellow—" "Avast, lass, avast! Stint thy clack, **a mercy's sake**, for I'm plaguey weary and must sleep." > (Ursula Revell & Japhet Bly, *Winds of Chance* 290)

Mother of Heaven [*Maahth/Mo'/Mudd-er o'\on 'eaven/'eav'n/heav'n*]

> "I would hang Belvedere and make you captain in his room—he wearies me, and would kill me were he man enough—ah, **Mother of Heaven**, what a sea!" (Captain Jo, *Martin Conisby's Vengeance* 87)

mother's love [*maahth/mo'/mudd-er's loohve/lub*]

> "**Mother's love**, Jack, you know better than to wake a man when he's sleeping!" (Joshamee Gibbs, "Pirates of the Caribbean: The Curse of the Black Pearl" 51:36)

my backside [*me/myee beck-sawd/syeede*]
my rear [*me/myee ree-arr/err*]

Used to dismiss or deride something (especially a statement, view, or idea) as absurd, inappropriate, unacceptable, or untrue.

> "Good luck, **me backside**!" (Long John Silver, *Dead Man's Chest* 8) < "You tolt me to keep a weather eye fer 'em to move them two cannons off the hill, and look! They're still there!" "Dark, **my rear**! You were sleepin' on watch!" (Henry Morgan & Joshua Smoot, *Dead Man's Chest* 212)

my socks [*me/myee sarrks*]
A sound-alike substitute for "my God."

> "Master Robert didn't tell you? **My socks**!" (Ben Gunn, *Dead Man's Chest* 139)

name of God [*nayeeme o'\on Garrd/Gott/Gud*]

> "**Name of God**! But didn't you tell this lackey from court that ..." (Peter Blood, *The Fortunes of Captain Blood* 65)

od rot me [*arrd rarrt me*]
A sound-alike substitute for "God rot me."

> "**Od rot me**! Ye're talking like a parson." (Tim, *The Fortunes of Captain Blood* 165)

> Note that the entries immediately below featuring the term "od's" can each be spelled several different ways: The first term may be spelled "ods," "'ods," "od's," "'od's," "odds," "'odds," "odd's," or "'odd's," and those without an apostrophe-"s" at the end may be conjoined with a second term (*e.g.,* "blood"; "bobs, hammer and tongs"; "body"; "fish"; "guts"; "life"; "'ooks"; "wounds") to form a single word (*e.g.,* "'odsblood," "oddslife"). The second term may also be kept separate from "blood" (*e.g.,* "ods fish," "'odd's wounds").

od's blood; 'odsblood [*arrd's bloohd/blut*]
A sound-alike substitute for "God's blood," a reference to Jesus' crucifixion.

> "'**Odsblood**! Here is a pretty coil!" (Andrew Murray, *Porto Bello Gold* 146)

od's bobs, hammer and tongs [*arrd's barrbs, 'am/hem-mer an'/'n' tarrngs*]
A sound-alike substitute for "God's blood, body, and wounds," a reference to Jesus' crucifixion.

> "Smee, this seat is hot. **Odds bobs, hammer and tongs** I'm burning." (James Hook, *Peter Pan* 61)

od's body [*arrd's bahee/barrdy*]
A sound-alike substitute for "God's body," a reference to Jesus' crucifixion.

> "'**Od's body**, Adam, —one would think you expect battle and bloody strife anon!"

(Benjamin Trigg, *Adam Penfeather, Buccaneer* 227)

od's fish [*arrd's fesh*]

A sound-alike substitute for "God's flesh" or "God's life."

"'Sdeath and **odds fish**, who is to bring me that doodle-doo?" (James Hook, *Peter Pan* 157)

od's life [*arrd's lawf/lyeefe*]

A sound-alike substitute for "God's life," a reference to Jesus' crucifixion, but arguably also a particularly bold oath sworn on God's very existence.

"**Odslife**, Peter, you'ld be wise to hold that Spanish gentleman." (Wolverstone, *The Fortunes of Captain Blood* 17)

od's my life [*arrd's me/myee lawf/lyeefe*]

A sound-alike substitute for "God's my life."

< "So now, Ben, you are leaving, I take it?" "Ay, **'od's my life**—that am I!" > (Adam Penfeather & Benjamin Trigg, *Adam Penfeather, Buccaneer* 264)

od's wounds [*arrd's woun's/wounts*]

A sound-alike substitute for "God's wounds," a reference to Jesus' crucifixion.

"**Ods wounds**, what's doing?" (Benjamin Trigg, seeing his friend Adam Penfeather pummeled to the ground, *Adam Penfeather, Buccaneer* 72)

odso [*arrd-so'oo*]

A sound-alike abridgement of "God's own" or "God's only son." Note the first syllable may be spelled four different ways: "ods," "'ods," "odds," "'odds."

"**Odso**! You're there, Isabelita?" (George Fairfax, *The Fortunes of Captain Blood* 150)

on my faith [*arrn/o' me/myee fayeeth*] my word; I swear

Used to swear on one's faith to the truth or certainty of the statement that precedes or follows.

"**On my faith**, you are well informed." (Peter Blood, *Captain Blood Returns* 269)

on my soul [*arrn/o' me/myee sool/so'ool*] my word; I swear

Used to swear on one's soul to the truth or certainty of the statement that precedes or follows.

"I thought that however things went it might prove useful. And **on my soul**, I believe it did." (Peter Blood, *Captain Blood Returns* 38)

on my soul's salvation [*arrn/o' me/myee sool's/so'ool's sal-vaah/vayee-shern/shoohn*] my word; I declare

Used to swear on one's soul's future place in heaven to the truth or certainty of the statement that precedes or follows.

"**On my soul's salvation**, Peter, there was a moment when I thought our sands were run." (Nathaniel Hagthorpe, *Captain Blood Returns* 37)

or I'm a __ [*arr I'eem a __*]

Used to declare a preceding statement to be as true or certain as the proposition that the speaker might be whatever thing he names is absurd or implausible.

"For here's scene o' domestic bliss to touch the heart o' poor, lorn sailorman and take him all aback, **or I'm a buttered parsnip**!" (Absalom Troy, *Adam Penfeather, Buccaneer* 105–6) "They do but rejoice, Adam, and not without due reason, **or I'm a curdog**!" (Benjamin Trigg, *Adam Penfeather, Buccaneer* 262) "He'll run foul o' trouble anon, **or I'm a flounder**!" (Absalom Troy, *Adam Penfeather, Buccaneer* 60)

or I'm a fool [*arr I'eem a foo'ell*]

Used to stake the speaker's own intelligence and credibility on the truth or certainty of a preceding statement.

"He's got the strength to enforce his will, and the will to play the rogue, **or I'm a** fool else." (Trenam, *Captain Blood Returns* 279)

or I'm a lubberly Dutchman [*arr I'eem a loohber/loohb'/lubb'-ly Darrtch/Doohtchman*]

Used to declare a preceding statement to be as true or certain as the proposition that the speaker might be a "lubberly Dutchman" is unlikely. English seamen traditionally had little regard for their Dutch counterparts; "lubberly" and "Dutchman" both telegraph "incompetence" in the average English-speaking pirate's mind.

> "There be more foul weather acoming, **or I'm a lubberly Dutchman**, which I ain't!" (Ned Bowser, *Adam Penfeather, Buccaneer* 162)

perish and plague me [*parrish/parsh/persh an'/'n' playeeg me*]

A milder alternative to "damn me" or "I'll be damned." Used for emphasis, especially to express surprise, disbelief, displeasure, or conviction.

> "Love my limbs! **Perish and plague me**, but who's the friend as be a rope's-ending o' ye, Andy lad—you as be cock o' the ship?" (Sam Spraggons, *Black Bartlemy's Treasure* 127)

INTERROGATIVE a\the plague [___ *a\ t' playeeg*] INTERROGATIVE the hell

Used for emphasis, especially to express surprise, disbelief, displeasure, or conviction. Modern speakers use "the hell" in the same way, *e.g.*, "What the hell does it matter?"

> "**What a plague** do it matter if it is an English settlement?" (Wolverstone, *Captain Blood: His Odyssey* 310) "Ho, George, **where a plague** are ye?" (Benjamin Trigg, *Adam Penfeather, Buccaneer* 207) "And how a-plague, **how the plague**, ma'm, shall I be dumb and yonder black rogue vaunting his rascality, twitting me with his villainy?" (Japhet Bly, *Winds of Chance* 271) "If ye wants the wench, **why the plague** don't ye go and fetch her?" (Wolverstone, *Captain Blood: His Odyssey* 309)

plague and confound me [*playeeg an'/'n' cahn/carrn/coohn/kern-foun'/fount/fowoon'/fowoond/fowoont me*]

A milder alternative to "I'll be damned."

> "Ha, **plague and confound me!**" (Benjamin Trigg, *Adam Penfeather, Buccaneer* 248)

plague on it [*playeeg arrn/o' ett/'n/'t*]

An arguably less blasphemous, though nevertheless potent, alternative to "damn it" or "to hell with it."

> "I tell you because ... Oh, **plague on it!**—so that ye may tell her ..." (Peter Blood, *Captain Blood: His Odyssey* 287) "Are you angry with me, Isabelita? **Plague on it!** I am like that. Hot and quick." (George Fairfax, *The Fortunes of Captain Blood* 156)

rip my jib [*rep me/myee jeb*]

Used in a similar way as, though obviously to much milder effect than, "damn me." A jib is a triangular sail at the head of a vessel.

> "Well! Well! **Rip me jib** if it isn't me old mate, Henry Morgan!" (Joshua Smoot, *Dead Man's Chest* 156)

rot me [*rarrt me*]

A milder alternative to "damn me" or "I'll be damned."

> "Ha—rot me! **Rot me** but you are afraid of me—afraid, yes!" (Captain Jo, *Martin Conisby's Vengeance* 33)

rot my bones [*rarrt me/myee boones/bo'oones*]

A milder alternative to "damn me," and perhaps a sound-alike substitute for "damn my soul."

> "Don't matter! **Rot my bones!** You lose a fortune; you spill thirty thousand ducats in the kennel, and you say it don't matter!" (George Fairfax, *The Fortunes of Captain Blood* 156)

's fish [*'s fesh*]

A sound-alike abridgement of "God's flesh" or "God's life."

"'S fish! Is this your Englishman, Jo?" (Captain Belvedere, *Martin Conisby's Vengeance* 59)

's heart ['s 'ahrrt/'eart/hahrrt]

An abridgement of "God's heart."

> < "But a sick man cannot give orders. Henceforth you should be Captain, for he is at present no more than our poor invalid." "'S heart! How sayst thou to this, Japhet, old lad?" > (Ursula Revell & Barnabas Rokeby, *Winds of Chance* 87)

saint's blood [*sayeent's bloohd/blut*]

An oath referring to a martyr's death. Used for emphasis, especially to express surprise, disbelief, displeasure, or conviction.

> < "We thought you were killed at Boco del Toro?" "**Saint's blood**, that's what I thought meself." > (Thomas Bartholomew Red, "Pirates" 1:01:05)

'sblood; 's blood [*'sloohd/'sblut*]

An abridgement of "God's blood," a reference to Jesus' crucifixion.

> "'**Sblood**, Aldbourne, you must hate our Japhet as I do, —almost." (Roger Snaith, *Winds of Chance* 317)

'sblood and death [*'sbloohd/'sblut an'/'n' dath/deff*]

An abridgement of "God's blood and death," a reference to Jesus' crucifixion.

> "'**Sblood and death**—what's here?" (Benjamin Trigg, seeing his friend Adam Penfeather pummeled to the ground, *Adam Penfeather, Buccaneer* 72)

'sblood and 'ounds [*'sbloohd/'sblut an'/'n' 'oun's/'ounts*]

An abridgement of "God's blood and wounds," a reference to Jesus' crucifixion.

> "'**Sblood and 'Ounds!** If ye wants the wench, why the plague don't ye go and fetch her?" (Wolverstone, *Captain Blood: His Odyssey* 309)

'sbud [*'sbarrd/'sboohd*]

A sound-alike substitute for "God's blood," a reference to Jesus' crucifixion.

> "We've reduced our inflammation but our fever little abates, we gain no strength, we languish, for, '**sbud**, mem, we refuse t'eat and we must eat t' give Nature a chance, demme." (Crabtree, *Winds of Chance* 89)

scupper, sink, and burn me [*scarr/skooh-per, senk, an'/'n' barrn me*]

To scupper something is to destroy or get rid of it. With respect to the "sink and burn" portion of the phrase, pirates often burned the ships they plundered. However, burning a ship did not necessarily sink it. Thus, to burn *and* sink something is to take pains to assure its complete obliteration. "Scupper, sink, and burn me" might therefore amount to something like "destroy me utterly."

> "Well, now, my poor orphan, I says you can **scupper, sink and burn me** if this an't a precious sorry business for any dutiful son, and mighty heart-breaking!" (Absalom Troy, *Adam Penfeather, Buccaneer* 4)

scuttle me [*scu'le me*]

"Scuttle" means to sink a vessel by opening a hole in her hull, and is used more broadly to mean to discard or get rid of something.

> "Well, **scuttle me** if it be none other'n me old ship mate, Jimmy Hawkins!" (Long John Silver, *Dead Man's Chest* 293)

'sdeath [*'sdath/'sdeff*]

An abridgement of "God's death," a reference to Jesus' crucifixion.

> "'**Sdeath!** 'Twould be the greatest haul in our time, Murray." (John Flint, *Porto Bello Gold* 88)

'sdeath and blood [*'sdath/'sdeff an'/'n' bloohd/blut*]

An abridgement of "God's death and blood," a reference to Jesus' crucifixion.

"But 's death and blood, Captain Troy, don't I tell ye ..." (Benjamin Trigg, *Adam Penfeather, Buccaneer* 44)

shiver my sides [*shevv/shibb/shi'-arr me/myee sawds/syeedes*]

A milder alternative to "damn me" or "I'll be damned." To "shiver" something is to cause it to shake or quiver. "Shiver my sides" is likely a derivation from "shiver my timbers" (referring to a forceful impact between cannon shot and wooden vessel) or "split my sides" (referring to a sensation of laughing so hard that one's abdomen feels as if it is being torn apart), or a combination thereof, and in any event is used in reference to something that, figuratively speaking, hits the speaker hard or shakes her up.

"Cross me, and you'll go where many a good man's gone before you, first and last, these thirty year back—some to the yard-arm, **shiver my sides!** and some by the board, and all to feed the fishes." (Long John Silver, *Treasure Island* 159, Chap. 28)

shiver my soul [*shevv/shibb/shi'-arr me/myee sool/so'ool*]

A milder alternative to "damn my soul." To "shiver" something is to cause it to shake or quiver. For pirates, the term is typically a reference to the impact made by a cannon ball or other kind of shot on a vessel.

"Scatter and look for them, dogs! Oh, **shiver my soul**, if I had eyes!" (Pew, *Treasure Island* 26, Chap. 5)

shiver my timbers [*shevv/shibb/shi'-arr me/myee tem-barrs*]

To shiver one's timbers, literally, means to fire a cannon ball or other kind of shot into a ship with such force that those on deck hear or feel the impact.

"**Shiver my timbers**, a land lubber I'll never be!" (Long John Silver, "Long John Silver's Return to Treasure Island" 51:58)

sink and burn me [*senk an'/'n' barrn me*]

A milder alternative to "damn me" or "I'll be damned." Pirates often burned the ships they plundered. However, burning a ship did not necessarily sink it. Thus, to burn *and* sink something is to take pains to assure its complete obliteration. "Burn and sink me" might therefore amount to something like "destroy me utterly."

< "I'll fight you or any man, kill or be killed and joy in it." **"Sink and burn me** but I believe you would." > (Adam Penfeather & Absalom Troy, *Adam Penfeather, Buccaneer* 32)

sink and drownd me [*senk an'/'n' drowoond me*]

A milder alternative to "damn me" or "I'll be damned." Used for emphasis, especially to express surprise, disbelief, displeasure, or conviction. As most pirates (and seamen of the seventeenth and eighteenth centuries) cannot swim, the reference is to a circumstance that many of them fear profoundly.

"Why **sink and drownd me**! I say drownd and sink me if it a'n't the little, crowing captain, the game-cock whiffler ..." (Roger Tressady, *Adam Penfeather, Buccaneer* 276)

sink and scuttle me [*senk an'/'n' scu'le me*]

A milder alternative to "damn me" or "I'll be damned." Used for emphasis, especially to express surprise, disbelief, displeasure, or conviction. To scuttle something is to discard or get rid of it.

"Now, now, shipmate, here's lubberly manners, **sink and scuttle me—**." (one-eared pirate, protesting Martin Conisby's shoving of a staff into his pirate comrade's stomach, *Black Bartlemy's Treasure* 22)

sink me [*senk me*]

A milder alternative to "damn me" or "I'll be damned." Used for emphasis, especially to express surprise, disbelief, displeasure, or conviction.

"Sink me! It's him, Roger; 'tis Martin sure as saved of us from Penfeather, curse him, on Bartlemy's Island three years agone—it's him, Roger, it's him!" (Abnegation Mings, *Martin Conisby's Vengeance* 155) "Sink me, but I like his spirit!" (John Sharkey, admiring Captain Scarrow's defiant refusal at knifepoint to beg for his life, *The Dealings of Captain Sharkey and Other Tales of Pirates* "How the Governor of Saint Kitt's Came Home" 23)

sink me in blood [*senk me i'/'n bloohd/blut*]
A reference to a desperately violent death.

"Let me perish, I say **sink me in blood** if I can get a word in edgewise!" (Benjamin Trigg, *Adam Penfeather, Buccaneer* 312)

sink me now [*senk me narr/nowoo*]

"But **sink me now** if I'd rot myself in rum on account of anything that wears a petticoat." (Wolverstone, *Captain Blood: His Odyssey* 310)

smite me __ [*smawt/smyeete me __*]
A milder alternative to "damn me" or "I'll be damned." To "smite" means to strike hard, injure, or kill, and the use of the term in biblical passages to refer to acts of punishment or destruction by God makes it particularly appropriate for use as an oath. The speaker fills in the blank with some adjective or phrase describing a state of incapacitation or some other unfortunate condition ("blind" [*blawnd/blin'/blyeen'/blyeend/blyeent/blynt*], "dumb" [*doohmb*], and "bleeding" [*a-bleedin'*] are frequently used). Used for emphasis, especially to express surprise, disbelief, displeasure, or conviction.

"Ha, **smite me blind and speechless** but she creeps like a slug, a very louse!" (Benjamin Trigg, bemoaning the slowness of the *Santissima Trinidad, Adam Penfeather, Buccaneer* 232) "**Smite me dumb**, George! D'ye think I don't know swagger from stride?" (Benjamin Trigg, *Adam Penfeather, Buccaneer* 208) "Why, **smite**

me stiff in gore if y' aren't all of a quake and pallid as a shark's belly!" (Benjamin Trigg, seeing inexplicable anxiety and agitation in Adam Penfeather's face, *Adam Penfeather, Buccaneer* 245)

snake sting me [*snayeeke steng me*]
A milder alternative to "damn me" or "I'll be damned." The reference to a snake is likely both literal and metaphorical, inspired by the traditional biblical and literary characterization of Satan or evil generally as a serpent.

"**Snake sting me**! This comes o' harbouring a lousy rogue as balks good liquor." (Abnegation Mings, *Black Bartlemy's Treasure* 32)

snoggers [*snarrgers*]
An expletive of indeterminate origin. The term is a minced oath allowing the speaker to avoid a more offensive formulation. Possible derivations include: a remote sound-alike substitute for "God rot it"; a playful reference to persons engaged in sexual intercourse (based on "snog," meaning to engage in affectionate play such as cuddling or smooching); or a pluralized nonsense oath like "shucks" or "bejeebers."

"**Snoggers**! So here's our rogue Johnny in association with God, eh, ma'm!" (Japhet Bly, exasperated by Ursula Revell's relentless efforts to describe Bly's hated enemy John Barrasdale as brave and admirable, *Winds of Chance* 332)

souse me for a gurnet [*soust/sowoose/sowoost me farr/fer a garr-n't*]
To "souse" is to pickle. A "gurnet" is a fish with a large, flat, spiny head.

"On my soul now a most learned and bloodthirsty disquisition—or **souse me for a gurnet**!" (Absalom Troy, *Adam Penfeather, Buccaneer* 101)

split me [*splet me*]
A milder alternative to "damn me" or "I'll be damned." Used for emphasis, especially

to express surprise, disbelief, displeasure, or conviction.

> "**Split me!** O blind me if I thought ye such a lubberly fool!" (Roger Tressady, *Black Bartlemy's Treasure* 303)

split my sides [*splet me/myee sawds/syeedes*]

A milder alternative to "damn me" or "I'll be damned." Traditionally, to "split one's sides" means to laugh so hard one feels as if her abdomen is being torn apart. However, the phrase might be used in any context in which the speaker experiences thoughts or feelings so violent or radical they might be said to endanger her body's integrity.

> "**Split my sides,** I've a sick heart to sail with the likes of you!" (Long John Silver, *Treasure Island* 60, Chap. 11)

split my skull [*splet me/myee skoohl*]

> "Well, **split my skull!**" (Henry Morgan, "Pirates of Tortuga" 1:10:04)

stab me [*starrb me*]

A milder alternative to "damn me" or "I'll be damned." Used for emphasis, especially to express surprise, disbelief, displeasure, or conviction.

> < "If we fail to agree terms, why, that's the end of the matter." "Oho! The end of the matter, eh? **Stab me,** but it may prove the beginning of it." > (Peter Blood & Captain Easterling, *Captain Blood Returns* 32)

stap me [*starrp me*]

A milder alternative to "damn me" or "I'll be damned." "To stap" means both to stop and to pierce or impale.

> "**Stap me,** but I might ha' known you would see it, Peter!" (Andrew Murray, *Porto Bello Gold* 98)

stap/step my vitals [*starrp me/myee vawt/vy'/vyeet-als*]

A milder alternative to "damn me" or "I'll be damned." "To stap" means both to stop and to pierce or impale. Vitals are one's in-

ternal organs. The phrase refers ultimately to the doing of violence to one's innards.

> "**Stap me vitals,** your brother, Captain, your brother?" (Benjamin Trigg, *Adam Penfeather, Buccaneer* 45) < "Should he not be bled, sir?" "**Step me vitals**—no, mem! 'Tis blood we lack! There's more fine lads killed by the dem'd lancet than all y'r rapiers and small swords, b'ged!" > (Ursula Revell & Crabtree, *Winds of Chance* 89)

strike me [*strawk/stryeeke me*]

A milder alternative to "damn me" or "I'll be damned." Used for emphasis, especially to express surprise, disbelief, displeasure, or conviction.

> "**Strike me,** you're a smart one." (Long John Silver, "Long John Silver's Return to Treasure Island" 40:17)

strike me ___ [*strawk/stryeeke me ___*]

A milder alternative to "damn me" or "I'll be damned." To "strike" is to hit with the intention of causing injury or pain. The speaker fills in the blank with some adjective or phrase describing a state of incapacitation or some other unfortunate condition ("blind" [*blawnd/blin'/blyeen'/blyeend/blyeent/blynt*], "dumb" [*doohmb*], and "bleeding" [*a-bleedin'*] are frequently used). Used for emphasis, especially to express surprise, disbelief, displeasure, or conviction.

> "**Strike me blind,** you have as much to say as a shoal of salmon!" (Thomas Bartholomew Red, astonished at the silence of his old company mates on seeing him for the first time in years, "Pirates" 1:00:06) "Well now, **strike me deaf, blind and bleeding** if I ever heard the like o' this!" (Benjamin Trigg, *Adam Penfeather, Buccaneer* 208) "Black Bartlemy for one and Roger Tressady for t'other and hell-fire roarers both or **strike me dumb!**" (Absalom Troy, *Adam Penfeather, Buccaneer* 6)

suffering catfish [*sarrff/soohff-erin'/'rin/'ring carrt-fesh*]

Used for emphasis, especially to express surprise, disbelief, displeasure, or conviction. American and English modern speakers have long used the phrase "suffering cats" (as well as, though less frequently, "suffering catfish"), and the use of "catfish" rather than "cats" is decidedly consistent with the pirate's preference—all other things being equal—for sea-themed expressions.

> "Oh, **suffering catfish**, how much longer are we goin' to put with Smollett and that windbag of a slob, Trelawney?" (Tom Morgan, "Treasure Island" [1960] 37:14)

sweet Jesus [*sweet Jaah/Jay-sus*]

Used for emphasis, especially to express surprise, sudden pleasure, exasperation, or displeasure.

> < "[I]f one of you doesn't start talking this very instant, then God save you!" "Oh God, **sweet Jesus**, holy Saviour! Don't, sir, please!" > (Arthur Ballard & hand aboard pirate schooner, *The Gun Ketch* 279)

sweet merciful heaven [*sweet marrciful 'eaven/'eav'n/heav'n*]

Used for emphasis, especially to express surprise, sudden pleasure, exasperation, or displeasure.

> "**Sweet, merciful heaven**, haven't you ears? Set the course for Port Royal!" (Peter Blood, "Captain Blood" 1:30:54)

'swounds and blood [*'swoun's/'swounts an'/'n' bloohd/blut*]

An abridgment of "God's wounds and blood," a reference to Jesus' crucifixion.

> "**'Swounds and blood**, Absalom, never tell me you'd 'list this little misery, this poor atomy?" (Benjamin Trigg, on seeing the slight Adam Penfeather for the first time, *Adam Penfeather, Buccaneer* 44)

ten thousand curses [*tan t'ou-san' carrses/coorses/curshes*]

An oath when used for emphasis, especially to express anger, displeasure, frus-tration, or some other negative, sharply felt sentiment, but also a curse when used to wish prodigious harm on another (see Chapter 7: Curses). The excerpt below possibly reflects both uses.

> < "'Tis mutinous rogue drew knife on me." "Tush and **ten thousand curses**! I tell ye this gentleman you outrage is friend o' mine." > (Captain Sharp & Benjamin Trigg, *Adam Penfeather, Buccaneer* 72)

(and) this I swear [(*an'/'n') dis/t'is I'ee swarr/swayarr/swayerr*]

Used before or after any representation or promise the speaker wishes to have believed as a sworn statement.

> "Japhet, old messmate, we offer ye quarters; here's terms, Japhet. Heave us down that you wot of, that same you stole from me—heave it to us, old shipmate, and we'll cry quits, ay—we'll up and stand away incontinent, and **this we swear**." (Roger Snaith, promising to leave Japhet Bly alone in exchange for Bly's bag of gems, *Winds of Chance* 355–56)

thunder [*t'und/tunn-er*] God; heaven

"Thunder" is an abridgment of "living thunder," which in turn is a phrase associated in Protestant Christian theology and verse with the Holy Spirit, or more generally with a powerful God-sent force animating its recipients with spiritual clarity and vigor.

> < "[D]id that doctor say how long I was to lie here in this old berth?" "A week at least." "**Thunder**! A week! I can't do that ..." > (Billy Bones & Jim Hawkins, *Treasure Island* 15, Chap. 3)

upon my life [*'parrn/'pon/uparrn me/myee lawf/lyeefe*]

The speaker swears on his own life to the truth or certainty of the statement that precedes or follows.

> < "Why did you so trick and marry me, Japhet?" "Ursula, **upon my life** I hardly know

... 'twas for divers reasons ... yet which o' these I'm not yet sure on." > (Ursula Revell & Japhet Bly, *Winds of Chance* 159)

upon my soul [*'parrn/'pon/uparrn me/myee sool/so'ool*]

The speaker swears on his own soul, and the eternal state thereof, to the truth or certainty of the statement that precedes or follows.

> "'Tis like you shall grow acquaint with dangers and, seeing pain o' wounds, you shall forget this mighty universe circles but about your puny self and come to know there be something better things than pretty-turned speech, gallantry o' bows and such fripperies. Thus and so, experience shall learn you to be a woman or, 'pon my soul, ma'm Ursula, though you be my wife, I'll none o' you." (Japhet Bly, *Winds of Chance* 40)

with a curse [*weth/wi'/wiff/witt a carrse/carrst/coorse/cursh/curst*]

An oath when used for emphasis, especially to express anger, displeasure, frustration, or some other negative, sharply felt sentiment, but also a curse when used to wish prodigious harm on another (see Chapter 7: Curses). The excerpt below reflects use of the phrase as an oath.

> "Lie you and rest, Johnny, sleep if you can against what's to do this night,

with a curse!" (Japhet Bly, *Winds of Chance* 357)

with a wannion [*weth/wi'/wiff/witt a warrn-yern*] with a vengeance

Used for emphasis, especially to express surprise, disbelief, displeasure, or conviction.

> "I say if fight we must, **with a wannion**, —fight we will, ay, and with a will, the closer the better!" (Benjamin Trigg, *Adam Penfeather, Buccaneer* 231)

ye gods [*ya/yer/you garrds/gotts/guds*] by God

> "That I should be here in fair lady's bedchamber and she, **ye gods**, my wife, and you so boldfaced crouching there, a very dragon o' virtue (swathed in bedclothes to be sure), —a sweetly frightful Gorgon." (Japhet Bly, *Winds of Chance* 288)

you can choke and let me rot [*ya/ye/yer cayn/kin chooke/cho'ooke an'/'n' laaht/le' me rarrt*]

> "And **you can choke and let me rot** if I ever seek the like!" (Abnegation Mings, *Adam Penfeather, Buccaneer* 16)

zounds [*zoun's/zounts/zowoonds/zowoon's/zowoonts*]

A sound-alike abridgement of "God's wounds," a reference to Jesus' crucifixion.

> < "They are under the tree yonder with John's sword and pistols." "**Zounds!** And why there?" > (Ursula Revell & Japhet Bly, *Winds of Chance* 339)

CHAPTER 7

Curses

At one in the morning, on May 27, 1726, Captain John Green of the merchant ship *Elizabeth* woke to find his boatswain, William Fly, and another crewman named Alexander Mitchel in his cabin. Green asked what was the matter.

This is what he heard: Fly was the ship's new captain, and Green now had a choice—to die where he lay, or to die above deck and save his mutinous crew the trouble of scraping blood out of the cabin floor.

Minutes later, Green found himself dangling over the side of the ship, one hand grasping a sail he had managed to catch as he was heaved overboard. He never let go, but his tenacity didn't save him. As he felt the sea swallow him up, he realized the ruthless Fly had chopped through his arm with an ax.

Ten days later, Fly and his new pirate company captured the *John and Betty*, sailing out of Barbados. Fly kept one of the passengers aboard, a sea captain named William Atkinson, to be his new pilot. When Atkinson protested, Fly exploded. Invective poured out of his mouth. The result is likely the finest piece of pirate profanity ever recorded:

> "Look ye, Captain Atkinson, it is not that we care a t[ur]d for your company, G[o]d d[am]n ye; G[o]d d[am]n my soul, not a t[ur]d by G[o]d, and that's fair; but G[o]d d[am]n ye, and G[o]d's b[loo]d and w[oun]ds, if you don't act like an honest man G[o]d d[am]n ye, and offer to play us any rogues'y tricks by G[o]d, and G[o]d sink me, but I'll blow your brains out; G[o]d d[am]n me, if I don't. Now, Captain Atkinson, you may do as you please, you may be a son of a whore and pilot us wrong, which, G[o]d d[am]n ye, would be a rascally trick by G[o]d, because you would betray men who trust in you; but, by the eternal J[esu]s, you shan't live to see us hang'd. I don't love many

words, G[o]d d[am]n ye, if you have a mind to be well used you shall, G[o]d's b[loo]d; but if you will be a villain and betray your trust, may G[o]d strike me dead, and may I drink a bowl of brimstone and fire with the D[evi]l, if I don't send you head-long to H[e]ll, G[o]d d[am]n me; and so there needs no more arguments, by G[o]d, for I've told you my mind, and here's all the ship's crew for witnesses, that if I do blow your brains out, you may blame no body but your self, G[o]d d[am]n ye." (For these and other facts about William Fly, see *General History of the Pyrates* 606–13; *Pirates of the New England Coast* 328–37; *Villains of All Nations* 1–4. Brackets in the quoted excerpt signify the restoration of full text in place of the profanity-softening omissions in the sources cited.)

This passage—with its thirteen oaths, six curses, and four threats—is impressive for its intensity, but it is not atypical in content. Fly's profanity likely was neither the sudden, inexplicable fit nor the unhinged, disproportionate response to provocation most often associated with the violent villains of history and literature. It was, rather, a calculated means of addressing a situation of critical practical importance to Fly and his company. This example makes the point that pirates were, above all, pragmatic people—men of questionable ends but considered means—and that their words, however colorful, were designed and deployed principally to advance those means.

The following are important points about curses.

- The curses listed in this chapter are listed in second person form. This is because curses are most often directed at the person addressed ("blast ye"). However, curses obviously can also be directed at third persons ("blast him") or at objects or circumstances ("blast it"), and the user should feel free to modify the curses below to suit such variable purposes.

- Curses fit nicely with epithets. A second-person curse ("blast you!") can be combined with an epithet ("chicken-hearted lubber!") by connecting them with the word "for": "blast you for a chicken-hearted lubber!" A third-person curse ("blast him!") can be combined with an epithet either by connecting them with "for" ("blast him for a chicken-hearted lubber!") or by replacing the third-person pronoun with the epithet ("blast the chicken-hearted lubber!").

- Curses that take an object of "you" can also be used with any of that word's variations. "Blast 'ee," "blast ya," "blast ye," and "blast yer" are all acceptable alternatives to "blast you."

- A curse is often an appendage to a full sentence, spoken immediately after referring to the person or thing cursed: "Who stole yarr gold, says you? It were Cap'n Parris and Quartermaster Ketchum, **devil take 'em**."

- A curse often takes as an object some part or aspect of the person cursed: "Suarez, them's the last warrds I'll be hearin' you speak wi' my blade still dry, **God rot yer lyin' tongue!**"

- Curses consisting of a verb and an object ("burn and sink you") are sometimes varied by adding terms like "devil," "fiend," or "hell" directly before the verb. Thus, "burn and sink you" can become "devil burn and sink you" or "hell burn and sink you."

- Every curse can be interjected at a sentence's opening or closing—with no modification ("Devil take you, the bosun's a thief!"); by adding "if" or "but" for use as an opener ("Devil take you, **but** the bosun's a thief!"); or by adding "else" or an "if" phrase for use as a closer ("The bosun's a thief, devil take you **else**," "The bosun's a thief, devil take you **if he bain't**").

- Many curses take the form of a verb and an object: "blast you" or "confound you." To convert a curse to an oath, replace "you" with "me": "**Blast me** if I don' cut his throat afore he sleeps agayn" or "**Confound me**, I seen enough of yer mischief." Conversely, turn an oath into a curse by replacing "me" with "you."

A final note: One should be careful whom one curses. On the afternoon of June 23, 1726, Atkinson, looking out over the ocean, claimed he could see three vessels. (In fact, he saw only one.) Fly also saw only one, but Atkinson insisted that Fly look closer. When Fly left the quarter-deck to take up his telescope, Atkinson ran up onto the quarter-deck and seized the weapons he rightly guessed Fly would leave behind. With the help of other prisoners, Atkinson secured Fly and the ship.

On July 12, 1726, Fly was hanged in Boston. His body was displayed in chains at the mouth of Boston harbor. Despite the effects of deterioration and the elements, Fly's gibbeted corpse—likely covered in preservative tar, as was customary—lasted longer than his 28-day career as a pirate.

bad cess may __ bring you [*bad sayss mayee __ breng 'ee/ya/ye/yer*]

"Bad cess" is bad luck, trouble, or a lack of success or good fortune.

> "Ye kin keep the bloody schooner, an' the loot, an' **bad cess may it bring ye**." (Billy Doyle, *The Gun Ketch* 159)

bad cess to you [*bad sayss t'/ta/ter 'ee/ya/ye/yer*] bad luck to you; may you fail; may you meet with misfortune

> < "Where's Finney!" "Woy, 'iz lordship's aft, Admiral. An' **bad cess t'the brainless bugger**, sez oy!" > (Alan Lewrie & pirate aboard the *Caroline*, *The Gun Ketch* 311)

battle, murder, shipwreck and hell-fire to you [*baah'ul, marr/mor-der, shep-wrack an'/'n' 'ell-farr/fyarr t'/ta/ter 'ee/ya/ye/yer*] may nothing but terrible things befall you

> "Drink **battle, murder, shipwreck and hell-fire to Adam Penfeather**, with a

curse!" (Roger Tressady, *Martin Conisby's Vengeance* 158-59)

be cursed to you [*be carrsed/coorsed/curshed t'/ta/ter 'ee/ya/ye/yer*]

A highly unspecific and accordingly all-purpose curse.

> "And who a plague are you and **be cursed to ye!**" (chair-leg wielding pirate, *Black Bartlemy's Treasure* 110)

be damned (to you) [*be damt (t'/ta/ter 'ee/ya/ye/yer)*]

> "Curse him! I'd give a handful o' gold pieces to see him dead and **be damned!**" (Captain Belvedere, *Martin Conisby's Vengeance* 67) "Silence and **be damned t'ye!**" (James Danvers, *Adam Penfeather, Buccaneer* 89)

be damned to you for a EPITHET [*be damt t'/ta/ter 'ee/ya/ye/yer farr/fer a ...*]

See Chapter 9 for a list of epithets with which to complete this curse.

> "**Be damned t'ye**, Joel, **for a lily-livered dog!**" (bony pirate, *Black Bartlemy's Treasure* 271)

be damned to you with all my heart [*be damt t'/ta/ter 'ee/ya/ye/yer weth/wi'/wiff/witt awrl me/myee 'ahrrt/'eart/hahrrt*]

A more potent and particularly passionate version of "damn you."

> "Aye, but she's off, slipped her moorings d'ye see, my good lad, and **be damned t' ye wi' all my heart.**" (one-eared pirate, *Black Bartlemy's Treasure* 23)

be off to hell [*be arrf t'/ta/ter 'ell*] go to hell

> "You may tell your scum that, if they has the impudence to refuse my offer they needn't trouble to send you here again. They can up anchor and **be off to hell.**" (Captain Easterling, *Captain Blood Returns* 283)

blast you [*blarrst/blass 'ee/ya/ye/yer*]

A milder alternative to "damn you." One condemned to eternal damnation is "blasted" to hell.

> "Women, women. **Blast all women**, they spell trouble." (member of Blackbeard's company, "Blackbeard the Pirate" 22:08)

blast your deadlights [*blarrst/blass ya/yarr/ye/yer/yere/yore dayd/deh'-lawts/ligheets*]
blast your eyes [*blarrst/blass ya/yarr/ye/yer/yere/yore eye'ees*]

A milder alternative to "damn you." "Deadlights" means "eyes."

> "We don't betray our poor messmates for to save our necks like yon Toby Drew, **blast his deadlights.**" (Sam Morris, *Adam Penfeather, Buccaneer* 214) "**Blast their eyes**. Who be on this island?" (Long John Silver, "Long John Silver's Return to Treasure Island" 1:15:00)

blind you [*blawnd/blin'/blyeen'/blyeend/blyeent/blynt 'ee/ya/ye/yer*]

A milder alternative to "damn you." Used for emphasis, especially to express surprise, disbelief, displeasure, or conviction.

> "**Blind you!** Go forward and turn out two o' the lads to draw this carcass aft!" (Captain Belvedere, *Martin Conisby's Vengeance* 69)

blind you for a EPITHET [*blawnd/blin'/blyeen'/blyeend/blyeent/blynt 'ee/ya/ye/yer farr/fer a ...*]

> "**Blind him for a dog**—a dog and murderous rogue as shall bite on this hook o' mine yet!" (Roger Tressady, *Martin Conisby's Vengeance* 158)

bloody end to you [*bloohd/bluh'/blutt-y aynd t'/ta/ter 'ee/ya/ye/yer*]

> "I'm telling ye she's our ship, and **bloody end to them** as shall gainsay us!" (Toby Drew, *Adam Penfeather, Buccaneer* 212)

bone-rot you [*boone/bo'oone rarrt 'ee/ya/ye/yer*]

A milder alternative to "damn you." Used for emphasis, especially to express surprise, disbelief, displeasure, or conviction.

"The man as won't take good rum hath the head of a chicken, the heart of a yellow dog, and the bowels of a w-worm, and **bone-rot him**, says I." (Abnegation Mings, *Black Bartlemy's Treasure* 32)

burn and blast your bones [*barrn an'/'n' blarrst/ blass ya/yarr/ye/yer/yere/yore boones/bo'oones*]

A milder alternative to "damn you." One condemned to eternal damnation is "blasted" to hell.

"I've a score agin him for this lick o' the eye he give me ashore—nigh blinded me, 'e did, **burn an' blast his bones**!" (Job, *Martin Conisby's Vengeance* 67–68)

burn you [*barrn 'ee/ya/ye/yer*]

A milder alternative to "damn you." The term "burn" arguably has double significance, referring principally to damnation but also to profound misfortune (as fire is easily the thing most dreaded among pirates, most of whom cannot swim and rely on the integrity of the wood underneath their feet for survival).

"**Burn him**! Is he drunk again, Tom?" (Absalom Troy, hearing of Abner's fit of drunken violence, *Adam Penfeather, Buccaneer* 14) "You had ought to tell me that—you and the rest, that lost me my schooner, with your interference, **burn you**!" (Long John Silver, *Treasure Island* 166, Chap. 29)

confound you [*cahn/carrn/coohn/kern-foun'/ fount/fowoon'/fowoond/fowoont 'ee/ya/ye/yer*]

"Confound" means to throw into confusion or disorder, but also to destroy or ruin.

"**Confound you**, Shadwell, you've drove the thought right out of me head, and it was an uncommon pretty one." (William Kidd, "Captain Kidd" 1:08:56)

a curse on you [*a carrse/carrst/coorse/cursh/ curst arrn/o' 'ee/ya/ye/yer*]

A very basic curse.

"Veer, Resolution, wear ship and man the larboard guns ... they are cool ... I must go tend my hurt—**a curst on't**!" (Captain Jo, *Martin Conisby's Vengeance* 110)

a curse out of Egypt on you [*a carrse/carrst/ coorse/cursh/curst arrt/ou'/owoot o'\on Ay-gyp'/ jept arrn/o' 'ee/ya/ye/yer*]

A reference to the plagues of Egypt. The speaker wishes on the addressee one of the ten disasters visited on Egypt by God in the biblical book of Exodus in order to compel the Pharaoh to release the Israelite slaves: rivers turned to blood, frogs, lice, beetles, diseased livestock, boils, hail and fire, locusts, darkness, and death of the firstborn.

"**A curse out o' Egypt on ya**, ye ungrateful daughter of a tavern hag!" (Long John Silver, *Dead Man's Chest* 9)

curse you [*carrse/carrst/coorse/cursh/curst 'ee//ya/ye/yer*]

This and "damn you" are the two most basic of curses.

"**Curse him**! I'd give a handful o' gold pieces to see him dead and be damned!" (Captain Belvedere, *Martin Conisby's Vengeance* 67)

curse you for a EPITHET [*carrse/carrst/co- orse/cursh/curst 'ee/ya/ye/yer farr/fer a ...*]

See Chapter 9 for a list of epithets with which to complete this curse.

< "Mr. Barnabas tells me you are sick." "Why then, you may **curse Barnabas for chatterbox** and go about your own concerns." > (Ursula Revell & Japhet Bly, *Winds of Chance* 85)

curse you for breathing [*carrse/carrst/coorse/ cursh/curst 'ee/ya/ye/yer farr/fer a-breev-in'*]

"**Curse ya for breathin'**, you slack-jawed idiot!" (Joshamee Gibbs, "Pirates of the Caribbean: The Curse of the Black Pearl" 51:30)

damn to you [*damn t'/ta/ter 'ee/ya/ye/yer*] damn you

"**D[am]n to him** who ever lived to wear a halter." (Bartholomew Roberts, *General History of the Pyrates* 244)

damn you [*damn 'ee/ye/ya/yer*]

This and "curse you" are the two most basic of curses.

> "Jesus an' Mary, wot kind o' King's officer they givin' commissions t'now, **damn ye**?" (Billy Doyle, shocked at Alan Lewrie's unconventional tactics, *The Gun Ketch* 163)

damn you altogether [*damn 'ee/ya/ye/yer awrl-t'/ter-gaahth/gayth/gedd/ge'-er*]

"Altogether" adds emphasis.

> "[B]ut **damn ye altogether**: damn them for a pack of crafty rascals, and you, who serve them, for a parcel of hen-hearted numskuls." (Captain Bellamy to the captain of a plundered Boston sloop, *General History of the Pyrates* 587)

damn you for a EPITHET [*damn 'ee/ya/ye/yer farr/fer a ...*]

See Chapter 9 for a list of epithets with which to complete this curse.

> < "Ye're light-headed, Captain." "Will you harp on that? **Damn you for a fool!**" > (Tim & George Fairfax, *The Fortunes of Captain Blood* 159) "[B]ut damn ye altogether: **damn them for a pack of crafty rascals, and you**, who serve them, **for a parcel of hen-hearted numskuls**." (Captain Bellamy to the captain of a plundered Boston sloop, *General History of the Pyrates* 587)

damn you to the depths [*damn 'ee/ya/ye/yer t'/ta/ter t' depfs/depps*] damn you to hell

The playful ambiguity of "depths" refers to the depths of both hell and the ocean.

> "Parlay?! **Damn to the depths** whatever mutton that thought up parlay!" (Pintel, "Pirates of the Caribbean: The Curse of the Black Pearl" 1:15:44)

damn your __ [*damn ya/yarr/ye/yer/yere/ yore __*]

The speaker completes this curse with a reference to some annoying aspect of the adressee. Thus, the speaker might rebuke a chatty deckhand with, "Damn your wagging tongue."

> "**Damn yer hands**, Ben!" (Long John Silver regarding Ben Gunn's inability to control a rope load, *Dead Man's Chest* 6)
> < "Find out anything yet, Davey?" "Find out anything?" "**Damn yer memory!** What the hell 'ave I been lookin' fer these past nine years!?" (Long John Silver & David Noble, *Dead Man's Chest* 26–27)

damn your blood [*damn ya/yarr/ye/yer/yere/ yore bloohd/blut*] damn you

> "**D[am]n your blood**, no preaching. Be damn'd an you will, what's that to us? Let him look out who has the watch." (Alexander Mitchel, *General History of the Pyrates* 607)

damn your eyes [*damn ya/yarr/ye/yer/yere/ yore eye'ees*] damn you

> "**Damn your eyes**, Marlowe! Don't you see that we're both dead if we don't work together, and it ain't going to be pleasant, I'll warrant." (Roger Press, *The Pirate Round* 290)

devil burn you [*daahv/dayv/debb/div-il barrn 'ee/ya/ye/yer*] damn you

> < "Will ye kill the fool?" "That will I!" "And hang for him?" "Nay—he's scarce worth it." "Then, **devil burn ye**—loose his windpipe!" > (Adam Penfeather & Martin Conisby, *Black Bartlemy's Treasure* 59)

the devil go with you [*t' daahv/dayv/debb/ div-il go'oo weth/wi'/wiff/witt 'ee/ya/ye/yer*]

The flip-side of the modern expression "go to hell," as the speaker urges instead that hell—or, more specifically, the devil—go with the addressee.

> "Then take one of the sloops, order your men aboard and put to sea, and **the devil go with you**." (Peter Blood, *Captain Blood: His Odyssey* 185)

devil take you [*daahv/dayv/debb/div-il tayeeke 'ee/ya/ye/yer*] damn you; go to hell

< "Do you surrender to me now, you bastard?" "**Devil take ye!**" > (Alan Lewrie & Billy Doyle, *The Gun Ketch* 164)

devil take you if [*daahv/dayv/debb/div-il tayeeke 'ee/ya/ye/yer an'\eff/eff'n/if'n*]

Used to emphatically negate the statement that follows.

"**Devil take you if** you haven't set me bleeding again." (George Fairfax, *The Fortunes of Captain Blood* 162)

devil take your __ [*daahv/dayv/debb/div-il tayeeke ya/yarr/ye/yer/yere/yore __*] damn your __

The speaker completes this curse with a reference to some annoying aspect of the addressee. Thus, the speaker might rebuke a chatty deckhand with, "Devil take your wagging tongue."

"Now, **devil take your lewdness!**" (Jeremy Pitt, *Captain Blood Returns* 192)

the devil with you [*t' daahv/dayv/debb/div-il weth/wi'/wiff/witt 'ee/ya/ye/yer*] damn you; go to hell

< "What about Blackbeard?" "**The devil with Black—.**" > (Ben Worley and another member of Blackbeard's company, interrupted in mid-sentence as Blackbeard suddenly appears on deck just in time to hear his name cursed, "Blackbeard the Pirate" 1:24:20)

eat that what falls from my tail [*eat tharrt wharrt/whorrt fawrls ferm me/myee tayell*] eat my shit

The speaker instructs the addressee not simply to "eat shit"—the modern equivalent—but specifically to eat the speaker's shit, thus urging on him not simply degradation but also humiliating submission.

*Doughty and his gentleman companions were kept on short rations. Doughty complained about this, the two men came to blows, and the master finally offered to give Doughty something to "**eat that falls from my tail.**"* (master

of Francis Drake's vessel the *Swan, The Queen's Pirate* 101)

flog off [*flarrg arrf*]

A milder alternatve to "fuck off" or "screw you," and likely a sound-alike substitute for "sod off".

"Oh, **flog off**. Just shut up." (Smee, "Hook" 43:59)

go to the devil [*go'oo t'/ta/ter t' daahv/dayv/ debb/div-il*] go to hell

< "Captain Blood, you disappoint me. I had hopes of great things for you." "**Go to the devil.**" > (Julian Wade & Peter Blood, *Captain Blood: His Odyssey* 234)

go to the devil when you please [*go'oo t'/ ta/ter t' daahv/dayv/debb/div-il whaahn 'ee/ya/ ye/yer pleess*] go to hell

The fanciful "when you please" lends a saucy note of breezy indifference that adds sting.

"They may **go to the devil when they please**." (Peter Blood, *Captain Blood: His Odyssey* 311)

God damn you [*Garrd/Gott/Gud damn 'ee/ ye/ya/yer*]

"G[o]d d[am]n ye, you are an obstinate villain, and your design is to hang us; but, b[loo]d and w[oun]ds you dog, you shan't live to see it." (William Fly, *General History of the Pyrates* 612)

God damn you to hell [*Garrd/Gott/Gud damn 'ee/ye/ya/yer t'/ta/ter 'ell*]

"**God damn you to hell!** God damn you!" (LeRois, screaming at the vessel firing cannon shot into his men, *The Guardship* 192)

God rot your bones [*Garrd/Gott/Gud rarrt ya/yarr/ye/yer/yere/yore boones/bo'oones*]

A milder alternatve to "God damn you." Used for emphasis, especially to express surprise, disbelief, displeasure, or conviction.

"**God rot your bones**, Tim, are you humouring me?" (George Fairfax, *The Fortunes of Captain Blood* 159)

gut you for a EPITHET [*garrt/gooht 'ee/ya/ ye/yer farr/fer a ...*]

See Chapter 9 for a list of epithets with which to complete this curse.

> < "Where's Billy Bones?" "Dhrunk under the cabin table." "**Gut him for the souse he is!**" > (John Flint & Darby McGraw, *Porto Bello Gold* 131)

hang you [*'ang 'ee/ya/ye/yer*]

An arguably less blasphemous, but equally potent alternative to "damn you."

> "Oh, **hang all doctors**. Give me rum!" (William Bones, "Treasure Island" [1950] 4:30) "It's gone—so's the money!" "**Hang the money!**" (Black Dog & Blind Pew, "Treasure Island" [1990] 21:36)

here's a black passage to you [*'ee'arr/'ee'err/ 'ere/hee'arr/hee'err is\be a bleck payssage t'/ta/ ter 'ee/ya/ye/yer*] you can go to hell

By wishing a "black passage" on the addressee, the speaker urges on him an ill or dark fate—most obviously a nightmarish life, death, damnation, or hell itself.

> "**Here's a black passage to Captain Penfeather**—curse him!" (pirate in Lady Brandon's stables, *Black Bartlemy's Treasure* 96)

I'll see you in hell [*I'ee'ull see 'ee/ya/ye/ yer i'/'n 'ell*]

> "**I'll see you in hell**." (Black Harry, "Cutthroat Island" 5:35)

kiss my arse [*kess me/myee ahrrse*] kiss my ass

> < "I think I shall have you write out the inventory of my treasure as it is swayed out. What say you?" "I say **kiss my arse**." > (Roger Press & Thomas Marlowe, *The Pirate Round* 268)

malediction [*malerdik-shern/shoohn*]

The word "malediction" means "curse." However, the term serves both as a curse, where used to wish harm on another, and as an oath, where used for emphasis, especially to express anger, displeasure, frustration, or some other negative, sharply felt sentiment (see Chapter 6: Oaths). The excerpt below possibly reflects both uses.

> "Desertion? Ha—**malediction!** What's the meaning o' this?" (Benjamin Trigg, on hearing news of the company's desertion, *Adam Penfeather, Buccaneer* 263)

may every curse ever cursed light on and blast you [*mayee ebber'/ebbry/e'ery/ever'/ev'ry carrse/carrst/coorse/cursh/curst ebber/e'er carrsed/coorsed/curshed lawt/ligheet arrn an'/'n' blarrst/blass 'ee/ya/ye/yer*]

> "[T]hink o' the devil wi' eyes like dim glass, flesh like dough and a sweet, soft voice, and you have Alexo Valdez inside and out, and **may every curse ever cursed light on and blast him**, says I!" (John, *Martin Conisby's Vengeance* 185)

od rot the __ of you [*arrd rarrt t' __ o'\on 'ee/ya/ye/yer*]

The speaker specifies some objectionable aspect of the person addressed. "Od" is a sound-alike abridgement of "God."

> "Ay, ay, '**od rot the lying tongues o' ye!**" (Ned, *Winds of Chance* 314)

od rot you [*arrd rarrt 'ee/ya/ye/yer*]

A sound-alike substitute for "God rot you."

> < "Ye've heard my order. Go about and lay a course for Cartagena." "But Cartagena ..." "**Od rot you!**" > (George Fairfax & Tim, *The Fortunes of Captain Blood* 159)

od rot your bones [*arrd rarrt ya/yarr/ye/yer/ yere/yore boones/bo'oones*]

A milder substitute for "God damn you," and perhaps a substitute for "damn your soul."

> "**Od rot your bones!**" (eye-patch wearing pirate, *Black Bartlemy's Treasure* 23)

plague and perish you [*playeeg an'/'n' parrish/persh/parsh 'ee/ya/ye/yer*]

The earthly equivalent of "damn you." The speaker wishes a horrific fate on the addressee not in the next life, but in this one.

> "**Plague and perish him**! Burn him, 'tis keelhaul 'im I would first and then give 'im to Pompey to carve up what remained ..." (Job, *Martin Conisby's Vengeance* 65–66)

a plague on your scurvy head [*a playeeg arrn/ o' ya/yarr/ye/yer/yere/yore scarrvy 'ead/hayd*]

A plague is a condition or calamity that causes intense and prolonged suffering. "Scurvy" means "rotten" or "lousy."

> "**A plague on your scurvy head**!" (Thomas Bartholomew Red, incensed at Dutch's refusal to purchase Red's hostages, "Pirates" 57:58)

plague seize you [*playeeg seize 'ee/ya/ye/yer*]

A curse used for emphasis, and especially to express anger, disgust, frustration, or intense displeasure. A plague is a condition or calamity that causes intense and prolonged suffering.

> "Jim, ho Jimmy. Jim—**plague seize ye**, show a leg, will 'ee ..." (Red Andy, *Black Bartlemy's Treasure* 126)

rot in hell [*rarrt in 'ell*]

> "**Rot in hell**!" (pirate yelling after a boat of fleeing Spaniards, "Pirates" 1:54:13)

rot you [*rarrt 'ee/ya/ye/yer*]

A milder alternative to "damn you."

> "But the jewels? Bah! **Rot the jewels**!" (George Fairfax, *The Fortunes of Captain Blood* 156–57)

sink you [*senk 'ee/ya/ye/yer*]

A milder alternative to "damn you."

> "Well, there's Montbars as they do call the Exterminator, and there's young Harry Morgan—a likely lad, and there's Roger Tressady and Sol Aiken and Pen-

feather—**sink him**!" (Abnegation Mings, *Black Bartlemy's Treasure* 31)

sink you for a EPITHET [*senk 'ee/a/ye/yer farr/fer a ...*]

See Chapter 9 for a list of epithets with which to complete this curse.

> "**Sink you for** a villain, do you dare to question my orders?" (John Sharkey, annoyed by his quartermaster's persistent suggestion that their prisoner be killed, *The Dealings of Captain Sharkey and Other Tales of Pirates* "How the Governor of Saint Kitt's Came Home" 24)

sod off [*sarrd arrf*] fuck off; get lost

Used both to express contempt for the addressee and to dismiss or urge him away. "Sod" is short for "sodomite."

> "**Sod off**, you bastard ..." (Peleg Dinwiddie, *The Pirate Round* 201) "No, he left me. Told me to **sod off**, you may recall." (Thomas Marlowe, *The Pirate Round* 336)

sod you [*sarrd 'ee/ya/ye/yer*] fuck you; screw you

Used to express contempt or reproach for the addressee. "Sod" is short for "sodomite."

> "[The tobacco convoy is g]lathering now, down by Hampton Roads, but **sod the fucking tobacco fleet**. We have all the fucking tobacco we needs." (Ezekiel Ripley, *The Guardship* 163)

ten thousand curses [*tan t'ou-san' carrses/ coorses/curshes*]

A curse used to wish prodigious harm on another, but also an oath when used for emphasis, especially to express anger, displeasure, frustration, or some other negative, sharply felt sentiment (see Chapter 6: Oaths). The excerpt below possibly reflects both uses.

> < "'Tis mutinous rogue drew knife on me." "Tush and **ten thousand curses**! I tell ye this gentleman you outrage is friend o' mine." > (Captain Sharp & Benjamin Trigg, *Adam Penfeather, Buccaneer* 72)

to blazes with you [*t'/ta/ter blayeezes weth/wi'/wiff/witt 'ee/ya/ye/yer*] go to hell; damn you

> "To blazes with the code!" (Ragetti, "Pirates of the Caribbean: The Curse of the Black Pearl" 34:41)

to the devil with you [*t'/ta/ter t' daahv/dayv/debb/div-il weth/wi'/wiff/witt 'ee/ya/ye/yer*] go to hell; damn you

> "Johnny pours coals o' fire on my head, you pour fulsome flatteries on his; ha, to the devil with Johnny ..." (Japhet Bly, *Winds of Chance* 331)

to hell with you [*t'/ta/ter 'ell weth/wi'/wiff/witt 'ee/ya/ye/yer*] go to hell; damn you

> "To hell with King James and all who serve him!" (Wolverstone, *Captain Blood Returns* 100)

to the devil with your black soul [*t'/ta/ter t' daahv/dayv/debb/div-il weth/wi'/wiff/witt ya/yarr/ye/yer/yere/yore bleck sool/so'ool*]

An especially emphatic version of "go to hell" or "damn you." The speaker purports not only to prescribe the addressee's destination, but also to define his character.

> "And he's bound for this place, to the devil with his black soul." (Thomas Marlowe, *The Guardship* 94)

with a curse [*weth/wi'/wiff/witt a carrse/carrst/coorse/cursh/curst*]

A curse when used to wish harm on another in an unspecific way, but also an oath when used for emphasis, especially to express anger, displeasure, frustration, or some other negative, sharply felt sentiment (see Chapter 6: Oaths).

> "We came on a burned village, the work of their damned Spanish allies—ay, and English, as I hear, with a curse!" (Japhet Bly, *Winds of Chance* 207)

you be damned [*ya/ye/yer be damt*] damn you

> < "John! Long John! They're headin' for shore in the jolly-boat!" "Ah, they be damned." > (member of Long John Silver's company & Long John Silver, "Treasure Island" [1972] 48:37)

you can up anchor and away to the devil [*ya/ye/yer cayn/kin arrp han-karr an'/'n' awayee/'way/'wayee t'/ta/ter t' daahv/dayv/debb/div-il*] you can go to hell

> "If that's their last word, my man, they can up anchor and away to the Devil." (Captain Easterling, *Captain Blood Returns* 285)

you can up anchor and be off to hell [*ya/ye/yer cayn/kin arrp han-karr an'/'n' be arrf t'/ta/ter 'ell*] you can go to hell

> "You may tell your scum that, if they has the impudence to refuse my offer they needn't trouble to send you here again. They can up anchor and be off to hell." (Captain Easterling, *Captain Blood Returns* 283)

you should be dead and quite beyond it [*ya/ye/yer shoood be dayd an'/'n' quieete b'-yarrn'/yarrnd/yon'/yont ett/'n/'t*] go to hell

> "Then, for another thing, ma'm, there be black villains alive, and apt for all manner of evil, that should be dead and quite beyond it." (Japhet Bly, *Winds of Chance* 292)

CHAPTER 8

Insults

This book teaches how to speak like a pirate. William Fly taught how to die like one.

After being taken prisoner by the resourceful William Atkinson (see Chapter 7), Fly was tried, convicted, and sentenced to hang. The next days of his life were likely the most principled he ever lived. In prison awaiting execution, Fly refused to eat. He insisted on New England rum instead.

Invited to Sunday church services before the execution, Fly's three condemned comrades accepted with eleventh-hour contrition. But Fly declined. No need to die a villain *and* a hypocrite. Arriving at the gallows, Fly sported a small bouquet of flowers, as if at a light social occasion, smiling and greeting breezily the young ladies in attendance. He leapt nimbly up the scaffold steps, like a schoolboy on holiday.

And when Fly looked up at the noose dangling above, he did not bite his lip in terror, or bleat out miserable expressions of regret, or attempt thoughtful pronouncements on the sinuous path his life had taken. Fly instead told the hangman he did not understand his trade, then fixed the knot himself and died with his own handiwork bearing him up. (*General History of the Pyrates* 606–13; *Pirates of the New England Coast* 328–37; *Villains of All Nations* 1–4; *Under the Black Flag* 239)

Sometimes an insult is the best last word.

What's the difference between an insult and an epithet (Chapter 9)? They are the same in that both identify something bad about the addressee. They are different in that insults are statements, whereas epithets are just name-calling. For example, one might call another a bad sailor by using an insult ("tailor is yer trade") or by using an epithet ("yer a lubber"). The insult is substantive and often observational. The epithet is quick and cookie-cutter.

Below is a list of insults. Definitions and explanations are provided only where meaning is not otherwise apparent. As the size of their respective lists in the *Primer* reflects, threats and curses are much more often deployed in pirate talk than insults for the purpose of antagonizing others. Why? One reason may be that insults depend in some part for their effectiveness on the speaker's knowledge of the addressee. When the speaker does not know the addressee well, an insult might ring hollow, but a threat or curse will still fly. (Another reason may be that sharp insults are simply harder to write well and therefore find themselves less often in the mouths of fictional characters.)

See Chapter 11: Retorts for standard methods of answering insults.

Beezelbub himself could hardly desire better company [*Bezzel-barrb/boohb 'im-seff coood 'ahrrd/'ard/hahrrd-ly der-zyee-arr/err be'er\gooder cahm/carrm/coohm-p'ny*]

Used to describe someone as profoundly evil or objectionable.

> "For my part, I don't know and I don't care what the Gospel does to them, but I know that when any o' the islands chance to get it, trade goes all smooth and easy; but where they ha'nt got it, **Beezelbub himself could hardly desire better company**." (pirate, *The Coral Island* 213–14)

the blood in your veins is (skim) milk [*t' bloohd/blut i'/'n ya/yarr/ye/yer/yere/yore vayeens be (skem) melk*]

> "I weep because I am woman, after all, but in my heart I hate you and with my soul I despise you, for you are but a mock man, —**the blood in your veins skim milk**!" (Captain Jo, *Martin Conisby's Vengeance* 33)

do you call that a head on your shoulders or a blessed dead eye? [*d'/does 'ee/ya/ye/yer cawrl tharrt a 'ead/hayd arrn/o' ya/yarr/ye/yer/yere/yore sho'/shool-ders arr a blass-erd/ert/ett dayd eye'ee?*]

> < "And what was he saying to you?" "I don't rightly know, sir." "**Do you call that a head on your shoulders, or a blessed dead eye?** Don't rightly know,

don't you! > (Long John Silver & Tom Morgan, *Treasure Island* 44, Chap. 8)

here's fine stuff for the gallows [*'ee'arr/'ee'err/ 'ere/hee'arr/hee'err is\be fawn/fyeene starrf/stoohf farr/fer t' gallowoos*]

> "I' faith! **Here's fine stuff for the gallows**!" (Adam Penfeather, looking over the twelve new men in his company, *Black Bartlemy's Treasure* 111)

hold your tongue and your whinin' for them that's at your beck and call, because I ain't [*hol'/hoold/ho'oold/'ol'/'old ya/yarr/ye/yer/ yere/yore toohngue an'/'n' ya/yarr/ye/yer/yere/ yore a-wawn/wyeen-in' farr/fer dem/'em/te'm\ dose/those/t'ose\dey/they tharrt's a'/hat ya/yarr/ ye/yer/yere/yore back an'/'n' cawrl, b'-carrse/ cawrse I'ee aren't/bain't/ben't/hain't/i'n't*]

> "Now you **hold your tongue and your whinin' for them that's at your beck and call, because I ain't**." (Purity Pinker, replying hotly to the supercilious Lady Harwood and her abusive comments, "The Adventures of Long John Silver: Dead Reckoning" 20:57)

I leave it to fancy where your mothers was that let you come to sea [*I'ee leaf ett/'n/'t t'/ta/ter fancy wayarr/wayerr/wharr ya/yarr/ ye/yer/yere/yore maahth/mo'/mudd-ers warss\ warr/were tharrt laaht/le' 'ee/ya/ye/yer cahm/ carrm/coohm t'/ta/ter sea*]

A brilliantly concise insult that indicts both the addressee's competence as a seaman and his mother's virtue (by its suggestion that she may have been where she should not have).

> "You've neither sense nor memory, and **I leave it to fancy where your mothers was that let you come to sea.**" (Long John Silver, denouncing George Merry and his colleagues, *Treasure Island* 164, Chap. 29)

I were wiser to have no truck with __, so I take my leave of you [*I'ee warr\warss/was waw/wyee-ser t'/ta/ter 'aff/'ave/ha'/haff no'oo troohk weth/wi'/wiff/witt __, so'oo I'ee tayeeke me/myee leaf o'\on 'ee/ya/ye/yer*]

To have truck with is to have any dealings or involvement with. The speaker fills in the blank by specifying a denigrating quality, characteristic, or phenomenon, then equates leaving the addressee's presence with ridding himself of it.

> "**I were wiser to have no truck with Iniquity. So, I take my leave of you**, Sir Roguery!" (Adam Penfeather, *Adam Penfeather, Buccaneer* 279)

I've seen street-walkers more womanly [*I'eev seen street-warrkers marr/moor womern/wom'n-ly*]

Used to deride a woman for ill-mannered behavior or some other lack of propriety.

> "What are you? A woman? Od's blood, ma'am, in London Town **I've seen poor street-walkers carted that were more womanly.**" (Peter Blood, *The Fortunes of Captain Blood* 100)

leave ships to men as can handle them [*leaf sheps t'/ta/ter men as cayn/kin 'andle dem/'em/t'em\dey/they*]

> "Faith, Doctor, ye were best to get back to your cupping and bleeding, and **leave ships to men as can handle them.**" (Captain Easterling, *Captain Blood Returns* 28–29)

the smell of you alone is enough to wrinkle the noses of pigs [*t' smaahl o'\on 'ee/ya/*

ye/yer aloone/alo'oone be enarrff/enow/'nough t'/ta/ter wrenkle t' noo/no'oo-sers o'\on pegs]

> "Why, **the smell of you alone is enough to wrinkle the noses of pigs.**" (Purity Pinker, "Long John Silver's Return to Treasure Island" 34:18)

tailor is your trade [*tayee-larr be ya/yarr/ye/yer/yere/yore trayeede*] you're not fit to be seaman or pirate

> "Sea! Gentlemen o' fortune! I reckon **tailors is your trade.**" (Long John Silver, denouncing George Merry and his colleagues, *Treasure Island* 164, Chap. 29)

that's not the only kind of fool you are [*tharrt's narrt t' on'y kin-da/der foo'ell 'ee/ya/ye/yer be*]

Used after a criticism or insult to introduce additional ones.

> "Ye can't be much of a hand at a bargain; and **that's not the only kind of fool you are.** How long did you think you'ld live to enjoy the money?" (Peter Blood, *The Fortunes of Captain Blood* 166)

there is more fire in a small, dead fish than in all your slow body [*tharr/theyarr/theyerr be marr/moor farr/fyarrr i'/'n a smawrl, dayd fesh 'n/thayn\nor i'/'n awrl ya/yarr/ye/yer/yere/yore slowoo bah'ee/barrdy*]

> "Oh, verily **there is more life, more fire and passion in a small, dead fish than in all thy great, slow body!**" (Captain Jo, *Martin Conisby's Vengeance* 48)

there is more of life in my little finger than in all your carcass [*tharr/theyarr/theyerr be marr/moor o'\on lawf/lyeefe i'/'n me/myee lil' feng/finn-er 'n/thayn\nor i'/'n awrl ya/yarr/ye/yer/yere/yore cahrr-cahss/cush/kerss*]

> "Ah, by God, **there is more of vigorous life in my little finger than in all your great, heavy, clod-like carcase.**" (Captain Jo, *Martin Conisby's Vengeance* 33)

what fool has broke adrift here? [*wharrt foo'ell 'as brooke/bro'ooke a-dreff/dreft/driff* 'ee'arr/'ee'err/'ere/hee'arr/hee'err?] what kind of idiot are you?

This insult is particularly effective for its dismissive treatment of the addressee as a third-party subject of mocking inquiry.

> "**What fool has broke adrift here?**" (watch aboard the *Dolphin*, losing patience after receiving nonsensical answers to his hails, *The Red Rover* 84)

yellow was never a pirate's color [*yaahller/lowoo warss\warr/were nebber/ne'er a pyeeret's/errt's/raaht's cahlerr*]

Used to express disdain for another's show of cowardice.

> "You've turned your hand against your Captain's back. **Yellow was never a pirate's color.**" (Captain Vallo, "The Crimson Pirate" 1:02:56)

you always was trouble [*ya/ye/yer al-way/wayees warss\warr/were troohble*]

> "**You always was trouble**, blast ya." (Mordachai Fingers, "Cutthroat Island" 34:34)

you are but a mock man [*ya/ye/yer be barrt a marrk man*]

> "I weep because I am woman, after all, but in my heart I hate you and with my soul I despise you, for **you are but a mock man**, —the blood in your veins skim milk!" (Captain Jo, *Martin Conisby's Vengeance* 33)

you got no more brain than a sea-turtle [*ya/ye/yer garrt no'oo marr/moor brayeen 'n/thayn\nor a sea-tarrtle*]

> "Israel, **you got no more brain than a sea-turtle.**" (Long John Silver, "Treasure Island" [1990] 46:32)

you have the head of a chicken, the heart of a yellow dog, and the bowels of a worm [*ya/ye/yer 'aff/'ave/ha'/haff t' 'ead/hayd o'\on a check-ern, t' 'ahrrt/'eart/hahrrt o'\on a yaahller/lowoo dahg/darrg/dorrg, an'/'n' t' bowoo-ells o'\on a warrm*]

> "The man as won't take good rum **hath the head of a chicken, the heart of a yellow dog, and the bowels of a w-worm**, and bone-rot him, says I." (Abnegation Mings, *Black Bartlemy's Treasure* 32)

you should be fed on pap and suckets [*ya/ye/yer shoood be fad arrn'/o' parrp an'/'n' sarrk/soohk-erts*] you are a child

Pap is soft baby food, and more specifically bread boiled in or softened with milk or water (though the insult arguably borrows on the fact that "pap" can also mean "nipple"). Suckets are syrupy or candied pieces of fruit, fruit peel, or vegetable.

> "I am used to outfacing men, but you—ha, **you should be fed on pap and suckets**, you that are no man!" (Captain Jo, *Martin Conisby's Vengeance* 30)

you should be more of man and less of fish [*ya/ye/yer shoood be marr/moor o'\on man an'/'n' lass o'\on fesh*]

Used variously to characterize another as spineless (*i.e.* weak or cowardly), slippery (*i.e.* untrustworthy or evasive or temperamental), or cold-blooded (*i.e.* without passion or mercy).

> "Ah, **had you been more of man and less of fish**, I had made you captain of this ship ..." (Captain Jo, *Martin Conisby's Vengeance* 70)

your master is the devil [*ya/yarr/ye/yer/yere/yore marrster be t' daahv/dayv/debb/divil*] you're evil

> "Paddle, rogue Johnny, paddle, —for **thy master the Devil**'s abroad ..." (Japhet Bly, *Winds of Chance* 273)

your mind's unhinged [*ya/yarr/ye/yer/yere/yore mawnd's/min's/myeen's/myeend's arrn/hun/oohn-henged/'inged*] you're crazy

> "**Your mind's un'inged.**" (Long John Silver, "The Adventures of Long John Silver: The Necklace" 19:02)

your mother turns an honest woman [ya/
yarr/ye/yere/yore maahth/mo'/mudd-er tar-
rns a hon-erst womern/wom'n]

This premise of an insult is folded easily
into various constructions, e.g.: "I'll be tellin'
ye where the gold's buried when your mother
turns an honest woman." "Faith, I believe ye.
As I believe your mother's turned an honest
woman, hah!"

> "Out with it, then, Jack Nasty-Face. Is
> it that **your mother's turning into an
> honest woman**?" (unnamed prisoner
> pirate, "Captain Kidd" 16:00)

you're a bold one in a calm [ya're/yer/ye're/
yore a bol'/boold/bo'oold 'un/woohn i'/'n a
carrm]

Used to disparage the addressee's confidence, commitment, or determination as in-
substantial and likely to evaporate when tested
by some actual event or circumstance.

> "Ay, **he's a bold 'un in a calm**." (hand
> aboard the Dolphin, mocking Harry Wilder,
> The Red Rover 335)

**you're as bone-headed as a backwards
blowfish** [ya're/yer/ye're/yore as boone/bo'oone-
'ead/hayd-ered as a OR azzer beck-wahrrds
blowoo-fesh]

> "Billy Bones, **you're as bone-headed as a
> backwards blowfish**." (Long John Silver,
> "Treasure Island" [1998] 3:33)

you're better fitted for __ than the sea [ya're/
yer/ye're/yore be'er\gooder fetted/fi'ed farr/fer __
'n/thayn\nor t' sea]

> "If the Spaniards on Hispaniola spare
> you when you land there, you can get
> back to your hunting and boucanning,
> **for which ye're better fitted than the
> sea**." (Peter Blood, Captain Blood Re-
> turns 61)

**you're not fit for a __ to wipe her\his feet
upon you** [ya're/yer/ye're/yore narrt fett farr/fer
a __ t'/ta/ter wawp/wyeepe 'er\'is feet 'parrn/'pon/
uparrn 'ee/ya/ye/yer]

> "What do you do here with this Yankee
> supercargo, **not fit for a gentlewoman
> to wipe her feet upon**?" (John Malyoe,
> The Book of Pirates "The Ghost of Captain
> Brand" 59)

you're not worth shiproom [ya're/yer/ye're/
yore narrt warrth shep-roohm]

> "Tush and curse it, Captain, 'tis no more
> than petty boy, a sickling, a lousy lad, a
> puling mannikin **not worth shiproom**!"
> (Benjamin Trigg, on seeing the slight
> Adam Penfeather for the first time, Adam
> Penfeather, Buccaneer 44)

you've a split tongue [ya've/ye've/yer've a
splet toohngue]

The speaker characterizes the addressee
as being false or duplicitous. The expression
is doubly effective for evoking the image of
a serpent's tongue and thereby equating the
addressee implicitly with a snake.

> "**You've a split tongue**, Silver." (Israel
> Hands, "Long John Silver's Return to
> Treasure Island" 1:16:38)

**you've eyes, but no more sight than a
blind puppy** [ya've/ye've/yer've eye'ees, barrt
no'oo marr/moor sawt/sigheet 'n/thayn\nor a
blawnd/blin'/blyeen'/blyeend/blyeent/blynt
parr/pooh-py]

> "Ye've eyes, Sam, **but no more sight than
> a blind puppy**." (Peter Blood, Captain
> Blood Returns 151)

you've neither sense nor memory [ya've/
ye've/yer've needer/nee'er/nyder/ny'er saahnse
narr/noor mamma/memb/mem'-ry]

> "Why, I give you my word, I'm sick to
> speak to you. **You've neither sense nor
> memory** ..." (Long John Silver, dressing
> down George Merry and his colleagues,
> Treasure Island 164, Chap. 29)

CHAPTER 9

Epithets

The epithet is the insult's shorter, quicker cousin. When one uses an insult, he is making a derogatory statement about someone else. When one uses an epithet, he is simply calling him a name. Epithets come in the form of simple nouns (*e.g.*, "lubber," "whoreson") or modifier-noun combinations (*e.g.*, "plaguey skulker," "bilge-sucking scallywag").

Listed separately below are epithet modifiers (Section 9.1) and epithet nouns (Section 9.2). Composing an epithet is as easy as selecting a modifier from Section 9.1 and a noun from Section 9.2. Or, for a short and simple epithet, one might use just a noun from Section 9.2 with no modifier.

Given the value pirates often place on conventionally negative qualities like malice and evil-doing, many terms and phrases used as epithets are sometimes also used to praise or to express admiration. Thus, the phrase "murderous cutthroat" can be used negatively as a hateful epithet ("I'll hang 'im by 'is 'eels when I catch 'im, the **murderous cutthroat**") or positively as a glowing characterization ("A rouse for our cap'n, the **murderous cutthroat!**").

One might expand his arsenal of epithets beyond the standard formula with various special constructions:

- **"You" Epithets:** A "You" Epithet is an epithet preceded by the word "you" or any version of "you" ("ye," "ya," "yer," "thou"): **"ye plaguey skulker!," "ya whoreson!".** "You" is often repeated at the end of a "You" Epithet: **"you dog, you!".**

- **"My" Epithets:** A "My" Epithet is an epithet preceded by the word "my": "You've no more gold than courage, **my yellow-livered cockroach.**" The usage radiates ironic warmth; a casual, bemused tone; and a sly knowingness, all of which convey confidence, condescension, and utter dismissiveness.

- **Name Epithets:** Both second-person and third-person epithets are often preceded by the name of the person denigrated: "I'll be goin' wherever **Blackbeard whoreson** goes." The close verbal association between name and aspersion adds potency to the epithet by telegraphing an identity or equivalence between the two. Note also the reverse name epithet: "You'll die, **rogue Jack**, where you stand."

- **Body Epithets:** Body Epithets juxtapose a part of a person's body with an epithet. One might use an epithet modifier and a body part ("I'll slit your **lubberly throat**") or an epithet noun in possessive form and a body part ("I'll slit your **lubber's throat**"). Body Epithets can be used in both second-person ("I'll slit **your lubber's throat**") and third-person ("I'll slit **that lubber's throat**"). The Body Epithet accomplishes the same as the Name Epithet: an uncomfortably close association between the person defamed and the defamation spoken.

- **Command Epithets:** One can combine a command ("avast") and an epithet ("scoundrel") by connecting the two with the word "for": "Avast for a scoundrel!"

- **Curse and Oath Epithets:** One can combine a curse ("blast you") or an oath ("blast me") with an epithet ("scoundrel") by using the word "for": "Blast you for a scoundrel!" "Blast me for a scoundrel!"

- **Epithet Helpers:** One might add any of several phrases to an epithet for a more dramatic delivery: "You're naught but a __," "I know you for a __," "I grieve to find you such a __," "Here's\There's a __," "Here's\There's no __'er __ than you," "OATH if you ain't a __," or "__ as ever was."

See Chapter 11: Retorts for ways of responding to an epithet.

9.1 MODIFIERS

accursed; accurst [ac-cars/coors/cursh-ed] contemptible; hateful

> "Loose me, **accursed** renegade, loose me, I say!" (Smy Peters, *Adam Penfeather, Buccaneer* 335)

barbarous [bahrr-beerous/b'rous] coarse; ignorant

Though the term also means "cruel" or "inhuman," pirates use it more frequently to disparage a person's worth than to characterize his conduct (as inhumanity and mercilessness are among the types of traits often prized by pirates).

> "The five English the **barbarous** Spaniards hanged up immediately, wounded as they were." (Captain Avery, *The King of Pirates* 50)

barnacle-covered [bahrr-n'cle/nerkle coohvert] encrusted with hard-shelled marine crustaceans

Used to suggest that another is so old, disused, or out of shape as to be decrepit, or so ugly as to be freakish-looking.

> "Raise that ugly claw to me once more and it'll be yer last, you **barnacle-covered** son-of-a-scab!" (Henry Morgan, *Dead Man's Chest* 10)

base [bayeese] contemptible; worthless

> "This **base** and scurvy traitor—guilty of foulest treason—." (pirate mate, "The Black Pirate" 1:04:31)

base-souled [bayeese sooled/so'ooled] contemptible; worthless

> "Then go! I am not so **base-souled** to weep and wheedle, to scheme and pray for thing that can never be truly mine, or to keep you here in hated bondage—go!" (Captain Jo, *Martin Conisby's Vengeance* 172)

bastard [barrs/bash-tahrrd]

Meaning literally "born out of wedlock," the term is used to characterize another as offensive, contemptible, or worthless.

< "[T]he Brethren of the Coast, the whole buccaneering fraternity, will be raised against you for this breach of faith." "Breach of faith! Breach of faith, ye **bastard** scum! D'ye dare stand before my face and say that to me?" > (Crosby Pike & Captain Easterling, *Captain Blood Returns* 286)

beastly [*beas'/behst-ly*] monstrous; extremely unpleasant; nasty

"As for their murderers yonder, these **beastly** rogues, I give them the clean sea and sailorly death here ..." (Adam Penfeather, *Adam Penfeather, Buccaneer* 237)

bile-laden [*byell-ladden*] disgusting; offensive

Bile has a detestable look and color, and the speaker associates those qualities with the person so described.

"I'm not thinking of Don Ilario, but of that **bile-laden** curmudgeon Don Clemente." (Wolverstone, *The Fortunes of Captain Blood* 19)

bilge-licking [*belge-leck-in'*]
bilge-sucking [*belge-sarrk/soohk-in'*]

"Bilge" is stagnant, foul-smelling water that accumulates at the bottom of a vessel.

"This should teach ya once an' fer all, ya **bilge-lickin'** swab!" (Henry Morgan, *Dead Man's Chest* 251) "At last we meet face to face, you **bilge-sucking** scum!" (Henry Morgan, *Dead Man's Chest* 10)

black (base) [*bleck (bayeese)*] evil

"To-night the city was attacked by pirates, led, they say, by that **black** rogue—Bartlemy, intent on plunder, murder, Adam, and ravishment." (Absalom Troy, *Adam Penfeather, Buccaneer* 330) < "How better are you to so cruelly entreat him?" "Oceans better, lass! Worlds better; with all my sins, I could never be so **black base** as vicious Johnny." > (Ursula Revell & Japhet Bly, *Winds of Chance* 156)

blackguard(ly) [*blaggahrrd(ly)*] reprehensible

"Besides, you are wrong in regard to the cargo being aboard; there's a good quarter of it lying in the woods, and that **blackguard** chief knows it and won't let me take it off." (pirate captain, *The Coral Island* 249) < "The *Santa Veronica* carries a sacerdotal cargo as rich as the plate in any ship that ever came out of Mexico." "I see. And it's your **blackguardly** notion that we should lay her board and board, and seize the Archbishop?" > (Yberville & Peter Blood, *The Fortunes of Captain Blood* 110–11)

black-hearted [*bleck-'ahrrt/'eart/hahrrt-ered*] evil; malicious

"And now him and Galloway—them two **black-hearted** bastards—is in such strength that Crosby Pike dursn't say a word o' protest." (Cunley, *Captain Blood Returns* 277)

blasted [*blarrsted*]
blasting [*blarrst-in'*] damned

An unspecific derogatory adjective.

"You **blasted** idiot!" (Henry Morgan, "Pirates of Tortuga" 50:13) < "Bill's dead!" "Well, search him for me, you **blasting** lubbers!" > (Pew, "Treasure Island" [1934] 20:19)

bleeding [*bleedin'*] damned

An unspecific derogatory adjective.

"Dirty **bleedin'** spy as deserves to swing." (pirate aboard the *Hispaniola*, muttering disgustedly about captain's mate Mister Arrow, "Treasure Island" [1960] 33:51)

blind [*blawnd/blin'/blyeen'/blyeend/blyeent/blynt*] idiotic; useless

Used to characterize another as foolish, and more specifically as fundamentally imperceptive or uncomprehending.

"Why, you **blind** sheep!" (Long John Silver, "Long John Silver's Return to Treasure Island" 1:25:33)

bloated [*bloot/blo'oot-ered*] swollen
Used especially in reference to a large or pompous person.

> "Not this pitiful, spineless, pasty, **bloated** codfish I see before me." (James Hook, "Hook" 44:33)

blood-thirsty [*bloohd/blut-tharrsty/thirshty*] excessively violent; mindlessly destructive

> "'Tis as I guessed ... this shrewish claw-cat, this **blood-thirsty** she-devil ... you love her, eh, my poor lad?" (Absalom Troy, *Adam Penfeather, Buccaneer* 110)

bloody [*bloohd/bluh'/blutt-y*]
(1) damned (An unspecific derogatory adjective.)

> "Come along, you **bloody** laggards, haul away all!" (William Darnall, *The Guard-ship* 37)

(2) excessively violent; mindlessly destructive

> "His sport is rape and slaughter of the defenceless, he is, in fine, a very **bloody**, vile rogue and damned rascal, —eh, Smy?" (Absalom Troy, *Adam Penfeather, Buccaneer* 19–20)

bloody-minded [*bloohd/bluh'/blutt-y mawnd/myeend-ered*] bent on violence; excessively inclined to inflict pain or injury

> "So ho, my beastly rogues and right **bloody-minded** villains, ye plot mutiny and murder, do ye!" (Adam Penfeather, *Adam Penfeather, Buccaneer* 214)

blooming [*bloomin'*]
An unspecific derogatory adjective milder than most.

> "Strike your colors, ya **bloomin'** cockroaches!" (Barbossa, "Pirates of the Caribbean: The Curse of the Black Pearl" 1:26:47)

blundering [*blarrn/bloohn-derin'*]

> "Merry, you **blunderin'** squid. Can you hear me?" (Long John Silver, "Treasure Island" [1950] 46:55)

bone-headed [*boone/bo'oone-'ead/hayd-ered*] thick-headed; dull; stupid

> "Billy Bones, you're as **bone-headed** as a backwards blowfish." (Long John Silver, "Treasure Island" [1998] 3:33)

bone-idle [*boone/bo'oone iy'eedle*] lazy

> "What, am I to be baulked by such **bone-idle**, misbegotten spawn?" (Benjamin Trigg, *Adam Penfeather, Buccaneer* 310)

boosy drunken

> "When did ever gentlemen of fortune turn astern to that much dollars for a **boosy** old seaman? And him dead, too." (Long John Silver, "Treasure Island" [1972] 1:24:34)

brainless [*brayeenless*] foolish; stupid

> < "Where's Finney!" "Woy, 'iz lordship's aft, Admiral. An' bad cess t'the **brainless** bugger, sez oy!" > (Alan Lewrie & pirate aboard the *Caroline*, *The Gun Ketch* 311)

butcherly [*barrtcher/butch'-ly*] violent; murderous

> "But one said, 'Damn him, let him go, he was a **butcherly** dog'; another said, 'Damn him, he was a merciless son of a bitch'; another said he was a barbarous dog, and the like." (Captain Avery, *The King of Pirates* 24)

chicken-hearted [*check-ern 'ahrrt/'eart/hahrrt-ered*] lacking courage or determination; cowardly; spineless

> "And if you're too **chicken-hearted** for this, I say depose yourself." (Old Stingley, "Long John Silver's Return to Treasure Island" 7:19)

chuckle-headed [*charrk/choohk-le 'ead//hayd-ered*] thick-headed; dull; stupid

> "[They] pin their faith upon a pimp of a parson; a squab, who neither practices nor believes what he puts upon the **chuckle-headed** fools he preaches to." (Captain Bellamy, *General History of the Pyrates* 587)

clod-like [*clarrd-lawk/lyeeke*] stupid; oafish

"Ah, by God, there is more of vigorous life in my little finger than in all your great, heavy, **clod-like** carcase." (Captain Jo, *Martin Conisby's Vengeance* 33)

cold [*coold/co'oold*] heartless; unfeeling

"By thunder, that Flint were a **cold** bastard." (Long John Silver, "Treasure Island" [1990] 1:52:22)

cold-gutted [*coold/co'oold garrt/gooht-ered*] heartless; unfeeling

< "You **cold-gutted** shark." "Ah, flatterer." > (Orange Povy & William Kidd, "Captain Kidd" 23:17)

confounded [*cahn/carrn/coohn/kern-fount/fowoond/fowoont-ered*]

"Confound" means to throw into confusion or disorder, but also to destroy or ruin. As an epithet, it means the addressee is meriting or destined for destruction or ruin.

"Here I have this **confounded** son of a Dutchman sitting in my own house, drinking of my own rum!" (Long John Silver, *Treasure Island* 45, Chap. 8)

cowardly [*carrd/cowahrrd/cowar'/cowart-ly*]

"Tho', damn ye, you are a sneaking puppy, and so are all those who will submit to be governed by laws which rich men have made for their own security, for the **cowardly** whelps have not the courage otherwise to defend what they get by their knavery ..." (Captain Bellamy to the captain of a plundered Boston sloop, *General History of the Pyrates* 587)

crass [*crarss*] dull; stupid

"See how the **crass** fools straggle!" (Japhet Bly, *Winds of Chance* 352)

craven [*cravv/crayeev-ern*] utterly without courage or determination; pathetically spineless

"Wipe the **craven** sweat from you!" (Captain Jo, *Martin Conisby's Vengeance* 13)

crawling [*crawrl-in'*]

Used to suggest that the person so described is a pathetic lowlife—a worm or insect, for example.

"You **crawlin'** squid! You dogfish!" (Long John Silver, "Treasure Island" [1934] 1:08:35)

cringing [*creng-in'*] weak or submissive; obsequious; wormlike

"And as for you, you **cringin'** bookworm, get your carcass out of this tavern!" (Long John Silver, "The Adventures of Long John Silver: Dead Reckoning" 23:39)

crooked [*crook-ered/ert/ett*] dishonest; corrupt

"Oh, a **crooked** rogue. So you have your price." (William Kidd, "Captain Kidd" 39:16)

crossgrained [*crarss-grayeend*] perverse; troublesome

"Yet ye're aggrieved, being a poor-spirited, **crossgrained** cur, and to vent your spite you're running straight upon destruction." (Peter Blood, *Captain Blood Returns* 141)

crowing [*crowin'*] pompous or arrogant without good reason; self-aggrandizing

"Why sink and drownd me! I say drownd and sink me if it a'n't the little, **crowing** captain, the game-cock whiffler ..." (Roger Tressady, *Adam Penfeather, Buccaneer* 276)

cuckoldy [*carrk/coohk-ooldy*] mean-spirited or underhanded, especially in a weak or undignified—rather than intimidating or menacing—way

"Squeeze it out of his **cuckoldy** head, my lads." (Peter Blood's impersonator, *The Fortunes of Captain Blood* 47)

curse and damn you [*carrse/carrst/coorse/cursh/curst an'/'n' damn 'ee/ya/ye/yer*]

A rare example of the colorful use of a curse as an epithet-modifier. There's no good reason not to use other curses as epithet-modifiers as well, so feel free to select among the curses listed in Chapter 7 when disparaging another.

> "Ha, and there ye may see Sir Benjamin, with Dodd the Master and William Sharp, our sharp-nosed, sharper-tongued, **curse and damn ye** fool of a captain." (Absalom Troy, *Adam Penfeather, Buccaneer* 60)

cursed; curst [*carrsed/coorsed/curshed*] contemptible; hateful

> "It's that **cursed** petticoat's making a coward of you." (Wolverstone, *Captain Blood: His Odyssey* 252)

cutthroat [*carrt/cooht-thro'oot*] ruthless; murderous

> "Innocent, d'ye say? A **cut-throat** gallows-bird, says I ..." (Absalom Troy, *Adam Penfeather, Buccaneer* 110)

daft [*daff/darrft/deft*] (1) mad; insane (2) stupid; foolish

> "You're **daft**, lady. You both are." (Anamaria, "Pirates of the Caribbean: The Curse of the Black Pearl" 1:24:07)

damned [*damt*]
An unspecific derogatory adjective.

> "**Damned** assassins!" (George Fairfax, *The Fortunes of Captain Blood* 148)

desperate [*daahss/darrss-peerate/p'rate*] outrageous; unredeemable

> < "We just saw torches inside!" "Thieves!" "**Desperate** cutthroats, without a doubt." > (Purity Pinker & Jim Hawkins, reporting suspicious activity to passing soldiers, "The Adventures of Long John Silver: Miss Purity's Birthday" 24:21)

devil(ish) [*daahv/dayv/debb/div-il(-ersh/esh)*] of or relating to the devil; evil; malicious

> "For yonder come two **devil** craft intent on our slaughter and destruction!" (Amos Perring, *Adam Penfeather, Buccaneer* 117)
> "A woeful end to both of us but for our damned Johnny! And there's the **devilish**

irony of it!" (Japhet Bly, conceding that his hated enemy has just saved his and his wife's lives, *Winds of Chance* 330)

devil's [*daahv/dayv/debb/div-il's*] of or relating to the devil; evil; malicious

> "See how yon **devil's** craft gains on us, she grows with every minute." (Benjamin Trigg, bemoaning the slowness of the *Santissima Trinidad*, *Adam Penfeather, Buccaneer* 232)

dirty [*darrty*] filthy; vile; despicable

> "Some **dirty** thievin' pirates got here before we did." (Trip Fenner, "The Adventures of Long John Silver: Sword of Vengeance" 6:30)

dishonoured [*des-hon-ertt*] disgraceful; shameful

> "It is probable that I shall have the satisfaction of hanging you from that yardarm, like the forsworn, **dishonoured** thief you are, you gentleman of Spain." (Peter Blood, *The Fortunes of Captain Blood* 137)

double-dealing [*darr/dooh-ble dealin'*] dishonest in a weak, furtive, or despicable way

> "Why, you **double-dealin'** swab! These dice be loaded!" (Long John Silver, "The Adventures of Long John Silver: Devil's Stew" 1:52)

doubly-damned [*darr/dooh-bly damt*]
An unspecific but emphatic derogatory adjective.

> "Villain! **doubly d[amne]d** villain! thou'lt die like a dog, and unrevenged!" (Cain, *The Pirate* 138, Chap. XVII)

driveling [*drev-erlin'/erling//'lin'/'ling'*]
drooling [*droolin'*]
Used to suggest mental incapacity, and often coupled with similarly themed epithet nouns such as "fool" and "idiot."

> "Now, I believe there's thousands o' the people in England who are sich born **drivelin'** *won't-believers* that they think

the black fellows hereaways at the worst eat an enemy only now an' then, out o' spite; whereas I know for certain ... that the Feejee Islanders eat not only their enemies but one another; and they do it not for spite, but for pleasure." (Bloody Bill, *The Coral Island* 219) "Well, what are they waiting for, **drooling** idiot?" (Humble Bellows, "The Crimson Pirate" 34:38)

drunken [*drarrnk/dronk-ern*]

"**Drunken** sot! Begone lest I send ye aloft to join yon carrion!" (Captain Jo, *Martin Conisby's Vengeance* 87)

dull(-witted) [*doohl(-wett/wih'-ered)*] stupid; unintelligent; idiotic

"But you were ever a **dull** fool, my pretty man, yes!" (Captain Jo, *Martin Conisby's Vengeance* 62) "You poor, **dull-witted** fool, would you match yourself against me?" (John Sharkey, *The Dealings of Captain Sharkey and other Tales of Pirates* "The Dealings of Captain Sharkey with Stephen Craddock" 36)

dung-souled [*darrng/doohng-sooled/so'ooled*] contemptible; despicable

"You **dung-souled** impostor!" (Peter Blood, *The Fortunes of Captain Blood* 50)

envenomed [*enven-ermed/omt*] so hateful or contemptible as to be toxic or corrosive

*Fly finding himself beyond Nantucket, and that his design was baulk'd, called to Atkinson, and told him, he was a rascally son of an **envenom'd** bitch, and d[am]n his blood it was a piece of cruelty to let such a son of a whore live, who design'd the death of so many honest fellows.* (attribution to William Fly, *General History of the Pyrates* 611)

eternal [*ay/iy-tarnal*] damned

An unspecific but emphatic derogatory adjective, meaning something equivalent to "eternally cursed" or "eternally damned."

"Well, then, you get on a horse, and go to—well, yes, I will!—to that **eternal** doctor swab, and tell him to pipe all hands ..." (Billy Bones, *Treasure Island* 15–16, Chap. 3)

everlasting [*ebber/ebbry/e'er/e'ery/ev'ry-lastin'*]

An unspecific but emphatic adjective amplifying the meaning of the noun modified.

"Wherefore I grieve to find ye such an **everlasting** fool, brother." (Resolution Day, *Martin Conisby's Vengeance* 89)

faithless [*fayeethless*] depraved; wicked

*[H]e openly declared, he was no longer the ally, but the profess'd enemy of **faithless** people.* (attribution to Nathaniel North, *General History of the Pyrates* 532)

false [*fawrlse*] lying; dishonest; treacherous

"'T[i]s a sin to suffer such a **false** traiterous dog as [you] to live." (John Russell, threatening George Roberts for toasting King George rather than his Roman Catholic rival James Edward Stuart, *Pirates of the New England Coast* 179)

false-tongued [*fawrlse-toohngued*] lying

"You were too curious in your inquiries of the dolt who declares he was robbed by us of his provisions and sails. The **false-tongued** villain!" (The Red Rover, *The Red Rover* 103–04)

fat [*fett*] overweight; plump

The term is also used figuratively in reference to a pompous or overindulgent person.

"He loves his life, does this **fat** rascal." (Peter Blood, *Captain Blood: His Odyssey* 283)

feckless [*fackless*] incompetent; ineffectual

"Go after her, you **feckless** pack of ingrates." (Barbossa, "Pirates of the Caribbean: The Curse of the Black Pearl" 1:14:44)

fiendly [*fien'ly*] depraved; wicked

< "What like is this Black Bartlemy?" "A smiling, **fiendly** gentleman, Adam, all niminy-piminy affectations, and, save for

lace ruffles, all sable black from trucks to keelson." > (Adam Penfeather & Absalom Troy, *Adam Penfeather, Buccaneer* 21)

filthy [*felthy*] vile; nasty

"You **filthy** pig, you'll be shot! Clap him in irons!" (El Toro Mendoza, "Long John Silver's Return to Treasure Island" 17:49)

fine-feathered [*fawn/fyeene fay-thert*]
Used to refer derisively to someone well or elaborately dressed or to a person of pretentious speech, manner, or attitude.

< "I'll give you just two seconds to get out of 'ere." "Belay. I'll tend to this **fine-feathered** upstart meself." > (Long John Silver & Purity Pinker, confronting the pompous Bellows and the soldiers flanking him, "The Adventures of Long John Silver: The Eviction" 7:01)

fishbait [*fesh-bayeete*] worthless
Used to characterize another as irrelevant or useless—*i.e.*, a lowlife with little value other than as food for fish after death.

"We need the manpower from the *Walrus* to help get the treasure, but after that, I'd be willin' to help the *Cloud* sink Pritchard an' the rest of them **fishbait** troublemakers." (Joshua Smoot, *Dead Man's Chest* 171)

fishy [*feshy*] sheepish; pathetic

"We looked out, and, by thunder! the old ship was gone. I never seen a pack o' fools look **fishier**; and you may lay to that, if I tells you that looked the **fishiest**." (Long John Silver, ridiculing his crew for having somehow misplaced the *Hispaniola*, *Treasure Island* 157, Chap. 28)

flogging [*flarrg-in'*]
An unspecific but emphatic adjective, used in much the same way as the modern speaker's "freakin'."

< "I'm ready for my nightcap." "Abso-**floggin'**-lutely." > (James Hook & Smee, "Hook" 1:04:00)

fo'c'sle [*fo'ook/fork-sull*] low-brow; common; brutish; insignificant

"Fo'c'sle" is a compressed form of the term "forecastle," meaning the portion of a vessel between its foremast and bow. The common, non-officer crew of a sailing vessel often worked and nearly always slept there, so the term came to be used figuratively to refer to anything relating to such common crew, and pejoratively to characterize the addressee as somehow inferior or unworthy of respect.

< "We wants the red'ead!" "Belay there, ya **fo'c'sle** swab." > (pirates in crowd at auction & pirate auctioneer, "Pirates of the Caribbean" Disney attraction)

fond [*farrnd/font*] foolish; silly; absurd

"Can the poor, **fond** wretch have sunk to wedlock when any woman may be had for the taking—by such as we?" (Black Bartlemy, *Adam Penfeather, Buccaneer* 257–58)

fond and feckless [*farrnd/font an'/'n' fackless*] foolish and incompetent

"Japhet, you're a stout captain, a prime sailorman, a good friend, but a **fond and feckless** fool, and there's for ye, Captain and sir!" (Crabtree, *Winds of Chance* 89)

fool(-headed) [*foo'ell(-'ead/hayd-ered)*] foolish; dull; stupid

"**Fool** wench, let be! Must you foul yourself with his vile blood ... such beastly contamination, —let be!" (Japhet Bly, urging Ursula Revell not to wipe clean the bloodied face of John Barrasdale, *Winds of Chance* 171) "He's that **fool-headed** beachcomber what thinks he's you." (Bullwinkle, "Blackbeard the Pirate" 46:50)

foppish [*farrp-ersh/esh*] affected and overly ostentatious in manner or appearance; dandyish

"He's no coward, this **foppish** little prick, I'll give him that." (Roger Press, *The Pirate Round* 266)

forsworn [*farr/foor-swarrn*] contemptible

To forswear is to reject or renounce utterly or determinedly. The term is accordingly used to suggest the speaker wants nothing to do with the person so described.

> "That land, you treacherous, **forsworn** Spanish dog, is the island of Hispaniola." (Peter Blood, *Captain Blood: His Odyssey* 126)

foul [*fowool*]

foul-advised [*fowool a'/erd-vawsed/viced/vyeesed*]

foul-lived [*fowool-levved/liffed/livt*] vile; loathsome

> < "Why, he can't die now!" "Not until he settles his score with that **foul** scum de Vegas." > (Patch & other member of Long John Silver's company, "The Adventures of Long John Silver: Sword of Vengeance" 10:23) "I don't know his infernal name, but 'tis that same ill-beseen, **foul-advised** hell-hound ..." (Benjamin Trigg, *Adam Penfeather, Buccaneer* 207) "... it behoveth me to very heartily reprove thee, Ursula, thy most unmaidenly frowardness to traffic wi' such notable villain and **foul-lived** dog as yon Ramirez, with a curse!" (Lovepeace Farrance, *Winds of Chance* 61)

gallowsy [*galler/galloo/gallowoo-sy*] deserving of execution; degenerate

> "I think, shipmate, that your doublet bloody and you the grimly, desperate, **gallowsy**, hell-fire rogue you strive so hard to appear, Martin, I say here's enough to hang you ten times over." (Adam Penfeather, *Black Bartlemy's Treasure* 144–45)

game-cock [*gayeeme-carrk*] fierce, but in a pathetic, ridiculous way

> "Why sink and drownd me! I say drownd and sink me if it a'n't the little, crowing captain, the **game-cock** whiffler ..." (Roger Tressady, *Adam Penfeather, Buccaneer* 276)

God-forsaken [*Garrd/Gott/Gud farr/fer-sayee-kered/kern*] damned

An unspecific derogatory adjective.

> "When you marooned me on that **God-forsaken** spit of land, you forgot one very important thing, mate: I'm Captain Jack Sparrow." (Jack Sparrow, "Pirates of the Caribbean: The Curse of the Black Pearl" 1:16:45)

grass-combing [*grarss-comb/coom-in'*] useless; incompetent

The suggestion is that the person so described is as worthless as someone given to grass-combing—an activity not overwhelmingly productive in any context, but especially pointless when at sea (and particularly odious to the true seaman for its landbound quality).

> "'Twere you that done it—you, George, and you, Tom Morgan, you infernal gang o' **grass-combing** lubbers!" (Long John Silver, "Treasure Island" [1990] 1:43:37)

great [*grayeet/grea'/grett*]

An unspecific but emphatic adjective amplifying the meaning of the noun modified.

> "Here, you **great** sons of whores, listen here!" (Henry Nagel, *The Pirate Round* 212)

grimly [*gremly*] grim; ghastly; savage

> "I think, shipmate, that your doublet bloody and you the **grimly**, desperate, gallowsy, hell-fire rogue you strive so hard to appear, Martin, I say here's enough to hang you ten times over." (Adam Penfeather, *Black Bartlemy's Treasure* 144–45)

half-masted ['*alf/harrf-marrst-ered*] inadequate; worthless

> "Mister Bellows, keep the rest of these **half-masted** monkeys below deck." (Captain Vallo, "The Crimson Pirate" 16:38)

half-witted ['*alf/harrf-wett/wih'-ered*] dim-witted; simple-minded; foolish

> "You're a [damned] pig-headed, **half-witted** fool." (Blueskin, *The Book of Pirates* "Blueskin, the Pirate" 166)

hell-fire ['*ell-farr/fyarr*]
hellish ['*ell-ersh/esh*] evil; awful

"We should ha' kept to the river and my boats, damme, 'stead o' this **hellfire** labour o' marching ..." (Rogerson, *Winds of Chance* 353) "Now if you mean our **hellish** rogues, these imps o' Satan and spawn o' the devil, our rascal crew, —eh Adam?" (Benjamin Trigg, *Adam Penfeather, Buccaneer* 224)

hen-hearted ['*en-'ahrrt/'eart/hahrrt-ered*] lacking courage or determination; spineless

"[B]ut damn ye altogether: damn them for a pack of crafty rascals, and you, who serve them, for a parcel of **hen-hearted** numskuls." (Captain Bellamy to the captain of a plundered Boston sloop, *General History of the Pyrates* 587)

ill [*ee'ull*] vile; offensive

"And there we fought, his dagger and hook against my dead comrade's knife, and thus as he sprang I, falling on my knee, smote up beneath raised arm, heard him roar and saw him go whirling over and down and splash into the sea. ... Aye, Martin, which was the end of an **ill** rogue and an evil thing." (Adam Penfeather, *Black Bartlemy's Treasure* 94)

ill-beseen [*ee'ull b'seen*] vile; offensive
The term "beseen," meaning "seen" or "perceived," suggests an element of disapproval or disapprobation by the speaker.

"I don't know his infernal name, but 'tis that same **ill-beseen**, foul-advised hell-hound ..." (Benjamin Trigg, *Adam Penfeather, Buccaneer* 207)

ill-conditioned [*ee'ull cahhn/carrn/coohn/kern-deh-sherned/shoohned*] vile; offensive
The term "conditioned" suggests there is something about another's constitution or character, persisting through time, that is "ill," and that the epithet is not simply something the speaker is tossing out without substantiation.

< "I sent Giles Tregenza to you this morning." "Ay, sir, which as-tonished me, for you'll mind him as one o' the worst aboard yon galley, a fur'ous, **ill-conditioned** raskell." > (Ned Bowser, *Adam Penfeather, Buccaneer* 210–11)

ill-look'd [*ee'ull look'd*] ugly; bad-looking

"Hearkee me, sirrah, you lousy, pittiful, **ill-look'd** dog; what have you to say why you should not be tuck'd up immediately, and set a sun-drying like a scare-crow?" (George Bradley, *General History of the Pyrates* 293)

impudent [*em-per/poo-dent*] impertinent; disrespectful in a casual or cavalier fashion

"You are an **impudent** dog." (Edward Low, rebuking a prisoner who repeatedly refused when asked three times—twice at gunpoint—to join Low's company, *Pirates of the New England Coast* 228)

incarnate [*en-cahrr/ker-naaht/nayte*]
Used in connection with the noun modified to suggest that the person so described is an actual embodiment of the noun.

"The South Sea Islanders are such **incarnate** fiends that they are the better of being tamed, and the missionaries are the only men who can do it." (Bloody Bill, *The Coral Island* 214–15)

indolent [*en-d'/dee/der-lernt*] lazy

"I may have tired of chasing your **indolent** Don, and of driving guarda costas into port." (The Red Rover, *The Red Rover* 347)

infernal [*en-farrnal*] damned
An unspecific derogatory adjective.

"'Twere you that done it—you, George, and you, Tom Morgan, you **infernal** gang o' grass-combing lubbers!" (Long John Silver, "Treasure Island" [1990] 1:43:37)

insolent [*en-ser/so'oo-lernt*] impudent; brazen

< "You have your warning." "You **insolent** dog!" > (Captain Tondeur & Jeremy Pitt, *Captain Blood Returns* 199)

lazy [*layeezy*] disinclined to work; slothful

"Faster, you **lazy** dogs! Bend your backs to it, you louts!" (George Fairfax, *The Fortunes of Captain Blood* 150)

lewd [*lood*] obscene; vile

"Man, I'm telling ye o' this same tall, great, ugly rascal, this scoundrelly, very **lewd** rogue provoked you lately to blooding him and very handsomely ye did it!" (Benjamin Trigg, *Adam Penfeather, Buccaneer* 208)

lily-livered [*lelly/li'y-levv/libb/li'-ered*] lacking courage or determination; cowardly

"Wait, you **lily-livered** scoundrel! Come back and fight like a man!" (The Frog, "Pirates" 1:53:12)

loathly [*loaf/loav/lo'ooth/looth-ly*] loathsome; disgusting

"Master, think o' the most sinful stench ever offended you, the most **loathly** corruption you ever saw and there's his soul; think o' the devil wi' eyes like dim glass, flesh like dough and a sweet, soft voice, and you have Alexo Valdez inside and out, and may every curse ever cursed light on and blast him, says I!" (John, *Martin Conisby's Vengeance* 185)

lousy [*lowoosy*] contemptible; nasty

"Pull, ye **lousy** dogs, pull." (Benjamin Trigg, *Adam Penfeather, Buccaneer* 310)

loutish [*lou'/lowoot-ersh/esh*] stupid; oafish

"There'll be more o' that to follow, my pullet, unless your **loutish** husband comes to his senses." (unnamed pirate impersonator of Peter Blood, *The Fortunes of Captain Blood* 48)

low-lived [*lowoo-levved/liffed/livt*] vulgar; worthless; contemptible

"Skulkers, they be—**low-lived** skulkers as ever was." (Long John Silver, *Porto Bello Gold* 48)

lubberly [*loohber/loohb'/lub'-ly*] (1) inexpert at sailing; lacking seamanship (2) generally incompetent or poorly suited to a task; useless

"[I]f ye were making for La Hacha ye'ld never be reaching so far on this westerly tack unless ye're a **lubberly** idiot, which I perceive ye're not." (Peter Blood, *The Fortunes of Captain Blood* 165)

lukewarm [*loohk-wahrrm*] lacking vigor, energy, or will; indifferent; passionless

"Shall I be in greater danger ashore than aboard, now that we've but fifty men left, and they **lukewarm** rogues who would as soon serve the King as me?" (Peter Blood, *Captain Blood: His Odyssey* 269)

mad crazy; insane

"**Mad** fool! why do you tempt me thus?" (Cain, *The Pirate* 45, Chap. VII)

malapert [*maller-parrt*] disrespectful in a mouthy, overassertive kind of way; impudent

"'Twould almost seem I am not wanted! Ay, and a saucy, **malapert**, young ruffler to tell me so!" (Absalom Troy, *Adam Penfeather, Buccaneer* 107)

mangy [*mayeengy*] filthy; contemptible

"What's it to me what any of your **mangy** followers may feel?" (Captain Easterling, *Captain Blood Returns* 282)

maudlin [*mawrd-ling*] foolish, especially as a result of intoxication or excessive emotion

"Ye're **maudlin**. We'll talk again tomorrow." (Wolverstone, *Captain Blood: His Odyssey* 308)

mealy-mouthed [*mealy-moutht/mowoothed*] unwilling to state something simply and straightforwardly; evasive

The term usually implies further that the person so described is being slippery or evasive as a result of weakness or cowardice.

"I'll bring my boot to ya, and I'll grind your **mealy-mouthed** jib into the dirt, I will!" (Blackbeard, "Blackbeard's Ghost" 1:03:25)

mean vulgar; worthless; contemptible

"For what poor, **mean** wretch is he that will set selfish prudence afore friendship and will not risk all for his messmate!" (Adam Penfeather, *Adam Penfeather, Buccaneer* 294)

milksop [*melk-sarrp*] lacking courage or determination; weak; spineless

"A **milksop** merchantman, the *Mermaid*. We boarded her and walked into a trap." (Montbars, "Pirates of Tortuga" 49:33)

misbegotten [*mes-ber-garrt-ered/ern*]

Meaning literally "born out of wedlock," the term is used to characterize another, depending on context, as offensive, contemptible, or worthless.

"What, am I to be baulked by such bone-idle, **misbegotten** spawn?" (Benjamin Trigg, *Adam Penfeather, Buccaneer* 310)

miserable [*mez-eeble/'rable/reeble*] inadequate; contemptible; worthless

"You **miserable** son of a whore!" (Long John Silver, "Treasure Island" [1990] 1:43:57)

murderous [*marrd/mord-eerous/'rous*]

"Blind him for a dog—a dog and **murderous** rogue as shall bite on this hook o' mine yet!" (Roger Tressady, *Martin Conisby's Vengeance* 158)

mutinous [*moot-'nous*]

Used by a senior member, especially a captain, in rebuking others inferior in command.

"The first swab ta make a move I'll blast to Kingdom Come. Back to yer posts, you **mutinous** dogs!" (Long John Silver, "The Adventures of Long John Silver: The Tale of a Tooth" 15:16)

nasty [*narrsty*] disgusting; offensive

"They'll be correcting the mistake I made last night when I saved your **nasty** life." (Peter Blood, *The Fortunes of Captain Blood* 172)

niminy-piminy [*nemme/nimmer-ny pemme/pimmer-ny*] dainty; mincing

< "What like is this Black Bartlemy?" "A smiling, fiendly gentleman, Adam, all **niminy-piminy** affectations, and, save for lace ruffles, all sable black from trucks to keelson." > (Adam Penfeather & Absalom Troy, *Adam Penfeather, Buccaneer* 21)

obstinate [*obs-'/tern-naaht/nayt*] powerfully stubborn; unyielding to persuasion

Used especially in reference to one whose disagreement the speaker finds baseless or exasperating.

"So you're blubbering, are you, you **obstinate** whelp?" (pirate captain, *The Coral Island* 201)

officious [*arr-fecious*] interfering; meddling

"**Officious** fool!" (Cain, berating his mate for murdering a Portuguese bishop before extracting from him the whereabouts of gold and silver religious ornaments, *The Pirate* 61, Chap. IX)

paltry [*pawrltry*] small; measly; trifling

"As for cowardice, you **paltry** rascal, that is the attribute of the rat to which I liken you." (Peter Blood, *Captain Blood Returns* 200)

parasitic [*pahrr/par'/parrer-setic*] pathetic, especially for one's dependence on or willing submissiveness to another; sycophantic

"Well, my stupid, sorry, **parasitic** sacks of entrails ..." (James Hook, "Hook" 40:31)

pasty [*paahs/payees-ty*] pale

Used literally to refer to an unnatural or unhealthy-looking white complexion and figuratively to suggest the person so described looks pathetically weak or unimposing.

"Not this pitiful, spineless, **pasty**, bloated codfish I see before me." (James Hook, "Hook" 44:33)

pestiferous [*pasti/pershti-farrous/f'rous*] annoying; bothersome

"But now, Ursula, needs must thou be chidden for thy naughty doing ... to stoop for such vile, **pestiferous** company as ..." (Ezekiel Penryn, *Winds of Chance* 61)

pestilent [*past/pesht-erlent/'lent*] odious; pernicious

"He is a lousy, **pestilent** fellow, a plague o' the seas, who will plunder and destroy any vessel weaker than his own—and of any nation." (Absalom Troy, *Adam Penfeather, Buccaneer* 19–20)

petty [*patty/peh'y*] small; measly; trifling

"Tush and curse it, Captain, 'tis no more than **petty** boy, a sickling, a lousy lad, a puling mannikin not worth shiproom!" (Benjamin Trigg, on seeing the slight Adam Penfeather for the first time, *Adam Penfeather, Buccaneer* 44)

pewling; puling [*pool-in'*] whining; whimpering

Used to suggest the person so described is so pathetically weak as to cry. Used especially in mocking reference to another's speech or way of speaking.

< "See how greatly the men favor you, sir?" "The **pewling** spawn—how I despise them." > (Smee & James Hook, "Hook" 40:17)

pimpish [*pemp-ersh/esh*] unscrupulous; worthless; contemptible; unseemly

"I've a mind to slit your **pimpish** ears so that they may see what happens to them as gets pert with Captain Easterling." (Captain Easterling, *Captain Blood Returns* 283)

pitiful [*petti/petty/pih'i-ful*] pathetic

"Hearkee me, sirrah, you lousy, **pittiful**, ill-look'd dog; what have you to say why you should not be tuck'd up immediately, and set a sun-drying like a scare-crow?" (George Bradley, *General History of the Pyrates* 293)

plaguey [*playeeguey*] vexatious; bothersome

"And what of my blood, then? Hasn't there been enough of that shed by him and his **plaguey** bullies?" (George Fairfax, *The Fortunes of Captain Blood* 155)

plausible [*plaah/plawr-seble/seeble*] untrustworthy, especially in a fast-talking, unctuous way; unscrupulous

"So! A runaway wife and a **plausible**, thrice damned villain! Well, these sort well together." (Japhet Bly, *Winds of Chance* 139)

poor-spirited [*parr-sperrit/sp'rit-ered*] cowardly; pathetic

"Yet ye're aggrieved, being a **poor-spirited**, crossgrained cur, and to vent your spite you're running straight upon destruction." (Peter Blood, *Captain Blood Returns* 141)

powder-brained [*parr/powoo-der brayeened*] dull; stupid

Used especially in reference to a gunner or other person who frequently handles gunpowder.

"They're not firing at us, you **powder-brained** ape." (Captain Vallo, "The Crimson Pirate" 16:20)

poxed [*parrxed*] damned

An unspecific derogatory adjective.

"How the hell do I get out of this **poxed** river?" (Roger Press, *The Pirate Round* 67)

pox-riddled [*parrx-redd-lered/ult*] loathsome

"Why, you **pox-riddled** villain, I can be as honest as any man if I have the incentive." (William Kidd, "Captain Kidd" 30:59)

poxy [*parrxy*] vile; loathsome

"**Poxy** ass! [I'll] get you!" (Black Dog, "Treasure Island" [1998] 37:28)

pretty [*preh'y*]

(1) Used mockingly and ironically.

"Ha, my **pretty** lambs! Will ye skulk then, will ye skulk with your fool's heads together?" (Roger Tressady, upon discovering members of his company conspiring to leave him to join Adam Penfeather, *Black Bartlemy's Treasure* 312)

(2) ridiculous; pathetic

"'Fore God, that merchant skipper has left his mark on us, and **pretty** fools we were to think that such a maid would be quarantined for the cause he gave." (Baldy Stable, realizing that a murdered merchant captain had avenged himself by leaving behind a leprous female prisoner, *The Dealings of Captain Sharkey and Other Tales of Pirates* "The Blighting of Sharkey" 57)

puny [*poony*] small; measly; trifling

"Die? Who—me? And by such **puny** wretch as you?" (Giles Tregenza, mocking the small-statured Adam Penfeather, *Adam Penfeather, Buccaneer* 203)

rank [*renk*] odious; disgusting

"This man—O'Brien were his name—a **rank** Irelander—this man and me got the canvas on here, meaning for to sail her back." (Israel Hands, *Treasure Island* 137, Chap. 25)

rascal(ly) [*rarrscal(ly)*] deceitful; treacherous

"So you are the Captain Adam Penfeather they call The Buccaneer, and more bloody and merciless than any **rascal** pirate in The Main ..." (Black Bartlemy, *Adam Penfeather, Buccaneer* 253) "[You're a] **rascally** son of a b[itch]." (John Russell, rebuking George Roberts for toasting King George rather than his Roman Catholic rival James Edward Stuart, *Pirates of the New England Coast* 179)

rogue [*roo/ro'oo-gue*]
roguesy [*roo/ro'oo-gsy*]
roguish [*roo/ro'oo-gesh/gersh*] offensive or objectionable, especially in a way threatening harm or danger to others

"Well, ma'm, he is the elder o' my two **rogue** cousins that, with their father, my villainous uncle, shipped me off whiles yet a lad and sold me into slavery." (Japhet Bly, *Winds of Chance* 219) "[I]f you don't act like an honest man G[o]d d[am]n ye, and offer to play us any **rogues'y** tricks by G[o]d ... I'll blow your brains out ..." (William Fly, *General History of the Pyrates* 610–11) "Also you refused to betray your fellow rogues to save that **roguish** neck o' yours." (Adam Penfeather, *Adam Penfeather, Buccaneer* 215)

ruffian [*raff/rarrf-ian*] cruel; brutal; barbaric

< "Oh, now, now, I'm sorry, Purity." "Sorry, he says. Sorry indeed. If it weren't for you and the **ruffian** manners of you and your crew this would never have happened." > (Long John Silver & Purity Pinker, "The Adventures of Long John Silver: The Eviction" 12:28)

ruination [*roo/rooer-nayee-shern/shoohn*] damned

An unspecific derogatory adjective.

"Now, that's about where we are, every mother's son of us, thanks to him, and Hands, and Anderson, and other **ruination** fools of you." (Long John Silver, *Treasure Island* 165, Chap. 29)

rumpot [*roohmpahrrt*] drink-addled

Used to characterize another as incapacitated with drink or with a tendency to drink excessively, and implicitly to dismiss the person so described as hopeless or no-good.

"So whose fault is it, really, that you've ended up a **rumpot** deckhand what takes orders from pirates?" (Jack Sparrow, "Pirates of the Caribbean 2: Dead Man's Chest" 1:51:39)

rutting [*rarrt-in'*] damned

To "rut" is to desire or engage in sexual intercourse.

"Stand off! Stand off, ya **rutting** bastards, the ship is ours!" (Duncan Honeyman, *The Pirate Round* 263)

sad pathetic; sorry; worthless

"[H]ere is a fellow before you that is a **sad** dog, a **sad sad** dog; and I humbly hope your Lordship will order him to be hang'd out of the way immediately." (pirate in Thomas Antsis' company, *General History of the Pyrates* 292)

saucy [*sarrcy*] rude; impertinent

"[S]hould a captain be so **saucy** as to exceed prescription at any time, why, down with him!" (Henry Dennis, *General History of the Pyrates* 194–95 & *The Pirates Own Book* 83)

scabrous [*scarr-broohss*] rotten; lousy
Literally meaning "scaly" or "scurfy" in reference to a person's skin or an animal's coat, the term is used figuratively to refer more broadly to another as disgusting or offensive.

"On deck, you **scabrous** dogs! Hands to braces!" (Jack Sparrow, "Pirates of the Caribbean: The Curse of the Black Pearl" 2:12:37)

scoundrel(ly) [*scowoondrel(ly)*] depraved; wicked

< "If the captain's son, why were you contending?" "Because just now I shot his **scoundrel** father." > (Edward Templemore & Hawkhurst, *The Pirate* 126, Chap. XVI) "Man, I'm telling ye o' this same tall, great, ugly rascal, this **scoundrelly**, very lewd rogue provoked you lately to blooding him and very handsomely ye did it!" (Benjamin Trigg, *Adam Penfeather, Buccaneer* 208)

scurvy [*scarrvy*] rotten; lousy

"The **scurvy** swabs'll die whether we lay a wager on their heads or not, little brother, so I don't see the harm in it." (Long John Silver, *Dead Man's Chest* 75)

shallow-pated [*shallowoo patered*] empty-headed; stupid; foolish

"Very well, it is agreed you are certainly abducted. But I have carried you away from the following evils, greater or less, to wit—a bibulous uncle, a **shallow-pated** aunt, divers sighful swains, a rascal that would ha' wed you for your aforesaid possessions and a life of useless, pampered ease ..." (Japhet Bly, *Winds of Chance* 39)

sharp-nosed [*shahrrp no'oosed/no'oost/nost*] irritating; meddlesome

"Ha, and there ye may see Sir Benjamin, with Dodd the Master and William Sharp, our **sharp-nosed**, sharper-tongued, curse and damn ye fool of a captain." (Absalom Troy, *Adam Penfeather, Buccaneer* 60)

shindly [*shend/shin'-ly*] weak; spindly

"I've got a **shindly** little beanrake with the shakes and the whimpers." (Blackbeard, "Blackbeard's Ghost" 26:41)

shirking [*sharrkin'*] avoiding or negecting work or duty; lazy; worthless

"Search him, some of you **shirking** lubbers, and the rest of you aloft and get the chest." (Pew, *Treasure Island* 25, Chap. 5)

shrewish [*shrew-ersh/esh*] bad-tempered; excessively complaining or nagging

"'Tis as I guessed ... this **shrewish** claw-cat, this blood-thirsty she-devil ... you love her, eh, my poor lad?" (Absalom Troy, *Adam Penfeather, Buccaneer* 110)

skulking [*skoohl-kin'*] slinking; cowardly

"'Tis sly, **skulking** rogue Abner!" (Adam Penfeather, *Black Bartlemy's Treasure* 328)

slab-faced [*slarrb fayeeced*] ugly
Used often in reference to someone with an especially large, flat, or plainly featured face.

"Belay for a — lackey, ye **slab-faced** chunk o' rotted seahorse!" (John Flint, *Porto Bello Gold* 83, omission in original)

slack-bellied [*slarrk belleet*] having a distended belly

Used literally to comment derisively on another's physique, or figuratively in reference to a lazy, sloppy, pompous, or overindulgent person.

"[Y]e lousy, **slack-bellied** swab ..." (John Flint, *Porto Bello Gold* 83)

slack-jawed [*slarrk jawered/jawrred/jawt*] foolish; dull; stupid; useless; lazy; weak-willed

"Curse ya for breathin', you **slack-jawed** idiot!" (Joshamee Gibbs, "Pirates of the Caribbean: The Curse of the Black Pearl" 51:30)

slammakey [*slarrmakey*]

slimy [*slaw/slyee-my*] vile; loathsome

"Of all the **slammakey** blackguards." (William Kidd, "Captain Kidd" 39:29) "Why, you—you **slimy** squid! If it weren't for you, our little Jim would be here now!" (Long John Silver, "The Adventures of Long John Silver: Dead Reckoning" 21:46)

slouching [*slou'oo-chin'*] lazy; slothful; oafish; useless

"[Y]e that are Englishmen all, —ye that were o' late right hardy mariners, prime seamen bold for all hardship, now show no better than so many whey-faced, spiritless, **slouching** wastrels!" (Adam Penfeather, *Adam Penfeather, Buccaneer* 301)

sluggard [*sloohg-gahrrd/gerd/gert*] lazy; slothful

"Oh, **sluggard** soul—how like, how very like thee, Martino!" (Captain Jo, *Martin Conisby's Vengeance* 49)

small [*smawrl*] measly; trifling

"A **small**, thieving rogue is Penfeather ..." (Roger Tressady, *Martin Conisby's Vengeance* 158)

smock-faced [*smarrk-fayeeced*] feminine-looking; girl-faced

"Damme, Adam, but thou'rt transforming this gentle, **smock-faced** brother o' thine into a perfect throat-slitting 'sdeath and blood bravo, a notable swashing, hell-fire, bully roarer, eh, Adam?" (Absalom Troy, *Adam Penfeather, Buccaneer* 101)

sneaking [*sneakin'*] lacking courage or determination; cowardly; spineless

"It's that whiner—**sneakin'** brat!" (Pew, "Treasure Island" (1934) 20:44)

sniveling [*snev-erlin'/erling//'lin'/'ling*] whining; whimpering

Used to suggest the person described is so pathetically weak as to cry. Used especially in mocking reference to another's speech or way of speaking.

"[T]here is no arguing with such **sniveling** puppies, who allow superiors to kick them about deck at pleasure ..." (Captain Bellamy, *General History of the Pyrates* 587)

sodden [*sarrd-dern*] drunken

"That ain't the point, you **sodden**, stupid wretch of a —" (Ezekiel Ripley, interrupted in mid-rebuke by LeRois' iron grip around his throat, *The Guardship* 238)

soft-headed [*sarrft/soff-'ead/hayd-ered*] foolish; dull; stupid

"What **soft-headed** lubber had a Bible?" (Long John Silver, *Treasure Island* 163, Chap. 29)

soft-hearted [*sarrft/soff-'ahrrt/'eart/hahrrt-ered*] despicably susceptible to emotional reaction, especially one of pity or sorrow; weak

"There's a set o' **soft-hearted** folk at home that I knows on who don't like to have their feelin's ruffled, and when you tell them anything they don't like—that shocks them, as they call it—no matter how true it be, they stop their ears and cry out, 'Oh, that is *too* horrible! We can't believe that!'" (Bloody Bill, *The Coral Island* 219)

sorry [*sahr/soo-ry*] pathetic; worthless

> "Well, my stupid, **sorry**, parasitic sacks of entrails ..." (James Hook, *Hook* 40:31)

sottish [*sarrt-ersh/esh*] dull; stupid

> "You've no home in England; you've a house there, you've lands and what not, but how then? It is not roof and walls that make home, no nor company of **sottish** uncle and witless aunt." (Japhet Bly, *Winds of Chance* 194)

soulless [*sool/so'ool-less*] depraved; wicked

> "Come back, Long John, you **soulless** devil!" (Purity Pinker, "Long John Silver's Return to Treasure Island" 1:42:12)

sour-faced [*sarr/sowarr-fayeeced*] (1) wearing an annoying or worrying look of anger, dissatisfaction, glumness, or resentment (2) ugly; ill-featured

> "Ah, there ya be, **sour-faced** as ever." (Thomas Bartholomew Red, "Pirates" 59:36)

spindle-shanked [*spend-ler/ly-shenked*] thin-legged; weak; frail

> "I want hearty fellows, seadogs and tarry mariners, not **spindle-shanked** whifflers!" (Benjamin Trigg, on seeing the slight Adam Penfeather for the first time, *Adam Penfeather, Buccaneer* 44)

spineless [*spawn/spyeene-less*] lacking courage or determination; weak-willed

> "[M]y ship is off the harbour. She carries two hundred of the toughest fighting-men, who would devour your **spineless** militia at a gulp." (Peter Blood, *Captain Blood Returns* 125)

spiritless [*sperrit/sp'rit-less*] lacking vigor, energy, or will; indifferent; passionless

> "[Y]e that are Englishmen all, —ye that were o' late right hardy mariners, prime seamen bold for all hardship, now show no better than so many whey-faced, **spiritless**, slouching wastrels!" (Adam Penfeather, *Adam Penfeather, Buccaneer* 301)

stinking [*stenk-in'*] rotten; lousy; nasty

> "Everyone wants to bargain with me, you and Mercy. Fire and thunder, what do you think I am, a **stinking** sausage merchant?" (William Kidd, "Captain Kidd" 55:23)

stump-winged [*stoohmp-wenged*] (1) clumsy; awkward (2) ineffectual

The speaker suggests the addressee is as adroit or effective as a bird with stumps for wings.

> "Can't you reach any further, you **stump-winged** bilge rat?!" (pirate prisoner, frustrated with his comrade's inability to secure jailhouse keys from a nearby dog, "Pirates of the Caribbean" Disney attraction)

stupid [*stoo-perd/pitt*]

> "Ah, here she comes, lads, right to us, the **stupid** bastard." (captain of Quail Island battery, *The Pirate Round* 351)

swag-bellied [*sweg-bellied*] having an oversized, protuberant, or overhanging belly

Used literally to comment derisively on another's physique or figuratively in reference to a lazy, sloppy, pompous, or overindulgent person.

> "A mite too fast these light-footed wenches be for the likes of an ol' **swag-bellied** pirate such as I." (libidinous pirate, "Pirates of the Caribbean" Disney attraction [2000])

swivel-tongued [*swev/swiff-el toohngued*] lying; double-talking; hypocritical; duplicitous

> "You're naught but a **swivel-tongued** liar, John Silver." (Purity Pinker, "The Adventures of Long John Silver: The Necklace" 8:23)

tender-hearted [*tenner/tenter-'ahrrt/'eart/hahrrt-ered*] despicably susceptible to emotional reaction, especially one of pity or sorrow; weak

> < "I thought the South Sea Islanders never ate anybody except their enemies."

"Humph! I s'pose 'twas yer **tender-heart-ed** friends in England that put that notion into your head." > (Ralph Rover & Bloody Bill, *The Coral Island* 219)

thick-headed [*theck-'ead/hayd-ered*]
thick-pated [*theck-patered*] dumb; stupid; dimwitted

"Pate" means "head" or "brain."

"You **thick-headed** swab." (Long John Silver, "Treasure Island" [1950] 40:24)

"You was ever a **thick-pated** fool, Rogerson my hearty!" (Roger Snaith, *Winds of Chance* 353)

thieving [*thievin'*] (1) given to thievery (2) generally dishonest, unscrupulous, or otherwise contemptible

Pirates, who value qualities like strength and courage above all, abhor the notion of the slippery pilferer, who gets ahead not by venturing forth boldly but by slinking about evasively. The terms "thieving" and "thief" are correspondingly potent and deliver an insult much more profound than when used in modern speech.

"Batten 'em down, and let 'em suffercate, the **thievin'** scum!" (Blackbeard, "Blackbeard the Pirate" 1:29:55)

thorough-going [*th'row/toro-goerrn/goin'*] utter; complete; consummate

An emphatic adjective amplifying the meaning of the noun modified.

"And **thorough-goin'** blackguards some o' them traders are; no better than pirates, I can tell you." (Bloody Bill, *The Coral Island* 220)

thrice-damned [*thrawce/thryeece damt*]

An unspecific but emphatic derogatory adjective.

"So! A runaway wife and a plausible, **thrice damned** villain! Well, these sort well together." (Japhet Bly, *Winds of Chance* 139)

traitorous [*traaht/trayeet-'/arr-rous*]
treacherous [*traah/tray-charr/ch'r-ous*] inclined to betray; traitorous; insidious; false

"'[Ti]s a sin to suffer such a false **traiterous** dog as [you] to live." (John Russell, threatening George Roberts for toasting King George rather than his Roman Catholic rival James Edward Stuart, *Pirates of the New England Coast* 179) "The **treacherous** dog will spare nothing to do us a mischief, pledge or no pledge." (Wolverstone, *The Fortunes of Captain Blood* 17)

twopenny [*ter/tuh-puhnee*] cheap; nearly worthless; trifling

"Influence—that's what I've got—in higher places than this **twopenny** governor's palace." (Henry Morgan, "Pirates of Tortuga" 1:33:10)

ugly [*arrgly*] unattractive; bad-looking

"Man, I'm telling ye o' this same tall, great, **ugly** rascal, this scoundrelly, very lewd rogue provoked you lately to blooding him and very handsomely ye did it!" (Benjamin Trigg, *Adam Penfeather, Buccaneer* 208)

unhung [*arrn/hun/oohn-harrng/hoohng/'ung*]

Used to refer deploringly to any degenerate criminal ("unhung" because he deserves but so far has evaded execution), and especially to one pirate by another. The usage is an example of the tendency of the pirate to deny his own piracy but condemn another's. See Section 16.1 for more on how pirates despise themselves and show it in the way they talk.

"As to you, Farnaby, muster the hands, and stand by to go aboard in half an hour—every **unhung** rascal." (Adam Penfeather, *Black Bartlemy's Treasure* 111)

unnatural [*arrn/hun/oohn-nat'ral/nayt'ral/naytural*] inhuman; deviant; monstrous

"I'll have my money if there's law in the land—ye bloody, **unnatural** thief ye, who'd go agin your dead father's will!"

(Blueskin, *The Book of Pirates* "Blueskin, the Pirate" 172)

useless good for nothing; worthless

"LeRois, you stupid son of a whore, you drunken **useless** madman!" (Thomas Marlowe, *The Guardship* 360)

verminous [*varrm-er-nous*] nasty; lousy

"And now what for these **verminous** dogs?" (Lovepeace Farrance, *Winds of Chance* 56)

very [*vaah/vay-ry*] real; true; utter

Used especially when identifying or characterizing some person or thing to emphasize or warrant the truth of the identification or characterization. Just as the modern speaker might say, "He's a real jerk," the pirate might say, "He's a very lubber."

< "And pray, what of Don Luiz da Ramirez?" "A **very** son o' Belial!" > (Ursula Revell & Lovepeace Farrance, *Winds of Chance* 46)

vile [*vawl/vyee'ell/vyell*] loathsome; disgusting

"Back, ye **vile** scum or I'll bring bloody death on ye." (Adam Penfeather, *Adam Penfeather, Buccaneer* 189)

villain(ous) [*vell-ay/er/y-n(ous)*] wicked

"And Ursula, here's news for thee, of their company is my **villain** cousin, our Johnny!" (Japhet Bly, *Winds of Chance* 302) "Well, ma'm, he is the elder o' my two rogue cousins that, with their father, my **villainous** uncle, shipped me off whiles yet a lad and sold me into slavery." (Japhet Bly, *Winds of Chance* 219)

water-hearted [*wahh/warr-ter 'ahrrt/'eart/ hahrrt-ered*] lacking strength of character, courage, or determination; weak-hearted

"You dogs—you poor, fond, **water-hearted** dogs—we hold you at the end of our pistols!" (John Sharkey, *The Dealings of Captain Sharkey and Other Tales of Pirates* "How the Governor of Saint Kitt's Came Home" 22)

weak-kneed lacking strength of character, courage, or determination

"Get up, Jim. Get up, ya **weak-kneed** sniveller or, by thunder, we'll leave you behind! Up with 'ee!" (Long John Silver, rousing Jim Hawkins to his feet, "The Adventures of Long John Silver: Pieces of Eight" 16:49)

whey-faced [*wheyee-fayeeced*]

Literally meaning "having a pale or chalk-white face," the term is used figuratively to suggest the person so described looks pathetically weak or unimposing.

"[Y]e that are Englishmen all, —ye that were o' late right hardy mariners, prime seamen bold for all hardship, now show no better than so many **whey-faced**, spiritless, slouching wastrels!" (Adam Penfeather, *Adam Penfeather, Buccaneer* 301)

white-livered [*wawt/whyeet levv/libb/li'-ert*] cowardly; without courage or character

"Ye're a **white-livered** cur when all is said." (Peter Blood, *Captain Blood: His Odyssey* 194)

witless [*wetless*] senseless; lacking intelligence; stupid; idiotic

"You've no home in England; you've a house there, you've lands and what not, but how then? It is not roof and walls that make home, no nor company of sottish uncle and **witless** aunt." (Japhet Bly, *Winds of Chance* 194)

wooden-headed [*woodern/woo'n-'ead/hayd-ered*] thick-headed; dull; stupid

"You're him that never bungled nothing, you **wooden-headed** lubber!" (George Merry, *Treasure Island* 185, Chap. 33)

worthless [*warrth/werf-less*] having no value; vile; undeserving

"Tasker, you **worthless** son of a bitch, letting those bastards go on a drunk." (Roger Press, *The Pirate Round* 284)

yellow(-livered) [*yal-ler/lowoo (levv/libb/li'-ert)*] lacking courage or determination; cowardly; spineless

"Why, the **yellow** scut! Fallin' it out and runnin'." (Patch, condemning the cowardice of an enemy ship for fleeing battle, "The Adventures of Long John Silver: Turnabout" 3:34) "Arrgh, we—we did 'em in! Err, we did 'em in! Every **yellow-livered** one of 'em." (Long John Silver, "Long John Silver's Return to Treasure Island" 1:38:51)

9.2 NOUNS

> The nouns in this section are masculine or gender neutral. Feminine epithets can be found in section 16.11: Women.

ape [*ayeepe*]
Used especially in reference to a physically imposing person to suggest he is of limited intelligence and of coarse or vulgar character.

"They're not firing at us, you powder-brained **ape**." (Captain Vallo, "The Crimson Pirate" 16:20)

arch-devil [*ahrrch/harch daahv/dayv/debb/div-il*]
arch-villain [*ahrrch/harch vell-ayn*] extremely depraved or wicked person

"And then it was that I fell in with that **arch-devil**, that master rogue whose deeds had long been a terror throughout the main, ... who hid his identity under the name of Bartlemy." (Adam Penfeather, *Black Bartlemy's Treasure* 83) "Ha, well now you'll bear witness, George, 'tis that cursed, red-headed, great rogue, Adam, that same **arch-villain** you fought at prayers ..." (Benjamin Trigg, *Adam Penfeather, Buccaneer* 207)

arsehole [*arse'ole/ho'oole/'o'oole*] asshole

"What in all hell are these **arseholes** about?" (Flanders, *The Pirate Round* 263)

ass [*arrss*] fool; idiot

"Poxy **ass**! [I'll] get you!" (Black Dog, "Treasure Island" [1998] 37:28)

atomy [*at-ermy/'my*] ridiculously small or weak person

"'Swounds and blood, Absalom, never tell me you'd 'list this little misery, this poor **atomy**?" (Benjamin Trigg, on seeing the slight Adam Penfeather for the first time, *Adam Penfeather, Buccaneer* 44)

babbler [*barrbler*] prattler
Used to refer to someone who speaks foolishly, excessively, or quickly but to little effect.

"Take that, **babbler**! for your intelligence; if these men are obstinate, we may have worked for nothing." (Cain, *The Pirate* 56, Chap. IX)

baboon [*barrboon*] (1) ridiculous person; fool (2) boorish person; brute

"Come on down, you little **baboon**." (Thomas Bartholomew Red, urging his lieutenant to climb down off a raft's mast, "Pirates" 5:44)

bard slab [*bard slarrb*] ridiculous-looking person, especially one who wears garish or incongruent clothing
The term "bard" or "bard slab" literally means a piece of armor used to shield or ornament a horse.

"You're supposed to be King's men, not **bard slabs**." (Captain Vallo, to his disguised crewmates, "The Crimson Pirate" 38:52)

barnacle [*bahrr-n'cle/nerkle*] hard-shelled marine crustacean
Used to suggest the person so described is a worthless low-life, in the same way as a modern speaker might call another a "worm" or an "insect."

"You **barnacle**! Next time I'll sever your gullet!" (Billy Bones, "Treasure Island" [1934] 14:23)

barracuda [*bahrr-acuda/acuder/'cuda/'cuder/ercuda/ercuder*] person who is fierce, vexatious, or odious in a dangerous or harmful way

"Dead or alive, he is my bait to catch the **barracuda** called Silver." (El Toro Mendoza, "Long John Silver's Return to Treasure Island" 1:35:23)

bastard [*barrs/bash-tahrrd*]
Meaning literally "a person born out of wedlock," the term is used to characterize another as offensive, contemptible, or worthless.

"Ya bloody **bastard**!" (Long John Silver, "Treasure Island" [1998] 1:12:58)

beanrake [*beanrayeeke*] excessively thin or weak person; beanpole

"I've got a shindly little **beanrake** with the shakes and the whimpers." (Blackbeard, "Blackbeard's Ghost" 26:41)

bilge rat [*belge rarrt*] rat living in bilge, or the stagnant, foul-smelling water that collects at the bottom of a vessel

"Speak up, you **bilge rat**! Where be the treasure?" (pirate overseeing repeated dunking of Spanish magistrate in village well, "Pirates of the Caribbean" Disney attraction)

bird o' price [*barrd o'\on prawce/pryeece*]
Used sarcastically to convey transparently false affection for someone whom the speaker actually disrespects or hates.

"And where, where might you ha' come from, my **bird o' price**?" (Sam Spraggons, *Black Bartlemy's Treasure* 128)

blackguard [*blaggahrrd*] unprincipled, dishonest, or unscrupulous person; scoundrel

"Be off this ship at once, and tell your **blackguards** that if the *Valiant* is still there by noon I'll blow her out of the water." (Captain Easterling, *Captain Blood Returns* 286)

bladder of air [*bla'/blarrd-er o'\on ay-arr/err*] self-important and overbearing individual

< "And what of the captain, Sir Rupert Dering?" "That, Martin! A very gentleman-like fool, d'ye see, a **bladder of air**—like his three fellows." > (Martin Conisby & Adam Penfeather, *Black Bartlemy's Treasure* 124)

blighter [*blarrt/blawt/bligh'-er*] (1) annoying person; jerk (2) guy; fellow

"Stupid **blighter**." (Ragetti, "Pirates of the Caribbean: The Curse of the Black Pearl" 1:42:06)

blockhead [*blarrk-'ead/hayd*] fool; idiot

< "I don't think so." "Oh, you don't, **blockhead**?" > (Big Eric & Long John Silver, "The Adventures of Long John Silver: The Eviction" 4:53)

bloke [*blooke/blo'ooke*]
A slightly disrespectful or dismissive term for a man.

"After the little **bloke**!" (pirate in Long John Silver's company, urging on his comrades in pursuit of Jim Hawkins, "Treasure Island" [1950] 48:49)

bloodsucker [*bloohd/blut-sarrker/soohker*] (1) person who extorts or exploits another (2) person who is shamelessly or invasively dependent on another (3) person who promotes himself and his own interests at the blatant expense of others

The term "bloodsucker" refers literally to a parasitic worm that attaches itself by means of a sucker to the flesh of its victim, but obviously has various figurative uses.

"Bloodsucker." (Thomas Bartholomew Red, upbraiding Dutch for resisting payment of 632 doubloons owed him, "Pirates" 54:54)

brat [*brarrt*] troublesome or annoying child

"It's that whiner—sneakin' **brat**!" (Pew, "Treasure Island" [1934] 20:44)

buffoon [*barrfoon*] fool; idiot; oaf

"You play-acting **buffoon**! Ye don't leave this ship." (Captain Easterling, *Captain Blood Returns* 35)

bugger [*bogger*] jerk; wretch

"[H]aul the bloody mainsheet, you damned **buggers**, I'll thank you to mind your work ..." (Peleg Dinwiddie, *The Pirate Round* 45)

bumboat [*barrm/boohm-bo'oot*]

A dismissive or derogatory term for any shabby, unimpressive, or otherwise inadequate or undesirable person or thing.

< "Pieces of eight! Pieces of eight!" "Who hailed you, you old **bumboat**?!" > (Cap'n Flint the parrot & Long John Silver, "Treasure Island" [1950] 21:39)

bungler [*boohngler*] bumbler; incompetent or ineffectual person

"You all mean well, but you're **bunglers**, here's a little delicate matter as none can handle like the Smiler." (Roger Tressady, *Black Bartlemy's Treasure* 306)

cake's dough [*cayeeke's do'oo*] hopeless, used up, or defeated person; failure

"Joanna's cocked her eye on this fellow and Belvedere's **cake's dough**—see him yonder!" (Diccon, *Martin Conisby's Vengeance* 66)

carcass [*cahrr-cahss/cush/kerss*] scumbag

Literally meaning "corpse of an animal," the term is used figuratively to refer in dehumanizing fashion to another or his person.

"Blind you! Go forward and turn out two o' the lads to draw this **carcass** aft!" (Captain Belvedere, *Martin Conisby's Vengeance* 69)

carrion [*cahrrion/cairn/carriern*] scumbag

Literally meaning "dead and decaying flesh," the term is used figuratively to refer in dehumanizing fashion to another or his person.

"So up wi' you, lass! Heave ahead, **Carrion**!" (Japhet Bly, ordering his two companions forward, *Winds of Chance* 155)

caterpillar [*carrt-ee/ri-peller*] worm; slug

"Were it not for this shift the lazy Spaniard could not grow so rich, but their insupportable cruelties to these poor natives I hope in due time will reach the almighty's ear, who will open the heart of a more Christian prince to deliver this people and drive away these **caterpillars** from their superbous seats of laziness." (Basil Ringrose, describing how the Spanish residents of Chuluteca require the natives to trade through them, under pretense of protecting them from fraud but in reality doing so in order to defraud the natives themselves, *The South Sea Waggoner* Chart 25)

catfish [*carrt-fesh*]

The term is used figuratively as one of disrespect or dismissiveness. The disparaging quality of the term likely borrows on negative associations arising from this fish's (1) omnivorous feeding, scavenging, and mud-burrowing, which may have contributed to its reputation among some as dirty or repulsive, and (2) whisker-like barbels, which have similarly promoted a perception of the fish as ugly or crude-looking.

"I said *when* you sees him, you crazy **catfish**." (Billy Bones, "Treasure Island" [1960] 5:15)

chunk of rotted seahorse [*charrnk/choohnk o'\on roh'-ered sea-'arrse/harrse/'orse*] scumbag

"Belay for a — lackey, ye slab-faced **chunk o' rotted seahorse**!" (John Flint, *Porto Bello Gold* 83, omission in original)

clam brain [*clam brayeene*] fool; idiot

"You **clam brain**!" (Long John Silver, "Treasure Island" [1934] 35:30)

clod(poll) [*clarrd(po'ool)*] idiot; fool

"Arrgh, mind ya, **clod**, have an eye to that chest." (Billy Bones, "Treasure Island" [1934] 5:08) "[W]e'll burn them bloody crafts of yours that we've took over yonder, and cut the weasand of every **clodpoll** aboard of 'em." (Captain Richards, threatening the governor of South Carolina into giving him a supply of medicines, *The Book of Pirates* "Buccaneers and Maroonners of the Spanish Main" 30)

cockerel [*carrk-erel/'rel*]

Literally meaning "young rooster," the term is used to refer mockingly to a man or boy who is fiercer, more aggressive, or more arrogant than his actual strength or capabilities might justify.

"Is that the kind of **cockerel** ye are, Master Ormerod or whatever ye may be called?" (John Flint, *Porto Bello Gold* 132)

cockroach [*cack/carrk-ro'ooch/rooch*] odious and insigificant person

"Strike your colors, ya bloomin' **cockroaches**!" (Barbossa, "Pirates of the Caribbean: The Curse of the Black Pearl" 1:26:47)

codfish [*carrd-fesh*]

Used figuratively as a term of disrespect or dismissivneess.

"Not this pitiful, spineless, pasty, bloated **codfish** I see before me." (James Hook, "Hook" 44:33)

corker [*carrker*] remarkable or astonishing person

Though the term might conceivably be used neutrally, or even favorably, the typical implication is that the person so described is remarkably or astonishingly objectionable or reprehensible. The usage is comparable to the modern expressions "You're unbelievable!" and "You're amazing!" Though the speaker does not specify how exactly the addressee might be "unbelievable" or "amazing," the reference is clearly an unfavorable, disapproving one.

"What a **corker**! What a ruddy **corker**!" (Long John Silver, defaming the captain in the voice of Silver's parrot Cap'n Flint, "Treasure Island" [1960] 30:30)

coward [*carrd/cowahrrd/cowar'/cowart*]

"Ah, damned **coward**, ye dare not slay me lest Belvedere torment ye to death—'tis your own vile carcase you do think of!" (Captain Jo, *Martin Conisby's Vengeance* 94)

craven [*cravv/crayeev-ern*] person utterly without courage or determination; pathetically spineless person

"Well, shoot if you will and end Black Bartlemy with **craven**'s pistol 'stead o' valiant steel." (Black Bartlemy, *Adam Penfeather, Buccaneer* 256)

craven-coward [*cravv/crayeev-ern carrd/cowahrrd/cowar'/cowart*]

A combination of "craven" and "coward" suitable for use with an initial modifier—e.g., "skulking craven-coward."

"**Craven-coward**!" (Smy Peters, condemning Absalom Troy for turning Spaniard and betraying himself to the Inquisition, *Adam Penfeather, Buccaneer* 290)

crow's-bait [*crowoo's bayeet*] scumbag

Used to characterize another as irrelevant or useless—*i.e.*, a lowlife with little value other than as food for crows after death.

"Hey, **crow's-bait**, if ye've the strength, bring hither the satchel." (Japhet Bly, *Winds of Chance* 177)

cur [*carr*]

Literally meaning "mongrel" or "dog," the term is used figuratively to suggest the person so described is vulgar or worthless.

"Yap not, **cur**." (Japhet Bly, *Winds of Chance* 165)

curmudgeon [*carr/coor-marr/mooh-jern*] (1) greedy, miserly person (2) difficult, ornery, ill-tempered person, especially an older man

"I'm not thinking of Don Ilario, but of that bile-laden **curmudgeon** Don Clemente." (Wolverstone, *The Fortunes of Captain Blood* 19)

curse to the Main [*carrse/carrst/coorse/cursh/curst t'/ta/ter t' Mayeen*] (1) pirate (2) pain in the ass

Literally a characterization of another as irksome to the Spanish ("Main" meaning mainland or other territories and/or adjacent waters held by Spain in the New World) and accordingly an implication that he is a pirate (see Section 16.1 on the use by pirates of "pirate" as a derisive reference). The term is also used to suggest the person so described is unwanted among, and a bane to, other pirates cruising the New World and especially the Caribbean.

"Ah, that one-legged black-hearted **curse to the Main** be here." (pirate at the Cask & Anchor, "The Adventures of Long John Silver: The Necklace" 2:08)

cutthroat [*carrt/cooht-thro'oot*] ruthless, murderous person

"Bloody Bill there was just such a fellow as you are, and he's now the biggest **cut-throat** of us all." (pirate, *The Coral Island* 202)

darling [*dahrr-lin'*]

A term of affection used ironically, most often to convey a smug dislike or a calm threat.

"My finger's on the trigger, Tim, and if ye were to move suddenly, ye might startle me into pulling it. Put your elbows back on the rail, Tim **darling**, while we talk." (Peter Blood, *The Fortunes of Captain Blood* 165)

dastard [*darr-stahrrd*] coward

"Must I consort with roguish **dastards**, hobnob with knaves, make fellowship wi' villainy and common cause with debauched rascaldom?" (Benjamin Trigg, *Adam Penfeather, Buccaneer* 313)

dawcock [*dawrr-carrk*] silly or ridiculous person; fool

"Some o' them **dawcocks** may believe that tale." (Wolverstone, *Captain Blood: His Odyssey* 255)

devil [*daahv/dayv/debb/div-il*]

"It's just what that **devil** Easterling desires." (Trenam, *Captain Blood Returns* 290)

dog [*dahg/darrg/dorrg*] vulgar or worthless person

"Upon deck, you **dog**, for we shall lose no more time about you." (Alexander Mitchel, *General History of the Pyrates* 607)

dogfish [*dahg/darrg/dorrg-fesh*]

A term of disrespect or dismissivneess.

"You crawlin' squid! You **dogfish**!" (Long John Silver, "Treasure Island" [1934] 1:08:35)

dog's breakfast [*dahg's/darrg's/dorrg's brayk/breff-farrst/fess*]

dog's leavings [*dahg's/darrg's/dorrg's leaf-in's*]

(hunk of) dog's meat [*(harrnk/hoohnk/'unk o'\on) dahg's/darrg's/dorrg's meat*] scumbag

"Well, you might take a mind to release my prisoner **Dog's-breakfast** yonder—" (Japhet Bly, *Winds of Chance* 147) "Pull, **dog's leavings**, —arms and legs and backs to it—pull, ye lubbers!" (Benjamin Trigg, *Adam Penfeather, Buccaneer* 310) "So there y'are, Johnny! and dying by inches! How doth it feel, **Dog's-meat**?" (Japhet Bly, doubling back to discover John Barrasdale trapped and sinking in a patch of quicksand, *Winds of Chance* 175) < "You mean ... the Earl of Aldbourne?" "Yea, lass, and no, lass, for I mean my Johnny, yon **hunk o' dog's meat**!" > (Ursula Revell & Japhet Bly, *Winds of Chance* 151)

dolt [*doolt/do'oolt*] idiot; fool

< "Because I had rather die solitary than live in your fellowship—" "**Dolt**! Clod!

Worm!" > (Martin Conisby & Captain Jo, *Martin Conisby's Vengeance* 25)

dumb arse [*darrm/doohm-ahrrse*] dumbass

The term is twofold, denoting in one epithet roughly the same objectionable properties as the terms "idiot" and "jerk."

"Lord, what a **dumb arse**." (Thomas Marlowe, *The Pirate Round* 288)

dunderhead [*darrnd/doohnd/dunn-er-'ead/hayd*] fool; dolt

"Lieutenant, you **dunderhead**." (Thomas Bartholomew Red, mocking The Frog's pining admiration for the young Spanish lady aboard the *Neptune*, "Pirates" 27:38)

fiend [*fien'*] evil or malicious person

"The South Sea Islanders are such incarnate **fiends** that they are the better of being tamed, and the missionaries are the only men who can do it." (Bloody Bill, *The Coral Island* 214–15)

focsle-head [*fo'ook/fork-sull-'ead/hayd*]

A derogatory term for a member of the regular, non-officer crew, implying an inability to think or perform more than mean labor.

< We're all sailors 'ere." "Aah, all **focsle-heads**, you mean. We can steer a course, but who's to set one?" > (George Merry & Long John Silver, "Treasure Island" [1998] 45:43)

fool [*foo'ell*] idiot; dullard; dope

"**Fool**! Could've had a fortune in your grasp!" (Henry Morgan, "Pirates of Tortuga" 1:31:57)

fop [*farrp*] person of affected, overly ostentatious appearance or manner; dandy

< "Why, I have three men-of-war in the harbor with metal enough aboard to sink any popinjay buccanner." "Popinjay, says you. Well, don't be fooled by his fine feathers and plumage. He may seem a **fop**, but underneath he's as wily as a vulture." > (Governor Strong & Long

John Silver, "Long John Silver's Return to Treasure Island" 11:22)

fresh-water sailor [*frash/fraysh wahh/warrter saah/sayee/sayor-larr*] weakling; coward

< "What's the use o' tryin' to kill the blackguards when it'll do us no manner o' good?" "Mate, you talk like a **fresh-water sailor**. I can only attribute this shyness to some strange delusion; for surely, surely I am not to suppose that *you* have become soft-hearted!" > (pirate mate & pirate captain, *The Coral Island* 249)

fuddler [*farrd/foohd-ler*] drunkard

< "A big, ugly, booze-soaked rummy!" "Hold on there! There be no call to put the **fuddler**'s name on your newfound shipmate." (Steve Walker & Blackbeard, "Blackbeard's Ghost" 30:18)

gallows bird\meat [*gallers/galloos/gallowoos barrd\meat*] person suitable for execution by hanging

Used to suggest the person so described is (1) degenerate (that is, so steeped in crimes and malice to be deserving of execution), (2) incompetent (and therefore vulnerable to apprehension and execution for piracy), or (3) not likely to live much longer for either or both reasons.

"Innocent, d'ye say? A cut-throat **gallowsbird**, says I ..." (Absalom Troy, *Adam Penfeather, Buccaneer* 110) "Satisfied, **gallows meat**?" (William Kidd, grudgingly allowing members of his company to verify the contents of a treasure chest before burying it, "Captain Kidd" 4:31)

git scumbag; lowlife

"Come to negotiate, eh, have you, you slimy **git**?" (Jack Sparrow, taunting Davy Jones, "Pirates of the Caribbean 2: Dead Man's Chest" 2:00:40)

half-man ['*alf/harrf-man*]

Used with derogatory reference to someone small or short.

"You poor, little **half-man**!" (Giles Tregenza, berating the small-statured Adam Penfeather, *Adam Penfeather, Buccaneer* 203)

(my) harem girl [(*me/myee*) '*arem gurrell*]

A term used to assert the speaker's absolute power over another, especially when the person so described is not a "girl," but rather a man.

"Run an' twist, **me** little **harem girl**!" (Alacan the Turk, referring to a seaman on an enemy ship during an attack, *Dead Man's Chest* 55)

hell-hound ['*ell-houn'/howoon'/howoond/ howoont/'oun'/'ound/'owoond/'owoont*] evil or malicious person

"We resolve, when we come to Bassora, to separate into three companies, as if we did not know one another; to dress ourselves as merchants—for now we look like **hell-hounds** and vagabonds, but when we are well-dressed, we expect to look as other men do." (Captain Avery, *The King of Pirates* 76)

hellion ['*ell-yern*] troublesome or mischievous person

"'Curse me if I like to bob and prance for the old **hellion**, Bill, but he has the skill o' the Fiend at our lay.'" (Billy Bones, quoting Captain Flint, *Porto Bello Gold* 50)

horse's arse [*arrse's/harrse's/'orse's arse*] fool; idiot

"The lads won't go back, long as that **horse's arse** is there." (Henry Nagel, *The Pirate Round* 215)

hound [*houn'/howoond/howoont/'oun'/'ound/ 'owoond/'owoont*] despicable person

"Ye mangy **hound**, d'ye dare come to me with such proposals?" (Peter Blood, *Captain Blood: His Odyssey* 310)

hulk [*harrlk/'ulk*] used-up, worthless, or hopeless person or thing

"Hulk" literally means a vessel without operable rigging—that is, a shell or bare hull of a vessel—or any vessel in a state of advanced age, disrepair, and/or deterioration.

"I'm just an old **hulk** wrecked on a lee shore." (Blackbeard, "Blackbeard's Ghost" 30:31)

idiot [*ed-ierrt*] fool; dope

"Curse ya for breathin', you slack-jawed **idiot**!" (Joshamee Gibbs, "Pirates of the Caribbean: The Curse of the Black Pearl" 51:30)

imp o' Satan [*emp o'\on Sayee/Seh/Sy-tan*] evil or malicious person

"Now if you mean our hellish rogues, these **imps o' Satan** and spawn o' the devil, our rascal crew, —eh Adam?" (Benjamin Trigg, *Adam Penfeather, Buccaneer* 224)

jackass [*jarrk-arse*] fool; idiot

"Ay, there he is, —hark to the bellowing **jackass**!" (Absalom Troy, *Adam Penfeather, Buccaneer* 43)

jellyfish [*jally-fesh*] (1) plump or overweight person (2) physically unimposing person (3) submissive, cowardly, or otherwise weak-willed person

"This **jellyfish** looks soft enough t'eat." (Montbars, mocking the captain of a would-be prize, "Pirates of Tortuga" 41:03) "And you've all turned to **jellyfish** now that we're so close to the gold that you've worked so hard for." (Tom Morgan, upbraiding his comrades for letting disembodied ghost voices distract them from their treasure-hunting, "Treasure Island" [1960] 1:08:45)

Judas (Iscariot) [*Juderss (Es-cahrr-ierrt)*] treacherous person; traitor

Judas Iscariot was the disciple who betrayed Jesus and turned him over to the authorities. His name is synonymous with "traitor."

"[Y]ou detest pirates and I have as lively a contempt for sanctimonious **Judases** ..." (Black Bartlemy, *Adam Penfeather, Buccaneer* 256) "Fie on you deserting our captain in this way, you scurvy traitors, you **Judas Iscariots**, you snakes in the grass, you wolves in sheep's clothing!" (Honesty Nuttall, "Captain Blood" 1:36:15)

knave [*knayeeve*] deceitful or unscrupulous person; scoundrel

"Overboard with him! overboard with them all! he and his **knaves** together!" (hands aboard the *Dolphin*, threatening to kill their new first mate Harry Wilder and his two sidekicks, *The Red Rover* 335)

knothead [*knarrt/kno'-'ead/hayd*] idiot

< "What good is a 'ostage, and 'im bad 'urt?" "Why, you **knothead**. With 'im bad hurt, they'll part with the map to save his life." > (George Merry & Long John Silver, "Treasure Island" [1950] 1:16:16)

knuckle brain [*knarrkle/knoohkle brayeen*] fool; idiot

"On him, you **knuckle brain**." (Henry Morgan, "Pirates of Tortuga" 1:09:18)

labberneck [*labbernack*]

A derogatory term for any sailor or seaman. "Labber" means "wet" or "splash."

"Fifty pound a head, you **labbernecks**." (MacTavish, setting the ransom on the crew of a plundered merchant ship, "The Black Pirate" 39:48)

lackey person of inferior position, especially one desirous of or scraping after approval or attention; toady

"Name of God! But didn't you tell this **lackey** from court that ..." (Peter Blood, *The Fortunes of Captain Blood* 65)

laggard [*laggahrrd*] slow or sluggish person

"Come along, you bloody **laggards**, haul away all!" (William Darnall, *The Guardship* 37)

lamb [*larrm/lemm*]

A term of affection used ironically, most often to convey a smug dislike or a calm threat.

"Ha, my pretty **lambs**! Will ye skulk then, will ye skulk with your fool's heads together?" (Roger Tressady, upon discovering members of his company conspiring to leave him to join Adam Penfeather, *Black Bartlemy's Treasure* 312)

land pirate [*lan' py-eeret/errt/raaht*] person who misappropriates things of value from others by force or threat of force

The person described is being characterized as a pirate not because his delinquencies occur on the seas, but rather because of the menacing or galling quality of his conduct.

"You—bloody **land pirate**!" (Blueskin, accusing his stepbrother of cheating him out of 500 pounds, *The Book of Pirates* "Blueskin, the Pirate" 171)

landlubber [*lan' looh-ber*]

A seaman's derogatory term for a landsman—that is, a person unknowledgeable of and oblivious to the seafaring life.

"Shiver my timbers, a **landlubber** I'll never be!" (Long John Silver, "Long John Silver's Return to Treasure Island" 51:58)

leech vile, disgusting person; parasite

"You sneaking **leech**, you college offal!" (Captain Easterling, *Captain Blood Returns* 36)

liar [*larr/lyarr*] deceitful, duplicitous person

"I know you for base **liar** would draw me to your design by contemptible trick." (Adam Penfeather, *Adam Penfeather, Buccaneer* 259)

lick-spittle(r) [*leck-speh'le/spettle/spih'le(\ spettler/spittlarr)*] person known for or inclined to obsequious, shamelessly flattering, or insincere but self-promoting behavior, or any conduct that is at once shameless and reprehensible

"Come on, let's have a proper sea-chan-
ty to put some guts into ya, ya mealy-
mouthed **lick-spittlers!**" (Billy Bones,
"Treasure Island" [1960] 7:42)

loggerhead [*larrger-'ead/hayd*] fool; dolt

"I am sure you never heard me say such
a word to such a **loggerhead** as you."
(William Kidd, cross-examining one of
his own former pirates at Kidd's trial,
The Pirate Hunter 375)

long-gone fool [*larrng-garrn foo'ell*] utter
idiot; complete dope

The term "long-gone" is technically a modifier but is not freely used with other epithet
nouns and is fairly considered as part of the
distinctive usage "long-gone fool." The suggestion here is that the mental incapacity of
the person so described is neither recent nor
temporary, but rather an inborn deficiency.

"Ya think old Morley Rowe's a **long-gone
fool**, don't ya?" (Morley Rowe, *Dead
Man's Chest* 252)

louse [*lowoose*] vile, disgusting person

"Throw those **lice** in the 'old!" (Blackbeard, cornering on deck the mutinous
members of his crew, "Blackbeard the
Pirate" 1:29:30)

lout [*lowoot*] awkward, stupid person; oaf

"Faster, you lazy dogs! Bend your backs
to it, you **louts!**" (George Fairfax, *The
Fortunes of Captain Blood* 150)

lubber [*loohber*] (1) person inexpert at sailing; poor seaman (2) generally incompetent
or unknowledgeable person

"Look alive, Tim! Can these **lubbers** of
yours move no faster?" (George Fairfax,
The Fortunes of Captain Blood 152)

lump o' roguery [*loohmp o'\on roo/ro'oo-
guery*] piece of crap; scumbag
"Roguery" is dangerous mischief.

"Now as to this **lump o' roguery**, have
him into the yard and heave a bucket

o' water over him." (Adam Penfeather,
Black Bartlemy's Treasure 111)

lunatic [*loon'/looner-teck*] insane person

"LeRois, you are a goddamned crazy son of
a whore. Fucking **lunatic**." (pirate aboard
the *Vengeance*, *The Guardship* 32)

lurcher [*larrcher*] one who lurks or skulks
about in furtive and undignified fashion;
coward; loser

"Easy, my pretty cut-throat **lurcher**,
and very gently now." (Absalom Troy,
confronting Antonia Chievely's pursuer,
Adam Penfeather, *Buccaneer* 26)

maggot [*maggert*] vile, offensive person

< "Hold fast! You'll obey orders from
your cap'n or you'll walk the plank!
You mutinous **maggot!**" > (Long John
Silver, "The Adventures of Long John
Silver: Execution Dock" 13:01)

mannikin [*mann'/manner-kin*] very small
person

"Tush and curse it, Captain, 'tis no more
than petty boy, a sickling, a lousy lad, a
puling **mannikin** not worth shiproom!"
(Benjamin Trigg, on seeing the slight
Adam Penfeather for the first time, *Adam
Penfeather, Buccaneer* 44)

master rogue [*marrster roo/ro'oo-gue*] extremely offensive or objectionable person; one
who threatens harm or danger to others

"And then it was that I fell in with that
arch-devil, that **master rogue** whose
deeds had long been a terror throughout the main ..." (Adam Penfeather, *Black
Bartlemy's Treasure* 83)

miscreant [*mes-cree'ernt/creent*] evil-doer; person lacking any moral impulse or restraint

"[T]hese **miscreants**, who so boldly sur-
round you, shall kneel, and be mute, as
beings whose souls are touched by the holy
rite." (The Red Rover, *The Red Rover* 499)

money-grabber\grubber [*mo'ey/moohny-grebber\groohbber*] grasping, greedy person; person concerned with money to an inordinate, offensive degree

> "Why, you **money-grabbers**." (Long John Silver, "Long John Silver's Return to Treasure Island" 1:13:26) < "I thought it'd be pearls we'd be starin' at." "You spyin' **money-grubber**. Bain't the happiness of a fine lad and a lovely girl enough payment for 'ee?" > (Ironhand & Long John Silver, "The Adventures of Long John Silver: The Pink Pearl" 24:11)

monkey [*marrn/moohn-key*] ridiculous person; person unworthy of respect

> "Apes! **Monkeys**, cease your chattering and list to Joanna." (Captain Jo, *Martin Conisby's Vengeance* 62)

motherless bastard [*maahth/mo'/mudd-er-less barrs/bash-tahrrd*]

Meaning literally a person born out of wedlock and unclaimed and uncared for by either mother or father, the term is used to characterize another as offensive, contemptible, or worthless.

> "Get out of here, you sons of a bitch, or I will shoot each one of you **motherless bastards**!" (Roger Press, *The Pirate Round* 223)

mountebank [*mon/mowoon-tee/ter-bank*] deceitful person; liar; charlatan

> "I've a mind to sling you up from your own yardarm for letting this **mountebank** slip through my blockade." (Henry Morgan, "Pirates of Tortuga" 50:16)

muckrake [*marrk/moohk-rayeeke*]

Sometimes used to refer to a person or institution intent on revealing or rooting out corruption, the term is used as an epithet in the opposite sense—to characterize a person as thoroughly mired in filth and corruption.

> "You should be marooned. It's what I intended for you in the end. But since you prefer it this way, ya **muckrake**, faith, I'll be humouring ya." (Peter Blood, provoked into swordfight with Levasseur, "Captain Blood" 1:24:59)

mumps [*marrmps/moohmps*]

A mocking reference to a sulking or conspicuously displeased person.

> "And you, ye lubberly **mumps**, yonder be quags, so tread warily." (Japhet Bly, warning John Barrasdale of patches of quicksand nearby, *Winds of Chance* 174)

murderer [*marrd/mord-eerer/erer/'rer*]

> "The Lord shall decide if such rogue **murderer** live or die!" (Smy Peters, *Adam Penfeather, Buccaneer* 24)

mutton(head) [*mooht/mu-'on-('ead/hayd)*] idiot

The speaker implies that the person so characterized is as intelligent as a sheep.

> "Parlay?! Damn to the depths whatever **mutton** that thought up parlay!" (Pintel, "Pirates of the Caribbean: The Curse of the Black Pearl" 1:15:44) "If—, if them **muttonheads** that slipped me the black spot gets here afore you come back, they won't find that on me." (William Bones, "Treasure Island" [1950] 9:01)

ninny [*nenny*]

(1) weakling

> "Weigh anchor! Hoist the sails! Spread quick, you **ninnies**!" (Anamaria, "Pirates of the Caribbean: The Curse of the Black Pearl" 1:16:30)

(2) bothersome or inconsequential girl

> "Will you spend your days moping and swilling 'cause a white-faced **ninny** in Port Royal'll have none o' ye?" (Wolverstone, *Captain Blood: His Odyssey* 309)

nit [*net*] small or inconsequential person; person of limited or no significance

"I'd rather spend a winter of eternities in limbo than knock knees a tick longer with a **nit** like you." (Blackbeard, "Blackbeard's Ghost" 1:14:29)

numbskull [*narrm/noohm-skoohl*] idiot

< "Gold will be your ruin, Cap'n ..." "Easier to live without a head than without gold, you **numbskull**." > (The Frog & Thomas Bartholomew Red, "Pirates" 9:05)

offal [*arrfal*] piece of crap; scumbag

"You sneaking leech, you college **offal**!" (Captain Easterling, *Captain Blood Returns* 36)

offscouring [*arrf-scourin'*] scumbag

< "Sir, do you warn me?" "Ay, I do, for yon poor rascals are the very **offscourings** of this motley crew. One wonders how you came in such ill company?" > (Ursula Revell & Barnabas Rokeby, *Winds of Chance* 57)

oyster-head [*o-eester 'ead/hayd*]

A derogatory term for any sailor or seaman.

< "Oh, and Slimey, give the Governor my compliments." "The Crimson Pirate's?" "No, you **oyster-head**, Baron Gruda's." > (Captain Vallo and Slimey, "The Crimson Pirate" 16:35)

parcel of __s [*pahrrcel o'\on __s*]

Used to refer in derogatory fashion to two or more persons. The speaker fills in the blank with an epithet of his choice.

*Captain Kidd, when he realized what had happened, was furious. He called them a "**parcel of** rogues."* (William Kidd, on learning some of his men had looted food, weapons, and equipment from the *Mary*, *The Pirate Hunter* 134) "[B]ut damn ye altogether: damn them for a pack of crafty rascals, and you, who serve them, for a **parcel of** hen-hearted numskuls." (Captain Bellamy, to the captain of a plundered Boston sloop, *General History of the Pyrates* 587)

pig [*peg*] beast; swine

"You filthy **pig**, you'll be shot! Clap him in irons!" (El Toro Mendoza, "Long John Silver's Return to Treasure Island" 17:49)

pimp [*pemp*] unscrupulous, worthless, contemptible, or unseemly person

Literally meaning a man who procures customers for whores, the term is used figuratively to refer to one with some fundamental deficiency of character.

"[They] pin their faith upon a **pimp** of a parson; a squab, who neither practices nor believes what he puts upon the chuckle-headed fools he preaches to." (Captain Bellamy, *General History of the Pyrates* 587)

pimple [*pemp-ler*]

Used figuratively to refer to a disgusting or offensive person, and especially one of little consequence.

"D'you mean they've roused themselves at home and kicked out that **pimple** James?" (Peter Blood, on first learning of William of Orange's ascension to the English throne, "Captain Blood" 1:42:12)

pip-squeak [*pep-squeak*] small or insignificant person

"A bargain? What kind, **pip-squeak**?" (Montbars, "Pirates of Tortuga" 41:19)

plague o' the seas [*playeeg o'\on t' seas*]

A phrase used to characterize a seaman as offensive or contemptible, so much so that he might fairly be said to infest or blight the sea or those who sail upon it.

"He is a lousy, pestilent fellow, a **plague o' the seas**, who will plunder and destroy any vessel weaker than his own—and of any nation." (Absalom Troy, *Adam Penfeather, Buccaneer* 19–20)

popinjay [*parr-pen-jayee*] person who resembles a parrot, either because of arrogance or an affected or ostenatious manner or appearance (analogous to a parrot's showy plumage) or because of a tendency to chatter annoyingly

The term is often used to refer to a uniformed sailor or soldier or to any person of real or purported authority.

> "Now you listen to me, you fine **popinjay**. Because you have the fine manners and the silks and satins don't mean you love your boy any more than I love mine." (Purity Pinker, replying hotly to the supercilious Lady Harwood's abusive comments, "The Adventures of Long John Silver: Dead Reckoning" 20:57)

prick [*preck*]

Literally meaning "penis," the term is used figuratively to refer derisively to a person, especially a man, who is obnoxious, offensive, or otherwise contemptible.

> "He's no coward, this foppish little **prick**, I'll give him that." (Roger Press, *The Pirate Round* 266)

princock [*pren-carrk*] a conceited, arrogant, or overbearing man or boy

> < "So we have four gentlemen aboard, Adam?" "Aye—**princocks** all that do nothing but vie in court to her ladyship!" > (Martin Conisby & Adam Penfeather, *Black Bartlemy's Treasure* 124)

puppy (dog) [*parr/pooh-ppy (dahg/darrg/dorrg)*] fool, especially a naively confident or otherwise immature one

Note that "puppy dog" is a derogatory term, while "pup" is a polite form of address conveying amiability and familiarity (see Chapter 10: Respectful Address).

> "All right, play it whatever way you like, ya **puppy**." (Blackbeard, "Blackbeard's Ghost" 1:03:14) "Ha, will ye squeak, rat! 'S fish, will ye yap, then, **puppy-dog**?" (Captain Belvedere, *Martin Conisby's Vengeance* 100)

ragamuffin [*rag'/ragger-moohfin/muf'n*] shabby-looking, inconsequential, or disreputable

> "A God's name what use is the ship to those poor **ragamuffins**?" (Captain Easterling, *Captain Blood Returns* 13)

rascal [*rarrscal*] deceitful or treacherous person

> "It's well, for had you been ill treated, I would have put all these **rascals** to the sword." (Captain Lewis, after his quartermaster reported good treatment during his imprisonment aboard another ship, *General History of the Pyrates* 596 & *The Pirates Own Book* 311)

rat [*rarrt*]

Used figuratively to refer to a despicable or contemptible person, especially one given to furtive, obsequious, or deceitful conduct.

> "Do as I say, you sniveling little **rat**." (Blind Pew, forcing Jim Hawkins to lead him to Billy Bones, "Treasure Island" [1960] 13:53)

renegade [*raah-nee/ner-gayeede*]
renegado [*raah-nee/ner-gayeedo*] person who is depraved or wicked, especially in a dangerous or threatening way; outlaw

> "Loose me, accursed **renegade**, loose me, I say!" (Smy Peters, *Adam Penfeather, Buccaneer* 335) "Damned **renegado**!" (Smy Peters, condemning Absalom Troy for turning Spaniard and betraying himself to the Inquisition, *Adam Penfeather, Buccaneer* 290)

rogue [*roo/ro'oo-gue*] deceitful or otherwise wicked person

The term suggests that the person so described engages in reprehensible conduct in a reckless fashion. See Chapter 10 for the use of the same term to convey affection for, familiarity with, joviality to, or mock condemnation of the person so described.

> "I knew you for a stout seaman, you **rogue**, before you took to this long-shore canting." (John Sharkey, *The Dealings of Captain Sharkey and Other Tales of Pirates*

"The Dealings of Captain Sharkey with Stephen Craddock" 37)

rogueling [*roo/ro'oo-glin'*] little rogue
Used to refer derisively to a small child.

"Child? Ha, is't this little **rogueling** ye mean, friend?" (Sam Spraggons, *Black Bartlemy's Treasure* 128)

ruffian [*rarr/rooh-ffian*]
ruffler [*rarr/rooh-ffler*] cruel or brutal person

"By swarming aboard her with a couple of score of his **ruffians** and taking the men here unawares at a time when there would be none to lead them." (Peter Blood, *Captain Blood Returns* 24) "'Twould almost seem I am not wanted! Ay, and a saucy, malapert, young **ruffler** to tell me so!" (Absalom Troy, *Adam Penfeather, Buccaneer* 107)

sack of entrails [*sack o'\on entrayells*] piece of crap; scumbag

"Entrails" are bowels or intestines. To the extent entrails contain excrement and are readily associated with its offensive qualities, this usage is nearly an exact equivalent to the modern speaker's epithet "sack of shit."

"Well, my stupid, sorry, parasitic **sacks of entrails**. ..." (James Hook, "Hook" 40:31)

scallywag [*scarrly-warrg*] deceitful or mischievous person

"He was a bloody pirate, a **scallywag**." (Jack Sparrow, "Pirates of the Caribbean: The Curse of the Black Pearl" 49:17)

scoundrel [*scowoondrel*] deceitful or wicked person

"Wait, you lily-livered **scoundrel**! Come back and fight like a man!" (The Frog, "Pirates" 1:53:12)

scratching [*scretch-in'*] person of little consequence

"Scratching" is both a mark produced by a scraping or scratching across the skin, and chicken feed. The epithet is likely derived from one or both of these literal usages.

"Haul off, cast about, stand off and on. If the woman's here, t'others should be skulking about—come, bouse about and stand away, and lively, ye **scratchings**!" (Ned, instructing Tom and Tony to look around for Ursula Revell's companions, *Winds of Chance* 314)

scug [*skarrg/skoohg*] contemptible person, especially one engaged in or inclined to furtive or deceitful conduct

To scug means to hide, and a scug is a cave or hollow. The epithet is likely derived from one or both of these literal usages.

"Quiet, you **scugs**, or I'll cast anchor in you." (James Hook, *Peter Pan* 148)

scum [*skarrm/skoohm*] despicable or worthless person

"You mean murder, you **scum**, and I mean to prevent it." (Peter Blood, *Captain Blood Returns* 202)

scum of the world [*skarrm/skoohm o'\on t' warrld*]

An emphatic phrase characterizing another as a despicable or worthless person.

"**Scum o' the world**!" (Captain Jo, berating three of her men for drunkenness, *Martin Conisby's Vengeance* 71)

scupperlout [*scarr/skooh-per-lowoot*] disgusting fool

The term is a combination of "scupper" (a drain leading water from a low point on a vessel's deck over its side and into the sea, which—when plugged or stopped—can contain stagnant, foul-smelling liquid and pieces of scummy trash) and "lout" (a doltish, oafish idiot). The epithet wraps into one efficient term the two most popular bases for calling someone a bad name—offensiveness and stupidity.

"I'm gonna disappear myself, that's what I'm gonna do—mister sanctimonious **scupperlout**." (Blackbeard, "Blackbeard's Ghost" 1:14:18)

scut [*skarrt/skooht*] coward; spineless person

Used literally to refer to the short, erect tail of a hare, deer, or other short-tailed, fast-moving animal (a tail often observed to perk up or twitch just before sudden flight), the term is used figuratively to refer to another's tendency to flee or evade, especially in a cowardly manner, or to characterize a person as lacking courage, determination, or conviction.

> "Why, the yellow **scut**! Fallin' it out and runnin'." (Patch, condemning the cowardice of an enemy ship for fleeing battle, "The Adventures of Long John Silver: Turnabout" 3:34)

sea lawyer [*sea law'/lawry-er*] seaman who challenges his captain's orders or organizes dissent among the crew; smart aleck; smartass; troublemaker

Used especially as a reference to assertive quartermasters by captains threatened by, resentful toward, or suspicious of them.

> "I should have reckoned Honeyman for a **sea lawyer**, damn his eyes." (Thomas Marlowe, *The Pirate Round* 74)

sea snake [*sea snayeeke*] treacherous, conniving, or deceitful person

> "Pack on all canvas, you fairy-tale **sea snakes**! (Captain Vallo, "The Crimson Pirate" 1:33:31)

sea wolf [*sea woolf*] vicious, brutal, or malicious seaman

> "And I would not have it other, for here's chance to prove me your mettle, to show these cursed **sea-wolves** that English sea-dogs can out-bite 'em." (Absalom Troy, *Adam Penfeather, Buccaneer* 119)

serpent [*sarr-paahnt*] treacherous, conniving, or deceitful person

> "Arrgh, yer haven't changed, Silver. A one-legged **serpent** ya were, a one-legged **serpent** ye are, a one-legged **serpent** you die." (Israel Hands, "Long John Silver's Return to Treasure Island" 1:17:29)

shark [*shahrrk/shairk*] ruthless person

> "You cold-gutted **shark**." (Orange Povy, "Captain Kidd" 23:17)

shark's-bait [*shahrrk's/shairk's-bayeet*] piece of **crap**; scumbag

Used to characterize another as irrelevant or useless—*i.e.*, having little value other than as food for sharks.

> "Well, it is just as I am being lectured thus on my marital duties, that you begin your creeping and colloguing with **Shark's-bait** yonder." (Japhet Bly, *Winds of Chance* 152)

sheep fool, especially one who is overly timid, complacent, dependent, or submissive

> "Why, you blind **sheep**!" (Long John Silver, "Long John Silver's Return to Treasure Island" 1:25:33)

shit [*shett*]

Literally meaning "excrement," the term is used to characterize another, depending on context, as offensive, contemptible, or worthless.

> "Go pick that up, you little **shit**." (Roger Press, *The Pirate Round* 354)

sickling [*seck-lin'*] weak, pathetic person

> "Tush and curse it, Captain, 'tis no more than petty boy, a **sickling**, a lousy lad, a puling mannikin not worth shiproom!" (Benjamin Trigg, on seeing the slight Adam Penfeather for the first time, *Adam Penfeather, Buccaneer* 44)

Sir Roguery [*Sarr Roo/Ro'oo-guery*] deceitful or otherwise wicked person

An elaborate version of "rogue," suggesting the person described engages in reprehensible conduct in a reckless fashion.

> "I were wiser to have no truck with Iniquity. So, I take my leave of you, **Sir Roguery**!" (Adam Penfeather, *Adam Penfeather, Buccaneer* 279)

sirrah; syrra [*sarrah*]

A contemptuous or dismissive term for an inferior man or boy.

> "Hearkee me, **sirrah**, you lousy, pittiful, ill-look'd dog; what have you to say why you should not be tuck'd up immediately, and set a sun-drying like a scare-crow?" (George Bradley, *General History of the Pyrates* 293)

skipjack [*skep-jarrk*]

Used literally to refer to a fish resembling the tuna, common to warm Pacific and Atlantic waters, and known for leaping out of the water vigorously and repeatedly, the term is used figuratively as one of disrespect or dismissiveness. The somewhat absurd image of a fish jumping out of water lends the usage a mocking, ridiculing overtone.

> "So ho now, ye hear him, Captain? This paltry **skipjack**, —ye hear him?" (Roger Tressady, *Adam Penfeather, Buccaneer* 253)

skulk(er) [*skoohlk(er)*]

Used literally to refer to a person who hides, lurks, or evades, the term is used figuratively to describe another as deceitful or contemptible, especially in a pathetic, weak way.

> < "There's Dirk again. Twice! We'll have to budge, mates." "Budge, you **skulk**! Dirk was a fool and a coward from the first—you wouldn't mind him." > (comrade of Pew's & Pew, *Treasure Island* 26, Chap. 5) "**Skulkers**, they be—low-lived skulkers as ever was." (Long John Silver, *Porto Bello Gold* 48)

slime [*slawm/slyeeme*] despicable person

> "The **slime** won't even fight like men. They run. It was easy." (Patch, "The Adventures of Long John Silver: Pieces of Eight" 7:01)

slug [*slarrg/sloohg*] despicable person

> "Ah, you drunken **slug**!" (Long John Silver, poking at one of his company with his crutch, "Treasure Island" [1960] 48:15)

slugabed [*slarrg/sloohg-er-bayd*] lazybones; sleepyhead

Literally meaning a person who stays too late or spends too much time in bed, the term is used figuratively to characterize another as lazy or laggard.

> "Up, **slugabed**! Rouse out, messmate, and stand by for breakfast!" (Japhet Bly, *Winds of Chance* 148)

sluggard [*slarrg/sloohg-gahrrd*] lazy, slothful person

> "Ha, d'ye stir at last, **sluggard**?" (Resolution Day, *Martin Conisby's Vengeance* 151)

smug [*smarrg/smoohg*] arrogant, self-righteous, or annoyingly self-satisfied person

> "So you are the Captain Adam Penfeather they call The Buccaneer ... a choice, hypocritical **smug** that calls on God and blasts poor sailormen to hell!" (Black Bartlemy, *Adam Penfeather, Buccaneer* 253)

snake (in the grass) [*snayeeke (i'/'n t' grarrs)*] treacherous, conniving, or deceitful person

> "Ah, the very thought of him turns me blood to boilin' oil. That **snake**." (Billy Bones, expressing his hatred of Long John Silver, "Treasure Island" [1960] 4:40) "Fie on you deserting our captain in this way, you scurvy traitors, you Judas Iscariots, you **snakes in the grass**, you wolves in sheep's clothing!" (Honesty Nuttall, "Captain Blood" 1:36:15)

sneak a person given to secretive, treacherous conduct undertaken in a cowardly or otherwise shameful manner

> "Jim—Jim Hawkins, eh? Captain Smollett's lily-livered **sneak**!" (Israel Hands, "Treasure Island" [1960] 59:44)

snip [*snep*] small or insignificant person

> "Are we going to stand by and see this little **snip** laugh at our captain?" (Henry Hagthrope, "Captain Blood" 1:35:58)

sniveller [*snev-erler/'ler*] whiner; person given to annoying, pathetic, or excessive crying or complaining

> "Get up, Jim. Get up, ya weak-kneed **sniveller** or, by thunder, we'll leave you behind! Up with 'ee!" (Long John Silver, rousing Jim Hawkins to his feet, "The Adventures of Long John Silver: Pieces of Eight" 16:49)

snood

Literally meaning a decorative bag-like net used to gather a woman's or girl's hair at the back of her head, the term is used figuratively to characterize another as insignificant or ridiculous, and especially to characterize a man as dainty, weak, or ineffectual.

> "That's the score, **snood**!" (Israel Hands, celebrating after putting a musket ball through one of Captain Smollet's men from a distance, "Treasure Island" [1934] 1:01:17)

sod [*sarrd*] obnoxious person; loser; jerk

> < "He's gettin' away!" "No he isn't, you **sod**!" > (unnamed pirates on Dead Man's Chest, *Dead Man's Chest* 269)

> Any of the entries below starting with "son of" can be modified to "daughter of" [*darrter/dawrrter/dotter o'\on*] for purposes of addressing a female.

son of a bastard [*soohn o'\on a barrs/bash-tahrrd*] offensive or contemptible person

> "No, no, no! **Son of a bastard**, no!" (Le-Rois, seeing his archenemy Malachias Barrett for the first time in years, *The Guardship* 192)

son of a bitch [*soohn o'\on a betch*] contemptible or vexatious person

> "Benner, you **son of a bitch**, where are you?" (Roger Press' guard, *The Pirate Round* 248)

son of a blundering ox [*soohn o'\on a blarrn/bloohn-derin' arrx*] foolish, incompetent, or worthless person

> "**Son of a blundering ox**, what did you do?" (El Toro Mendoza, "Long John Silver's Return to Treasure Island" 17:29)

son of a dog [*soohn o'\on a dahg/darrg/dorrg*] foolish, incompetent, or worthless person

> "We should never ha' put our trust in that **son of a dog**." (Trenam, *Captain Blood Returns* 284)

son of a (double) Dutchman [*soohn o'\on a (darr/dooh-ble) Darrtch/Doohtch-man*] contemptible or ridiculous person

English seamen of the sixteenth and seventeenth centuries were known to ridicule their Dutch counterparts based on certain sterotypically negative qualities, such as dishonesty, miserliness, shabbiness of appearance, personal uncleanliness, and bumbling oafishness. (The Dutch had a reputation for industry and economy, such that one might argue such ridicule was fundamentally a sour reflection of the grudging admiration they inspired.) A "son of a Dutchman," therefore, is someone who possesses these same qualities; the reference to parentage gives the characterization a judgmental, dismissive air. A "double Dutchman" is one of full Dutch parentage ("double" meaning both mother and father), though the phrase was likely a figurative one even in early usage, meaning someone particularly absurd or despicable.

> "Here I have this confounded **son of a Dutchman** sitting in my own house, drinking of my own rum!" (Long John Silver, *Treasure Island* 45, Chap. 8) "If I was sure of you all, **sons of double Dutchmen**, I'd have Cap'n Smollett navigate us halfway back again, before I struck." (Long John Silver, *Treasure Island* 60, Chap. 11)

son of a double-eyed whore from the reeking gutters of Rotterdam [*soohn o'\on* *a darr/dooh-ble eye'eed harr/'ore ferm t' reekin' garr/gooh-ters o'\on Rarrter-dem*] extremely offensive, contemptible, or worthless person

The length and vivid detail of this epithet lend it special vituperative power. The addressee in the below excerpt (Dutch, the island tavern-keeper) happens to be a Dutchman, but—given the much-maligned status of the Dutchman in the English-speaking pirate's figurative world—the characterization is applicable to anyone, regardless of heritage.

"Holy poker! You **son of a double-eyed whore from the reekin' gutters of Rotterdam!**" (Thomas Bartholomew Red, incensed at Dutch's refusal to purchase Red's hostages, "Pirates" 57:53)

son of a rum puncheon [*soohn o'\on a rarrm/roohm parrn/poohn-chern*]

A "rum puncheon" is a large wooden cask used to hold rum. "Son of a rum puncheon" is a nonsensical phrase. The fact that the speaker does not even put herself to the trouble of forming a cogent or fitting epithet itself implies dismissiveness and exasperation.

"Have I lived this many years, and a **son of a rum puncheon** cock his hat athwart my hawse at the latter end of it?" (Long John Silver, eager to crush any insolent upstart daring to question his authority, *Treasure Island* 159, Chap. 28)

son of a scab [*soohn o'\on a scarrb*] offensive, insignificant, or worthless person

"Raise that ugly claw to me once more and it'll be yer last, you barnacle-covered **son-of-a-scab!**" (Henry Morgan, *Dead Man's Chest* 10)

son of a sea cook [*soohn o'\on a sea cook*] insignificant person; person of little worth or meriting little consideration

Ship's cooks were often recruited from the ranks of crippled and aging seamen; though tight galley spaces and hot stoves may have created certain physical challenges, the posi-

tion required little exertion or agility. Important to the smooth operation of any vessel, the sea cook was nevertheless a marginal member of the crew—often isolated from his comrades, and contributing nothing to the handling of the vessel. One might refer to another as a "son of a sea cook," therefore, for the same reasons one might call an opposing player a "bat boy" on the baseball diamond: The association with a subsidiary and servile function works to disparage.

"Do but give me the word, Your Honor, and I'll put another bullet through the **son of a sea cook.**" (John Malyoe's sailing master, *The Book of Pirates* "The Ghost of Captain Brand" 51)

son of a sea hag [*soohn o'\on a sea 'ag*] offensive, contemptible, or vexatious person

"Morgan! Where is that **son-of-a-sea-hag?**" (Joshua Smoot, *Dead Man's Chest* 222)

son of a tavern hag [*soohn o'\on a tabbern/tav'n 'ag*] offensive, contemptible, or worthless person

"Tavern hag" is a close approximation of "whore."

Compare: "A curse out o' Egypt on ya, ye ungrateful **daughter of a tavern hag!**" (Long John Silver, *Dead Man's Chest* 9)

son of a whore [*soohn o'\on a harr/'ore*] offensive, contemptible, or worthless person

< "Must I hit her?" "Yes, you dog, you **son of a whore**, why are you so long about it?" > (gunner of the *Margaret* & Samuel Burgess, *The Pirate Hunter* 292)

son of Belial [*son o'\on Balial*] malicious, irredeemable, or contemptible person

"It is my constant prayer that I may be so blest to let out his evil soul by incision of steel beneath his fifth rib, or—watch him hang, for 'tis very **son o' Belial.**" (Smy Peters, *Adam Penfeather, Buccaneer* 21)

sot [*sarrt*] drunkard

"Drunken **sot**! Begone lest I send ye aloft to join yon carrion!" (Captain Jo, *Martin Conisby's Vengeance* 87)

Spaniard-lover [*Span-iahrrd/isher/nerd loohv/lubb-er*] traitor; scoundrel

In the below excerpt, Patch uses the term somewhat literally—given that Salamander the Greek was known for having betrayed Henry Morgan's company to the Spanish. However, the term works well as a potent epithet among any English-speaking pirates, for whom the Spaniard was arguably the most despicable of all things contemptible.

> "Here's something to lift your heavy heart, Long John. I found this slimy **Spaniard-lover** by the waterfront." (Patch, dragging Salamander the Greek into the Cask & Anchor, "The Adventures of Long John Silver: Pieces of Eight" 2:17)

spark [*spahrrk*] ridiculous or contemptible man; jerk

Literally meaning a man who affects elegance in appearance or dress, or whose manner is contrived, supercilious, or overbearing, the term is used figuratively to refer mockingly or derisively to any man, especially for the manner in which he comports himself.

> "Last night one Michael Jones and James Brown, two Irish landmen, run into the woods, thinking to get away from us; th[e] two such **sparks** run away the 25th from the Dutchess, and in the night were so frighted with tygers, as they thought, but really by monkeys and baboons, that they ran into the water, hollowing to the ship till they were fetch'd aboard again." (Woodes Rogers, *A Cruising Voyage Round the World* 28)

spawn [*spawrrn*] offensive, insignificant, or worthless person

> < "See how greatly the men favor you, sir?" "The pewling **spawn**—how I despise

them." > (Smee & James Hook, "Hook" 40:17)

spawn o' the devil [*spawrrn o'\on t' daahv/dayv/debb/div-il*] malicious or evil person

> "Now if you mean our hellish rogues, these imps o' Satan and **spawn o' the devil**, our rascal crew, —eh Adam?" (Benjamin Trigg, *Adam Penfeather, Buccaneer* 224)

sprat little piece of crap

Literally meaning a small fish of northeast Atlantic waters, the term "sprat" is used figuratively to refer dismissively to another as one of little consequence or deserving little respect.

> < "Aye, ye'r a hellish crafty **sprat**, ye are, Capt'n Lewrie. Pulled it off sweet as a ..."
> "Damn your blood, Doyle." > (Billy Doyle & Alan Lewrie, with Doyle delaying talk of surrender by lavishing praise on Alan Lewrie's battle tactics, *The Gun Ketch* 159)

sprits'l [*spret/spris-sel*] small or insignificant person

"Sprits'l" is a contraction of "spritsail," a small sail hung under a vessel's bowsprit. Used figuratively to characterize another as small or insignificant. Though most often used dismissively to convey disrespect, the term can also be used affectionately as a diminutive.

> "March, now, you little **sprits'l**." (Long John Silver, "Treasure Island" [1950] 1:25:56)

squab [*squarrb*] short, plump person

The term is also used figuratively in reference to a pompous or overindulgent person.

> "[They] pin their faith upon a pimp of a parson; a **squab**, who neither practices nor believes what he puts upon the chuckle-headed fools he preaches to." (Captain Bellamy, *General History of the Pyrates* 587)

squid [*squedd*] offensive or contemptible person

> "Devil burn ya, you one-legged **squid**. I'll heave ya to the shore." (Billy Bowlegs,

"Long John Silver's Return to Treasure Island" 15:48)

stockfish [*starrk-fesh*]

Literally meaning a fish (especially a codfish) cured not by being salted but by being split open and air-dried, the term is used figuratively to deride someone for inappropriate silence or excessive reticence.

> < "Oh, be silent!" "As any stockfish, an' ye will, ma'm." > (Ursula Revell & Japhet Bly, *Winds of Chance* 19)

swab [*swarrb*] low, vulgar, insigificant, or worthless person

Literally meaning one who cleans or washes, especially a vessel's decks ("deckswab"), the term is used figuratively to minimize the worth or significance of the person so described.

> "This should teach ya once an' fer all, ya bilge-lickin' swab!" (Henry Morgan, *Dead Man's Chest* 251)

swabby [*swarrby*]

The diminutive form of "swab," "swabby" might be used as a mild and even amiable or affectionate reproof—just as a modern speaker might refer to a mischievous friend as a "rascal" or "knucklehead."

> "Weigh anchor now, ya swabbies." (pirate auctioneer, goading the crowd into bidding, "Pirates of the Caribbean" Disney attraction)

swine [*swawn/swyeene*] offensive or contemptible person; beast

> < "You! Your sword. Lower it, you big, black ape!" "In a pig's eye, you swine!" > (Nick Debrett, "Swashbuckler" 1:09:16)

tern [*tarrn*] weakling; pansy; coward

Literally meaning a small, slender gull with narrow wings, the term is used figuratively to characterize another as weak, submissive, lacking courage, or too easily yielding.

> "Come back 'ere, you lubberly terns!" (Long John Silver, yelling as his company

mates abandon the attack on the stockade, "Treasure Island" [1950] 1:03:08)

thief [*teef*] contemptible person, especially one inclined to or engaged in stealing; degenerate

Pirates, who value qualities like strength and courage above all, abhor the notion of the slippery pilferer, who gets ahead not by venturing forth boldly but by slinking about evasively. The term "thief" is correspondingly potent and delivers an insult much more profound than when used in modern speech.

> "There's honour among buccaneers and we hold him to his pledge, to the articles upon which the dirty thief enlisted us." (pirate aboard the *Valiant*, *Captain Blood Returns* 284)

toad [*tood/to'ood*] offensive, contemptible, or worthless person

> "Forgive my slow-wittedness, Skipper, but are thee asking us to spare this sweet-smelling toad?" (Humble Bellows, "The Crimson Pirate" 11:23)

traitor [*traah/trayee-tarr*]

> "This base and scurvy traitor—guilty of foulest treason—." (pirate mate, "The Black Pirate" 1:04:31)

turncoat [*tarrn-co'oot/coot*] treacherous person; one engaged in or inclined to betrayal

> "And when ya touch down next time, it'll be me crutch to yer back, just like the turncoat, John Mary!" (Long John Silver, *Dead Man's Chest* 9)

two-legged beast [*two-lagg-ered beasht*] offensive or contemptible person

> "Now forrard two o' ye and take me up this two-legged beast." (Adam Penfeather, *Adam Penfeather, Buccaneer* 189)

tyke [*tawk/tyeeke*] vulgar or barbarous person

> "He's a treacherous tyke, Sam, as I should know." (Peter Blood, *Captain Blood Returns* 151)

upstart [*arrp-stahrrt*] arrogant, overreaching, or self-promoting person

> < "I'll give you just two seconds to get out of 'ere." "Belay. I'll tend to this fine-feathered **upstart** meself." > (Long John Silver & Purity Pinker, confronting the pompous Bellows and the soldiers flanking him, "The Adventures of Long John Silver: The Eviction" 7:01)

urchin [*arr-choohn*] impertinent, mischievous, or vexatious child

> "The **urchin** is mad!" (The Red Rover, exasperated with his opinionated cabin boy, *The Red Rover* 475)

varmint [*vahrr-maahnt/ment/mit*] obnoxious, offensive, or contemptible person

Literally meaning a wild animal despised for its predatory or disease-carrying tendencies, the term is used figuratively to refer derisively to any despicable person.

> "You young **varmint**. Why, I'll break you of these insolent ways." (Long John Silver, "Long John Silver's Return to Treasure Island" 22:16)

vermin [*varr-men*] obnoxious, offensive, or contemptible person

Literally meaning an insect, rodent, or other pest, the term is used figuratively to refer derisively to any despicable person.

> "Die he must, but in proper fashion and time, not by such **vermin** as you—so put up that knife!" (Captain Jo, *Martin Conisby's Vengeance* 60)

villain [*vell-ayn*] depraved or wicked person

> "**Villain**! doubly d[amne]d **villain**! thou'lt die like a dog, and unrevenged!" (Cain, *The Pirate* 138, Chap. XVII)

wanton [*warrn-tern*] sexually promiscuous or dissolute person, especially a woman

> "My Silver Woman! This priceless **wanton**!" (Black Bartlemy, showing Adam Penfeath-er his silver woman-shaped dagger, *Adam Penfeather, Buccaneer* 256)

wastrel [*waah/wayee-strell*] wasteful, self-indulgent, or lazy person; good-for-nothing

> "[Y]e that are Englishmen all, —ye that were o' late right hardy mariners, prime seamen bold for all hardship, now show no better than so many whey-faced, spiritless, slouching **wastrels**!" (Adam Penfeather, *Adam Penfeather, Buccaneer* 301)

weasel [*wezzel*] person given to secretive, treacherous conduct undertaken in a cowardly or otherwise shameful manner

> "Oh, that **weasel**. He tricked us all into stayin' here, then made off in the ship, he did." (Ben Gunn, condemning Captain Flint for his duplicity, "Treasure Island" [1960] 49:50)

weevil [*weebull*] offensive, insignificant, or worthless person

> "Haul that **weevil** to his feet!" (bosun aboard the *Flying Dutchman*, "Pirates of the Caribbean 2: Dead Man's Chest" 1:13:12)

whale [*waahl/wayell*]

A disparaging term for a large, overweight, or oafish person.

> < "What insolence! That throne belongs to the Spanish crown." "No longer, you ol' **whale**. I want it! At once!" > (Thomas Bartholomew Red, "Pirates" 1:22:03)

whale's bile [*waahl's/wayell's by-ell/ool*] offensive or contemptible person

> "**Whale's bile**, that's what you be." (Long John Silver, "Long John Silver's Return to Treasure Island" 7:26)

wharf rat [*wahrrf rarrt*] offensive, contemptible, or insignificant person

> "You blasted **wharf rat**! Mutiny, will 'ee?" (Long John Silver, "Long John Silver's Return to Treasure Island" 39:53)

whelp [*whalp*]

Literally meaning a very young dog, the term is used figuratively to refer dismissively or derisively to a young person or to characterize a person as offensive or insignificant.

> "So you're blubbering, are you, you obstinate **whelp**?" (pirate captain, *The Coral Island* 201)

whiffler [*weffler*]

Literally used to refer to a person who sporadically changes his view or course of action, the term is used figuratively to characterize another as indecisive, weak-willed, pathetic, or lacking courage or determination.

> "I want hearty fellows, seadogs and tarry mariners, not spindle-shanked **whifflers**!" (Benjamin Trigg, on seeing the slight Adam Penfeather for the first time, *Adam Penfeather, Buccaneer* 44)

whiner [*wawn/wyeen-er*] person given to annoying or excessive crying or complaining

> "It's that **whiner**—sneakin' brat!" (Pew, "Treasure Island" [1934] 20:44)

whoreson [*harr/'ore-soohn*] son of a whore

Used to characterize another as offensive, contemptible, or worthless.

> "Don't you play it coy with me, you **whoreson**, or I'll have you impaled here and now." (Elephiant Yancy, *The Pirate Round* 315)

worm [*warrm*] offensive, worthless person

> "Crawl into the boat, **worm**, and wait till I'm minded to patch up your hurt—Go!" (Captain Jo, *Martin Conisby's Vengeance* 61)

worm's-meat [*warrm's-meat*] scumbag

Used to characterize another as irrelevant or useless—*i.e.*, having little value other than as flesh for consumption by worms after death.

> < "Nay, Sir Villainy, let not my presence check your natural ferocity; wreak your brutish pleasure on your weeping victim, I'll twiddle my thumbs or—" "Peace, **Worm's-meat**!" > (John Barrasdale & Japhet Bly, *Winds of Chance* 162)

wretch [*wratch*] depraved or wicked person, especially one who is pathetically or desperately given to reprehensible conduct

> "Die? Who—me? And by such puny **wretch** as you?" (Giles Tregenza, mocking the small-statured Adam Penfeather, *Adam Penfeather, Buccaneer* 203)

yellow dog [*yal-ler/lowoo dahg/darrg/dorrg*] one lacking courage or determination; spineless person; coward

> "Get back here, you bloody **yellow dog**!" (Long John Silver, "Treasure Island" [1990] 1:23:33)

CHAPTER 10

Respectful Address

Chapter 9 introduced the use of epithets—modifier-noun combinations used to deride or denigrate. This chapter sets out modifiers and nouns for use in opposite circumstances: to express respect, praise, or appreciation. One might refer to a particularly competent member of a company as a "brisk hand," for example, or convey in hearty terms one's fondness or admiration for another by proclaiming him a "roaring bully."

The mix and match of modifiers (Section 10.1) and nouns (Section 10.2) should be a creative, freewheeling enterprise governed only by taste and circumstance. Note, however, that certain modifiers and nouns tend to be used with each other with disproportionate frequency. Note also the following important points about respectful address:

- Respectful address, like the epithet, is often a tool for manipulation or influence. In the scheming, two-faced world of piracy, there might be occasion for both an epithet *and* respectful address to be used in the same sentence: "You was ever **a thick-pated fool**, Rogerson **my hearty**!" (Roger Snaith, *Winds of Chance* 353)

- The same term can be used as epithet in certain circumstances and as respectful address in others. One example is the term "hell-fire." Just as the modern English speaker might use the phrase "from hell" both to condemn ("my sixth-grade teacher was from hell") and to express admiration ("that middleweight's right hook is from hell"), pirates might use "hell-fire" in the same way—both negatively and positively depending on context. ("Hell-fire" and other such terms are accordingly listed as both epithets in Chapter 9 and forms of respectful address in this chapter.)

> In the world of piracy, it's good to be *bad*. Traits like ruthlessness, hedonism, and borderline insanity are often admired. As a result, the same words used to condemn one's enemies are often used to praise one's leaders or comrades.

- The word "my" is often used with nouns of respectful address, as in "Come here, **my** hearty." The term connotes familiarity with, affection for, or amiability toward the addressee. However, "my" is not always used in respectful address. Indeed, certain nouns are almost never used with "my." This is a matter of convention; nothing governs the use or omission of "my" except what happens to be customary. The following is a quick summary for easy reference:

    Certain nouns used in respectful address are almost *always* used with the word "my"—as in "my beauty," "my bird," "my cull," and "my roarer." One rarely would say "Avast, beauty" or "Ahoy, roarer," but rather "Avast, **my** beauty" or "Ahoy, **my** roarer."

    Other nouns are almost *never* used with the word "my." These include "mate," "shipmate," and "sonny." One would not say, "Belay, my shipmate!" Rather, the customary form is "Belay, shipmate!"

    Finally, most nouns are sometimes used with "my" and sometimes used without. These include "boy," "bucko," "bully," "bully boy," "cock," "cove," "friend," "hearty," "lad," "lass," "man," "master," and "matey." Accordingly, one might say either "Forward, buckos!" or "Forward, my buckos!"

    Keep in mind, however, that in pirate speech there are no absolute rules, and even the strongest of conventions may submit to individual preference.

- The addressee's name is often used immediately before a respectful address:

    "Come now, **Jim lad**, time be wastin'." (Long John Silver, "Treasure Island" [1950] 21:02) "What, are ye hurt, Jo? Ha, **Joanna lass**, are ye hit indeed?" (Resolution Day, *Martin Conisby's Vengeance* 108) "Hallo, **Ralph boy**! rouse up, lad; we're safe now." (Bloody Bill, waking Ralph Rover up from his feverish swoon, *The Coral Island* 256)

    The addressee's name is also—though less frequently—used immediately *after* a term of respectful address:

    "**Friend Adam**, I was captured and slave to 'em once ..." (Amos Perrin, *Adam Penfeather, Buccaneer* 117) "But is the matter thus, why yet, **fellow John**, I pray thee let me live until I come into England." (Thomas Doughty, *The Queen's Corsair* 52) **"Ma'm Ursula**, you show a strange inclination to the company of rogues and damned rascals ..." (Japhet Bly, *Winds of Chance* 113)

10.1 MODIFIERS

able [*abble/ayeeble*] capable; competent

"And if they would do this, said I, they can ask no reasonable sum but our General might advance it, besides getting home such a body of stout **able** seamen as we were, such a number of ships and such a quantity of rich goods." (Captain Avery, *The King of Pirates* 71)

ardent [*ahrr-daahnt/dernt*] passionate; zealous

"Here we be, two hundred and fifty choice lads, **ardent** souls and very eager, and— a marvellous rich city." (Benjamin Trigg, *Adam Penfeather, Buccaneer* 332)

bawcock(y) [*bawrr-carrk(y)*] deserving or inviting respect or approval; fine; admirable

"Eye him over, lads! View him well, **baw-cock** boys!" (Resolution Day, inviting the pirates aboard the *Happy Despatch* to witness Captain Belvedere's mutilated corpse, *Martin Conisby's Vengeance* 111) "Clear the guns, **bawcocky** boys; 'tis our turn next—but stand by till she comes about ..." (Resolution Day, rallying the pirates of the *Happy Despatch* after a devastating surprise broadside from Adam Penfeather's ship, *Martin Conisby's Vengeance* 105)

ben [*ban/bayn*] good; fine

Used as a amiable term in referring to another, as with "good" in the modern phrase "my good sir," or "fine" in "my fine friend."

"And look'ee, my **ben** cull, if I was to offer ye all Bartlemy's treasure—which I can't, mark me—still you'd never gather just what manner o' hook that was."

(Abnegation Mings, *Black Bartlemy's Treasure* 32)

blood-and-beef [*bloohd/blut-an'/'n'-biff*] red-blooded; strong; hearty; vigorous

"Aye, 'tis pity, for I do like you more and more, such a fine **blood-and-beef**, dare-and-be-damned, gibbet-like figure of a rogue, shipmate, as would grace a cross-roads better than most ..." (Adam Penfeather, *Black Bartlemy's Treasure* 47–48)

bold [*bol'/boold/bo'oold*] fearless; daring

"I have singled out about twelve or thirteen **bold** brave fellows, with whom I have resolved to venture to the Gulf of Persia." (Captain Avery, *The King of Pirates* 76)

brave [*brayeeve*] courageous; valiant

"[O]ur number increased so, especially at first, that we were once 800 men, stout **brave** fellows and as good sailors as any in the world." (Captain Avery, *The King of Pirates* 63)

bright [*brawt/brigheet*] splendid; admirable

"There never was such a murderer born into this wicked world as Adam Penfeather, with a curse! 'Twas he as murdered Black Bartlemy and nine sweet, **bright** lads arter him, murdered 'em here one by one, and wi' a parchment rove about the neck of each poor corpse, Marty." (Roger Tressady, *Black Bartlemy's Treasure* 302–3)

brisk [*bresk/brishk*] (1) vigorous; energetic (2) industrious; diligent (3) competent; able (4) fine; admirable

"Z[oun]ds, his mate is a lusty young **brisk** man, and has been upon the account before ..." (John Russell, *Pirates of the New England Coast* 184–85)

bull-bodied [*bull-bah'/barrd-eed*] having a large and muscular physique; big and strong

"'Tis a fine, **bull-bodied** boy, Job, all brawn and beef—witness your eye, Lord love me!" (Diccon, *Martin Conisby's Vengeance* 65)

bully (1) admirable (2) vigorous; energetic

"You're a **bully** cock, I could see that in two shakes." (Thomas Bartholomew Red, "Pirates" 40:42)

buxom [*barrx/boohx-arrm*] fine; admirable

The term "buxom" is used to stand for some combination of the positive qualities often associated with youth: health, vigor, and beauty.

"Lord love me, but I've seen many a better throat than yours slit ere now, my **buxom** lad!" (Abnegation Mings, *Black Bartlemy's Treasure* 32)

case-hardened [*cayeese-'ard/hahrrd-erned*] hard-boiled; tough-as-nails

Used in reference to someone able to heartily and impressively endure or overcome challenge or adversity, especially as a result of long, colorful, and dangerous experience.

"[T]here was on board 160 stout fellows, as bold and as **case-hardened** for the work as ever I met with upon any occasion whatever." (Captain Avery, *The King of Pirates* 11)

choice [*ch'ice/choyeece*] of a superior kind

"Here we be, two hundred and fifty **choice** lads, ardent souls and very eager, and—a marvellous rich city." (Benjamin Trigg, *Adam Penfeather, Buccaneer* 332)

crafty [*crarrfty*] smart; clever

Used especially to refer to another's skill in outwitting or deceiving.

< "Aye, ye'r a hellish **crafty** sprat, ye are, Capt'n Lewrie. Pulled it off sweet as a ..." "Damn your blood, Doyle." > (Billy Doyle

& Alan Lewrie, with Doyle delaying talk of surrender by lavishing praise on Alan Lewrie's battle tactics, *The Gun Ketch* 159)

cunning [*coohn-in'*] resourceful; clever

"O a right **cunning**, fierce rogue was Adam, and none to match him but me." (Roger Tressady, *Black Bartlemy's Treasure* 304)

dainty [*daahn/dayeen-ty*]

A mildly ironic term of fondness by which the speaker conveys a degree of familiarity with and affection or admiration for the person so described.

"And look'ee, my **dainty** cull, when you've seen as much o' death as Abnegation Mings you'll know as Death's none so bad a thing, so long as it leaves you alone." (Abnegation Mings, *Black Bartlemy's Treasure* 31)

dare-and-be-damned [*darr/dayarr/dayerr an'/'n' be damt*] courageous and iron-willed; daring and resolute

The term is used to refer to someone as both willing to take risks and confronting them with fierce determination.

"Aye, 'tis pity, for I do like you more and more, such a fine blood-and-beef, **dare-and-be-damned**, gibbet-like figure of a rogue, shipmate, as would grace a crossroads better than most ..." (Adam Penfeather, *Black Bartlemy's Treasure* 47–48)

delicate [*daahl-er-cayte/kert*]

A mildly ironic term of fondness by which the speaker conveys a familiarity with and affection or admiration for the person described.

"[T]here be none of all the coastwise Brotherhood quicker or readier when there's aught i' the wind than Abnegation, and you can lay to that, my **delicate** cove!" (Abnegation Mings, *Black Bartlemy's Treasure* 31)

desperate [*daahss/darrss-peerate/p'rate*] extremely courageous; willing to take great risks

"A wildish company, Martin, **desperate** fellows as ever roved the Main, as I do love no more than they love me." (Roger Tressady, *Black Bartlemy's Treasure* 305)

doglike [*dahg/darrg/dorrg-lawk/lyeeke*] relentlessly loyal; devoted

"Mistress Ursula, in saving yon poor rogues, you have broke all 'stablished rules and precedents among the Coast Brethren and won you as many **doglike** friends shall bark to your bidding—yet such dogs bite." (Barnabas Rokeby, *Winds of Chance* 57)

fierce [*fee-arrce*] possessing fearsome degrees of strength and intensity

"O a right cunning, **fierce** rogue was Adam, and none to match him but me." (Roger Tressady, *Black Bartlemy's Treasure* 304)

fine [*fawn/fyeene*] superior; admirable

< "Should he not be bled, sir?" "Step me vitals—no, mem! 'Tis blood we lack! There's more **fine** lads killed by the dem'd lancet than all y'r rapiers and small swords, b'ged!" > (Ursula Revell & Crabtree, *Winds of Chance* 89)

fire and blood [*farr/fyarr an'/'n' bloohd/blut*] tough and dangerous

Used to refer to someone well-acquainted with—and hardened by exposure to or immersion in—fight, death, and danger.

"What o' yourself, friend? There's a regular **fire-and-blood**, skull-and-bones look about ye as liketh me very well." (Resolution Day, *Martin Conisby's Vengeance* 72)

fire and fury [*farr/fyarr an'/'n' fee'oo/foo-ree*] violently intense; extremely fierce

"Hast transformed timid-bleating ewe lamb into roaring lion, meek-eyed, whispering coyness into this **fire and fury** young Bobadil!" (Absalom Troy, *Adam Penfeather, Buccaneer* 107)

gibbet-like [*gibbert/gib't-lawk/lyeeke*] having a deeply intimidating, threatening, or foreboding appearance or demeanor

"Aye, 'tis pity, for I do like you more and more, such a fine blood-and-beef, dare-and-be-damned, **gibbet-like** figure of a rogue, shipmate, as would grace a cross-roads better than most ..." (Adam Penfeather, *Black Bartlemy's Treasure* 47–48)

good(ly) fine; admirable

The term has little or no substantive content when used as a modifier in respectful address, but rather radiates the speaker's familiarity with, amiability toward, or affection for the person so described.

"To it, lads, sa-ha—at him then, **good** bullies!" (Captain Jo, urging her pirates to beat Martin Conisby, *Martin Conisby's Vengeance* 63) "Which agreement we have come to after proper discussion and with the consent of each member of our **goodly** company." (pirates' ransom note, "The Black Pirate" 43:04)

great [*grayeet/grea'/grett*] fine, admirable; impressive

*And he gave in for evidence, that the prisoner [John Walden] was looked on as a brisk hand (*i.e.,* as he farther explained it, a stanch pyrate, a **great** rogue) ...* (attribution to Henry Glasby, *General History of the Pyrates* 270)

gut-cutting [*garrt/gooht carrt/cooht-in'*] (1) dangerous (2) capable; effective

"He'll take a lot for a sizzlin', **gut-cuttin'** fire-eater." (Long John Silver, *Porto Bello Gold* 49)

hard-favoured [*'ahrrd/'ard/hahrrd-fayee-varred*] hard- or stern-looking; having a threatening or intimidating appearance or demeanor

"They are tall, well made, raw-boned, lusty, strong, and nimble of foot, long-visaged, lank black hair, stern of look, **hard-favoured**, and of a dark copper-coloured complexion." (William Dampier, describing the Moskito Indians traveling with his company, *A New Voyage Round the World* 11)

hardy [*'ar/'ahrr/hahrr-dy*] strong; resolute

"[Y]e that are Englishmen all, —ye that were o' late right **hardy** mariners, prime seamen bold for all hardship, now show no better than so many whey-faced, spiritless, slouching wastrels!" (Adam Penfeather, *Adam Penfeather, Buccaneer* 301)

hearty [*'ahrrt/'eart/hahrrt-y*] vigorous; zealous

"Look'ee my **hearty** boys, the first man as setteth foot atwhart this line I send to hell-fire along o' Tom Purdy yonder!" (Roger Tressady, *Black Bartlemy's Treasure* 313)

hell-fire [*'ell-farr/fyarr*] fierce, violent, or dangerous

< "Is he well?" "Well-ish, brother—fairly bobbish, all things considered, mate—though not such a **hell-fire**, roaring lad o' mettle as yourself, comrade." > (Martin Conisby & Resolution Day, *Martin Conisby's Vengeance* 89)

honest [*hon-erst*] good; decent

"Honest fellow" is a phrase used to depict someone in a generally positive light. Modern equivalents to "He's an honest fellow" might include "He's a nice person" or "He's a good guy." Note, however, that the phrase "honest gentleman" is typically used to refer specifically to someone who is not a pirate, in the same way the term "civilian" is used in modern English to distinguish those who are not soldiers.

"Except for rum, yon noisy fellows be **honest** lads and right sailormen." (Japhet Bly, *Winds of Chance* 81)

jolly [*jarrly*] good; great

"His accursed savages! Four o' my best and **jolliest** lads dead and scalped since we came ashore." (Roger Snaith, *Winds of Chance* 317)

likely [*lawk/lyeeke-ly*] pleasant; decent

"Well, there's Montbars as they do call the Exterminator, and there's young Harry Morgan—a **likely** lad, and there's Roger Tressady and Sol Aiken and Penfeather—sink him!" (Abnegation Mings, *Black Bartlemy's Treasure* 31)

lovesome [*loohve/lub-sahm/sarrm/soohm*] romantically or sexually desirable; lovely

< "My name is Ursula." "Well, I like thee, Ursula, and shall doubtless like thee better anon, for thou'rt a **lovesome** thing, I vow and protest." > (Roger Snaith, *Winds of Chance* 316)

lusty [*larrsty*] (1) vigorous; energetic (2) powerful; strong (2) competent; effective

"'Twas I (and my good comrade Nick Frant) with sixteen **lusty** lads took sea in an open pinnace and captured the great treasure galleon *Dolores del Principe* off Carthagena ..." (Adam Penfeather, *Black Bartlemy's Treasure* 83)

merry [*maah/mahr/may-ry*] delightful

"You, Tom Purdy, step forward—so! Now where's the prisoner as I set i' your charge, where, my **merry** bird, where?" (Roger Tressady, *Black Bartlemy's Treasure* 312)

of (right) mettle\metal [*o'\on (rawt/righeet) meh'le*] courageous; determined; spirited

Used in a sentence after, not before, the noun modified.

"I am glad to see that you are man enough to enter thus into an affair, though you can't see to the bottom of it. For it shows me that you are a man **of mettle**, and are deserving of the fortune that is to befall you to-night." (Abraham Dawling, congratulating Barnaby True on his willingness to join Dawling despite True's uncertainty, *The Book of Pirates* "The Ghost of Captain Brand" 46) "Curse me, if she is not a lass **of metal**!" (John Sharkey, pleased and surprised at his female prisoner's contrived friendliness, *The Dealings of Captain Sharkey and Other Tales of Pirates* "The Blighting of Sharkey" 55) "Come, you are indeed **of right mettle**, and I like your spirit." (Abraham Dawling, laughing on seeing young Barnaby True brandish his pistol, *The Book of Pirates* "The Ghost of Captain Brand" 48)

old [ol'/oold/o'oold]

Used by the speaker to convey familiarity with, affection for, or amiability toward the person so described.

"Japhet, **old** messmate, 'tis joy to see thee again! Come alongside ..." (Will, *Winds of Chance* 207)

pretty [pratty/preh'ee] fine; admirable

The term "pretty" is an inherently diminutive term, however favorable, and implies a dismissiveness or playfulness consistent with a superiority of station of the speaker over the person being described.

"Now, my **pretty** lads, d'ye give us room or do I make ye—which?" (Japhet Bly, *Winds of Chance* 14)

prime [prawm/pryeeme] excellent; terrific

"Step forward, Abner. Come, you'll do— you're a **prime** sailor-man, you're my bo'sun henceforth." (Roger Tressady, *Black Bartlemy's Treasure* 308)

rare [rarr/rayarr/rayerr] unusually or exceptionally good

"Well done, lad! you're a brick, and I have no doubt will turn out a **rare** cove." (pirate, lauding fifteen-year-old Ralph Rover for his aggressive boldness, *The Coral Island* 202)

right [rawt/righeet] (1) good; fine; decent (2) competent; effective

"Except for rum, yon noisy fellows be honest lads and **right** sailormen." (Japhet Bly, *Winds of Chance* 81)

roaring [rarr-in'] impressively vigorous; dashing

Used literally to refer to a loud or noisy person, especially one creating a public disturbance of some kind, the term is used figuratively to refer to a dynamic individual.

"Come speak up, my **roaring** boy!" (Roger Tressady, *Black Bartlemy's Treasure* 307)

ruddy [roohdy/ruh'ee] strong; vigorous

Literally meaning "having a healthy, red- or pink-skinned color," the term is used figuratively to refer to another as powerful or dynamic.

"Last o' the — **ruddy**-boys is comin' aboard, sir." (Martin, *Porto Bello Gold* 176, omission in original)

sailorly [saah/sayee/sayor-larr/luh-ly] deserving or inviting respect or approval from seamen; displaying qualities admired by seamen

The term is often used as a loose equivalent for positive modifiers like "brave," "competent," "determined," and "vigorous."

"Ay, ay, my lady, and venturing your own body along of ours, my lady, so bold and **sailorly** ..." (Ben, praising Ursula Revell's insistence on staying abovedecks with the ship's crew during a recent violent storm, *Winds of Chance* 130)

'sdeath and blood ['sdath/'sdeff an'/'n' bloohd/blut] tough and dangerous

Used to refer to someone well-acquainted with—and hardened by exposure to or immersion in—fight, death, and danger.

"Damme, Adam, but thou'rt transforming this gentle, smock-faced brother o' thine into a perfect throat-slitting **'sdeath and blood** bravo, a notable swashing, hellfire, bully roarer, eh, Adam?" (Absalom Troy, *Adam Penfeather, Buccaneer* 101)

sizzling [sezz-lern/lin'] fiery; fierce

Used to characterize another favorably as dynamic, resolute, or impressively capable.

"He'll take a lot for a **sizzlin'**, gut-cuttin' fire-eater." (Long John Silver, *Porto Bello Gold* 49)

skull-and-bones [skoohl-an'/'n'-boones/bo'oones] tough and dangerous

Used to refer to someone well-acquainted with—and hardened by long exposure to or immersion in—fight, death, and danger.

> "What o' yourself, friend? There's a regular fire-and-blood, **skull-and-bones** look about ye as liketh me very well." (Resolution Day, *Martin Conisby's Vengeance* 72)

sober [*soo/so'oo-ber*] prudent; judicious

> "But for the rest, they be all tried and **sober** men, well beknown to me and to each other ..." (Absalom Troy, *Adam Penfeather, Buccaneer* 12)

staunch [*stanch/starrnch*] (1) powerful; strong (2) confident; resolute (3) trustworthy; reliable

> *And he gave in for evidence, that the prisoner [John Walden] was looked on as a brisk hand (*i.e.* as he farther explained it, a **stanch** pyrate, a great rogue) ...* (attribution to Henry Glasby, *General History of the Pyrates* 270)

stout [*stowoot*] (1) powerful; strong (2) resolute; determined (3) worthy or admirable, especially in the sense of being effective, competent, or reliable

> "We are gathered together to bid farewell to a gallant seaman and a **stout** comrade." (William Kidd, "Captain Kidd" 34:25)

stout of heart [*stowoot o'\on 'ahrrt/'eart/ hahrrt*] brave; courageous

> "Well, 'twas good fight, John, and thou a ... notable good comrade ... **stout o' heart**, d'ye see." (Japhet Bly, *Winds of Chance* 362)

sturdy [*starrdy*] (1) powerful; strong (2) resolute; determined (3) worthy or admirable, especially in the sense of being effective, competent, or reliable

> "A **sturdy** soul, Job, and of a comfortable conversation!" (Diccon, commenting on a barely conscious and profanity-sputtering Martin Conisby, *Martin Conisby's Vengeance* 65)

swashing [*swarrsh-in'*] swaggering; bold; dashing

> "Damme, Adam, but thou'rt transforming this gentle, smock-faced brother o' thine into a perfect throat-slitting 'sdeath and blood bravo, a notable **swashing**, hell-fire, bully roarer, eh, Adam?" (Absalom Troy, *Adam Penfeather, Buccaneer* 101)

sweet fine; decent; admirable

> "There never was such a murderer born into this wicked world as Adam Penfeather, with a curse! 'Twas he as murdered Black Bartlemy and nine **sweet**, bright lads arter him, murdered 'em here one by one, and wi' a parchment rove about the neck of each poor corpse, Marty." (Roger Tressady, *Black Bartlemy's Treasure* 302–3)

tarry [*taah/tay-ry*] possessing the prodigious skills and long experience of a veteran seaman; experienced; seasoned

The term "tarry," meaning covered with tar, is a reference to the use of tar in coating the rope lines of sailing vessels to protect them from the disintegrating effects of seawater and sunlight. A "tarry" hand, therefore, is a seaman who has spent so much time working on sailing vessels that he might be said figuratively to be covered with tar.

> "I want hearty fellows, seadogs and **tarry** mariners, not spindle-shanked whifflers!" (Benjamin Trigg, on seeing the slight Adam Penfeather for the first time, *Adam Penfeather, Buccaneer* 44)

throat-slitting [*thro'oot slet-tin'*] dangerous; menacing

> "Damme, Adam, but thou'rt transforming this gentle, smock-faced brother o' thine into a perfect **throat-slitting** 'sdeath and blood bravo, a notable swashing, hell-fire, bully roarer, eh, Adam?" (Absalom Troy, *Adam Penfeather, Buccaneer* 101)

tried [*trawwed/tryeed*] (1) experienced; seasoned (2) trustworthy; reliable

"But for the rest, they be all **tried** and sober men, well beknown to me and to each other ..." (Absalom Troy, *Adam Penfeather, Buccaneer* 12)

true [*troo*] decent; honest

> < "Why, then, so is it my prayer to watch my enemy die and I do live to none other purpose—" "Spoke like **true**, bully lad, Martino!" > (Martin Conisby & Captain Jo, *Martin Conisby's Vengeance* 48)

trusty [*traahs/trarrs-ty*] reliable; solid

> "[I]t was left to me to name my men, so I chose me out forty stout fellows, and among them several who were **trusty** bold men, fit for anything." (Captain Avery, *The King of Pirates* 38)

valiant [*varrl-iernt*] bold; courageous

> "[W]ee lost **valiant** Capt[ain] Sawkins by an ambuscade." (Basil Ringrose, *The South Sea Waggoner* Chart 35)

wildish [*wawld-ersh/esh*] wild; fierce

> "A **wildish** company, Martin, desperate fellows as ever roved the Main, as I do love no more than they love me." (Roger Tressady, *Black Bartlemy's Treasure* 305)

10.2 NOUNS

> The terms in this section are either masculine or gender neutral. For feminine nouns of respectful address, see section 16.11: Women.

amigo [*arr-mee-go'oo*] friend

"Amigo" is the Spanish word for "friend." Used especially by buccaneers who spent time in and around the Spanish-speaking territories of the New World.

"So stand by to let go the halyard and ship oars when I give word, *amigo*." (Resolution Day, *Martin Conisby's Vengeance* 151)

barracuda [*bahrr-acuda/acuder/'cuda/'cuder/ercuda/ercuder*] violent or dangerous person

> "I'm Montbars, the **barracuda** of Sir Henry Morgan's flotilla." (Montbars, "Pirates of Tortuga" 40:45)

beauty [*bee'ooty*]

(1) Used by a man to refer showily or slyly to a woman.

> "Share this one amongst ya, me **beauties**." (Blackbeard, blowing a kiss to the ladies of Godolphin, "Blackbeard's Ghost" 1:44:41)

(2) Used, often ironically or mockingly, to refer to another amiably or affectionately.

> "Come in, come in, me **beauties!**" (Thomas Bartholomew Red, parading his hostages before a prospective buyer, "Pirates" 57:25)

Bobadil [*Bober/Bo'ooba/Bo'oober-dell*]

A term used either as a straightforward reference to a fierce or dangerous person, or as a mocking or sarcastic reference to someone who thinks he is more fierce or dangerous than he really is. "Boabdil" (notice the slightly different spelling) was the last Moorish king of Granada, who invaded Castile and later refused to surrender Granada to Ferdinand and Isabella. Captain "Bobadil," on the other hand, is a character in Ben Jonson's 1598 play *Every Man in His Humour*, a pompous and irascible braggart of a military man who makes himself out to be more impressive than he is.

> "Hast transformed timid-bleating ewe lamb into roaring lion, meek-eyed, whispering coyness into this fire and fury young **Bobadil!**" (Absalom Troy, *Adam Penfeather, Buccaneer* 107)

boy [*boyee*] young man

"I know you to be roaring **boys** who would go with me against the devil himself if I bid you." (John Sharkey, *The Dealings of Captain Sharkey and Other Tales of Pirates* "The Blighting of Sharkey" 48)

bravo [*brarr-vo'oo*] evil or dangerous person; villain; killer

"Damme, Adam, but thou'rt transforming this gentle, smock-faced brother o' thine into a perfect throat-slitting 'sdeath and blood **bravo**, a notable swashing, hellfire, bully roarer, eh, Adam?" (Absalom Troy, *Adam Penfeather, Buccaneer* 101)

brethren [*brayth/bredd/breeth/breff/bre'-ren*] brothers

Used by pirates to refer to their comrades.

"**Brethren**, you'll have been wondering why I altered course for yon island which yet is no island." (Japhet Bly, to the crew of the *Joyful Deliverance*, *Winds of Chance* 152)

brick [*breck*] good or decent fellow; nice guy

"Well done, lad! you're a **brick**, and I have no doubt will turn out a rare cove." (pirate, lauding fifteen-year-old Ralph Rover for his aggressive boldness, *The Coral Island* 202)

brother [*brarr/brooh-der/'er*]

A respectful term used between pirates.

< "Liar! Liar!" "Peace, **brother**, peace! From any other man this were a fighting word, but as it is, let us reason together, **brother**!" > (Martin Conisby & Resolution Day, *Martin Conisby's Vengeance* 168)

brother-adventurer [*brarr/brooh-der/'er a'van/ a'ven/arrdvan/arrdven/'van/'ven-charr/terr-arr*]

A respectful term used between pirates.

"To my well-loved, trusty friend, comrade and **brother-adventurer** Martin ..." (letter from Adam Penfeather to Martin Conisby, *Black Bartlemy's Treasure* 163)

bucko [*boohk-o'oo*] (1) young man (2) friend

"Here, me **buckos**. Go below and break out some rum." (Blackbeard, "Blackbeard the Pirate" 1:31:28)

bully (boy) [*bully (boyee)*] admirable, capable, or dashing man

"Now then, me **bullies**, would you rather do the gallows dance and hang in chains till the crows pick your eyes from your rotting skulls, or would you feel the roll of a stout ship beneath your feet again?" (William Kidd, recruiting a crew from among condemned prisoners, "Captain Kidd" 16:19) 92) "So fight, **bully boys**, fight for a chance o' life and happy days— here stand I to fight wi' you and Diccon 'twixt decks and Captain Jo everywhere." (Resolution Day, *Martin Conisby's Vengeance* 111)

camarado (mio) [*carrm-eerah/eerarr/errah/ errarr/'rah/'rarr-do'oo (mio'oo)*] (my) comrade; (my) colleague

"Camarado" and "mio" are Spanish for "comrade" and "my," respectively. Both connote familiarity with, affection for, or amiability toward the person so described.

"Aha, and are ye there, **camarado**! 'Tis well, for I am a-seeking ye." (Resolution Day, *Martin Conisby's Vengeance* 88) "So, Ben, **camarado mio**, we be committed to it now!" (Roger Tressady to his comrade Ben, after the two slaughter four members of their own company, *Black Bartlemy's Treasure* 90)

cock [*carrk*]
cockerel [*carrk-'rel*] fine young man

"Cock" literally means "rooster" ("cockerel" is "young rooster") and is used figuratively to refer to a man (or young man) notable for boldness, arrogance, or pugnacity, or more broadly as an aggrandizing term used to refer to any male, in the same way the modern speaker might refer to a man as "chief" or "big guy."

"I always wanted you to jine and take your share, and die a gentleman, and now, my **cock**, you've got to." (Long John Silver, *Treasure Island* 156, Chap. 28) "Is that the kind of **cockerel** ye are, Master Ormerod or whatever ye may be called?" (John Flint, *Porto Bello Gold* 132)

comrade [*carrm-rayeede*] friend; colleague; companion

Used typically to refer to a fellow member of one's company or crew.

"Easy all, brother! Soft it is, **comrade**!" (Resolution Day, urging Martin Conisby to stay quiet as he unfastens his restraints, *Martin Conisby's Vengeance* 78)

cove [*co'oove*] guy; dude; fellow

"Well done, lad! you're a brick, and I have no doubt will turn out a rare **cove**." (pirate, lauding fifteen-year-old Ralph Rover for his aggressive boldness, *The Coral Island* 202)

cull(y) [*cull(y)*] friend; companion

Used in the same way as the modern speaker might use "pal" or "buddy"—that is, to refer to another in an amiable manner, regardless of the actual existence or depth of any familiarity or friendship between the speaker and the person so described.

"And look'ee, my dainty **cull**, when you've seen as much o' death as Abnegation Mings you'll know as Death's none so bad a thing, so long as it leaves you alone." (Abnegation Mings, *Black Bartlemy's Treasure* 31) "His throat, **cully**—quick's the word!" (black-eyed pirate, *Black Bartlemy's Treasure* 127)

cutthroat [*carrt/cooht-thro'oot*] evil or dangerous person; villain; killer

"You're big enough and wild enough and as likely a **cut-throat** as another—what's the lay?" (Abnegation Mings, *Black Bartlemy's Treasure* 30)

fellow [*faahl-owoo*] guy; dude

A reference to a person that, while itself neutral, is very often used in conjunction with adjectives of praise or other modifiers positively characterizing the person described.

"I proposed to our men to remove ourselves and all our goods into the great ship and the sloop, and so take the honest **fellows** into the frigate ..." (Captain Avery, *The King of Pirates* 26)

fire-eater [*farr/fyarr-ea'er/etter*] tough and dangerous person

Used to refer to someone well-acquainted with—and hardened by exposure to or immersion in—fight, death, and danger.

"He'll take a lot for a sizzlin', gut-cuttin' **fire-eater**." (Long John Silver, *Porto Bello Gold* 49)

friend [*fraynd/frien'*]

"My sympathies, **friend**—you've no manner of luck at all!" (unnamed pirate escaping from prison, *Pirates of the Caribbean* 35:41)

gent [*jant*]

A jaunty, familiar term.

"**Gents**, you all remember Captain Jack Sparrow." (Barbossa, "Pirates of the Caribbean: The Curse of the Black Pearl" 1:17:01)

gentleman [*jan-'leman*]

Used to convey polite respect or deference to the person so characterized.

"Ay, and 'twill be noble venture besides, —to save from the hell o' slavery divers goodly **gentlemen**, poor souls and woeful prisoners, bound for the plantations." (Absalom Troy, *Adam Penfeather, Buccaneer* 12)

great rogue [*grayeet/grea'/grett roo/ro'oo-guel*] good guy; terrific son of a gun

A phrase of condemnation used in the rough, hard-bitten way of pirates to praise or characterize favorably, just as the modern phrase "son of a bitch" is more often used in a negative sense ("That son of a bitch stole my car") but occasionally in a positive one ("That Tiger Woods is the most talented son of a bitch I've ever seen").

> *And he gave in for evidence, that the prisoner [John Walden] was looked on as a brisk hand (*i.e.*, as he farther explained it, a stanch pyrate, a **great rogue**) ...*

hands [*'ands/'an's/han's*] members of a vessel's crew

The term is not used in the singular form to address another (*i.e.*, "hand, go aloft!"), only in the plural ("hands, go aloft!").

> "**Hands**, stand ready to come about!" (Thomas Marlowe, *The Guardship* 278)

hearty [*'ahrrt/'eart/hahrrt-y*] good fellow; comrade

> "**Hearties** all, the moon sinketh apace and 'twill be ill shooting for 'em i' the dark, so with dark 'tis us for the boats— muffled oars—we clap 'em aboard by the forechains larboard and starboard, and the ship is ours, bullies—ours!" (Roger Tressady, *Black Bartlemy's Treasure* 314)

hell-hound [*'ell-houn'/hount/howoon'/howoond/howoont/'ound/'owoond/'owoont*] fierce, violent, or dangerous person

> *[O]ne of the **hell-hounds** asked if he had rather take a leap like a brave fellow, or to be toss'd over like a sneaking rascal.* (attribution to pirate in William Fly's company, *General History of the Pyrates* 607–8)

jolly dog [*jarrly dahg/darrg/dorrg*] good guy

> "We be three lorn mariners, d'ye see—**jolly dogs**, bully boys, shipmate—a little fun wi' a pretty lass—nought to harm d'ye see, sink me!" (one-eared pirate, *Black Bartlemy's Treasure* 22)

lad [*lad*]

(1) any male person

> < "You're back, right?" "That be about the measure of it, **lad**." > (Steve Walker & Blackbeard, "Blackbeard's Ghost" 30:00)

(2) boy; male child

> "Here, what's gotten into 'ee, **lad**?" (Long John Silver, to Jim Hawkins, who has cried out at the dinner table upon been kicked in the shin by Algy Harwood, "The Adventures of Long John Silver: Dead Reckoning" 8:35)

(3) fellow member of one's company or crew

> "All right, **lads**, quiet now. Quiet. Listen to your captain." (Ned Lynch, "Swashbuckler" 28:04)

laddy [*lah'y*] (1) any male person (2) boy; male child

> "D'ye think I'm joshin' ye, now, **laddy**?" (Billy Doyle, threatening to kill his women prisoners if Alan Lewrie attacks, *The Gun Ketch* 161)

lamb [*larrmb/lemm*]

Used to refer sarcastically, and usually approvingly or admiringly, to someone rough, powerful, or dangerous.

> "Martin, 'twill be a plaguy business carrying women aboard ship—along o' these **lambs** o' mine—there's scarce a rogue but cheats the gallows with his every breath!" (Adam Penfeather, *Black Bartlemy's Treasure* 108)

little master [*lil' marrster*]

Used to refer familiarly or affectionately to a young man or boy.

> "Now, this here's a grog shop, **little master**. Looking for a dram, ey?" (Long John Silver, on seeing Jim Hawkins for the first time, "Treasure Island" [1972] 23:55)

mackie [*marrkie*] man; dude

"Mack," variously meaning "pimp" or "fellow," has a more familiar (for use with friends or persons toward whom the speaker wishes to convey amiability or affection) or diminutive (for use in referring to a young man or boy) version in the word "mackie."

> "It's m' old sea chest they're after, **mackie**." (Billy Bones, "Treasure Island" [1990] 13:23)

man

> "**Man**, ye'll never leave Tortuga alive." (Peter Blood, *Captain Blood Returns* 152) "If that's their last word, my **man**, they can up anchor and away to the Devil." (Captain Easterling, *Captain Blood Returns* 285)

man of spirit [*man o'\on sperrit/sp'rit*] man of notable courage or determination

> "There's a **man of spirit**, and one of my own kidney, and he's going to make a very pretty death of it!" (John Sharkey, *The Dealings of Captain Sharkey and Other Tales of Pirates* "How the Governor of Saint Kitt's Came Home" 22)

master [*marrster*]

Used to address a male person with polite respect or deference.

> "Howsoever, come life or death, here's Abnegation doth wish ye a fair wind ever and always, **master**." (Abnegation Mings, *Black Bartlemy's Treasure* 319)

mate [*mayeete*]
matey [*ma'ey*] friend; pal; buddy

> "You need to find yourself a girl, **mate**." (Jack Sparrow, "Pirates of the Caribbean: The Curse of the Black Pearl" 24:45) "Jim, you'll bring me one noggin of rum, now, won't you, **matey**?" (Billy Bones, *Treasure Island* 14, Chap. 3)

mate o' mine [*mayeete o'\on mawn/myeene*] my friend; my pal

> "How now, **mate o' mine**, shall dog bite dog then?" (eye-patch wearing pirate to Martin Conisby as Conisby holds him and his comrades at pistol-point, *Black Bartlemy's Treasure* 22)

mates [*mayeetes*] fellow members of one's company or crew

> "Map or no map, we ain't givin' up no 'ostage till we lays hands on the treasure itself. Am I right, **mates**?" (George Merry, "Treasure Island" [1950] 1:20:18)

men [*men*]

Used to address fellow members of one's company or crew.

> "My **men**! you demand justice, and you shall have it." (Cain, *The Pirate* III, Chap. XV)

messmate [*mass-mayeete*] friend; pal

A term implying warm familiarity and especially close acquaintance between the speaker and the addressee. While the term "shipmate" literally refers to anyone in the same company or crew, "messmate" literally refers to one with whom the speaker regularly chooses to share his meals. The figurative use of the term is correspondingly more familiar.

> "Will you taste, **messmate**? Well, I'll take a drain myself, Jim.'" (Long John Silver, offering Jim Hawkins cognac, *Treasure Island* 161, Chap. 28)

monkey [*marrn/moohn-key*] member of a vessel's crew responsible for ascending into a ship's rigging and adjusting its sails; topman

> "Up that rigging, you **monkeys**! Aloft!" (Peter Blood, making preparations to sail out of Port Royal aboard the *Cinco Llagas*, "Captain Blood" 1:01:40)

my NAME [*me/myee ...*]

As it does when used with conventional, nonproper nouns of respectful address, the term "my" here connotes familiarity with, affection for, or amiability toward the person described.

> < "Now if you mean our hellish rogues, these imps o' Satan and spawn o' the devil, our rascal crew, —eh Adam?" "Ay, ay, **my Benjamin**." > (Benjamin Trigg & Adam Penfeather, *Adam Penfeather, Buccaneer* 224)

old lad [ol'/oold/o'oold lad]

A term connoting fond familiarity and close acquaintance or friendship between the speaker and the man so described.

> < "But a sick man cannot give orders. Henceforth you should be Captain, for he is at present no more than our poor invalid." "'S heart! How sayst thou to this, Japhet, **old lad**?" > (Ursula Revell & Barnabas Rokeby, *Winds of Chance* 87)

pigtail [peg-tayell] veteran seaman

Men at sea, without access to a neighborhood barber, grew their hair long and, to keep it out of their eyes (unobstructed sight was at a premium on windy days when scaling a vessel's rigging and performing intricate tasks dexterously and efficiently were urgent matters), braided and tarred it into a single pigtail. The term "pigtail" is accordingly used in reference to any seasoned sailor.

> "Howbeit, lass, what with climbing mountains, swimming rivers and what not, ye shall presently get you such legs they shall bear you well as mine own: ay, and once aboard the *Deliverance*, you shall run up the weather rigging in gale o' wind, speedy and sure as any tarry **pigtail**—" (Japhet Bly, *Winds of Chance* 153)

roarer [rarrer] dashing man; vigorous fellow

Literally meaning a loud or noisy person, especially one creating a public disturbance of some kind, the term is used figuratively to refer to a dynamic individual.

> "Well so, my bully **roarer**, and what now?" (one-eared pirate, *Black Bartlemy's Treasure* 22)

rogue [roo/ro'oo-gue]

Used ironically to convey affection for, familiarity with, joviality to, or mock condemnation of the person addressed.

> "You old **rogue**. Ye play upon my vanity, do you?" (Peter Blood, *Captain Blood: His Odyssey* 199)

rooster [rooshter] fine young man

Used to refer to a man, especially a young one, notable for boldness, arrogance, or pugnacity, or more broadly as an aggrandizing term used to refer to any male, in the same way the modern speaker might refer to a man as "chief" or "big guy."

> "This young **rooster**, my good friend, he played a modest part in your delivery from disaster." (Blackbeard, "Blackbeard's Ghost" 1:42:42)

sailorman [saah/sayee/sayor-larr/lee-man] seaman

> < "Well, how say you, friend, will ye sail with me?" "With you, yet who beside?" "Certain lusty fellows, well chosen and prime **sailormen** all ..." > (Absalom Troy & Adam Penfeather, *Adam Penfeather, Buccaneer* 12)

sea dog [sea-dahg/darrg/dorrg] veteran seaman; seasoned sailor

> "To it, lads ... at 'em, old **seadogs**, point and edge ... sa-ha!" (Absalom Troy, *Adam Penfeather, Buccaneer* 129)

shipmate [shep/shi'-mayeete] friend

Often used as a term of mild condescension or deliberate over-politeness.

> < "Some wine? Far better. Will you have white or red?" "Well, I reckon it's about the blessed same to me, **shipmate**, so it's strong, and plenty of it, what's the odds?" > (Jim Hawkins & Israel Hands, *Treasure Island* 140, Chap. 26)

son of a gun [sonva OR soohn o'\on a garrn/goohn]

A term used in modern English, but nevertheless worth noting as a figure of pirate speech for its nautical, albeit mythical, origins. Seafaring men (pirates and honest sailors alike) visited with women—occasionally wives, more often women of a less permanent relation—aboard their own vessels, such that a woman giving birth to a male infant on the vessel's gun deck might be said to have borne a "son of a gun." Consequently, the phrase "son of a gun" is technically a disparaging comment on one's parentage (that is, the oblique equivalent of "son of a whore"), but is used as a benign, colorful, and fundamentally amiable term of address.

> "You ol' **son of a gun**." (Ned Shill, "Long John Silver's Return to Treasure Island" 1:41:42)

son of a sea dog [*sonva* OR *soohn o'\on a sea dahg/darrg/dorrg*]

A term of mild and often affectionate derision, as in the phrase "son of a gun."

> "You are a **son of a sea dog**." (Long John Silver, "Treasure Island" [1998] 1:28:01)

son of a Yorkshire steer [*sonva* OR *soohn o'\on a 'ork/Yarrk/Yor'-sharr/sherr stee-arr/err*] big guy

> < "Didn't I tell you I was a gunner, sir?" "You did that, you **son of a Yorkshire steer**!" > (Henry Hagthorpe & Peter Blood, "Captain Blood" 56:48)

sonny [*soohnny*] young man; boy

> < "What might I get for you, sir?" "Rum, **sonny**. Rum'll do." > (Jim Hawkins & Black Dog, "Treasure Island" [1990] 8:00)

tar [*tahrr*]

tarry-breeks [*taah/tay-ry breeks*] seaman, especially a seasoned one

The term "tar" is traditionally associated with sailors and sailing vessels as a result of tar's long-time use in coating rope lines to protect them from the disintegrating effects of seawater and sunlight.

"Hearts of oak are our ships/Jolly **tars** are our men." (song sung by Blackbeard, "Blackbeard's Ghost" 1:26:14) "Flint had the secret of it from a **tarry-breeks** who claimed to have sailed on the *Adventure* galley." (Andrew Murray, *Porto Bello Gold* 104)

wildcat [*wawld/wil'-ket*] (1) person of fierce determination or dynamic resourcefulness; person not easily restrained or defeated (2) dangerous person, especially one who threatens danger in an irrational or unpredictable manner

> < "Captain Silver, where's the French lieutenant?" "He escaped! He's a **wildcat**!" > (guard sergeant & Long John Silver, "The Adventures of Long John Silver: Turnabout" 23:14)

youngster [*yarrng/yoohng/yun'-ster*]

> "Now, go, make a fire on that point; and hark'ee, **youngster**, if you try to run away, I'll send a quick and sure messenger after you." (pirate, brandishing his gun, *The Coral Island* 196) "Now then, do you hear, **youngster**? the captain wants you." (Bloody Bill, *The Coral Island* 204)

your honour [*ya/yarr/ye/yer/yere/yore hon-ry*]
Used to refer to another with conspicuous respect or deference.

> < "You are Samuel Morris, I think?" "That same, **your honour**." > (Adam Penfeather & Sam Morris, *Adam Penfeather, Buccaneer* 215)

CHAPTER 11

Retorts

The cruelest pirate that ever lived took up piracy because he lacked a command of retorts.

Edward Low left Boston in 1719 after losing both his wife (who died after giving birth to a daughter) and his job. He shipped aboard a sloop headed for the Bay of Honduras. Once there, he was put in charge of the boat crew, responsible for loading and unloading logwood and shuttling between sloop and shore.

One day, Low and his hard-laboring men arrived at the sloop with a loaded boat just before dinner time. They were hungry, and wanted to stay and eat. The captain told them to make one more run to shore, and ordered a bottle of rum for them instead.

Low's response was, let us say, firm. He fired a musket at the captain, but missed, instead shooting a sailor in the head. Low and his twelve-man boat crew immediately fled. Taking their first vessel the very next day, their turn to piracy was as quick as Low's trigger finger. (*General History of the Pyrates* 318–19; *Pirates of the New England Coast* 141–43)

One wonders how Low's life—let alone merchant shipping in the Caribbean and Atlantic in the early eighteenth century—might have played out had he set aside his musket in favor of a verbal response like "Don't give me that bilge" or "I do my possible, which that ain't" or "What daftness be this?"

This chapter introduces available retorts to insults and epithets; retorts used to express surprise, ridicule, indignation, or agreement; and all-purpose responses. Direct replies—both affirmative and negative—to questions and requests are covered in Chapter 12: Questions & Replies.

There are, of course, infinite numbers of ways to reply to a comment, including reciprocation (answering an insult or epithet with an insult or epithet of one's own), escalation (answering an insult or epithet with a threat or curse), and spicing any answer with an oath.

However, there are certain retorts that are sufficiently routine in pirate speech (and sufficiently unusual in modern English) that they merit special attention. Some afford the respondent a challenging, dismissive air, while permitting him to stall for time and prepare a more substantive retort. Others permit him to endorse or concur with what someone else has just said. All of these are listed below.

Note that every command meaning "shut up" or "quiet"—such as "belay," "cease your chattering," or "stint your clack"—is a potentially appropriate retort to any comment. Those terms are listed and explained in Chapter 4: Commands.

Note also that any curse works as a sharp, dismissive, unyielding retort: < "Do you surrender to me now, you bastard?" "**Devil take ye**!" > (Alan Lewrie & Billy Doyle, *The Gun Ketch* 164). See Chapter 7 for a list of curses.

Finally, one can use nearly all of the Affirmative Replies listed in section 12.2 as a retort—that is, not simply to reply affirmatively to another's question, but also as an affirmation used to agree with another's statement.

SUBJECT+VERB, VERB+SUBJECT?

The speaker repeats the subject (or equivalent pronoun) and verb (or the equivalent form of "do") of the statement being responded to, then reverses them to form a question.

> < "The man tried to horsewhip me." "Oh, **he did, did he?**" > (Jim Hawkins & Long John Silver, "The Adventures of Long John Silver: The Eviction" 5:19)

ain't you the ADJECTIVE one? [*aren't/b'ain't/ben't/hain't/i'n't/isn't 'ee/ya/ye/yer t' ... 'un/woohn?*]

Used with an adjective that mocks the addressee—depicting him, for example, as foolish, ridiculous, extreme, or unreasonable—and usually in connection with a statement he has made or an action he has taken.

> < "Son of a double Dutchman! Son of a double Dutchman!" "Belay! **Ain't you the pretty one**. Swearin' blue fire in front of a gentleman." > (Cap'n Flint & Long John Silver, with Silver castigating his parrot for its penchant for profanity, "Treasure Island" [1950] 21:41)

__ am I? [*__ arrm/em\be I'ee?*]

Used in response to an insult or epithet, or some other unfavorable comment about the speaker. The speaker repeats the objectionable term, then adds "am I?"

> < "Yer daft, Morley!" "**Daft, am I?**" > (Dick Walpole & Morley Rowe, *Dead Man's Chest* 248)

and VERB+SUBJECT so? [*an'/'n' ... so'oo?*]

The speaker repeats, between "and" and "so," the subject and verb of the statement to which she responds. Thus, the retort to "Wynn'll use yer skin fer a sack when 'ee's done with 'ee" is, "And will he so?"

> < "I pray God utterly destroy this accursed ship and all aboard her!" "**And do ye so?**" > (Martin Conisby & Resolution Day, *Martin Conisby's Vengeance* 104)

and willing [*an'/'n' a-well-in'*]

Used in response to a threat or some otherwise unpleasant or discouraging statement. By responding with "and willing," the speaker claims that, far from displeasing him, the statement he has just heard is consistent with his own preferences. The speaker thereby conveys defiance and bold invitation. Rough modern equivalents might include "That's fine with me" and "Sounds good to me."

> < "Belvedere be our Cap'n—we want Belvedere!" "Why then, take him, bullies, take him **and willing!**" > (pirates aboard the *Happy Despatch* & Resolution Day, with Resolution heaving Captain Belvedere's corpse onto the lower deck, *Martin Conisby's Vengeance* 111)

as I say [*as I'ee sayee*]

Used to simply re-assert what a speaker has said before, usually in response to a challenge or retort by the addressee that merits no acknowledgment.

> < "And I have been expecting you ever since I anchored and no sign of you until now." "Expecting me? Ha, the devil you have!" "**As I say,** sir." > (Adam Penfeather & Black Bartlemy, *Adam Penfeather, Buccaneer* 321)

as is well [*as be waahl*] that's good; that's the way it should be

> < "Where's your mother, boy?" "She's not here. She's in the village, at the market." "**As is well.**" > (Jim Hawkins & Black Dog, "Treasure Island" [1990] 8:45)

bah [*barr*]

Used to express dismissiveness ("yeah, right," "please"); incredulity ("nonsense," "bullshit"); indifference ("whatever," "it doesn't matter"); or contempt.

> < "Barrett's dead." "How do you know?" "Last I heard, his men killed him. I ain't heard another word about him in three years. If he was around, I'd know." "**Bah!** He is not dead." > (Ezekiel Ripley & Le-Rois, *The Guardship* 131)

be this a jest? [*be dis/t'is a jast/jayst?*] are you joking?; is this some kind of joke?

> "Here, **be this a jest?**" (Long John Silver, to the Governor's soldiers as they march into the Cask & Anchor and seize Silver's diamond necklace, "The

Adventures of Long John Silver: The Necklace" 10:13)

be you out of your head? [*be 'ee/ya/ye/yer arrt/ou'/owoot o'\on ya/yarr/ye/yer/yere/yore 'ead/hayd?*] are you out of your mind?; are you crazy?

> "Here, **be you out of your head?** He'll put out to sea!" (Blackbeard, "Blackbeard the Pirate" 52:54)

curse your prating insolence [*carrse/carrst/ coorse/cursh/curst ya/yarr/ye/yer/yere/yore prayee-tin' en-ser/so'oo-laahnce*]

Suitable for use in response to nearly any objectionable statement, but especially one in which the addressee has said something annoyingly inappropriate, and particularly something beyond his competence or station, such that he might relevantly be accused of "insolence."

> < "You, being once a gentleman, should know better than affront so basely one so helpless, and this I will permit by no means." "Permit? Now **curse your prating insolence** ..." > (Adam Penfeather & Absalom Troy, *Adam Penfeather, Buccaneer* 110)

damme, but VERB + SUBJECT so? [*damn, barrt ... so'oo?*]

Used for a mocking, jeering effect. The speaker repeats, between "damme, but" and "so," the subject and verb of the statement to which she responds. Thus, the retort to "Wynn'll use yer skin fer a sack when 'ee's done with 'ee" is, "Damme, but will he so?"

> < "I liked you better in your grime and shackles!" "Eh! Now **damme, but did ye so,** Tony?" > (Antonia Chievely & Absalom Troy, *Adam Penfeather, Buccaneer* 107)

dare you say it? [*darr/dayarr/dayerr 'ee/ya/ ye/yer sayee ett/'n/'t?*]

This retort is actually an indirect threat, suggesting the addressee has imperiled himself by saying what he has just said.

> < "[Y]ou thing shaped like a man, must ye cringe at the word 'love'?" "Aye! On

your lips 'tis desecration!" "Desecration—desecration? Ha, **dare ye say it, dog?**" > (Captain Jo & Martin Conisby, *Martin Conisby's Vengeance* 29–30)

the devil SUBJECT+VERB [*t' daahv/dayv/ debb/div-il* ...]

A way of categorically contradicting some proposition. The speaker responds with "the devil," then either repeats the verb in the statement being responded to, or an equivalent form of "do." Thus, the retort to "They scaled the walls of that fort three years agone" is, "The devil they did."

> < "And I have been expecting you ever since I anchored and no sign of you until now." "Expecting me? Ha, **the devil you have!**" > (Adam Penfeather & Black Bartlemy, *Adam Penfeather, Buccaneer* 321)

do I offend? [*d' I'ee arr-fand/fen'?*]

An appropriate retort where the addressee has expressed some annoyance or displeasure with the speaker.

> "**Do I offend?** Ah, prithee, why art grown so strange to me?" (Captain Jo, probing the reasons for Conisby's increasingly morose disposition, *Martin Conisby's Vengeance* 169)

don't give me that bilge [*don'/doon't/dorrn't gi'/giff me tharrt belge*] don't give me that crap; don't give me that garbage

> < "Tell ya what. If me crew agrees, and mind ya they're not ..." "**Don't give me that bilge!** Your crew does exactly what you say, ever since the Turk was killed two winters ago!" > (Henry Morgan, *Dead Man's Chest* 158)

(and) don't you forget 'n [(*an'/'n*) *don'/ doon't/dorrn't 'ee/ya/ye/yer farr/fer-git ett*]

> < "My revenge is sweeter than betraying you." "Arrgh, and **don't you forget 'n.**" > (Salamander the Greek & Long John Silver, "The Adventures of Long John Silver: Pieces of Eight" 4:26)

do you dare ...? [*d'/does 'ee/ya/ye/yer darr/ dayarr/dayerr ...?*] how dare you ...?

> "Ye mangy hound, **d'ye dare** come to me with such proposals?" (Peter Blood, *Captain Blood: His Odyssey* 310)

do you play with me? [*d'/does 'ee/ya/ye/yer playee weth/wi'/wiff/witt me?*]

An all-purpose retort. It can be said coolly with arched brow to suggest menacingly, or hotly with furrowed brow to protest angrily, that the addressee has said something inappropriate, offended the speaker, or otherwise gone too far.

> < "I can say nothing until I have taken the wishes of my followers." "Oh, s'death! **Do you play with us?**" > (Peter Blood & Captain Easterling, *Captain Blood Returns* 31)

__ do you say? [__ *d'/does 'ee/ya/ye/yer say- ee?*]

The speaker throws back the key word in another's statement and follows it with "do you say?" Thus, the retort to "Wynn'll use yer skin fer a sack when 'ee's done with 'ee" is, "Sack, do you say?"

> < "No, I do but make him so able in his own defence that none shall affront him with impunity." "Oho! **Affront, d'ye say?**" > (Adam Penfeather & Absalom Troy, *Adam Penfeather, Buccaneer* 101)

do you say so? [*d'/does 'ee/ya/ye/yer sayee so'oo?*] you think so?; is that what you think?

> < "I heard tell of it last night in a cave from a sailor-man." "How? A sailor-man—hereabouts?" "Damme! the country seems thick o' sailor-men." "Ha! **D'ye say so?** And what like was this one?" > (Martin Conisby & Adam Penfeather, *Black Bartlemy's Treasure* 61)

do you think I ain't heard of nothing? [*d'/ does 'ee/ya/ye/yer fink/thenk/t'ink I'ee bain't/ ben't/hain't/ha'n't 'arrd/'eard/harrd o'\on nuff/ nutt-in'?*] do you think I'm stupid?; do you think I was born yesterday?

"Err, **do you think I ain't heard of noth-in'?**" (Blackbeard, "Blackbeard the Pi-rate" 11:58)

do you threaten? [*d'/does 'ee/ya/ye/yer thrat/thray-ten?*]

Used in response to a threat, or to any statement that could be so interpreted.

< "It'll be the worse for you, Captain, if they go." "**D'ye threaten**, by God!" > (Crosby Pike & Captain Easterling, *Captain Blood Returns* 285)

enough (of this) [*enarrff/enow/'nough (o'\on dis/t'is)*] that's enough

< "Would to God—" "**Enough!** you shall accompany your friend." > (Mrs. Wyl-lys & The Red Rover, *The Red Rover* 455) < "Indeed, and there's the pity of it, for this poor wretch might be a great earl and man truly noble." "**Enough o' this**, ma'm. Say no more ..." > (Ursula Revell & Japhet Bly, *Winds of Chance* 251)

explain your meaning [*es/iks-playeen ya/yarr/ye/yer/yere/yore meanin'*] what do you mean?

< "[S]he would have fared but badly in her own navigation." "**Explain your mean-ing.**" > (Richard Fid & The Red Rover, *The Red Rover* 391)

flatterer [*flarrt/flatt-erarr/'rarr/'rer*]

Used in response to an insult or epithet. The speaker pretends that the disparaging remark is actually a compliment, thus remov-ing its sting and suggesting a smug immunity to any attempt at offense.

< "You cold-gutted shark." "Ah, **flatterer.**" > (Orange Povy & William Kidd, "Captain Kidd" 23:17)

from any other man these were fighting words [*ferm a'y o'er/udder man dese/t'ese warr fawt/figh'-in' warrds*]

"Fighting words," of course, are words so offensive as to require or justify a violent re-sponse. The retort is accordingly used where

such offense has been given, but where the addressee is spared the ugly consequence because of his identity or special relation-ship with the speaker. Note, however, the mischievous possibilities: One might respond with "From any other man this were a fighting word," encouraging the addressee to think all's well, then take a surprising turn with something like "But from you it's a killin' word, bein' as how bilge rats can't fight."

< "Liar! Liar!" "Peace, brother, peace! **From any other man this were a fighting word**, but as it is, let us reason together, brother!" > (Martin Conisby & Resolution Day, *Martin Conisby's Vengeance* 168)

ha [*harr*] indeed; yeah, right

< "D'ye know aught of navigation, Mar-tin?" "No whit, Adam, but I'll handle a boat with any man." "**Ha!**" > (Adam Pen-feather & Martin Conisby, *Black Bartlemy's Treasure* 109)

have done [*'aff/'ave/ha'/haff doohn*] enough; that's enough; stop that

< "[T]he Lord hath set you here i' this flowery garden like Adam and her like Eve—" "And yourself like the serpent!" "**Ha' done**, Martin, **ha' done!** 'The Lord shall root out deceitful lips and the tongue that speaks proud things!' mark that!" > (Resolution Day & Martin Conis-by, *Martin Conisby's Vengeance* 168)

have you done? [*'aff/'ave/ha'/haff 'ee/ye/ya/yer doohn?*] are you finished speaking?

Thinking two steps ahead, should the speaker say "Have you done?" and the ad-dressee respond "No, I have not," the speaker might further retort "Then spare me the rest" (as Peter Blood does immediately following the exchange excerpted below).

< "Your fool letter it have seal' the doom of us all." "**Have ye done?**" > (Cahusac & Pe-ter Blood, *Captain Blood: His Odyssey* 197)

have you gone daft? ['*aff*/'*ave*/*ha*'/*haff* '*ee*/ *ya*/*ye*/*yer garrn daff*/*darrft*/*deft?*] have you gone crazy?; have you lost your mind?

> < "You and your evil ways, caring not for law and order, rippin' and cuttin', and layin' his hands to anything that belongs not to him. Where else could it end?" **"Have you gone daft?"** > (Purity Pinker & Long John Silver, "The Adventures of Long John Silver: Dead Reckoning" 3:42)

the hell you say [*t*' '*ell* '*ee*/*ya*/*ye*/*yer sayee*] what?!; what the hell are you saying?

> < "Them ain't our men, Govn'r! The bonfires belong to the *Cloud*'s men." **"The hell you say!"** > (Joshua Smoot, *Dead Man's Chest* 225)

here's paltry invention ['*ee*'*arr*/'*ee*'*err*/'*ere*/ *hee*'*arr*/*hee*'*err is**be pawrltry en-vaahn*/*vaynshern*/*shoohn*] that's a lie

> < "Look you, Mossoo, this fellow here, this Blood, this doctor, this escaped convict, made believe that he would enter into articles with us so as to get from me the secret of Morgan's treasure. Now that he's got it, he makes difficulties about the articles ..." "Why, **here's paltry invention!**" > (Captain Easterling & Peter Blood, *Captain Blood Returns* 32–33)

here's unchancy talk, ill and unmannered ['*ee*'*arr*/'*ee*'*err*/'*ere*/*hee*'*arr*/*hee*'*err is**be arrn*/ *hun*/*oohn-charrncy tarrk, ee*'*ull an*'/'*n*' *arrn*/ *hun*/*oohn-mannert*/*maynerd*/*maynert*]

A great example of a retort that takes the high road, comparable to modern retorts like "That's uncalled for" or "I won't reduce myself to your level." The best part is the reference to "unmannered," which—coming from the typical rum-belching, blood-soaked pirate—is patently ridiculous.

> < "What's your quarrel lad, what?" "Quarrel enough, what with your drugging me and murder aboard ship—" "Avast, lad! **Here's unchancy talk, ill and unman-**

nered!" > [Roger Tressady & Martin Conisby, *Black Bartlemy's Treasure* 302)

hum [*harrm*/*hoohm*] humph

A dismissive expression of annoyance, spite, incredulity, or indignation.

> < "[I]f you are to load at this port, it will be some days before you put to sea." **"Hum!** I don't think we shall be long after our neighbor." > (Harry Wilder & officer aboard the *Dolphin*, *The Red Rover* 87)

I admire your spirit much more than your discretion [*I*'*ee a*'/*erd-marr*/*myarr ya*/*yarr*/*ye*/ *yer*/*yere*/*yore sperrit*/*sp*'*rit marrch*/*moohch marr*/ *moor* '*n*/*thayn**nor ya*/*yarr*/*ye*/*yer*/*yere*/*yore dee*/ *der-scraah*/*scray-shern*/*shoohn*]

An appropriate response to any statement so bold or assertive as to be arguably foolhardy.

> < "If it is to be a slave, and, like one of the bolts, a fixture in the vessel, that you need me, our bargain is at an end." "Hum! **I admire your spirit, sir, much more than your discretion.**" > (Harry Wilder & The Red Rover, *The Red Rover* 104)

I begs to differ [*I*'*ee bags t*'/*ta*/*ter deffer*/*diffy*]

Used to express disagreement with or objection to a statement.

> < "With all the hemming and hawing that goes on, you'd think there wasn't an honest seaman to be had in Bristol." **"I begs to differ,** sir." > (Squire Trelawney & Long John Silver, "Treasure Island" [1950] 18:38)

I do my possible, which that ain't [*I*'*ee d*'/*does me*/*myee poss*'/*posser-ble, whech tharrt aren*'*t*/*b*'*ain*'*t*/*ben*'*t*/*hain*'*t*/*i*'*n*'*t*/*isn*'*t*] I can't do that; that's out of the question

> < "Silver!—I'll give you a piece of advice, don't you be in any great hurry after that treasure." "Why, sir, **I do my possible, which that ain't.**" > (Doctor Livesey & Long John Silver, *Treasure Island* 172, Chap. 30)

I don't care a louse [*I'ee don'/doon't/dorrnt carr/cayarr/cayerr a lowoose*] I don't care one bit; I don't give a crap

> "For **I don't care a louse** what may happen to the blackguard, and I'm not by nature a vindictive man." (Peter Blood, *The Fortunes of Captain Blood* 168)

I don't know so much [*I'ee don'/doon't/dorrnt knowoo so'oo marrch/moohch*] I don't know about that; I wouldn't go that far

Used in response to a compliment or statement of praise which the speaker wishes to wave off modestly, a statement more extreme than the speaker thinks accurate, or any other kind of statement with which the speaker does not quite agree.

> < "How silly of him." "**I don't know so much!** He wasn't too far wrong!" > (Edward & Otto, *A High Wind in Jamaica* 124)

I fear not [*I'ee fee-arr/err narrt*] I don't think so; I think not

> < "Surely I know the advantages of my native country." "**I fear not.**" > (Harry Wilder & The Red Rover, *The Red Rover* 355)

I __ for no man, few women, and take orders from neither [*I'ee __ farr/fer no'oo man, foo womern/wom'n, an'/'n tayeeke arrders ferm needer/nee'er/nyder/ny'er*]

Used to respond defiantly to a command. The speaker fills in the blank with a verb corresponding to some action or behavior he is unwilling to undertake.

> < "Sir, you may now remove yourself." "Anon, sir, anon. **I hurry myself for no man, few women, and take orders from neither.**" > (Adam Penfeather & Black Bartlemy, *Adam Penfeather, Buccaneer* 254)

I know not [*I'ee knowoo narrt*] I don't know about that

> < "You would forfeit the good opinions of knaves, to gain a reputation among those whose commendations are an honour."

"**I know not.**" > (Harry Wilder & The Red Rover, *The Red Rover* 354)

I see it not [*I'ee see ett/'n/'t narrt*] I don't agree; I see it differently; I don't understand it

> < "Gut me, but ye bargain like a Jew, Murray!" "And like a Jew I pay well and surely, offering good security." "**I see it not.**" > (John Flint & Andrew Murray, *Porto Bello Gold* 93)

I'll choke those words down your throat [*I'ee'ull chooke/cho'ooke dose/t'ose\dem/'em/them\dey/they warrds dowoon ya/yarr/ye/yer/yere/yore thro'oot*]

A threat that doubles as a concise retort to any unpleasantry.

> < "You're a wily bird, Silver. But this time you've overreached yourself. The harbormaster has reported to me concerning your interest in the *Rachel*, and your use of the boy in whatever scheme you're planning." "If you weren't the Governor of Porto Bello, **I'd choke those words down your throat.**" > (Governor Strong & Long John Silver, "The Adventures of Long John Silver: Ship o' the Dead" 8:09)

I'm captain here [*I'eem cap'n 'ee'arr/'ee'err/'ere/hee'arr/hee'err*]

A pirate captain's retort to any impudent, presumptuous, or overbold statement by a member of his company.

> < "We'll destroy them all if it takes the life of every last man aboard this ship." "'Ere, hold fast, **I'm Cap'n 'ere!**" > (Richard Thorpe & Long John Silver, "The Adventures of Long John Silver: The Pink Pearl" 17:29)

I'm damned if I do [*I'eem damt an'\eff/eff'n/if'n I'ee do*] damned if I will; I'll be damned if I do that; I'll never do that

> < "Let him be, Bill." "**I'm [damned] if I do.**" > (Long John Silver & Billy Bones, *Porto Bello Gold* 68)

in a pig's eye [en/i' a peg's eye'ee] never; absolutely not

An emphatic, categorical way to say no.

> < "You! Your sword. Lower it, you big, black ape!" "**In a pig's eye**, you swine!" > (Nick Debrett, "Swashbuckler" 1:09:13)

indeed [endeed] really; you don't say

A one-word retort that suggests suprise at, disbelief of, or difficulty comprehending a statement, with the subtle corollary that the addressee is being fatuous or absurd.

> < "It must be, sir; or you will no longer command this vessel. I am desired to say so." "Indeed! Perhaps you have already chosen my successor?" > (Hawkhurst & Cain, The Pirate 63–64, Chap. IX)

__ indeed [__ endeed]

A retort to a command or comment, wherein the key word is repeated back and followed with the word "indeed," which itself conveys the speaker's doubt, incredulity, superciliousness, or defiance.

> < "Oh, now, now, I'm sorry, Purity." "Sorry, he says. **Sorry indeed**. If it weren't for you and the ruffian manners of you and your crew this would never have happened." > (Long John Silver & Purity Pinker, "The Adventures of Long John Silver: The Eviction" 12:28)

indeed, and ... [endeed, an'/'n' ...]

Used to contradict another's statement by asserting the opposite after the words "indeed, and." Thus, the retort to "The Marina's not ready to sail with the rest of the fleet" is, "Indeed, and she is" or "Indeed, and sail she will."

> < "This amounts to a declaration of war." "You may so regard it if you choose. It is not material." "**Indeed, and it's most material**. Since you declare war on me, war you shall have ..." > (Peter Blood & Colonel Courtney, Captain Blood Returns 124)

__, is it? [__, be ett/'n/'t?]

(1) A very common retort to a command, threat, insult, or epithet. The key word or phrase is repeated and followed with the question "is it?"

> < "But as for you, Tressady, pray if you can, for this hour you hang." "**Hang is it**, Adam? And who's to do it—who?" > Adam Penfeather & Roger Tressady, Black Bartlemy's Treasure 316)

(2) Can also be used to express doubt or incredulity with respect to any assertion.

> < "Peter, by what miracle do you happen here?" "**Miracle, is it?** Now didn't ye suppose that sooner or later one or another of us would be coming to look for you?" > (Tom Hagthorpe & Peter Blood, The Fortunes of Captain Blood 100)

is it blowing a gale of wind, you can't hear me—what did I say? [be ett/'n/'t a-blowoo-in' a gayell o'\on win'/wint, 'ee/ya/ye/yer carrn't/cayn't/kint 'ear/'ee'arr/'ee'err/hee'arr/hee'err me—wharrt/whorrt ded I'ee sayee?]

A mocking reply to any stalling retort, such as "what did you say?" or "are you talking to me?" or "you didn't say what I think you said, did you?"

> < "Silence there, between decks!" "Were you addressing me, sir?" "**Is it blowing a gale o' wind, you can't hear me? What did I say?**" > (Billy Bones & Doctor Livesey, "Treasure Island" [1934] 10:46)

(and) is it like that? [(an'/'n') be ett/'n/'t lawk/lyeeke tharrt?] so that's how it is?; so that's how things are?

> "**And is it like that?** Well, well, it's a pity now that the Admiral's so headstrong." (Peter Blood, responding to Don Miguel and his hard-line message from the Spanish Admiral, Captain Blood: His Odyssey 196)

is that seamanly behavior? [be tharrt seamanly be-'ay/haah/hayee-viarr?]

Used in response to any statement that could be construed as profane, uncouth, or uncivil.

"Is that seamanly behavior, now, I want to know?" (Billy Bones, condemning the efforts of Black Dog and Pew to take from him a treasure map, *Treasure Island* 15, Chap. 3)

it is no business of yours [*ett 's\be* OR *'tes/'tis no'oo bez-nass o'\on yarrs/yer'n/yourn\ theys*] it is none of your business

< "What do you want?" "I'll tell you, but **it's no business of yours.**" > (watchman aboard pirate ship at Smith Island & Thomas Marlowe, *The Guardship* 89)

it is of no account\matter [*ett 's\be* OR *'tes/'tis o'\on no'oo accarrnt/accowoont/'carrnt/'cowoont\ ma'er*] it doesn't matter; it is irrelevant

< "[I]f you've no great pride on your own behalf, just tell his—" "It is of no account; take the glass yourself, and pass an opinion on the sail in sight." > (Richard Fid & The Red Rover, *The Red Rover* 405) < "Smith Island, *oui*?" "I reckon. That's where she bears." "It is of no matter." > (LeRois & William Darnall, guessing at the location of distant gunfire, *The Guardship* 100)

it is so [*ett 's\be* OR *'tes/'tis so'oo*] that's right; you're correct

< "Heard you nothing?" "I thought a rope had fallen into the water." "Ay, **it is so.**" > (The Red Rover & Harry Wilder, *The Red Rover* 350)

it is well [*ett 's\be* OR *'tes/'tis waahl*] that's good; that's fine

< "You want service?" "One should be ashamed of idleness in these stirring times." "**It is well.**" > (The Red Rover & Harry Wilder, discussing Wilder's desire to join the *Dolphin*'s crew, *The Red Rover* 93)

let it be forgotten [*laaht/le' ett/'n be farr/fer-garrt-ered/ern*] forget it; don't worry about it

< "I would he might be pardoned. I can venture to promise, in his name, 't will be the last offence—" "**Let it be forgotten.**" >

(Harry Wilder & The Red Rover, with the Red Rover deciding not to punish a bumbling hand, *The Red Rover* 412–13)

let's have no harsh words [*laaht's/less 'aff/ 'ave/ha'/haff no'oo 'arsh/hahrrsh warrds*]

< "I'll see you hanging on Execution Dock before I'm through with you, Mister Silver." "**Let's have no harsh words**, Mister Smollett.**" > (Captain Smollett & Long John Silver, "Treasure Island" [1960] 55:18)

meaning what by that last? [*a-meanin' wharrt/ whorrt byee tharrt larrst?*] what's that supposed to mean?; what are you trying to say?

< "Well, now, don't ye worry about Jim. There be no better schoolmaster than being master at your own helm." "**Meanin' what by that last?**" > (Long John Silver & Purity Pinker, "The Adventures of Long John Silver: Ship o' the Dead" 2:42)

mind your language [*mawnd/min'/myeen'/ myeend ya/yarr/ye/yer/yere/yore lang'age*]

< "Damnation take you, you black-livered ..." "**Mind your language**, Squire. You mustn't upset my parrot." > (Squire Trelawney & Long John Silver, "Treasure Island" [1960] 55:39)

nay nay [*nayee nayee*] no, no
Used to emphatically contradict, dispute, or disagree with another's statement.

< "[H]e expects miracles to be wrought for him, or he never would have chosen what he hath." "**Nay, nay**, if he be such a one, he will do well enough ..." > (John Russell & another member of Edward Low's company, *Pirates of the New England Coast* 196)

nay now [*nayee narr/nowoo*] no; absolutely not; uh-uh

< "This damnable evil that can so pervert and corrupt the best and bravest—" "**Nay now**, sir! Belay, Master Adam, I was but saying, seeing as how we'm rich, one and all, —why run chance o' losing

all?" > (Adam Penfeather & Ned Bowser, *Adam Penfeather, Buccaneer* 228)

never doubt it [*nebber/ne'er darrt/dowoot ett/ 'n*] don't you worry; you better believe it

Used defiantly to turn another's command or unpleasantry against him. Just as a modern speaker might respond to "Stay away from me" with "Don't worry, I will," a pirate might respond to "Keep the likes o' ye out o' me sight" with "Never doubt it."

< "Get you to farthest corner out of my sight and trouble me no more." "**Never doubt it!**" > (Ursula Revell & Japhet Bly, *Winds of Chance* 290)

never say it [*nebber/ne'er sayee ett/'n/'t*] don't say it; hold your tongue

Used to gently castigate another for referring to something dreadful, inconceivable, or implausible.

< "Oh, Japhet, it were strangely terrible if, despite all your cunning stratagems and care of me, I should end by killing myself, as did your poor Spanish lady and for the same ... shameful reason—" "God's death! **Never say it** ... never think such vile thing ..." > (Ursula Revell & Japhet Bly, *Winds of Chance* 304)

no matter [*no'oo ma'er*] it doesn't matter; it's not important

< "That will bring us within range." "**No matter.** We'll run the gantlet of his fire." > (Trenam & Peter Blood, *Captain Blood Returns* 292)

no matter for this [*no'oo ma'er farr/fer dis/t'is*] that doesn't matter; that's not important

"**No matter for this**, sir, there be divers o' my bully lads do need your care ..." > (Matthew Swayne & Roger Snaith, *Winds of Chance* 323)

no matter for you [*no'oo ma'er farr/fer 'ee/ ya/ye/yer*] don't worry about it; that's none of your concern

< "What is it you will do?" "**No matter for you**, sweetheart." > (Isabel de Sotomayor & George Fairfax, *The Fortunes of Captain Blood* 160)

not? [*narrt?*] you don't?; no, really?

Used to express disbelief of, surprise at, or curiosity about another's negative statement.

< "Well, my limbs are not stout!" "A pity, lass, a pity. Yet constant labour shall harden 'em—" "But I don't want them hardened." "**Not?**" > (Ursula Revell & Japhet Bly, *Winds of Chance* 153)

not so [*narrt so'oo*]

Used to contradict another's statement.

< "Besides, my company's complete—" "**Not so**, your damned company will lack Captain Smy Peters, John Fenn, Nicholas Cobb, Abnegation Mings, with myself and others, except my comrade Adam be signed on." > (Benjamin Trigg & Absalom Troy, *Adam Penfeather, Buccaneer* 44)

not so hot [*narrt so'oo harrt/'ot*]

(1) don't get so excited; calm down (2) no need to be so harsh; don't be so hard on me; ease up

< "Sink you for a villain, do you dare to question my orders?" "Nay, nay, Captain Sharkey, **not so hot**, sir!" > (John Sharkey & Roaring Ned Galloway, with Galloway attempting belatedly to mollify his captain, *The Dealings of Captain Sharkey and Other Tales of Pirates* "How the Governor of Saint Kitt's Came Home" 24)

nothing doing [*nuff/nutt-in' a-doin'*] no way; absolutely not; not on your life

< "And just where, pray tell, does this ransom o' three kings lie?" "**Nothing' doin**, Govn'r! Not till we strike our bargain first." > (Joshua Smoot & Henry Morgan, *Dead Man's Chest* 157)

VERB+SUBJECT now? [*... narr/nowoo?*]

The speaker repeats the verb and subject of the statement to which he is responding, then adds "now?"

> < "And I don't think you're stupid enough to kill them, when they're the only things keeping you and your bully-bucks alive." "**Don't ye, now?**" > (Alan Lewrie & Billy Doyle, debating the significance of Doyle's women prisoners as hostages, *The Gun Ketch* 161)

now is that friendly? [*narr/nowoo be tharrt fraynd/frien'-ly?*]

Used in response to any challenging or antagonistic statement.

> "Oh, **now is that friendly**, soldier?" (Patch, encountering a soldier and his threateningly pointed rifle, "The Adventures of Long John Silver: The Necklace" 20:03)

oh, will you? [*o'oo, well 'ee/ya/ye/yer?*]

Used in response to any representation by the addressee about what he might do in the future, especially a hollow threat, worthless promise, or otherwise implausible intention.

> < "And if you don't keep off it I'll fire the cannon and get a proper watch aboard." "**Oh, will ya?**" > (Israel Hands & Haggott, "Treasure Island" [1950] 1:07:00)

one more word of your sauce and ... [*woohn marr/moor warrd o'\on ya/yarr/ye/yer/yore sarrce an'/'n' ...*]

Used in making a threat in response to any impertinent or disrespectful statement.

> < "Mighty pretty. But how are we to get away with it, and us no ship?" "Now I give you warning, George. **One more word of your sauce, and I'll call you down and fight you.**" > (George Merry & Long John Silver, *Treasure Island* 166, Chap. 29)

passion is an ill word to steer by [*pa-shern/shoohn be an ee'ull warrd t'/ta/ter stee-arr/err byee*]

A sailorly retort to any hot-tempered, sharp-tongued, or precipitous remark.

> < "I being a quiet soul—" "And a pirate, like as not!" "Easy, shipmate, easy. **Passion is an ill word to steer by.**" > (Adam Penfeather & Martin Conisby, *Black Bartlemy's Treasure* 48)

pish [*pesh*] nonsense; that's absurd; quiet, you're embarassing yourself

A condescendingly dismissive retort to any statement, but particularly to any earnestly or firmly expressed assertion.

> < "[T]hen you must turn the man adrift in the sloop without a mainsail." "**Pish**, the same miraculous power that is to bring him provisions, can also bring him a sail." > (member of Edward Low's company & John Russell, *Pirates of the New England Coast* 196)

__, say you? [*__ sayee 'ee/ya/ye/yer?*]

The speaker throws back the key word in another's statement and follows it with "say you?" or "say ye?" Thus, the retort to "Wynn'll use yer skin fer a sack when 'ee's done with 'ee" is, "Sack, say ye?"

> < "Ay, some better purpose than tormenting; one hath troubles enough and to spare." "**Tormenting, say you?**" > (Adam Penfeather & Absalom Troy, *Adam Penfeather, Buccaneer* 109)

say you so? [*sayee 'ee/ya/ye/yer so'oo?*] you don't say?

A retort that suggests surprise at, disbelief of, or difficulty comprehending a statement, with the subtle corollary that the addressee is being fatuous or absurd.

> < "I tell you to your face, if you were to toss me over yonder cliff into the sea, I would not tell you where my companions are, and I dare you to try me!" "**Say you so?** Here, lads, take him by the legs and heave him in—quick!" > (Ralph Rover & pirate captain, *The Coral Island* 198)

__ **says you** [__ *sayees/sayz 'ee/ya/ye/yer*]
A retort to a command or assertion of any kind. The speaker repeats the key word of the statement to which he is responding, then adds "says you."

> < "Oh, barbarous!" "**Barbarous, says you!** You that have experienced nothing of barbarity all your smugly sheltered, easeful days!" > (Ursula Revell & Japhet Bly, *Winds of Chance* 228)

VERB + SUBJECT so? [... *so'oo?*]
The speaker repeats the verb and subject of the statement being responded to, then follows with "so?" The subject can be replaced with a pronoun, and the verb with an appropriate form of "do." Thus, the retort to "Those Spanishers have twice the guns" is, "Do they so?"

> < "You've killed him at last." "**Have I so**, ma'm?" > (Ursula Revell & Japhet Bly, *Winds of Chance* 171)

so be it [*so'oo be ett/'n/'t*] fine; that's alright

> "Who give me'll a hand, I say? [No response.] **So be it.** But afore an hour's out, you'll be beggin' 'elp from me." (Long John Silver, "Treasure Island" [1950] 1:00:13)

so I trust [*so'oo I'ee trarrst/troohst*] I'm assuming as much; I'm counting on it

> < "They'll follow." "Why, **so I trust**." > (Trenam & Peter Blood, *Captain Blood Returns* 290)

so is it very well [*so'oo be ett/'n/'t vaah/vay-ry waahl*] that's fine; that's very good

> "Ah, ah! do I then vex you a little, *amigo mio*? **So is it very well**." (Captain Jo, *Martin Conisby's Vengeance* 26)

so now you're ..., are 'ee? [*so'oo narr/nowoo ya're/yer/ye're/yore ..., be 'ee/ya/ye/yer?*]
The speaker characterizes the addressee as being or doing something (typically in a way that reflects poorly on the addressee) based on what she has just said: < "That's

the gold, but where be the silver?" "**So now you're** interrygatin' me, Lavin, **are 'ee?**" >

> < "Now show us the color of ya money." "Do you think I keep it on me person?" "**So, now you're askin' me to trust you, are 'ee?**" > (Long John Silver & Purity Pinker, "The Adventures of Long John Silver: The Necklace" 9:56)

soft [*sarrft/soff*] oh, stop; calm down; oh, hush; enough of that; quiet down

> < "Deal with them as Magellan did. Hang them up to be an example to the rest!" "Nay, **soft**! His authority is none such as Magellan's was ..." > (John Saracold & Thomas Doughty, *The Queen's Corsair* 56)

stint this foolery [*stent dis/t'is foo'ell/fool'-ry*] stop this nonsense; enough of this crap

> "Ha, damnation! **Stint this foolery**, Adam ..." (Absalom Troy, *Adam Penfeather, Buccaneer* 114)

stow that [*stowoo tharrt*] forget that; never mind that

> "Jot this down. 'I, Archibaldo ...,' ah, what's your name?" "Archibaldo Esteban." "'I, Archibaldo,' it says, an' the rest of it, 'Governor of Maracaibo' ..." "Knight of the Holy Sepulchre." "**Stow that**. Write 'Maracaibo.'" (Thomas Bartholomew Red & the Governor of Maracaibo, drafting a letter authorizing Red to carry away Spanish treasure, "Pirates" 1:24:41)

that'd be so? [*tharrt'd be so'oo?*] really?; is that right?

> < "Nay, all the servants have a holiday. Mr. Wainright 'n' 'is wife be dinin' at the Governor's." "**That'd be so?** Then Mrs. Wainwright's jewels'll be left unguarded." > (pirates at the Cask & Anchor, "The Adventures of Long John Silver: The Necklace" 1:49)

that's a trifle [*tharrt's a traw/tryee-fle*] that's unimportant; that's not really the issue

"[Y]ou'd have starved, too, if I hadn't—but that's a trifle! you look there—that's why!" (Long John Silver, *Treasure Island* 165, Chap. 29)

that\this is as (it) may be but [*tharrt's\dis/t'is as (ett/'n/'t) mayee be barrt*] that may be, but; that may be true, but; be that as it may

> < "Sir, if you wait much longer you'll be too dead to see em at all." "That's as may be, Ned, **but** when we do fire it shall be point blank to do their business perfectly." > (Ned Bowser & Adam Penfeather, *Adam Penfeather, Buccaneer* 235) < "Japhet, you rush upon destruction." "**This is as may be**, ma'm, **but** for the nonce, sweet poppet, be seen and not heard." > (Ursula Revell & Japhet Bly, *Winds of Chance* 334) < "I may live to rip you the length of your vest for this night's work." "**That is as it may be**, Captain Sharkey, **but** if you will look up you will see that I have those at my back who will not see me mishandled." > (John Sharkey & Birthmark Sweetlocks, *The Dealings of Captain Sharkey and Other Tales of Pirates* "The Blighting of Sharkey" 49)

that's my affair [*tharrt's me/myee arr/err-farr/fayarr/fayerr*] that's my business; that's for me to worry about

> Thus: < "How the b'jesus will the *Rachel* be sailin' wi' the tide an' you wiff no crew?" "**That's my affair**. Favor, show me your **stern** and budge now." >

> Compare: "So ye've friends among the buccaneers? Well, well! **That's your affair**, to be sure." (George Fairfax, *The Fortunes of Captain Blood* 158)

that's the tune, is it? [*tharrt be t' toon, be ett/'n/'t?*] that's how it is?; that's what you think?; that's what you want?

> < "Barbecue for ever! Barbecue for cap'n!" "So **that's the toon, is it?**" > (Silver's company mates & Long John Silver, with Silver's

mates suddenly celebrating his leadership on discovering the treasure map in his possession, *Treasure Island* 166, Chap. 29)

that's the way you be, hey? [*tharrt's t' wayee 'ee/ya/ye/yer be, 'ey/'eyee/heyee?*] that's how it is?; that's how you're going to be?

> < "Damn your blood, Doyle. Surrender or die." "Ah, **that's the way ye be, hey?**" > (Alan Lewrie & Billy Doyle, *The Gun Ketch* 159)

that's your sort, is it? [*tharrt be ya/yarr/ye/yer/yere/yore sarrt, be ett/'n/'t?*] (1) that's what you're made of?; that's what you're like?; that's what you're all about? (2) that's the way you want it? that's where you come out?; that's your story?; that's your decision?

> "Or would any man jack of ye care to give me an argument to the con'ary? So, **that's your sort, is it?**" (Long John Silver, challenging his company mates to defy him, then reproving them for their cowardly silence, "Treasure Island" [1950] 1:16:38)

there be no call to ... [*tharr/theyarr/theyerr be no'oo cawrl t'/ta/ter ...*] there's no need to ...; you have no good reason to ...

> < "A big, ugly, booze-soaked rummy!" "Hold on there! **There be no call to** put the fuddler's name on your newfound shipmate." (Steve Walker & Blackbeard, "Blackbeard's Ghost" 30:18)

there's reason in that [*tharr/theyarr/theyerr is\be reasern/reas'n i'/'n tharrt*] that makes sense; that stands to reason

> < "'An eye for an eye,' reverend sir." "Why, **there's reason in that**, look you!" > (Japhet Bly & Ezekiel Penryn, *Winds of Chance* 31)

there's the truth of it [*tharr/theyarr/theyerr is\be t' troof o'\on ett/'n/'t*] that's the truth; that's for sure

> < "Well, salvagin' is saving, in a manner of speaking." "**There's the troof of it!**" >

(Ragetti & Pintel, "Pirates of the Caribbean 2: Dead Man's Chest" 32:00)

the thing is like enough [*t' fing/theng/thin'/ t'in'/t'ing 's\be lawk/lyeeke enarrff/enow/'nough*] that's likely the case; that's probably true

> < "I believe he has made many voyages; and I dare say has long since paid the proper tribute to your majesty." "Well, well; **the thing is like enough** ..." > (Harry Wilder & the captain of the *Dolphin's* forecastle, *The Red Rover* 328)

this does not suit [*dis/t'is does narrt soot*] that's unacceptable; that's not good enough

> < "It shall be done—" "Mañana! **This doth not suit** when I am aboard, no! The new yard must be rigged now, at once, for we sail with the flood—voila!" > (Captain Belvedere & Captain Jo, *Martin Conisby's Vengeance* 68)

this here gets away from me clean [*dis/t'is 'ee'art/'ee'err/'ere/hee'arr/hee'err gits awayee/ 'way/'wayee ferm me clean*] I don't understand it; this is beyond me; this blows my mind

> "I see you were smart when first I set my eyes on you; but **this here gets away from me clean**, it do." (Long John Silver, *Treasure Island* 156, Chap. 28)

this is rich [*dis/t'is be rech*] that is unbelievable; that is really something

> "Oh, Yancy, **this is rich**! I bring you four ships, I bring you the Great Mogul's treasure and Marlowe and his bitch to boot, and you piss it all away!" (Roger Press, *The Pirate Round* 354)

this is spleen [*dis/t'is be spleen*] you've got some nerve; how dare you

> < "Vile man, there be worse things than death and you are one of these—go!" "Hum! **This is spleen!** A megrim or fit o' your ladylike vapours! Easy, lass, take that hoity-toity look off our face and bid me stay and—" "Go—go!" >

(Ursula Revell & Japhet Bly, *Winds of Chance* 182)

this is talking [*dis/t'is be a-tawrrk-in'*] now you're talking; you said it

Used to express affirmation or approval of, or admiration or enthusiasm for, what another has just said.

> < "[I]f you will take your sword and pistols and come upon a sand-bank with me, then the world will be rid of a damned villain whichever way it goes." "Now, **this is talking!**" > (Copley Banks & John Sharkey, *The Dealings of Captain Sharkey and Other Tales of Pirates* "How Copley Banks Slew Captain Sharkey" 69)

'tis a foul tongue yours [*ett/it 's\be OR 'tes a fowool toohngue yarrs/yer'n/yourn\theys*]

Used in response to any statement that could be construed as profane, uncouth, or uncivil.

> < "Why, there be rogues for you a-plenty hereabouts shall fit ye better than I—" "Oh, **'tis a foul tongue yours**, Martino!" > (Martin Conisby & Captain Jo, *Martin Conisby's Vengeance* 93)

'tis an ill word [*ett/it 's\be OR 'tes an ee'ull warrd*]

A retort to an insult or epithet. The speaker may, but need not, repeat the key word in the objectionable statement before saying "'Tis an ill word." The effect is the same as a modern speaker responding with "That's not very nice."

> < "I do take ye for a very rogue and so I'm done with you henceforth." "Rogue? **'Tis an ill word!**" > (Martin Conisby & Adam Penfeather, *Black Bartlemy's Treasure* 325)

'tis joy to me [*ett/it 's\be OR 'tes joyee/j'y t'/ta/ ter me*] I like that; that makes me happy

A phrase said defiantly or to goad when the addressee has done or said something to hurt or antagonize the speaker.

> "Ha, scowl, fool Martino, scowl and grind your teeth; **'tis joy to me** and shall never

bring back your little axe." (Captain Jo, *Martin Conisby's Vengeance* 26)

'tis well [*ett/it 's\be* OR *'tes waahl*] that's good; that's fine

< "Struck the bell six or seven?" "Seven ..." "'Tis well. I feared the time had passed." > (The Red Rover & Harry Wilder, *The Red Rover* 348)

to me? [*t'/ta/ter me?*]

Really an abbreviated form of "You dare say that to me?"

< "And now, leave me—begone lest I thrash you again for the evil child you are." "Child? Child—and to me, fool, to me? All along the Main my name is known and feared." > (Martin Conisby & Captain Jo, *Martin Conisby's Vengeance* 13)

the tongue of woman is very disquiet-ing member, being tipped with a viper-ish gall [*t' toohngue o'\on womern/wom'n be vaah/vay-ry des-quier-tin' mamber, a-bein' tepped weth/wi'/wiff/witt a vaw/vyee-parr/p'r-ersh/esh gawrl*]

Obviously a retort appropriate only in an exchange with a woman.

"And the tongue of woman is very dis-quieting member, being tipped with a viperish gall." (Smy Peters, *Adam Pen-feather, Buccaneer* 33)

trifles [*traw/tryee-fulls*] the things you men-tion don't matter; you speak of insignificant or irrelevant details

< "We are very much alike, you and I. I and you. Us." "Oh. Except for a sense of honor, and decency, and—and a moral center. And personal hygiene." "Trifles. You will come over to my side, I know it." > (Jack Sparrow & Elizabeth Swann, "Pirates of the Carib-bean 2: Dead Man's Chest" 1:40:26)

what daftness be this? [*wharrt/whorrt daff/darrft/deft-ness be dis/t'is?*] are you crazy?; have you lost your mind?

< "I tell ya, I've seen Slygo." "Where be?" "Hid. And nobody but meself knows where." "What daftness be this, woman?!" > (Purity Pinker & Long John Silver, "The Adventures of Long John Silver: The Necklace" 18:56)

what kind of a fool do you think I be? [*wharrt/whorrt kawnd/kin'/kyeen'/kyeend o'\on a foo'ell d'/does 'ee/ya/ye/yer fink/thenk/t'ink I'ee be?*]

"Well, now what kind of a fool do you think I be?" (Blackbeard, "Blackbeard the Pirate" 50:51)

what mean you by this? [*wharrt/whorrt mean 'ee/ya/ye/yer byee dis/t'is?*] what's that sup-posed to mean?; what are you saying?

< "I quarrel with no just law, Captain Absalom, more especially such law of stern hounour as can aid a man to gov-ern and discipline himself!" "What mean ye by this now, —what mean ye?" > (Adam Penfeather & Absalom Troy, *Adam Penfeather, Buccaneer* 99)

what of it? [*wharrt/whorrt o'\on ett/'n/'t?*] so what?; what about it?

"Now you've run me down. What of it?!" (Billy Bones, "Treasure Island" [1998] 12:52)

what talk is this? [*wharrt/whorrt tarrk be dis/t'is?*] what are you talking about?

< "You come to see punishment properly done, sir?" "No, Mr. Danvers, mere jus-tice." "Justice, sir? What talk is this?" > (James Danvers & Adam Penfeather, *Adam Penfeather, Buccaneer* 89)

what the devil do you mean? [*wharrt/whorrt t' daahv/dayv/debb/div-il d'/does 'ee/ya/ye/yer mean?*]

what the devil mean you? [*wharrt/whorrt t' daahv/dayv/debb/div-il mean 'ee/ya/ye/yer?*] what the hell is that supposed to mean?; what the hell are you talking about?

< "And we're not here to play, but to agree terms. And, by God, we'll agree them be-

fore you leave." "Or not, as the case may be." "Or not? **What the devil do you mean with your 'or not'?"** > (Captain Easterling & Peter Blood, *Captain Blood Returns* 32)

what the devil may you chance to be talking about? [*wharrt/whorrt t' daahv/dayv/debb/div-il mayee 'ee/ya/ye/yer charrnce t'/ta/ter be a-tarrk-in' abarrt/abowoot/'barrt/'bout/'bowoot?*] what the hell are you talking about?

> < "[Y]ou are verily so much other than you show, that I am, as I say, wondering if you ever permit yourself to lay by these affectations, when alone of course, and become the creature you truly are?" "Pray be more explicit to let me know **what the devil you may chance to be talking about."** > (Adam Penfeather & Black Bartlemy, *Adam Penfeather, Buccaneer* 277)

what then? [*wharrt/whorrt thayn?*] so what?; what of it?

> "I heard what you said. Well, **what then?** D'ye think I mind it at all? Spottiswood is going to send his bullies down here after me. That's what you were saying. Well, **what then?"** (Blackbeard, *The Book of Pirates* "Jack Ballister's Fortunes" 133)

what's that to me? [*wharrt/whorrt is\be tharrt t'/ta/ter me?*] why should I care?; so what?

> "D[am]n your blood, no preaching. Be damn'd an you will, **what's that to us?** Let him look out who has the watch." (Alexander Mitchel, *General History of the Pyrates* 607)

what's this? [*wharrt/whorrt is\be dis/t'is?*] what was that?; what did you say?

> < "However, sir, I desire you shall hear a word on this man's behalf." "Eh—**what's this?"** > (Adam Penfeather & James Danvers, *Adam Penfeather, Buccaneer* 89)

who be you? [*'oo be 'ee/ya/ye/yer?*] who do you think you are?

"Who be you, George Merry?" (Long John Silver, stopping George Merry as he charges toward Jim Hawkins with a knife, "Treasure Island" [1990] 1:39:**55**)

why do you tempt me thus? [*whyee d'/does 'ee/ya/ye/yer tampt/temp' me tharss/thoohss?*]

Used to suggest that the addressee is tempting the speaker to violence, and that the speaker therefore should not be held responsible for the consequences.

> < "As you please; it matters little whether I am brained by your own hand, or launched overboard as a meal for the sharks; it will be but one more murder." "Mad fool! **why do you tempt me thus?"** > (Francisco & Cain, *The Pirate* 45, Chap. VII)

..., will you? [*..., well 'ee/ya/ye/yer?*]

The speaker characterizes the addressee as being or doing something (typically in a way that reflects poorly on the addressee) based on what she has just said.

> "Sing out your ribaldries afore a lass, **will ye!"** (Japhet Bly, answering John Barrasdale's string of profanities by scolding him for uttering them in Ursula Revell's presence, *Winds of Chance* 156)

will you dare me? [*well 'ee/ya/ye/yer darr/dayarr/dayerr me?*]

Used especially in exchanges with someone who is being defiant, overly insistent, contradictory, or provocative. The speaker suggests the addressee is driving him to violence.

> < "And, sir, I tell you 'tis murderous villain would ha' knifed me!" "Od's my life, Captain, **will ye dare me?"** > (Captain Sharp & Benjamin Trigg, *Adam Penfeather, Buccaneer* 72)

will you squeak, rat? [*well 'ee/ya/ye/yer squeak, rarrt?*]
will you yap, (puppy) dog? [*well 'ee/ya/ye/yer yarrp, (parrpy) dahg/darrg/dorrg?*]

Two wonderfully obnoxious retorts to anything another might say—anything at all.

< "And I say 'tis foul murder in the sight of God and man!" "Ha, **will ye squeak, rat!** 'S fish, **will ye yap**, then, **puppy-dog**?" > (Martin Conisby & Captain Belvedere, *Martin Conisby's Vengeance* 99–100)

would you match yourself against me? [*woood 'ee/ya/ye/yer metch ya/yarr/ye/yer/yere/yore-seff agaynst/agin/'gainst/'gaynst me?*]

Used in facing down a challenge from someone the speaker is implicitly characterizing as inferior.

"You poor, dull-witted fool, **would you match yourself against me?**" (John Sharkey, *The Dealings of Captain Sharkey and Other Tales of Pirates* "The Dealings of Captain Sharkey With Stephen Craddock" 36)

you become offensive [*ya/ye/yer b'-cahm/carrm/coohm arrf-aahn-sev/siff*] you're out of line; that's uncalled for

< "And a very haphazard, piratical, bloody botch you'll make on't!" "Captain Penfeather, **you become offensive**." > (Adam Penfeather & Black Bartlemy, *Adam Penfeather, Buccaneer* 322)

you crow like small bantam cock on his own dunghill [*ya/ye/yer crowoo lawk/lyeeke smawrl barrn-term carrk arrn/o' 'is arrn/owoon darrng/doohng-hell/'ill*]

A nice retort to any strident, provocative, or threatening statement.

< "First, I would say if your mannerless rogue fouls my deck with his beastly spittle again, or flaunts that hook of his, he shall be kicked overboard, —and secondly, Black Bartlemy, I invite you now to leave in fashion more seemly." "Ha, Captain, he crows! **He croweth like very small bantam cock on his own dunghill**, —he crows and be damned." > (Adam Penfeather & Roger Tressady, *Adam Penfeather, Buccaneer* 254)

you may well ask [*ya/ye/yer mayee waahl aks/arrsk*] that's a good question; funny you should ask

< "Son of a blundering ox, what did you do?" "**You may well ask**." > (El Toro Mendoza & Long John Silver, "Long John Silver's Return to Treasure Island" 17:32)

you needn't be so husky with a man [*ya/ye/yer needern't/nee'n't be so'oo harr/hooh-sky weth/wi'/wiff/witt a man*]

Used to chide another coyly for any rude or aggressive remark.

< "We know what you meant to do, Silver—only now you can't do it." "Well, **you needn't be so husky with a man**." > (Alexander Smollett & Long John Silver, "Treasure Island" [1990] 1:15:35)

you pain\wound me to my\the marrow [*ya/ye/yer payeen\woun'/wount me t'/ta/ter me/myee\t' mahr/may-rowoo*] you hurt me; you wound me

Used, often ironically, to claim injury to one's feelings as a result of another's speech or actions.

"Ben, ye **pain me to me marrow**, ya do." (Long John Silver, *Dead Man's Chest* 279)

"Oh, Jimmy, ye **wound me to the marrow**, ya do." (Long John Silver, *Dead Man's Chest* 296)

you say true [*ya/ye/yer sayee troo*] you're right; you speak the truth

< "If I took a turn too many of the gasket off the yard, it is a fault I am ready to answer for." "**You say true**, and dearly shall you pay the forfeit." > (Richard Fid & The Red Rover, *The Red Rover* 412)

you shall VERB with the devil [*ya/ye/yer shawrl ... weth/wi'/wiff/witt t' daahv/dayv/debb/div-il*] go VERB in hell

The speaker takes the verb in the statement to which he is responding and, no matter how *non sequitur* the resulting formulation might prove (indeed, the more illogical, the better), exhorts the addressee to "VERB with the devil."

< "Japhet—ahoy! A parley ere we begin, a parley, Japhet!" "Snaith, **you shall parley with the devil** ere all's done." > (Roger Snaith & Japhet Bly, respectively requesting and declining a negotiation before battle, *Winds of Chance* 355)

you speak in vain [ya/ye/yer speak i'/'n vayeen] you're wasting your breath

< "They tell me you are but half lost to feeling for your kind ..." "Peace! **You speak in vain**." > (priest aboard the *Dart* & The Red Rover, *The Red Rover* 500)

you weary me [ya/ye/yer wee-arr/err-y me] you bore me; you grow tiresome

< "You—killed him?" "Aye—**he wearied me**. So do all my lovers, soon or late." > (Martin Conisby & Captain Jo, *Martin Conisby's Vengeance* 6)

you were wiser [ya/ye/yer warr waw/wyee-ser] you're smarter than that; you know better

"Aye, truly, **you were wiser**, Martin!" (Abnegation Mings, winking and tapping his pistol as warning to Martin Conisby not to move, *Martin Conisby's Vengeance* 160)

you'd try that [ya'd/ye'd/yer'd tryee tharrt] Used in responding to threats to convey defiant invitation. Modern equivalents include "try it" and "I'd like to see that."

"[B]y G[o]d **he'd try that**." (drunk gunner aboard the *Whidaw*, after mistaking the lines of a pirate play being performed on deck for a threat to a crewmate, and just before throwing a lit grenade among the actors, *General History of the Pyrates* 588)

you'll go whining to __, will you? [ye'll go'oo a-wawn/wyeen-in' t'/ta/ter __, well 'ee/ya/ye/yer?] Used to respond to any threat to complain to, request redress or assistance from, or otherwise seek involvement by a third party.

< "You'll have Captain Blood to deal with for this." "Captain Blood? **You'll go whining to Captain Blood, will you?**" >

(Crosby Pike & Captain Easterling, *Captain Blood Returns* 286)

you're a diamond [ya're/yer/ye're/yore a dy'ee-moohnd] you're the best; you're fantastic
Used to express extreme pleasure with or approval of another's statement or the view or sentiment conveyed thereby, often to flatter for self-serving purposes.

< "One hundred souls, three days." "**You're a diamond**, mate." > (Davy Jones & Jack Sparrow, "Pirates of the Caribbean 2: Dead Man's Chest" 1:03:40)

your mind's unhinged [ya/yarr/ye/yer/yere/yore mawnd's/min's/myeen's/smyeend's arrn/hun/oohn-henged/'inged] you've lost your mind

< "I can save ya, or stand by and see ya hanged." "**Your mind's un'inged**!" "Me mind never worked better." > (Purity Pinker & Long John Silver, "The Adventures of Long John Silver: The Necklace" 19:02)

you're a EPITHET to give me those words [ya're/yer/ye're/yore a ... t'/ta/ter gi'/giff me dose/t'ose\dem/'em/them\dey/they warrds] See Chapter 9 for a comprehensive list of epithets with which to fill the blank.

< "You have brought us to ruin. We are desolate." "Have I brought you to ruin? I have not brought you to ruin. I have not done an ill thing to ruin you. **You are a dog to give me those words**." > (William Moore & William Kidd, debating Kidd's responsibility for the crew's sad condition just before Kidd's bludgeoning of Moore with a bucket, *The Pirate Hunter* 149)

you're full of prating [ya're/yer/ye're/yore full o'\on a-prayee-tin'] you're full of it; you're babbling; you're talking nonsense

< "It is necessary that it should be here shewed." "Well, you shall not see it. But well, my masters, **this fellow is full of prating**!" > (Thomas Doughty & Francis Drake, debating Drake's possession of

any commission to hold criminal proceedings, *The Queen's Corsair* 85)

you're neither mad nor a fool and yet talk like both [*ya're/yer/ye're/yore needer/nee'er/nyder/ny'er mad narr a foo'ell an'/'n' yat tarrk lawk/lyeeke bofe/bo'ooth*]

A colorful and efficient way of characterizing another's statement as both crazy and stupid.

> < "And what say you, Adam?" "Take her with us." "Smy, you heard him, **he's neither mad nor a fool and yet talks like both**—or I'm a stockfish, damme!" > (Absalom Troy & Adam Penfeather, with Troy ridiculing Penfeather's insistence that Antonia Chievely accompany them, *Adam Penfeather, Buccaneer* 41)

you're not talking to low sailor hand [*ya're/yer/ye're/yore narrt a-tarrk-in' t'/ta/ter lowoo saah/sayee/sayor-larr 'an'/'and/han'*]

Used to respond to any statement suggesting condescension or disrespect. A comparable modern counterpart is, "Who do you think you're talking to?"

> < "Why, the smell of you alone is enough to wrinkle the noses of pigs." "Arrgh, belay, Purity." "Belay, indeed. **You're not talkin' to low sailor hand**." (Purity Pinker & Long John Silver, "Long John Silver's Return to Treasure Island" 34:24)

you're overly apt with your tongue [*ya're/yer/ye're/yore ober/o'er-ly ap'/arrpt weth/wi'/wiff/witt ya/yarr/ye/yer/yere/yore toohngue*] you talk too much

> "Belay now! Easy all and softly by reason of our Martha for, though good soul, she's a woman and therefore **overly apt with her tongue**." (Absalom Troy, pre-

paring to enter the Mariner's Joy with Antonia Chievely despite the owner's prohibitions against women guests, *Adam Penfeather, Buccaneer* 33)

you're surely crazed [*ya're/yer/ye're/yore sharr/shorr-ly crayeezed*] you must be out of your mind

> < "You old rogue. Ye play upon my vanity, do you?" "Upon your honour, Captain." "The honour of a pirate? Ye're **surely crazed**!" > (Peter Blood & Don Francisco, *Captain Blood: His Odyssey* 181)

you're trepanning me [*ya're/yer/ye're/yore a-ter/tree-pannin' me*] you're bullshitting me; you're trying to pull one over on me

To "trepan" is to trick or deceive.

> < "That stuff he says I stole, it was mine, it weren't never his ..." "That a lie! **Son of a bitch is trepanning you**, Your Honor, and I can have a dozen witnesses say that's a fact!" (unnamed pirate claimant before Elephiant Yancy, *The Pirate Round* 93)

you're wasting words [*ya're/yer/ye're/yore a-waahst/wayeest-in' warrds*] you're wasting your time; save your breath; don't bother

> "**You're wasting words**, I say. Hang him!" (John Wolverstone, "Captain Blood" 1:00:06)

you've the tongue of some fouled scupper [*ya've/ye've/yer've t' toohngue o'\on sahm/sarrm/soohm fowooled scarr/skooh-per*] you have a filthy mouth

> "And just because our adopted father, or should I say owner, taught you the king's English, an' **I've the tongue of some fouled scupper**, it don't make me yer lesser." (Long John Silver, *Dead Man's Chest* 14)

CHAPTER 12

Questions & Replies

In 1680, a band of buccaneers marched from the Atlantic to the Pacific across the Panamanian isthmus. They captured Spanish vessels, making the finest their flagship. They terrorized settlement after settlement along the Spanish coastline. Then, leaving the Pacific behind, they became the first Englishmen to sail from west to east around Cape Horn. They also left behind the story of one of the biggest blunders in pirate history.

These men, led by Captain Bartholomew Sharp, captured a Spanish vessel in July 1681 off Cape Passao (now Cabo Pasado, Ecuador). The *El Santo Rosario* (or *The Holy Rosary*) carried brandy, oil, wine, and fruit. She also carried 700 crude ingots of a gray-colored metal.

The buccaneers examined these, ran their hands over them, struck them with their blades. Sharp decided these rough lumps were mere tin and not valuable enough to transport. He took the rest of the cargo and left the ship and all but one of its ingots behind, keeping a single specimen as a souvenir.

When one third of that ingot later sold for 75 English pounds, the truth became clear. Sharp had discarded a treasure trove of silver worth about 150,000 pounds. For comparison, the booty from Henry Morgan's celebrated sack of Panama ten years earlier was worth about 100,000 pounds.

Knowledge may be priceless, but questions—in this case, a few incisive ones that might have been posed forcefully to the sailors aboard *El Santo Rosario*—can be worth exactly a small fortune. (*Bucaniers of America* Part III, Chap. XII [account of William Dick] 349–50)

This chapter introduces distinctive questions (Section 12.1) and replies (Section 12.2).

12.1 QUESTIONS

am I explicit? [*arrm/em\be I'ee ess/iks-pless-ert?*] do I make myself clear?; am I understood?

> "I do here and now pronounce and will maintain him innocent! **Am I explicit,** sir?" (Benjamin Trigg, *Adam Penfeather, Buccaneer* 75)

as how? [*as howoo/'ow/'owoo?*] how so?; in what way?; what do you mean?

> < "Because I am your responsibility and intend to be even more so." "**As how,** Ursula?" "Thus, sir, —if to any purpose good or ill you jeopardize your life henceforth, you shall peril mine also." > (Ursula Revell & Japhet Bly, *Winds of Chance* 197)

be that plain enough? [*be tharrt playeen enarrff/enow/'nough?*] is that understood?

> "We're waitin' till I decides the time be right. **Be that plain enough,** George Merry?" (Long John Silver, "Treasure Island" [1950] 44:31)

do I speak in reason? [*do I'ee speak i'/'n reasern/reas'n?*] does what I'm saying make sense?; am I right?

> "[W]here a brave man reposes his confidence, he has a right to hope it will not be abused. **Do I speak in reason?**" (The Red Rover, entrusting his ship and men to Harry Wilder in the event of his death, *The Red Rover* 408)

do you fancy ...? [*d'/does 'ee/ya/ye/yer fancy ...?*] do you think ...?

> "Do you imagine that glasses were forgotten in the inventory of this ship? or, **do you fancy** that we don't know how to use them?" (officer aboard the *Dolphin*, *The Red Rover* 86)

do you glimpse aught? [*d'/does 'ee/ya/ye/yer glempse awrrt?*] do you see anything?

> "**D'ye glimpse aught,** Martin?" (Adam Penfeather, *Black Bartlemy's Treasure* 119)

had your tongue pruned? [*'ad ya/yarr/ye/ yer/yere/yore toohngue pruned?*] cat got your tongue?

Used to taunt another who has fallen suddenly or uncharacteristically silent.

> "What ails ya all? **Had your tongues pruned,** like that Dago lawyer?" (Thomas Bartholomew Red, "Pirates" 1:00:22)

how? [*howoo/'ow/'owoo?*] what?; what was that?

> < "So ye've heard tell of it then, along the Spanish Main?" "I heard tell of it last night in a cave from a sailor-man." "**How?** A sailor-man—hereabouts?" > (Adam Penfeather & Martin Conisby, *Black Bartlemy's Treasure* 61)

how an' ...? [*howoo/'ow/'owoo eff/eff'n/if/if'n ...?*] what if ...?

> "Yourself! Always and forever you, yours, or yourself. **How an'** I too should think but of myself?" (Japhet Bly, *Winds of Chance* 194)

how be ...? [*howoo/'ow/'owoo be ...?*] how is it that ...?; how does it happen that ...?

> "**How be** ye gonna find the treasure wi'out the map?" (Long John Silver, "Treasure Island" [1950] 1:20:23)

how comes it ...? [*howoo/'ow/'owoo cahms/ carrms/coohms ett/'n/'t?*] how is it that ...?; how does it happen that ...?

> "And talking of him, **how cometh it** you aren't blown t'hell along wi' him and the rest?" (Roger Tressady, *Black Bartlemy's Treasure* 303)

how do you say to this? [*howoo/'ow/'owoo d'/does 'ee/ya/ye/yer sayee t'/ta/ter dis/t'is?*] what do you say to that?; what do you have to say about that?; what do you think about that?

> "And talking o' Japhet, daughter, —lookee, whom the Lord hath joined in holy wedlock let no man, nor yet woman, put asunder?

And **how d'ye say to this?**" (Lovepeace Farrance, *Winds of Chance* 124–25)

how does __ go forward? [*howoo/'ow/'owoo d'/do __ go'oo farr-ad/ard/edd/erd?*] how is __ coming along?; how is __ proceeding?

> < "Boy! **how does** the dinner **go forward?**" "Very well, sir." > (Edward Low and Low's cabin boy, *Pirates of the New England Coast* 167)

how if ...? [*howoo/'ow/'owoo an'\eff/eff'n/if'n ...?*] what if ...?

> "But **how if** she slip her cable and stand from us ..." (Sam Spraggons, *Black Bartlemy's Treasure* 314)

how it be ...? [*howoo/'ow/'owoo ett/'n/'t be ...?*] how is it that ...?; how does it happen that ...?

> "Say, **'ow it be** ya knows me name, Govn'r?" (Henry Morgan, *Dead Man's Chest* 128)

how now? [*howoo/'ow/'owoo narr/nowoo?*]
(1) what?; what was that?

> "**How now**, mate o' mine, shall dog bite dog then?" (eye-patch wearing pirate to Martin Conisby as Conisby holds him and his comrades at pistol-point, *Black Bartlemy's Treasure* 22)

(2) what's going on?; what's up?; what's happening?

> "**How now**, Martino? What troubleth your sluggish brain now?" (Captain Jo, *Martin Conisby's Vengeance* 26)

(3) what's the meaning of this?; what's going on here?

> "**How now!** who has dared to let yonder top-gallant-sail fly?" (The Red Rover, aghast at seeing one of his hands unfurl a sail despite the crew's careful efforts to remain unseen by an approaching ship, *The Red Rover* 411)

how of __? [*howoo/'ow/'owoo o'\on __?*] what about __?; what happened to __?; tell me about __; how is __?

< "Then I'll none of him." "Ay, but **how of this woeful marriage?**" "I'll to England and take out bill of divorcement, or better, proceed against him for abduction." > (Ursula Revell & Japhet Bly, *Winds of Chance* 293)

how of it? [*howoo/'ow/'owoo o'\on ett/'n/'t?*] what about it?; what do you think?

> "Well, Adam, well? **How of it?**" (Absalom Troy, pointing Adam Penfeather into a mirror so that he can see for himself his black hair turned white overnight, *Adam Penfeather, Buccaneer* 9)

how say you (of\to __)? [*howoo/'ow/'owoo sayee 'ee/ya/ye/yer (o'\on\t'/ta/ter __)?*] what do you say (about __)?; what do you think (of __)?

> "[Y]onder, six odd leagues, is Viracocha, the city of my father; march wi' me and ye shall find a fortun' o' gold—or graves. **How say ye?**" (Will, *Winds of Chance* 212) "Well, Ned man, how think ye of our ship? ... **How say you of her, Ned?**" (Adam Penfeather, *Adam Penfeather, Buccaneer* 197) "**How say'st thou to** a noggin, shipmate?" (Absalom Troy, *Adam Penfeather, Buccaneer* 98)

how then? [*howoo/'ow/'owoo thayn?*]
(1) what then?; what happens then?; what about that?

> "Ha, and when he brings his like rogues down 'pon us to slit our throats, **how then?**" (Benjamin Trigg, *Adam Penfeather, Buccaneer* 208)

(2) so what?

> "You've no home in England; you've a house there, you've lands and what not, but **how then?** It is not roof and walls that make home, no nor company of sottish uncle and witless aunt." (Japhet Bly, *Winds of Chance* 194)

(3) what?

< "Oh, girl, you were never such crass fool to tell John this—no, no—" "Ay, but I did. Well, why not?" "**How then**, are ye so blind, Ursula; don't you see it?" > (Japhet Bly & Ursula Revell, discussing Revell's dangerous advertisement of herself to John Barrasdale as able to swear to Bly's true identity, *Winds of Chance* 252)

(4) what's new?; what's going on?

"Ha, Ben! **How then**, lad, **how then?** Hast found what we sought?" (Roger Tressady, confronting Ben after spying on him and witnessing his discovery of Black Bartlemy's dagger, *Black Bartlemy's Treasure* 92)

how's for __? [*howoo's/'ow's/'owoo's farr/fer __?*] how about __?; how would you like __?

"Good morning, Mister Arrow, sir. **How's for** a cup o' tea this morning?" (Long John Silver, "Treasure Island" [1934] 45:07)

how's her head? [*howoo/'ow/'owoo is\be 'er 'ead/hayd?*]

A question asked of a helmsman to inquire generally about a vessel's management, especially her current heading and any difficulties experienced in maintaining it.

"Aft there, **how's her head?**" (Japhet Bly, *Winds of Chance* 63)

how's she lie? [*howoo's/'ow's/'owoo's she lyee?*] what's the vessel's heading?; on what course does the vessel sail?

< "**How's she lie** now, Penryn?" "... West and by south, sir!" > (Japhet Bly & Ezekiel Penryn, *Winds of Chance* 62)

how's this? [*howoo/'ow/'owoo 's\be dis/t'is?*] what's going on here?; what's this?

"Well, since your captain there cannot save you, I suppose I must; but **how's this?** We are out of the passage already." (Hawkhurst, guiding the *Avenger* through a maze of island coral reefs, *The Pirate* 121, Chap. XVI)

is not this the truth of it? [*be narrt dis/t'is t' troof o'\on ett/'n/'t?*] isn't that true?; isn't that the case?; isn't that what's going on here?

"And you alone here, longing but for her return, through weeks and months and years waiting for her to come back to you: **is not this the truth of it**, yes?" (Captain Jo, *Martin Conisby's Vengeance* 10)

is the __ fit on you? [*be t' __ fet arrn/o' 'ee/ya/ye/yer?*]

A sarcastic, mocking, goading way of asking about some anomaly in or objectionable aspect of another's behavior, speech, or disposition, as if to suggest it may be the result of disease or mysterious phenomena. The speaker inserts an adjective descriptive of the quality being observed.

"Ha, won't ye talk? **Is the sullen fit on you?**" (Captain Jo, *Martin Conisby's Vengeance* 70)

mutiny, is it? [*moot-erny/'ny, be ett/'n/'t?*]

The phrase with which pirate captains confront shows of insolence or disobedience from members of their companies.

"Ha, will ye fight agin my orders, then—**mutiny is it?**" (Adam Penfeather, *Black Bartlemy's Treasure* 110)

said I well? [*sayd I'ee waahl?*] am I right?; do you agree?; does what I'm saying make sense?

"I, for one, would rather lower the pride of the minions of King George, than possess the power of unlocking his treasury! **Said I well**, general?; **said I well**, in asserting there was glorious pleasure in making a pennant trail upon the sea?" (The Red Rover, voicing his American revolutionary sympathies, *The Red Rover* 410)

see the course I lay? [*see t' carrse/coorse I'ee layee?*] catch my drift?; get what I'm saying?; understand where I'm coming from?

< "I'm all a-tremble with pleasure at seeing you restored to life, my dear captain." "Your best affidavy to that would be my

632 doubloons. **See the course I lay?**" > (Dutch & Thomas Bartholomew Red, "Pirates" 55:09)

today or tomorrow? [t'/ter-dayee arr t'/ter-mahrr-owoo?] sometime today?; any day now?

A sarcastic way of prodding someone causing delay, moving slowly, or acting in laggardly fashion.

"Hey, Scratch, that rum, do we get it **today or tomorrow?**" (Thomas Bartholomew Red, "Pirates" 1:01:36)

what(ever) ails you? [wharrt/whorrt(-ebber/e'er) ayells 'ee/ya/ye/yer?] what's the matter with you?; what's wrong?

"**What ails ya all?**" (Thomas Bartholomew Red, frustrated with the stubborn silence kept by his old company mates on seeing them for the first time in years, "Pirates" 1:00:18) "**Whatever ails you**, Peter? I've never known ye scared before." (Wolverstone, *Captain Blood: His Odyssey* 251)

what are you about? [wharrt/whorrt be 'ee/ya/ye/yer abarrt/abowoot/'barrt/'bout/'bowoot?] what do you think you're doing?; what are you up to?

"And **what are ye about**, within the sweep of my hawse?" (watch aboard the *Dolphin*, suspicious after hearing a nonsensical answer to his hail, *The Red Rover* 84)

what be yon? [wharrt/whorrt be yarrn?] what is that?

"Ben! **What be yon?**" (Roger Tressady, pointing to a fresh mound of sand on what they had believed to have been an uninhabited island, *Black Bartlemy's Treasure* 91)

what be your poison? [wharrt/whorrt be ya/yarr/ye/yer/yere/yore p'i/poyee-son?] what would you like to drink?

The pirate version of the barkeep's time-honored query.

< "I'm sure your wine's the finest in the colonies, Mister Bridger, but there's another I'd fancy if you have it, good sir." "Aye! I knew ye were a man of distinction, I did! **What be your poison?**" (John Paul & Long John Silver, *Dead Man's Chest* 27–28)

what beside? [wharrt/whorrt b'-sawd/syeede?] what else?

"As for you, Martin, Lord Wendover, there is your enemy, ha?—bloody vengeance and murder and **what beside?**" (Adam Penfeather, *Black Bartlemy's Treasure* 81)

what course (should we steer next)? [wharrt/whorrt carrse/coorse (shoood we stee-arr/err nex')?] what next?; what do we do now?

"**What course now, sir?**" (Ned Bowser, as he and Adam Penfeather's company march away from the palace of Santo Domingo into the neighboring savannah, *Adam Penfeather, Buccaneer* 334) "Being thus made surprisingly rich, we began to think **what course we should steer next.**" (Captain Avery, *The King of Pirates* 24)

what cozening is here? [wharrt/whorrt a-coz-enin'/'nin'/'ning 's\be 'ee'arr/'ee'err/'ere/hee'arr/hee'err?] what's going on here?; what are you trying to pull?

Used to express suspicion of trickery or wrongdoing.

"Brimstone and gall, **what cozening is here?**" (James Hook, *Peter Pan* 94)

what do you think you're about? [wharrt/whorrt d'/does 'ee/ya/ye/yer fink/thenk/t'ink ya're/yer/ye're/yore abarrt/abowoot/'barrt/'bout/'bowoot?] what do you think you're doing?

"LeRois, you stupid drunk bastard, goddamn your eyes, **what do you think you're about?**" (Ezekiel Ripley, *The Guardship* 237)

what fool('s) __ is this? [wharrt/whorrt foo'ell('s) __ 's\be dis/t'is?]

Question derisively asked in reference to anything absurd, nonsensical, idiotic, short-sighted, or otherwise ill-conceived. "Fool," where used without the apostrophe-"s", functions as an adjective.

> "Lord love me! **What** new **fool craze is this**?" (Adam Penfeather, *Black Bartlemy's Treasure* 318) "Lord love me, now **what fool's ploy is this**?" (Adam Penfeather, *Black Bartlemy's Treasure* 318)

what ho? [*wharrt/whorrt ho'oo?*] what's up?; what's going on?

> "**What ho**, gentlemen?" (Elizabeth Marlowe, *The Pirate Round* 234)

what is __ about? [*wharrt/whorrt 's\be __ abarrt/ abowoot/'barrt/'bout/'bowoot?*] what's up with __?; what's the story with __?

Used to express puzzlement with, bewilderment by, or confusion about something. The question is typically reserved for occasions in which the speaker is more than simply curious or inquisitive, but rather frustrated by or exasperated with his inability to comprehend.

> "**What are those guns about**?" (Scribner, *The Pirate Round* 314)

what like is __? [*wharrt/whorrt lawk/lyeeke be __?*] what is __ like?

Modern speakers save the word "like" for the end of the question, while pirates use it toward the beginning, immediately after the word "what." Thus, "What was Madagascar like?" becomes "What like was Madagascar?"

> < "And these other rogues?" "**What like were** they, shipmate?" > (Martin Conisby & Adam Penfeather, *Black Bartlemy's Treasure* 62)

what luck? [*wharrt/whorrt larrk/loohk?*] how did things turn out?; how did it go?

The thrust of the question is whether the addressee accomplished what he set out to do or otherwise met with success.

> "Ye're soon returned. **What luck**?" (Peter Blood, *Captain Blood Returns* 183)

what maggot's burrowing under your periwig? [*wharrt/whorrt maggert's a-burrowin' arrn/hun/oohn-darr/'ner ya/yarr/ye/yer/yere/ yore parri/payri-weg?*] what's the matter?; what are you worried about?; what's wrong?

Note with respect to the excerpt below that Captain Blood actually does wear a periwig, and Wolverstone may intend this at least in part somewhat literally. A purely metaphorical use, however, is also effective—arguably more so.

> "**What maggot's burrowing under your periwig**, Peter?" (Wolverstone, *Captain Blood Returns* 23)

what matter __? [*wharrt/whorrt ma'er __?*] what does __ matter?; what difference does __ make?

> "I would, Wilder, that we had known each other earlier. But **what matter** vain regrets?" (The Red Rover, *The Red Rover* 408)

what mean you by ...? [*wharrt/whorrt mean 'ee/ya/ye/yer byee ...?*] what do you think you're doing by ...? why are you ...?

> "**What mean you by** entering my cabin as though it were a Wapping alehouse?" (John Sharkey, rebuking his boatswain and gunner for rushing into his cabin, *The Dealings of Captain Sharkey and Other Tales of Pirates* "The Blighting of Sharkey" 47)

what o'clock is it? [*wharrt/whorrt o'clarrk be ett/'n/'t?*] what time is it?

> < "Hey, Frog. **What o'clock is it**?" "Six, or eight." > (Thomas Bartholomew Red & The Frog, "Pirates" 1:54:42)

what of __? [*wharrt/whorrt o'\on __?*] what about __?; what happened to __?; tell me about __?; how is __?

> < "**What of** Cecco?" "He's as dead as Jukes." > (Noodler & James Hook, *Peter Pan* 158)

what remains? [*wharrt/whorrt remayeens?*] what next?; what do we do now?

> "And now, Captain? **What remains?**" "To go about again." (Trenam & Peter Blood, *Captain Blood Returns* 292)

what say you that ...? [*wharrt/whorrt sayee 'ee/ya/ye/yer tharrt ...?*] what would you say if ...?; what do you think if ...?

> "I know every able-bodied seafaring man in the town of Bristol. **What say you that** I fetch a flock of 'em right down here to you?" (Long John Silver, "Treasure Island" [1934] 28:00)

what say you to this? [*wharrt/whorrt sayee 'ee/ya/ye/yer t'/ta/ter dis/t'is?*] what do you have to say?; what do you think?

> "Well, Smy, **what say ye to this?**" (Absalom Troy, asking his comrade what he thinks of Adam Penfeather's decision to bring Antonia Chively along, *Adam Penfeather, Buccaneer* 28)

what should move you thus to ...? [*wharrt/whorrt shoood move 'ee/ya/ye/yer tharss/thoohss t'/ta/ter ...?*] what would make you ...?; why would you ...?

> "Why, Ned Bright, **what should move thee thus to** belie me?" (Thomas Doughty, *The Queen's Corsair* 86–87)

what signifies ___? [*wharrt/whorrt seg-nee/ner-faws/fyees ___?*] what is the meaning or purpose of ___?

> "Captain, **what signifies** this trouble of yo hope, and straining in hot weather; there are more anchors at London, and besides, your ship is to be burnt." (John Walden, *General History of the Pyrates* 270)

what then? [*wharrt/whorrt thayn?*]

(1) what is it?; what's going on?

> "**What then**, d'ye sweat, Johnny, d'ye sweat?" (Japhet Bly, mocking John Barrasdale's efforts to carry his heavy burden through the jungle, *Winds of Chance* 158)

(2) what about it?; what of it?; so what?

> < "Don Federigo is governor of the town, I think?" "Verily and so he is. And **what then?**" > (Martin Conisby & Resolution Day, *Martin Conisby's Vengeance* 88)

(3) what next?; so what do we do?

> "Well-a, my Tom, she is the prize—no? And to us. How say-a you, Tom? **What then?**" (Tony, on seeing Ursula Revell hidden in the brush, on *Winds of Chance* 313)

what thing are you? [*wharrt/whorrt fing/theng/thin'/t'in'/t'ing be 'ee/ya/ye/yer?*] who do you think you are?

> "**What thing are you** that seeming man must blench at a little blood? Are you yourself so innocent, you that know Tressady o' the Hook?" (Captain Jo, *Martin Conisby's Vengeance* 9)

what though ...? [*wharrt/whorrt thoughoo ...?*] what if ...?

> < "Us do be but contriving o' ways and means seein' as Penfeather do ha' took our ship, curse him!" "And **what though** he has?" > (Sam Spraggons & Roger Tressady, *Black Bartlemy's Treasure* 312)

what troubles your brain? [*wharrt/whorrt troohbles ya/yarr/ye/yer/yere/yore brayeen?*] what's the matter?; what's wrong?

> "How now, Martino? **What troubleth your** sluggish **brain** now?" (Captain Jo, *Martin Conisby's Vengeance* 26)

what was yon? [*wharrt/whorrt warss\warr/were yarrn?*] what was that?

> "**What was yon!**" (Abnegation Mings, hearing Roger Tressady cry out at a distance, *Martin Conisby's Vengeance* 161)

what would you? [*wharrt/whorrt woood 'ee/ya/ye/yer?*]

(1) what do you want?

> "Well, who are you and **what would you** with us?" (Japhet Bly, challenging Mat-

thew Swayne to identify himself more plainly, *Winds of Chance* 266)

(2) what would you have done?

"Oh, but after all, **what would you?** There was a lady in the case—his little Indian wife." (Yberville, *Captain Blood Returns* 185)

(3) what are you doing?

"Easy, shipmate, easy! Lord love you, Martin, **what would you** now?" (Adam Penfeather, upon being surprised by a delusional and knife-wielding Martin Conisby, *Black Bartlemy's Treasure* 130)

what's acting? [*wharrt/whorrt is\be hact-in'?*] what's happening?; what's going on?

"**What's acting?**" (battery captain on Quail Island, demanding news from a freshly arrived reinforcement, *The Pirate Round* 350)

what's all this to the point? [*wharrt/whorrt is\be awrl dis/t'is t'/ta/ter t' p'int/poyeent?*] what's your point?; so what?

< "Gunners like Ogle are like poets; they are born, so they are. He'll put you a shot between wind and water, will Ogle, as neatly as you might pick your teeth." "**What's all this to the point?**" > (Peter Blood & Captain Easterling, *Captain Blood Returns* 30)

what's doing? [*wharrt/whorrt is\be a-doin'?*] what's going on?; what happening?

"Ods wounds, **what's doing?**" (Benjamin Trigg, seeing his friend Adam Penfeather pummeled to the ground, *Adam Penfeather, Buccaneer* 72)

what's for you? [*wharrt/whorrt is\be farr/fer 'ee/ya/ye/yer?*] what's up with you?; what's the matter?

< "Stop!" "Avast, Johnny! Belay, John! **What's for thee**, lass?" "My shoe heel." > (Ursula Revell & Japhet Bly, with Ursula

stopping the group's progress because of a broken heel, *Winds of Chance* 154)

what's here? [*wharrt/whorrt is\be 'ee'arr/'ee'err/ 'ere/hee'arr/hee'err?*] what's going on?; what's happening?; what's up?; what's the matter?

"**What's here**, Martin, are ye sick?" (Adam Penfeather, to Martin Conisby as Conisby suddenly swoons dizzily and grips the table, *Black Bartlemy's Treasure* 125)

what's in your head? [*wharrt/whorrt is\be i'/'n ya/yarr/ye/yer/yere/yore 'ead/hayd?*] (1) what are you thinking? (2) what's gotten into you?; what's wrong?

"**What's in your head** has put ya in such a fine mood, Cap'n?" (Joshamee Gibbs, "Pirates of the Caribbean: The Curse of the Black Pearl" 1:03:58)

what's that to the matter? [*wharrt/whorrt is\be tharrt t'/ta/ter t' ma'er?*] what difference does that make?; why does that matter?; so what?

< "Who are you, sir?" "**What's that to the matter?**" > (Peter Blood, *Captain Blood Returns* 267)

what's the lay? [*wharrt/whorrt is\be t' layee?*] what's the situation?; what's going on?; what are you up to?

"You're big enough and wild enough and as likely a cut-throat as another—**what's the lay?**" (Abnegation Mings, *Black Bartlemy's Treasure* 30)

what's the odds? [*wharrt/whorrt is\be t' arrds?*] what's the difference?

< "Some wine? Far better. Will you have white or red?" "Well, I reckon it's about the blessed same to me, shipmate, so it's strong, and plenty of it, **what's the odds?**" > (Israel Hands, *Treasure Island* 140, Chap. 26)

what's the word? [*wharrt/whorrt is\be t' warrd?*]

(1) what's up?; what's going on?

"Well, **what's the word?**" (Abnegation Mings, on sitting down across a campfire from Martin Conisby, *Black Bartlemy's Treasure* 30)

(2) what do you say?; what do you think?; how about it?

< "I've no knowledge of navigation." "But I've enough for the two of us, Martin. 'Tis a comrade at my back I need. **What's the word?**" > (Martin Conisby & Adam Penfeather, *Black Bartlemy's Treasure* 112)

what's to do (here)? [*wharrt/whorrt is\be t'/ta/ter do ('ee'arr/'ee'err/'ere/hee'arr/hee'err)?*] what's going on?; what's happening?

< "Here, matey, **what's to do?**" "Oh, the Captain ordered us to move our bunks aft." > (Long John Silver & Jim Hawkins, "Treasure Island" [1934] 38:57) "How now, my hearty! **What's to do here?**" (Benny Willitts, *The Book of Pirates* The Ruby of Kishmoor" 235)

what's yon? [*wharrt/whorrt is\be yarrn?*] what's that?

"Aha, but Adam's dead at last, curse him! Unless he can't be killed either, unless he is—. Ha—**what's yon!**" (Roger Tressady, cowering in terror at some fictional object behind Martin Conisby in order to fool Conisby into turning around, *Black Bartlemy's Treasure* 303)

what's your mind? [*wharrt/whorrt is\be ya/yarr/ ye/yer/yere/yore mawnd/min'/myeen'/myeend?*] what's your view?; what are your thoughts?

"And women aboard ship mean strife, bloodshed, Japhet, and all the sins in the calendar; so, comrade, **what's your mind?**" (Ezekiel Penryn, *Winds of Chance* 33)

what's your trouble? [*wharrt/whorrt is\be ya/yarr/ye/yer/yere/yore troohble?*]

(1) what's wrong?; what's the matter?: A sincere inquiry into the cause of another's complaint or displeasure.

(2) what's your problem?; what's your story?: A gruff challenge to another to speak up and explain himself.

"**What's your trouble**, Murray?" (John Flint, *Porto Bello Gold* 123)

where d'ye lay\lie? [*wayarr/wayerr/wharr d'/ does 'ee/ya/ye/yer layee\lyee?*] where are you?

Note that "does" is often replaced with an apostrophe-"s", as in "where's he lay" or "where's it lie."

"Ha, 'tis plaguey dark, the pit o' Acheron ain't blacker, **where d'ye lay**—speak soft for there's ears a-hearkening very nigh us." (Resolution Day, *Martin Conisby's Vengeance* 78) "**Where's he lie?**" (Roger Tressady, asking Lady Brandon's footman about Adam Penfeather's whereabouts, *Black Bartlemy's Treasure* 97)

where lays your course? [*wayarr/wayerr/ wharr layees ya/yarr/ye/yer/yere/yore carrse/ coorse?*] where are you?

< "A small, thieving rogue is Penfeather—" "And the likest man to make an end o' the Brotherhood that ever sailed!" "**Where lays his course?**" "Who knows!" > (Roger Tressady & Captain Jo, *Martin Conisby's Vengeance* 158)

where would be the use? [*wayarr/wayerr/ wharr woood be t' use?*] what would be the use?; what would be the point?

< "What—Resolution?" "That same, friend, brought somewhat low, comrade, yet soon, it seems, to be exalted—on a gallows, d'ye see, yet constant in prayer, steadfast in faith and nowise repining— for **where would be the use?**" > (Martin Conisby & Resolution Day, in a surprise reunion aboard Adam Penfeather's ship, *Martin Conisby's Vengeance* 137–38)

where you be heading of? [*wayarr/wayerr/ wharr 'ee/ya/ye/yer be a-'ead/hayd-in' o'\on?*] what are you talking about?; what do you mean?; what are you trying to say?

"**Where be you heading of** now, Smiler? Where's the wind? Talk plain!" (pirate in Roger Tressady's company, asking Sam Spraggons to explain more clearly what he is proposing, *Black Bartlemy's Treasure* 311)

whereaway (...) ? [*wayarr/wayerr/wharr awayee/'way/'wayee (...)?*]

(1) where?; where ... ?

"**Whereaway** is he that answers?" (watch aboard the *Dolphin*, suspicious after hearing a nonsensical answer to his hail, *The Red Rover* 84)

(2) where to?; where to ... ?

< "Yo-ho! **Whereaway**, Adam?" "The prison of the Holy Office. Lead on, Joel." > (Benjamin Trigg & Adam Penfeather, *Adam Penfeather, Buccaneer* 328)

where's the wind? [*wayarr/wayerr/wharr is\be t' win'/wint?*] what are you talking about?; what do you mean?; what are you trying to say?

"Where be you heading of now, Smiler? **Where's the wind?** Talk plain!" (pirate in Roger Tressady's company, asking Sam Spraggons to explain more clearly what he is proposing, *Black Bartlemy's Treasure* 311)

where's your hide? [*wayarr/wayerr/wharr is\be ya/yarr/ye/yer/yere/yore hawd/hyeede/'ide?*] where are you?

"Blast ye, woman! **Where's your hide?** Rum! And scupper all this!" (pirate from El Toro Mendoza's company at the *Cask and Anchor*, "Long John Silver's Return to Treasure Island" 1:38)

who comes\goes? [*'oo cahms/carrms/coohms\ go'ooes?*] who's there?; who goes there?

"Yonder—look yonder! **Who comes?**" (Roger Tressady, *Black Bartlemy's Treasure* 309)
"**Who goes?**" (Long John Silver, waking on hearing his parrot Captain Flint announce an intruder, *Treasure Island* 151, Chap. 27)

who hailed you? [*'oo 'ailed/'ayulled/hayulled 'ee/ya/ye/yer?*] who asked you?

< "Pieces of eight! Pieces of eight!" "**Who hailed you**, you old bumboat?!" > (Cap'n Flint the parrot & Long John Silver, "Treasure Island" [1950] 21:39)

who may tell? [*'oo mayee taahl?*] who knows?; who can say?

"[T]hese scum are a means to an end, d'ye see?" "How so?" "Just that, Martin, a means to an end." "What end?" "Ah, **who may tell**, Martin?" > (Adam Penfeather & Martin Conisby, *Black Bartlemy's Treasure* 111–12)

will you be pleased to ...? [*well 'ee/ya/ye/yer be pleast t'/ta/ter ...?*] would you ...?; would you like to ...?

"Good friend, **will you be pleased to** walk with me?" (Absalom Troy, *Adam Penfeather, Buccaneer* 97)

12.2 REPLIES

Below are affirmative replies (12.2.1), negative replies (12.2.2), and noncompliant replies (12.2.3) a pirate can use to answer questions or requests. They may come in handy when you're out of powder and shot.

12.2.1 AFFIRMATIVE REPLIES

PREDICATE + SUBJECT + HELPING VERB

The speaker replies with an affirmative statement but reverses the usual order of the words—that is, starting with the predicate and ending with the subject (or equivalent pronoun) and helping verb. Thus: < "Thatcher make off with the treasure?" "Make off with it he did." >

"I am here to say that since you are so desperate earnest to be wed eftsoons,—**wed you I will**, and so be done." (Japhet Bly, *Winds of Chance* 51)

an' you will [*eff/eff'n/if'n 'ee/ya/ye/yer well*] as you will; if you so desire

< "And now, I humbly beseech you'll suffer me a word." "**An' you will**, sir, and what then?" > (Japhet Bly & Crabtree, *Winds of Chance* 89)

and with a will [*an'/'n' weth/wi'/wiff/witt a well*] I'm all for it; I'm with you one hundred percent; absolutely

< "If 'tis a duel you mean, give me sword and let's to it!" "Ay, ay, Johnny man, **and with a will!**" > (John Barrasdale & Japhet Bly, *Winds of Chance* 141)

arrgh aye; yes

Though "arrgh" has multiple meanings (set out in Chapter 15), when used as a reply it invariably means "aye" or "yes."

< "Why, woman, he loved you with passion to the end." "End?" "**Arrgh**, 'ee died with your name on his lips." "Richard died?" "**Arrgh**, an 'ero's death." > (Long John Silver & Miss Willoughby, "The Adventures of Long John Silver: The Orphans' Christmas" 20:31)

arrgh, that SUBJECT+VERB [*arrgh, tharrt ...*]

An emphatic affirmation. The speaker replies with "arrgh, that," then repeats the subject of the statement being affirmed (or an equivalent pronoun) plus the appropriate form of the verb "be" or of a helping verb like "do," "will," or "would." Thus: < "Will we be attackin' at sunup, then?" "Arrgh, that we will." >

< "You cut away his tops'ls!" "**Arrgh, that I did.**" > (Ben Worley & Blackbeard, "Blackbeard the Pirate" 1:20:01)

as you say [*as 'ee/ya/ye/yer sayee*]

A way of affirming what the addressee has just described or proposed without saying much more. Used often by a speaker who is accepting another's statement grudgingly or without enthusiasm or who is wary of committing himself thereby.

< "[A]t first glimpse of strange sail, you'll bear up and stand away on opposite course, like wise man and prudent com-

mander, eh, Adam, eh?" "**As you say**, Ben." > (Benjamin Trigg & Adam Penfeather, *Adam Penfeather, Buccaneer* 225)

aye (aye) [*aheee/arrgh (aheee/arrgh)*] yes

"Aye" can stand alone or be used to preface any affirmative response.

< "So you've slaved at an oar, then?" "**Aye**, shipmate!" "Endured the shame of stripes and nakedness and filth?" "**Aye**, shipmate." > (Martin Conisby & Adam Penfeather, *Black Bartlemy's Treasure* 47)
< "Gentlemen, the master, I must needs say, has spoke nothing but what is very reasonable, and I think he ought to have his sloop. What do you say gentlemen?" "**Ay, ay**, by G[od] ..." > (Edward Low & members of his company, debating the fate of a prisoner, *Pirates of the New England Coast* 177) < "Sir, do you warn me?" "**Ay, I do**, for yon poor rascals are the very offscourings of this motley crew. One wonders how you came in such ill company?" > (Ursula Revell & Barnabas Rokeby, *Winds of Chance* 57) < "And so, so Captain Penfeather gave you medicine for her?" "**Aye, did he!**" > (Martin Conisby & Resolution Day, *Martin Conisby's Vengeance* 145)

beyond all peradventure [*b'-yarrn'/yarrnd/yon'/yont awrl parr-a'van/a'ven/arrdvan/arrdven/'van/'ven-charr/terr*] without a doubt

< "Are these indeed pirates, Smy?" "Ay, **beyond all peradventure**, Adam!" > (Adam Penfeather & Smy Peters, *Adam Penfeather, Buccaneer* 116)

certain, SUBJECT+VERB [*sarrten, ...*]

The speaker replies with "certain," followed by the subject of the statement being affirmed (or an equivalent pronoun), plus the appropriate form of the verb "be" or of a helping verb like "do," "will," or "would." Thus: < "Are the boatmen still sleepin' in the hold?" "Certain, they are." >

< "We'll always be mates, won't we?" "**Certain, we will.**" > (Jim Hawkins & Long John Silver, "Treasure Island" [1934] 43:56)

even so [*eeben/e'en so'oo*] that's correct

< "You must have been wounded." "**Even so,** lad." > (Ralph Rover & Bloody Bill, *The Coral Island* 257)

I'll warrant __ [*I'ee'ull waah/weh-runt __*]

Used to express the speaker's absolute certainty about something. "I'll warrant" is followed by a pronoun corresponding to the person or thing in question. Thus: < "Be the treasure buried still?" "I'll warrant it." >

< "Snaith? Dead? Is he?" "**I'll warrant ... him!**" > (John Barrasdale & Japhet Bly, with Bly believing he has fatally strangled Roger Snaith as he and Barrasdale run from Snaith's limp body, *Winds of Chance* 328)

VERB it is [*... ett/'n/'t be*]

The speaker repeats back the verb in the statement being replied to, then adds "it is."

< "You ... you will dare abduct me?" "Ay, ay, ma'm, **abduct it is** and more's the pity." > (Ursula Revell & Japhet Bly, *Winds of Chance* 19)

just so [*jast/jarrst/jarrs'/joohst/jus' so'oo*] exactly; precisely

< "The *Maria Gloriosa*? What are you telling me? Why, you captured her yourself at San Domingo and came back here in her when you brought the treasure-ships." "**Just so.**" > (Monsieur d'Ogeron & Peter Blood, *The Fortunes of Captain Blood* 81)

like enough [*lawk/lyeeke enarrff/enow/'nough*] in all likelihood; it's likely

< "And hark to yon scream! One surely died then, eh, Japhet?" "Ay, **like enough.**" > (John Barrasdale & Japhet Bly, *Winds of Chance* 333)

never doubt it [*nebber/ne'er darrt/dowoot ett/'n*] of course

A solid, reassuring answer to any question, especially a request.

< "Oh, Master Penryn, be my good friend." "Mistress Revell, **never doubt it.**" > (Ursula Revell & Ezekiel Penryn, *Winds of Chance* 48)

now there was a true word as ever was heard spoke [*narr/nowoo tharr/theyarr/theyerr warss\warr/were a troo warrd as ebber/e'er warss\warr/were 'arrd/'eard/harrd spooke/spo'ooke*] that's the truth; you speak the truth

< "Your name wouldn't be Henry Morgan, would it?" "**Now there was a true word as ever was heard spoke!**" > (David Noble & Henry Morgan, *Dead Man's Chest* 128)

so SUBJECT+VERB [*so'oo ...*]

The speaker replies with "so," then repeats the subject of the statement being affirmed (or an equivalent pronoun) plus the appropriate form of the verb "be" or of a helping verb like "do," "will," or "would." Thus: < "Will we be attackin' at sunup, then?" "So we will." >

< "It was liker somebody else' voice now—it was liker—" "By the powers, Ben Gunn!" "Ay, and **so it were.** Ben Gunn it were!" > (George Merry, Long John Silver, & Tom Morgan, correctly identifying a ghostlike voice as Ben Gunn's, *Treasure Island* 182, Chap. 32)

so I think [*so'oo I'ee fink/thenk//t'ink*] I think so; I think that's right; I think you're right

< "Yon should be Snaith's villains." "Ay, **so I think.**" > (John Barrasdale & Japhet Bly, hearing distant shouting and gunshots, *Winds of Chance* 333)

that SUBJECT+VERB [*tharr ...*]

The speaker replies with "that," then repeats the subject of the statement being affirmed (or an equivalent pronoun) plus the appropriate form of the verb "be" or of a helping verb like "do," "will," or "would." Thus: < "Thatcher make off with the treasure?" "That he did." >

< "You sailed under the Admiral?" "**That I did**, sir." > (Squire Trelawney & Long John Silver, "Treasure Island" [1950] 17:54)

that VERB+SUBJECT [*tharrt ...*]

The speaker replies with "that," then follows with the appropriate form of the verb "be" or of a helping verb like "do," "will," or "would," plus the subject of the statement being affirmed (or an equivalent pronoun). Thus: < "Thatcher make off with the treasure?" "That did he." >

> < "So now, Ben, you are leaving, I take it?" "Ay, 'od's my life—**that am I**!" > (Adam Penfeather & Benjamin Trigg, *Adam Penfeather, Buccaneer* 264)

SUBJECT+VERB that [*... tharrt*]

The speaker repeats the subject of the statement being affirmed (or an equivalent pronoun), plus the appropriate form of the verb "be" or of a helping verb like "do," "will," or "would." The speaker then finishes with "that." Thus: < "Thatcher make off with the treasure?" "He did that." >

> < "Are you an Englishman?" "**I am that**! Born within sound o' Bow Bells ..." > (Martin Conisby & John, *Martin Conisby's Vengeance* 181)

that be about the measure\shape of it [*tharrt is/'s abarrt/abowoot/'barrt/'bout/'bowoot t' maysure\shayeepe o'\on ett/'n/'t*] that's about the size of it; that's about right

> < "You're back, right?" "**That be about the measure of it**, lad." > (Steve Walker & Blackbeard, "Blackbeard's Ghost" 30:00) < "You mean, no one can see you except me?" "**That's about the shape of it**, son." > (Steve Walker & Blackbeard, "Blackbeard's Ghost" 25:50)

that's a true word [*tharrt's a troo warrd*] that's the truth

> < "He were an ugly devil, that blue in the face, too!" "That was how the rum took him. Blue! well, I reckon he was blue. **That's a**

true word." > (unnamed pirate & George Merry, *Treasure Island* 180, Chap. 32)

that's the verity of it [*tharrt's t' vaah/vay-rity o'\on ett/'n/'t*] that's the truth

> < "And indeed, Mr. Troy, your play is even more reckless than I expected, so loose and wild I might have killed you all too easily. So let's be done." "The which is gospel true." "Ay, body o' me, **that's the verity on't**, sirs!" > (Adam Penfeather, Smy Peters, & Benjamin Trigg, *Adam Penfeather, Buccaneer* 115)

there's reason\sense in that [*tharr/theyarr/theyerr is\be reasern/reas'n\sanse i'/'n tharrt*] that makes sense; that stands to reason

> < "'An eye for an eye,' reverend sir." "Why, **there's reason in that**, look you!" > (Japhet Bly & Ezekiel Penryn, *Winds of Chance* 31) "**There's sense in what he tells us—**." (MacTavish, endorsing the idea of holding the plundered merchant ship for ransom, "The Black Pirate" 38:44)

there's the truth on't [*tharr/theyarr/theyerr is\be t' troof o'/of ett/'n/'t*] that's the truth of it

> "So **there's the truth on't**, ma'm, a yarn as aren't nowise fit for a pretty lady's years ..." (Jeremy Jervey, *Winds of Chance* 229)

'tis well bethought on [*ett/it 's\be OR 'tes waahl b'-tharrt arrn*] that's a good idea

> < "By your grace, Master Slave Driver, shall we not eat?" "Ay, Johnny, **'tis well bethought on**." > (John Barrasdale & Japhet Bly, *Winds of Chance* 166)

true as death [*troo as dath/deff*] absolutely true

> "Which is marvellous strange yet **true as death**, Adam." (Absalom Troy, *Adam Penfeather, Buccaneer* 135)

true for you [*troo farr/fer 'ee/ya/ye/yer*] that's true; that's right

< "Ay, but bethink you, Captain; such caresses should savour sweeter were they enjoyed before my damned cousin Japhet's very face." "Aha—**true for you**, my lord! Passion o' Venus—yes!" > (John Barrasdale & Roger Snaith, *Winds of Chance* 317)

verily (and __) [*vaah/vay-rily (an'/'n' __)*] indeed (and ...); certainly (and ...)

> < "[A] notable swordsman, eh, Smy?" "**Verily**, brother." > (Absalom Troy & Smy Peters, *Adam Penfeather, Buccaneer* 21) < "And 'tis to sink, burn and destroy Bartlemy's accursed ship and make an end of him that Smy and I are pledged and sworn." "**Verily and indeed!**" > (Absalom Troy & Smy Peters, *Adam Penfeather, Buccaneer* 21) < "Don Federigo is governor of the town, I think?" "**Verily and so he is**. And what then?" > (Martin Conisby & Resolution Day, *Martin Conisby's Vengeance* 88) < "He is dead?" "**Verily and thoroughly!** And a moist end he made on't." > (Captain Jo & Resolution Day, *Martin Conisby's Vengeance* 109)

the which is gospel true [*t' whech be garrspel troo*] which is absolutely true; which is certainly right

> < "And indeed, Mr. Troy, your play is even more reckless than I expected, so loose and wild I might have killed you all too easily. So let's be done." "**The which is gospel true**." > (Adam Penfeather & Smy Peters, *Adam Penfeather, Buccaneer* 115)

yes, faith\verily [*yahss, fayeeth\vaah/vay-rily*] yes, indeed

> < "To kill men and ... cut off their heads!" "**Yes, faith!** The head of Cap'n Tobias Ingleby—one o' three, ma'm that shall have like end, though I die for 't." > (Ursula Revell & Japhet Bly, *Winds of Chance* 228) < "Oh, Japhet and you, Mr.

John, the evils committed, the harms endured are past and done with, so let them be forgot betwixt ye and think only of the future." "Why, Ursula, so I do, and very evil future I am promised." "**Yes, verily!**" > (Ursula Revell, John Barrasdale, & Japhet Bly, *Winds of Chance* 255–56)

you have it [*ya/ye/yer 'aff/'ave/ha'/haff ett/'n/'t*] you said it; you've got that right

> < "The Primate of the New World is still at sea. Let him pay for the sins of his countrymen." "Faith, **ye have it**. It's like burning candles to Satan to be delicate with a Spaniard just because he's an archbishop." > (Yberville & Wolverstone, *The Fortunes of Captain Blood* 118–19)

you have the right of it [*ya/ye/yer 'aff/'ave/ha'/haff t' rawt/righeet o'\on ett/'n/'t*]
you're in the right of it [*ya're/yer/ye're/yore i'/'n t' rawt/righeet o'\on ett/'n/'t*] you're right; you're correct

> < "[I]t's him, Roger, it's him!" "Bleed me! But you're i' th' right on't, Abny. You **ha' th' right on't**, lad." > (Abnegation Mings & Roger Tressady, *Martin Conisby's Vengeance* 155) "That's you, Bill, you**'re in the right of it**, Billy." (Black Dog, *Treasure Island* 11, Chap. 2)

you said right [*ya/ye/yer sayd rawt/righeet*] you said it; you've got that right

> < "Troth, say I to meself, if the captain must talk with Murray he'll ha' a bad taste in the mouth o' him to be washed out, and I'd best ha' a sup o' sugar-juice handy for his needin's." "**You said right**, my lad." > (Darby McGraw & John Flint, *Porto Bello Gold* 131)

12.2.2 NEGATIVE REPLIES

I'm damned if I do [*I'eem damt an'\eff/eff'n/if'n I'ee do*] I'll be damned if I do that; never

< "Let him be, Bill." "I'm [damned] if I do." > (Long John Silver & Billy Bones, *Porto Bello Gold* 68)

nay [*nayee*] no

"Were you shipwrecked?" "**Nay**, mate, marooned." (Ben Gunn, *Treasure Island* 80, Chap. 15)

nenny [*nanny/neh'ee*] nope; nah; uh-uh

A casual, dismissive version of "no."

< "I thank you gratefully, yet think I may better despatch alone." "**Nenny**, messmate, no, no!" > (Adam Penfeather & Absalom Troy, *Adam Penfeather, Buccaneer* 19)

never think it [*nebber/ne'er fink/thenk/t'ink ett/'n/'t*] don't even think it

An especially colorful and emphatic way of saying no.

< "Hath Joanna ordered this?" "**Never think it**, mate—she's ashore and I swam aboard, having my suspicions." > (Martin Conisby & Resolution Day, *Martin Conisby's Vengeance* 78)

OATH no [... *no'oo*]

The speaker uses any oath (see Chapter 6) plus the word "no" for a very emphatic way of replying in the negative.

< "Japhet, if you should indeed be so mad to attempt any attack on Captain Snaith and his men, I'll be mad also, for I shall go with you—" "'**Sdeath—no!**" > (Ursula Revell & Japhet Bly, *Winds of Chance* 310)

not PRONOUN [*narrt ...*]

A speaker who might otherwise reply "no" instead says "not," plus the pronoun equivalent of the subject used in the question. Thus: < "Are the boatmen still sleepin' in the hold?" "Not they." >

< "Are you aware whom you are addressing?" "**Not I!** nor do I care." > (Clara d'Alfarez & Cain's mate, *The Pirate* 113, Chap. XV)

not a whit [*narrt a whet*] not a bit; not in the least

< "Have you—oh, Japhet, have you no thought of forgiveness?" "**Not a whit**, ma'm, **not a whit**." > (Ursula Revell & Japhet Bly, *Winds of Chance* 235)

not by no manner o' means [*narrt byee no'oo manner o' means*] no way, no how; not under any circumstances

< "Could you but get me speech with him—" "**Not by no manner o' means** whatsoever, amigo!" > (Martin Conisby & Resolution Day, *Martin Conisby's Vengeance* 89)

that bite won't take [*tharrt bawt/byeete won't/woon't tayeeke*] that won't work; that dog won't hunt; nice try, but no dice

"Ay, G[o]d d[am]n ye, to live and hang us, if we are ever taken: No, no, walk up and be damn'd, **that bite won't take**, it has hanged many an honest fellow already." (William Fly, answering Captain Green's desperate plea for his own life and offer to remain in irons until put ashore, *General History of the Pyrates* 607)

12.2.3 NONCOMPLIANT REPLIES

how shall I know? [*howoo/'ow/'owoo shawrl I'ee knowoo?*] how should I know?

< "What, what can it be ... Japhet—" "**How shall I know?**" > (Ursula Revell & Japhet Bly, *Winds of Chance* 258)

no matter [*no'oo ma'er*] no reason

< "And where lieth this Troy prisoned?" "In dungeon of the Holy Office at— Pray why would you know, Sir Buccaneer?" "**No matter!** I was curious to learn if his wife was prisoned with him ..." > (Adam Penfeather & Black Bartlemy, *Adam Penfeather, Buccaneer* 257)

no matter for this [*no'oo ma'er farr/fer dis/t'is*] that doesn't matter; that's not important

"Well, now, there lieth Conscience shall nevermore denounce me—now what shall this portend?" **"No matter for this, sir, there be divers o' my bully lads do need your care ..."** (Matthew Swayne & Roger Snaith, *Winds of Chance* 323)

('tis) no matter for you [*(ett/it 's\be OR 'tes) no'oo ma'er farr/fer 'ee/ya/ye/yer*] don't worry about it; it's none of your business; that's none of your business

> < "What is it you will do?" **"No matter for you**, sweetheart." > (Isabel de Sotomayor & George Fairfax, *The Fortunes of Captain Blood* 160) < "Aye, but what o' Joanna, what o' that she-snake, ha?" **"'Tis no matter for her."** > (Captain Belvedere & Job, *Martin Conisby's Vengeance* 68)

some might say one thing and some another [*sahm/sarrm/soohm mawt/migheet sayee woohn fing/theng/thin'/t'in'/t'ing an'/'n' sahm/sarrm/soohm ano'er/anudder/'no'er/'nother/'nudder*]

Typically used either to defuse a disagreement or, as in the below excerpt, to evade a question.

> < "To whom do you owe your present position?" **"Some might say one thing and some another."** > (Andrew Murray & John Flint, *Porto Bello Gold* 85)

that's a trifle [*tharrt's a traw/tryee-fle*] that's unimportant; that's not really the issue

> "[Y]ou'd have starved, too, if I hadn't—but **that's a trifle!** you look there—that's why!" (Long John Silver, *Treasure Island* 165, Chap. 29)

'tis no matter [*ett/it 's\be OR 'tes no'oo ma'er*] it doesn't matter

> < "And what I ask is, how a sailor-man comes to know the patter o' the flash coves!" **"'Tis no matter**, but since you're o' the Brotherhood sit ye and welcome, 'tis dry enough here in this cave." > (Martin Conisby & Abnegation Mings, *Black Bartlemy's Treasure* 30)

'tis no matter for __ [*ett/it 's\be OR 'tes no'oo ma'er farr/fer __*] __ doesn't matter

> "Below there! Ho, John, **'tis no matter for** the castle batteries, they'll soon be out o' range, man our stern-chase guns, for we're pursued." (Adam Penfeather, ordering his gunner to shift his target from the fort ashore to the pursuing ship, *Adam Penfeather, Buccaneer* 186)

CHAPTER 13

Toasts & Declamations

In 1669, off the Caribbean island of Savona, Henry Morgan and the captains of his buccaneer fleet held a war council aboard Morgan's thirty-six-gun flagship. After deciding on a new venture against the Spanish, they drank, toasted the health of the King of England, and drank some more. Morgan's crew also celebrated, rioting around the ship and firing off her cannon.

Until a few sparks landed in the gunpowder.

The ship exploded. Only thirty of the three hundred Englishmen aboard survived. Miraculously, Morgan was one of them. Just six weeks later, Morgan led his men in the sacking of Gibraltar and Maracaibo. (*Buccaneers of America* 141–63; *Under the Black Flag* 48–49)

Had Morgan died in the explosion, just after raising a glass, he might have died a martyr. Or he might have died a fool, with fickle history viewing the incident as oafish absurdity. One thing is for sure: If you're going to die with a toast on your lips, it should be as eloquent as possible.

Section 13.1 lays out a list of toasts. The examples cited were uttered, in every instance, with drink in hand. Boldness and drink are cornerstones of pirate life; the two merge neatly when strong words are spoken over raised cups.

Section 13.2 sets out a list of declamations. These are sweeping but pithy statements memorable for their catchy encapsulations of pirate life. They often convey—and are intended to convey—as much about the strength and bent of the speaker's character as about the subject being expounded upon. Most declamations are easily used as toasts but are listed separately here because they were not originally spoken in that specific context.

13.1 TOASTS

"Clear the decks for pleasant action!"
[clee-arr/err t' dacks farr/fer playsant hack/ack-shern/shoohn]

(Billy Bones, sitting down with rum at a long table of tavern-goers at the Admiral Benbow Inn, "Treasure Island" [1934] 7:19)

"[Curse] the head of him who ever lived to wear a halter." [carrse/carrst/coorse/cursh/ curst t' 'ead/hayd o'\on 'im 'oo ebber/e'er levved/liffed/livt t'/ta/ter warr/wayarr/wayerr a 'alter/harrlter]

(Bartholomew Roberts, *The Pirates Own Book* 95)

"Curse the King and all the higher powers."
[carrse/coorse/cursh t' Keng an'/'n' awrl t' harr/'igher parrs/powarrs]

(Charles Vane's crew, *Villains of All Nations* 93 & *Under the Black Flag* 93)

"Damn the Governour." [damn t' Goohv/ Gub-'ner]

(Charles Vane's crew, likely referring to Woodes Rogers, the former privateer who re-established royal authority as governor of the Bahama Islands, *Villains of All Nations* 93 & *Under the Black Flag* 93)

"Damnation to him who ever lived to wear a halter." [dam-may/mayee/nayee-shern/shoohn t'/ta/ter 'im 'oo ebber/e'er levved/liffed/livt t'/ta/ter warr/wayarr/wayerr a 'al/harrl-ter]

(Bartholomew Roberts, *Villains of All Nations* 149–50)

"Damnation to King George." [dam-may/mayee/nayee-shern/shoohn t'/ta/ter Keng Jarrge]

(Charles Vane's crew, *Villains of All Nations* 93 & *Under the Black Flag* 93)

"Damnation to the Governour and confusion to the colony ..." [dam-may/mayee/nayee-shern/shoohn t'/ta/ter t' Goohv/Gub-'ner an'/'n' cahn/carrn/coohn/kern-foo-zhern t'/ta/ter t' carrl-erny/'ny]

(one of eight members of Bartholomew Roberts' crew at their place of execution, raising a glass of wine in bitter condemnation of the colony of Virginia and its pirate-hunting governor Alexander Spotswood, *Villains of All Nations* 12)

"Drink battle, murder, shipwreck and hellfire to ..." [drenk baah'le, marrder, shep-wrack an'/'n' 'ell-farr/fyarr t'/ta/ter ...]

(Roger Tressady, *Martin Conisby's Vengeance* 158–59)

"[D]rink hearty ..." [drenk 'ahrrt/'eart/hahrrt-y]

(Roger Tressady, *Martin Conisby's Vengeance* 158)

"Drink up, me hearties, yo ho!" [drenk arrp my/myee 'ahrrt/'eart/hahrrt-ies, yo'oo ho'oo]

(carousing pirates, "Pirates of the Caribbean" Disney attraction)

"Fair voyage and success ..." [farr/fayarr/fay-err vaw/v'y-'ge an'/'n' sarrk/soohk-sess]

(Long John Silver, toasting the *Hispaniola* at the Spyglass Inn, "Treasure Island" [1960] 26:56)

"Fill that pretty belly with grog and that's what makes the world spin on its poles, say I." [fell tharrt preh'y belly weth/wi'/wiff/witt grarrg an'/'n' tharrt's wharrt/whorrt mayeekes t' warrld spen arrn/o' etts po'ooles, sayee I'ee]

(Billy Bones, "Treasure Island" [1934] 7:23)

"[F]or old Friendship's noble sake." [farr/fer ol'/oold/o'oold Fraynd/Frien'-shep's nooble/no'ooble sayeeke]

(Benjamin Trigg, *Adam Penfeather, Buccaneer* 311)

"Good success to ..." [good sarrk/soohk-sess t'/ta/ter]

(John Augur, toasting the Bahama Islands and their governor with a last glass of wine at the Nassau gallows just before being hanged for piracy, *Under the Black Flag* 154)

"Here's luck." [*'ee'arr/'ee'err/'ere/hee'arr/hee'err be loohk*]

    (Israel Hands, *Treasure Island* 141, Chap. 26)

"[H]ere's luck and long life to each and all on us." [*'ee'arr/'ee'err/'ere/hee'arr/hee'err be larrk/loohk an'/'n' larrng lawf/lyeefe t'/ta/ter each an'/'n' awrl o'/of arrss*]

    (Roger Tressady, *Martin Conisby's Vengeance* 159)

"[H]ere's to a bloody shirt and the Brotherhood o' the Coast." [*'ee'arr/'ee'err/'ere/hee'arr/hee'err be t'/ta/ter a bloohd/bluh'/blutt-y sharrt an'/'n' t' Brudder/Bru'er/Bruvver-'ood of\on t' Coost/Co'oost*]

    (Abnegation Mings, *Black Bartlemy's Treasure* 32)

"[H]ere's to a good, hot fight ... and the best dog on top!" [*'ee'arr/'ee'err/'ere/hee'arr/hee'err be t'/ta/ter a good harrt/'ot fawt/figheet an'/'n t' bast dahg/darrg/dorrg arrn/o' tarrp!*]

    (Blackbeard, toasting with tavern patrons on the eve of his show-down with Virginia privateers, *The Book of Pirates* "Jack Ballister's Fortunes" 137)

"[H]ere's to our better acquaintance." [*'ee'arr/'ee'err/'ere/hee'arr/hee'err be t'/ta/ter arr/owarr be'er\gooder acquayeen/akayn/'kayn/'quayeen-ternce*]

    (Captain Jo, putting Roger Tressady's liquor bottle to her mouth, *Martin Conisby's Vengeance* 157–58)

"Here's to ourselves, and hold your luff, plenty of prizes and plenty of duff." [*'ee'arr/'ee'err/'ere/hee'arr/hee'err be t'/ta/ter arr/owarr-seffs/selfs, an'/'n' hol'/hoold/ho'oold/'old ya/yarr/ye/yer/yere/yore larrf/loohff, plen'y o'\on praw/pryee-zes an'/'n' plen'y o'\on darrf/doohff*]

    (Long John Silver, *Treasure Island* 62, Chap. 12)

"[H]ere's you and me agin world and damn all, says I." [*'ee'arr/'ee'err/'ere/hee'arr/hee'err be 'ee/ye an'/'n' me against/agaynst/'gainst/'gaynst warrld an'/'n' damn awrl, sayee I'ee*]

    (Roger Tressady, *Martin Conisby's Vengeance* 158)

"I now takes off my glass to ..." [*I'ee narr/no-woo tayeeke arrf me/myee glass t'/ta/ter ...*]

    (Ned Bowser, *Adam Penfeather, Buccaneer* 295)

"The King of England's health." [*t' Keng o' Ayng-lan's/lun's 'ealth/helf*]

    (Henry Morgan and his men, just before blowing themselves up by inadvertently igniting the ship's gunpowder, *The Buccaneers of America* 142) (John Russell and other members of Edward Low's company, referring not to King George but rather to his Roman Catholic rival, James Francis Edward Stuart, son of James II, *Pirates of the New England Coast* 178)

"The King of France." [*t' Keng o'\on France*]

    (John Russell and other members of Edward Low's company, *Pirates of the New England Coast* 178)

"[L]et us drain a goblet, clink cannikin and toss a pot to ..." [*laaht/le' arrss drayeen a garrblet, clenk cannerkin an'/'n' tarss a parrt t'/ta/ter ...*]

    (Benjamin Trigg, *Adam Penfeather, Buccaneer* 246)

"[L]et us forthwith toss a pot, twirl a can, and drain a beaker to ..." [*laaht/le' arrss farrt/farrth/fort/foort/foorth-weth/wi'/wiff/witt tarss a parrt, twirell a can, an'/'n' drayeen a beaker t'/ta/ter ...*]

    (Benjamin Trigg, *Adam Penfeather, Buccaneer* 311)

"Prosperity to trade." [*prahrrs-per'ty t'/ta/ter trayeede*]

    (John Russell and other members of Edward Low's company, *Pirates of the New England Coast* 178)

"Sluice the ivories, drink deep and drink oft ..." [*sluice t' aw/iyee-varr/v'r-ies, drenk deep an'/'n' drenk arrft*]

> (Absalom Troy, *Adam Penfeather, Buccaneer* 6)

"Success to [our] undertaking." [*sarrk/soohk-sess t'/ta/ter arr/owarr arrn/hun/oohn-darr/'ner-tayee-kin'*]

> (John Russell and other members of Edward Low's company, *Pirates of the New England Coast* 178)

"Take what you can. Give nothing back." [*tayeeke wharrt/whorrt 'ee/ya/ye/yer cayn/kin, gi'/giff nuff/nutt-in' back*]

> (Jack Sparrow & Joshamee Gibbs, "Pirates of the Caribbean: The Curse of the Black Pearl" 53:53)

"[T]o ... a good voyage, and a safe return." [*t'/ta/ter ... a good vaw/v'y-'ge an'/'n' a sayeefe retarrn*]

> (officers aboard the *Duke, A Cruising Voyage Round the World* 61)

"[T]o a happy sight of ..." [*t'/ta/ter a 'appy/harrpy sawt/sigheet o'\on ...*]

> (Woodes Rogers and his officers, toasting the fair ladies of Bristol, *A Cruising Voyage Round the World* 191)

"[T]o all my many shipmates lost at sea." [*t'/ta/ter awrl me/myee meh'y shep-mayeetes lorrst a'/hat sea*]

> (Jack Sparrow, "Pirates of the Caribbean" Disney attraction [2006])

"To luck." [*t'/ta/ter loohk*]

> (Israel Hands, *Treasure Island* 62, Chap. 12)

"[T]o Old England, ourselves and the golden Future ..." [*t'/ta/ter Ol'/Oold/O'oold Ayng-lan'/lun', arr-seffs/selfs an'/'n' t' goold/go'oold-ern Foo-charr*]

> (Benjamin Trigg, *Adam Penfeather, Buccaneer* 246)

"[T]o our better friendship." [*t'/ta/ter arr/owarr be'er\gooder fraynd/frien'-shep*]

> (John Sharkey, putting an arm around the waist of his female prisoner, *The Dealings of Captain Sharkey and Other Tales of Pirates* "The Blighting of Sharkey" 55)

"To [our] fortunate proceedings and good success." [*t'/ta/ter arr/owarr farr/foor-chern/tern/t'n-ayte per/pree-ceedin's an'/'n' good sarrk/soohk-sess*]

> (members of Edward Low's company, *Pirates of the New England Coast* 193)

"To [our] next merry meeting." [*t'/ta/ter arr/owarr nex' maah/mahr/may-ry meetin'*]

> (Edward Cheeseman toasting a merchant sloop's boatswain and master just before murdering them, *General History of the Pyrates* 349)

"[T]o ... success on our venture." [*t'/ta/ter ... sarrk/soohk-sess arrn/o' arr/owarr van-charr/terr*]

> (Adam Penfeather, *Adam Penfeather, Buccaneer* 295)

"To the health of the Pretender." [*t'/ta/ter t' 'ealth/helf o'\on t' Parr/Per-tendarr*]

> (Stede Bonnet's crew, raising glasses to King George's Roman Catholic rival, James II, *Villains of All Nations* 93)

13.2 DECLAMATIONS

better days ahead [*be'er\gooder dayees a'ead/ayahd/'head*] things will get better; tomorrow's another day

Words of consolation and encouragement spoken to the sad or defeated.

> "Good luck, Major Folly. **Better days ahead**." (Ned Lynch, "Swashbuckler" 24:26)

curse all rovers who should ever give quarter to an Englishman [*carrse/carrst/coorse/cursh/curst awrl rob/roov/ro'oov-ers* 'oo shoood ebber/e'er gi'/giff quahrr/quaht-ter t'/ta/ter a Ayng-lersh/lesh-man]

A colorful and passionate condemnation of all Englishmen. A speaker might substitute for "an Englishman" any description, characterization, or category of persons.

> "Curse all rovers who should ever give quarter to an Englishman." (William Fly, *Pirates of the New England Coast* 335)

curse all Spanishers [carrse/carrst/coorse/cursh/curst awrl Span-iahrrds/ishers/nerds]

As Spain claimed the entirety of the New World as its possession and viewed any trespass (let alone any act of plunder or violence on its subjects) as an act of war, pirates generally had only contempt for the Spanish.

> "A land o' milk and honey given over to devils—**curse all Spanishers**, say I!" (John, *Martin Conisby's Vengeance* 186)

eye for eye, tooth for tooth, blood for blood—'tis a good law and just [eye'ee farr/fer eye'ee, toof farr/fer toof, bloohd/blut farr/fer bloohd/blut—ett/it 's\be OR 'tes a good lawr an'/'n' jast/jarrst/jarrs'/joohst/jus']

A colorful articulation of the pirate's penchant for revenge and ruthless retribution.

> "Eye for eye, Martino. **Tooth for tooth, blood for blood: 'tis a good law and just**, yes!" (Captain Jo, *Martin Conisby's Vengeance* 48)

a fair wind [a farr/fayarr/fayerr win'/wint]

Used to wish another seaman a good journey or to wish any person well in his future endeavors.

> "But good luck t'ye and **a fair wind**, say I!" (Roger Tressady, *Black Bartlemy's Treasure* 302)

a fair wind, a quick eye, and no favor [a farr/fayarr/fayerr win'/wint, a queck eye'ee, an'/'n' no'oo faah/fayee-varr]

The phrase is a seaman's play on the older, better-worn expression "a fair field and no favour," a reference to the notion that one

fares best not by preferential treatment but by equitable treatment and opportunity to rely on his own resources and capabilities.

> "Aye, Cap'n, by cock, them was the days, **a fair wind, a quick eye an' no favour**, aye, them was the days, by cock's-body!" (Joel Bym, *Black Bartlemy's Treasure* 80)

Fortune with you and yours [Farr-chern/toon weth/wi'/wiff/witt 'ee/ya/ye/yer an'/'n' yarrs/yer'n/yourn\theys]

An expansive way of wishing one luck.

> "Good lad. Bide where you are, Jo, and **Fortune with you and yours**." (Adam Penfeather, saying farewell to Joel Bym, *Black Bartlemy's Treasure* 107)

good fortune attend you [good farr-chern/toon arr-tand/ten' 'ee/ya/ye/yer] good luck to you

> "So now, Martin, **good Fortune attend you**." (farewell in letter from Adam Penfeather to Martin Conisby, *Black Bartlemy's Treasure* 164)

good luck to you and a fair wind [g' loohk t'/ta/ter 'ee/ya/ye/yer an'/'n' a farr/fayarr/fayerr win'/wint]

Used to wish another seaman a good journey or to wish any person well in their future endeavors.

> "But **good luck t'ye and a fair wind**, say I!" (Roger Tressady, *Black Bartlemy's Treasure* 302)

having lost my all, I'll take all that I may ['av/haff-in' larrst me/myee awrl, I'ee'ull tayeeke awrl tharrt I'ee mayee]

A determined expression of resilience and ambition after total defeat or failure.

> < "And what says you, Japhet man?" "That **having lost my all, I'll take all that I may**." > (Barnabas Rokeby & Japhet Bly, *Winds of Chance* 32–33)

here's luck and a fair wind to you ['ee'arr/'ee'err/'ere/hee'arr/hee'err be loohk an'/'n' a farr/fayarr/fayerr win'/wint t'/ta/ter 'ee/ya/ye/yer]

Used to wish another seaman a good journey, or to wish any person well in his future endeavors.

> "Here's luck and a fair wind t'ye, Marty!" (Roger Tressady, upon recognizing Martin Conisby after years of not having seen him, *Martin Conisby's Vengeance* 155)

here it is about gentlemen of fortune— they lives rough, and they risk swinging, but they eat and drink like fighting-cocks [*'ee'arr/'ee'err/'ere/hee'arr/hee'err ett/'n/'t be OR 'tes/'tis abarrt/abowoot/'barrt/'bout/'bowoot jan'lemen o'\on farr/chern/toon—dey\dem/them levvs/liffs rarrf/roohff, an'/'n' dey\dem/them resk a-swengin', barrt dey\dem/them eat an'/'n' drenk lawk/lyeeke fawt/figh'-in'-carrks*]

A colorful summary of the pirate's life.

> "Here it is about gentlemen of fortune. They lives rough, and they risk swinging, but they eat and drink like fighting-cocks." (Long John Silver, *Treasure Island* 58, Chap. 11)

I wish you a fair wind ever and always [*I'ee wersh/wesh 'ee/ya/ye/yer a farr/fayarr/fayerr win'/wint ebber/e'er an'/'n' al-way/wayees*]

An expansive way of wishing someone well luck in his future endeavors.

> "Howsoever, come life or death, here's Abnegation doth **wish ye a fair wind ever and always**, master." (Abnegation Mings, *Black Bartlemy's Treasure* 319)

it's a pirate's life [*ett be OR 'tes/'tis a py-eeret's/errt's/raaht's lawf/lyeefe*]

Used to characterize an event, circumstance, or condition—particularly an unfortunate or unforeseeable one—as simply another aspect or consequence of life as a pirate.

> "Once you shed blood and dole out cruelty, it's hard to stop. **It's a pirate's life**, my lad!" (James Hook, "Hook" 1:49:38)

it's the world against us, and us against the world [*ett is\be OR 'tes/'tis t' warrld agaynst/agin/'gainst/'gaynst arrss, an'/'n' arrss agaynst/agin/'gainst/'gaynst t' warrld*]

Pirates typically see themselves as hunted down by and warring against the rest of the world—trusting only in their company mates. This strident declaration approaches an oath of brotherhood and is appropriate for use by any pirate in reference to his allegiance to the company in the hardest of times.

> "**It's the world against us, and us against the world!**" (Peter Blood, just after setting out the articles for his new company of pirates, "Captain Blood" 1:04:56)

life's a bed of roses [*lawf/lyeefe is\be a bad o'\on roo/ro'oo-sers*] life is wonderful

> "Drinks are on the house! **Life's a bed of roses!**" (Thomas Bartholomew Red, "Pirates" 1:00:34)

(to) the luck of the Brotherhood [*(t'/ta/ter) t' loohk o'\on t' Bro'er/Brudder/Bruvver-'ood*]

An expression consistent with the self-congratulatory tendency among pirates to consider themselves favored by fortune.

> "Ha, 'tis so—'tis our Jo—our luck! Shout for Cap'n Jo and the **luck o' the Brotherhood!**" (pirates aboard the *Happy Despatch, Martin Conisby's Vengeance* 106)

a merry life and a short one [*a maah/mahr/may-ry lawf/lyeefe an'/'n' a sharrt 'un/woohn*]

An endorsement of the dissipative, raucous, devil-may-care ways of pirates, especially when in port and with plunder to spend. Rough modern equivalents include "Eat, drink, and be merry, for tomorrow we die" and "Better to burn out than fade away."

> "No, **a merry life and a short one**, shall be my motto." (Bartholomew Roberts, *General History of the Pyrates* 244)

of all liquor commend me to rum [*o'\on awrl likkerr cahm/carrm/coohm/kerm-mand me t'/ta/ter roohm*]

A resonant expression of the pirate's prizing of rum above all other liquors.

"[T]here's nought like liquor for putting the devil into a man, and **of all liquor commend me to rum** with a dash o' tobacco or gunpowder, d'ye see." (Adam Penfeather, *Black Bartlemy's Treasure* 158)

the only trade where a pretty fellow can pick up a living [*t' on'y trayeede wayarr/wayerr/wharr a preh'y fellowoo cayn/kin peck arrp a levv/liff-in'*]

"Pretty" here is likely used as a double entendre, meaning both "clever" and "terrible." The phrase is a frank characterization of piracy as a profession appropriate for those with more cunning than conscience.

"You've saved your skin, Scarrow, and it's a pity so stout a man should not take to **the only trade where a pretty fellow can pick up a living**." (John Sharkey, *The Dealings of Captain Sharkey and Other Tales of Pirates* "How the Governor of Saint Kitt's Came Home" 23)

a pirate's life for me [*a py-eeret's/errt's/raaht's lawf/lyeefe farr/fer me*]

A pirate's enthusiastic endorsement of life as a pirate, implying an appreciation of it as admirable, pleasurable, or otherwise rewarding.

"Yo ho, yo ho, **a pirate's life for me!**" (carousing pirates, "Pirates of the Caribbean" Disney attraction)

a pirate's life is the only life for a man of any spirit [*a py-eeret's/errt's/raaht's lawf/lyeefe be t' on'y lawf/lyeefe farr/fer a man o'\on a'y sperrit/sp'rit*]

An enthusiastic endorsement of the life of a pirate as a good and admirable one.

*Bunce and Macarty began to rattle, and talk with great pleasure, and much boasting of their former exploits when they had been pyrates, crying up **a pyrate's life to be the only life for a man of any spirit**.* (attribution to Phineas Bunce and Dennis Macarty, *General History of the Pyrates* 628)

pirates have no God but their money, nor saviour but their arms [*py-eerets/errts/raahts 'aff/'ave/ha'/haff no'oo Garrd/Gott/Gud barrt tharr/theyarr/theyerr moohny/muh'ey, narr saah/sayeevyarr barrt tharr/theyarr/theyerr ahrrms*]

"Pirates ha[ve] no God but their money, nor saviour but their arms." (members of Edward Low's company, *Pirates of the New England Coast* 174)

share and share, 'tis the law of the Coast [*sharr/shayarr/shayerr an'/'n' sharr/shayarr/shayerr, ett/it/'n/'t is/'s\be OR 'tes t' lawr o'\on t' Co'oost/Coost*]

Used to emphasize the importance and tradition of dividing plunder fairly.

"**Share and share!** 'Tis the law of the Coast." (Adam Penfeather, *Black Bartlemy's Treasure* 82)

some fight, 'tis for riches—some fight, 'tis for fame ... [*sahm/sarrm/soohm fawt/figheet, ett/'n/it is\be OR 'tes farr/fer reches—sahm/sarrm/soohm fawt/figheet, ett/'n/it is\be OR 'tes farr/fer fayeeme ...*]

A line from a song that colorfully articulates the pirate's penchant for revenge and ruthless retribution.

"Some fight, 'tis for riches—some fight, 'tis for fame:/The first I despise, and the last is a name./I fight, 'tis for vengeance! I love to see flow,/At the stroke of my sabre, the life of my foe." ("Pirate's Song", *The Pirates Own Book* 465)

there's nought like liquor for putting the devil into a man [*tharr/theyarr/theyerr is\be narrt lawk/lyeeke likkerr farr/fer a-puttin' t' daahv/dayv/debb/div-il in-ta/terr a man*]

A reference to the close association between drunkenness and evil-doing in pirate life.

"[T]here's nought like liquor for putting the devil into a man, and of all liquor commend me to rum with a dash o' tobacco or gunpowder, d'ye see." (Adam Penfeather, *Black Bartlemy's Treasure* 158)

they rob the poor under the cover of law, and we plunder the rich under the protection of our own courage [*dey\dem//them rarrb t' poo'err arrn/hun/oohn-darr/'ner t' co'/cooh/cubb-er o'\on lawr, an'/'n' we ploohn-darr/'ner t' rech arrn/hun/oohn-darr/'ner t' per/pree-tak-shern/shoohn o'\on arr/owarr owoon carr-'ge*]

An expression inspired by the pirate's romantic vision of himself as a warrior against the world of oppressive society.

> "They villify us, the scoundrels do, when there is only this difference, **they rob the poor under the cover of law, forsooth, and we plunder the rich under the protection of our own courage ...**" (Captain Bellamy to the captain of a captured Boston sloop, *General History of the Pyrates* 587)

'tis give and take, share and share [*ett/it is/'s\be* OR *'tes gi'/giff an'/'n' tayeeke, sharr/shayarr/shayerr an'/'n' sharr/shayarr/shayerr*]

(1) A reference to the practice among members of a pirate company of sharing all plunder. (2) An aspirational expression characterizing the extent to which pirates consider themselves members of a single brotherhood.

> < "Then, Adam Penfeather, I'm your debtor." "Nay, there be no debts 'twixt comrades o' the Brotherhood, **'tis give and take, share and share!**" > (Martin Conisby & Adam Penfeather, *Black Bartlemy's Treasure* 60)

'tis my trade—sinkin's, burnin's, kidnaps, murder, the fine art o' profit—but larceny above all [*ett/it 's\be* OR *'tes me/myee tray-eede—senk-in's, barrn-in's, ked-narrps, marrder, t' fawn/fyeene ahrrt o'\on prarrf-ert—barrt lahrr-cerny 'bove awrl*]

An acknowledgment that, at the heart of it all, piracy is about taking things that belong to someone else.

> < "A little private larceny, huh?" "Arrgh, **'tis my trade. Sinkin's, burnin's, kidnaps, murder. The fine art o' profit. But larceny**

above all." > (Edward Maynard & Blackbeard, "Blackbeard the Pirate" 48:25)

to win fortune and power or six foot of earth [*t'/ta/ter wen farr-chern/toon an'/'n' parr/powarr arr sex foot o'\on arrth*]

A determined expression presenting a pirate's choice as one between success and death. If pirates had a creed, this might be it.

> "So Absalom, I'll with thee, —**to win fortune and power or six foot of earth ...**" (Adam Penfeather, *Adam Penfeather, Buccaneer* 13)

your foes and woes are mine and mine are thine [*ya/yarr/ye/yer/yere/yore fo'oos an'/'n' wo'oos be mawn/myeene an'/'n' mawn/myeene be yarrs/yer'n/yourn\theys*]

An expression of brotherhood.

> "Well now, henceforth **thy foes and woes are mine and mine are thine ...**" (Absalom Troy, explaining to Adam Penfeather the significance of their blood brotherhood, *Adam Penfeather, Buccaneer* 36)

your true buccaneer has but two enemies— himself by reason of drink and the devil, and the accursed Spaniard [*ya/yarr/ye/yer/yere/yore troo barka/barker/buccarr/bucker-nee-arr 'as/ha' barrt two aahn-ermies—'im-seff byee reasern/reas'n o'\on drenk an'/'n' t' daahv/dayv/debb/div-il, an'/'n' t' ac-cars/coors/cursh-ed Span-iahrrd/isher/nerd*]

An indication of the profound contempt pirates have for gentlemen of Spain.

> "On the other hand, messmate, **your true buccaneer hath but two enemies**, to wit—**himself by reason of drink and the devil, and the accursed Spaniard** with his hellish slave-galleys, cruel *autos da fe* the which are public burnings ... and the most horrid torments of his Inquisition." > (Absalom Troy, *Adam Penfeather, Buccaneer* 19–20)

CHAPTER 14

Contractions

Contractions are quick and dirty ways of spitting out larger words: "**You are** to be trusted not to kill me because **I have** the map" becomes "**You'm** to be trusted not to kill me because **I've** the map." Pirates love using contractions, both because they're always in a hurry to get to the main idea of what they're saying and because they'd like to do so as unconventionally as possible.

Below is a list of contractions frequently used by pirates, listed by their full word equivalents (appearing in capital letters) in alphabetical order.

The list includes common abridgements of single words ("o'" for "of") as well as contractions of two or more words ("'twere" for "if it were"). Note that there is often more than one contraction for a given term.

AM = 'm

"It may be knowledge to you, but how**'m** I to know of it as never heard it?" (John Flint, *Porto Bello Gold* 87)

AM NOT = ain't; bain't

"I'm not stayin' 'ere to be cut up piecemeal. Not me, I **ain't**. I'm for runnin' for it." (Frogger, "Long John Silver's Return to Treasure Island" 1:19:31) "I **b'ain't** no coward, doctor. But the thought of them there gallows gives me the shakes." (Long John Silver, "Treasure Island" [1950] 1:23:11)

AND = an'; 'n'

"Ye kin keep the bloody schooner, **an'** the loot, **an'** bad cess may it bring ye." (Billy Doyle, *The Gun Ketch* 159) < "Be she not wanted for service at the house?" "Nay, all the servants have a holiday. Mr. Wainright **'n'** 'is wife be dinin' at the Governor's." > (pirate at the Cask & Anchor, "The Adventures of Long John Silver: The Necklace" 1:42)

ARE = 'm; 're

"You**'m** great 'ands to talk, you are. But when it comes to fightin', that boy there be a better man than any two of ye." (Long John Silver, "Treasure Island" [1950] 1:16:40) "Ye touch off yer cannon an' these**'re** dead, an' so**'re** the others." (Billy Doyle, threatening to kill his women prisoners if attacked, *The Gun Ketch* 160)

ARE NOT = ain't; ben't

"**Ain't** you forgettin', Mister Bowlegs, I'm now cap'n here." (Long John Silver, "Long John Silver's Return to Treasure Island" 15:51) "If you **ben't** dead, it'd be my duty to rescue 'ee." (Long John Silver, "Long John Silver's Return to Treasure Island" 1:16:41)

AS = 's; 'z

"Might be sportin' agin, soon**'s** ye scrub her up, an' put some rum in 'er." (Billy Doyle, talking of a woman prisoner he's mistreated, *The Gun Ketch* 161) "Ain't they a handsome pair o' young pieces, squire's son? Pretty**'z** yer sister, I wager." (Billy Doyle, bringing out two women prisoners for Alan Lewrie to see, *The Gun Ketch* 159)

BE = b'

"**B'**you standin' for cap'n, agayn?" (Long John Silver, "Treasure Island" [1950] 1:28:36)

DARE(S) NOT = dursn't

"Ye know I **dursn't** accept your offer. Ye know my men would tear me in pieces if I did so without consulting them." (Crosby Pike, *Captain Blood Returns* 283)

DID NOT HAVE = hadn't

"Ye're not by any means the first to do that. But they've mainly been Spaniards, and they **hadn't** your luck." (Peter Blood, *Captain Blood: His Odyssey* 244)

DID YOU = d'ye

"**D'ye** hear that? Him sailing under Hawke?!" (George Merry, "Treasure Island" [1950] 17:54)

DO NOT = ain't; bain't

"Argh, medallion there be, but medallion I **ain't** got nor knows who has." (Long John Silver, "Long John Silver's Return

to Treasure Island" 8:20) "**B'ain't** you no love in your hearts for the peace and beauty of this here tropical island?" (Long John Silver, "Long John Silver's Return to Treasure Island" 1:13:29)

DO NOT HAVE = haven't

"You **haven't** got a bit of cheese on ya, have ya? 'Course, you haven't." (Ben Gunn, "Treasure Island" [1998] 54:11)

DO YOU = d'ya; d'ye

"How **d'ya** sail with your mate and quartermaster in jail?" (Ironhand, "The Adventures of Long John Silver: The Pink Pearl" 7:38) < "What now?" "Smoke! **D'ye** not smell it?" > (Ursula Revell & Japhet Bly, *Winds of Chance* 273)

HAD = 'ad; 'd

"Cabin boys. None of 'em be any good. I remember one we **'ad** when I sailed with Flint." (Long John Silver, "Long John Silver's Return to Treasure Island" 22:29) < "I should never have married him, Japhet!" "Howbeit, ma'm, **I'd** word 'twas all arranged." > (Ursula Revell & Japhet Bly, *Winds of Chance* 238)

HAD NOT = 'adn't; han't

"In no coffeehouse in London or any other where, shall you drink coffee the like o' this, taken from a Spanish galleass out o' Java. **Ha'n't** you noticed its excellence aboard the Deliverance?" (Japhet Bly, *Winds of Chance* 150)

HAS = 'as; 's

"This here sauce **'as** a nice flavor." (Long John Silver, "The Adventures of Long John Silver: Turnabout" 19:02) "She**'s** a swivel gun on 'er poop, and nothin' more." (Alacan the Turk, *Dead Man's Chest* 52)

HAVE = 'a'; ha'; 've

"He can't **'a'** found the treasure, for that's clean a-top." (Tom Morgan, *Trea-*

sure Island 177, Chap. 31) "We should never **ha'** put our trust in that son of a dog." (Trenam, *Captain Blood Returns* 284) "Now, youngster, listen to me. I**'ve** no time to waste here." (pirate captain, threatening fifteen-year-old Ralph Rover with a cocked pistol, *The Coral Island* 198)

HAVE NOT = ain't; hain't; han't

"You **ain't** let no one see it, have ye?" (Long John Silver, "Treasure Island" [1950] 32:22) "[Y]ou **hain't** got the invention of a cockroach." (Long John Silver, *Treasure Island* 166, Chap. 29) "I **ha'n't** fought and hunted with Indians without learning me some o' their craft." (Japhet Bly, *Winds of Chance* 300)

HE = 'e

"He don't fool me, **'e** don't." (Ironhand, "The Adventures of Long John Silver: The Pink Pearl" 20:31)

HE IS = 'tis

"Flint may well make trouble. **'Tis** a determined dog, and a greedy." (Andrew Murray, *Porto Bello Gold* 104)

HER = 'er

"Damn me buttons. There's a thin slice o' luck. See **'er** colors?" (Thomas Bartholomew Red, on spotting a rescuing ship hoist the Spanish flag, "Pirates" 8:07)

HIM = 'im

"One of them swabs. After **'im**, all of ye. Run **'im** down." (Long John Silver, "Treasure Island" [1950] 23:26)

HIS = 'is

"Have ye the kidney fer cuttin' a man open fer **'is** purse?" (Long John Silver, *Dead Man's Chest* 11)

IF = i'

"A man might as well be in the King's own navy **i'** 'e's aboard ship with Miss Purity

there." (Patch, "The Adventures of Long John Silver: The Eviction" 15:10)

IN = i'; 'n

"There be three lying **i'** the cave yonder." (Roger Snaith, *Winds of Chance* 323)

IS IT = is't

"Good lack, **is't** thee, child?" (Lovepeace Farrance, encountering Ursula Revell unexpectedly on Farrance's gun deck, *Winds of Chance* 75)

IS NOT = ain't; bain't; ben't

"Now **ain't** it a shame to see you in such ill condition, Perch." (Long John Silver, "Long John Silver's Return to Treasure Island" 4:07) "It **bain't** mutiny, Long John, to refuse to be ruled by a man what lets a piddlin' toothache drive him daft." (Patch, "The Adventures of Long John Silver: The Tale of a Tooth" 15:23) "There be no votin' till the business o' this here map be disposed of. Till then I'm still cap'n, and your black spot **ben't** worth a biscuit." (Long John Silver, "Treasure Island" [1950] 1:20:09)

IT = 'n; 't

"Now, put**'n** in your pocket and keep**'n** there at half cock." (Long John Silver, letting Jim Hawkins keep an impressive-looking pistol, "Treasure Island" [1950] 24:56) "This here crew'll lay a sight more confidence in a cap'n as'll allow**'t** our say about enemy pris'ners." (George Merry, "Treasure Island" [1950] 1:16:05)

IT HAS = 'tis

< "Are we safe, sir?" "Ay, ma'm, **'tis** blown out sooner than I expected, so I am here to your service." > (Ursula Revell & Japhet Bly, *Winds of Chance* 128)

IT IS = 'tis

"And I say **'tis** foul murder in the sight of God and man!" (Martin Conisby, *Martin Conisby's Vengeance* 99)

IT IS NOT = 'tain't

"**Tain't** right, Master Ormerod, and don't follow in nature nowhow." (Ben Gunn, *Porto Bello Gold* 144)

IT WAS = 'twas; 'twere

"I want their captain, Peter Pan. **'Twas** he cut off my arm." (James Hook, *Peter Pan* 60) "Ay, and what's more, so soon as **'twere** known as he's a-marching—these here Ayamaras and Chachapuyas must be for marching wi' him." (Jeremy Jervey, *Winds of Chance* 248)

IT WAS NOT = 'tweren't; 'tworn't

"'**Tweren't** no ghost what fired that shot." (Long John Silver, "Long John Silver's Return to Treasure Island" 1:15:51)

IT WILL = 'll; 'twill

"Cut me a quid, as **'ll** likely be the last, lad; for I'm for my long home, and no mistake." (Israel Hands, *Treasure Island* 141, Chap. 26) "In another hour **'twill** be dark and what then?" (Roger Snaith, *Winds of Chance* 320)

IT WOULD = 'twould

"If you'll forgive my pointing it out, Skipper, we can't leave a pretty woman unmolested aboard ship. **'Twould** give piracy a bad name." (Humble Bellows, "The Crimson Pirate" 53:08)

IT WOULD BE = 'twere

< "So then ... wouldst murder me, Japhet?" "Ay, as I would any other ravening beast—**'twere** but natural!" > (John Barrasdale & Japhet Bly, *Winds of Chance* 259)

LITTLE = lil'

"We could make the **lil'** buggers love ya." (Smee, "Hook" 1:05:01)

MIGHT NOT = mightn't

"You **mightn't** happen to have a piece of cheese about you, now?" (Ben Gunn, *Treasure Island* 80, Chap. 15)

OF = o'

"Curse him! I'd give a handful **o'** gold pieces to see him dead and be damned!" (Captain Belvedere, *Martin Conisby's Vengeance* 67)

ON ACCOUNT OF = 'count o'

"But my mates most generally calls me 'Barbecue' **'count o'** my being held a monstrous fine cook." (Long John Silver, *Porto Bello Gold* 20–21)

ONE = 'n

"This**'n** here, she wuz right good sport, once she got me ideer." (Billy Doyle, boasting of his mistreatment of a woman prisoner, *The Gun Ketch* 161)

OR = 'r

"I give ye me Bible-oath no harm**'ll** come t' these young tits, an' I'll leave 'em safe an' sound on French Cay**'r** West Caicos." (Billy Doyle, offering Alan Lewrie the lives of his women prisoners in exchange for a clean getaway, *The Gun Ketch* 160)

SHALL NOT = shan't

"[B]ut, by the eternal J[esu]s, you **shan't** live to see us hang'd." (William Fly, *General History of the Pyrates* 611)

SHE IS = 'tis

"Lord love thee, John, Ursula would never leave thee so—**'tis** plaguey wilful spouse." (Japhet Bly, *Winds of Chance* 345)

SHOULD = 'd

< "What if the worst **'d** happen?" "Keep to the Code." "Aye, the Code." > (Joshamee Gibbs & Jack Sparrow, "Pirates of the Caribbean: The Curse of the Black Pearl" 1:07:50)

THAN = 'n

"It's a fool's errand. Why, you know better**'n** me the tales of the *Black Pearl*." (Joshamee Gibbs, "Pirates of the Caribbean: The Curse of the Black Pearl" 52:44)

THAT IS = 's

"It's that cursed petticoat's making a coward of you." (Wolverstone, *Captain Blood: His Odyssey* 252)

THE = t'

"Well, Jim. You seem t' likely lad. Have ya noticed a sea-farin' man along this here grog shop?" (Black Dog, "Treasure Island" [1950] 3:01)

THEM = 'em

"We'll sweep around 'em and cut 'em down." (Patch, "The Adventures of Long John Silver: Sword of Vengeance" 19:14)

THIS = 'tis

Though technically the apostrophe should replace the "h" and intervene between "t" and "i" (spelled "t'is"), the abridgement of "this" in written pirate dialogue is more often spelled "'tis."

< "And I perish with cold, sir." "Yet 'tis tropic sun might soon dry thee." > (Ursula Revell & Japhet Bly, *Winds of Chance* 128)

TO = t'

"Wot say I cut this sweet little dug off, jus' t'prove t'ye 'tis that seryus I am. Still, I got me five more t'offer ye, so this 'un won't be missed." (Billy Doyle, threatening to cut off his woman prisoner's breast to make clear he's prepared to kill her and two others, *The Gun Ketch* 161)

WILL = 'll

"It's done, skipper. We set 'em adrift. The morning tide'll take 'em out to sea." (Slimey, "The Crimson Pirate" 1:05:26)

WILT = 'lt

"I've a message for thee to give to him. Do it, and when I'm skipper, thou'lt be first mate." (Humble Bellows, "The Crimson Pirate" 55:22)

WOULD = 'd; 'ld

"I never tharrt the day'd come I'd need this pistol against them cutthroats." (Long John Silver, "Treasure Island" [1950] 24:01) "There'ld be no harm in having the men stand to their arms on the island tonight." (Wolverstone, *The Fortunes of Captain Blood* 18)

YOU = 'ee

"Cap'n, could I have a word with 'ee about the galley stores?" (Long John Silver, "Long John Silver's Return to Treasure Island" 1:03:00)

CHAPTER 15

𝕬𝖗𝖗𝖌𝖍

There is no term in the pirate language better known than "arrgh." The following is the most comprehensive treatment to date of the term and its uses.

Section 15.1 provides an overview of the term. Section 15.2 lists the forty-four different meanings of the term, with representative excerpts. Section 15.3 lists thirteen other "noise terms"—along with definitions and accompanying excerpts—used by pirates in ways and contexts very similar to those in which "arrgh" is used.

15.1 OVERVIEW

PRONOUNCIATION

"Arrgh" is pronounced "arrr," not "arg." The "gh" at the end represents not a hard "g," but rather the guttural growling quality with which the sustained "rr" should be pronounced.

SPELLING

There are many ways of spelling "arrgh." One common alternative is "argh," and two excerpts given in Section 15.2 spell it "ar." There is no single correct spelling. The *Primer* uses the spelling "arrgh" because that variation faithfully reflects the two *sine qua non* aspects of its pronunciation: (1) a sustained "rr" (the sound is an extended one, such that spelling it with one "r" is really inadequate) and (2) a back-of-the-throat growl (hence the "gh" ending).

NEWTONIZATION

The term "arrgh"—and certainly its notoriety as a term in pirate speech—is almost totally attributable to a single person. Of the 223 instances of "arrgh" in film, television, and literature, all but eight were spoken by characters played by actor Robert Newton. Newton most famously played Long John Silver in "Treasure Island" (1950), reprising the role in "Long John Silver's Return to Treasure Island" (1954) and television's "The Adventures of Long John Silver" (1955), and moreover starred as Blackbeard in "Blackbeard the Pirate" (1952).

Of the eight non-Newtonian instances of the use of "arrgh," four were spoken by actors during scenes

Non-Newtonian Instances of Arrgh

<"I'll set the fire." "Arrgh, they'd see the hulk of ye, no matter how dark it is."> (Patch & Trip Fenner, "Long John Silver's Return to Treasure Island" 1:06:17) **(2)** "Arrgh, yer haven't changed, Silver. A one-legged serpent ya were, a one-legged serpent ye are, a one-legged serpent you die." (Israel Hands, "Long John Silver's Return to Treasure Island" 1:17:29) **(3)** <"Now we'll have no more grumblin'. And up anchor." "Arrgh."> (Long John Silver & Patch, "The Adventures of Long John Silver: The Pink Pearl" 24:25) **(4)** <"You two, stand guard here. The rest of us, ta the house!" "Arrgh."> (Long John Silver & Patch, "The Adventures of Long John Silver: Sword of Vengeance" 19:47).

Of the four remaining instances, one was spoken by Billy Bones (played by Lionel Barrymore) in "Treasure Island" [1934] at time mark 5:08: "**Arrgh**, mind ya, clod, have an eye to that chest." Two were spoken by Ned Bowser, bo'sun aboard the *Bold Adventuress*, in Chapters XII and XVI, respectively, of Jeffery Farnol's *Adam Penfeather, Buccaneer* (1940) (and spelled "ar" on both occasions). The fourth was spoken by a gluttonous pirate in the "Pirates of the Caribbean" Disney attraction who wore a feather hat, professed an affection for "fried salted pork" and "pork loin," and was heard to say, among other things, "Me belly be feelin' like a galleon with a load o' treasure in 'er hold, **arrgh**." The gluttonous pirate was installed sometime after 2000 at the U.S. attractions in place of a character with more libidinous inclinations (*e.g.*, "Oh, I tell you true, it's sore I be to hoist me colors on the likes of that shy little wench") and was himself replaced in 2006 by a pirate brandishing a key and treasure map (*e.g.* "What I wouldn't dare to see the look on Jack Sparrow's face when he hears tell 'tis only me what got the goods!").

or exchanges with Newton in films or television episodes starring Newton.

While Newton obviously did not invent the term (which is spoken in both the 1934 film version of "Treasure Island" and the 1940 book *Adam Penfeather, Buccaneer*), the actor—and the lasting popularity of the 1950 production of "Treasure Island" in which he appeared—cemented "arrgh" into the pirate classic it is today. Newton relied heavily on a dark, throaty delivery and also peppered his pirate characters' speech liberally with "arrgh" and other noise terms to show off that guttural style.

The frequent use of noise terms by Newton's pirate characters only accelerated in his later films. While Newton's 1950 Long John Silver ("Treasure Island") used "arrgh" only nine times in that ninety-six-minute film, for instance, his 1954 Long John Silver ("Return to

Treasure Island") used "arrgh" twenty-seven times in 102 minutes, and his 1952 Blackbeard ("Blackbeard the Pirate") used the term fifty times in ninety-eight minutes—an average of more than twice a minute.

MEANINGS

"Arrgh" can mean a variety of different things. Its uses in film, television, and literature reflect forty-four different meanings. The term's single most popular meaning is "aye" (expressing affirmation, as in "yes"). This "aye" meaning accounts for approximately 37 percent of all instances of the term's use. (The distant runners-up are "aahh" [impatience, mild exasperation, or dismissal—7 percent], "all right" [acknowledgment or mild affirmation—4 percent], and "hey" [4 percent].) That fact is instructive, suggesting that "arrgh" fundamentally may be the result of darkening the word "aye" and bringing it down to a guttural growl.

The vast majority of the other meanings are expressible in modern English as vowel-driven noise terms similar to "arrgh"—such as "ahh," "aww," "hey," "huh," "oh," "ugh" and "uh"—suggesting further that "arrgh" is not some contrivance out of left field, but rather a dark and grunting equivalent of noise terms we use all the time in modern English.

MULTIPLE USAGES

The many meanings of "arrgh" allow a speaker to use the word in different ways, with different meanings, in a single sentence or piece of conversation. The following are a few excerpts illustrating such variable usage. Each excerpt is followed by a run-down of what each "arrgh" in the excerpt means.

- < "Do I make meself clear? Now name the day of our weddin' or be hanged." "**Arrgh**." "Now ya have till the mornin' to make up ya mind, Long John." "**Arrgh!** Ah!" > (Purity Pinker & Long John Silver, "The Adventures of Long John Silver: The Necklace" 19:31)

  "ohh" (sullen or resentful displeasure; definition #30) and "ugh" (anger, exasperation, or acute frustration; definition #34)

- < "**Arrgh**." "You are indeed a master chef." "**Arrgh**." > (Long John Silver & Lieutenant Leon, with Silver uttering "arrgh" first upon sitting himself down for dinner and again to acknowledge the lieutenant's compliments, "The Adventures of Long John Silver: Turnabout" 11:11)

  "ahh" (relaxation, satisfaction, or contentment; definition #4) and "aye" (affirmation; definition #12)

- "**Arrgh!** No grog, no tobacky, no excitement! **Arrgh**, Jim lad, they, they might as well throw me to the sharks now and

'ave done with 'n." (Long John Silver, protesting the doctor's strict instructions for Long John Silver's convalescence, "The Adventures of Long John Silver: Execution Dock" 4:54)

  "ugh" (anger, exasperation, or acute frustration; definition #34) and "ohh" (disappointment, resignation, defeat, or helplessness; definition #29)

OTHER NOISE TERMS

Section 15.3 lists thirteen other noise terms comparable to "arrgh." "Err" and "ha-harr," in particular, are broadly used in many of the same ways as "arrgh" and—though their less frequent use means far fewer documented meanings—they likely can be used in place of "arrgh" in nearly every context.

15.2 DEFINITIONS

Below are the forty-four definitions of "arrgh," each consisting of the closest modern English equivalents and a summary description of the state of mind, attitude, sentiment, reaction, or expression that particular usage of "arrgh" is intended or understood to convey. They are listed, for ease of reference, in the alphabetical order of their modern English equivalents.

(1) **aahh**

Impatience; mild exasperation; dismissal.

< "Gold, Long John, the gold." "What are we waiting for?" "Where is the gold?" "Ay, the medallion, where's the treasure?" "**Arrgh**, belay!" > (various pirates in Long John Silver's company & Long John Silver, quieting their nagging questions as they approach Flint's hidden treasure, "Long John Silver's Return to Treasure Island" 1:26:12) < "What's the matter with her, Long John? I think she was crying." "**Arrgh**, she'll get over it." > (Jim Hawkins & Long John Silver, "The Adventures of Long John Silver: Miss Purity's Birthday" 11:02)

(2) **ah**

Interest or an eagerness to know more.

> < "This here sauce 'as a nice flavor." "That, Monsieur, that is a wine sauce hollandaise." "**Arrgh**, you don't say." > (Long John Silver & Lieutenant Leon, "The Adventures of Long John Silver: Turnabout" 19:02)

(3) **ahh**

Calm pleasure.

> < "And I ask your forgiveness, love." "**Arrgh**, say those golden words agayn." > (Purity Pinker & Long John Silver, "The Adventures of Long John Silver: The Necklace" 9:19)
>
> "**Arrgh**, my glist'nin' darlin's." (Blackbeard, running his hands through strings of pearls, "Blackbeard the Pirate" 48:17)

(4) **ahh**

Relaxation, satisfaction, or contentment.

> "**Arrgh**." (Long John Silver, letting out a sigh as he sits down at a table at the Cask & Anchor, *The Adventures of Long John Silver* 7:53) "And when you comes back aboard, I'll have a nice goat stew waitin' for 'ee to warm your honest bellies. Here, now, get goin'. **Arrgh**." (Long John Silver, cheerfully seeing off his comrades, "The Adventures of Long John Silver: Devil's Stew" 15:15)

(5) **ahh**

Boredom or listlessness.

> "**Arrgh**. Purity and the Reverend should be up at the orphanage by now." (Long John Silver, growing restless as he and an unfriendly Miss Willoughby pass the time together, "The Adventures of Long John Silver: The Orphans' Christmas" 8:05)

(6) **ah-hah**

Sharp realization, discovery, or epiphany.

> < "And this be his picture?" "I kept it like a foolish old maid." "**Arrgh**!" (Long John Silver & Miss Willoughby, with Silver recognizing the old picture of Miss

Willoughby's once boyfriend as fellow seaman Richard Carstairs, "The Adventures of Long John Silver: The Orphans' Christmas" 20:04)

(7) **ah-hah; so there; in your face**

Gleeful or spiteful gloating.

> < "Ahoy there! Have Patch run out the plank!" "Yes, Captain!" "**Arrgh**!" > (Long John Silver & Jim Hawkins, with Silver threatening an intransigent Angus MacAllister with death and turning to him to growl an intimidating "**Arrgh**!," "The Adventures of Long John Silver: The Tale of a Tooth" 22:15)

(8) **all right; okay**

Acknowledgement or mild affirmation.

> < "Not a word was spoken except what I've already told ya." "**Arrgh**. Well, thankee, uh, you've done a fine job of work." "Thank you, Captain." "**Arrgh**, now, if you just fetch Patch and Stingley, we'll carry out my plan." "Aye-aye, Captain." "**Arrgh**." > (Ironhand & Long John Silver, "The Adventures of Long John Silver: Devil's Stew" 14:06)

(9) **anyway; in any event; so; now then**

Used to preface a statement that is apropos of nothing or does not necessarily follow from what has been said before.

> < "At your service, captain." "**Arrgh**, I've just been samplin' your cookin'. And mighty tasty it be, too." > (Lieutenant Leon & Long John Silver, "The Adventures of Long John Silver: Turnabout" 18:51)

(10) **aww**

Show sympathy or give comfort, assurance, or consolation.

> < "Oh, I couldn't let him go." "**Arrgh**, but it be for his good." "Oh, it'd break my heart." "**Arrgh**, and mine too. But 'tis the right thing to do." > (Purity Pinker & Long John Silver, "The Adventures of Long John Silver: Dead Reckoning" 5:17)

(11) **aww, it was nothing**

A friendly dismissal of thanks.

< "Much as I hate to say it, I'm in your debt." "**Arrgh**, 'twas nothin'." > (Angus MacAllister & Long John Silver, "The Adventures of Long John Silver: The Tale of a Tooth" 20:21)

(12) **aye**
Affirmation.

< "Why, woman, he loved you with passion to the end." "End?" "**Arrgh**, 'ee died with your name on his lips." "Richard died?" "**Arrgh**, an 'ero's death." > (Long John Silver & Miss Willoughby, "The Adventures of Long John Silver: The Orphans' Christmas" 20:31)

Note that a speaker might use "arrgh" as an affirmation of what he himself has said: "Me belly be feelin' like a galleon with a load o' treasure in 'er hold, **arrgh**." (gluttonous pirate, "Pirates of the Caribbean" Disney attraction [2005])

Note the use of both "aye" and "arrgh" by the same speaker in a single exchange:
< "I've bad news for your Excellency. Mendoza, he tricked me and sacked your warehouse." "The warehouse sacked?" "**Aye**, and sack it well, he did." "But there was a fortune stored there." "**Arrgh**, I know. But I did stay 'im from gettin' away with the ransom." > (Long John Silver & Governor Strong, "Long John Silver's Return to Treasure Island" 30:30)

(13) **aye!; yes; that's excellent**
Elation, celebration.

"**Arrgh**, we—we did 'em in! Err, we did 'em in! Every yellow-livered one of 'em." (Long John Silver, "Long John Silver's Return to Treasure Island" 1:38:51)

(14) **do it now**
Punctuates an imperative.

"Now get movin'! Get movin', I say! **Arrgh**!" (Long John Silver, forcing at gunpoint a reluctant Salamander the Greek

to walk alone into a Spanish ambush, "The Adventures of Long John Silver: Pieces of Eight" 18:34)

(15) **hah!**
Triumph, vindication.

"**Arrgh**, only the devil and I know where you are now." (Blackbeard, after hiding a treasure chest under a pile of rocks, "Blackbeard the Pirate" 54:32)

(16) **hey; now**
Used to preface a command, instruction, exclamation, or any especially sharp or definitive statement.

< "Ned! Ned!" "**Arrgh**, mind your noise!" > (Ben Worley & Blackbeard, with Worley waking up Blackbeard with urgent news of missing men, "Blackbeard the Pirate" 56:25)

(17) **hey!**
Calls another's attention.

"**Arrgh**, mind ya, clod, have an eye to that chest." (Billy Bones, "Treasure Island" [1934] 5:08)

(18) **hmm**
Observation, assessment, deliberation.

< "You girls—gather 'round!" "What is it, Captain?" "**Arrgh**. **Arrgh**, you'll do. I want you to change clothes with this gentleman here." > (Long John Silver & serving girl at the Cask & Anchor, with Silver sizing up her physical dimensions before having her switch clothes with Lieutenant Leon, "The Adventures of Long John Silver: Turnabout" 22:37)

(19) **hmph!; huff!; tsk!**
Annoyance, irritation, frustration.

< "I've been goin' ashore for thirty years in my shirtsleeves." "Not while I be about. Now you'll put your coat on." "**Arrgh**." > (Long John Silver & Purity Pinker, "The

Adventures of Long John Silver: The Eviction" 14:09)

(20) huh?; yes?; what is it?
Elicitation.

< "Oh, uh, Silver?" "**Arrgh**?" "Is there some other reward, something more substantial you'd rather have?" "No. If you'd been aboard the *Faithful* with me the last week, you'd've found out as I did, there be more important things to a man than the jingle of gold." > (Governor Strong & Long John Silver, "The Adventures of Long John Silver: The Eviction" 24:31)

(21) huh?; what?; what did you say?; what are you saying?
Inquiry or request for explanation.

< "Gold, silver, jewels. That's what he's sittin' on up there." "I bet he isn't." "**Arrgh**?" "Morgan's at sea." > (Blackbeard & Edward Maynard, "Blackbeard the Pirate" 10:26)

(22) huh?!; what?!; what are you talking about?!
Shock, confusion, bewilderment.

< "Jubel, where be that 'and we took aboard at Port Royal?" "You mean Briggs, sir?" "**Arrgh**, that's it." "Disappeared. No trace, sir." "**Arrgh**?!" > (Blackbeard & Jubel, "Blackbeard the Pirate" 41:57)

(23) I see
Soft discovery, realization, epiphany.

< "Here, be there any room at the tavern that's been locked up and you been told not to enter?" "Ironhand says the best bedroom was shut and locked this mornin', and only Miss Purity has the key." "**Arrgh**. Here, come on." > (Long John Silver & Old Stingley, "The Adventures of Long John Silver: The Necklace" 22:32)

(24) oh
Gratitude; acknowledgement of generosity; hospitality; show of benevolence.

< "Come in, Monsieur Silver." "**Arrgh**, thank 'ee kindly, sir." > (Lieutenant Leon & Long John Silver, "The Adventures of Long John Silver: Turnabout" 10:57)

(25) oh!
Pleasure or surprise.

< "Sail ho! Black she be!" "**Arrgh**, I, I do believe that's Uncle Harry." > (lookout in Blackbeard's company and Blackbeard, spotting the black sails of Henry Morgan's ship, "Blackbeard the Pirate" 45:15)

(26) oh, all right; I guess you're right
Grudging acknowledgment or acceptance.

< "Patch, you an' I've sailed many a sea together. And I swear by the blood in my heart that if anything 'appens to this lad, I—I'd as soon give myself to the sharks." "He'll be shipshape, Long John. I know he will." "**Arrgh**." > (Long John Silver & Patch, at the side of Jim Hawkins' sickbed, "The Adventures of Long John Silver: Pieces of Eight" 22:20)

(27) oh, boy!
Excitement, anticipation.

"**Arrgh**, we got a good fight comin' up!" (Blackbeard, *Blackbeard the Pirate* 57:42)

(28) ohh
Relief.

"**Arrgh**, Doc, you, you've come in the nick o' time." (Long John Silver, "The Adventures of Long John Silver: Execution Dock" 24:50)

(29) ohh
Disappointment; resignation; defeat; helplessness.

< "Long John, I've come to crave your pardon for misdoubtin' your word." "**Arrgh**, 'tis too late. I'll soon be mountin' the steps to the gibbet." > (Purity Pinker & Long John Silver, "The Adventures of Long John Silver: The Necklace" 18:49)

(30) ohh

Sullen or resentful displeasure.

< "And Ironhand will go along to watch my interest." "**Arrgh**." > (Purity Pinker & Long John Silver, "The Adventures of Long John Silver: The Pink Pearl" 8:24)

(31) ohh

Mournful sadness; melancholy.

"**Arrgh**, black is the day, heavy is my heart, that I should live to see stout Ben Worley turn on ol' Ned Teach, what's always trusted him like a brother. Heavy is my heart, **arrgh**. It breaks my heart." (Blackbeard, "Blackbeard the Pirate" 49:39)

(32) oww!; ouch!: pain; discomfort

"**Arrgh**, belay! My, my head be throbbin' fit to burst." (Long John Silver, feeling pain at the touch of Purity Pinker's wash cloth on the back of his head, "The Adventures of Long John Silver: Devil's Stew" 2:51)

(33) that's good; that's right

A positive endorsement.

< "Where be the money?" "Here." "**Arrgh**. They'll never get this. This be my first honest voyage, and I pledge I'll finish it honest." > (Long John Silver & Ironhand, "The Adventures of Long John Silver: Devil's Stew" 16:48)

(34) ugh

Anger; exasperation; acute frustration.

"**Arrgh**, you clumsy little bungler, you." (Long John Silver, "Long John Silver's Return to Treasure Island" 22:06)

(35) ugh

Disgust or extreme distaste.

< "All right, then, stew in your own juice, ungrateful swab." "**Arrgh**, women. Ironhand, they be queer cattle. I never could fathom 'em." > (Purity Pinker & Long John Silver, "The Adventures of Long John Silver: Devil's Stew" 4:13)

(36) ugh

Focused or strained effort.

"**Arrgh**. Shoulder to 'er, Jim." (Long John Silver, straining to pry his boat free from the sand in time to make an escape, "Treasure Island" [1950] 1:33:47)

(37) uh

Used to stall or as a pause in speech, especially by a cautious, reluctant, or confused speaker.

< "And my guess would be, if I were asked, that she'd be willin' to put up the two hundred sovereigns." "Ha-harr, most interestin'. **Arrgh**, I, I—I'll give it a thought." > (Ironhand & Long John Silver, "The Adventures of Long John Silver: Devil's Stew" 9:36)

(38) uh-huh; that's it

Encouragement, positive reinforcement.

"Shoulder to 'er, Jim. **Arrgh**, that's it." (Long John Silver, straining to pry his boat free from the sand in time to make an escape, "Treasure Island" [1950] 1:33:47)

(39) uh-uh; uh, no

Prefaces a contradiction.

< "I was told I could find some men here that might sign on." "**Arrgh**, there be faint hope o' that." > (Asa MacDougal & Long John Silver, "Long John Silver's Return to Treasure Island" 45:04)

(40) well; you know

Subdeclarative prefatory used to preface a suggestion, impression, or other soft statement—that is, any statement the speaker wishes to express gently, tentatively, or without presumption.

< "Here, lad, you be twelve year old now, ain't 'ee?" "That's right." "**Arrgh**, that's still a bit young to know the treacheries o' women." > (Long John Silver & Jim Hawkins, "The Adventures of Long John Silver: The Eviction" 16:05)

(41) well, just a moment; wait a minute
Correction or qualification.

> < "You have a plan!" "**Arrgh**, a good cap'n never makes a plan until he's spied out the lay of the land." > (Jim Hawkins & Long John Silver, "The Adventures of Long John Silver: The Orphans' Christmas" 9:03)

(42) whoo
Relief after cessation of intense activity or effort.

> "**Arrgh**. Heh-heh." (Long John Silver, after jumping down from the rail to the deck of the *Cordoba*, "Long John Silver's Return to Treasure Island" 16:29)

(43) yeah, right!
Derisive dismissal, disbelief.

> < "And the ghost ship?" "She was real!" "**Arrgh**, like the *Flying Dutchman*!" > (Long John Silver & Jim Hawkins, "The Adventures of Long John Silver: Ship o' the Dead" 7:17)

(44) you know what; I'll tell you what
Used to preface any statement, especially a firm assertion.

> "**Arrgh**, she ain't near so cheap to keep as she were to take." (Blackbeard, bemoaning the trouble that Edwina Mansfield's presence on board is causing him, "Blackbeard the Pirate" 23:31)

15.3 OTHER NOISE TERMS

Below are thirteen noise terms used in pirate speech in addition to "arrgh." Included in each entry are the closest modern English equivalents and a summary description of the state of mind, attitude, sentiment, reaction, or expression the term is intended or commonly understood to convey.

All of these thirteen terms originated with pirate characters played by Robert Newton in film or television. Note that the only definitions given for each noise term are those corresponding to the meanings with which Newton happened to use it in the original source(s). You should feel free, however, to use each term in other ways (using, perhaps, the definitions of "arrgh" as a guide). In particular, the use of the terms "err" and "ha-harr"—which Newton's characters spoke with a broad variety of meanings—certainly need not be confined to the definitions specified here.

ah-harr
Used to preface any statement, especially a firm assertion, such as "you know what" or "I'll tell you what," or used to preface a command, instruction, exclamation, or any especially sharp or definitive statement, such as "hey" or "now."

> "**Ah-harr**, Mistress Alvina, have a little gulp." (Blackbeard, giving Alvina another drink, "Blackbeard the Pirate" 31:41)

airr
(1) you know what; I'll tell you what
Used to preface any statement, especially a firm assertion.

> "**Airr**, medallion there be, but medallion I ain't got nor knows who has." (Long John Silver, "Long John Silver's Return to Treasure Island" 8:20)

(2) tell me; let me ask you

> "**Airr**, **airr**, Jubel, where be that 'and we took aboard at Port Royal?" (Blackbeard, "Blackbeard the Pirate" 41:51)

bink wha—; the hell—
Shocked disbelief or utter bewilderment, laced with acute displeasure or frustration with one's situation.

> < "So you did steal it. And the charge be thievin'." "And cold-blooded murder." "**Arrgh! Bink! Harr-yy! Arrgh.**" > (Purity Pinker, soldier & Long John Silver, "The Adventures of Long John Silver: The Necklace" 10:44)

darr
Used to preface any statement, especially a firm assertion, such as "you know what"

or "I'll tell you what," or used to preface a command, instruction, exclamation, or any especially sharp or definitive statement, such as "hey" or "now."

> "**Darr**, you'd be slaughtered like hogs in springtime." (Long John Silver, "Long John Silver's Return to Treasure Island" 1:19:38)

err

(1) aahh

Impatience; mild exasperation; dismissal.

> < "I'm looking for Captain Silver." "**Err**, well I be Silver, but I—I'm busy now." > (Evan Frost & Long John Silver, "The Adventures of Long John Silver: Dead Reckoning" 21:37)

(2) all right; okay

Acknowledgment.

> < "Lookout reports wreckage on the starboard bow." "**Err**." > (Jim Hawkins & Long John Silver, "The Adventures of Long John Silver: The Tale of a Tooth" 11:05)

(3) aye!; yes!; that's great; that's excellent

Elation; celebration.

> "Arrgh, we—we did 'em in! **Err**, we did 'em in! Every yellow-livered one of 'em." (Long John Silver, "Long John Silver's Return to Treasure Island" 1:38:51)

(4) hey; now

Used to preface a command, instruction, exclamation, or any especially sharp or definitive statement.

> "**Err**, and put the ladies in the Dutchman's cabin." (Blackbeard, "Blackbeard the Pirate" 8:11)

(5) huh?; yes?; what is it?

> < "Long John." "**Err**?" "Long John, we was betrayed." "What?!" "Patch and Stingley was seized." > (Ironhand & Long John Silver, "The Adventures of Long John Silver: Devil's Stew" 16:41)

(6) huh?; what?; what did you say?; what are you saying?

Inquiry or request for an explanation.

> < "Here's some letters from her to Bellamy." "**Err**?" > (Ben Worley & Blackbeard, "Blackbeard the Pirate" 28:40)

(7) huh?!

Sharp confusion; perturbation.

> < "Now you tell us all about the treasure." "What treasure?" "**Err**?!" > (Blackbeard & Alvina, "Blackbeard the Pirate" 31:54)

(8) oh

Exertion or discomfort.

> "**Err. Err. Err**, but the doctor said only liquid. **Err, err, err, err, err**, water." (Long John Silver, protesting the bread he's been given, then drinking water instead, "The Adventures of Long John Silver: Execution Dock" 10:14)

(9) ohh

Sullen or resentful displeasure.

> "What was he doin' 'ere, I'd like to know. **Err**. Sharks like him, they'll give my 'ouse a bad name. **Err**." (Long John Silver, pretending for Jim Hawkins' benefit to react angrily to Black Dog's sudden appearance at his inn, "Treasure Island" [1950] 23:37)

(10) tell me; let me ask you

> < "What be he payin' for my head?" "He's offered five hundred pounds." "Only five hundred? **Err**, you work cheap, don't you?" (Blackbeard & Edward Maynard, "Blackbeard the Pirate" 40:40)

(11) ugh

Focused or intense effort.

> "Eh. **Err. Err**. Why, I—I've got 'n on." (Long John Silver, making considerable effort at dinner with the Harwoods to tuck his napkin under his collar, then protesting Purity Pinker's signal to put it on his lap

instead, "The Adventures of Long John Silver: Dead Reckoning" 7:38)

(12) uh

Used to stall or as a pause in speech, especially by a cautious, reluctant, or confused speaker.

> "**Err**, I—I suppose you've heard the terrible news." (Long John Silver, "The Adventures of Long John Silver: Dead Reckoning" 3:26)
>
> Note the use of both "uh" and "err" by the same speaker: < "How do you spell 'excellent,' Long John?" "**Err**, now, let's see, **uh**, e-x-s-l ..." > (Jim Hawkins & Long John Silver, "The Adventures of Long John Silver: The Eviction" 3:54)

(13) uh-uh; uh-no

Contradiction.

> < "He'll have to die in the end, Ned." "**Err**, not on this deck he won't." > (Ben Worley & Blackbeard, "Blackbeard the Pirate" 43:05)

(14) well, just a moment; wait a minute

Prefaces a correction or qualification.

> < "Perhaps you would take me to my brother." "**Err**, it's a costly business to outfit and provision a ship." > (Richard Thorpe & Long John Silver, "The Adventures of Long John Silver: The Pink Pearl" 6:48)

(15) you know what; I'll tell you what

Used to preface any statement, especially a firm assertion.

> < "Fortunate I be that you fell in my hands when you did." "I don't understand." "**Err**, you will. You will." > (Blackbeard & Edward Maynard, "Blackbeard the Pirate" 21:15)

(16) growling threat

> "You lay a finger on Mister Arrow and you'll answer to me. **Err**." (Long John Silver, "Treasure Island" [1950] 33:51)

ha-harr

The term "ha-harr," like "arrgh" and "err," is notable for the wide variety of meanings it has. Note in the following excerpt, for example, the multiple meanings with which Newton's Long John Silver uses "ha-harr" in a single exchange—specifically, "ha" (laughter or amusement, definition #5), "you know what" (definition #13), and "hey" (definition #6).

> < "**Ha-harr**, you took your time a-comin'." "But we're going to save you from death." "**Ha-harr**, you're saving me from a fate worse than death. **Ha-harr**, me bucko, let's get movin'." > (Long John Silver & Patch, "The Adventures of Long John Silver: The Necklace" 21:29)

The term is also notable as that with which every episode of "The Adventures of Long John Silver" commenced. The opening sequence of the television show featured Newton's Long John Silver standing silently in silhouette, then suddenly illuminated and brandishing cutlass and bellowing: "Ha-harr, ha-ha, ha-harr!"

(1) ah

Interest; eagerness to know more.

> < "And my guess would be, if I were asked, that she'd be willin' to put up the two hundred sovereigns." "**Ha-harr**, most interestin'. Arrgh, I, I—I'll give it a thought." > (Ironhand & Long John Silver, "The Adventures of Long John Silver: Devil's Stew" 9:36)

(2) aww, it was nothing

Friendly dismissal of thanks.

> < "I owe you my life. I have little to offer in return." "**Ha-harr**. 'Twas nothin'." > (Sean O'Flaherty & Long John Silver, "The Adventures of Long John Silver: Sword of Vengeance" 11:22)

(3) aye

Affirmation.

> < "He'll sink her at anchor while she can't fight back." "**Ha-harr**, you'll fight back."

"Me?" **Ha-harr**. I've left 'ee four cannon aboard." > (Ben Worley & Blackbeard, "Blackbeard the Pirate" 43:44)

(4) aye!; yes!; that's excellent
Elation; celebration.

"**Ha-harr**! Fortune 'as smiled on us at last!" (Long John Silver, "The Adventures of Long John Silver: Sword of Vengeance" 3:22)

(5) ha
Laughter, used to show amusement.

< "He looked like a drowned rat when I finished with him." "**Ha-harr**, excellent! Excellent, indeed!" > (Big Eric & Long John Silver, "The Adventures of Long John Silver: The Eviction" 5:24)

(6) hey; now
Used to preface a command, instruction, exclamation, or any especially sharp or definitive statement.

"**Ha-harr**, put 'n down here." (Long John Silver, motioning Big Eric to place the pot of stew on his table, "The Adventures of Long John Silver: Devil's Stew" 18:34)

(7) not so fast; wait a minute
Prefaces a correction or qualification.

< "Maybe I know." "**Ha-harr**, maybe you think you do." > (Edward Maynard & Blackbeard, "Blackbeard the Pirate" 10:42)

(8) that's right; that's it
Emphasis or conviction.

"Now off you go, my little rabbits, scamper! **Ha-harr**." (Blackbeard, dismissing three island native girls, "Blackbeard the Pirate" 46:36)

(9) ugh
Anger; exasperation; acute frustration.

"**Ha-harr**. She sails like a brick smokehouse right now." (Blackbeard, on announcing the discovery of a leak and four feet of water in the ship's hold, "Blackbeard the Pirate" 41:43)

(10) uh-huh; that's it
Encouragement; positive reinforcement.

"**Ha-harr**, that's right, my little chicken." (Blackbeard, encouraging Alvina to have another drink, "Blackbeard the Pirate" 27:16)

(11) uh-uh; uh, no
Contradiction.

"John Silver, I owe you an apology." "**Ha-harr**, there'll be no need for that." (Governor Strong & Long John Silver, "The Adventures of Long John Silver: The Necklace" 24:36)

(12) well; you know
Used to preface a suggestion, impression, or other soft statement—that is, any statement the speaker wishes to express gently, tenatively, or without presumption.

< "Aw, a fine show he'd make of himself in such company." "**Ha-harr**, Purity's right. I'm no good at birthdays and such frivolities." > (Purity Pinker & Long John Silver, "The Adventures of Long John Silver: Miss Purity's Birthday" 10:02)

(13) you know what; I'll tell you what
Used to preface any statement, especially a firm assertion.

"**Ha-harr**, a right pretty lot of Frenchmen they be." (Long John Silver, watching a boarding party from a French warship approach, "The Adventures of Long John Silver: Turnabout" 4:04)

ha-hurr that's right; that's it
Emphasis or conviction.

"Four and twenty bilge rats rottin' in an 'old. When the hatch was opened, away had gone the gold. **Ha-hurr**." (Blackbeard, "Blackbeard the Pirate" 1:31:18)

harr
(1) hey; now

Used to preface a command, instruction, exclamation, or any especially sharp or definitive statement.

> "**Harr**, listen to this, ha-harr, 'tis a cackle." (Blackbeard, "Blackbeard the Pirate" 28:58)

(2) oh!

Pleasure, surprise.

> "**Harr**, here comes Purity! Arrgh, Jim lad!" (Long John Silver, seeing Purity Pinker and Jim Hawkins return to the Cask & Anchor from Government House, "The Adventures of Long John Silver: Miss Purity's Birthday" 9:11)

(3) you know what; I'll tell you what

Used to preface any statement, especially a firm assertion.

> < "Ironhand!" "Yes, sir!" "**Harr**. Ah, I've got a little job for 'ee." > (Long John Silver & Ironhand, "The Adventures of Long John Silver: Devil's Stew" 12:23)

harr-yy damn it

Angry frustration.

> < "So you did steal it. And the charge be thievin'." "And cold-blooded murder." "Arrgh! Bink! **Harr-yy**! Arrgh." > (Purity Pinker, soldier & Long John Silver, "The Adventures of Long John Silver: The Necklace" 10:44)

hurr

(1) I see

Soft realization or discovery.

> "**Hurr**, so you be 'ob-nobbin' with the gentry, have 'ee?" (Long John Silver, teas-

ing Purity Pinker on her return from an evening at Government House, "The Adventures of Long John Silver: Miss Purity's Birthday" 9:28)

(2) ugh

Anger; exasperation; acute frustration.

> < "Oh, so you doubt my word, woman?" "Aye." "The word of Long John Silver?" "Aye." "**Hurr**." > (Long John Silver & Purity Pinker, "The Adventures of Long John Silver: The Necklace" 8:32)

orr oh

Gratitude, acknowledgement of generosity, hospitality, or any show of benevolence.

> < "Sit down, mon ami." "**Orr**, that's very nice of 'ee." > (Lieutenant Leon & Long John Silver, "The Adventures of Long John Silver: Turnabout" 11:05)

rarr oh, please; come on

Glum or impatient dubiousness.

> < "You could make you a rich man." "**Rarr**, how?" "I make me fortune carryin' livestock to the nearby islands." > (Bartholemew Roberts & Long John Silver, "The Adventures of Long John Silver: Devil's Stew" 6:46)

rarrr-yy aaaaaah!

Shock laced with intense dread or terror.

> "Look, Long John, I'm a bride." "**Rarrr-yy**!" (Purity Pinker & Long John Silver, with Pinker showing off her new wedding dress to the commitment-phobic Silver, "Long John Silver's Return to Treasure Island" 51:46)

CHAPTER 16

Cultural Terms

Certain items excite interest and provoke activity in the average pirate's life more so than other things. Money, drink, and women are prime examples. The closer a given interest or activity to the core of pirate culture, the more likely it is that a rich sub-vocabulary of unique terms has proliferated around it.

One such activity is piracy itself. Section 16.1 covers in detail the strange way in which pirates refer (or, rather, artfully avoid referring) to piracy.

Sections 16.2 through 16.11 list terms relating to discrete cultural categories central to pirate life. Those sections introduce terms associated with, respectively: pirate companies and crews, weapons and armament, torture and punishment, food, drink, currency, time, distance, other units of measurement, and women.

16.1 PIRACY

Eskimos supposedly have multiple words for "snow." Similarly, pirates have at least twenty words for "pirate," eleven words for the plural form "pirates," and eighteen words meaning "to engage in piracy." Why?

Pirates generally do not call themselves "pirates" or refer to their profession as "piracy" for both practical and cultural reasons. Piracy traditionally has been a crime punishable by death—and more specifically, in England, by hanging at low tide. Pirates are rational beings, however intemperate, and generally are not in the business of advertising themselves as gallows-meat. Moreover, the centuries of condemnation to which pirates have been subjected by lawful society have infused the term "pirate," to a certain extent, with a cultural opprobrium that even pirates themselves cannot ignore. As a result, even the most cool-headed acknowledgment by a pirate of his pirate's identity comes grudgingly: "Their minds are but half made up to piracy. 'Tis a coarse word, Mr. Wilder, but I fear we earn it." (The Red Rover, *The Red Rover* 419)

Instances in which pirates take offense—pretended and otherwise—to being called "pirate" are as plentiful as they are amusing:

> < "'Tis said they be no better than pirates—." "Would ye call me a pirate then?" > (Martin Conisby & Abnegation Mings, *Black Bartlemy's Treasure* 32)

> < "I being a quiet soul—" "And a pirate, like as not!" "Easy, shipmate, easy. Passion is an ill word to steer by." > (Adam Penfeather & Martin Conisby, *Black Bartlemy's Treasure* 48)

Watch the film "Captain Blood" for a striking example of a pirate's disavowal of his pirate identity. An hour in, Peter Blood stridently declares himself a pirate as he and his friends draw up company articles, then just twenty-five minutes later reacts with hurt indignation when called exactly that:

> "Desperate men, we go to seek a desperate fortune. Therefore, we do here and now band ourselves into a brotherhood of buccaneers, to practice the trade of piracy on the high seas." (Peter Blood, "Captain Blood" 1:03:01)

> < "I often wondered why I bothered to save all these things. Tonight I know it's because one day you'd be here in this cabin to wear them." "I'll never wear them, never! Those nor any other plunder gotten by a thief and pirate." "*Thief* and *pirate*?!" "I've seen your pirate ways. I've seen myself bargained for and fought over. A combat between jackals." "But I thought you understood!" > (Peter Blood & Arabella Bishop, "Captain Blood" 1:28:47)

Job Bayley, a pirate on trial in Charleston in 1718, put an amusing spin on the traditional denial of pirate identity. When asked by South Carolina's attorney general why he and his pirate comrades defied and fought the government vessel sent to apprehend them, Bayley did not let a possible death sentence crimp his sense of humor. He replied, "We thought it had been a pirate." The judge ordered him executed. (*Villains of All Nations* 161)

On those rare occasions when they do call themselves "pirates," pirates do so only (a) around other pirates—who, of course, threaten neither penal consequences nor credible disdain as a result, or (b) in special, compelling contexts.

Around other pirates—

> "I may be British by birth, but my soul is **pirate**, and we Brothers of the Coast have but one loyalty, and that's to the brotherhood." (Long John Silver, *Dead Man's Chest* 44)

to persuade credibly on the subject of one's own character otherwise—

> "She was, in a manner, covered with diamonds, and I, like a true **pirate**, soon let her see that I had more mind to the jewels than to the lady." (Captain Avery, *The King of Pirates* 56)

> "**Pirate**. Why, **pirate** it is. But look'ee, there never was pirate the like o' me for holiness—'specially o' Sundays!" (Resolution Day, on hearing Martin Conisby call him a pirate rogue, *Martin Conisby's Vengeance* 72)

to save another from unjust punishment—

> "I am the **pirate** Cain, and was the captain of the Avenger!" (Cain, announcing himself to the judge in a court of law in order to testify on his step-son's behalf, *The Pirate* 137, Chap. XVII)

and in taking a long view of life—

> "Aye, ye took me when I was an honest young man and made a **pirate** o' me." (John Flint, *Porto Bello Gold* 129)

< "What [do you] propose by so much noise and devotion?" "Heaven, I hope." "Heaven, you fool, did you ever hear of any **pyrates** going thither? Give me hell, it's a merrier place." > (Thomas Sutton, asking a fellow prisoner about his praying, *General History of the Pyrates* 246)

Pirates themselves also use the term "pirate" to condemn or express disdain for others:

> "For, d'ye see, Ned, though we must needs sail with these **pirates** we'll have little truck with 'em as may be." (Adam Penfeather, *Adam Penfeather, Buccaneer* 319)

> "They're turnin' tail and goin' in around the point. **Pirates**. Aaah." (Long John Silver, expressing disgust with a strange ship flying the Jolly Roger, "The Adventures of Long John Silver: Turnabout" 3:25)

> "Damn your eyes! He's no queen's officer, he is a bloody **pirate**!" (Thomas Marlowe, *The Pirate Round* 84)

> < "They're stealin' our ship!" "Bloody **pirates**!" > (Pintel & Ragetti, "Pirates of the Caribbean: The Curse of the Black Pearl" 1:58:39)

How do pirates do it? That is, how can pirates pretend indignation on being called "pirate," or even use the term to insult others, when they know full well they are pirates themselves? The answer is that most pirates define "piracy" broadly enough to include others whom they despise, but just narrowly enough to exclude themselves. Note the following passage, in which Absalom Troy and Smy Peters educate Adam Penfeather on the supposed difference between noble buccaneers (which, of course, they consider themselves) and loathsome pirates:

> < "Well then, Adam, you'll have heard tell of the Buccaneers and Pirates of the Main?" "Yes." "Good! Then, first and foremost—a buccaneer is no pirate." "The Lord forbid!" "A pirate, Adam, lives for murder

by murder. He is a lousy, pestilent fellow, a plague o' the seas, who will plunder and destroy any vessel weaker than his own—and of any nation. His sport is rape and slaughter of the defenceless, he is, in fine, a very bloody, vile rogue and damned rascal, —eh, Smy?" "Ah, 'tis even so, friend Adam. He is an abomination, a rank offence whose iniquities reek to heaven." "On the other hand, messmate, your true buccaneer hath but two enemies, to wit—himself by reason of drink and the devil, and the accursed Spaniard with his hellish slave-galleys, cruel *autos da fe* the which are public burnings—crowds of poor men, ay and women too, —and the most horrid torments of his Inquisition." > (Absalom Troy & Smy Peters, *Adam Penfeather, Buccaneer* 19–20)

One can slice the term "pirate" to include any number of meanings, but there are four classes of pirate that merit close attention. They include, in ascending order of iniquity:

(1) **Privateer:** The privateer holds a letter of marque (an official document authorizing the bearer to attack and plunder ships of enemy nations on behalf of a country's government) and sails only against vessels of enemy nations upon which war has been declared.

(2) **Paperless Privateer:** The paperless privateer has no letter of marque but—rather than attack any vessel he can get his hands on—shows some restraint and sails only against vessels of enemy nations upon which war is declared. Such a person is often termed a "buccaneer" if he sails against Spanish vessels; the term has traditionally been used in (though is not strictly limited to) reference to a Frenchman or Englishman.

(3) **Peacetime Privateer:** The peacetime privateer has no letter of marque and sails against vessels of traditional enemy na-

tions even when no war has been declared. Again, the term "buccaneer" is often used to refer to such a person, particularly if he is a Frenchman or Englishman preying on vessels flying the Spanish flag.

(4) **Pirate:** This seaman has no letter of marque and sails against any and all vessels, including those of his own nation. Seamen who attack their own countrymen—an Englishman who takes English vessels, an American who plunders American vessels—are pirates of the worst kind. While reasonable minds might differ on the above three classes of seamen, most would agree this indiscriminate breed definitely qualifies as pirate.

Pirates often use the above distinctions to separate themselves from real "pirates." However, pirates are shameless. They'll use any reason to condemn others as pirates while purporting themselves to be mere merchants or adventurers. For notable example, the line between pirate and non-pirate might shift inside a seaman's head based on the type of treatment to which he subjects his "trading partners." Does he kill a plundered vessel's crew, forcibly enlist them, or let them go after their cargo is taken? If he kills them, does he do so only if they've resisted, or in every circumstance? If he kills them, does he torture them first? If he releases them, does he let them go in the plundered vessel? In the plundered vessel but without sails or masts? In the plundered vessel but without any crew skilled in navigation (whom he might selectively enlist)? In the plundered vessel burned down to a floating hulk? Not in the plundered vessel but rather in a boat with oars? In a boat without oars? A pirate might use any or all of, and more than, these considerations to distinguish himself as a good and merciful citizen of the seas, rather than an odious "pirate."

The bottom line is that pirates need plenty of euphemisms, synonyms, and benign equivalents to avoid using the term "pirate" or "piracy" except around other pirates or in very special circumstances. The rest of Section 16.1 sets out those terms.

16.1.1 TERMS FOR "PIRATE"

Below are various terms for "pirate" used by pirates. Note that some are strong synonyms rarely used in reference to anyone other than pirates ("Brotherhood boy," "gentleman of fortune"); others are weak euphemisms often used to refer to persons other than pirates and, for that very reason, are preferred heavily by some pirates ("fighting man," "sailor-man"); and still others suggest specific kinds of pirates ("buccaneer," "filibuster," "Roundsman").

adventurer [a'van/a'ven/arrdvan/arrdven/ 'van/'ven-charr/terr-arr]

> "Are you such a fool as to expect 'im to send a lad o' quality to follow in the footsteps of an **adventurer** with no roots?" (Purity Pinker, "Long John Silver's Return to Treasure Island" 36:55)

blade o' fortune [blayeede o'\on farr-chern/toon]
A "blade" is a swordsman. The term is also used to refer to any dashing young man.

> < "Name." "Adam Mercy, sir." "Oh, so it's you. 'Mercy,' that's a comical handle for a **blade of fortune**, 'Mercy'." > (William Kidd & Adam Mercy, "Captain Kidd" 18:44)

buccaneer [barka/barker/buccarr/buckernee-arr]

A term used to refer favorably to any pirate but, more specifically, to refer to any English, French, or Dutch pirate of the late seventeenth century preying on Spanish vessels or settlements in the Caribbean or along the Atlantic or Pacific coasts of Mexico or South America. The term is derived from the French word "boucaner" (meaning to dry or cure meat by slow smoking), because the first buccaneers were originally hunters of wild cattle and pigs on the island of Hispaniola who were known for smoking meat over open wood-frame barbecues ("boucans") and who increasingly turned to piracy in the 1620s.

> "In all the Caribbean there is no **buccaneer** so strong as me, except you." (Levasseur, "Captain Blood" 1:13:30)

corsair [*carr/coor-say-arr/err*]

A term used to refer to any pirate but originally employed to refer to any of the pirates of the Barbary Coast, based out of ports in North Africa and preying on shipping in the western Mediterranean Sea between the twelfth and early nineteenth centuries.

> "At two o'clock at night the buccaneers came up with the Spaniards, who hailed them, asking if they had seen the **corsairs**. The buccaneers answered, 'No—warned of your coming, they have fled.'" (former buccaneer Alexander O. Exquemelin, recounting one of pirate Francois L'Olonnais' encounters with the Spanish, *The Buccaneers of America* 91)

desperado [*daahs/dayss-parr/p'r-adoo*]

Literally meaning an outlaw, the term is also used to refer to any pirate, especially (as suggested by the term's Spanish origin) to a buccaneer preying on Spanish vessels in the late seventeenth century.

> "However, this troop of **desperadoes** had alarmed all the coast, and expresses both by sea and land were dispatched to warn the towns on the coast to be upon their guard ..." (Captain Avery, *The King of Pirates* 21)

fighting man [*fawt/figh'-in' man*]

A term for any man skilled at and experienced in battle but also a weak euphemism for "pirate."

> "[M]y ship is off the harbour. She carries two hundred of the toughest **fighting-men**, who would devour your spineless militia at a gulp." (Peter Blood, *Captain Blood Returns* 125)

filibuster [*fel'/feller/fil'/filler-barrster/boohster*]

Used to refer to any pirate, especially a seventeenth-century French or Dutch pirate of the Caribbean. The term is likely derived from the word "fly-boat," the light craft that island-based pirates often used to harass Spanish shipping and/or from the Dutch word for "freebooter."

> "I know nothing of **filibuster** customs." (Baron de Rivarol, *Captain Blood: His Odyssey* 341)

freebooter [*freeboo'er*]

The term emphasizes the plundering ways of pirates—that is, their defining habit of appropriating things by force or threat of force.

> "Another **free-booter** living on the island was Michel the Basque, a man who had won so much by marauding he no longer went to sea." (former buccaneer Alexander O. Exquemelin, *The Buccaneers of America* 93)

gentleman adventurer [*jan'leman a'van/a'ven/ arrdvan/arrdven/'van/'ven-charr/terr-arr*]

> "We'll show you the life of real **gentlemen adventurers** aboard the *Walrus*." (John Flint, *Porto Bello Gold* 93)

gentleman of fortune [*jan'leman o'\on farr-chern/toon*]

The term most frequently used among pirates themselves to refer to a pirate.

> < "Are you telling me you let yourself be led away by that stinkin' mess of swabs?" "Smells sweeter with gold in their pockets, don't it?" "But pirates!" "**Gentlemen of fortune**." > (Tom & Long John Silver, "Treasure Island" [1972] 45:46)

marooner [*maah/mahr-rooner*]

Though typically used to refer to someone left behind by a vessel on a desolate island, the term is also used to refer to any pirate and emphasizes the wandering, nationless, self-sufficient aspects of pirate life.

> "If at any time we should meet another **marooner**, that man that shall sign his Ar-

ticles without the consent of our company, shall suffer such punishment as the captain and company shall think fit." (fourth of the Articles of John Phillips' company, *General History of the Pyrates* 342)

of the Brotherhood [o'\on t' Bro'er/Brudder/Bruvver-'ood]

The "Brotherhood" is a term used to refer to the pirates of the late seventeenth century operating in the Caribbean, especially those based out of the pirate strongholds at Tortuga, Port Royal, and Petit Goave, and less frequently to the eighteenth-century pirates of the Atlantic seaboard.

> < "Then, Adam Penfeather, I'm your debtor." "Nay, there be no debts 'twixt comrades **o' the Brotherhood**, 'tis give and take, share and share!" > (Martin Conisby & Adam Penfeather, *Black Bartlemy's Treasure* 60)

one\man who flies no\any flag [woohn\man 'oo flaws/flyees no'oo\a'y flarrg]

A reference arising from pirates' traditional refusal to fly over their vessels the flag of their country of origin (consistent with nautical custom) and their practice instead of flying no flag, a flag of their own creation, or the flag of a country with which it becomes expedient to claim sudden affiliation (flying a Spanish flag when approaching a Spanish vessel, for example) in order to invite trust or discourage pursuit.

> "Sir, to be frank with you, I am of **those who fly any flag** that the occasion may demand." (Peter Blood, *The Fortunes of Captain Blood* 76)

one\man who has sold his nation [woohn\man 'oo ha'/'as soold/so'oold 'is naah/nayee-shern/shoohn]

> *Some pirates explained to captives that they had "**sold their nation**" for booty.* (*Villains of All Nations* 8)

privateer [praw/pree/pryee-vateee/verteee-arr/err]

This term technically refers to one who holds a letter of marque issued by a nation-state, or some governmental subunit or authorized representative thereof, licensing the bearer to take ships of one or more enemy nations. However, pirates are notorious for their loose use of the term to refer to themselves and their comrades, regardless of whether they bear any official commission. Indeed, pirates often carry commissions to allow themselves some pretense of legitimacy, regardless of the scope or validity of the commission; the French-language commissions issued by the Governor of Petit Goave were popular among English buccaneers in the 1670s and 1680s, for example, but to the extent their bearers did not speak or read French, they may not have known that many of these commissions were, in fact, mere hunting and fishing licenses. Nor would they have cared to know.

> "[H]e had no intention of being a **privateer** in the East Indies, but, as he has often assured me with his own mouth, he resolved to take the first opportunity of returning to England. So he feigned compliance with some of his men, who were bent upon going to cruise at Manila, so that he might have leisure to take some favourable opportunity of quitting the **privateer** trade." (William Dampier, recounting the reluctant buccaneer Captain Swan's efforts to stall his company from pirating, *A New Voyage Round the World* 129)

Roundsman [Roun's/Rowoon's/Rowoondsman]

This term came from the pirates sailing and preying on ships in the Red Sea and Indian Ocean, an area which—together with the route around the Cape of Good Hope and past Madagascar—was known as the Pirate Round, especially during the peak period of pirating activity there in 1690–1705. See James L. Nelson's *The Pirate Round*.

"That is the way of the **Roundsmen**. I could do nothing about it. Dinwiddie wanted to sail the Pirate Round, and that is a part of it. Ship's articles, vote of the men, all of it." (Thomas Marlowe, *The Pirate Round* 229)

rover [*rob/roov/ro'oov-er*]

"I told them the Romans themselves were, at first, no better than such a gang of **rovers** as we were, and who knew but our General, Captain Avery, might lay the foundation of as great an empire as they." (Captain Avery, *The King of Pirates* 75)

roving adventurer [*roo/ro'oo-vin' a'van/a'ven/ arrdvan/arrdven/'van/'ven-charr/terr-arr*]

"For, Martin, I have here the secret of a treasure that hath been the dream and hope of **roving adventurers** along the Main this many a year—a treasure beyond price." (Adam Penfeather, *Black Bartlemy's Treasure* 82)

sailor-man [*saah/say'ee/say'or-larr/lee-man*]

A generic (and somewhat playful, as a result of the double noun) term for any seaman but often used specifically to refer to a pirate.

< "Damme! Was it to read me homilies that you had me here?" "Aha, shipmate, there spake the young divine, the excellent divinity student who committed a peccadillo long years agone and, sailing to the Golden West, gave place to one Adam Penfeather a **sailor-man**—as you shall hear tell of at St Kitt's, Tortuga, Santa Catalina and a score o' places along the Main." > (Martin Conisby & Adam Penfeather, *Black Bartlemy's Treasure* 80)

scavenger o' the seas [*scarr-vaahnger o'\on t' seas*]

< "Thou'rt an odd, mournful soul for such vastly fortunate buccaneer, victorious captain and merciless fighter." "Not merciless—no! Say rather—a worker for Justice and Law in wild places, —a **Scav-**

enger o' the Seas." > (Benjamin Trigg & Adam Penfeather, *Adam Penfeather, Buccaneer* 245–46)

sea-wolf [*sea-wahlf*]

This term is inspired not by the pirate's tendency to characterize himself favorably or ambiguously, but by the related impulse to condemn other pirates as vehemently as possible. To the extent a "wolf" makes a feared and formidable adversary, however, the term inevitably conveys a note of admiration as well.

"[Y]onder come pirate rogues to destroy us— if they can. And I would not have it other, for here's chance to prove me your mettle, to show these cursed **sea-wolves** that English sea-dogs can out-bite 'em." (Absalom Troy, *Adam Penfeather, Buccaneer* 119)

seafaring man [*seafahrrin' man*]

A term for any seaman, also used as a euphemism for "pirate."

"Ye wouldn't be of a mind to be helpin' an old **seafarin' man** ashore, would ya?" (Long John Silver, *Dead Man's Chest* 11)

wanderer [*waahn/warrn-d'rer*]

"They took us into their boat, and afterwards carried us on board their ship. When we came there we found they were a worse sort of **wanderers** than ourselves." (Captain Avery, *The King of Pirates* 10)

16.1.2 TERMS FOR "PIRATES"

Below are various terms for the plural noun "pirates" used by pirates.

the Ancient Brotherhood [*t' Ayn-shernt Bro'er/Brudder/Bruvver-'ood*]

"Billy 'Bones,' they names me. Capt'n Billy Bones, o' **the Ancient Brotherhood**, like." (Billy Doyle, introducing himself to Alan Lewrie, *The Gun Ketch* 159)

brethren [*brayth/bredd/breeth/breff/bre'-ren*]

Used to refer to pirates generally but also to a particular company of pirates.

"Cap'n, look, here's why they've run! She must have seventy guns aboard. That's why the **brethren** left." (Patch, pegging a nearby warship as the cause of a pirate ship's retreat, "The Adventures of Long John Silver: Turnabout" 3:50)

the Brethren of the Coast [*t' Brayth/Bredd/ Breeth/Breff/Bre'-ren o'\on t' Coh-oost/Coost*]
the Brotherhood of the Coast [*t' Bro'er/Brud-der/Bruvver-'ood o'\on t' Coh-oost/Coost*]
the Coast Brethren [*t' Coh-oost/Coost Brayth/ Bredd/Breeth/Breff/Bre'-ren*]
the Coast Brotherhood [*t' Coh-oost/Coost Bro'er/Brudder/Bruvver-'ood*]
the coastwise Brotherhood [*t' coh-oost/coost-wawse/wyeese Bro'er/Brudder/Bruvver-'ood*]

Used in reference to the pirates of the late seventeenth century operating in the Caribbean, especially those based out of the pirate strongholds at Tortuga, Port Royal, and Petit Goave, and less frequently to the eighteenth-century pirates of the Atlantic seaboard. Also used are the abbreviated forms "the Brethren," "the Brotherhood," and "the Coast."

"They insist that the treasure itself be produced and weighed in their presence, as is the custom among **the Brethren of the Coast**." (Peter Blood, *Captain Blood: His Odyssey* 341) < "Hast ever heard tell o' **the Brotherhood o' the Coast**, Adam?" "Never." "Ah well, 'tis a staunch company, and powerful in the Indies and along the Main, and made up of English, French, Scots, Hollanders and others, good, bad and indifferent, —like Life itself, Adam." > (Absalom Troy & Adam Penfeather, *Adam Penfeather, Buccaneer* 12) "Mistress Ursula, in saving yon poor rogues, you have broke all 'stablished rules and precedents among **the Coast Brethren** and won you as many doglike friends shall bark to your bidding—yet such dogs bite." (Barnabas Rokeby, *Winds of Chance* 57) "The captain o' **the Coast Brotherhood** is Joanna

here—Captain Jo, by the Brotherhood so ordained; 'tis Captain Jo commands here ..." (Resolution Day, *Martin Conisby's Vengeance* 156) "First, there's Abnegation Mings as you shall hear tell of on the Main from Panama to St Catherine's, aye, by the horns of Nick there be none of all **the coastwise Brotherhood** quicker or readier when there's aught i' the wind than Abnegation, and you can lay to that, my delicate cove!" (Abnegation Mings, *Black Bartlemy's Treasure* 31) < "We boarded her and walked into a trap." "Aye, that it was, Sir Henry. As bloodthirsty a crew as any in **the Brotherhood**." > (Montbars & Montbars' mate, "Pirates of Tortuga" 49:33) "'Tis a rule o' **the Coast** to shoot or hang the like o' you!" (Resolution Day, having just caught Martin Conisby preparing to launch the boat and thereby leave Captain Jo and Resolution Day stranded, *Martin Conisby's Vengeance* 171)

the Fellowship [*t' Faah-ler/lowoo-shep*]
Used to refer to pirates generally but also (often with a small "f," as in "fellowship") to a particular company of pirates.

< "She be only a woman, when all's said, Cap'n. ..." "Nay, Job. She's Joanna and behind her do lie Tressady and Sol and Rory and Abnegation Mings—and all **the Fellowship**." > (Job & Captain Belvedere, *Martin Conisby's Vengeance* 67)

the Flying Gang [*t' Flaw/Flyee-in' Gang*]
Pirates based in the Bahama Islands in 1716–20, following the end of the War of Spanish Succession and preceding Governor Woodes Rogers's re-establishment of royal authority there in 1720–21. Note that the same phrase (uncapitalized) can also be used to refer to pirates generally.

*The Bahama Islands, undefended and un-governed by the Crown, began, in 1716, to attract pirates by the hundreds. Governor Alexander Spotswood noted that pirates

---

The Pirate Company

The pirate company is an incredibly unique and important element of pirate culture. Pirate companies were democracies, not masses of unthinking drones under the thumb of a single strong-willed thug. Decisions affecting the company were made by majority vote among its members. Pirate captains generally had authority over a company only in fight, chase, or retreat; the members themselves were otherwise in charge, could depose or replace the captain at any time other than during battle or pursuit, and even appointed their own representative—called a quartermaster—to voice their interests, oversee company discipline and dispense punishment, and keep the captain in check.

Pirate companies conducted their affairs in accordance with rules and principles that the company's members themselves drew up and signed, known as articles (among French buccaneers, *chasse partie*). The articles of various pirate companies in history, literature, and film are set out in Appendix C. They allow a fascinating look into the lives of pirates.

---

used the Bahamas as a "General Rendezvous & seem to look upon those Islands as their own." These pirates called themselves **the Flying Gang.*** (*Villains of All Nations* 30) *Pirates acted the part of a floating mob, a "flying gang," as they called themselves, with its own distinctive sense of popular justice.* (*Villains of All Nations* 86)

the Fraternity [*t' Farr/Fer/Fraah/Frarr-tarr-netty*]

Used to refer to pirates generally but also to a particular company of pirates.

> < "Where do we make for, Resolution?" "To a little island well beknown to **the Fraternity**, comrade ..." > (Martin Conisby & Resolution Day, *Martin Conisby's Vengeance* 146)

those who fly no\any flag [*dose/t'ose\dey/they\dem/them 'oo flaw/flyee no'oo\a'y flarrg*]

A reference arising from pirates' traditional refusal to fly over their vessels the flag of their country of origin (consistent with nautical custom) and their practice instead of flying no flag, a flag of their own creation, or the flag of a country with which it becomes expedient to claim sudden affiliation (flying a Spanish flag when approaching a Spanish vessel, for example) in order to invite trust or discourage pursuit.

"Sir, to be frank with you, I am of **those who fly any flag** that the occasion may demand." (Peter Blood, *The Fortunes of Captain Blood* 76)

16.1.3 TERMS FOR "BAND OF PIRATES"

Pirates operate in bands or groups in order to effectively man pirate vessels and their labor-intensive sails and rigging. Also, though pirate vessels are generally speedy and carry heavy firepower, the pirate's best weapon is superior numbers. The outcome of a boarding depends, more than anything else, on the raw numbers of bodies on the respective ships' decks.

The preferred, and by far most frequently used, term for a group of pirates is a "company." Several other terms are also used, however, and those are listed below.

brotherhood [*bro'er/brudder/bruvver-'ood*]

Used to refer to a particular company of pirates, but also to pirates generally, with "brotherhood" often (but not always) meaning a particular company and "Brotherhood" often (but not always) meaning pirates generally.

> < "We boarded her and walked into a trap." "Aye, that it was, Sir Henry. As bloodthirsty a crew as any in the **Brotherhood**." > (Montbars & his mate, "Pirates of Tortuga" 49:33)

company [*cahm/carrm/coohm-perny/p'ny*]

Easily the preferred term among pirates for a group of pirates or for the crew aboard a pirate ship.

> "He that shall be found guilty of taking up any unlawful weapon on board the privateer, or any prize, by us taken, so as to strike or abuse one another, in any regard, shall suffer what punishment the Captain and majority of the **company** shall think fit." (second of the Articles of George Lowther and company, *General History of the Pyrates* 307)

confederacy [*cahn/carrn/coohn/kern-fed-dercy/fed'racy*]

> "And the men who were of our **confederacy**, who were not with me at my country house, were twelve in number." (Captain Avery, *The King of Pirates* 78)

Fellowship [*Faah-ler/lowoo-shep*]

Used to refer (1) to a particular company of pirates ("fellowship") but also (2) to a smaller group of pirates forming the core or most senior members of a company or (3) to pirates generally ("Fellowship").

> "Japhet, you being now the only married man o' the **Fellowship**, why not settle down and beget a family as a man should?'" (Barnabas Rokeby, *Winds of Chance* 151–52)

following [*a-fol-ler/lowoo-in'*]

> < "What boats does she carry?" "Three with the cock-boat." "That should be enough to accommodate your **following**." > (Peter Blood & Captain Easterling, *Captain Blood Returns* 61)

16.1.4 TERMS FOR "PIRACY"

The following are various terms for "piracy" or, more broadly, the pirate life.

the account [*t' accarrnt/accowoont/'carrnt/'cowoont*]

> "I reckon she is a Red Sea Rover, here on **the account**." (Thomas Marlowe, *The Pirate Round* 231)

the cruising trade [*t' croos-in' trayeede*]

> "I would try my fortune in **the cruising trade**, but would be sure not to prey upon my own countrymen." (Captain Avery, *The King of Pirates* 9)

the game [*t' gayeeme*]

> *In pursuance of **the game**, and beating up for the Windward Islands, the *Scowerer* met with a ship from New-England, bound to Jamaica ...* (account of the depredations of John Evans' company in the Caribbean, *General History of the Pyrates* 338)

(this) merry trade of ours [*(dis/t'is) maah/mahr/may-ry trayeede o'/on arrs/owarrs*]

> "You are new, sir, to **this merry trade of ours**, or you would know that size is a quality we greatly esteem." (The Red Rover, *The Red Rover* 401)

ripping and cutting [*a-rep-pin' an'/'n' a-carrt/cooht-tin'*]

A reference (1) to swordplay, (2) to violence or battle of any kind, or (3) to piratical pursuits of a violent nature.

> "You and your evil ways, caring not for law and order, **rippin' and cuttin'**, and layin' his hands to anything that belongs not to him. Where else could it end?" > (Purity Pinker & Long John Silver, "The Adventures of Long John Silver: Dead Reckoning" 3:40)

roving [*a-rob/roov/ro'oov-in'*]

> "I had long before this repented of that **roving** course of life, but never with such concern as now." (William Dampier, reflecting morosely on his piratical past as he braces for death on heavy seas, *A New Voyage Round the World* 237)

the runaway account [*t' roohn-awayee accarrnt/accowoont/'carrnt/'cowoont*]

Used especially to refer to a captain or crew having taken over, absconded with, or otherwise misappropriated from her rightful owner or captain a vessel for their own use.

> *Two seamen of the settlement, William Crew and John Pigot, were invited to join the ship. Certain signs indicated that she was on the **"runaway account,"** according to Pigot's testimony later, "for the fish was not stowed properly, but carelessly tossed about, and the hatch cover was missing.* (John Pigot, recalling his suspicions that the fishing schooner *Three Sisters* had turned pirate when he joined her crew, *Pirates and Buccaneers of the Atlantic Coast* 258–59)

the running trade [t' *roohn-nin' trayeede*]

Most immediately a reference to smuggling, but also used euphemistically to refer to piracy.

> "I have had her in port; she has undergone some improvements, and is now altogether suited to a **running trade.**" (The Red Rover, referring to his ship *Dolphin*, *The Red Rover* 121)

the Sport [t' *Sparrt*]

> "[I] could like **the Sport,** were it lawful." (George Wilson, *General History of the Pyrates* 277)

the sweet trade [t' *sweet trayeede*]

> "I urge you to abandon this ugly business and join us in the **sweet trade.**" (Gasparilla, *Gasparilla: Pirate Genius* 233)

the trade [t' *trayeede*]

> "[S]ome of our men were young in **the trade** and had seen nothing; and they lay at me every day not to lie still in a part of the world where, as they said, such vast riches might be gained." (Captain Avery, *The King of Pirates* 45)

16.1.5 TERMS FOR "ENGAGE IN PIRACY"

The following are verbs and verb phrases that describe what pirates do. All or nearly all do double duty. That is, they can be used narrowly to refer to a particular piratical undertaking ("We'll **seek our fortune** after waterin' at Berenguer Key") or broadly to refer to piracy as a pursuit or way of life ("I'll **seek my fortune** till the brine swallow me whole-like").

account, be on\upon the [*be arrn/o'\'parrn/'pon/ uparrn t' accarrnt/accowoont/'carrnt/ 'cowoont*]

> *For nearly twenty years he had **been on the account,** an extraordinarily long career for a pirate.* (*The Guardship* 31)

account, be on\upon the runaway [*be arrn/ o'\'parrn/'pon/uparrn t' roohn-awayee accarrnt/accowoont/'carrnt/'cowoont*]

Used especially to refer to a captain or crew sailing a vessel misappropriated from her rightful owner or captain.

> *Two seamen of the settlement, William Crew and John Pigot, were invited to join the ship. Certain signs indicated that she was on the **"runaway account,"** according to Pigot's testimony later, "for the fish was not stowed properly, but carelessly tossed about, and the hatch cover was missing.* (John Pigot, recalling his suspicions that the fishing schooner *Three Sisters* had turned pirate when he joined her crew, *Pirates and Buccaneers of the Atlantic Coast* 258–59)

account, go on\upon the [*go'oo arrn/ o'\'parrn/'pon/uparrn t' accarrnt/accowoont/ 'carrnt/'cowoont*]

> *Captain Bellamy and Paul Williams, in two sloops, had been upon a Spanish wreck, and not finding their expectation answered, as has been mentioned in former parts of this history, they resolved not to lose their labour, and agreed to **go upon the account,** a term among the pyrates, which speaks their profession.* (explanation by author Captain Charles Johnson, *General History of the Pyrates* 585)

account, pursue the [*parr-soo t' accarrnt/accowoont/'carrnt/'cowoont*]

> *Lowther received them as friends, and treated them with all imaginable respect, inviting them, as they were few in number, and in no condition to **pursue the account**, (as they called it) to join their strength together ...* (account of how Edward Low and his company joined George Lowther's, *General History of the Pyrates* 312)

adventure [*a'van/a'ven/arrdvan/arrdven/'van/'ven-charr/terr-arr*]

> "[W]hen we're wed I'll go no more **adventuring**. I'll be done with the sea." (Absalom Troy, *Adam Penfeather, Buccaneer* 157)

be listed in the service of the devil [*be les/lish-ted i'/'n t' sarrvice o'\on t' daahv/dayv/debb/div-il*]

> "[W]e never offered to rob any of our other European nations, either Dutch or French, much less English—but now we **were listed in the service of the Devil** indeed, and like him were at war with all mankind." (Captain Avery, *The King of Pirates* 10)

buccaneer [*barka/barker/buccarr/buckernee-arr*]

> "Capt. Davis, an Englishman, who was **a buckaneering** in these seas, above 20 years ago, lay some months and recruited here to content." (Woodes Rogers, *A Cruising Voyage Round the World* 114)

cruise [*croose*]

> "When I came to look about me here, I found our men had increased their number, and that a vessel which had been **cruising**, that is to say pirating on the coast of Arabia, having seven Dutchmen, three Portuguese and five Englishmen on board, had been cast away upon the northern shore of that island ..." (Captain Avery, *The King of Pirates* 44)

cruise abroad [*croose abrarrd*]

> "For this reason we civilly declined them, told them we had wealth enough and therefore did not now **cruise abroad** as we used to do unless we should hear of another wedding of a king's daughter, or unless some rich fleet or some heathen kingdom was to be attempted ..." (Captain Avery, *The King of Pirates* 74–75)

cruise, be on\upon the [*be arrn/o'\'parrn/'pon/uparrn t' croose*]

> "We sought no purchase, for I had fully convinced our men that our business was not to appear as we were used to **be upon the cruise**, but as traders." (Captain Avery, *The King of Pirates* 38)

cruise for booty [*croose farr/fer boo'y*]

> "For though we had the sloop, we could propose little advantage by her, for as to **cruising for booty** among the Arabians or Indians, we had neither room for it nor inclination to it ..." (Captain Avery, *The King of Pirates* 35)

cruise, go abroad to [*go'oo abrarrd t'/ta/ter croose*]

> "Our number decreased afterwards upon several occasions, such as the **going abroad to cruise**, wandering to the south part of the island, (as above) getting on board European ships, and the like." (Captain Avery, *The King of Pirates* 63)

cruise upon all nations [*croose 'parrn/'pon/uparrn awrl naah/nayee-sherns/shoohns*]

> *[T]hey took a clear contrary course, and resolved to station themselves upon the coasts of Spain and Portugal, and to **cruise upon all nations** ...* (account of John Gow's first measures as a pirate captain after successfully leading a mutiny, *Lives of the Most Remarkable Criminals* 580)

cruising, go a- [*go'oo er-croos-in'*]

*[T]hey were told by Gow what his resolution was, viz., to **go a-cruising** or to go upon the account.* (account of John Gow's statement to crew members who did not join his mutiny, *Lives of the Most Remarkable Criminals* 579)

dare Fortune on one's own account [*darr/dayarr/dayerr Farr-chern/toon arrn 'un's/woohn's owoon accarrnt/accowoont/'carrnt/'cowoont*]

dare Fortune on the golden quest [*darr/dayarr/dayerr Farr-chern/toon arrn t' goold/go'oold-ern quast*]

"So now, will ye 'list with us, wilt hazard thy life—first to the rescue of these doomed prisoners and thereafter **dare Fortune on thine own account?**" (Absalom Troy, *Adam Penfeather, Buccaneer* 12)

"This ship that was the *London Merchant* is now the *Bold Adventuress* to **dare Fortune on the golden quest.**" (Absalom Troy, *Adam Penfeather, Buccaneer* 76)

dare with Jolly Roger [*darr/dayarr/dayerr weth/wi'/wiff/witt Jarrly Raah/Rarr-ger*]

"Here's never a man, woman or child **dared** so much **wi' Jolly Roger** all his days—oh, sink me!" (Roger Tressady, *Martin Conisby's Vengeance* 158)

do exploits [*do ess-ployeets*]

"We had after this three pirate ships come to us, most English, who had **done** some **exploits** on the coast of Guinea, had made several good prizes and were all tolerably rich." (Captain Avery, *The King of Pirates* 62)

follow privateering [*fol-ler/lowoo a-praw/pree/pryee-vatee/vertee-arrin'/errin'*]

"The next morning the Spaniards killed one of our tired men. He was a stout old grey-headed man, aged about 84, who had served under Oliver in the time of the Irish Rebellion. After this he was at Jamaica, and had **followed privateering**

ever since." (William Dampier, *A New Voyage Round the World* 117)

go a-roguing [*go'oo er-roo/ro'oo-guin'*]

"You left my ship, with 95 more men, and **went a-roguing** afterwards." (William Kidd, cross-examining one of his own former pirates at Kidd's trial, *The Pirate Hunter* 375)

maraud [*mahrr/mer/m'r-rard*]

"Morgan was made captain, and they went **marauding** along the coast of Campeche, where they captured several ships." (former buccaneer Alexander O. Exquemelin, recounting Henry Morgan's first ventures as captain of his own ship, *The Buccaneers of America* 119)

maroon [*maah/mahr-roon*]

*[F]or the fifty years that **marooning** was in the flower of its glory it was a sorrowful time for the coasters of New England, the middle provinces, and the Virginias ...* (*The Book of Pirates* "Buccaneers and Marooners of the Spanish Main" 22)

pillage [*pell-ayge/'ge*]

"But this was only a pretence of ours, to get out of them what intelligence we could as to their shipping, strength and the like, under colour of seeking a trade: for our business was to **pillage.**" (William Dampier, explaining the company's reasons for discussing with four passing natives the possibility of trade with the Spanish, *A New Voyage Round the World* 178–79)

plunder [*ploohnder*]

"[T]he inhabitants of Mindanao being then, as we were told (though falsely), at wars with the Spaniards, our men, who, it should seem, were very squeamish of **plundering** without licence, derived hopes of getting a commission there ..." (William Dampier, *A New Voyage Round the World* 140)

ramble

> *[D]uring Tew's stay at Bermuda "it was a thing notoriously known to everyone that he had before then been a pirate"; and a sailor who had known him well testified [at the trial of Governor Fletcher of New York] that he "had been **rambling**."* (attribution to seaman acquaintance of Thomas Tew's, *Pirates of the New England Coast* 84)

rove (on the account) [roove/ro'oove (arrn/o' t' accarrnt/accowoont/'carrnt/'cowoont)]

> "Why, look'ee all, if Penfeather wants men, as wants 'em he doth, what's to stay or let us from rowing out to Penfeather soft and quiet and 'listing ourselves along of Penfeather, and watchin' our chance t' heave Penfeather overboard and go a-**roving on our own account**?" (Sam Spraggons, *Black Bartlemy's Treasure* 312)

sail with a roving commission [sayell weth/ wi'/wiff/witt a roo/ro'oo-vin' cahm/carm/coohm/ kerm-meh-shern/shoohn]

> "The Dons are said to run this passage often in order to escape speaking us gentlemen who **sail with roving commissions**." (hand aboard the *Dolphin*, *The Red Rover* 401)

seek one's fortune [seek 'un's/woohn's farr-chern/toon]

Said often to express one's ultimate goal in engaging in piracy or to inspire others to engage in piracy.

> "But the truth of the thing was that at first our commission was made only for the space of three months ... whereas among ourselves we had contrived to make it last for three years—for with this we were resolved to **seek our fortunes**." (William Dick, *Bucaniers of America* 325)

try one's (good) fortune [tryee 'un's/woohn's (good) farr-chern/toon]

Though the phrase literally means to risk one's luck in adventurous pursuits, it is a well-worn euphemism for engaging more specifically in the pirate trade.

> "Upon these considerations we came to this resolution: that they should go out to sea and cruise the height of Lima and **try their fortune** ..." (Captain Avery, *The King of Pirates* 27–28) "In a word, I was overcome with these new proposals, and told the rest of my people I was resolved to go to sea again and **try my good fortune** ..." (Captain Avery, *The King of Pirates* 45)

16.1.6 TERMS FOR "PIRATE SHIP"

The following are terms pirates use in reference to their own vessels. The paucity of entries is a reflection of two truths:

(1) Pirates are intensely interested in the unique features and capabilities of a given vessel and, consequently, are more likely to refer to it by name or type than by a more generic term.

(2) Pirates are typically proud of their own vessels and often admiring of others' and, consequently, are less likely to associate these honored things with the opprobrium and self-loathing that compel their description of everything else piratical in wildly indirect, euphemistic terms.

corsair [carr/coor-say-arr/err]

A term used to refer to any pirate vessel, especially to a ship used by pirates of the Barbary Coast, based out of ports in North Africa and preying on shipping in the western Mediterranean Sea between the twelfth and early nineteenth centuries.

> "I lay yard-arm and yard-arm, once, under that very bit of bunting, with a heavy **corsair** from Algiers ..." (The Red Rover, *The Red Rover* 100)

cruiser [crooser]

"[W]here there are no courts on shore to protect us, nor any sister **cruisers** to look after our welfare, no small portion of power is necessarily vested in the commander." (The Red Rover, *The Red Rover* 118)

free ship [*free shep*]

"I says she's our ship, and therefore a **free ship**, and us to 'lect our own captain!" (Toby Drew, *Adam Penfeather, Buccaneer* 212)

pirate [*py-eeret/errt/raaht*]

"[I'll] cut [you] in sunder if [you] d[o]n't make haste to go on board the **pirate** with [your] books and instruments." (William White, forcing navigator Henry Gyles to join John Phillips' company, *Pirates of the New England Coast* 320)

privateer (vessel) [*praw/pree/pryee-vateee/vertee-arr/err (vassel)*]

A "privateer," strictly speaking, is a ship whose commander is authorized by a nation's government to attack and plunder ships of enemy nations, but the term is used more broadly to refer to any pirate ship.

"He that shall be found guilty of taking up any unlawful weapon on board the **privateer**, or any prize, by us taken, so as to strike or abuse one another, in any regard, shall suffer what punishment the Captain and majority of the company shall think fit." (second of the Articles of George Lowther and company, *General History of the Pyrates* 307) "I heard also that these men were taken by a **privateer-vessel** which came thither a year or two after; and that one of them is since come to England." (Lionel Wafer, *Isthmus of America* 192)

Red Sea Rover [*Red Sea Rob/Roov/Ro'oov-er*]

A pirate vessel used to sail the Pirate Round (the area of the Red Sea and the Indian Ocean, and the route leading around the Cape of Good Hope and past Madagascar, frequented by pirates preying on shipping bound from and to India and the Arabian peninsula in 1690–1705). See James L. Nelson's *The Pirate Round*.

"Sloop's fair shot up, but I reckon she'd make a fine **Red Sea Rover**." (Henry Nagel, *The Pirate Round* 355)

16.2 COMPANY & CREW

Were pirates any good at sailing? Were they lubbers or prime seamen?

The truth, as usual, is case-by-case. Pirates were roughly as good as the larger population of seamen, who in turn varied widely in skill and experience. Edward Low once impressively evaded an English man-of-war by sailing over an uncharted shoal, causing his pursuer to run aground (*Pirates of the New England Coast* 203). On the other hand, pirate captain Stede Bonnet's knowledge of the sea was so rudimentary that Blackbeard persuaded him he'd be better off handing over his ship and sailing aboard it as Blackbeard's guest. Bonnet reportedly shipped with Blackbeard for nearly a year, an idle passenger, padding about the deck in his "morning gown" and spending hours with books from his shipboard library (*Under the Black Flag* 18; *General History of the Pyrates* 72, 95–97).

Section 16.2 identifies the cast of characters aboard a pirate vessel—the various members of a pirate company or ship's crew that played distinctive and often essential roles.

This list of company and crew terms constitutes only a subset of the larger universe of nautical terms and phrases used by the seafaring. There are several good comprehensive treatments of nautical language; a few are William Falconer, *An Universal Dictionary of the Marine* (1780); Peter Kemp, *The Oxford Companion to Ships and the Sea* (Oxford University Press 1976); Robert McKenna, *The Dictionary of Nautical Literacy* (International Marine 2001); and Thompson

Lenfestey with Captain Thompson Lenfestey, Jr., *The Sailor's Illustrated Dictionary* (The Lyons Press 2004).

anchor watch [*han-karr warrtch*] one or more members of a vessel's crew on duty and on deck when a vessel is at anchor, typically at night or during bad weather conditions

armourer [*aahmourer/aahm'rer/ahrrmourer/ ahrrm'rer*] member of a vessel's crew responsible for storing, maintaining, and distributing small arms—weapons such as pistols and muskets—aboard a vessel

The gunner, not the armourer, is responsible for the ship's guns or cannons and the equipment and ammunition for them.

armourer's mate [*aahm/ahrrm-arrer/'rer's mayeete*] member of a vessel's crew responsible for assisting the armourer in storing, maintaining, and distributing small arms—weapons such as pistols and muskets—aboard a vessel

artist [*ar'/ahrrt-est*] (1) seaman skilled in piloting or navigation (2) seaman with special skill or knowledge (3) any person with special skill or knowledge

barbecue [*bah/bahrr-bercue*] common nickname for a company's cook (and the legendary nickname of *Treasure Island*'s Long John Silver)

before the mast [*afarr/afore/befarr/'farr/'fore t' marrst*] of or relating to common crew or "hands," as opposed to officers or persons of authority within a company

This usage reflects that common crew sleep and work (in forecastle and waist) toward the front of a vessel (and are accordingly known as "focslehands" or "men before the mast" or "men forward"), while officers sleep (in cabins) and generally work (on poop and quarterdeck) closer to the rear of a vessel.

boatswain [*bo'oos/bos-'n*] member of a vessel's crew in charge of the deck; of the crew, equipment, and work being performed there; and often of other miscellaneous affairs concerning the company

Always pronounced "bosun." The spellings "bo's'n," "bosun," and "bo'sun" are more frequently used. One of the boatswain's duties is to call out commands across the expanse of a vessel's deck by playing distinctive tones or cadences (that corresponded to particular instructions) on a shrill-sounding pipe or whistle.

Note the various roles and responsibilities of the bosun in the following excerpts:

- **disciplinarian:** "Ha, **Bo'sun**, strip and seize him up for punishment!" (Absalom Troy, *Adam Penfeather, Buccaneer* 91

- **foreman:** "Bosun, set the lads to building me a lodge to shelter her ladyship's grace to-night, and thereafter make camp and double the watch." (Roger Snaith, *Winds of Chance* 320)

- **jailer:** "Absalom, take me this dog and chain him up in the lazarette ... secure him well, **Bosun**!" (Japhet Bly, *Winds of Chance* 113)

- **nurse:** "Me being **Bo'sun** and therefore ship's nurse, I'll away and tend her." (Ned Bowser, *Adam Penfeather, Buccaneer* 132)

- **steward:** < "As for you, **Bo'sun**, have up a flask o' the Spanish wine—the black seal!" "Aye, cap'n!" > (Adam Penfeather & Joel Bym, *Black Bartlemy's Treasure* 78–79)

- **undertaker:** "**Bo'sun**, send two men for this body, let it be prepared for burial." (Adam Penfeather, *Adam Penfeather, Buccaneer* 215)

bosun's mate; bo'sun's mate [*bo'oos/bos-'n's mayeete*] member of a vessel's crew responsible for assisting the boatswain and typically most concerned with implementing and ensuring compliance by the deck crew with the boatswain's orders

The bosun's mate was often selected for force of personality as much as for shiphandling skills and, as the most immediate overseer of what went on upon deck, was often either a very well-liked individual or an extremely gruff and intimidating one.

cabin boy [*carrb-'n boyee*] boy serving as valet and assistant to a vessel's captain

cape-merchant [*cayeepe marrch-oohnt*] crew member responsible for a vessel's cargo and transactions

Also known as a "supercargo."

carpenter [*caah/cahrr-pernter*] crew member responsible for inspection, maintenance, and repair of the vessel's decks, masts, and other wooden equipment, and for supervision of careening (hauling a vessel onto shore, turning her on her side, and cleaning and/or repairing the bottom of her hull)

carpenter's mate [*caah/cahrr-pernter mayeete*] member of a vessel's crew responsible for assisting the carpenter

chirurgeon [*chir'-jin*] member of a vessel's crew responsible for treating the sick and injured

Also known as a "surgeon."

cooper [*coo-parr*] member of a vessel's crew responsible for the repair and maintenance of wooden casks, used for various shipboard purposes and especially to store food, water, and other provisions

coxswain [*cox-ern/in*] crew member responsible for maintaining and deploying the boats carried aboard a vessel

first mate [*farrst/firs'/firsht/fust mayeete*] a captain's second-in-command

Also known as "master's mate" or simply "mate," the first mate is traditionally someone closely allied with the captain and frequently depicted as dealing gruffly with those he commands. The company's favorite is the quartermaster, not the first mate (the quartermaster is the company's choice, while the first mate is the captain's choice), such that the quartermaster often takes over on a captain's death or incapacitation. Consequently, though a first mate is second-in-command, he is typically not second-in-line. Pirate vessels—particularly those where the balance of power lay with the quartermaster and company, and not with an iron-fisted or charismatic captain—often sailed without a mate altogether.

fo'c'sle; forecastle [*fork-sell*] members of, matters concerning, or things associated with the regular, non-officer crew

"Forecastle" or "fo'c'sle" means literally the portion of a vessel between its foremast and bow, but is used more loosely to refer to that part of a crew whose activities are closely associated with that forward part of a vessel.

fo'c'sle hand [*fork-sell 'an'/'and/han'*] member of a vessel's regular, non-officer crew; deck hand

fo'c'sle head [*fork-sell 'ead/hayd*] member of a vessel's regular, non-officer crew; deck hand

"Fo'c'sle head" is a derogatory term (unlike the more neutral "fo's'cle hand," "fo'c'sle jack," and "foremast jack"), implying an inability to think or perform anything more than mean labor.

fo'c'sle jack [*fork-sell jarrk*]
foremast jack [*farr/foor-marrst jarrk*] member of a vessel's regular, non-officer crew; deck hand

forward [*farr/forr-ad/ard/edd/erd*] of, relating to, or in connection with regular, non-officer crew or "hands," as opposed to officers or persons of authority within a company

This usage reflects the fact that common crew sleep and work (in forecastle and waist) toward the front of a vessel (and are accordingly known as "fo'c'slehands" or "men before the mast" or "men forward"), while officers sleep and work closer to the rear of a vessel.

gun crew [*garrn/goohn croo*] members of a vessel's crew responsible for cleaning, maintaining, loading, firing, and storing shot used with a vessel's cannons

gunner [*garrn/goohn-er*] (1) abridgement of "master gunner" or (2) any member of a vessel's gun crew

gunner's mate [*garrn/goohn-er's mayeete*] member of a vessel's crew responsible for assisting the gunner in overseeing the gun crew and the vessel's guns

helmsman [*'elmsman*] member of a vessel's crew in charge of steering the vessel by adjusting the vessel's rudder with a wheel, whipstaff (pole connected to the rudder), or tiller

Also known as a "steersman." In close sea-battle, an enemy vessel's helmsman is a premium target for gunners or pirates equipped with small-arms, as incapacitating him both (1) renders the vessel unmaneuverable, and therefore more easily boarded and unable to position optimally its shipboard cannon and (2) invites members of the enemy crew to attempt serially to take the helm from their fallen comrade, furnishing a steady parade of easy pot-shot targets for the same marksmen who mowed him down in the first place.

interpreter [*ayn/en-tarr/tree-parr/per/pree/puh-tarr*]

linguist [*len-gist/guisht/guiss/gwest*] member of a vessel's crew responsible for undertaking and translating communications with persons speaking other languages

master [*marrster*] (1) sailing master; senior member of a crew responsible for the navigation and steering of a vessel; (2) captain of a merchant vessel or of any vessel other than a naval vessel

The term "captain" was originally used to refer specifically to the ranking military officer aboard a naval warship, responsible for the pursuit and completion of the mission, as distinguished from (a) the senior seaman aboard a warship, responsible for the handling of the vessel and the administration of her crew or (b) the commander of any kind of vessel other than a naval warship. The term "master" was reserved for anyone falling into the latter two categories. Thus, in its narrowest sense, only a ranking naval officer aboard a naval vessel may be called a captain. Pirates made a point of calling their commanders "captain," therefore, in part to defy that strict naval convention and in part to promote the notion that they were warriors themselves.

master gunner [*marrster garrner/goohner*] member of a vessel's crew in charge of her gun crew, in turn responsible for cleaning, maintaining, loading, firing, and storing shot used with the vessel's guns

master's mate [*marrster's mayeete*] a captain's second-in-command

Also called "first mate" or simply "mate."

mess [*maahss*] (1) cabin, compartment, or other space aboard a vessel where the crew take their meals; (2) group of seamen aboard a vessel who eat together

musketeer [*moohs/mush-ker-tee-arr*] member of a vessel's company specially trained in the use of muskets and other firearms (particularly in long-range marksmanship), and deployed as part of a vessel's armament and defenses against other vessels, especially when boarding or being boarded

powder boy [*parr/powoo-der boyee*] boy employed on a vessel to assist the gunners with loading, cleaning, and maintaining the guns aboard

prize crew [*prawze/pryeeze croo*] members of a pirate company assigned to man a vessel taken and kept by the company

quartermaster [*quahrr/quaht-ter-marrster*] member of a company selected by his comrades to represent and voice their interests in dealings with the captain and mate, and often the most articulate, assertive, trusted, or popular member of the company

The quartermaster typically oversees company discipline, the handling of prize vessels and crews once taken, the safekeeping and allocation of plunder, and the dispensing of food and other ship's stores among the crew.

rope-maker [*ro'oope-mayeeker*] member of a vessel's crew responsible for the making, splicing, and repair of a vessel's rope lines

sea-artist [*sea ar'/ahrrt-est*] seaman skilled in piloting or navigation, or more generally possessing any special skill or knowledge

skipper [*skepper*] captain or master of a vessel

stand-by watch [*stan'/starrn'/starrnd-byee warrtch*] small portion of a vessel's crew, often only two or three seamen, assigned to watch over a vessel while the rest of the crew goes ashore

steersman [*stee-arrs/errs-man*] member of a vessel's crew in charge of steering the vessel by adjusting the vessel's rudder with a wheel, whipstaff (pole connected to the rudder), or tiller
Also known as a "helmsman."

supercargo [*suparr-cahrr-go'oo*] member of a crew responsible for a vessel's cargo and transactions
Also known as a "cape-merchant."

surgeon [*sarr-jin*] member of a vessel's crew responsible for treating the sick and injured
Also known as a "chirurgeon."

topman [*tarrp-man*] member of a vessel's crew who works aloft in the vessel's rigging

watch [*warrtch*] (1) one or more members of a vessel's crew on duty and on deck at a given time; (2) subgroup of crew members aboard who work half of the crew's shifts
The crew aboard a pirate (or any other sailing) vessel was typically divided into two watches—the "larboard watch" and the "starboard watch." A hand was usually assigned to either larboard or starboard watch according to the side of the vessel on which he berthed, but sometimes the designation was arbitrary—in the same way that children at play might be assigned odd and even numbers, or troops on training exercises assigned to "red" and "blue" teams, to achieve a quick and random allocation into two groups.

16.3 ARMS

For pirates, weapons do more than kill. They are symbols of mission. When John Phillips formed a pirate company with a lowly crew of four fish-splitters, the men—having no Bible, nor much of anything else—swore to their new articles on a hatchet (*Pirates of the New England Coast* 315). When Nathaniel North was voted captain of his company, he was solemnly escorted to the great cabin, seated at the head of the table, and then given a sword by the quartermaster, who, nodding to the blade, intoned, "This is the commission under which you are to act, may you prove fortunate to yourself and us."(*General History of the Pyrates* 525)

Sometimes, however, the baser, cutting edge of the weapon is the more immediately relevant. In Jeffrey Farnol's *Black Bartlemy's Treasure*, Adam Penfeather and Martin Conisby prepare themselves in one scene for a stealthy and perilous escape past Roger Tressady and his deadly comrades. Penfeather turns to Conisby and asks: "As to arms, Martin, ha' ye aught beside your knife?" (106)

Below are all the items Martin Conisby might have identified in response. The following are various terms relating to the weapons and ammunition routinely used and encountered by pirates, both at sea and on land.

(h)arquebus [(*h*)*ahrr-kee/ker-barss*] (1) light handgun with a long smooth-bored barrel used in the sixteenth and seventeenth centuries; (2) musket equipped with a wheel lock (mechanism by which pyrites are applied against a fast-spinning serrated wheel in order to produce sparks to ignite the charge), rather than a matchlock (as featured on a musket) or flintlock (as featured on a fusil or fuzil)

ball [*bawrl*] (1) small spherical piece of iron for use as a round of ammunition with a pistol; (2) type of projectile fired from a ship-board cannon consisting of spherical pieces of iron, cannon balls, or round shot; (3) single cannon ball or piece of round shot

bar (shot) [*bahrr (sharrt)*] type of projectile fired from a shipboard cannon, in the form of two cannon balls with an iron bar between them

Bar shot is generally used to inflict maximum damage on a vessel's crew or rigging (that is, "soft" targets), rather than on a vessel's hull (for which round shot is typically best suited). The iron bar expands the amount of surface area likely to be damaged, while the twin balls tend to increase the severity of damage, as an impact by one ball may cause the other to whip around at that much more vicious a velocity.

barker [*bahrrker*] pistol

basilisk [*bas'-lesk*] shipboard cannon firing twelve-pound shot and itself weighing about two thousand pounds

belaying pin [*b'-layin' pen*] pin typically made of hard wood, inserted vertically and down into one of several holes in a pinrail, and equipped with a neck or thickness toward the top preventing the pin from falling all the way through

A rope line can be turned or wrapped around the ends of a belaying pin protruding from the top and bottom of the rail (as well as around the circumference of the rail itself), then quickly released by simply pulling the pin out of the hole, causing the line to drop onto the deck. In pirate narratives, the belaying pin is often featured as an improvised weapon. See "Treasure Island" (1934) 1:38: Long John Silver knocks Ben Gunn over the head with a belaying pin before escaping off the *Hispaniola*; "Treasure

Island" (1972) 49:28: members of Long John Silver's company take over the *Hispaniola* after arming themselves with belaying pins and incapacitating Redruth by throwing one at his head.

blade [*blayeede*] (1) sword or any long-bladed variation; (2) knife

blunderbuss [*blarrn/bloohn-darr/dee/ner-barrss*] gun between one and three feet in length, equipped with a short stock and firing several small pieces of shot simultaneously

The blunderbuss was designed to inflict damage across a large area with a single discharge.

boarding axe [*barrdin'/barrding/boardin' ar-rxe*] axe equipped with a spike opposite the axehead and often with a wrist strap on the handle, used for boarding other vessels and close combat

bottle [*bah'/bahrr-tle*]

Bottles served as weaponry in at least two ways: as crude grenades or *grenadoes* when filled with gunpowder and iron scraps and fitted with burning matches or fuses, and as passive but effective armament against bare-footed boarding parties when shattered and spread across a defending vessel's decks.

bow chase(r) [*bowoo chayeese(r)*] cannon positioned at a vessel's bow and used to fire on a pursued vessel, typically in order to damage its rigging and compromise its speed

brace of barkers [*brayeece o' bahrrkers*] pair of pistols

brass gun [*brarss garrn/goohn*] cannon made of brass, which is more expensive to make but lighter and more durable (less suceptible to corrosion, fracture, or explosion) than its iron counterparts

broadsword [*brarrd-sarrd/swarrd*] straight, double-edged, single-handed, basket-hilted sword, typically measuring between 2½ and 3½ feet in length and weighing three to four pounds, designed for slashing and hacking rather than stabbing or piercing

buck-shot [*boohk-sharrt*] one or more balls of lead used as ammunition, measuring approximately one-quarter to one-third of an inch in diameter, designed for use in hunting animals larger than fowl

caliver [*cal-'barr/'ber/ibarr/iber/'ver*] light handgun with a long smooth-bored barrel used in the sixteenth and seventeenth centuries, eventually replaced by the musket

The term "caliver" is likely derived from the phrase "arquebus of calibre" (meaning an arquebus equipped with a barrel of standard or average bore or diameter), but as a practical matter, is used in reference to any arquebus generally.

canister [*carrn-eh/er-starr*] type of projectile fired from a shipboard cannon consisting of bags or, more typically, metal cases containing musket balls

cannon [*cannern*] large, heavy gun, typically mounted on a carriage

cannon-petro [*cannern petro'oo*] shipboard cannon firing twenty-four pound shot and itself weighing about three thousand pounds

cannon-royal [*cannern ro'/royee/r'y-al*] shipboard cannon firing forty-eight pound shot and itself weighing about six thousand pounds

cannon shot [*cannern sharrt*] type of projectile fired from a shipboard cannon consisting of spherical balls of iron; round shot

Round shot is the most accurate type of projectile that can be fired from a vessel's guns and is particularly suitable for inflicting maximum damage on another vessel's hull.

carbine [*cahrr-bawn/byeen*] short, light musket

carcass [*cahrr-cahss/cush/kerss*] thinly constructed iron case perforated with several holes and containing combustible materials,

designed to be fired by a small cannon and to set fire to enemy vessels or defenses

carronade [*cahrr-ernade/ernayeede/'nade/nayeede*] light, short-barreled cannon first manufactured by the Carron Iron Founding and Shipping Company in 1778, mounted on a slide (rather than wheeled) carriage, and firing cannon balls at lower velocity, and inflicting resultingly greater damage on wooden hulls at short range than other, higher-velocity guns that produced smaller, cleaner holes

cartouche (box) [*cahrr-tooch (bahrrx)*] cartridge, typically one made of paper

cartridge [*cahrr-tredge*] complete charge for a firearm (shot and powder) contained in a case or shell made of metal, paper, or other material

case (shot) [*cayeese (sharrt)*] type of projectile fired from a shipboard cannon, consisting of musket balls, other lead balls or pellets, pieces of iron scrap, or other bits of metal—or of metallic cylinders packed with these—and particularly suitable for inflicting maximum damage on persons assembled on another ship's deck

chain shot [*chayeen sharrt*] type of projectile fired from a shipboard cannon consisting of two cannon balls with a chain between them

Used for the same purpose as bar shot.

chaser [*chayeeser*] cannon positioned at a vessel's bow or stern and used to fire on a pursued or pursuing vessel, typically in order to damage rigging and compromise the targeted vessel's speed

A "chaser" is also known more specifically as a "bow chaser" or "fore-chase" (if placed at the bow) or a "stern chaser" (if at the stern).

cohorn mortar [*co'oo-harrn/'orn marrter*] small bronze mortar (high-angle gun with a short barrel for use with short-range targets) mounted on a block or other piece of wood equipped with handles, such that it might be moved and re-positioned by two men

cold steel [*col'/coold stee'ell*] a reference to one or more swords and knives or to the use thereof, particularly as distinguished from firearms

cross-bar (shot) [*crarss-bahrr (sharrt)*] type of projectile fired from a shipboard cannon, consisting of round cannon balls with iron bars crossing through them and extending six to eight inches on either side

Cross-bar shot is designed to inflict damage on a vessel's crew or rigging (the iron bars claw at and cut through a larger target area along the shot's trajectory) without compromising the shot's capacity to damage a vessel's hull.

culverin [*coohl-varrin/lv'rin*] shipboard cannon firing eighteen-pound shot and itself weighing about twenty-five hundred pounds

cutlass; cutlash [*carrt/cooht-lerss/lish*] thick, heavy, slightly curving sword with a flat, single-edged, relatively short blade

The blade of choice for most pirates, the cutlass (with its sturdy feel, conservative length, and slight curve) is designed for use in small spaces—such as close combat on a crowded deck—and for slashing and hacking, rather than thrusting and piercing.

dagger [*darrger*] short knife with a double-edged blade designed for stabbing (rather than slashing) and equipped with a hilt or guard protecting the wielding hand

demi-cannon [*daahmi-cannern*] shipboard cannon firing thirty-two pound shot and itself weighing about four thousand pounds

demi-culverin [*daahmi-coohlverin/coohlv'rin/ culv'rin*] shipboard cannon firing nine-pound shot and itself weighing about fifteen hundred pounds

double round\shot [*darr/dooh-ble roun'/ rount/rowoon'/rowoond/rowoont\sharrt*] type of projectile, consisting of two cannon balls loaded together and fired in a single discharge, for use with a shipboard cannon

Dutch knife [*Darrtch/Dootch knawf/knyeefe*] sharp-pointed knife with a down-curved blade and handle, such that the knife's profile is that of a gentle arc

The curving is optimal both for skinning and other close cutting work and for knife-fighting using quick, downward slashes.

falconet [*felk-ernet/'net*] small cannon using shot typically weighing two to three pounds

fire-ball [*farr/fyarrr bawrl*] pot filled with oil or other flammable materials set aflame and launched like a bomb from the deck or rigging of a vessel at another

The real tactical benefit from launching a fire-ball is not so much destruction as diversion: the noise, explosion, and rapid spread of flames following the impact of a fire-ball invite members of the enemy crew to stop battling and start fire-fighting. The fire-ball carries some risk, however, to the extent that (1) flames might spread back onto the deploying vessel, especially on a windy day, and (2) the fire-ball might counterproductively drive the enemy crew to fight that much harder—knowing in win-or-die fashion that the only escape from their inferno of a ship is to seize control of the other. Use of the fire-ball declined after the start of the eighteenth century, as the practice of firing red-hot or explosive iron shot from a vessel's cannons became more common.

firelock [*farr/fyarrr-larrk*] musket

"Firelock" technically refers to a gun's flint-equipped hammer, which produces a spark that ignites a charge.

fore-chase (gun) [*farr/foor chay-eese (goohn)*] cannon positioned at a vessel's bow and used to fire on a pursued vessel, typically in order to damage its rigging and compromise its speed

fusee; fuzee [*foo-see/zee*]
(1) musket
"Fusee" technically refers to a gun's igniting mechanism.
(2) fusil or fuzil

fusil; fuzil [*foo-sell/zell*] (1) an alternative term for any type of musket; (2) smoothbore long gun fired from the shoulder and equipped with a flintlock (mechanism by which flint is struck against steel in order to produce sparks to ignite the charge) as opposed to a matchlock (as featured on a musket) or wheel lock (as featured on an arquebus)

grape (shot) [*grayeepe (sharrt)*] type of projectile, consisting of small iron balls packed in canvas bags, fired from a shipboard cannon

Grape shot is generally used to inflict maximum damage on a vessel's crew, rather than on its hull (for which round shot is typically best suited). The advantage of firing grape shot from a cannon is similar to that of firing buck shot from a shotgun: The likelihood of hitting one or more objects within range is increased, and the damage to a given object within particularly close range (such as a threatening boarder) is enhanced, though at the expense of penetrative power.

great gun [*grayeet/grea'/grett garrn/goohn*] cannon

great shot [*grayeet/grea'/grett sharrt*] round shot of large size, especially shot weighing thirty-two pounds or more

grenado [*ger/graah-nayee-do'oo*] grenade

Also known as a "grenado shell" or "powder flask." "The grenades used by pirates were hollow balls weighing about two ounces. They were made of iron or wood and filled with gunpowder. They had a touch hole and a fuse which was lit before the grenade was thrown among the seamen on the deck of the merchant ship. The resulting explosion was designed to cause death and injury, and could totally demoralize a crew with no experience of battle." (*Under the Black Flag* 120)

gun [*garrn/goohn*] cannon

Pirates almost always use the term "gun" in reference to cannon, and not to smaller firearms like muskets or pistols.

half-pike [*'alf/harff-pawk/pyeeke*] short spear

The half-pike's compact length is useful in close combat, where a longer instrument could easily be caught or obstructed.

handspike; hand spike [*'and/'an'/han' spawk/spyeeke*] bar or lever made of wood or metal and fitted in a windlass or capstan for the purpose of grasping hold and applying heavy force when heaving an anchor

hanger [*'anger*] short, single-edged, slightly curved sword

The term is derived from the practice of hanging the weapon from one's belt.

iron shot [*iy'ee-arrn sharrt*] round shot

land gun [*lan' garrn/goohn*] cannon or other piece of artillery mounted on land, typically as part of a fort or embattlement guarding a port or harbor

langrage [*la'/larrn-grage/gerrge*] type of projectile consisting of nails, bolts, and odd (and preferably twisted and jagged) pieces of scrap iron (or cases loaded with these) fired from a shipboard cannon

Langrage is generally used to inflict maximum damage on a vessel's crew or rigging (that is, "soft" targets), rather than on a vessel's hull (for which round shot is typically best suited).

long gun [*larrng/lon' garrn/goohn*] long-barreled cannon designed to project shot over large distances

long tom [*larrng/lon' tarrm*] long-barreled cannon designed to project shot over large distances, especially one mounted on a rotating base

machet(e) [*mahrr-chetter/shetter*] large, heavy knife with a curving blade that broadens toward the tip and features a bottom edge shorter than the top edge, used for clearing vegetation

marlin spike [*mahrr-lern spawk/spyeeke*] pointed iron hand tool used to separate a rope's strands while splicing or to loosen tight rope knots, often with an eye at the top to which a lanyard is fastened

metal [*maaht/meh'-al*] potency of armament or firepower, especially the size of the cannons (typically expressed in terms of the weight of the round shot fired from them) aboard a vessel, as distinguished from their number

minion [*men-yern*] shipboard cannon firing four-pound shot and itself weighing about eight hundred pounds

murdering piece [*marrder-in' peesh*] small cannon designed for targeting a vessel's own deck in order to clear it of enemy boarders, typically mounted on a rotating base or positioned at an elevation—on the poop or quarterdeck, for example—or toward the center of a vessel and not its perimeter

musket [*moohs/mush-kert*] smoothbore long gun fired from the shoulder and equipped with a matchlock (mechanism by which a lighted match is applied to priming powder in order to produce sparks to ignite the charge) as opposed to a wheel lock (as featured on an arquebus) or flintlock (as featured on a fusil)

musket ball\bullet [*moohs/mush-kert bawrl\ bullert/bul't*] round of ammunition, typically a ball or pellet of lead, for use with a musket and therefore of a larger size than that fired from a pistol

musketoon; musquetoon [*moohs/mush-kertoon*] musket with a shortened barrel

partridge(s) [*pahrr-treh-dger(s)*]
partridge shot [*pahrr-tredge shahrrt*] type of projectile consisting of bags of small balls or pellets of lead, optimal for use in saturating a target area (especially a vessel's crew or rigging) with multiple projectiles at some expense to the force of impact, fired from a shipboard cannon

paterero [*parr-tee/tree-rarr/ray-ro'oo*]
pedrero [*paah/parr/pee/per-drayee-ro'oo*] small gun mounted on a rotating base on a vessel's

poop deck or railing, designed to strafe and repel boarding enemies; swivel gun

piece [*peesh*] (1) shipboard cannon; (2) firearm of any kind, especially a musket

pike [*pawk/pyeeke*] spear

pike-staff [*pawk/pyeeke starrf*] shaft of a pike

pinking thing [*penk-in' fing/theng/thin'/t'in'/ t'ing*] sword or any long blade, especially one made for piercing as opposed to hacking and slashing

pistol [*peh-shtol*] handgun

pistol ball [*peh-shtol bawrl*] round of ammunition, typically a ball or pellet of lead, for use with a pistol and therefore of a smaller size than that fired from a musket

pole-ax [*po'oole arrxe*] ax equipped with a hammer head opposite the blade, such that one might hack with one face and bludgeon with the other

powder [*parr/powoo-der*] gunpowder

powder and ball\shot [*parr/powoo-der an'/'n' bawrl\sharrt*] ammunition; gunpowder and projectiles necessary for the discharge of an early firearm, such as a musket

powder barrel [*parr/powoo-der bahrrel*] cask filled with gunpowder and suspended on the end of one of a vessel's yards (wood poles supporting square sails)

Powder barrels were used to deter other vessels from approaching too closely, as they might be dropped and detonated on the offending vessel's deck. Of course, the tactical advantage of a powder barrel—the closest pirate equivalent of a bomb—had to be weighed against the risk that a careful musket shot from the enemy vessel might detonate the cask pre-deployment and set the defending ship's sails and rigging on fire.

rapier [*raah-pier*] (1) long, thin, two-edged sword with a cup-shaped hilt; (2) any sword

round shot [*roun'/rount/rowoon'/rowoond/ rowoont sharrt*] type of projectile, consisting of spherical balls of iron, fired from a shipboard cannon

Round shot is the most accurate type of projectile that can be fired from a vessel's guns and is particularly suitable for inflicting maximum damage on another vessel's hull.

sabre; saber [*sabber*] (1) heavy, one-edged, slightly curved sword; (2) light, one-edged, tapered sword with an arched guard protecting the hand

saker [*sack/sayeek-er*] shipboard cannon firing six-pound shot and itself weighing about one thousand pounds

seaman('s) knife [*seaman('s) knawf/knyeefe*] small blunt-ended knife with a serrated blade, typically measuring five inches or less in length, and usually carried on a lanyard or in a sheath

serpent [*sarr-pant*] shipboard cannon firing forty-two pound shot and itself weighing about five thousand pounds

shot [*sharrt*] ammunition; projectile for use with or discharged from a cannon or firearm of any kind

shot and shell [*sharrt an'/'n' shayell*] (1) projectiles fired from shipboard cannons; (2) a phrase used more generally to refer to battle or conflict, especially a battle at sea between ships

shot and steel [*sharrt an'/'n' stee'ell*] (1) weapons; (2) a phrase used more generally to refer to battle or violence, especially hand-to-hand combat.

small arm [*smawrl ahrrm*] any firearm capable of being held, such as a pistol, musket, arquebus, etc.

small shot [*smawrl sharrt*] projectiles fired from pistols, muskets, or other held firearms—that is, from weapons other than mortars or cannons

Spanish knife [*Span-ersh/esh knawf/knyeefe*] navaja, or folding clasp knife that ratchets open to any of multiple blade positions with a menacing chattering sound, developed in the seventeenth century

steel [*stee'ell*] (1) any type of sword; (2) use of a sword or swords; swordfight

steel o' proof [*stee'ell o' proof*] armor made of steel and "proofed" by being shot at with a firearm, with the non-penetrating dent circled or otherwise limned by an engraving as evidence of the armor's effectiveness

stern chase(r) (gun) [*starrn chayeese(r) (garrn/goohn)*] cannon positioned at a vessel's stern and used to fire on a pursuing vessel, typically in order to damage its rigging and compromise its speed

swivel (gun) [*swe-bbel/'el (garrn/goohn)*] small gun mounted on a rotating base on a vessel's poop deck or railing, designed to strafe and repel boarding enemies

Also known as a "paterero" or "pedrero."

tree ram [*tree rem*] hollowed tree packed with gunpowder and sealed, propped against a door, gate or other barrier, then ignited in order to destroy or force a passage through such object

trundle shot [*troohnd/trun'-le sharrt*] type of projectile, consisting of iron spikes or bolts sharpened on both ends and measuring one to two feet long, fired from a shipboard cannon

tuck [*tarrk/toohk*] (1) long, straight, especially rigid sword with a point but no cutting edge, used for thrusting and piercing; (2) any sword

whinger [*whenger*] long knife or short stabbing sword

yatagan [*yat'/yatter-gern*] long knife or short sabre with a steel cutting edge and an iron top edge, and with a slightly S-shaped blade curving down toward the cutting edge along the middle portion of its length, then curving up at the pointed tip

16.4 TORTURE & PUNISHMENT

In this section you'll find terms associated with various types of torture and punishment administered by pirates.

What cannot be catalogued are the infinite intimidations, degradations, and psychological persecutions short of torture to which pirates expertly subjected their victims.

In 1718, Blackbeard blockaded Charleston harbor, demanding a supply of medicines in exchange for the lives of several elite townspeople he had kidnapped. On receiving the medicines, he sent the notables ashore in only their underclothes (*Under the Black Flag* 166; *General History of the Pyrates* 74–75, 87–92).

In 1722, Bartholomew Roberts took a Dutch ship and found a supply of fine sausages aboard. When Roberts' men learned the Dutch captain's wife had made them, they strung them around their necks and cavorted around as ridiculously as possible, then threw the sausages overboard to confirm their contempt for them (*General History of the Pyrates* 231, 234).

Then there were your more involved humiliations. In June 1721, on encountering a French ship, George Lowther's crew disguised their own ship as a merchant so that one of them—John Massey, dressed in a wealthy trader's finery—could stroll about the decks of the French ship with her captain and make light conversation about the cargo aboard. Having established a warm rapport, Massey turned to his host, confessed he had a secret, then whispered in his ear: "We must have it all without money." Any confusion on the Frenchman's part dissolved on seeing Lowther's men emerge from their hiding places and swarm the vessel. After the pirates carried away the expensive liquors and textiles, Lowther thanked the Frenchman and handed him five pounds (*Villains of All Nations* 162–63).

But when various mental harassments grew tiresome, or proved inadequate for more practical purposes, pirates turned to cruelties of the flesh. An inventory follows. While most of the terms in this section were names recognized and used by pirates for types of torture or punishment (*e.g.*, "sweat," "cat o' nine tails"), other terms (*e.g.*, "hoisting," "target shooting") are not terms of art, but rather only words that functionally identify certain practices. Pirates may or may not have used uniformity in proposing or describing them.

bilbo [*bel-bowoo*] long iron bar with sliding shackles attached, used to secure a prisoner's feet at the ankles

> "This morning two persons being accus'd of concealing a peruke of the plunder in the *Canary* bark, two shirts, and a pair of stockings; and being found guilty, I order'd them into the **bilboes**. ..." (Woodes Rogers, *A Cruising Voyage Round the World* 25)

boiling water in the ears [*boilin' wahh/warrter i'/'n t' ee-arrs/errs*]

> "Or **boiling water poured in his yeres** might serve." (Sam Spraggons, describing possible methods of torturing Martin Conisby, *Black Bartlemy's Treasure* 307)

bottles [*barrt/boh'-les*]

Bottles are thrown forcefully enough to break on impact and cut the victim's skin.

> *[W]hen Scarfield had tied the skipper of the *Baltimore Belle* naked to the foremast of his own brig he had permitted his crew of cutthroats (who were drunk at the time) to throw **bottles** at the helpless captive, who died that night of the wounds he had received.* (account of John Scarfield's cruelties, *The Book of Pirates* "Captain Scarfield" 193)

bowel [*bowoo-ell*] cut into another's abdomen and remove the intestines

"Disembowel" and "eviscerate" are modern terms referring to the same action. By far the most horrific examples of boweling (and arguably of any pirate-inflicted tortures) are the atrocities reportedly committed by French pirate Montbars of Languedoc. Montbars, called the "Exterminator," was known for slicing open a victim's abdomen just enough to get hold of one end of his bowels, nailing that end to the wall, then beating on his back with a burning log in order to force him to uncoil his own bowels and dance himself to death (*Under the Black Flag* 132).

> "Avast, sons o' dogs, stand off or **I'll bowel ye**." (Ned, brandishing a long knife, *Winds of Chance* 313)

burning [*a-barrn-in'*]

Burning is both a form of execution, where a victim's entire body is burnt—

> "Shoot the dog! Nay, hang him up! Aye, by his thumbs. Nay, **burn him—to the fire wi' the bloody rogue!**" (Captain Jo's company, *Martin Conisby's Vengeance* 59)

—and a form of torture, where only one or more parts of the victim's body are exposed to flame at a given time (often allowed to blister from the heat before being thrust directly into the fire), thus inflicting pain but not death.

> "Still not satisfied, they put a stone weighing at least two hundred-weight on his loins and lit a fire of palm leaves under him, **burning his face and setting his hair alight**—yet despite all these torments he would not confess to having money." (former buccaneer Alexander O. Exquemelin, describing the prolonged torture of a Spaniard at Gibraltar by Henry Morgan's men, *The Buccaneers of America* 150)

burst guts with water [*barrst garrts/goohts weth/wi'/wiff/witt wahh/warr-ter*]

There are several torture methods featuring the forced consumption of massive amounts of water, all ending with the painful rupture of the victim's stomach. They include, for example: pouring water into a funnel inserted down the victim's throat, while pinching his nostrils and thus forcing him to swallow; forcing the victim to swallow a knotted cord along with large amounts of water, then ripping the cord out of the victim's mouth—and the victim's esophagus along with it; forcing the victim to swallow uncooked rice or grain (which expands upon saturation) along with large amounts of water, thus speeding the stomach-bursting process; hammering or beating on the victim's tender, water-engorged abdomen in order to cause his stomach to burst; and forcing the victim to consume large amounts of water while secured to a rack or slab elevating his feet to a point higher than his head, so as to subject the lungs to pressure from the liquid-filled stomach, thus simulating a feeling of drowning or suffocation.

> "I mind too as Lollonais had a trick o' **bursting a man's guts wi' water**. ...." (Sam Spraggons, describing possible methods of torturing Martin Conisby, *Black Bartlemy's Treasure* 307)

by inches [*byee en-chers*] a phrase used in reference to any form of slow, prolonged torture

> < "[S]o 'twas Mr. John that saved us—?" "Ay, faith, ma'm; but for him, my wife would now be shamed to death and myself **dying by inches** in torment ... but for Johnny!" > (Ursula Revell & Japhet Bly, *Winds of Chance* 330)

by the board [*byee t' barrd*]

"By the board" means overboard or over the side of a vessel. The side of a vessel is sometimes referred to as the "board." Setting film and fiction aside, the pirates of history probably threw persons overboard more often than they engaged in more elaborate forms of execution, as it was the quickest and easiest way to eliminate an unwanted person.

> "Cross me, and you'll go where many a good man's gone before you, first and last, these thirty year back—some to the yard-arm, shiver my sides! and some **by the board**, and all to feed the fishes." (Long John Silver, *Treasure Island* 159, Chap. 28)

cane [*cayeene*]

A hollow interior and an extremely hard exterior make the cane a preferred instrument of corporal punishment or torture. The hollow interior shifts the weight of the shaft to the perimeter, allowing a quicker and sharper whipping action, while the hard exterior delivers a painful impact.

> < "The order is—twenty-five with the cat." "Ax pardon, sir, but might I suggest the **cane** or rope's end?" "You may not." > (James Danvers, *Adam Penfeather, Buccaneer* 88)

carbonado [*cahrr-bern/b'n-ayee-do'oo*] a form of torture wherein the victim's body is treated as a piece of meat for broiling—*i.e.*, cut across or scored, then placed over flames

> < "'Tis said he died at your hands, Senor Capitan—" "Not mine, Don, not mine. We gave him to Black Pompey to **carbonado**." > (Don Federigo & Captain Belvedere, *Martin Conisby's Vengeance* 60)

cashier [*carrsh-ee-arr/err*] demote or dismiss from a position of authority or responsibility, or expel from a larger group or unit, for disciplinary reasons, incompetence, or unfitness to perform one's duties

> "As for Gronet, he said his men would not suffer him to join us in the fight. But we were not satisfied with that excuse, so we suffered him to go with us to the Isles of Quibo, and there **cashiered** our cowardly companion." (William Dampier, recounting the explusion of Captain Gronet and his French pirates from the

larger company on grounds of cowardice, *A New Voyage Round the World* 111)

cat (o' nine tails) [*ket (o' nawn/nyeen tayells)*] set of nine knotted leather cords or thongs fastened to a single handle and used for whipping

The instrument was termed a "cat" because the marks it leaves on a victim's back were fancifully thought to resemble cat scratches.

> < "No man shall be flogged aboard my ship, —except he earn it, and then, 'stead o' one lash shall be nine!" "Ha, so you'll dare threaten us wi' the **cat**, eh?" "The cat, yes, Tobias, and thereafter plenty o' salt to heal bloody backs ..." > (Adam Penfeather & Toby Drew, *Adam Penfeather, Buccaneer* 212) "The same day I was carried on board the pirate sloop, tied to the gears and received two hundred lashes with a **cat o' nine tails** which the prisoner Upton had made for that purpose; after which they pickled me ..." (Dimmock, describing his torture at the hands of the pirate crew of the *Night Rambler*, *Lives of the Most Remarkable Criminals* 476)

Cobbey [*Carrbey*] the spanking of one's buttocks with a paddle

> * As might have been expected, the crew gave him the sort of ribald welcome that sailors reserve for mates not seen for a while. They "offered hym a **Cobbey**," which is to say that some of the men held him while others beat him on the buttocks with a paddle.* (account of the rough but good-natured welcome received by Francis Drake's trumpeter aboard the *Pelican*, *The Queen's Pirate* 98–99)

cord [*carrd*]

Used as a means of both securing a victim's limbs and applying sudden, bone-jarring force thereto.

> "He still would not confess, so they tied long **cords** to his thumbs and his big toes and spreadeagled him to four stakes.

Then four of them came and beat on the cords with their sticks, making his body jerk and shudder and stretching his sinews." (former buccaneer Alexander O. Exquemelin, describing the torture of a Spaniard at Gibaltrar by Henry Morgan's men, *The Buccaneers of America* 150)

crucifixion [*cru-cer/see-fek/fik-shern/shoohn*] execution of a victim by binding or nailing his hands and feet to a wooden cross

> "Yet even this man had not suffered all the torments which the buccaneers inflicted on the Spaniards to make them divulge their hidden wealth. ... Others they **crucified**, with burning fuses between their fingers and toes." (former buccaneer Alexander O. Exquemelin, recounting the torture of Gibraltar's Spanish residents by Henry Morgan's men, *The Buccaneers of America* 151)

cut off eyelids [*carrt/cooht arrf eye'ee-leds*]

In addition to causing short-term pain and discomfort as a result of the unobstructed passage of irritants to the corneal surface, the removal of one's eyelids has been said to make it difficult or impossible for a victim to fall or stay asleep for any significant period of time, causing all the typical consequences of sustained sleep deprivation—including hallucination, irrational impulses cascading into full-blown insanity, and death.

> "Look, Japhet man, —nay, damn ye, open your eyes and watch now or Pompey shall **cut off thine eyelids**, old messmate, —so open and watch, I say. ..." (Roger Snaith, forcing Japhet Bly to watch him rape Bly's wife, *Winds of Chance* 326)

Dead Man's Nag [*Dayd Man's Narrg*]

A form of humiliation and torture wherein two victims are forced to ride on each other's shoulders and engage in swordfight to the death with one or more other pairs of victims. If the participants fail to kill anyone,

all are hanged; if one pair kills a member of another, the winning "rider" and "nag" both are spared.

> "Well, I have it in mind to play a little game we never tire of, me mates an' I, which I meself call "**Dead Man's Nag**." (Thomas Bartholomew Red, forcing his Spanish prisoners to mount each other and fight, *Pirates* 1:03:21)

drub [*droohb*] beat or thrash with a stick or other hard, long object; cudgel

> *[A]n elderly logwood-cutter ... had fallen into the pirate's hands, and in some freak of drunken benevolence had been allowed to get away with nothing worse than a slit nose and a **drubbing**.* (account of an erstwhile prisoner of Captain Sharkey's, *Dealings of Captain Sharkey* "The Dealings of Captain Sharkey with Stephen Craddock" 28)

eat candles [*eat kendles*]

The victim is forced to ingest candles.

> *A bonfire was made of his ship, however, and a little later, desiring more diversion, the unfortunate Hawkins was sent down to the cabin for supper. This turned out to be a dish of **candles** which he was forced to swallow and then, in order to aid digestion, the poor man was thrown about the cabin until he was covered with bruises and afterward sent forward amongst the other prisoners.* (account of Captain Hawkins' mistreatment at the hands of Francis Spriggs' men, *Pirates of the New England Coast* 280)

eat oneself [*eat 'un/woohn-seff*]

The pirate Edward Low was famous for forcing his victims to eat pieces of flesh cut from their own bodies or those of their associates, sometimes after roasting and seasoning.

> "Some day, Abny, some day, I shall cut out that tongue o' yourn and watch ye eat it, lad, eat it—hist, here cometh Gregory at

last—easy all." (Roger Tressady, *Black Bartlemy's Treasure* 96)

flog [*flahrrg*] beat or thrash severely with a whip, rod, or cane

> "The rule o' the sea is—for strife aboardship, **flogging**, and aboard this ship, twenty-five lashes, and by Captain Troy's order." (James Danvers, *Adam Penfeather, Buccaneer* 89)

genital hanging [*genertal 'ang-in'*]

A victim is suspended from ropes or cords tied around his genitals, which causes not only excruciating pain but often his genitals to be ripped from his body.

> "Yet even this man had not suffered all the torments which the buccaneers inflicted on the Spaniards to make them divulge their hidden wealth. Some they **hung up by their genitals**, till the weight of their bodies tore them loose." (former buccaneer Alexander O. Exquemlin, recounting the torture of Gibraltar's Spanish residents by Henry Morgan's men, *The Buccaneers of America* 151)

give to the fish\sharks [*gi'/giff t'/ta/ter t' fesh\shahrrks/shairks*]

A colorful way to describe throwing a man overboard.

> "If Long Tom does not speak presently I'll **give myself to the sharks**." (pirate mate, assuring the crew that their captain will avenge the island natives' aggression with firepower, *The Coral Island* 216)

hang [*'ang*] execute by suspending from a rope tied around the neck

> "The mulatto, because he said he was in the fireship that came to burn us in the night, was immediately **hanged**." (William Dampier, reporting the immediate execution of a prisoner found to have assisted a treacherous Spanish merchant in attempting to set Dampier's ship afire, *A New Voyage Round the World* 105)

hang by the thumbs [*'ang byee t' thoohms/ t'umbs*]

The victim is suspended from a rope or cord tied around his thumbs, which causes not only excruciating pain buy also typically the dislocation of, and permanent damage to, his thumbs.

> "Shoot the dog! Nay, **hang him up**! Aye, **by his thumbs**." (Captain Jo's company, *Martin Conisby's Vengeance* 59)

hang from the yardarm [*'ang ferm t' yahrrd-erm*] be hanged by the neck and thereby killed almost instantly by being suspended, then dropped, from the end of one of a vessel's yards (wood poles supporting a square sail)

The yardarm figures much more prominently in the pirate narratives of history and fiction as a makeshift, seagoing gallows than as a part of a vessel's rigging.

> "Morgan made all the prisoners understand they must persuade the general to agree to let the buccaneers pass the fort unmolested; if he would not consent they should all be **hanged from the yard-arm**." (former buccaneer Alexander O. Exquemelin, describing how Henry Morgan ensured a safe escape from Maracaibo by keeping Spanish hostages aboard, *The Buccaneers of America* 161)

hang over the end of a gun [*'ang ober/o'er t' aynd o'\on a garrn/ goohn*]

Whereas someone forced to "kiss the gunner's daughter" would lean forward and over the butt end of a cannon to be caned or whipped on the buttocks, someone "hanged over the end of a gun" would be draped over the front end of the cannon barrel, such that fired shot would put one large hole or several small ones (depending on the type of ammunition) through his abdomen.

> *[T]hey carried Sharkey to the gun and they **triced him** sitting over the porthole, **with his body about a foot from the muzzle**.

... And then at last there came the dull thud of a gun, and an instant later the shattering crash of the explosion.* (account of Copley Banks' dramatic murder of John Sharkey, *Dealings of Captain Sharkey* "How Copley Banks Slew Captain Sharkey" 73, 76)

heave overboard ['*eave/heeff ober/o'er-barrd*]

"Over the side with him, men!" (Peter Blood, ordering his crew to heave Colonel Bishop overboard, *Captain Blood* 1:00:25)

hock and heave [*harrk/'ock an'/'n' 'eave/heeff*]

To "hock" a person is to sever his hamstrings by slicing across them with a blade, and to thereby deprive him of the use of his legs. A prisoner might be hocked before being thrown overboard to prevent him from swimming or treading water.

> *When all the plunder was gathered, the passengers and crew were dragged to the waist, and under the cold smile of Sharkey each in turn was thrown over the side—Sweetlocks standing by the rail and ham-stringing them with his cutlass as they passed over, lest some strong swimmer should rise in judgment against them.* (description of John Sharkey's cruel disposition of the crew and passengers aboard the *Portobello*, *Dealings of Captain Sharkey* "The Blighting of Sharkey" 51)

hoist [*hoyeest/'oist*]

The term "hoist" generally means to lift or raise something, usually with the assistance of a line (rope), block, or other intermediary device. Hoisting as a form of torture or punishment is a preparatory phase: the victim is suspended over the deck, so that something painful can be done to him in that vulnerable position. He may be suddenly dropped onto the deck, for example, or struck or otherwise physically compromised while still hovering in the air. The only surprising aspect of this use of "hoisting" is that the rigging and other equipment aboard pirate vessels did not figure more frequently in improvised barbarities.

> *The plunder of the vessel didn't amount to much so the pirates thought they would amuse themselves by fastening a rope around the men's bodies, one by one, and after **hoisting** them as high as the main-and-foretops by letting go of the ropes the unfortunate wretches would fall tumbling to the deck with force enough to break skins and smash bones. After the men were well crippled by this usage Captain Trot was given his sloop and told to clear out.* (account of the mistreatment by Francis Farrington Spriggs' company of the crew of a sloop taken near St. Christopher's, *Pirates of the New England Coast* 282)

hot iron in the eyes [*hahrrt/'ot iy-arrn i'/'n t' eye'ees*]

The application of red-hot iron against the victim's eyes both causes him excruciating pain and blinds him.

> "Or a **hot iron close agen his eyes** is good." (Sam Spraggons, describing possible methods of torturing Martin Conisby, *Black Bartlemy's Treasure* 307)

irons [*iy-arrns*] metal shackles used to secure a prisoner's hands and legs

> "An officer aboard our ship, and other officers and men aboard Capt. Courtney, began to be mutinous, and form a conspiracy against us; but we prevented it, by chastising their leaders, whom we put in **irons**, on board different ships, to break the knot, which might otherwise have ruin'd the voyage." (Woodes Rogers, *A Cruising Voyage Round the World* 201)

keel [*kee'ell*]

Securing a seaman to a vessel's keel and getting the vessel under way so as to drag him behind or underneath is a distant cousin of keelhauling (see immediately below) and a surer cause of death by drowning.

"I'll have you chained to the **keel**!" (El Toro Mendoza, *Long John Silver's Return to Treasure Island* 19:43)

keelhaul [*kee'ell-'awrl/hawrl*] subject to keel-hauling; haul on a rope under a vessel's hull from one side to another or (less typically) from one end to another

> < "And what did I order done to him, Master Bones?" "**Keel-hauled**, he was." "Correct. **Keel-hauled**. A most expressive phrase, Robert. Technically, I should explain, it involves drawing a man under the keel of a vessel. It has—shall we say?—unpleasant consequences." > (Andrew Murray & Billy Bones, *Porto Bello Gold* 69–70)

knife under fingernails\toenails [*knawf/knyeefe arrn/hun/oohn-darr/'ner fenger/finner\to'oo-nayells*]

> The victim's fingernails or toenails are removed slowly so as to maximize both physical pain and psychological discomfort.

> "See now—a good sharp **knife 'neath the finger or toe-nails**—drew slow, mates, slow!" (Sam Spraggons, describing possible methods of torturing Martin Conisby, *Black Bartlemy's Treasure* 307)

lash athwart\over a gun [*larrsh ay/er-thwahrrt\ober/o'er a garrn/goohn*]

> The victim is tied to the butt end of a cannon so as to secure him and thereby prevent him from dodging or shrinking from the blows of a cane or whip. A seaman forced to "kiss the gunner's daughter" is either secured to, or forced to lean over, the butt end of a cannon and his buttocks repeatedly struck or whipped.

> "You shall be rove to a gun and flayed with whips. ..." (Captain Jo, *Martin Conisby's Vengeance* 94)

lose one's passage [*loose 'un's/woohn's parr-sayge*]

> An ironic reference to a person being thrown overboard.

> < "And suppose I will not?" "Then you **lose your passage**, that's all. Is it not so, my lads?" "Yes; either take us safe in, or —overboard." > (Hawkhurst, boatswain aboard the *Avenger*, and other crew members aboard the *Avenger*, *The Pirate* 121, Chap. XVI)

maroon [*maah/mahr-roon*] place on a remote island as a form of punishment

Pirates sometimes refer wryly to marooning as appointing the victim the "Governor of an Island." (*Villains of All Nations* 75) Practices vary with respect to what a person is given before being marooned. (See Section 20.3.)

> "They **marooned** Jack on an island and left him to die, but not before he'd gone mad with the heat ... When a pirate's marooned, he's given a pistol with a single shot." (Joshamee Gibbs, "Pirates of the Caribbean: The Curse of the Black Pearl" 1:06:19)

matches\fuses between fingers\toes [*marrtches\fooses/fusers 'tween\betwixt/'twixt fengers/finners\to'oos*]

Matches and fuses are pieces of cord saturated with saltpeter; once ignited, they smolder and burn slowly. A match or fuse placed between a victim's fingers or toes burns off the victim's flesh and exposes the bone.

> *They cut and whipped some and others they burnt with **matches between their fingers** to the bone to make them confess where their money was.* (account of the tortures inflicted by Edward Low's company on the captain and crew of a New England vessel, *Pirates of the New England Coast* 206)

Moses' law [*Moo/Mo'oo-ses' lawr*] form of punishment whereby the victim was lashed or flogged with thirty-nine strokes of a rod, cane, whip, or cat o' nine tails

The rules announced by Moses in the Bible prescribe thirty-nine lashes as the maximum number permissible as punishment for any guilty man incurring the penalty of flogging: "Forty stripes he may give him, and not exceed: lest, if he should exceed, and beat him above these with many stripes, then thy brother should seem vile unto thee." (Deuteronomy 25:3) The suggestion is that more than forty strokes would go beyond punishment and amount to impermissible degradation—so thirty-nine lashes should be the maximum in case of a miscount.

> "That man that shall strike another whilst these Articles are in force, shall receive **Moses' law** (that is, 40 stripes lacking one) on the bare back." (fifth of the Articles of John Phillips' company, *General History of the Pyrates* 342)

overboard; overside [*ober/o'er-barrd\sawd/syeede*]

Note that pirates sometimes take additional measures—such as binding hands and feet or wrapping in a sail—in the course of throwing their victims over a ship's side, either to ensure their drowning or to aggravate their terror.

> "Into the sea with him! **Overboard** with the upstart! Into the sea with him!" (hands aboard the *Dolphin*, threatening to kill their new first mate Harry Wilder, *The Red Rover* 335)

quarter [*quahrr/quaht-ter*] subject to a form of torture and execution whereby a victim's four limbs are torn off his body, with adjoining pieces of torso accompanying them

> < "I were a-saying to Job that here was a fellow to match Pompey at last." "Tush! Pompey would **quarter** him wi' naked hands." > (Diccon & Captain Belvedere, *Martin Conisby's Vengeance* 67)

the rack [*t' reck*] wooden frame on which a victim is laid and tied at the wrists and ankles to bolts at either end (which in turn are connected to wheels or rollers), then slowly and forcibly stretched with the turning of cranks or pulling of levers, causing the rupture of bone, cartilage, tendons, and ligaments

> "When l'Olonnais had a victim on **the rack**, if the wretch did not instantly answer his questions he would hack the man to pieces with his cutlass and lick the blood from the blade with his tongue, wishing it might have been the last Spaniard in the world he had thus killed." (former buccaneer Alexander O. Exquemelin, describing the torture of Puerto Cavallo's Spanish residents at the hands of pirate Francois l'Olonnais, *The Buccaneers of America* 102)

roast alive [*roas'/ro'oost/roost '/er-lawv/lyeeve*]

The difference between being roasted alive and burned alive is time and distance: roasting requires exposure to dry heat, and denotes the cooking of meat or flesh at some distance from—and typically directly over—the cooking flame.

> "He perpetrated the greatest atrocities possible against the Spaniards. Some of them he tied or spitted on wooden stakes and **roasted them alive** between two fires, like killing a pig—and all because they refused to show him the road to the hog-yards he wanted to plunder." (Alexander O. Exquemelin, describing the depredations of the pirate Rock the Brazilian, *The Buccaneers of America* 80)

rope's end [*roope's/ro'oope's aynd*]

Used in reference to the use of a rope to whip another, and specifically to the end of the rope that actually makes painful contact with the victim's body.

> "One of our men, in the midst of these hardships, was found guilty of theft, and condemned for this, to have three blows from each man in the ship, with a two and a half inch rope on his bare back." (William Dampier, *A New Voyage Round the World* 133)

rosary of pain [*ro'oos/roos-ahrry/'ry o'\on payeen*] length of knotted cord wrapped around a victim's head at the forehead and temples, tightened either by pulling the ends in opposite directions or more often by inserting a long, thin, hard object (*e.g.*, a rigid stick, one leg of a compass, the stem of a large key) into the space between the rope and the head and twisting it, thus causing intense pain and possibly forcing the victim's eyeballs out of his skull.

The use of a rosary of pain on a victim's skull is known as "woolding."

> "You know this? It is the **rosary of pain**. It is possible to screw a man's eyes out of his head." (Levasseur, showing Lord Willoughby a small length of knotted rope, "Captain Blood" 1:19:47)

sew lips together [*sowoo leps t'/ter-gaahth/ gayth/gedd/ge'-er*]

A gratuitously painful way of quieting someone.

> *Now Sawbridge, facing the loss of yet another ship, ranted and cursed at Shivers and Hore to mend their ways and spare his ship. "They ordered him to hold his tongue," recounted a local sea captain, "but he continuing his discourse they took a sail-needle and twine and **sewed his lips together**, and so kept him several hours with his hands tied behind him."* (account of the definitive silencing of merchant captain John Sawbridge by the followers of pirate captains Shivers and Hore, *The Pirate Hunter* 127)

shoot

While heaving a prisoner overboard is the quickest and easiest way of ending someone while at sea, pirates on land—whether engaged in raiding settlements or repairing their vessels—often opt for a fast-moving bullet as an equivalently efficient means of execution.

> "This morning on board the ship we examined one of the old men, who were taken prisoners upon the island the day before. But finding him in many lies, as

we thought, concerning Arica, our commander ordered him **shot** to death, which was accordingly done." (Basil Ringrose, *Bucaniers of America* Part IV Chap. XVI)

skin [*sken*] flay or peel the skin off another's body with some kind of blade

> "**Skin** 'im from the neck, mate." (Tom Morgan, "Treasure Island" [1990] 1:39:48)

slice off [*slawce/slyeece arrf*]
slit nose [*slet no'oose/noose*]
trim ears [*trem ee-arrs/errs*]

The cutting, and cutting off, of another's facial features are popular among pirates for being quick and easy ways to radically disfigure and thereby dehumanize a victim.

> "Since he still would not admit where the coffer was, they hung him up by his male parts, while one struck him, another **sliced off** his nose, yet another an ear, and another scorched him with fire—tortures as barbarous as man can devise." (former buccaneer Alexander O. Exquemelin, describing the prolonged torture of a Panama citizen by Henry Morgan's men, *The Buccaneers of America* 200)

slit throat [*slet throh-oot*]

Slitting another's throat is a particularly bloody affair and an effective form of execution for the perpetrator, who counts on inspiring immediate and committed cooperation in all observers.

> "He should walk overboard wi' **slit** weasand, or better—he's meat for Pompey, and wherefore no?" (Job, advocating Martin Conisby's death, *Martin Conisby's Vengeance* 67)

Spanish torture [*Span-ersh/esh tarrture*]

The phrase "Spanish torture" can be used to refer to any number of seventeenth- and eighteenth-century torture methods closely associated with or distinctive to the Spanish, in particular: the rack, whereupon a victim's back and limbs are slowly stretched to breaking; the mouth pear, a metal bulb with a screw and shaft on one end, the bulb end of which is inserted into a victim's mouth and the screw turned so as to cause the bulb to unfold slowly but powerfully (thus destroying the lower part of the victim's face); hoisting, in which a victim's hands are bound and looped over a rope that is then raised such that the victim's body is suspended in the air (with excruciating pain to wrists, shoulders, and back, and constriction of chest); and the whipping of the soles of one's feet.

> "Give 'im the Spanish torture!" (member of Long John Silver's company, "Treasure Island" [1990] 1:39:50)

stones [*stoones/sto'oones*]

Stones are used as improvised instruments of torture, specifically as weights to be hung from various parts of the victim's body—

> "Again they took him and bound him, hanging **stones** from his neck and his feet." (former buccaneer Alexander O. Exquemelin, recounting the torture of a Spaniard at Gibraltar by Henry Morgan's men, *The Buccaneers of America* 107)

—or to be placed on the body.

> "Still not satisfied, they put a **stone** weighing at least two hundred-weight on his loins ..." (former buccaneer Alexander O. Exquemelin, recounting the torture of a Portuguese resident of Gibraltar by Henry Morgan's men, *The Buccaneers of America* 107)

strappado [*strarrp/sterp-parr-do'oo*] subject to a form of torture whereby a victim's hands are tied behind his back, then his body repeatedly raised off the ground by a rope tied to his wrists and dropped until the fall is stopped by a painful upward jerking on the same rope

Consequences include the dislocation of the victim's shoulders and slow suffocation.

> "This old man was seized and asked where his money was. He swore by ev-

ery oath that all the money he'd had in the world was a hundred pieces of eight, and that a young man who lived near him had taken this money and run off with it. The rovers did not believe him, but **strappado**'d him so violently that his arms were pulled right out of joint." (former Buccaneer Alexander O. Exquemelin, describing the torture of a Spaniard at Gibraltar by Henry Morgan's men, *The Buccaneers of America* 150)

sweat [*swayt*] method of torture or physical intimidation whereby a group jabs at a victim with swords or knives and thereby forces him to move constantly to avoid deeper penetrations

> *In 1724, merchant captain Richard Hawkins described another form of retribution, a torture known as the 'Sweat': "Between decks they stick candles round the mizen-mast, and about twenty-five men surround it with points of swords, penknives, compasses, forks &c in each of their hands: Culprit enters the circle; the violin plays a merry jig; and he must run for about ten minutes, while each man runs his instrument into his posteriors."* (*Villains of All Nations* 87)

target shooting [*tahrr-gert shootin'*]

The victim is suspended over a vessel's deck—especially from a yardarm so as to keep the victim clear from the center mass of rigging—and shot at.

> *The pirates tortured the passengers to find out where every last valuable was hidden; they hung up the tindall (lascar overseer) and enjoyed some drunken **target shooting**, whizzing shots close to his head and groin.* (account of the cruel treatment of the foreman aboard the *Great Mohammed* at the hands of the pirate companies of Culliford and Shivers, *The Pirate Hunter* 197)

tear out one's heart [*tarr/tayarr/tayerr arrt/ ou'/owoot 'un's/woohn's 'ahrrt/'eart/hahrrt*]

Obviously a form of execution and not torture, as victims do not live long after having their hearts removed, except to the extent third party observers might be forced to witness such a brutal act.

> "L'Olonnais then took them aside one at a time, and asked if there were any other road to take to avoid the ambushes, and they each answered no. ... Then l'Olonnais, being possessed of a devil's fury, ripped open one of the prisoners with his cutlass, tore the living heart out of his body, gnawed at it, and then hurled it in the face of one of the others, saying, 'Show me another way, or I will do the same to you.'" (former buccaneer Alexander O. Exquemelin, describing Francois l'Olonnais' torture of Spanish prisoners taken from Puerto Cavallo, *The Buccaneers of America* 107)

tear twixt trees [*tarr/tayarr/tayerr 'tween\ betwixt/twixt trees*]

The pimento tree (which bears the dried fruit known as allspice) mentioned in the below excerpt figures prominently in pirate literature, being a tree indigenous to the Caribbean islands and perhaps second only to the palm in evoking the sun-drenched, breeze-dappled tropical settings where buccaneer life often transpired. The torture being threatened would seem to involve the fastening of the victim's limbs to two young trees, and either the stretching or cutting of the victim's body once suspended.

> "See, my Dolores, for two days he shall be our slave and thereafter, for thy joy, shall show thee how to die, my sweet—**torn 'twixt pimento trees** or Tressady's hook— thou shalt choose the manner of't." (Black Bartlemy, *Black Bartlemy's Treasure* 87)

throw to the fish\sharks [*t'r-owoo t'/ta/ter t' fesh\shahrrks/shairks*] kill by heaving overboard

Being thrown overboard meant two perils: drowning, and being eaten by sharks or other predatory fish, including barracudas.

> "**Throw** the girl **to the sharks!**" (Cain, *The Pirate* 59, Chap. IX)

thumb screws [*thoohmb/t'umb scroos*] torture device consisting of two slats of wood joined to each other sandwich-style by a pair of screws (with space enough that a person's thumbs might be inserted between them) and lined on their interior surfaces with small iron spikes or studs, used to crush a victim's thumbs

Turning the screws forces the slats of wood closer together and compresses the victim's thumbs between the studs.

> "The **screws**—the **screws!** quick! we'll have the secret from him." (Cain, ordering the torture of a Portuguese bishop to extract from him the whereabouts of gold and silver religious ornaments, *The Pirate* 61, Chap. IX)

triangle [*tr'a/traw/tryee'a-ngle*] tripod of wooden beams from the top of which an offender is suspended by a rope tied around his wrists for the purpose of being whipped or flogged

> "Ye don't want poor Ben Gunn to be screamin' on the **triangle**." (Ben Gunn, *Porto Bello Gold* 144)

twist thumbs [*twest thoohms/t'umbs*]

Arguably a more debilitating form of punishment than thumb screws, as the pain experienced on having one's thumbs twisted is more closely coincident with the dislocation and breaking of bones than that inflicted by crushing them. A torturer intent on inflicting pain, therefore, might crush thumbs—but might not so easily twist thumbs—without inevitably doing permanent damage.

> "**Twist** his **thumbs**, Cap'n!" (first of three proposals from Roger Tressady's company for extracting from a silent Martin Conisby the whereabouts of Bartlemy's treasure, *Black Bartlemy's Treasure* 306)

Walking the Plank

Walking the plank certainly figures more prominently aboard the pirate ships of fiction than those of history. However, it has been claimed that ancient Mediterranean pirates often fooled Roman prisoners into thinking they were honored guests, then—after these came to take for granted such premium treatment—gleefully showed them a ladder over the vessel's side and hospitably advised they were free to leave the ship that way (*Pirates of the New England Coast* 361–62).

A rare recorded instance of real pirates employing the plank occurred in 1829, when a pirate schooner flying Buenos Aires colors took a Dutch brig off of Cuba. The pirates blindfolded the Dutch crewmen and fastened cannon shot to their feet before forcing them to walk into the sea (*Under the Black Flag* 130–31). The late date of the incident—one hundred years after the golden age of piracy—strongly suggests this was an instance of life imitating art, of Argentine sea-thugs subjecting their victims to a fatal ceremony they had read or heard about in fictional contexts.

walk the plank; run out the plank [*warrk t' plenk; roohn arrt/ou'/owoot t' plenk*]

To walk the plank is to be forced, as a method of execution, to walk along and off the far end of a small wood beam with one end suspended from a vessel's deck and the other overhanging the ocean. To run out the plank is to set up a wood beam in preparation for execution; the action of running out the plank has the same sinister and threatening implications as tying a noose or sharpening a blade.

See the following excerpt for a detailed description of both running out the plank and walking it:

> *[D]ivers men began rigging a wide plank out-board from the gangway amidships, whiles others hasted to pinion these still supplicating wretches. This done, they seized upon one, and hoisting him up on the plank with his face to the sea, betook them to pricking him with sword and pike, thus goading him to walk to his death. So this miserable, doomed man crept out along the plank, whimpering pleas for mercy to the murderers behind him and prayers for mercy to the God above him, until he was come to the plank's end and cowered there, raising and lowering his bound hands

in his agony while he gazed down into the merciless sea that was to engulf him. All at once he stood erect, his fettered hands uprasied to heaven, and then with a piteous, wailing cry he plunged down to his death and vanished 'mid the surge; once he came up, struggling and gasping, ere he was swept away in the race of the tide.* (describing pirates aboard the *Happy Despatch* making a Spanish prisoner walk the plank, *Martin Conisby's Vengeance* 98–99)

whip [*whep*] lash or flog with leather cord

> "We got other pilots at Puna, and left him aboard the bark, where I punish'd one that I brought aboard drunk from Puna, and had him severely **whipt** before the whole company as a terror to the rest." (Woodes Rogers, *A Cruising Voyage Round the World* 92)

whip and pickle [*whep an'/'n' peckle*] lash or flog with leather cord, then douse the resulting wounds with any briny or acidic fluid, such as salt water or vinegar, so as to cause a burning sensation

> *Here [Captain Condent] took upon him the administration of justice, enquiring into the manner of the commanders' be-

haviour to their men, and those, against whom complaint was made, he **whipp'd and pickled**.* (reference by author Captain Charles Johnson, *General History of the Pyrates* 582)

16.5 FOOD

Pirates and table manners just don't go together.

George Roberts, a merchant captain imprisoned by Edward Low's company for ten days, was disgusted to see how his captors ate. "More like a kennel of hounds, than like men, snatching and catching the victuals from one another." This was no accident. The pirates told Roberts they deliberately ate like animals because it "look'd martial-like." (*Pirates of the New England Coast* 168)

In fairness, pirates went with so little food so often that any impulse to feast decadently when possible shouldn't be blamed. On the hard nine-day march from the river Chagre to Panama City, Henry Morgan's men found evidence of a tactical retreat: The cunning Spaniards had taken with them or destroyed everything conceivably edible along the way. After four days of hard trekking on empty stomachs, the men broke down and ate the only thing they found—a pile of leather bags, which they cut into bite-size pieces and roasted over hot embers. (*Buccaneers of America* 186–88)

Shipboard diets could also disappoint. In March 1686, Captain Swan and his privateer company determined to sail from Baja California to Guam despite limited rations, steeling themselves to endure the next sixty days on just eight spoonfuls of boiled corn a day. Only after the ship reached Guam with three days of rations left was it discovered that the crew had decided, should stores run out, that they would kill and eat their own leadership—starting with Swan and proceeding with other company members in order of

rank and influence. (*A New Voyage Round the World* 131–34)

Below are types of food notable for their place in pirate life—some more exotic than others, but all more typical than the odd steak of high-ranking human flesh.

alligator [*arr-leh/ler-ga'or/gayeetor*]

> "**Alligator's** and guano's, which are also very good meat, especially the tail of the **alligator**, I have eaten in several parts of the West-Indies ..." (Lionel Wafer, *Isthmus of America* 116)

apple [*arrple*]

Large amounts of fresh fruits were not found aboard the typical seventeenth- or eighteenth-century sailing ship and certainly were not among the provisions routinely doled out to common hands. Though the link between scurvy and the consumption of fruits like apples, oranges, and lemons was known by the early 1700s, some years passed before ship's stores adjusted to include those relatively expensive and perishable items. It was not until 1865, for example, that the British Board of Trade required lemon and orange juice concentrates to be carried aboard vessels as mandatory rations.

> "When you shipped with the Admiral, you never took scurvy from the salt pork and hardtack. Not with a barrel of **apples** aboard for the men to chew on." (Long John Silver, "Treasure Island" [1950] 17:59)

bread [*brayd*]

Soft bread, also known as "English bread" or "soft tack," is less often served in the seamen's mess than hardtack or ship's biscuit, as its preparation is work-intensive and the final product is highly perishable. The more a ship's stores consist of flour rather than other types of rations, and thus the more heavily bread figures in a crew's diet, the more likely it is that bread might be boiled (to save on time, effort, and wood fuel) rather than baked.

"This day [September 29, 1679] our allowance was shortened, and reduced to three pints and a half of water, and one cake of boiled **bread** to each man for a day." (Basil Ringrose, *Bucaniers of America* Part IV Chap. XIII)

cassava; casavio [*carr-sarr-varr\vierr*] starchy, stringy root vegetable comparable (after drying and cooking) in color and density to, but more granular and less creamy in texture than, a potato

Also known as "yuca" or "manioc."

"He had all the food supplies—such as maize and **cassava**—put on board his vessels for the maintenance of the garrison he intended to leave in Fort Chagre." (former buccaneer Alexander O. Exquemelin, of Henry Morgan's preparations for his campaign against Panama, *The Buccaneers of America* 184)

chocolate [*charrk-lert/lit*]

"[F]or three days before we parted, we sifted as much flour as we could well carry, and rubbed up 20 or 30 pounds of **chocolate**, with sugar to sweeten it." (William Dampier, describing his company's preparations before striking out for the River of Santa Maria, *A New Voyage Round the World* 7)

cockle [*carrkle*] bivalve mollusk, many species of which are edible clams

"There was a monstrous sort of **cockle** here, the meat of one of which would suffice seven or eight men. It was very good wholesome meat." (Basil Ringrose, describing a delicacy found off the coast of the island of Celebes, *A New Voyage Round the World* 211)

coconut [*co'oo-co'oo/ker-nooht*]

"[W]e saw an abundance of **coconuts** swimming in the sea, and we hoisted out our boat and took up some of them. The nuts were very sound, and the kernel sweet, and in some the milk or water in them was sweet and good." (William Dampier, *A New Voyage Round the World* 224)

coconut rice [*co'oo-co'oo/ker-nooht rawce/ry-eece*] rice cooked in coconut-steeped water

"Our food now was rice and the meat of the coconuts, rasped and steeped in water, which made a sort of milk into which we put our rice, making a pleasant enough mess." (William Dampier, *A New Voyage Round the World* 225)

deer [*dee-arr/err*]

"They have considerable store of **deer** also, resembling most our red deer; but these they never hunt nor kill. ... [W]hen they saw some of our men killing and eating of them, they not only refus'd to eat with them, but seem'd displeas'd with them for it." (Lionel Wafer, recounting the Darien natives' displeasure at their pirate visitors' consumption of deer, *Isthmus of America* 111)

dog-fish [*dahg/dahrrg/dorrg-fesh*] small shark found in the Atlantic, Pacific, and Mediterranean and consisting of several species, some of which resemble larger species of shark and others of which are thin and eel-like

"There is a fish there like the shark, but much smaller and sweeter meat. Its mouth is also longer and narrower than the shark[']s; neither has he more than one row of teeth. Our seamen us'd to call this the **dog-fish**." (Lionel Wafer, *Isthmus of America* 126)

dolphin [*darrl-phen*]

Though seamen have long been said to respect dolphins as good omens at sea and to believe that bad luck will plague any who harmed them, starving pirates sometimes allow nutrition to trump superstition.

"On the 26th we caught a couple of fine **dolphins**, which were very acceptable to us, having had but very indifferent luck of fish in this long passage." (Woodes Rogers, *A Cruising Voyage Round the World* 191)

doughboy [*do'oo-booyee*] dumpling generally made of flour and suet (animal fat, especially beef fat), congealed with cold water and balled into dough, then dropped into boiling soup or stew and left to puff up on the broth's surface, half-boiled and half-steamed

The finished doughboy is dense and moist on the outside, light and airy on the inside, and carries a milder version of the flavor of the broth in which it is cooked. The soup or stew also benefits from being cooked with doughboys, as some of the flour in the latter leeches out and acts as a thickening agent.

"The men that were landed had each of them three or four cakes of bread (called by the English **dough-boys**) for their provision of victuals; and for drink, the rivers afforded enough." (Basil Ringrose, *Bucaniers of America* Part IV Chap. I)

(plum) duff [(*plarrm/ploohm*) *darrff*] pudding consisting of a dough formed from some combination of prunes, raisins, currants, flour, butter, rum, milk, eggs, salt, brown sugar, molasses, and yeast, which is allowed to rise before being wrapped in a cloth and boiled

Also known among landsmen (but never referred to as such by pirates) as "spotted dick" or "Christmas pudding."

*[T]here was **duff** on odd days, as, for instance, if the squire heard it was any man's birthday ...* (Jim Hawkins, recounting the items among the *Hispaniola*'s stores popular with the crew, *Treasure Island* 55, Chap. 10) < "I knows what'll do 'im. **Plum duff**." "Oh, my mother made that." "Tasted proper on a cold night, didn't it? Did, uh, did your mother ever put a drop o' rum in it?" "Good and strong, so the smell went up your nose." "Aye, 's too bad we ain't got none. **Plum duff** bake no better 'n bilge water wi'out rum." > (Long John Silver & Jim Hawkins, "Treasure Island" [1950] 34:27)

English bread [*Ayng-lersh/lesh*] bread made with yeast and allowed to rise before being baked (as opposed to unleavened bread, also known as "hardtack" or "ship's biscuit")

English bread or "soft tack" is less often served in the seamen's mess than hardtack or ship's biscuit, as its preparation is work-intensive and the final product is highly perishable. The more a ship's stores consist of flour rather than other types of rations, and thus the more heavily bread figures in a crew's diet, the more likely it is that bread might be boiled (to save on time, effort, and wood fuel) rather than baked.

"The little **English bread** we have left is eaten as hollow as a honeycomb, and so full of worms, that it's hardly fit for use." (Woodes Rogers, *A Cruising Voyage Round the World* 120)

fat [*fett*]

Used when warm as a sauce or dressing in which meat is dipped.

"They cook two meals a day of this meat, without rationing. When it is boiled, the **fat** is skimmed off the cauldron and put into little calabashes, for dipping the meat in." (former buccaneer Alexander O. Exquemelin, describing the customs of the pirates of the Caribbean, *The Buccaneers of America* 70)

flamingo [*flarr/fler-men-goh-oo*]

"I saw a few **flamingos** ... The flesh of both young and old is lean and black, yet very good meat, tasting neither fishy, nor in any way unsavoury. Their tongues are large, having a large knob of fat at the root, which is an excellent bit, a dish of flamingos' tongues being fit for a prince's table." (William Dampier, *A New Voyage Round the World* 43)

flour [*flowoo-arr*]

The most basic of a pirate's shipboard provisions. Flour is more efficiently stowed in large quantities than biscuits or bread and can either be formed into dough and baked or boiled, or simply mixed with water or grog and eaten as a paste.

> "Having made this island, we resolved to go thither and refit our rigging, and get some goats which there run wild up and down the country. For, as was said before, at this time we had no other provision than **flour** and water." (Basil Ringrose, *Bucaniers of America* Part IV Chap. XI)

goat [go'oot]

The goat figures prominently in island-based pirate narratives and makes relatively easy prey for musket-equipped land parties.

> "From this cape 4 leagues S[outh]W[est] is an island called Plata w[hi]ch is soe called from S[i]r Francis Drake his share-ing of plate there. I have been here twise and have founde good turtle, **goates**, & fish." (Basil Ringrose, *The South Sea Wag-goner* Chart 54)

hardtack ['ahrrd/'ard/hahrrd-teck] very hard type of cracker or unleavened bread made from flour, water, and salt; shaped like a thick wafer; and, when kept dry, lasting for long periods of time

Also known as "ship's biscuit."

> "When you shipped with the Admiral, you never took scurvy from the salt pork and **hardtack**. Not with a barrel of apples aboard for the men to chew on." (Long John Silver, "Treasure Island" [1950] 17:59)

horse [harrse/'orse]

Like leather, the horse figures in pirate narratives as a food of last resort for starving pirates on long overland passages.

> "As there were few provisions on the vessel, they slaughtered some of their **horses** and salted the flesh with salt they found on board, to live on till they came across better fare." (former buccaneer Alexander O. Exquemelin, describing the diet of pirate

Rock the Brazilian and his company, *The Buccaneers of America* 81)

iguana [ee-gwanner]
guano [gwanner] lizard, various species of which are found in North, Central, and South America, with flat plates protruding along its back like a spine

The tropical iguana grows to between four and six feet long.

> *[I]t supports great numbers of **iguanas**, a kind of lizard that grows to a length of about five feet and is very good to eat; in fact, the pirates used to go there to catch them, as was well-known at the time.* (account of George Lowther's visit to the island of Blanco, *Pirates of the New England Coast* 139) "Blanco, a pretty large island almost north of Margarita ... is plentifully stored with **guanoes**, which are an animal like a lizard, but much big-ger. ... Their flesh is much esteemed by privateers, who commonly dress them for their sick men, for they make very good broth." (William Dampier, *A New Voyage Round the World* 37)

iguana eggs [ee-gwanner aygs]

> "The **guano** is all over very good meat, prefer'd to a pullet or chicken, either for the meat or broth. Their **eggs** also are very good; but those of the alligator have too much of a musky flavour, and sometimes smell very strong of it." (Lio-nel Wafer, *Isthmus of America* 116)

junk [jarrnk/joohnk] salted pork or beef

> "Just then a man hailed us from the fire that breakfast was ready, and we were soon seated here and there about the sand over biscuit and fried **junk**." (Jim Hawkins, using the pirate terminology of his dining companions, *Treasure Island* Chap. 31)

lampert [larrm-pert]
limpet [lem-pert] mollusk having a rough cone-shaped shell with an opening at one

end and clinging to rocks in areas between low and high tides

The meat of the limpet can be eaten raw, is tasty but tough, and typically grows even tougher if cooked more than a few seconds.

> "Wee lay there a month and every day took **lamperts** off the rocks, enough to serve 100 men ..." (Basil Ringrose, of the food enjoyed off the Pacific coast of South America just north of the Strait of Magellan, *The South Sea Waggoner* Chart 104) "This evening we brought on board great store of **limpets**, of which we made a kettle of broth that contained more than all our company could eat." (Basil Ringrose, *Bucaniers of America* Part IV Chap. XXIII)

land-crab [*lan' crab*] any of several species of crab—found in the Caribbean islands and coastal areas in the southern United States, parts of Mexico, and Central and South America—that live in underground burrows, typically close to water and often among tree roots, with white, fleshy, sweet-tasting meat comparable to that of the blue crab

> "On the Samballoe's I think there are also **land-crabs**, tho' but few: But in the Caribee-Islands, among which I have been cruising, and especially on Anguilla, they are very numerous, and some very large, as big as the largest sea-crabs that are sold at London. ... They are excellent good meat, and are the main support of the inhabitants ..." (Lionel Wafer, *Isthmus of America* 115–16)

leather [*laath/ledd/le'-er*]

Like the horse, leather figures in pirate narratives as a food of last resort for starving pirates on long overland passages. Pirates sufficiently malnourished to reduce themselves to the consumption of leather were almost certainly malnourished enough to be experiencing symptoms of scurvy and beri-beri, which included the loosening of teeth. Thus, the biting and swallowing of tough leather may have represented for many a choice between starvation and toothlessness.

> "Food and drink were extremely scarce among them, and at Torno Caballos they hoped to find both in abundance. ... But the birds had flown, leaving the nest empty apart from about 150 leather bags which had once contained meat and bread. ... They tore apart the huts put up by the Spaniards, but, since they found nothing better, the buccaneers ate the **leather** bags, with as much gusto as if leather were meat—and so it was, in their imagination. ... They beat the leather between two stones at the water's edge, made it wet, and scraped off the hair while it was soft. Then, having roasted it on hot embers, they cut it up in small pieces which they swallowed whole." (former buccaneer Alexander O. Exquemelin, recounting the hard march to Panama by Henry Morgan and his company, *The Buccaneers of America* 187–88)

maize [*mayeeze*] corn

> "[W]e had not sixty days provision, at a little more than half a pint of **maize** a day for each man ..." (William Dampier, *A New Voyage Round the World* 131)

manatee [*mayn-narr/ner-tee*] plant-eating aquatic mammal having paddle-like flippers and a flattened tail, found in coastal waters of Florida, northern South America, West Africa, and the Caribbean, growing to between eight and fourteen feet in length and a weight of about one thousand to fifteen hundred pounds, and known for a gentle, slow-moving disposition

> "Moskito Indians ... always bear arms amongst the privateers, and are much valued by them for striking fish, turtle (or tortoise), and **manatee** (or sea-cow) ..." (William Dampier, describing the Moski-

to Indians in his expedition party, *A New Voyage Round the World* 7)

marrow [*mahr/may-rowoo*] soft, fatty tissue found inside most bone cavities

Marrow generally has a slightly sweeter but much milder flavor than meat found outside the bone and contains substantial amounts of iron, calcium, and protein.

"In the meantime, trouble broke out between the French and the English because an Englishman had shot a Frenchman dead on account of a marrow-bone. I have recounted earlier how the *boucaniers*, when they have killed a beast, suck out the **marrow**, and these men did the same thing. The Frenchman had flayed an animal and the Englishman came up and helped himself to the marrow-bones. This started the quarrel. ..." (former buccaneer Alexander O. Exquemeling, identifying marrow-eating as a custom common to both the pirates of Henry Morgan's company and the wild-cattle hunters of Hispaniola, *The Buccaneers of America* 132)

monkey [*marrnkey*]

"These monkeys are tasty and very nourishing; every day we boiled and roasted so much **monkey**-flesh we became used to it, and to us it tasted better than pheasant." (former buccaneer Alexander O. Exquemelin, describing how he and his fellows survived on monkey meat while cleaning and refitting their ship in Bleeckveldt Bay, *The Buccaneers of America* 216)

mussels [*marrss/moohss-els*]

"We lay there a month and every day took ... **mussells**, some 6 inches long, all most pure and ex[c]ellent good." (Basil Ringrose, of the food enjoyed off the Pacific coast of South America just north of the Strait of Magellan, *The South Sea Waggoner* Chart 104)

pad(d)y [*pah'y*] unhusked rice

"I sent the pinnace aboard the *Marquiss* ... and in their way order'd 'em to speak with the *Batchelor* and *Dutchess*, to be satisfy'd what allowance of **pady** (being rice in the husk) their men were at ..." (Woodes Rogers, *A Cruising Voyage Round the World* 197)

paracood [*pahrra/parer-cood*] type of fish

"They have **paracoods** also, which are a long and round fish, about as large as a well-grown pike, but usually much longer. They are generally very good meat ... I have known several men poison'd with them, to that degree as to have their hair and nails come off; and some have died with eating them. The antidote for this is said to be the back-bone of the fish, dried and beaten to a powder, and given in any liquor ..." (Lionel Wafer, *Isthmus of America* 127)

parrot [*parrert/parr't*]

"They have **parrots** good store, some blue and some green, for shape and size like the generality of the parrots we have from Jamaica. There is here great variety of them, and they are very good meat." (Lionel Wafer, *Isthmus of America* 119–20)

pec(c)ary [*paah-cahrry/c'ry*] wild pig-like mammal with short, straight tusks and dark gray, dark brown, or black bristly hair, growing to between three and four feet in length and a weight of about forty to eighty pounds, feeding principally on roots and grasses, often living in herds, and found in the southwestern United States and Central and South America

Peccaries are also known as musk hogs for the glands they use to mark territory with a powerful skunk-like odor.

"The country has of its own a kind of hog, which is call'd **pecary**, not much unlike a Virginia hog. 'Tis black, and has little

357

short legs, yet is pretty nimble. It has one thing very strange, that the navel is not upon the belly, but the back: And what is more still, if upon killing a **pecary** the navel be not cut away from the carkass within three or four hours after at farthest, 'twill so taint all the flesh, as not only to render it unfit to be eaten, but make it stink insufferably." (Lionel Wafer, *Isthmus of America* 110)

penguin [*pan-guern*]

Many of the buccaneers of the late 1600s, intent on plundering the New World's Pacific shores and who accordingly spent time navigating the Strait of Magellan, Cape Horn, and the inhospitable coasts and near-Antarctic climes of Tierra del Fuego, encountered substantial populations of penguins—a species which, of course, would have been utterly alien to the typical Caribbean-/North Atlantic-/and Africa-bound pirate of the 1700s.

> "Some few **penguins** wee caughte (w[hi]ch are a most exellent fowle but there wings are not large enough to beare there bodyes soe they live amongst the rocks and in the water)." (Basil Ringrose, of the food enjoyed off the Pacific coast of South America just north of the Strait of Magellan, *The South Sea Waggoner* Chart 104)

pippin [*pep-pen/pern*] apple

> "When the thirst is on 'ee, hah-hah, bite into a **pippin** real savage. Hah, hah, hah, hah. It staves off the desire." (Long John Silver, "Treasure Island" [1950] 41:04)

plantain [*plarrn-tayeen*] banana-like fruit that is starchier, slightly denser, and typically larger than the banana

Plantains are eaten cooked when green and unripe (when they have a neutral flavor similar to, but more savory than, the potato), and either raw or cooked when ripe (when they have a soft, mushy texture and a sweet, fruity flavor similar to, but fuller than, the banana).

> "We there fed plentifully on **plantains**, both ripe and green, and had fair weather all day and night." (William Dampier, describing his company's two-course feast on the fifteenth day of a twenty-three-day journey across Panama, *A New Voyage Round the World* 20)

pork [*parrk*]

> "On the ship, they first discuss where to go and get food supplies. This means meat—for they eat nothing else on their voyages, unless they capture other foodstuffs from the Spaniards. The meat is either **pork** or turtle, which is also salted." (former buccaneer Alexander O. Exquemelin, describing the customs of the pirates of the Caribbean, *The Buccaneers of America* 70)

pottage [*parrt/pah'-age*] (1) soup or stew of vegetables and sometimes meat; (2) hot meal or gruel made of grain (typically oat or wheat) and hot water; porridge

> "I think, nay, I'm sure this **pottage** is ready, so let us eat." (Japhet Bly, *Winds of Chance* 159)

rice [*rawce/ryeece*]

> "[O]n making a strict rummage there, we found more **rice** than we expected; so that with the shortest allowance we may subsist at sea above 3 weeks longer." (Woodes Rogers, *A Cruising Voyage Round the World* 198)

salt beef [*sarrlt biff*]

Salt beef on sailing ships—between the desiccating effects of salt and the hardening effects of age—was far from tender. William Dampier once used a hunk of salt beef to plug a leak in the side of his ship, the *Roebuck*.

> "[W]e must soon fare otherwise, and take to our old food of almost decay'd **salt** pork and **beef**, which we must prize, and heartily wish we had more on't."

(Woodes Rogers, *A Cruising Voyage Round the World* 150)

salt fish [*sarrlt fesh*]

"[W]e had not sixty days provision, at a little more than half a pint of maize a day for each man, and no other provision except three meals of **salted** jew-**fish**." (William Dampier, *A New Voyage Round the World* 131)

salt pork [*sarrlt parrk*]

"I can make **salt pork** taste just like roast pheasant." (Long John Silver, "Treasure Island" [1934] 27:10)

sea-gull [*sea gole*]

"There are a great many **sea-gulls** ... '[T]is tolerable good meat, but of a fishy tast[e], as sea-fowl usually are. Yet to correct this tast[e], when we kill'd any **sea-gulls**, sea-pies, boobies, or the like, on any shore, we us'd to make a hole in the hot sand, and there bury them for eight or ten hours, with their feathers on, and guts in them: And upon dressing them afterwards, we found the flesh tenderer, and the tast[e] not so rank nor fishy." (Lionel Wafer, *Isthmus of America* 123–24)

seal [*see-ell*]

"The 15th day we went ashore, and found abundance of penguins and boobies, and **seal** in great quantities. We sent aboard all of these to be dressed, for we had not tasted any flesh in a great while, and some of us ate very heartily. Captain Swan, to encourage his men to eat this coarse flesh, would commend it for extraordinary food, comparing **seal** to a roasted pig, the boobies to hens, and the penguins to ducks." (William Dampier, *A New Voyage Round the World* 78)

shark [*shahrrk/shairk*]

"While we lay in the calms we caught several great **sharks**, sometimes two or three in a day, and ate them all, boiling and squeezing them dry and then stewing them with vinegar, pepper, &c., for we had little flesh aboard." (William Dampier, *A New Voyage Round the World* 47–48)

ship's biscuit [*shep's bes/bish-kert*] very hard type of cracker or unleavened bread made from flour, water, and salt; shaped like a thick wafer; and, when kept dry, lasting for long periods of time

Also known as "hardtack."

"So I've tended Johnny's needs; he sitteth even now guzzling sweet water and gnawing on a **ship's biscuit**." (Japhet Bly, *Winds of Chance* 151)

soldier-insect [*so'ool-jarr en-seck*] insect about a half-inch long with a wide, oval shell and feeding on other insects, especially worms, beetles and caterpillars

"There is a sort of insect like a snail in great plenty among the Samballoe's, which is call'd the **soldier-insect** ... [O]ne third part of his body, about his head, which is out of the shell, is in shape and colour like a boil'd shrimp, with little claws, and 2 larger like those of a crab. That part within the shell, the tail especially, is eatable, and is good food, very well tasted and delicious, like marrow. We thrust a skuer through this part, and roast a pretty many of them in a row." (Lionel Wafer, *Isthmus of America* 114)

tarpon [*tahrr-pern*]
tarpom [*tahrr-perm*] large coastal fish native to the Atlantic Ocean, green or blue on top and silver on the sides, growing up to between three and six feet in length, and known for having very bony, extremely coarse, and not particularly flavorful flesh

"The **tarpom**, which is a large and firm fish, eating in flakes like salmon or cod. They are some of 50 or 60 pound weight and upwards. One of them afforded a good dinner once to about ten of us, as we were cruising towards the coast of Cartagene ..." (Lionel Wafer, *Isthmus of America* 126)

tortoise [*tahrr-terss/tiss*]

"[T]he sea affords the best meate w[hi]ch is **tortoise**, very large, fatt, & sweete ..." (Basil Ringrose, *The South Sea Waggoner* Chart 36)

turtle [*tarrtle*]

"Our pinnace came aboard and brought about 18 bushells of salt, and 18 land **turtle** more; the men commend them for excellent food, especially the land **turtle**, which makes very good broth, but the flesh never boils tender ..." (Woodes Rogers, *A Cruising Voyage Round the World* 142)

turtle-dove [*tarrtle-doohve/dub*] small species of dove with brown wing feathers, a black-and-white striped marking on the side of its neck, and a wedge-shaped tail

The bird Dampier describes in the below excerpt was likely not a turtle-dove, but another comparably-sized species of bird—perhaps the mourning dove, found throughout the Americas including Central America and the Caribbean—as the turtle-dove is native to Europe, Africa, and Asia, but not any part of the Western Hemisphere.

"There are great plenty of **turtle-doves**, so tame that a man may kill 5 or 6 dozen in a forenoon with a stick. They are somewhat less than a pigeon, and are very good meat, and commonly fat." (William Dampier, *A New Voyage Round the World* 60)

turtle oil [*tarrtle oyee-ell*]

Turtle oil or fat is used for cooking as well as for caulking or waterproofing boat hulls.

"There he found such plenty of **land-turtle** that he and his men ate noth-

ing else for the three months that he stayed there. They were so fat that he saved sixty jars of oil out of those that he spent. This **oil** served instead of butter ..." (William Dampier, describing Captain Davis' company's encounter with the nutritious land-turtle, *A New Voyage Round the World* 61)

warree [*wahrree*] wild pig-like mammal with tusks and dark gray, dark brown, or black bristly hair, found in Central America, and similar to the peccary

"The **warree** is another kind of wild-hog they have, which is also very good meat. It has little ears, but very great tusks. ... The warree is fierce, and fights with the pecary, or any other creature that comes in his way." (Lionel Wafer, *Isthmus of America* 111)

16.6 DRINK

The next time you have a drink, raise a glass to the pirate Richard Hains. For if drinkers had to choose a guardian saint, surely Hains would be in the running.

In 1723, off St. Michael's Island in the Azores, Edward Low plundered a Portuguese bark. He and his pirates were in a good mood: They only slashed at the crewmen with cutlasses and burned their vessel before releasing them in a boat.

The grateful sailors scrambled to get under way before the psychopathic Low changed his mind. As they started rowing, something heavy dropped into the boat. It was Richard Hains, a member of Low's company. Whether because he had been forced to join Low's crew, or because he had seen enough of Low's barbarity, Hains was seizing this chance to make his getaway. As soon as Hains hit the boat's bottom, he stretched himself out and hid, keeping as still and quiet as possible. If any on Low's ship saw him, he would die, and his new Portuguese comrades would likely be slaughtered as well.

Then Hains realized something. Just minutes earlier he had been drinking out of a silver tankard, but he had left it behind, next to the gun port above him. Going back for it could mean death.

But leaving it behind was apparently worse. Hains quietly leapt up to the port, grabbed his tankard, and clambered back down, but—notwithstanding what were likely looks of utter horror from the Portuguese sailors—with no one the wiser. (*General History of the Pyrates* 335–36; *Pirates of the New England Coast* 214–15)

In three seconds, Hains had achieved immortality. Almost three hundred years later, we remember the creed he scrawled out across the air with a drop, a leap, and a tumble: A life without liberty is not worth living. But a life with liberty and no beer mug ain't much better.

Below find a list of the various kinds of drink around which pirate life transpired.

ale [*ay-ell*] alcoholic beverage made from fermented barley and flavored with hops; beer

> "[N]ext to rum, there's nought for trouble o' mind or body, like nappy **ale**, 'tis a true Englishman's panacea." (Absalom Troy, *Adam Penfeather, Buccaneer* 4)

arrack [*ahrr/ay-rack*] potent alcoholic beverage made from fermented fruits (especially coconut or other tropical fruit juice), grains (especially rice), saps (especially from palm trees), and/or sugar or sugarcane
Also known as "rack."

> "[W]e took in our way a small bark laden with **arrack** and rice, which was good sauce to our other purchase. For if the women made our men drunk before, this **arrack** made them quite mad." (Captain Avery, recalling the taking of a ship bearing a cargo of liquor just after having taken a ship bearing the granddaughter of the Great Mogul and her female retinue, *The King of Pirates* 60)

beer [*bee-arr*] alcoholic beverage made from fermented barley and flavored with hops

> "They sail two foot to our one ... our bread and **beer** is all most expended." (Christopher Goffe, the pirate turned privateer, making a report to the governor of Masschusetts Bay Colony on his pursuit of two pirate ships, *Pirates of the New England Coast* 32)

bitter wine [*better/bi'er wawn/wyeene*] alcoholic beverage consisting of a mixture including beer, liquor, and raw eggs

> *And they were all drinking, all those who were still conscious—drinking **bitter wine** or 'kill devil' rum or rumfustian, made of beer, gin, sherry, raw eggs, and whatever else happened to be available.* (*The Guardship* 30)

black strap [*bleck strep*] alcoholic beverage consisting of a combination of rum, chowder beer (made by boiling tree pitch or gum—especially that of the black spruce—in water, adding molasses, and allowing the brew to ferment), and still more molasses

> *Fishing, splitting and drying fish was hard labor and as the nights were chill, "**black strap**" was in great demand. This was a villainous combination of rum, molasses and chowder beer and before the season was over it usually caused many to "outrun the constable" and compelled them to agree to articles of servitude that kept them on the island during the winter. ... This made men willing converts to the Articles signed on board pirate vessels or caused them to run away with shallops and boats and begin piratical exploits on their own account.* (account of why Newfoundland and its fishing vessels were fertile recruiting ground for pirates, *Pirates of the New England Coast* 339–40)

brandy [*brayn/bren-dy*]

"We lay at this isle until Tuesday following, and in the meanwhile gave our vessel a pair of boots and tops, being very merry all the while with the wine and **brandy** we had taken in the prize." (Basil Ringrose, *Bucaniers of America* Part IV Chap. XXI)

bumbo; bomboo [*barrm/boohm-bo'oo/boo*] alcoholic beverage consisting of some combination of rum, sugar, water, lemon juice, lime juice, and nutmeg

> *But he recovered all his heat and fury when they came to sit about the table, on which the Negro steward had set Canary sack and Nantes brandy and a jug of **bumbo**, brewed of rum and sugar, water and nutmeg, and it roared in him as he related what he had endured.* (*The Fortunes of Captain Blood* 113)

chocolate [*charrk-lert/lit*] non-alcoholic beverage consisting of cocoa and water, typically served hot

> "I order'd a large kettle of **chocolate** to be made for our ship's company (having no spiritous liquor to give them) ..." (Woodes Rogers, recounting the drinking of chocolate as among his company's preparations for battle, *A Cruising Voyage Round the World* 158)

Goa arack [*Goer/Go'oo-a ahrr/ay-rack*] potent alcoholic beverage made from fermented fruits (especially coconut or other tropical fruit juice), grains (especially rice), saps (especially from palm trees), or sugar or sugarcane

Goa is a small region on the Arabian Sea at the center of India's western coast, under Portuguese influence since Vasco da Gama first landed there in 1498 and a permanent Portuguese merchant-driven settlement was established in 1510.

> "Arack is also distilled from rice, and other things in the East Indies, but none is so esteemed for making punch as the sort

made of toddy, or the sap of the coconut tree, for it makes a most delicate punch. But it must have a dash of brandy to hearten it, because this arack is not strong enough to make good punch of itself. This sort of liquor is chiefly used about Goa, and therefore it has the name of **Goa arack**." (William Dampier, *A New Voyage Round the World* 277)

grape wine [*grayeepe wawn/wyeene*] alcoholic beverage made from fermented grapes; wine made from grapes

> "It is also agreed to allow the following particulars for t[h]e use of the officers in the great cabbin of each ship, *viz.* ... the third part of a lea[gue]r of g[r]ape wine ..." (resolution by officers aboard *Duke* and *Dutchess*, *A Cruising Voyage Round the World* 209)

grog [*grarrg*] liquor, especially rum, mixed with water

> "Give the men an extra glass of **grog**, and don't forget the buck-shot." (pirate captain, preparing for the company's assault on the island natives, *The Coral Island* 250)

gunpowder rum [*garrn/goohn-parr/powooder roohm*] rum mixed with gunpowder

Gunpowder is a mixture of saltpeter, sulphur, and charcoal. It has long been suggested, though without scientific substantiation, that consuming saltpeter (potassium nitrate or sodium nitrate) deadens sexual desire but inspires fearlessness and aggressiveness. Mutineering sailors sometimes drank gunpowder in rum or water as a ritualistic preparation for rebellion (a practice also observed among slaves).

> "[T]here's nought like liquor for putting the devil into a man, and of all liquor commend me to **rum with a dash o' tobacco** or **gunpowder**, d'ye see." (Adam Penfeather, *Black Bartlemy's Treasure* 158)

Hangman's Blood [*'angman's Bloohd/Blut*] potent alcoholic beverage made by combining various liquors and other alcoholic beverages (such as beer and wine), and typically including rum and gin

> *Captain Jonsen ... went on board, and mixed several gallons of that potion known in alcoholic circles as **Hangman's Blood** (which is compounded of rum, gin, brandy, and porter).* (*A High Wind in Jamaica* 101–02)

Hollands [*Harrl/ol'-lan's*] Dutch gin made of fermented barley malt and redistilled with juniper berries or juniper berry oil, and having a sweet, robust flavor

The term distinguishes this spirit from the other principal type of gin, known as "London gin," "English gin," or "British gin." Hollands is also known as "geneva gin," "genever gin," or jenever gin."

> "He's no more right to come blustering down here into Governor Eden's province than I have to come aboard of your schooner here, Tom Burley, and to carry off two or three kegs of this prime **Hollands** for my own drinking." (Blackbeard, protesting the Governor of Virginia's effort to apprehend Blackbeard in North Carolina, *The Book of Pirates* "Jack Ballister's Fortunes" 133–34)

kill-devil rum [*kell-daahv/dayv/debb/div-il roohm*] alcoholic beverage consisting of a mixture including beer, liquor, and raw eggs

> *And they were all drinking, all those who were still conscious—drinking bitter wine or '**kill devil**' rum or rumfustian, made of beer, gin, sherry, raw eggs, and whatever else happened to be available.* (*The Guardship* 30)

Madeira [*Madayee/Madee/Marrdayee/Marrdeera*] wine from the island of Madeira, situated in the Atlantic along a latitude just south of the

Strait of Gibraltar and roughly along the longitude of the western-most edge of Africa

A white wine (though there are lesser known red-grape varieties), Madeira was highly prized because of its ability to survive long sea-going voyages. Its flavor only improved when stored in hot temperatures and did not deteriorate when left opened and exposed to air.

> "An' I've a score bottles of **Madeira** wine on me shelf what would wash yer throat clean as a maiden's soul, it would." (Long John Silver, *Dead Man's Chest* 27)

Nantes [*Naahn/Narrn-tees*] wine from the port city of Nantes or the surrounding Loire Valley region in western France, especially a dry, tart white wine known as "muscadet"

> "When the fierceness of the weather was over, and they had recovered their spirits, by the help of a little **Nantes**, they bore away to the West Indies. ..." (Philip Ashton, a prisoner of Edward Low's company, describing the men's methods of coping with rough weather, *Pirates of the New England Coast* 235)

palm wine [*parrm wawn/wyeene*] alcoholic beverage made from the fermented sap of various species of palm tree; toddy

> "The houses are low and ordinary, with one great house in the midst of it, where their chief men meet and receive strangers, and here they treated us with **palm-wine**." (William Dampier, *A New Voyage Round the World* 47)

pine-drink [*pawn/pyeene drenk*] alcoholic beverage made from fermented pineapple juice

> "Pine-apples ... is the main thing they delight in, for with these they make a sort of drink which our men call **pine-drink**, much esteemed by these Moskitos, and to which they invite each other to be merry, providing fish and flesh also." (William Dampier, describing a beverage

introduced to the buccaneers by Central American natives, *A New Voyage Round the World* 12–13)

punch [*parrnch/poohnch*] any improvised alcoholic beverage consisting of a combination of liquors and other beverages, particularly rum, wine, and fruit juice (especially lemon or lime juice), typically sweetened with sugar or honey, often spiced (especially with nutmeg), and sometimes served hot

> "This being New-Year's Day, every officer was wish'd a merry New-Year by our musick; and I had a large tub of **punch** hot upon the quarter-deck, where every man in the ship had above a pint to his share ..." (Woodes Rogers, *A Cruising Voyage Round the World* 61)

rum [*roohm*] alcoholic liquor distilled from fermented sugar cane molasses

Rum is the preferred drink of pirates, and—like sailing ships and gold—a *sine qua non* of pirate life.

> "I lived on **rum**, I tell you. It's been meat and drink, and man and wife, to me; and if I'm not to have my **rum** now I'm a poor old hulk on a lee shore. ..." (Billy Bones, *Treasure Island* 14, Chap. 3)

rumfustian [*roohm-farrss/foohss-chern/tern*] alcoholic drink consisting of a mixture including beer, liquor, and raw eggs

> *And they were all drinking, all those who were still conscious—drinking bitter wine or 'kill devil' rum or **rumfustian**, made of beer, gin, sherry, raw eggs, and whatever else happened to be available.* (*The Guardship* 30)

sack [*seck*] dry, strong white wine from Spain or the Canary Islands

> "Oho, landlord, —**sack**! Sack and plenty on't! Sack-ho!" (Benjamin Trigg, ordering drinks all around, *Adam Penfeather, Buccaneer* 46)

small beer [*smawrl bee-arr/err*] beer containing little alcohol; weak ale

> "However, he brewed us very good **small beer**, for present use, and instead of hops he found some wild wormwood growing on the island, which gave it no unpleasant taste ..." (Captain Avery, *The King of Pirates* 28)

Spelman's Neep [*Spaahlman's Neep*] kind of arrack

> "It is also agreed to allow the following particulars for t[h]e use of the officers in the great cabbin of each ship, *viz.* ... half a leaguer of **Spelman's Neep**, or the best sort of arrack ..." (resolution by officers aboard *Duke* and *Dutchess*, *A Cruising Voyage Round the World* 209)

stout [*stowoot*] dark beer made from roasted malt or roasted barley

> "But don't go wavin' it in the face of every man who asks for a glass of **stout**." (Long John Silver, giving Jim Hawkins an impressive pistol and a few words of caution, "Treasure Island" [1950] 25:00)

sweet water [*sweet wahh/warr-ter*] fresh water, as distinguished from saltwater

> "So I've tended Johnny's needs; he sitteth even now guzzling **sweet water** and gnawing on a ship's biscuit." (Japhet Bly, *Winds of Chance* 151)

tipple [*tepple*] liquor

> *Bellamy swore he was sorry he could not run out his guns to return the salute, meaning the thunder, that he fancy'd the gods had got drunk over their **tipple**, and were gone together by the ears.* (attribution to Captain Bellamy, *General History of the Pyrates* 586)

tobacco rum ['*bacco/'baccoo/backer/backy* OR *ter/too-'bacco/'baccoo/'backer/'backy roohm*] rum mixed with tobacco

The addition of tobacco gives rum an earthy, smoky, and (depending on how stale the tobacco) bitter flavor.

> "[T]here's nought like liquor for putting the devil into a man, and of all liquor commend me to **rum with a dash o' tobacco** or gunpowder, d'ye see." (Adam Penfeather, *Black Bartlemy's Treasure* 158)

toddy [*tarrdy/toh'y*] alcoholic beverage made from the fermented sap of various species of palm tree

Also known as "palm wine."

> "Beside the liquor or water in the fruit, there is also a sort of wine drawn from the [coconut] tree, called **toddy**, which looks like whey. It is sweet and very pleasant, but it is to be drunk within 24 hours after it is drawn, for afterwards it grows sour." (William Dampier, *A New Voyage Round the World* 277)

(honey) toke [(*harr/hooh/ooh-ny*) *tooke/to'ooke*] alcoholic beverage made from fermented honey

> *Here Cornelius lost 70 men by their excesses, having been long without fresh provision, the eating immoderately, drinking **toke** (a liquor made of honey) to excess, and being too free with the women, they fell into violent fevers, which carry'd them off.* (account of Captain Cornelius' company's troubles while in Madagascar, *General History of the Pyrates* 604)

16.7 CURRENCY

"Pirates have no God but their money, nor saviour but their arms."

So declared members of Edward Low's company in September 1721. A few of their comrades had been so impressed with the eloquence of a well-spoken prisoner that they proposed he preach them a sermon. But other members of the company strenuously objected. Though conscience rarely stayed these sea-wolves, their pious worship of money made unthinkable the acknowledgment of any other divinity.

Around January 1723, Low captured a Portuguese ship—the *Nostra Signiora de Victoria*. He tortured her crew to force disclosure of where the ship's money was hidden. The Portuguese crewmen finally blurted out that their captain, on seeing Low's pursuit, had lowered out of his cabin window a canvas bag containing eleven thousand gold moidores—worth about fifteen thousand English pounds. When the ship was captured, the captain sliced the rope from which the bag dangled, letting a small fortune plummet seaward.

Minutes later, the Portuguese second-in-command was eating a hot meal: his superior's lips, freshly cut off from the captain's face and broiled over a fire. (*General History of the Pyrates* 326; *Pirates of the New England Coast* 174, 201)

It was his last supper. After the last mouthful (pun intended), Low slaughtered all thirty-two members of the crew.

Below are terms for various coins and units of precious metal, significant (perhaps divinely so) in the lives of pirates both as objects of plunder and as specie for and by which other plunder was hurriedly sold and squandered in the next port.

bar [*bahrr*]

(1) solid piece of gold or silver shaped into a bar

> "And in the cave lie yet fifty and four **bars** of gold and others of silver, with store of rix-dollars, doubloons, moidores and pieces of eight—gold coins of all countries." (Adam Penfeather, *Black Bartlemy's Treasure* 328)

(2) a quantity of such pieces

Note the modifier "gold" or "silver" is almost always used either before or after "bar" in a sentence.

"Now, you didn't get all of that **bar** silver on that island, now did ya?" (Long John Silver, "Treasure Island" [1934] 1:41:00) < "Gold and silver." "And jewels too, I recollect." "Aye, jewels by the bushel baskets." "And silver **bar**." > (Long John Silver, George Merry, & Dick, "Treasure Island" [1990] 1:56:28)

broad piece [*brarrd peesh*] gold English coin issued before 1663 and worth between twenty and thirty shillings (or between one and one-and-a-half pounds), depending on year of issue

The term came into use after the introduction of the guinea in 1663 to refer to gold coins issued before that date that were worth the same as, but broader and thinner than, the guinea.

"For there's never a man o' them but hath two thousand, five hundred **broad pieces** to his share ..." (Benjamin Trigg, *Adam Penfeather, Buccaneer* 262)

castellano [*carrs/cayss-ter-llarr-no'oo*] gold Spanish coin worth approximately four-fifths of an escudo or one-tenth of a doubloon (a castellano equaling about 450 maravedis, an escudo equaling about 544), and a bit more valuable than a Spanish ducat (about 375 maravedis)

"I'll lay ye a **castellano** there was a whole watch awake on her the night long." (Jemmy, *Porto Bello Gold* 139)

Spanish coins struck in the New World (gold from 1622 until 1732, and silver from 1572 until 1732) were cobs—rough, irregularly-shaped chunks that, for expediency's sake, were simply cut off bars and hammered between crude dies. Spanish mints in the New World did not begin stamping proper coins from sheets of metal until 1732. The cruder production method was finally phased out in 1750 (gold) and 1773 (silver).

crown [*crowoon*] gold or silver (depending on year of issue) English coin worth five shillings, or one-quarter of a pound, and issued between 1526 and 1751 (when war shrank radically the supply of available silver), then again from 1818 through 1965

*Tew didn't sight a vessel until in the Atlantic, north of the Cape of Good Hope, where he fell in with a Dutch East Indiaman of eighteen guns which he took with the loss of but one man and secured several chests filled with English **crowns**.* (description of the adventures of Thomas Tew, *Pirates of the New England Coast* 87)

(copper) doit [(*cahrrper*) *doyeet*] small copper coin issued by the Dutch East India Company, worth between half and a quarter of an English penny

Referenced in phrases like "not a copper doit" or "ne'er a single copper doit" to emphasize an extreme scarcity of money or value of some kind.

"There ain't a thing left here, not a **copper doit** nor a baccy box." (George Merry, *Treasure Island* 178, Chap. 31)

doubloon [*darrb/doohb-loon*] gold Spanish coin

The doubloon, worth eight escudos, was the basic gold coin of Spain. One gold escudo was worth sixteen silver reales. In 1759, a doubloon was worth about three-and-a-half English pounds. Pirates occasionally, and redundantly, refer to the coin as a "gold doubloon," as a means of emphasizing or celebrating its worth.

"Dying! Dying—aye, am I! And wi' two thousand **doubloons** hid away as I shall ne'er ha' the spending on ..." (Diccon, *Martin Conisby's Vengeance* 115)

ducat [*doohk-ert*]

(1) gold or silver coin issued by various states in mainland Europe, likely first by Sicily in 1140

Gold ducats were much more common (and obviously more valuable) than silver ones, and the most popular and probably widely circulated ducat was that issued by the Netherlands, first struck in 1589. The Spanish ducat was worth a bit less than a castellano—that is, just under four-fifths of an escudo or one-tenth of a doubloon (a ducat equaling about 375 maravedis, and an escudo equaling about 544).

"I could not, without disrespect to his eminence the Primate of New Spain, set his ransom at less than a hundred thousand **ducats**." (Peter Blood, *The Fortunes of Captain Blood* 134)

(2) piece of eight

"Ducat" was often used loosely as a proxy term for any principal unit of currency, particularly the piece of eight.

"We shewed him our commission, which was now for three years to come. This we had purchased at a cheap rate, having given for it only the sum of ten **ducats**, or pieces-of-eight." (William Dick, *Bucaniers of America* 325)

Dutch dollar [*Darrtch/Doohtch darr-lahrr*] silver Dutch coin known in the Netherlands as the "leeuwendaalder" or "lion dollar" and among English speakers as a lion dollar or Dutch dollar

The "lion dollar," issued between 1575 and 1713, depicted a knight on the obverse and a lion on the reverse and saw regular use throughout the American colonies. The value of the lion dollar was standardized in New York in 1708 at five-and-a-half shillings.

"[W]e sold her to Cape. John Opey, Commander of the Oley frigate, lately arriv'd from London, for 575 **Dutch dollars**, being an extraordinary bargain ..." (Woodes Rogers, *A Cruising Voyage Round the World* 210)

farthing [*fahrr-thin'*] small English coin made of copper or bronze and worth one-quarter of a penny

The smallest denomination of English coin until 1827.

"But 'ow would you feel to be goin' back to England to stand trial without a **farthin'** to your name?" (Long John Silver, "Long John Silver's Return to Treasure Island" 1:09:56)

florin [*flarrin/flarrn/flor'n*]

(1) gold medieval English coin worth six shillings issued and withdrawn from circulation in 1344; (2) silver English coin worth two shillings, or one-tenth of a pound, first issued in 1849

The florin does not figure prominently in pirate life, as neither the medieval florin nor the modern florin was contemporaneous with the golden age of piracy of the late 1600s and early 1700s.

"This cargo will bring fifty thousand gold **florin** from any rebels worth the name." (Captain Vallo, "The Crimson Pirate" 10:32)

george [*jarge*] a type of guinea (gold English coin) worth twenty-one shillings and issued between 1714 and 1799 (with a final version struck in 1813) under the reigns of Georges I, II, and III

"Take the **Georges**, Pew, and don't stand there squalling." (comrade of Pew's, *Treasure Island* 26, Chap. 5)

groat [*gro'oot*] silver English coin worth four pence

"The Frenchman took Moon's knife in the throat—/Yo-ho-ho, and a bottle of rum!/ But all they found was a rusty **groat**—/Yo- ho-ho, and a bottle o' rum!" (song sung aboard the *Walrus, Porto Bello Gold* 126)

guinea [*gui'ea/guinee-er*] gold English coin issued between 1663 and 1813 and worth be- tween twenty and thirty shillings (or between one and one-and-a-half pounds), depending on year of issue (its value was not fixed at twenty-one shillings until 1717)

The term "guinea" was used originally to refer to the place in Africa from which the Africa Company imported much of the gold used to make the coin. Pirates occasionally, and redundantly, referred to the coin as a "golden guinea," as a means of emphasizing or celebrating its worth.

"Ten **guineas** for the lad first sights her." (Japhet Bly, *Winds of Chance* 98)

louis [*looer*] gold French coin of varying value issued between 1640 and 1795, known for- mally as a "Louis d'or," depicting the king on the obverse and the French royal coat of arms on the reverse, and worth approximately between sixteen and nineteen English shil- lings (just under a pound)

"Why, there is one little hoard of trea- sure Prince Charles had to leave behind him—the Loch Arkaig treasure they call it. ... And it not more than forty thousand **louis** at the beginning, and dribbling fast before it was turned to account." (An- drew Murray, *Porto Bello Gold* 100)

moidore [*moy-darr/derr*] gold Portuguese coin issued between 1640 and 1732, but continu- ing in regular circulation long after

In 1759, a moidore was worth about one- and-a-half English pounds, or just under half a doubloon. It was worth only a bit less in 1722–23, according to the account of Edward Low's piracies: "[T]he Portuguese captain had hung out of a cabin window, a canvas bag containing about eleven thousand gold moidores, the equivalent of nearly fifteen thousand English pounds ..." (*Pirates of the New England Coast* 201)

"Well, accardin' to the recipe, I would say that two helpings would contain twenty gold **moidores**." (Long John Silver, "The Adventures of Long John Silver: Devil's Stew" 20:21)

onza [*honza/honzer/onzer*] doubloon

"I would have all lookouts notified that I shall give ten **onzas** to him who first hails the deck for a large Spaniard of forty-four guns coming from the west." (Andrew Murray, *Porto Bello Gold* 149)

pagoda [*parr/per-go'oo-darr/der*] main coin of southern (Hindu) India in the sixth through nineteenth centuries

The pagoda was a small gold coin worth roughly seven or eight English shillings and struck by the Vijayanagar Kingdom, the East India Company at Madras, the Dutch at Tu- ticorin, and occasionally the French at Pon- dicherry.

"John Oliver had a greater respect paid him than the rest, and whereas their pay was ten **pagodas** a month each (a **pagoda** is two dollars or 9s. English), his pay was twenty **pagodas**." (William Dampier, *A New Voyage Round the World* 245)

peseta [*per-seeter*] silver Spanish coin worth four reales, or one-quarter of an escudo, or one-thirty-second of a doubloon

"Not a penny, not a doubloon. There's not a bent or damaged **peseta**." (Blackbeard, "Blackbeard's Ghost" 40:15)

piece (of eight) [*peesh (o'\on ayeet/ett*)] silver Spanish coin known as a peso and worth eight reales, or half of an escudo, or one- sixteenth of a doubloon

In 1722, a piece of eight may have been worth roughly five shillings or one-quarter of one pound sterling (based, for example, on the fact that pirate George Lowther's articles promised any company member who lost a limb 150 pounds sterling, while the articles of his former lieutenant Edward Low promised 600 pieces of eight for the same injury; see Appendix C).

> "I'll outbid the Spanish Admiral's blood money by forty thousand **pieces**. I offer you fifty thousand pieces of eight for my life." (Peter Blood, *Captain Blood Returns* 146) "You will give me up, of course, my Colonel. And the British Government will pay you the reward of a thousand pounds—five thousand **pieces of eight**." (Peter Blood, *Captain Blood Returns* 254)

pistole [*peh-shto'ool*] gold Spanish coin
The pistole was worth two escudos, or one-fourth the value of a doubloon.

> *Pirate Jeremiah Huggins claimed that he had been given 14 gold **pistoles**, 7½ ounces of gold dust, 82 pieces of eight, and 17 ounces of silver bullion "by reason of his being wounded among them."* (*Villians of All Nations* 73)

plate [*playeete*] silver, especially in bulk quantities and in the possession of (or after appropriation from) Spanish vessels or settlements
The term is derived from "plata," the Spanish word for silver.

> "Silence! the **plate**! the money for the troops—where are they?" (Cain, interrogating a Portuguese ship's supercargo about the plunder aboard, *The Pirate* 56, Chap. IX)

Note the term "plate" is usually, though not always, used to refer to silver in some raw form—such as bars, lumps, or nuggets—as opposed to, and purposely to distinguish it from, silver coins:

> "In the meanwhile we took out of the prize much **plate**, and some money ready coined, besides six hundred and twenty jars of wine and brandy, and other things."

(Basil Ringrose, describing the plundering of a Spanish vessel near Cape Passao, *Bucaniers of America* Part IV Chap. XXI)

pound (sterling) [*poun'/pount/powoon'/powoond/powoont (starr-lin')*] unit of English currency worth twenty shillings

> "It be a counterpart to a map I found in the sea chest I took away from Treasure Island. It points the way to more of Flint's gold still buried there. Nine hundred thousand **pounds**." (Long John Silver, "Long John Silver's Return to Treasure Island" 38:24) "He that shall have the misfortune to lose a limb, in time of engagement, shall have the sum of one hundred and fifty **pounds sterling**, and remain with the company as long as he shall think fit." (sixth of the Articles of George Lowther and company, *General History of the Pyrates* 308)

real [*ree-erl*] unit of Spanish currency
Sixteen silver reales were worth one gold escudo, and the gold Spanish coin known as the "doubloon" was worth eight escudos. Eight reales in the American colonies were worth approximately five or six shillings (though the value varied depending on the year and the colony). Historians have estimated that approximately half the coins in circulation in colonial America were Spanish reales.

rix-dollar [*rex darr-lahrr*] silver Dutch coin known in the Netherlands as "Nederlandse Rijksdaalder," depicting the country's ruler on the obverse and a shield on the reverse, and familiar to seventeenth-century American colonists because of its broad use in the Dutch colony of New Amsterdam
The value of the rix-dollar was standardized in Massachusetts in 1642 as worth five shillings and in 1686 as worth six shillings (and on both occasions as worth eight silver Spanish reales).

> "And in the cave lie yet fifty and four bars of gold and others of silver, with store

of **rix-dollars**, doubloons, moidores and pieces of eight—gold coins of all countries." (Adam Penfeather, *Black Bartlemy's Treasure* 328)

shilling [*shell-in'*] silver English coin worth twelve pence, or one-twentieth of a pound

> "You let me an' me lads go, take our boats an' steal off, an' it be all yer'n, ev'ry **shillin'**." (Billy Doyle, attempting to bribe Alan Lewrie, *The Gun Ketch* 159)

sovereign [*sarr-verrn/vren/vrin*] gold English coin worth between twenty and thirty shillings (or between one and one-and-a-half pounds), depending on year of issue

Sovereigns were issued between 1489 and 1604, then again from 1817 through the present. The coin got its name from the first sovereign's depiction on its obverse of the King on his throne. Note the occasional, and redundant, reference to the coin as a "gold sovereign," often for emphasis.

> < "What do you want?" "Them **gold sovereigns** to pay for the life of the Governor's little daughter. I've come to fetch her." > (Billy Bowlegs & Long John Silver, "Long John Silver's Return to Treasure Island" 15:21)

spade-guinea [*spayeede gui'ea/guinee'er*] gold English coin worth twenty-one shillings issued between 1787 and 1799, known as a "spade-guinea" for the spade-like shape of the shield displayed on the reverse side

> "You'll learn fast, you will, Master Ormerod. I'll lay four **spade-guineas** to that." (Long John Silver, *Porto Bello Gold* 64)

stiver [*steever*] Dutch coin worth one-twentieth of a gulden or guilder, equal in value to an English penny or two

Stivers were generally silver coins, though some stivers struck in the Dutch colonies were copper.

> "A flask of wine, which holds three quarts, will cost eighteen **stivers**, for I paid so much

for it." (William Dampier, complaining of the inflated liquor prices charged at Dutch establishments at the Cape of Good Hope, *A New Voyage Round the World* 262)

16.8 TIME

Time, like space, is relative. Even for pirates.

When William Dampier and his fellow buccaneers reached the East Indies, they encountered several Europeans who were one day behind—that is, who believed the date was one day earlier than Dampier and his comrades were observing. Other European seamen, however, were keeping the same calendar. Who was right?

The buccaneers ultimately determined that those who had sailed eastward around the southern tip of Africa were a day behind, and those who had sailed westward around the southern tip of South America were a day ahead—basically because of the failure to observe the equivalent of today's international date line. Dampier learned, weirdly, that even permanent colonies kept different times based on the direction from which they had been settled: the Spaniards at Guam, for example, were a day ahead simply because their original settlors had arrived westward via America. (*A New Voyage Round the World* 178)

Time may be relative, but—for pirates who work in four-hour shifts, who sail on tides coming twelve hours and twenty-five minutes apart, and for whom the number of seconds they re-load cannon faster than their enemy separates victory from death—it often must be a cold, hard, objectively measurable fact.

Below are terms associated with time and its measurement.

NUMBER bell(s) [... *bayulls*]

A shipboard day is divided into seven watches: middle watch (midnight–4 A.M.), morning watch (4 A.M.–8 A.M.), forenoon watch (8 A.M.–noon), afternoon watch (noon–4 P.M.), first dog watch (4 P.M.–6 P.M.), second dog watch (6

P.M.–8 P.M.), and first watch (8 P.M.–midnight). A ship's bells are struck every half-hour, with one bell at the start of every watch, one bell added each half-hour, and eight bells at the end. (Four bells are traditionally struck at the end of the first dog watch, while eight bells at the end of the second—even though the second dog watch also lasts only two hours and is marked by one, two, and three bells through its first hour-and-a-half—to signal that both halves of the dog watch have been completed.) Thus "six bells," for example, can mean 3 A.M., 7 A.M., 11 A.M., 3 P.M., or 11 P.M., depending on the time of day and which watch is in effect.

> "Tomorrow, when the for'ard new watch strikes **eight bells**, and the sun be at its highest, I'll be comin' to have a talk polite-like with the cap'n." (Long John Silver, *Long John Silver's Return to Treasure Island* 59:20) "And when? says you. Why, from about noon observation to about **six bells**." (Ben Gunn, *Treasure Island* 101, Chap. 19)

NUMBER bell(s) is made [… *bayulls be mayeede*]

Used to specify shipboard time, by identifying the number of bells that have been struck or "made." Note the use of the singular verb "is" even when the number of bells specified is plural (*e.g.*, "three bells is made"). See the above entry for a discussion of how the number of bells specified corresponds to the time of day.

> "I'm late as it is. **Eight bells was made** an hour ago and more." (Peter Blood, *Captain Blood Returns* 141)

the bell has struck NUMBER [*t' bayull 'as stroohk* …]

Used to specify shipboard time, by identifying the number of bells that have been struck. See the first entry in this section ("NUMBER bell(s)") for a discussion of how the number of bells specified corresponds to the time of day.

> Compare: < "Hush! **Struck the bell six or seven**?" "Seven." > (The Red Rover & Harry Wilder, *The Red Rover* 348)

fortnight [*farrt/foort-nawt/nigheet*] period of fourteen consecutive days or two weeks

> "[T]he whole ship's crew was drunk for above a **fortnight** together, till six or seven of them killed themselves …" (Captain Avery, *The King of Pirates* 60)

glass [*gless*]

(1) hour; period of sixty minutes

> "Go to your father, and tell him I must meet with him at his home in half a **glass**." (Long John Silver, *Dead Man's Chest* 28)

(2) any increment of time, the size of which is specified by the speaker with an adjective phrase ("five-minute glass") or a possessive phrase ("five minutes' glass")

> "And sailing up the west shore between the island and the coast of Africa, [we] came to an anchor over against our settlement, about two leagues' distance, and made the signal of our arrival with firing twice seven guns at the distance of a two-minute **glass** between the seven; when, to our infinite joy, the fort answered us and the longboat, the same that belonged to our former ship, came off to us." (Captain Avery, *The King of Pirates* 43)

(3) any short period of time; a while

> "You good sirs'll hafta 'scuze me fer a **glass** while I have a word with Charley, here." (Long John Silver, *Dead Man's Chest* 75)

half-glass [*'alf/harrf-gless*] half-hour

> "Maybe then ye'd add a mite to your kindness and let me borry his time for a **half-glass** or so for to show me a couple o' landmarks I must make in the town." (Long John Silver, *Porto Bello Gold* 23)

NUMBER the morning\forenoon\afternoon\ evening\night [... *t' marrn-in'\farr/foor-noon\ arrfter/arter/hafter-noon\evenin'\nawt/nigheet*]

"Yesterday at **twain the afternoon** we weigh'd again, with a breeze at N.E. but at five a gale came up at S.S.W. and blew very strong ..." (Woodes Rogers, *A Cruising Voyage Round the World* 33)

NUMBER of the clock [... *o'\on t' clarrk*]

The term "o'clock" is an abbreviation of "of the clock."

"On the 1st of October, about 11 **of the clock** we came to an anchor in the Downs, where several of our owners came aboard ..." (Woodes Rogers, *A Cruising Voyage Round the World* 224)

NUMBER+INCREMENT space [... *spayeece*]

The speaker specifies a number and an increment of time (*e.g.*, "two hours," "three days," "four months"), then says "space" (*e.g.*, "two hours space," "three days space," "four months space"). The term "space" means the same thing as "a period of." Thus, if the modern speaker says "a period of three days," a pirate might say "three days space."

"But we were **four or five days space** before we could get our sails dry, so as to be able to take them from the yards, there falling a shower of rain almost every hour of the day and night." (Basil Ringrose, *Bucaniers of America* Part IV Chap. X)

the space of NUMBER+INCREMENT [*t' spayeece o'\on ...*] a period of ...; an amount of time equal to ...

"We persisted in our course **the space of eight or ten days**, in all which time nothing remarkable happened unto us ..." (William Dick, *Bucaniers of America* 338)

tide [*tawd/tyeede*] period of time equal to that between consecutive high tides, or approximately twelve-and-a-half hours

"Yesterday afternoon I left Cap[t]. Courtney and Capt. Dampier at Puna, and went inquest of the barks admiring they did not come in sight, they being now **a tide** and a half behind." (Woodes Rogers, *A Cruising Voyage Round the World* 92)

NUMBER tide's\tides' time [... *tawd's/tyeede's\ tawds'/tyeedes' tawm/tyeeme*] period of time equal to that between consecutive high tides, or approximately twelve-and-a-half hours, multiplied by the specified number of such tides

"[T]hey could go from there aboard the guard-ship in half **a tide's time**." (William Dampier, *A New Voyage Round the World* 14)

what o'clock is it? [*wharrt/whorrt o'clarrk 's\be ett/'n/'t?*] what time is it?

< "Hey, Frog. **What o'clock is it?**" "Six, or eight." > (Thomas Bartholomew Red & The Frog, "Pirates" 1:54:42)

16.9 DISTANCE

After canoeing all night and hiking three miles, Henry Morgan's men weren't backing down. They were proceeding with their plan to attack the Spanish town of Porto Bello, despite the fact that gunfire from lookout sentries had destroyed their element of surprise and alerted soldiers manning the guns of Santiago Castle. *And* despite the fact that Morgan's men had to cross the open ground in front of Santiago Castle to get to the town.

The castle's frontage that morning on July 11, 1668, must have looked like a yawning expanse. Cross it, and the men were bloody pulp. Don't cross it, and the men were cowards—efforts wasted, hopes dashed—and penniless cowards at that.

Eighth-graders know the name Henry Morgan in part because of what happened next. Morgan gave the order to charge. His men bolted across that naked distance, yelling and screaming, waiting for death to rain down. But it never came. Only a single shot came from the fort, and the cannonball sailed harmlessly into the sea behind them. By nightfall the following day, Morgan had taken the town and its three forts. Thirty days later, Morgan and his men were 250,00 pieces of eight the richer, having made good on their promise not to burn the town on receiving a ransom from the governor of Panama. (*Under the Black Flag* 44–46)

Distance can be a help as well as a hindrance. Pirates used the distance kept by other vessels as a gauge for determining whether they might make good prizes. A vessel carrying more gold than cannon would display caution, shying away when sighting an unidentified vessel, while a man-of-war would be more likely to pursue a suspicious vessel, or at least proceed undeterred along its initial course. Evasion, the pirate calculated, is consciousness of weakness and wealth.

This truth that distance is a functional, and not just spatial, phenomenon is reflected in the entries below. Most of them involve the speaker specifying a time period—typically a number of hours, days, weeks, or months—in stating a distance. Thus, when a pirate is asked, "How far is it to Porto Bello?" he might reply with "Eight days' cruise" or "A two months' run." Other entries below use the range of a weapon or a throwing arm, or the number of nights' sleep required to traverse a given distance, as a proxy measurement.

NUMBER+INCREMENT's cruise [...'s *croose*]

> "We met with no less than five prizes more here in about **twenty days' cruise** ..." (Captain Avery, *The King of Pirates* 16)

NUMBER+INCREMENT's journey [...'s *jarrney*]

> "Thence we departed with our entire little camp, the Emperor, and his son, in quest of the town of Santa Maria, as yet distant from there no less than **four**

or **five days journey**." (William Dick, *Bucaniers of America* 331)

NUMBER+INCREMENT's march [...'s *mahrrch*]

> "After supper we agreed with one of these Indians to guide us **a day's march** into the country, towards the north-side." (William Dampier, *A New Voyage Round the World* 14–15)

NUMBER+INCREMENT's run [...'s *roohn*]

> < "Name your price, captain." "For **an hour's run**, half a crown, in advance." > (Angus MacAllister & Long John Silver, "The Adventures of Long John Silver: The Tale of a Tooth" 26:05)

NUMBER+INCREMENT's sail [...'s *sayell*]

> "Our Island lieth scarce **twenty-four hours' sail** due south-westerly." (letter from Adam Penfeather to Martin Conisby, *Black Bartlemy's Treasure* 163)

NUMBER+INCREMENT's start [...'s *stahrrt*]

Used to describe the extent to which a vessel (at sea) or a person or group of persons (on land) has been traveling longer, or is farther along a particular course, than another.

> "The *Rachel* has **two hours' start** and Jim's aboard." (Long John Silver, "The Adventures of Long John Silver: Ship o' the Dead" 19:36)

cable (length) [*caah/cayee-ble (lenf)*] measure of length or distance equal to 100 fathoms (or about 183 meters)

Modern standardizations defined the "cable" as equivalent to 608 feet (one-tenth of a nautical mile or about 185 meters) in England, especially in the Royal Navy, and 720 feet (120 fathoms or about 220 meters) in the U.S., especially in the U.S. Navy.

> < "How much cable have you veered, Mr. Dinwiddie?" "**Cable** and a half, sir. We was to moor, you'll recall." > (Thomas Marlowe and Peleg Dinwiddie, *The Pirate*

Round 80) "Another two **cable lengths** and we have them." (John Sharkey, *The Dealings of Captain Sharkey and Other Tales of Pirates* "The Dealings of Captain Sharkey with Stephen Craddock" 42)

cast of a stone [*carrst o'\on a stoone/sto'oone*] length or distance equal to the specified number of distances one might throw a stone

"The island on this side thereof makes two great bays, in the first of which we watered, at a certain pond not distant above the **cast of a stone** from the bay." (Basil Ringrose, describing the south-east side of the island of Cayboa, *Bucaniers of America* Part IV Chap. IX)

furlong [*farr/foor-larrng*] measure of length or distance equal to 220 yards, 660 feet, or one-eighth of a mile

"Near the eastern point of the bay, which is not above three or four **furlongs** distant from Golden Island, there is a rivulet of very good water." (Lionel Wafer, *Isthmus of America* 75)

league measure of length or distance that can be covered in an hour's walk, or about three miles or five kilometers

"Look, there's the island. It can't be more than two or three **leagues** off." (Morgan Adams, "Cutthroat Island" 58:54)

(within) TYPE OF GUN-shot [*(weth/wi'/wiff/witt-in) … sharrt*]

The speaker names a type of gun before the word "shot, and uses the phrase to express a measure of length or distance equal to the range of the gun specified. See Section 16.3 for a list of various types of weapons, including shipboard cannons and other firearms. The most common examples of this usage include "pistol-shot," measuring about twenty-five to fifty yards, and "musket-shot," meaning about one hundred yards.

"It was too late in the evening to go into battle, so Morgan dropped anchor about a **cannon-shot** from the enemy … " (Alexander O. Exquemelin, describing Morgan's preparations for his attack on Spanish men-of-war off Maracaibo, *The Buccaneers of America* 156) "The river at this place was not above **pistol-shot** wide, and the banks pretty high on each side …" (William Dampier, describing the River St. Jago, *A New Voyage Round the World* 124) "We shall let them charge within close **pistol-shot** ere we give fire …" (Adam Penfeather, *Adam Penfeather, Buccaneer* 339)

A "half shot" is a unit of length or distance equal to half the range of a vessel's guns:

"We got possession of the Spanish ship about two yesterday in the afternoon. … They would not strike till within **half-shot** of our ships." (Woodes Rogers, *A Cruising Voyage Round the World* 89) "We got possession of the Spanish ship about two yesterday in the afternoon. … They would not strike till **within half-shot** of our ships." (Woodes Rogers, *A Cruising Voyage Round the World* 89)

sleep day's journey; distance covered in a journey requiring the specified number of overnights

"Being asked where now the priest was, they answered that he was gone to a great Spanish town, which was distant thence four **sleeps** up in the country." (Basil Ringrose, recalling the interrogation of three natives about nearby Spaniards, *Bucaniers of America* Part IV Chap. XIX)

stone's cast [*stoone's/sto'oone's carrst*] length or distance equal to that across which one might throw a stone

"[B]etween this shoale and the maine is 17 fathom water. It is two good **stone[']s casts** from the maine." (Basil Ringrose, *The South Sea Waggoner* Chart 68)

within hail [*weth/wi'/wiff/witt-in 'ail/hayell*] close enough to be audibly spoken or shouted to

> ## The Hierarchy of the Cask
>
> Wooden casks came in various sizes, their names denoting the casks themselves ("we lugged aboard a puncheon o' Madeira") as well as the measures of volume they contain ("we drank down a puncheon o' Madeira"). From smallest to largest, these various casks are: bumpkin, barrel, tierce, hogshead, puncheon, butt, and leaguer.

"Ezekiel Penryn waits within hail to do our business; do I summon him? Ay or no?" (Japhet Bly, *Winds of Chance* 82)

16.10 OTHER UNITS OF MEASUREMENT

William Dampier was the most well-rounded pirate of all time. He was a buccaneer, but also an accomplished explorer, navigator, mapmaker, and naturalist. It was a prodigious talent for observation and inference that powered those pursuits. And it was that same talent that likely led Dampier to discover the Dutch spice trick.

Dampier reported that Dutch seamen would routinely sail to the East Indies and fill their cargo holds to bursting with spices. The Dutch merchants would then sail homeward, selling off a few tons along the way. Yet when these merchants finally reached home port (or a popular offloading depot at Batavia, known today as Jakarta, Indonesia), the cargo holds would be full again—though no additional cargo had been loaded.

Dampier revealed the secret in his book *A New Voyage Round the World*:

> [T]hey will pour water among the remaining part of their cargo, which will swell them to such degree that the ship's hold will be as full again as it was before any were sold. They use this trick whenever they dispose of any clandestinely. For when they first take the cloves in, they are extraordinarily dry, and so will imbibe a great deal of moisture. (144)

For the price of just a few buckets of water, captains could discreetly and repeatedly bilk their oblivious ship owners of valuable merchandise. Dampier also revealed the sophisticated business method by which Dutch merchants preserved their trade secrets:

> [N]othing will persuade them to discover one another. For should any do it, the rest would certainly knock him on the head. (144)

In a world of precious cargoes and limited shipboard provisions, units of measurement were important. Listed below are a variety of such units—some more precise than others—on which pirates depended.

barrel [*bahrrel/bar'l*] small cask made of wooden staves and iron hoops, with a flat top and bottom of equal diameter

The capacity of a barrel as a unit of volume varies with its contents—a barrel of wine, for example, holds 119 liters, and a barrel of beer holds 157 liters.

> "I sent the pinnace aboard the *Marquiss* with 12 hogsheads and a **barrel** of water, their stock being almost spent ..." (Woodes Rogers, *A Cruising Voyage Round the World* 197)

bumpkin [*barrm'/barrmp/boohm'/boohmp-ken/kern*] very small cask made of wooden staves and iron hoops, with a flat top and bottom of equal diameter

> "The morning of this day was rainy, and thereupon with good diligence we saved a **bumpkin** of water." (Basil Ringrose, *Bucaniers of America* Part IV Chap. XXV)

butt [*barrt*] very large cask made of wooden staves and hoops, with a flat top and bottom of equal diameter

The capacity of a butt as a unit of volume varies with its contents—a butt of wine, for example, holds 477 liters, and a butt of beer holds 749 liters.

> "The masts were also in great danger of being rolled by the board, but no harm happened to any of us, besides the loss of three or four **butts** of water ..." (William Dampier, *A New Voyage Round the World* 267)

fathom [*farr-tharrm*] unit of length or depth equal to six feet

> "The bar silver is in the north cache; you can find it by the trend of the east hummock, ten **fathoms** south of the black crag with the face on it." (Captain Flint, in instructions written on his treasure map, *Treasure Island* 33, Chap. 6)

hogshead ['*arrgs/harrgs/'ogs-'ead/hayd*] medium-sized cask made of wooden staves and iron hoops, with a flat top and bottom of equal diameter

The capacity of a hogshead as a unit of volume varies with its contents—a hogshead of wine, for example, holds 239 liters, and a hogshead of beer holds 236 liters.

> "[T]hey had not tasted good salt beef for a long time—and with it we sent them two **hogsheads** of rum." (Captain Avery, *The King of Pirates* 26)

horn [*harrn*] drinking cup or beaker, especially a tall and thin one

> "We had a smooth sea; and now we were come to only three **horns** of water a day, which made in all but a quart allowance for each man." (Basil Ringrose, *Bucaniers of America* Part IV Chap. XXV)

hundred-weight [*arrn/oohn/'un-derd wayeet*] unit of weight equal to about 50 kilograms or 110 U.S. pounds

The term was traditionally employed in England to mean 8 stone, or 4 quarters, roughly equal to 50 kilograms, which in turn equals about 110 U.S. pounds. The unit was later standardized in the U.S., however, as equaling 100 pounds.

> "But bad as the place was, our fortune was much worse. For we came only three days too late to meet with three **hundred weight** of gold ..." (Basil Ringrose, mourning the removal of the gold at Santa Maria to Panama just three days before his company's arrival, *Bucaniers of America* Part IV Chap. III)

leaguer huge cask made of wooden staves and hoops, with a flat top and bottom of equal diameter

The capacity of a leaguer as a unit of volume varies with its contents—a leaguer of wine or water, for example, holds 723 liters.

> "It is also agreed to allow the following particulars for t[h]e use of the officers in the great cabbin of each ship, *viz.* ... half a **leaguer** of Spelman's Neep, or the best sort of arrack[;] ... the third part of a **lea[gue]r** of g[r]ape wine ..." (resolution by officers aboard *Duke* and *Dutchess*, *A Cruising Voyage Round the World* 209)

pace [*payeece*] unit of length equal to the measure of a grown man's full stride from where his heel leaves the ground to where it is next planted, or about two-and-a-half feet or thirty inches

> < "Blowpipe?" "Aye—this! The Indians use 'em longer than this—aye, six foot I've seen 'em, but then, Lord! they'll blow ye a dart from eighty to a hundred **paces** sometimes, whereas I never risk shot farther away than ten or twenty at most; the nearer the surer, aha!" > (Martin Conisby & John, showing off his poison-dart blowpipe, *Martin Conisby's Vengeance* 183)

pound weight [*poun'/pount/powoon'/pow-oond/powoont*] pound or pounds

Note that "pound" is singular whether one pound or more than one pound is intended.

"On the isthmus grows that delicious fruit which we call the pine-apple. ... The fruit is ordinarily about six **pound weight** ..." (Lionel Wafer, *Isthmus of America* 99–100)

puncheon [*parrn/poohn-charrn/chern*] large cask made of wooden staves and hoops, with a flat top and bottom of equal diameter

The capacity of a puncheon as a unit of volume varies with its contents—a puncheon of wine, for example, holds 318 liters.

"While we lay here we scrubbed the bottom of our ship, and then filled all our water-casks, and bought up 2 **puncheons** of rice for our voyage." (William Dampier, *A New Voyage Round the World* 47)

sail (of ships) [*sayell (o'\on sheps)*]

"Sail" or "sail of ships" is often used instead of "ships" when specifying a certain number of them. The phrase serves to emphasize that it is purely the raw count of vessels that is being described, not their quality or nature (as when a modern English speaker uses the phrase "head of cattle").

"At this island we met, being in all seven **sail**, on April 3rd, 1680." (Basil Ringrose, *Bucaniers of America* Part IV Chap. I)
"[T]hey were told at London that we were no less than 5,000 men; that we had built a regular fortress for our defence by land, and that we had twenty **sail of ships**." (Captain Avery, *The King of Pirates* 61)

score [*scarr/scoor*]
(1) set of twenty things

"And yet, I have often heard you say that hook was worth a **score** of hands, for combing the hair and other homely uses." (Smee, *Peter Pan* 60)

(2) period of twenty years

"Flint accused Rip Rap, The treasure ye've stold./Ye took it to the Isle called Dead Man's Chest,/Where ye laid it by fer half a **score**'s rest." (song sung by unnamed drunken pirates aboard the *Eagle*, *Dead Man's Chest* 253)

(3) twenty

"An' I've a **score** bottles of Madeira wine on me shelf what would wash yer throat clean as a maiden's soul, it would." (Long John Silver, *Dead Man's Chest* 27)

NUMBER+score [*... scarr/scoor*] NUMBER times twenty

"There's a deal to be done in keeping **twelvescore** men from fighting on this chunk o' earth and rock!" (John Flint, *Porto Bello Gold* 123)

tierce [*tee-arrce*] small- to medium-sized cask made of wooden staves and iron hoops, with a flat top and bottom of equal diameter

The capacity of a tierce as a unit of volume varies with its contents, though a tierce of wine holds 159 liters.

"We slavers carry little else, you know, than our shackles and a few extra **tierces** of rice; the rest of our ballast is made up of these guns, and the stuff to put into them." (officer aboard the *Dolphin*, *The Red Rover* 87)

16.11 WOMEN

It was 1720, the peak of the golden age of piracy. The pirate was king of the sea.

But when the pirates aboard the *William* were overtaken off Jamaica's Negril Point by a privateer sloop bristling with cannon, they lost all pretense at anything resembling royal composure. Almost as one body, they scrambled down into the ship's hold and cowered in terror.

Only three hands remained on deck, determined to fight. Two were women. One of them, Mary Read, was so disgusted with her comrades that she opened fire—not at the enemy, but down into the hold, hoping to destroy as many of the cowards as possible.

The other, Anne Bonny, later attended the hanging of the craven crew's captain—who also happened to be her lover, Calico Jack Rackham. When it came time for last partings, Bonny was at no loss for words. She looked straight at Rackham and said, "If you had fought like a man, you need not have been hanged like a dog." (*General History of the Pyrates* 151, 156, 165; *Villains of All Nations* 107; *Under the Black Flag* 58–59)

History sometimes gets it wrong. The pirate—at least where 1720 is concerned—was *queen* of the sea.

Below you'll find terms used by pirates to address, refer to, and characterize women. They cover a broad spectrum of meanings and connotations, as they reflect the disparate roles women played in the history and literature of piracy—sometimes queen, often less than that.

On the one hand, women figure in many pirate narratives as mere props. They are plunder to be taken, hostages to be mistreated, forbidden fruit to be craved. Piratical tradition and the articles of many pirate companies prohibited the presence of women aboard—but even these prohibitions, dehumanizingly enough, were not acknowledgment of what the women themselves might do, but rather of the passive peril they posed as prized commodities amidst a conflict-prone crew. Indeed, the alpha and omega of pirate narratives—Robert Louis Stevenson's *Treasure Island*—features no women whatsoever, with only a few plot-neutral references to Jim Hawkins' mother at the start to kick things off. It should come as no surprise, therefore, that many of the pirate terms associated with women are mere proxies for misogyny, conveying dismissive indifference, patronizing disrespect, debasing objectfication, or utter contempt.

On the other hand, women number among the most memorable and charismatic characters in pirate lore. Anne Bonny and Mary Read are significant examples, and their stories catapulted the most important pirate history ever—Captain Charles Johnson's *General History of the Pyrates*—to near-instant popularity in the 1720s (*Villains of All Nations* 104–05). But there are others: Grace O'Malley made Ireland's western coast her personal plundering ground in the late sixteenth century (*Villains of All Nations* 113; *Under the Black Flag* 72–75). Cheng I Sao rose from Canton prostitute to command a pirate fleet of hundreds of vessels and some 50,000 pirates that dominated the South China Sea in 1807–10 (*Under the Black Flag* 75–78).

The women pirates of fiction are no less marginal, including both the bold protagonist (*e.g.*, Captain Joanna in Jeffrey Farnol's *Martin Conisby's Vengeance*, Morgan Adams in "Cutthroat Island") and the critical supporting player (*e.g.*, Purity Pinker in "Long John Silver's Return to Treasure Island" and "Adventures of Long John Silver," Elizabeth Marlowe in James L. Nelson's *The Pirate Round*).

Nothing equalizes like one's hand on a glinting cutlass. Long live the queen.

You'll recall from Chapter 9: Epithets and Chapter 10: Respectful Address that "my" is often used immediately before a term of characterization or address—or "of mine" immediately after it—in order to convey a sly or ironic tone (if the term is meant to disparage) or an amiable or affectionate tone (if the term is neutral or admiring). The same is true of the terms listed below. Thus, one might say "Stop aboard, Lady Scarozza, **my bit of daintiness**" or "Come your ways, Jennifer Lane, **me pearl o' woman-ware**."

armful [*ahrrmful*] an objectifying, sexualized term for a woman or girl

The usage implies that the speaker considers the person so described as someone he would like to or should put his arm around, and accordingly is often used suggestively or lewdly.

> "So—this is she, eh, my lord! This prime **armful** of beauty is your Japhet's woman, ha?" (Roger Snaith, *Winds of Chance* 316)

bag [*barrg*]

A derogatory term for a woman, used to suggest she is ugly or sloppy-looking.

> "Who be this ol' **bag** Willoughby? (Long John Silver, "The Adventures of Long John Silver: The Orphans' Christmas" 4:08)

baggage [*barrgage*]

A derogatory term for a woman or girl. Literally meaning "prostitute," the term is used figuratively to characterize a female—especially a young woman—as impudent, bothersome, or otherwise offensive.

> < "I cry you shame and—" "How then, will ye dare impeach my honour so lightly—and for this—this runaway **baggage**, this murderous shrew?" > (Adam Penfeather & Absalom Troy, *Adam Penfeather, Buccaneer* 110)

bird [*barrd*] a term of affection or endearment for a woman or girl, especially a small, slender, or otherwise physically delicate one, often used ironically or suggestively

> "Come, **my bird**, and drink to our better friendship." (John Sharkey, putting an arm around the waist of his female prisoner, *The Dealings of Captain Sharkey and Other Tales of Pirates* "The Blighting of Sharkey" 55)

bit of a girl [*bet o'\on a gurrell*]
bit of daintiness [*bet o'\on daahn/dayn-terness*]
bit of fluff [*bet o'\on flarrf/floohff*] a diminutive term for a woman or girl

The usage implies the speaker's perception of the person so described as small in some way—whether literally as small-statured, figuratively as cute or fine-featured, or still more metaphorically as appealing in any manner that inspires tenderness or affection.

> "Oh, not for their sake. For the sake of my pledged word, and that **bit of an** Indian **girl** with her baby." (Peter Blood, *Captain Blood Returns* 180) "Here's us cheated of a **bit o' daintiness**, here's Abner wi' all the wind knocked out o' him and now here's you for thieving and robbing three poor lorn sailor-men as never raised hand agin ye—shame, shipmate." (one-eared pirate, *Black Bartlemy's Treasure* 23) "Baron Gruda and his **bit of fluff** left enough clothes onboard to fool the King himself." (pirate in Captain Vallo's company, "The Crimson Pirate" 40:24)

bitch [*betch*] contemptuous term for a woman

Literally meaning "female dog," the term is used figuratively to refer to a woman whom the speaker wishes to disparage or treat or address dismissively.

> "And the great Sargasso Sea, where the seaweed grows living arms that can reach out and strangulate a man-of-war, like crushing a **bitch**'s throat." (Billy Bones, reaching toward the neck of a horrified woman patron of the Admiral Benbow, "Treasure Island" [1960] 7:06)

bunter [*barrn/boohn-ter*] cheap, vulgar woman or girl

The term "bunter" was used literally to refer to a woman who picks up rags and trash in the streets before it came to be used more figuratively to refer to any woman or girl in a demeaning, disparaging way.

> "And none of your nonsense, or I shall shoot you before you are two steps gone. And I shall shoot this little **bunter** first. Or save her for my men." (Roger Press, *The Pirate Round* 61)

chick [*check*] young woman, girl

> < "If I had love' you less, I would have think more of the casket." "To be sure you would, **chick**. To be sure." > (Isabel de Sotomayor & George Fairfax, *The Fortunes of Captain Blood* 157)

claw-cat [*clawrr-carrt*] vicious or dangerous woman or girl

> "'Tis as I guessed ... this shrewish **claw-cat**, this blood-thirsty she-devil ... you love her, eh, my poor lad?" (Absalom Troy, *Adam Penfeather, Buccaneer* 110)

dainty bit [*daahn/dayn-ty bet*] a diminutive term for a woman or girl

> "O mate, yon's a rare **dainty bit**—a sweet armful, Smiler ..." (Red Andy, *Black Bartlemy's Treasure* 139)

damsel [*darrm/daym-sell*] young woman, girl

> "If, as report goes, my pretty **damsel**, you have seen blue water before this passage, you may be able to recollect the name of the vessel ...?" (the captain of the *Dolphin*'s forecastle, addressing young Gertrude, *The Red Rover* 328)

daughter [*darr/dawrr/dott-er*]
A term of fatherly affection for a woman or girl, regardless of relation.

> < "Was I singing? Nay, surely not." "Ay, but you was so! Happy as a bird, merry as any grig, **daughter**." > (Ursula Revell & Lovepeace Farrance, *Winds of Chance* 60–61)

dearie [*'dee-arr/err-ee*]
A term of endearment for a woman.

> "Shift your cargo, **dearie**." (pirate auctioneer, asking a female prisoner to turn around for the crowd, "Pirates of the Caribbean" Disney attraction)

doxy [*darrxy*] a term for a young woman connoting feminine charm, sexual allure, or a tendency toward sexual promiscuity

> "Bishop's girl; the Governor of Jamaica's niece. ... We want her as a hostage for our safety. ... Then let them know that if they attempt to hinder our sailing hence, we'll hang the **doxy** first and fight for it after." (Ogle, *Captain Blood: His Odyssey* 255)

fair piece [*fayarr/fayerr peesh*] an objectifying, sexualized term for an attractive woman

> "Stap me, a **fair piece**, this!" (Andrew Murray, *Porto Bello Gold* 162)

fluttering dove [*flooht/flu'-erin' doohve/dub*] a term of affection or endearment for a woman or girl

The implausibly saccharine descriptor "fluttering" makes it difficult for a speaker to use the term without some irony—that is, without sounding sly, flirtatious, or lewd.

> "Well, here's my little **flutterin' dove**." (member of Blackbeard's company, blocking Edwina Mansfield's path, "Blackbeard the Pirate" 21:55)

gal
An informal term for any young woman or girl.

> "What be your name, **gal**?" (Blackbeard, "Blackbeard the Pirate" 6:38)

girl [*gurrell*]

> "Ye'll have a home somewhere in the world, no doubt. This will help you back to it, my **girl**." (Peter Blood, offering his gold and jewels to a poor young woman, *Captain Blood Returns* 156)

hag [*'ag/harrg*]
A derogatory term for a woman, especially an old one, used to suggest she is ugly, evil, or otherwise offensive.

> "Bottle of rum, you ol' **hag**!" (Billy Bones, "Treasure Island" [1934] 9:54)

hussy [*harr/hooh-ssy*] (1) promiscuous or immoral woman; (2) pert or impudent woman or girl

"Mercy, you **hussy!** you are surely a good twenty years too old for that." (John Sharkey, ridiculing an older, grey-haired woman among his prisoners before heaving her overboard, *The Dealings of Captain Sharkey and Other Tales of Pirates* "The Blighting of Sharkey" 52)

jade [*jayeede*] a contemptuous term for a woman, implying she is a prostitute or an adulteress

"Ask her—go ask Joanna, the curst **jade**." (Captain Belvedere, *Martin Conisby's Vengeance* 67)

lady [*la'y/layeedee*]
Used to refer to a woman with respect or deference.

< "Are you the Ben that gave a gold cross to my maid Deborah?" "Ay, I be so, **lady**." > (Ursula Revell & Ben, *Winds of Chance* 75)

(your) ladyship [(*ya/yarr/ye/yer/yere/yore*) *la'y/layeedee-shep*]
Used to refer to a woman with intense and conspicuous respect or deference.

"The which do mind me as Japhet bid me keep a weather eye on you, likewise, 'for,' says he, 'Jerry,' says he, 'my lady's forever a-standing off and on, backing and filling, plying here and there when least expected, so Jerry,' says he, 'should you run athwart her hawse,' he says, 'take **her** in tow lest she run foul of aught'—them's his orders consarning **your ladyship** ..." (Japhet Bly, as quoted to Ursula Revell by Jeremy Jervey, *Winds of Chance* 231)

lass(ie) [*larrss(ie)*] young woman, girl
< "Fancy the **lass**?" "Aye, that I do." "No wonder. A lovely thing she is." > (Nick Debrett & bald pirate aboard the *Blarney Cock*, "Swashbuckler" 46:59) "Were ya plannin' on makin' yourself clean for the little **lassie**?" (Ben Gunn, *Dead Man's Chest* 258)

maid(en) [*mayeed-(ern)*] young woman or girl, especially an unmarried one; miss

"Moreover, he is young and this **maid** uncommon comely!" (Lovepeace Farrance, *Winds of Chance* 49) "Nay, blench not from me, **maiden**, evil must be driven hence though it be by the sword." (Lovepeace Farrance, *Winds of Chance* 47)

ma'm [*marrm/mem*]
"Ma'm" is a form of address often followed immediately by the name of the addressee.

"For, **ma'm** Ursula, with your every look and gesture it becomes to me the more certain that for your own future good I must presently marry you!" (Japhet Bly, *Winds of Chance* 15)

milady [*mi-la'y/layeedee*]
An elision of "my lady." Used to refer to a woman with intense and conspicuous respect or deference.

"Beggin' yer pardon, **milady**, but might I make so bold as to say yer as wise as you be beautiful?" (Long John Silver, "Long John Silver's Return to Treasure Island" 10:59)

missus [*mers/mess-us*]
A phonetic representation of "Mrs."

"Good evenin', **missus**, lad." (Billy Bones, "Treasure Island" [1990] 3:21)

missy [*messy*] a familiar term for a young woman or girl, typically used either sincerely to express affection or endearment, or mockingly to disparage or reprove

"There's none can save you now, **missy**." (Robert Mullins, *Peter Pan* 160)

pearl o' woman-ware [*payurrl o'\on womern/wom'n-warr/wayarr/wayerr*] an objectifying term for an attractive woman
The usage implies both that the person so described is attractive, and that she is an item or thing to be owned, used, or admired.

"Is she not a **pearl o'** dainty **woman-ware**, Captain, a sweet and luscious piece, a passionate, proud beauty worth the taming—ha, Captain?" (Black Bartlemy, *Black Bartlemy's Treasure* 86)

petticoat [*peh'i/petter-coot/co'oot*] young woman, girl

The term objectifies the woman by characterizing her in the implicitly dismissive terms of what she wears.

> "It's that cursed **petticoat**'s making a coward of you." (Wolverstone, *Captain Blood: His Odyssey* 252)

piece [*peesh*] an objectifying term for a woman or girl

> "Ain't they a handsome pair o' young **pieces**, squire's son?" (Billy Doyle, bringing out two women prisoners for Alan Lewrie to see, *The Gun Ketch* 159)

pigeon [*peh-jern*] a term of affection or endearment for a woman or girl, often used ironically or suggestively

> "But seeing thou is selling these **pigeons** to Baron Gruda anyway, I thought 'twould be no harm to sport with 'em a bit first." (Humble Bellows, "The Crimson Pirate" 53:16)

poppet [*parr-pert*] used to refer to a young woman or girl, often ironically or suggestively, and especially to refer to a thin, small, or attractive one

> "We know you're here, **poppet**." (Pintel, "Pirates of the Caribbean: The Curse of the Black Pearl" 33:46)

pretty [*preh'y*] an admiring, and typically lewd or suggestive, term used to address a woman or girl

> "Tell me, **my pretty**, why you were so mishandled and laid in the bilboes aboard yonder craft?" (John Sharkey, *The Dealings of Captain Sharkey and Other Tales of Pirates* "The Blighting of Sharkey" 55)

pullet [*pullert/pul't*] used to refer to a young woman or girl, often ironically or suggestively

> "There'll be more o' that to follow, my **pullet**, unless your loutish husband comes to his senses." (unnamed pirate impersonator of Peter Blood, *The Fortunes of Captain Blood* 48)

puss young woman or girl

> "Come, my proud witch, sweet **puss**, be seated here betwixt us—sit, I say!" (Roger Snaith, *Winds of Chance* 318)

she-devil [*she-daahv/dayv/debb/div-il*] depraved or wicked woman or girl

> "'Tis as I guessed ... this shrewish clawcat, this blood-thirsty **she-devil** ... you love her, eh, my poor lad?" (Absalom Troy, *Adam Penfeather, Buccaneer* 110)

she-snake [*she-snayeeke*] treacherous, conniving, or deceitful woman or girl

> "Aye, but what o' Joanna, what o' that **she-snake**, ha?" (Captain Belvedere, *Martin Conisby's Vengeance* 68)

shrew [*shroo*] ill-tempered, nagging, troublesome, or vicious woman

> < "I cry you shame and—" "How then, will ye dare impeach my honour so lightly—and for this—this runaway baggage, this murderous **shrew**?" > (Adam Penfeather & Absalom Troy, *Adam Penfeather, Buccaneer* 110)

slip of a TERM FOR WOMAN OR GIRL [*slep o'\on a* ...] a diminutive term for a woman or girl

The speaker inserts after "slip of a" a noun referring to the person described, whether a generic description (*e.g.*, "woman," "girl"), a more colorful characterization (*e.g.*, "dove," "lass," or some other term listed here in this section), or a specific identification (*e.g.*, "wife," "nurse").

> "He's said more to his **slip of a murderess** in this short while than to me since I

hauled him to his spindle-shanks." (Absalom Troy, *Adam Penfeather, Buccaneer* 31)

strumpet [*stroohm-pert*] a contemptuous term for a woman, implying she is a prostitute or an adulteress

> "Or perhaps the reason you practice three hours a day is that you already found one, and are otherwise incapable of wooing said **strumpet**." (Jack Sparrow, "Pirates of the Caribbean: The Curse of the Black Pearl" 24:54)

sweet soul [*sweet sool/so'ool*]
sweetlips [*sweetleps*] honey; sweetheart

> < "How woundily you misjudged your humble, gentle Japhet!" "Because he was nowise humble or gentle." "Howbeit you shall never tremble at him again, **sweet soul**." > (Japhet Bly & Ursula Revell, *Winds of Chance* 309) "No, no, this place is very well and here we camp, at the least I and my lady **Sweetlips**; your lordship may camp where he will." (Roger Snaith, *Winds of Chance* 320)

termagant [*tarrme-gernt*] ill-tempered or malicious woman

> "Now curse your prating insolence ... to flout and give me the lie ... and all for this **termagent**. ..." (Absalom Troy, *Adam Penfeather, Buccaneer* 110)

tit [*tet*] a contemptuous and highly objectifying, sexualized term for a woman

The term overtly objectifies the woman by equating her with one of her (secondary) sexual organs.

> "I give ye me Bible-oath no harm'll come t' these young **tits**, an' I'll leave 'em safe an' sound on French Cay'r West Caicos." (Billy Doyle, offering Alan Lewrie the lives

of his women prisoners in exchange for a clean getaway, *The Gun Ketch* 160)

vixen [*vex-ern/ing*] a term for a fierce, harsh, cross, or malicious woman

> "Let me blast that buzzing **vixen** to pixie hell." (Smee, "Hook" 48:34)

wench [*wanch*]

The term was used literally to refer to a prostitute before it came to be used more figuratively to refer demeaningly to any young woman or girl.

> "Ain't she a handsome **wench**, Navy?" (Billy Doyle, knifing his woman prisoner's gown away from her body, *The Gun Ketch* 161)

white ewe lamb [*wawt/whyeete ewer larrmb/lemm*] young woman or girl; a term of affection or endearment for a woman or girl, often used ironically or suggestively

> "So hast found the damsel, Brother, this **white ewe lamb** that young Japhet hath reft hither so ungently." (Ezekiel Penryn, *Winds of Chance* 47)

witch [*wetch*] a hyperbolic term for a fierce, harsh, cross, or malicious woman

> < "Oh, I very much doubt if Miss Willoughby will let the children accept your gifts." "She'd better, or else I'll keel-'aul the ol' **witch**." > (Reverend Monaster & Long John Silver, "The Adventures of Long John Silver: The Orphans' Christmas" 6:03)

woman [*womern/wom'n*]

> < "I told you before and I say it again: half the Cask & Anchor be yours the day you lead me to the altar." "That's bribery and corruption! I will not be pushed around, **woman**!" > (Purity Pinker & Long John Silver, "The Adventures of Long John Silver: Devil's Stew" 4:07)

CHAPTER 17

Pronunciation

Pirates come from all over.

A fifth of those afloat in 1716–26 were Irish, Scottish, and Welsh; a quarter from the Americas (many from Jamaica and the Bahamas); and seven percent from places like Holland, France, Portugal, Denmark, Belgium, Sweden, Calabar, Sierra Leone, and Whydah. Black men sailed on nearly every pirate vessel (*Villains of All Nations* 52–54). Henry Morgan's men during the 1668 attack on Porto Bello included Italians, Dutchmen, and Portuguese (*Under the Black Flag* 15).

The pirates of fiction were similarly diverse. The crew aboard the *Red Rover* included eleven non-British/American ethnicities, including Russian, German, and Native American Indian. Captain Jo in *Martin Conisby's Vengeance* was the daughter of a Spanish governor and his English wife, raised by Indians from childhood, then abducted and raised by "white men" of undisclosed ethnicity.

Indeed, the *Primer* itself excerpts the speech of pirates from Ireland (Peter Blood, *Captain Blood*), Scotland (MacTavish, "The Black Pirate"), Wales (Crabtree, *Winds of Chance*), the Orkney Islands (John Gow, *General History of the Pyrates*, *Lives of the Most Remarkable Criminals*), France (LeRois, *The Guardship*; Cahusac, *Captain Blood Returns*), Greece (Salamander the Greek, "The Adventures of Long John Silver"), Italy (Tony, *Winds of Chance*), Holland (Bullwinkle, "Blackbeard the Pirate"), Denmark (Captain Jonsen, *A High Wind in Jamaica*), Austria (Otto, *A High Wind in Jamaica*), and even the Incan empire (Yupanaqui, a.k.a. Will, *Winds of Chance*).

Differences in education tended further to widen the language gap among pirates. Though the typical pirate, like the typical seaman, was poor and illiterate, Peter Blood was a Trinity College-trained doctor, Henry Mainwaring a lawyer, Stede Bonnet a Barbados gentleman, and both *Peter Pan*'s Captain James Hook and *Dead Man Chest*'s Long John Silver were graduates of Oxford.

So did all pirates talk the same? Carrse not. But there were common tendencies. After all, fully half of pirates sailing in the early eighteenth-century were English (*Villians of All Nations* 52–53). To the extent most of them hailed from port towns specifically, and from the West Country (southwestern England) generally, they shared certain speech patterns. Pirates perpetuated those speech patterns with their frequent visits to fishing waters to recruit new blood—usually the low-wage earners manning West Country fishing vessels (*Pirates of the New England Coast* 339; *General History of the Pyrates* 347–48). And many of the rest had incentive to tend toward the vocabularies and pronunciations of the majority in their effort to assimilate themselves as respected members of their respective companies.

Pirate speech is distinctive not only for the words used (as explored in Part I) but also for the ways in which those words are pronounced. Take, for example, the following excerpt:

"I don't 'member speakin' to yer likes 'afore." (Henry Morgan, *Dead Man's Chest* 128)

Morgan drops an entire syllable ("'member" instead of "remember"), omits letters ("speakin'" instead of "speaking," "'afore" instead of "before"), and—even when he decides to keep his syllables and letters—pronounces some of them very differently ("yer" instead of "your"). Those habits are quite typical of pirates everywhere.

This chapter is the definitive guide to how pirates pronounce their syllables (Section 17.1), their consonants (Section 17.2), and their vowels (Section 17.3).

See also Appendix B at the back of the *Primer* for a complete English-Pirate dictionary of sounds: a great way of seeing at a glance how pirates turn the English language, letter by letter, sound by sound, into something else entirely.

☠

17.1 SYLLABLES

17.1.1 STARTING SYLLABLES

Omit the first syllables of words. Do so especially (1) when the starting syllable consists entirely of a single vowel or vowel sound or (2) when what remains is a consonant-vowel-consonant combination, such that it is easily recognized as a stand-in for the full word.

Thus, words like "against," "above," and "escape" are almost never pronounced in their entirety. Pirates are more likely to pronounce them: "'gainst," "'bove," and "'scape."

- "This is jus' like what the Greeks done at Troy. 'Cept they was in a horse, 'stead of dresses." (Ragetti, "Pirates of the Caribbean: The Curse of the Black Pearl" 1:49:07)

- "Seems I 'member you sayin' that once ya reached Bristol, ye'd never set foot 'board a ship again." (Long John Silver, *Dead Man's Chest* 295)

- "I do 'spect yer lads're thirsty, hey?" (Billy Doyle, attempting to bribe Alan Lewrie out of demanding surrender by offering him liquor and loot, *The Gun Ketch* 159)

17.1.2 MIDDLE SYLLABLES

Omit middle syllables of words. Do so especially when a middle syllable consists wholly or principally of a single vowel or vowel sound.

- "And you don't have to ask the **Gov'nor** for no permission, neither." (Israel Hands, "Treasure Island" [1998] 40:10)

- "Here, where at did you learn your **doct'rin**'?" (Blackbeard, interviewing his new ship's surgeon, "Blackbeard the Pirate" 11:41)

- "It's a very favourite lark with these **'xtr'or'nary** critters." (Bloody Bill, explaining the island native custom of surf-swimming, *The Coral Island* 236)

17.2 CONSONANTS

17.2.1 EXTREME CONSONANTS

Intensify consonants by pronouncing them harder and longer. Where consonants involve lips or teeth or throat, snap or click them more sharply, harshly, and loudly. Where they involve blowing or hissing, blow or hiss more vigorously. If possible, extend them by intoning, blowing, rolling, or hissing them longer than a modern speaker ordinarily might.

Do so especially with the consonants "r" (pronounced as a rolling growl) and "t" (pronounced with a hard, spitting sound).

- "You'll see, lad: Willoughby won't refuse them pretty presents. Err, but if she do, why then **ou-rr parr-ty**'ll fall flatter than a serpent's stomach." (Long John Silver, "The Adventures of Long John Silver: The Orphans' Christmas" 8:19)

- < "Them that live'll have a tale to tell." "If anyone does live." "It's that or stay here and be **slaugh-tt-ered**." > (Long John Silver & Old Stingley, discussing a proposed trek through the Panamanian

jungle, "The Adventures of Long John Silver: Pieces of Eight" 8:09)

17.2.2 STARTING CONSONANTS

Omit consonants or consonant blends at the beginning of words. Do so especially with the consonant "h."

- < "What good is a **'ostage**, and **'im** bad **'urt**?" "Why, you knothead. With **'im** bad hurt, they'll part with the map to save his life." > (George Merry & Long John Silver, "Treasure Island" [1950] 1:16:16)

- "We'll **'eave** to and wait for **'em**, and thank **'em** for runnin' off the pirates." (Long John Silver, planning a friendly encounter with a French warship, "The Adventures of Long John Silver: Turnabout" 3:55)

Note that, while pirates tend to omit starting consonants, they do so inconsistently.

- "**Here**, how did you get in **'ere**?" (Long John Silver, "The Adventures of Long John Silver: The Pink Pearl" 17:16)

17.2.3 MIDDLE CONSONANTS

Consecutive Consonants

Pronounce consecutive consonant sounds ("frightful", "captain") as if one were missing ("frigh'ful", "cap'n").

- "Top o' the marnin', **gen'lemen**." (Long John Silver, "Treasure Island" [1950] 16:42)

- "We wants the **red'ead**, we wants the **red'ead**!" (pirates at auction, "Pirates of the Caribbean" Disney attraction)

- "Stop your clapper, Jack. Give the boy a junk o' meat. Don't you see he's **a'most** going to kick the bucket?" (pirate, *The Coral Island* 201–02)

Inter-Vowel Consonants

Omit consonants or consonant combinations intervening between vowels that might be pronounced together.

- "You hand it over, and we'll put your town to our rudder, and ne'er return." (Barbossa, "Pirates of the Caribbean: The Curse of the Black Pearl" 40:11)

- "[A]nd you bein' on watch o'er him, an' all!" (Long John Silver, *Dead Man's Chest* 7)

- "Who knows when that evil curse will strike the greedy be'olders of this bewitched treasure." (foreboding pirate voice, "Pirates of the Caribbean" Disney attraction)

17.2.4 ENDING CONSONANTS

Omit consonants at the end of words. Do so especially when the penultimate consonant is "n" (*e.g.*, "found," "praying"), such that the last consonant's omission results in the word ending with this "n" sound instead ("foun'," "prayin'").

- "Go an' bring help. And don' peach. And I'll go shares." (William Bones, "Treasure Island" [1950] 8:45)

- "Listen, are we goin' to stand aroun' growin' older, or attack the stockade an' get the treasure map?" (George Merry, "Treasure Island" [1998] 1:17:48)

- "Aye, aye, we'm wi' you! Gi'e us the word, Cap'n!"(pirates in Roger Tressady's company, *Black Bartlemy's Treasure* 314)

Note that the practice of omitting ending consonants is an inconsistent one.

"Ursula, there be eyes o' poor wretches that, groaning 'neath the lash, beholding this flag, ha' forgot their agony, have shouted for joy, because they knew it brought them deliverance from their cruel bondage, back to life or quick and merciful death."(Ezekiel Penryn, *Winds of Chance* 48)

17.3 VOWELS

17.3.1 EXTREME VOWELS

Intensify vowels by exaggerating their tone (away from the neutral schwa and deeper into

their distinctive mouth position), lengthening their duration, or both.

- "Mind what I say, Mas'r Hawkins, and don't try to fly the coop agayn." (Long John Silver, "Treasure Island" [1950] 1:25:44)

- "This one he hauled here and laid down by compass to point the way to the doublooooons." (Long John Silver, "Treasure Island" [1950] 1:27:14)

- "To Jim Hawkins, who's beeeen like a son ta me, an equal share in all the booty the *Faithful* collects until he be eighteen years of age." (Long John Silver, composing his will, "The Adventures of Long John Silver: Execution Dock" 8:34)

17.3.2 STARTING VOWELS

Dropped Starting Vowels

Omit vowels at the beginnings of words. Do so especially when the starting vowel or vowel sound alone constitutes the first syllable of a word.

- "He wasn't dead when I got round to him, not he." (Long John Silver, *Treasure Island* 107, Chap. 20)

- "P'r'aps you can understand King George's English. I'm cap'n here by 'lection." (Long John Silver, *Treasure Island* 159, Chap. 28)

- "Aye, an' I'd wear 'is ears 'bout me neck fer a right fine trophy, I would." (Henry Morgan, *Dead Man's Chest* 11)

Breathy Starting Vowels

Add an "h" sound to the start of a word beginning with a vowel, so that it begins with a breathy sound.

- < "Err, and put the ladies in the Dutchman's cabin." "You mean you trust the Dutchman in the same cabin with—." "No, throw the Dutchman in the horlop

[orlop]." > (Blackbeard & Ben Worley, "Blackbeard the Pirate" 8:17)

- "These are some precious family **hair-looms [heirlooms]**, what I've always refused to be parted from, even in times of direst adversity." (Thomas Bartholomew Red, attempting to bribe the *Neptune*'s carpenter into repairing his wooden leg, "Pirates" 23:29)

17.3.3 MIDDLE VOWELS

Dropped Middle Vowels

Omit vowels intervening between consonants that might be pronounced together.

- "Try **reas'n'n'** first, says I. I never was one to see poor seamen shot down needlesslike." (Long John Silver, "Treasure Island" [1950] 58:55)
- "**P'r'aps** you'll be able to conjure up another miraculous escape, but I doubt it." (Barbossa, "Pirates of the Caribbean: The Curse of the Black Pearl" 1:34:07)
- < "Ned ... is my brother here?" "No, sir. **Bleeve** he was took aboard the Cap'n's boat ... the longboat, sir." > (Ned Bowser, *Adam Penfeather, Buccaneer* 165)

Sweet Middle Vowels

Replace vowels or vowel sounds that intervene between consonants with the sweeter sound "ee" or "y". The closer the original vowel or vowel sound to "ee" or "y" to begin with, the more likely it is to be sweetened.

- "Too bad an **uneddycated** seaman can't open his head and see just what he's got in it." (Long John Silver, "Treasure Island" [1934] 40:13)
- < "I would join your Company." "Wud ye, now? An' what are your **qualeefee-cations**?" > (Michel & MacTavish, "The Black Pirate" 20:45)

- "We'd oughter take him to the South Seas and sell him to the **canneybals**." (Billy Bones, *Porto Bello Gold* 59)

Dark Middle Vowels

Add "r" or "rr" to vowels or vowel sounds that intervene between consonants. Modify the vowel sound to allow that darkening.

- "Batten 'em down, and let 'em **suffer-cate**, the thievin' scum!" (Blackbeard, "Blackbeard the Pirate" 1:29:55)
- < "I promise you, Long John Silver, should you ever venture beyond the breakwater, I will peel your skin like a mango." "You make it sound real **ap-pertizing**." > (El Toro Mendoza & Long John Silver, "Long John Silver's Return to Treasure Island" 28:26)
- < "Since the day you give him that sloop, the lad's not been himself anymore." "Arrgh, he be Christopher **Cer-lumbus**, watching America loom up through the mist." > (Purity Pinker & Long John Silver, "The Adventures of Long John Silver: Ship o' the Dead" 1:48)

17.3.4 ENDING VOWELS

Sweet Ending Vowels

Replace vowels or vowel sounds at the ends of words with the sweeter sound "ee" or "y".

- "If I may make so bold, sir, I'll **borry** your boat, I ain't takin' you to Jamaiker." (Long John Silver, "Treasure Island" [1950] 1:32:09)
- "It was main hot, and the **windy** was open, and I hear that old song comin' out as clear as clear—and the death-haul on the man a'ready." (unnamed pirate, *Treasure Island* 178, Chap. 31)
- "I'll lay you a piece of eight the captain never so much as sarves out a **extry** noggin o' rum." (Long John Silver, *Porto Bello Gold* 48)

Dark Ending Vowels

With words that end in vowels, add the "r" or "rr" sound at the end. Modify the vowel sound to allow that darkening.

- "Yonder lies **Jamaiker** and straight we sail for it!" (Peter Blood, "Captain Blood" 1:36:30)

- "No, his best men were we and ecod, Deb, 'twas me as roared and **bellered** and sang out loudest." (Ben, *Winds of Chance* 101)

- "Another **swaller** may well be sendin' me to Davy Jones." (gluttonous pirate, "Pirates of the Caribbean" Disney attraction [2005])

17.3.5 DIPHTHONGS

A diphthong is a pair of vowel sounds pronounced smoothly and continuously. The word "pie," for example, consists of the letter "p," then a diphthong featuring (1) the vowel sound "ah" and (2) the vowel sound "ee." The sounds "ah" and "ee" are pronounced continuously, such that they constitute almost a single sound with two phases. Pirates do one of two things with diphthongs: They either intensify the constituent vowel sounds or drop one vowel sound and keep the other.

Extreme Diphthongs

Intensify diphthongs by exaggerating the tone of either or both of the vowel sounds, by lengthening the duration of either or both of the vowel sounds, or by doing both. Thus, "pie" becomes "pah-eee."

- "Then it'd go hard with Long John if you was to turn it in **now-oo**." (Long John Silver, "Treasure Island" [1950] 32:24)

- "Shiver my timbers, a land lubber **I-ee-ull** never be!" (Long John Silver, "Long John Silver's Return to Treasure Island" 51:58)

- "**How-oo** can you stand **by-ee** and **al-low-oo** such things, Reverend?" (Long John Silver, "The Adventures of Long John Silver: The Orphans' Christmas" 5:01)

Dropped Diphthongs

Drop one of the vowel sounds of a diphthong—typically, but not always, the first of the two—while keeping the other.

- "Here's Tom and John and Bess and Jarge and Caroline and Mary and Ben and Ruth and Dick and Mercy and James and **Willum**, and all on 'em ready." (Jeremy Jervey, showing off his artillery to visitor Ursula Revell, *Winds of Chance* 213)

  Not "Will-ee-am."

- "Well, sir, by your leave, sir, John Silver's come back to do his **dooty**." (Long John Silver, "Treasure Island" [1950] 1:30:02)

  Not "d-ee-ooty."

- "Then we barges off from an **ekally** safe lay on the Main." (Long John Silver, *Porto Bello Gold* 49)

  Not "equally," which in reality is a highly continuous "eek-oo-a-lly."

CHAPTER 18

Wrong Talk

Blackbeard was the most famous pirate in history. Francis Drake and Bartholomew Roberts were the most successful. But the cruelest and most depraved pirate of all time, by a long sea-mile, was an Englishman by the name of Edward Low.

> For the facts reflected in the following narrative, and more on Edward Low, see *General History of the Pyrates* 334–35; *Pirates of the New England Coast* 214; and *The Pirates Own Book* 250.

One afternoon in June 1723, Low captured two whaling sloops near Rhode Island. Low cut off the ears of one of the captains, roasted and sprinkled them with salt and pepper, and then forced the man to eat them.

The other captain had his chest split open and his heart torn out—which, like his colleague's ears, was roasted. Of course, he did not survive long enough for further torture.

So Low instead gave the cooked heart to the victim's first mate to eat.

Low's reputation for brutality was prodigious. Once, when he took a Virginia ship, he greeted her captain with a bowl of rum punch. Captain Graves, so terrified he could not swallow, apologetically declined the drink. Low immediately whipped out a pistol, cocked it, then—holding punch in one hand and gun in the other—said: "Either take one or the other."

In the next moment, Graves did two smart things: He guzzled down a quart of punch. And he did not correct Low's grammar by saying something like, "It's 'Either take one or take the other,' not 'Either take one or the other.' Your sentence lacks parallel construction."

The single most important principle of pirate grammar is this: Pirates talk wrong. Whatever the rules of English grammar and syntax, pirates don't respect them.

This is not to say that they violate every rule at every opportunity—that would be too predictable, too conventional. The real rule of pirate grammar is that there are no rules. This chapter explores "Wrong Talk," the principle of pirate speech that the only right way of speaking is speaking wrong well. After outlining some basic Wrong Talk in Section 18.1, the *Primer* will cover four particularly important kinds of Wrong Talk: Redundancy (18.2), Double Negative (18.3), Malapropism (18.4), and Inconsistency (18.5).

18.1 BASIC WRONG TALK

One example of Wrong Talk is "switching." Pirates often "switch" their way into Wrong Talk by using the grammatical opposite of the correct form of speech. Take, for example, the sentence, **"I know they boldly sailed three ships through the channel last week."** That shiny sentence would never make its way out of a pirate's mouth. A pirate would instead do any or all of the following:

- **Replace the first-person verb with third-person.**

  "I ~~know~~ **knows** they boldly sailed three ships through the channel last week."

- **Replace the past tense verb with present (singular or plural).**

  "I knows they boldly ~~sailed~~ **sail** three ships through the channel last week."

- **Replace a plural verb with a singular, and/or a plural noun with a singular.**

  "I knows they boldly ~~sail~~ **sails** three ~~ships~~ **ship** through the channel last week."

- **Replace a nominative pronoun with its objective counterpart.**

  "I knows ~~they~~ **them** boldly sails three ship through the channel last week."

- **Replace an adverb with an adjective.**

  "I knows them ~~boldly~~ **bold** sails three ship through the channel last week."

A pirate might further drop the article "the," and use the pirate equivalent of "last week," so our sentence finally reads:

"I knows them bold sails three ship through channel this last week."

A pirate might choose any of the above alternative sentences, depending on how "wrong" he wants to talk and how much switching he wants to do. Pirate speech is a highly creative and highly violent (to the English language) process. In addition to switching (which will be covered more later), pirates also take random advantage of the rules of grammar. Below are a few examples of their miscellaneous transgressions. Each example sets out a pirate's "wrong" way of talking, then the "right," grammatically correct, version. The point of these examples is not to encourage mimicry, but awareness and inspiration.

Read them, then be wrongful and multiply.

- **misplaced contraction**

  Wrong: "Who give me**'ll** a hand, I say?" (Long John Silver, "Treasure Island" [1950] 1:00:13)

  Right: "Who**'ll** give me a hand, I say?"

- **wrong verb**

  Wrong: "Reckon we **got** more important things to talk about here." (Ezekiel Ripley, *The Guardship* 131)

  Right: "Reckon we **have** more important things to talk about here."

- **non-parallelism**

Wrong: "We're in no case either **to run or fight**." (Ogle, *Captain Blood: His Odyssey* 254)

Right: "We're in no case either **to run or to fight**."; "We're in no case to either **run or fight**."

- **wrong comparative adjective**

Wrong: "[K]now me for Lovepeace Farrance the gunner, once cornet of Oliver's horse, and one that helped to slay a wicked king. But there came a **wickeder** that tore poor Noll from 's grave, hanged him on gibbet and buried his poor bones shamefully." (Lovepeace Farrance, introducing himself to Ursula Revell, *Winds of Chance* 47)

Right: "... there came a **more wicked** that tore ..."

- **wrong superlative adjective**

Wrong: "My lord, it is a very hard sentence. For my part, I am the **innocentest** person of them all, only I have been sworn against by perjured persons." (William Kidd, on hearing his sentence of death after conviction on charges of piracy and murder, *Under the Black Flag* 189)

Right: "... I am the **most innocent** person of them all ..."

- **"less" vs. "fewer"**

Wrong: < "We can't leave yet, Captain. We haven't put enough food on board." "We need **less** mouths." > (pirate aboard *Reaper* & Dawg Brown, just before Dawg Brown shoots another pirate, "Cutthroat Island" 44:42)

Right: "We need **fewer** mouths."

- **"much" vs. "many"**

Wrong: < "Arrgh, mutiny, ey?" "Aye, one stupid order too **much**." > (Blackbeard & Ben Worley, "Blackbeard the Pirate" 52:34)

Right: "Aye, one stupid order too **many**."

18.2 REDUNDANCY

Redundancy is a type of overstatement in which an idea is needlessly expressed in more than one way. For example, in the movie "Captain Kidd," two of William Kidd's enemies—Adam Mercy (whom Kidd suspects of being some kind of double-dealing spy) and Jose Lorenzo (who knows where Kidd's treasure is buried, confound him)—are discovered aboard the *Adventure* engaged in brutal swordfight. Kidd's sidekick, Orange Povy, lurches forward as if to intervene, but Kidd stops him, muttering: "Use your head, Mister Povy. Luck's with us tonight. **Which of either of them** would you like to see survive?"

The phrase "Which of either of them" is a redundancy. That is, the term "which" already implies a choice, rendering the term "either" unnecessary. Kidd could and should have said "**Which** of them would you like to see survive?" or "Would you like to see **either** of them survive?"

18.2.1 INCIDENTAL REDUNDANCY

The following are examples in which pirates use redundancy incidentally. That is, the redundancy is likely not deliberate and does not in any way intensify or make more colorful the main idea of the sentence.

Incidental redundancy, though typically not a conscious choice, is nevertheless an interesting—and sometimes comical—example of the ungrammatical speech of pirates.

- "**Your** modern life **of yours** seems to have got small." (Blackbeard, "Blackbeard's Ghost" 37:14)

- "It's a key!" "No! Much **more better**. It is a drawring of a key." (Marty & Jack Sparrow, "Pirates of the Caribbean 2: Dead Man's Chest" 8:15)

- < "Do you seek any one in especial?" "Why, not **especially in particklar**, sir." >

(Bob Ormerod & Long John Silver, *Porto Bello Gold* 23)

- "And back comes Flint, **all alone**, and **by hisself**, aye." (Ben Gunn, "Treasure Island" [1990] 59:49)
- "This is a very difficult channell and **many severall** wayes are given to saile it, but few good ones ..." (Basil Ringrose, describing the difficulty of sailing from Lapuna to Guayaquil, *The South Sea Waggoner* Chart 56–57)

18.2.2 STYLISTIC REDUNDANCY

Pirates often use redundancy deliberately to make a point more firmly, more colorfully, and more memorably. Saying "I'll be with you **ever and always**," for example, cues the imagination in a way that the bland "I'll be with you **always**" simply does not. Below are notable examples of stylistic redundancy.

- "[T]hose that desires to go ashore and **enjoy their ease in comfort** can look to receiving free pardons." (Long John Silver quoting Andrew Murray, *Porto Bello Gold* 50)
- "You'll accept a noggin or two **free, gratis and for nothin'**, won't ya?" (Purity Pinker, "The Adventures of Long John Silver: The Necklace" 9:10)
- "I volunteered for blind curiosity, hopin' for to discover what he was up to, and I'm free to say **I've had my trouble for my pains**." (Long John Silver, *Porto Bello Gold* 50)
- "'Tis all **right and straight** as it should be." (Abraham Dawling, satisfied on examining the letter verifying Barnaby True's identity, *The Book of Pirates* "The Ghost of Captain Brand" 47)
- And I'll give you my affidavy, upon my **word and honor**, that we'll set ya down safe and sound at the first point o' civilization." (Long John Silver, "Treasure Island" [1934] 1:04:44)

18.3 DOUBLE NEGATIVE

By November 1718, the governor of Virginia had had enough. Blackbeard had taken twenty ships in two years, and showed no signs of slowing. Governor Spotswood turned to the Virginia Station of the Royal Navy.

Five days later, at dawn, off North Carolina's Okracoke Island, Lieutenant Robert Maynard's sloop crept toward Blackbeard's. Having ordered most of his crew into the hold, only Maynard and his helmsman remained on deck. Blackbeard, seeing so few men aboard, urged his men to do what pirates do best: "Let's jump on board, and cut them to pieces."

Maynard's men rushed the deck from below, taking Blackbeard's men by surprise. The two leaders squared off. Blackbeard fought hard with pistol and cutlass, even after Maynard shot him. Even after Maynard shot him again. Only after being shot five times and receiving twenty sword wounds—the twentieth lifting his head and beard clean off his body—did the legendary Blackbeard fall. (*General History of the Pyrates* 77–82; *Under the Black Flag* 194–99)

Two hundred and thirty-four years later, the 1952 film "Blackbeard the Pirate" showed Blackbeard seeking medical attention for a gunshot wound. When the ship's surgeon learns the bullet in his patient's neck lodged there at daybreak, he asks in wonder: "You carried this all day and stayed on your feet?" The pirate's answer:

"Why not? A bullet don't weigh nothin'." ("Blackbeard the Pirate" 12:26)

The response is solid comedy, and moreover a satisfying reference to the real Blackbeard's iron constitution. The response also reflects a figure of speech near and dear to the heart of pirates everywhere: the Double Negative.

The Double Negative (*e.g.*, "there **ain't nothing** wrong with me") is the king of wrong talk. Modern English speakers tend to associate the Double Negative with exceptionally bad grammar. Why? Three reasons:

1. The Double Negative is a type of redundancy—two negatives in place of one. Like all redundancies, it suggests the speaker is a bumbler who pays no attention to what he has said or is about to say.

2. The Double Negative isn't just a problem of form. It's a problem of substance, meaning the exact opposite of what the speaker intends to say. Taken literally, "there ain't nothing wrong with me" means, of course, that there is indeed something wrong with me.

3. Finally, the Double Negative is painful to hear in the same way that a sermonizing preacher with an unzipped fly is painful to see. The speaker is simultaneously passionate (the Double Negative is almost always used for emphasis or to convey a definitive position) and thoroughly oblivious, and watching someone proceed in utter ignorance yet steely conviction is absurd, discomfiting stuff.

Thus, the Double Negative is the calling card of the hopeless ne'er-do-well. Use it, therefore, and use it often.

Here are some good examples of the pirate's Double Negative.

- "**B'ain't** you **no** love in your hearts for the peace and beauty of this here tropical island?" (Long John Silver, "Long John Silver's Return to Treasure Island" 1:13:29)

- "You'll have to risk that. You **can't** land them **no** other place." (Otto, *A High Wind in Jamaica* 220)

- "But we was talkin' o' cripples and how a blind man can steer, which is a long way off from Bill, who **isn't neither** crippled nor blind ..." (Long John Silver, *Porto Bello Gold* 65)

- < "Alligators?" "Ay, lady, you'll see plenty o' they. But, Lord, they **won't nowise** trouble you, if you don't go a-troubling o' they." > (Ursula Revell & Jeremy Jervey, *Winds of Chance* 248–49)

Note also the occasional use by pirates of the Triple Negative:

- "No, no!, you can't quarrel wi' me, the Smiler **don't never** quarrel wi' **none**." (Sam Spraggons, *Black Bartlemy's Treasure* 128)

- "Lord love ee, there **couldn't never** be such mutinous riot on **no** ship commanded by Cap'n Japhet and you can lay to that!" (Ben, *Winds of Chance* 101)

- "Lookee now, when I goes for to kiss a woman, she ain't agoin' for to deny me, no nor **nobody** else **ain't neither**, and anybody as says me different ..." (Abner, raving in a drunken fit, *Adam Penfeather, Buccaneer* 14)

Finally, it is a pleasure to introduce in these pages the four-minute mile, the Hope diamond, the *tour de force* of pirate speech. Impressive for its sheer excess, and nearly incomprehensible as a logical matter, it is, ladies and gentlemen—the Quadruple Negative:

- < "And why must ye scowl on the lady, Absalom?" "Why, sir, I **never** knowed **no** manner o' luck on **no** ship **nowhen** and **nowhere**, wi' unmarried fe-males aboard." > (Lovepeace Farrance & Absalom Troy, *Winds of Chance* 49)

(Note the last negative term in the above excerpt—"nowhere"—is parallel with and not additive to "nowhen" and, therefore, regretfully does not result in a Quintuple Negative.)

18.4 MALAPROPISM

By 1660, the island of Tortuga was the greatest buccaneer stronghold in history. It goes without saying, therefore, that Tortuga was a lawless, riotous, chaotic place. Attacked four times by the Spanish between 1629 and 1654, and fractured by perennial infighting between English and French buccaneers, Tortuga was a roiling cauldron of war and upheaval. The capital of Cayonne was little more than a collection of taverns, with a harbor to bring in the patrons and houses to shelter them between drinking bouts. In 1645, Tortuga's governor imported fifteen hundred prostitutes from Paris—hoping they would have a steadying effect on the unruly population.

Jack Sparrow must have been speaking figuratively, therefore, when he ambled through the heart of harborfront Cayonne and mused:

> "I pity indeed the sad lot that 'as never breathed deep the sweet **proliferous** bouquet that is Tortuga, savvy? (Captain Jack Sparrow, "Pirates of the Caribbean: The Curse of the Black Pearl" 50:53)

"Proliferous"—the scientific term used by botanists and zoologists to mean "reproducing by means of buds, branches, or offshoots"—is no more appropriate an adjective here than "sweet" is to describe the smells of filthy Tortuga—of bloody war, constant alarm, sweaty carousing, and vomitous drinking. Sparrow was likely thinking of many words at once (perhaps "*pro*digious," "*de*licious," and "*odiferous*") and, combining them, came up with one that sounds impressive but is nonsense.

Malapropism is the practice of using the wrong word, or a made-up word, to refer to something—often to comical effect. Pirates are often guilty of malapropism, both inadvertently and deliberately. Here are some examples.

- "One thing ol' Blackbeard don't take kindly to it's them sort of **insinuendos**." (Blackbeard, combining in a spasm of inadvertent genius the terms "insinuation" and "innuendo," "Blackbeard's Ghost" 26:18)

- "[S]o, as he was going on a war-expedition in his canoe, he left her to think about it, sayin' he'd be back in six months or so, when he hoped she wouldn't be so **obstropolous**." (Bloody Bill, meaning "obstreperous," *The Coral Island* 238–39)

- "It was now about the **heighth** of summer here; for I remember that upon Christmas day, 1687 we were just clear of the storm …" (Lionel Wafer, of his company's month-long voyage near Tierra del Fuego, *Isthmus of America* 192–93)

- "Why then, first, sir, here's poor Cap'n Absalom's noble plantation **ruinated** by weather, by cock! So he tries for to right hisself by cards and horses, and **ruinates** his money affairs. So then he begins **ruinating** hisself wi' rum, by cock!" (Joel Bym, confusing "ruinate" for "ruin," *Adam Penfeather, Buccaneer* 285)

Note the following examples of malapropism that are deliberate invention, intended either to create a word for a specific meaning where no real one exists, or to make a point playfully or zestfully.

- "He's just been away from Neverland so long, his mind's been **junktified**." (Smee, "Hook" 47:20)

- "'Tis con-sarned with the sun sure-ly, also arks and merry deans, but **prezackly** how I dunno." (Ned Bowser, speculating on the meaning of the term "azimuth" and, while doing so, combining the words "precisely" and "exactly," *Adam Penfeather, Buccaneer* 96)

18.5 INCONSISTENCY

The pirate practice of keelhauling was painful. That fact—and the tying of the victim to a rope and hauling him through the ocean under a ship's keel—were the only standard aspects of the practice. Everything else was a variable.

Sometimes the victim was hauled from one side of the ship to the other and sometimes from one end to the other—with a longer period of time underwater and a correspondingly greater risk of drowning. Sometimes the rope was kept loose and handled casually and sometimes it was kept taut and held up tight against the ship's bottom as it was hauled, causing the victim to scrape bloodily against the hull's jagged barnacles. Sometimes a lead weight was tied to the victim's ankles, and sometimes not. Sometimes the dragging was quick and rough so that the hull caused serious injury, and sometimes it was slow, making lack of air the real danger.

This improvised, no-rules nature of keelhauling was consistent with the rest of pirate life: fluid, freewheeling, impulse-driven. The same is true of pirate speech. Lots of patterns, sure, but no rules. You say "toh-may-ee-ter" (I'll cut ya opern liker ...), I say "ter-mah-toh-oo" (I be cuttin' ye hoopen like a ...). Even the same speaker can say something two different ways in the same sentence. When Tom Morgan confesses to Long John Silver that he and his drinking partners "was a-**talkin'** of keel-**hauling**" (*Treasure Island* 44, Chap. 8), Morgan does not choose between dropping his "g"s from the ends of words or keeping them. He is a pirate. Pirates do not have to choose.

Pirates speak inconsistently. They often use a term or structure in one way, then use a different version a different way in the same conversation, or even (as Morgan does) in the same sentence. Inconsistency is a pirate's clearest sign of respect for the no-rules rule of pirate speech.

Note in each of the following excerpts, for example, the use of both a switched verb and a correct verb in the very same sentence.

- "And **does** you **do** this the whole, live-long night?" (Long John Silver, *Porto Bello Gold* 48)

- "It fair **gives** me a chill, it **do**." (Old Stingley, "Long John Silver's Return to Treasure Island" 1:24:32)

- "[T]hose that **desires** to go ashore and **enjoy** their ease in comfort **can look** to receiving free pardons." (Long John Silver quoting Andrew Murray, *Porto Bello Gold* 50)

Below is a sampling of the ways pirates engage in inconsistent speech.

- "I know it and the lads forrad know it, and Belvedere he knows it and is mighty **feared** of her and small blame either—aye, and mayhap you'll be **afeard** of her when you know her better." (Diccon, *Martin Conisby's Vengeance* 69)

- "Next thing we knew, everybody's yellin' an' cursin' **and** then we're droppin' anchor on the north coast of Hispaniola." (Ben Gunn, *Dead Man's Chest* 137)

- < "I'm looking for Captain Silver." "Err, well I **be** Silver, but I—**I'm** busy now." > (Evan Frost & Long John Silver, "The Adventures of Long John Silver: Dead Reckoning" 21:37)

- < "Lord love me! Aft with him—to the coach ..." "Coach, **Cap'n**? And why theer?" "Because I say so!" "And because, because women will be women, eh, **Captain**?" > (Captain Belvedere & Job & Diccon, *Martin Conisby's Vengeance* 66)

- "I **were** a-saying to Job that here **was** a fellow to match Pompey at last." (Diccon, *Martin Conisby's Vengeance* 67)

- "[A]s our powers increased, **we** took more ships until **us** had four ..." (Jeremy Jervey, *Winds of Chance* 212)

CHAPTER 19

Conversions

Conversions are easy, one-step ways of turning a modern English sentence into a pirate sentence. The sections in this chapter introduce three kinds of conversions: the Start (19.1), the Echo (19.2), and the Sternfirst (19.3).

☠

19.1 THE START

You are drifting in an open boat on the Caribbean Sea with twenty-eight men. Your food is almost gone, your rotting boat is leaking, and your men are miserable.

Then you catch sight of a Spanish ship so large and powerful that it strays freely from the rest of the fleet without apparent concern. Indeed, this one carries the vice-admiral of the Spanish armada. You manage to get your sorry boat close enough to do something.

But what will you do? How can you, a pathetic sea-vagrant, possibly go about taking such a powerful ship?

In 1602, Pierre le Grand faced this very situation. After making his crew swear an oath to fight to the death, he ordered one of them to bore a hole in the bottom of the boat. With the in-streaming water washing away any chance of retreat, the pirates scampered up the ship's side, dropped onto her decks with absolute will, and quickly overpowered the Spaniards aboard. (*The Buccaneers of America* 67–68)

Almost 400 years later, in the film "Pirates," Thomas Bartholomew Red employs the same tactic. As he and his men approach the Spanish galleon *Neptune*, Red points the brig's swivel gun inward, blasts a hole in her bottom, then announces, "That's just to put some fire in your bellies. **No going back now!** 'Tis victory or death!" (1:45:09)

Red's exhortation is typical piratese, both for its do-or-be-damned character and for his use ("No going back now!," rather than "There will be no going back now!") of the Chopped Start—the pirate's way of chopping off the starts of sentences. The Chopped Start is covered in more detail in section 19.1.1, and other types of starts—the Double-Subject Start (19.1.2), the "But" Start (19.1.3), the "If It Not" Start (19.1.4), the "It's" Start (19.1.5), and the Contraction Start (19.1.6)—follow.

19.1.1 CHOPPED START

Start sentences abruptly. More specifically, eliminate subjects, articles, and conjunctions (especially "if") at the beginnings of sentences. The effect is a strong-but-silent, no-nonsense speech style. Tough-guy talk.

- < "Sloop's fair shot up, but I reckon she'd make a fine Red Sea Rover." "Brig, too. Could work together." "Reckon we can put it to a vote, who captains what, quartermasters and the like." > (Henry Nagel & Israel Clayford, cautiously agreeing to join forces and cruise together, *The Pirate Round* 355)

- "Weren't for Morgan's orders, I'd throw a broadside into his hull." (Montbars, "Pirates of Tortuga" 1:04:08)

- "Looks of things, they've long been out of business. Probably have your bloody friend Norrington to thank for that." (Jack Sparrow, marooned on a desert island and disappointed to find a smugglers' supply depot abandoned, "Pirates of the Caribbean: The Curse of the Black Pearl" 1:36:10)

19.1.2 DOUBLE-SUBJECT START

Add a pronoun subject immediately after the subject of a sentence. Thus, "Captain Peter was the finest man I ever knew" becomes "**Cap'n Peter, he** were t' finest man ever I knowed."

- "Pew, **he** got a thousand pounds, which same he blowed in three nights in St. Pierre." (Long John Silver, *Porto Bello Gold* 65)

- "Some of them **lads**, the ones come from Press's ship, **they** say there's the treasure of the Great Mogul hisself aboard them ships." (Henry Nagel, *The Pirate Round* 317)

- "'Beware,' cried me shipmates. 'Sheer off. That **girl, she** be a true witch.'" (Blackbeard, "Blackbeard's Ghost" 23:48)

19.1.3 "BUT" START

Add "but" at the start of any sentence to express sharp reaction or emotion or, more generally, to lend emphasis or conviction to the statement.

The modern speaker says: "Yes, Patrick O'Connor was the wickedest rogue on the Spanish Main by far." A pirate says: "Aye, **but** Patrick O'Connor were the wickedest rogue on the Spanish Main by a long sea mile."

- "Oh, **but** enough of this shilly-shallying." (Tom Morgan, "Treasure Island" [1960] 37:49)

- "Ah, **but** you are cruel!" (Captain Jo, *Martin Conisby's Vengeance* 93)

- "Oh, **but** ye're a hard'un, squire's son. Worse'n a Dublin publican t'deal with." (Billy Doyle, on hearing Alan Lewrie doubt Doyle's willingness to kill his women hostages, *The Gun Ketch* 161)

Feel free to add a "But" Start to a sentence that already contains an opening oath, by adding "but" just *after* the oath. "**Holy poker, but** Bill Kane had the skill o' the devil when it come to layin' a yarn."

- "Dear heart, **but** he died bad, did Flint!" (bandaged John, *Treasure Island* 178, Chap. 31)

- "Dear God, **but** that is good." (Elephiant Yancy, *The Pirate Round* 246)

- "Stap me, **but** you have a low mind!" (Andrew Murray, *Porto Bello Gold* 90)

19.1.4 "IF IT NOT" START

Piratize any sentence by adding "if" before the subject and making the verb negative. Thus, "Peter the Big shows like a prince but fights like a demon" becomes "If Peter the Big **don't** show like a prince but fight liker demon."

- "Well, by the Holy Eternal, Hi, **if** that **isn't** a piece of your tarnal luck." (Blueskin, *The Book of Pirates* "Blueskin, the Pirate" 161–62)

- "If it **don't** make me cold inside to think of Flint." (Long John Silver, *Treasure Island* 178, Chap. 31)

19.1.5 "IT'S" START

For any sentence consisting of subject, verb, and predicate, rearrange the sentence by starting it with the word "it's," then proceeding with predicate, subject, and verb—in that order. Thus, "Andrew Thatcher is brave and bold" becomes "It's brave and bold Andrew Thatcher is."

- "Look you, Cahusac: **it's** sick and tired I am of your perpetual whining and complaining when things are not as smooth as a convent dining-table." (Captain Peter Blood, *Captain Blood: His Odyssey* 194)

- "**It's** wasting good time ye are, my friend." (Captain Peter Blood, *The Fortunes of Captain Blood* 130)

- "**It was** a great while I spent with hunting after a ship but was every way disappointed ..." (Captain Avery, *The King of Pirates* 41)

The negative form of the "It's" Start is constructed in the same manner—only with a negative verb.

- "**It ain't** piracy I'm proposing." (Captain Easterling, *Captain Blood Returns* 20)

The word "'tis" is a contraction of, and means the same thing as "it's." The "'Tis" Start is a variation on the "It's" Start. Begin the sentence with "'tis," then continue with predicate, subject, and verb.

- "Aye, by cock! **'Tis** 'witched he be!" (Joel Bym, *Black Bartlemy's Treasure* 104)

- "Plague and perish him! Burn him, **'tis** keelhaul 'im I would first and then give 'im to Pompey to carve up what remained ..." (Job, *Martin Conisby's Vengeance* 65–66)

- "Ah, damned coward, ye dare not slay me lest Belvedere torment ye to death—**'tis** your own vile carcase you do think of!" (Captain Jo, *Martin Conisby's Vengeance* 94)

19.1.6 CONTRACTION START

Add any of the contractions "here's," "there's," "it's," or "'tis" to the start of a sentence. "Jode the Scissor will slaughter you where you stand" becomes "**Here's** Jode the Scissor will slaughter ye wharr ye stand" or "**It's** Jode the Scissor will slaughter ye wharr ye stand."

The contracted form is not mandatory. One might instead say "here is" or "here was," for example, to start the sentence. "**Here is** Jode the Scissor will slaughter ye wharr ye stand."

> Note that relative pronouns like "that" and "who," used to introduce relative clauses, are often omitted in pirate speech. The Contraction Start is really just a reflection of that practice of omitting relative pronouns. Thus, when a pirate says "**It's** Jode the Scissor will slaughter ye wharr ye stand," he's really saying "**It's** Jode the Scissor **who** will slaughter you where you stand." He's just deleting the relative pronoun along the way. The Contraction Start, therefore, is particularly appropriate where the speaker wants to emphasize the subject of the sentence.

- "Howsoever, come life or death, **here's** Abnegation doth wish ye a fair wind ever and always, master." (Abnegation Mings, *Black Bartlemy's Treasure* 319)

- "**There's** never a man looked me between the eyes and seen a good day a'terwards, Tom Morgan, you may lay to that." (Long John Silver, *Treasure Island* 159, Chap. 28)

- "I've tried my fling, I have, and I've lost, and **it's** you has the wind of me." (Israel Hands, *Treasure Island* 137, Chap. 25)

- "Indeed, **'tis** you are my only and abiding anxiety, though a mighty precious one." (Captain Japhet Bly, *Winds of Chance* 304)

19.2 THE ECHO

In the 1934 film version of "Treasure Island," Israel Hands declares proudly, indignantly: "And I likes rum, I does." The isolation, danger, and dreary hardships of life on the account drove pirates to more-or-less perpetual drunkenness, when liquor provisions allowed. (And they often did.)

Rum was popular aboard sailing vessels as a drink of default. Pure, clean water was (1) hard to come by (empty casks would have to be loaded into a boat; the boat rowed to shore; a fresh water source located; the casks filled and rolled or carried to shore, re-loaded into the boat, and rowed to and hoisted onto the main vessel), and (2) difficult to store reliably (casks used to hold water were often recycled through different uses, and "warm, dark, and moist" is the best descriptor for both the inside of a water cask in a ship's hold and the microbe's ideal environment).

The pirate's fondness for rum would have only grown after experience of certain alternatives. Buccaneer Lionel Wafer tells how the natives of Darien made a special corn drink by having their old women chew up corn and spit it into a larger corn-water mixture so as to cause it to ferment, and how the paralyzing effects of coconut milk consumed in large quantities rendered his comrades unable to walk for four or five days (*Isthmus of America* 148, 176). Small beer (a lightly fermented barley drink) was condemned by a pirate in Thomas Antsis' company as insufficiently po-

tent, based on what he suggested was the obvious formulation that "there never was a sober fellow but what was a rogue." (*General History of the Pyrates* 293)

Rum. The drink so nice Israel Hands praises it twice: "And I likes rum, **I does.**" The repetitive "I does" at the end is a kind of "echo"—a quick and easy way of emphasizing a point. The Echo permits a pirate to stress what he's saying without using additional words that might dilute his strong, plain-spoken style. Sections 19.2.1 through 19.2.11 introduce the types of Echo.

19.2.1 FULL ECHO

At the end of a sentence, repeat the subject and verb, and in the same order.

- "You're a fine doctor, **you are.** You could have killed him!" (Gilly, "Blackbeard the Pirate" 15:00)

- "We're a respectable ship's crew, **we are.**" (Otto, *A High Wind in Jamaica* 95)

- "'Tis music to me ears, **it is.**" (one-eared Morley Rowe, *Dead Man's Chest* 251)

19.2.2 HALF ECHO

When a sentence contains a verb consisting of more than one word, repeat at the end of the sentence only the first word of the verb phrase. And where that first word happens to be a contraction (*e.g.* "'ve"), repeat it in full, non-contracted form ("have").

- "I'll bring my boot to ya, and I'll grind your mealy-mouthed jib into the dirt, **I will!**" (Blackbeard, "Blackbeard's Ghost" 1:03:25)

- "But I'll tell you I was sober; I was on'y dog tired; and if I'd awoke a second sooner I'd a' caught you at the act, **I would.**" (Long John Silver, *Treasure Island* 107, Chap. 20)

- "I be lookin' for a fine pork loin, I be." (gluttonous pirate, "Pirates of the Caribbean" Disney attraction [2005])

The Half Echo includes the use of "do" or "does" after any present-tense verb, or "did" after any past-tense verb.

- "Asking his pardon for bein' that familiar, but Squire, he's told me so much about the two of ye, it comes natural to call ye by name, it do." (Long John Silver, "Treasure Island" [1950] 17:19)

- "I sneaked in there one night, thinkin' to kill 'im, I did." (Gilly, "Blackbeard the Pirate" 15:25)

Note also the Bad Half Echo. The Bad Half Echo is a Half Echo in which the echo verb does not agree with the main verb. Thus, if the main verb is singular, use a plural echo verb ("The *Paul and Ellen* was a fine ship, she were"). If the main verb is plural, use a singular echo verb ("They're fightin' men, they is"). If the main verb is first-person, use a third-person echo verb ("I want rum, I does"). If the main verb is third-person, use a first-person echo verb ("She kills two pris'ners a day wi' that whip o' hers, she do").

- "It fair gives me a chill, it *do*." (Old Stingley, "Long John Silver's Return to Treasure Island" 1:24:32)

19.2.3 DOUBLE ECHO

The Double Echo is a Full or Half Echo, plus a Subject Echo. That is, repeat the subject and the verb, then the subject again, at the end of the sentence.

- "And there be many worse things than a mere pirate, brother. And what? You'll go for to ask. Answer I—Spanishers, Papishers, the Pope o' Rome and his bloody Inquisition, of which I have lasting experience, *camarado*—aye, I have I!" (Resolution Day, *Martin Conisby's Vengeance* 72)

19.2.4 CHOPPED ECHO

The Chopped Echo is a sentence that begins with a Chopped Start (Section 19.1.1) but ends with a Half Echo. "Shot me in the head, he did." The subject is omitted from the first part of the sentence but included in the echo at the end, along with some form of the verb "to do."

Thus, one can piratize the modern English sentence "We burned that Spanish fort to the ground" using either a Half Echo ("We burned that Spanisher fort to the ground, we did") or a Chopped Echo ("Burned that Spanisher fort to the ground, we did").

- "Ya can't be too careful comin' in through them mud flats, ya know. Only measured two fathoms at high tide, it did." (Morley Rowe, *Dead Man's Chest* 250)

- "Took ye for a ghost, I did, the ghost of a shipmate o' mine, one as do lie buried yonder ..." (Roger Tressady, *Black Bartlemy's Treasure* 301)

- "Bloody high-handed as a Protestant squire. Squire's son, are ye? Thought so, I did." (Billy Doyle, taunting Alan Lewrie, *The Gun Ketch* 159)

Note the following excerpt containing both a Half Echo and a Chopped Echo, in that order:

- < "He gave a fop an excellent dunking this afternoon, he did." "Yeah, put his head in a barrel of water, I did." > (Old Stingley & Big Eric, "The Adventures of Long John Silver: The Eviction" 4:57)

19.2.5 DELUXE ECHO

At the end of a sentence, repeat the subject and verb in the same order, but first adding the word "that" or "so." Thus, "April Gibson's the a-fearsomest pirate queen tharr ebber were, that she be."

- "I'd help you sail her up to Execution Dock, by thunder! **so I would**." (Israel Hands, *Treasure Island* 137, Chap. 25)

- "Sir, by cock but I'm glad for to clap eyes on ee again, ay, **that I am**, sir—and my lady too!" (Joel Bym, *Adam Penfeather, Buccaneer* 284)

- "Gunners like Ogle are like poets; they are born, **so they are**." (Captain Peter Blood, *Captain Blood Returns* 30)

A variation is the Late Deluxe Echo. The speaker waits until the very end of the sentence to add "that" or "so"—that is, only after repeating the subject and verb.

- "There'll be a surprised awakening for him; **there will so**." (George Fairfax, *The Fortunes of Captain Blood* 160)

Note the expert use in the following excerpt of both a Deluxe Echo and an "It's" Start:

- "She has a beckoning eye, **so she has**, and **it's** the uneasy husband I should be at sea if she were my wife." (Peter Blood, *Captain Blood Returns* 192)

19.2.6 OATH ECHO

At the end of a sentence, add an oath—with or without the word "but" following it—then repeat the subject and verb. "I've sailed many a ship" becomes "I've sailed many a ship, **by thunder, I have**" or "I've sailed many a ship, **by thunder, but I have**."

- "And I shall count it more heroic in thee, ay, **damme, but I shall**!" (Absalom Troy, *Adam Penfeather, Buccaneer* 122)

- "I've come down to working in the cane-brakes along o' poor black slaves, sir, ay, **by cock, I have**!" (Joel Bym, *Adam Penfeather, Buccaneer* 284)

- < "[W]hat is it all mariners do most fear at sea?" "... Why, sir, I du reckon as it be fire, —ay, **by cock, I du**!" > (Adam

Penfeather & Joel Bym, *Adam Penfeather, Buccaneer* 67)

19.2.7 REVERSE ECHO

At the end of a sentence, repeat the subject and verb of the sentence in reverse order. "The *Fearless Robin*'s the fastest bottom in all the New York colony, **is the *Fearless Robin***."

- "Now William is a lay reader in the church, **is William**." (Long John Silver, "Treasure Island" [1934] 31:00)

- "And me, I stood your friend so much as I might—aye, **did I**!" (Diccon, *Martin Conisby's Vengence* 92)

- "By your leave, Captain Jo, but your luck's wi' us—aye, **is it**! A fine large ship a-plying to wind'ard of us ..." (Diccon, happily announcing the sighting of a prize, *Martin Conisby's Vengeance* 95)

19.2.8 PRONOUN ECHO

When the subject of a sentence is a personal pronoun ("he," "she," "they"), end the sentence by more specifically naming the person referenced.

- "He's no friend o' mine, **Murray**; but he's kept me in rum and 'backy and spendin'-money since I joined up with him." (Billy Bones, *Porto Bello Gold* 50)

- "He's no common man, **Barbecue**. He had good schooling in his young days, and can speak like a book when so minded ..." (Israel Hands, *Treasure Island* 54, Chap. 10)

- "Oh, he's a fine gentleman, **the Squire**. A noble mind and very high-principled." (Long John Silver, "Treasure Island" [1960] 22:32)

Note also the Verb-Pronoun Echo, wherein the sentence similarly ends with naming, but only after repeating the verb.

- "Why, truly, Thomas Ford, remember Pompey, but forget not Job as died so sudden—in the midst o' life he were in death, **were Job!**" (Resolution Day, *Martin Conisby's Vengeance* 90)

- "Gunners like Ogle are like poets; they are born, so they are. He'll put you a shot between wind and water, **will Ogle**, as neatly as you might pick your teeth." (Peter Blood, *Captain Blood Returns* 30)

19.2.9 NEGATIVE ECHO

Where the verb of the sentence is negative, do not simply repeat the subject and verb. Rather, the proper Negative Echo is "not" followed by the subject of the sentence. Thus, a pirate would say "He weren't cap'n long, **not 'im**" or "He weren't cap'n long, **not 'ee**," rather than "He weren't cap'n long, **ee weren't**."

- "He didn't care about savin' his little matey's life, **not him**." (Long John Silver, "Treasure Island" [1950] 1:22:53)
- "Look, Jim, how my fingers fidget. I can't keep 'em still, **not I**." (Billy Bones, *Treasure Island* 14, Chap. 3)
- "Penfeather aren't to be caught so—**not him!**" (Sam Spraggons, *Black Bartlemy's Treasure* 311)

Consistent with the no-rules rule of pirate speech, however, there will always be a pirate who ignores the preferred Negative Echo form:

- "Never went to sea again, **he didn't**; started growing cocoa-nuts." (Otto, *A High Wind in Jamaica* 124)

19.2.10 QUESTION ECHO

When asking a question, repeat the subject and verb of the main question, but in reverse order. (This is more or less the Reverse Echo, but in the form of a question.)

- "So it's a mutiny, **is it**?" (Joshua Smoot, *Dead Man's Chest* 254)

- "So he thinks he's got us trapped, **does he**? Well, the laugh is on him." (Gilly, "Blackbeard the Pirate" 1:30:34)

The word "now" is often used before the echo phrase for emphasis.

- "[H]e wouldn't think twice 'bout bein' ordered back to Andros Island, **now would he**?" (Long John Silver, *Dead Man's Chest* 295)

One variation of the Question Echo is to use a negative form of the verb (or any form of "ain't," including "ain't," "bain't," "ben't," and "hain't") at the end of the question, rather than repeating the verb itself.

- < "Aye, but he've murdered Pompey, **ain't 'e**?" "Aye, aye—an' so 'e have, for sure!" "Well an' good—murder's an 'anging matter, **ain't it**?" > (Job & another pirate aboard the Happy Despatch, *Martin Conisby's Vengeance* 84)
- "Besides, you've made friends with the devil himself, **haven't you**? And that's no mean achievement." (Long John Silver, referring to himself, "Treasure Island" [1960] 1:16:25)

Alternatively, one can do the opposite—that is, make the main verb negative and the echo verb affirmative. "There bain't a more beautiful vessel than the *Hannah* out of New York, is there?"

- "You **never seen** a man hanged aboard ship, **did ya**—run up to the end of the yardarm by his own messmates ...?" (Long John Silver, "Treasure Island" [1990] 2:04:40)

19.3 THE STERNFIRST

Piracy was a dangerous proposition, especially for pirates themselves. Even short of battle and capture, the pirate's life was a merciless struggle for survival against multiple foes—hard living, malnutrition, inadequate or injuriously counterproductive medical care, constant exposure to the elements, and the perils of even routine service aboard a sailing vessel.

For most pirates, moreover, the only thing that separated them from quick and certain death was the wood underneath their feet. Most pirates could not swim. On October 12, 1681, Captain Sharp and his company approached the shore of a mysterious island in the south Pacific, which they named Duke of York's Island. As Sharp prepared to anchor, a crewman named Henry Shergall—making his way up to the sprit-sail top against heavy winds—lost his footing and plunged into the ocean. Shergall drowned before anyone could help him. His shipmate Basil Ringrose wrote in his firsthand account: "This incident several of our company interpreted as a bad omen of the place ..." (*Bucaniers of America* Part IV, Chap. XXIII)

Ringrose's sentence is a reminder that pirates, despite their penchant for hard practicality, were a superstitious bunch. The sentence also reminds us that pirates, like Ringrose, routinely employed a certain usage known as inversion, or the Sternfirst. Ringrose says, "This incident several of our company interpreted as a bad omen," rather than, "Several of our company interpreted this incident as a bad omen."

A cornerstone of pirate speech, the Sternfirst features the reversal of sentences containing subject, verb, and predicate—the predicate first, then the subject and verb last. That is, the speaker flips a sentence and starts with the back end first. Thus, "he is a blundering idiot" becomes "a blunderin' idiot he is."

- "What be I offered for this winsome wench? **Stout-hearted and corn-fed, she be.**" (pirate auctioneer, "Pirates of the Caribbean" Disney attraction)

- "While I was walking here, **comes up one of my comrades** and one who I always took for my particular friend." (Captain Avery, *The King of Pirates* 82)

One might even use the Sternfirst when asking questions—

- "Me holds are burstin' with swag. **That bit of shine matters to us—why?**" (Barbossa, "Pirates of the Caribbean: The Curse of the Black Pearl" 39:06)

or with subsidiary clauses or phrases that are parts of a larger sentence—

- "At none other place is any foothold or chance of escalade, d'ye see—no, not even for an Indian, if **Indians they have**, which God forbid." (Japhet Bly, *Winds of Chance* 351)

CHAPTER 20

Structural Forms

This chapter introduces various structural forms—that is, ways in which pirates put together sentences differently than speakers of modern English—including the Split Phrase (20.1), Split Adjective (20.2), varied word order (20.3), Tmesis (20.4), and Closing Repetition (20.5).

☠

20.1 SPLIT PHRASE

In the firsthand account of his exploits, titled *A New Voyage Round the World*, William Dampier praises buccaneers like himself as especially effective people. Average Englishmen, he says, "proceed usually too cautiously, coldly and formally to compass any considerable design." Buccaneers, on the other hand, are "inured to hot climates, hardened by many fatigues, and in general, daring men, **and such as would not be easily baffled.**" (164)

Dampier's last phrase—"and such as would not be easily baffled"—is a Split Phrase. Pirates often extend their thoughts by adding Split Phrases to the ends of their sentences as an addendum or appendix, typically starting with "and" or "or." This information

is split off from, but tacked onto, the rest of a statement.

The Split Phrase is an emphatic way of conveying a two-idea message. Its "and another thing"-style delivery is like a whip crack at the end of a sentence.

- "[Y]ou see afore you Jeremy Jervey, as sailed out o' Falmouth twenty odd year ago as gunner's mate aboard the *Falcon*, with Captain Amos Trevoe and seventy-odd stout lads **and all of 'em dead.**" (Jeremy Jervey, *Winds of Chance* 210)

- "It's Cap'n Sparrow we're after, **and a fortune in gold.**" (Barbossa, "Pirates of the Caribbean" Disney attraction [2006])

- "And ashamed o' myself I oughter be, says you, **and with rea-**

son, too." (Long John Silver, *Porto Bello Gold* 29)

Note, finally, that while Split Phrases almost always begin with "and" or "or," they occasionally do not.

- "I seen him grapple four, and knock their heads together—**him unarmed**." (Israel Hands, *Treasure Island* 54, Chap. 10)

20.2 SPLIT ADJECTIVE

The Split Adjective is identical to the Split Phrase, except that it consists only of the word "and" or "or" plus an adjective. It is a way of postponing one of a sentence's two adjectives until the end of a sentence for dramatic effect and emphasis. "The Lizzard's a bold and bloody she-devil" becomes "The Lizzard's a bold she-devil, **and bloody**" or "The Lizzard's a bold she-devil, **and a bloody**."

- < "Still interested in the *Rachel*, I see?" "Arrgh, she's a trim little craft, **and speedy**." > (Long John Silver & Governor Strong, "The Adventures of Long John Silver: Ship o' the Dead" 11:53)
- "Flint may well make trouble. 'Tis a determined dog, **and a greedy**." (Andrew Murray, *Porto Bello Gold* 104)
- "[Y]ou have all known me as a good man **and true**, and it's not likely that I shall desert you now." (Hawkhurst, *The Pirate* 121, Chap. XVI)

One might also add "that" before the Split Adjective:

- "On the 21st, we had very little wind, and all along as we went we could descry high land, **and that barren**." (Basil Ringrose, *Bucaniers of America* Part IV Chap. XVI)

20.3 WORD ORDER

We modern folk often ask each other playfully: If you had to live on a desert island,

what would you bring? Pirates often asked the same question. For them, however, the question was neither playful nor hypothetical, and the answer was far from speculative.

Marooning was a very popular punishment among pirates, imposed on both prisoners captured by the company and transgressors within. The basic protocol was simple: The condemned was placed on a remote island and abandoned.

What the maroon was allowed to take with him, however, varied widely. The most popular marooning kit was probably a gun, a few shot, a bottle of water, and a bottle of powder. Some were only allowed a pistol with a single shot, or a cask of rum, or nothing at all—not even clothing. (For a detailed account of each pirate captain's marooning kit, see Appendix C: Pirate Company Articles.)

When faced with the malevolent question, the modern speaker might say, "I'd **just** take **enough** tequila and margarita mix to last me a thousand sunsets." A pirate, however, would invert the word order and reply, "**Just** I'd take rum and punch **enough** ter last me a t'ousand soohnsets."

Words that routinely find themselves in a different sequence when spoken by pirates are listed below. Each entry includes a brief explanation of how, precisely, the term is ordered differently. Remember that these constructions are typical but not used in every instance.

all (1) Place "all" after—not before—the verb modified.

"It would not be fair to my men to put about now, for they have **all** an interest in the trade." (pirate captain, *The Coral Island* 206)

(2) Where the predicate of a sentence is quite short, place "all" after both verb and predicate—at the very end of the sentence.

"We were King's men **all**. ..." (Wolverstone, *Captain Blood: His Odyssey* 306)

all ... over Split the phrase "all over" so that "all" precedes the term modified and "over" follows it.

> "[T]hey had not tasted good salt beef for a long time—and with it we sent them two hogsheads of rum. This made them so hearty to us that they sent two of their company ... to go with us all the world over." (Captain Avery, *The King of Pirates* 26)

always Place "always" after—not before—the verb modified.

> "In all those prizes we got also about fifty-six men, ... including the carpenters and surgeons, who we obliged always to go." (Captain Avery, *The King of Pirates* 16)

early When using "early" with two-word phrases like "last month," "this week," "next year," or "tomorrow night," place "early" after—not before—the phrase.

> "This morning early the rogue Benjamin Denton, venturing within my fire-zone, took a bullet in his midriff, whereof he suddenly perished." (entry in Adam Penfeather's journal, *Black Bartlemy's Treasure* 239)

enough Place "enough" after—not before—the noun modified.

> "We have done him injury enough already." (John Phillips, *General History of the Pyrates* 348)

ever Place "ever" before—not after—the subject of any phrase, clause, or sentence.

> "In this place are a multitude of wolves, which are the boldest that ever I met with. ..." (Lionel Wafer, describing his experiences at the Gulf of Amapalla, *Isthmus of America* 174)

first When using the word "first" as an adverb, place "first" before—not after—the subject of any phrase, clause, or sentence.

> "One thousand two hundred and three poor souls ha' we freed one way or t'other, since first we took and named this ship *Joyful Deliverance* ..." (Ezekiel Penryn, *Winds of Chance* 48)

just When using the word "just" as an adverb, place "just" before—not after—the subject of any phrase, clause, or sentence.

> "An' if ya don't believe old Jack Bridger, just you ask about." (Long John Silver, *Dead Man's Chest* 26)

little When using the word "little" as an adverb, place "little" before—not after—the verb modified.

> "We've reduced our inflammation but our fever little abates, we gain no strength, we languish, for, 'sbud, mem, we refuse t'eat and we must eat t' give Nature a chance, demme." (Crabtree, *Winds of Chance* 89)

more (1) When using the word "more" as an adjective, place "more" after—not before—the noun modified.

> "And in this service I spent four years more of my time." (Captain Avery, *The King of Pirates* 11)

(2) When using the word "more" as an adverb, place "more" before—not after—the verb modified.

> "And no two men in the world more rejoiced than we as we clasped hands and embraced each other as only comrades may." (Adam Penfeather, *Black Bartlemy's Treasure* 88–89)

never When using the word "never" with a verb phrase—that is, a verb consisting of more than one word (*e.g.*, "have been," "has seen," "had gone," "will tell," "would say," "should have done")—place "never" after the verb phrase, not within it.

> "Shipmate, an we sail as brothers and comrades there must be never a secret betwixt us—speak!" (Adam Penfeather, *Black Bartlemy's Treasure* 79)

next When using the word "next" as an adjective, place "next" after—not before—the noun modified.

> "Don't reckon he'll live till morning **next**." (Henry Nagel, *The Pirate Round* 210)

now Place "now" after—not before—the verb modified.

> "We had **now** wealth enough not only to make us rich but almost to have made a nation rich. ..." (Captain Avery, *The King of Pirates* 60)

still When using the word "still" as an adverb, place "still" after—not before—the verb modified.

> "And though they had lost so great a part of their booty, yet they had **still** left a vast wealth, being six or seven tons of silver, besides what they had gotten before." (Captain Avery, *The King of Pirates* 51)

there When using the word "there" as an adverb, place "there" before—not after—the verb modified.

> "If a man conceal any treasure captured or fail to place it in the general fund, he shall be marooned—set ashore on a deserted island, and **there** left with a bottle of water, a loaf of bread, and a pistol with one load." (Peter Blood, setting out the articles of his new company of pirates, "Captain Blood" 1:04:21)

well When using the word "well" as an adverb, place "well" before—not after—the verb modified.

> "When I came in, she rose up and paid me such respect as I did not **well** know how to receive. ..." Captain Avery, *The King of Pirates* 58)

20.4 TMESIS

For centuries, bells have been rung to mark the time of day. One ring for every hour between one o'clock and twelve o'clock. Simple,

straightforward. But not always effective. Anything later than four o'clock means a blurring series of internally indistinguishable tones that require active cognitive memory (counting), not simply passive auditory memory (snapshot), to keep track. Anything later than seven o'clock, and the average listener has an equal chance of apprehending the correct time as she does a time that is one hour too many or too few.

Leave it to the multitalented buccaneer William Dampier—pirate, anthropologist, explorer, mapmaker, navigator—to discover a better way to ring the time. During his time in the Philippines, Dampier noted that the residents of the island of Mindanao rang out the time of day on a gong—not with steady, even strokes, but rather starting with slow strokes, speeding up the strokes in the middle, then ending with slow strokes.

Slow-fast-slow is more easily counted than steady-steady-steady. Why? Because putting something in the middle that contrasts with what's on either side is more memorable. A green valley between two black mountains focuses the mind in a way that flat gray sky cannot.

It is for the same reason that modern speakers use tmesis every day—that is, insert words inside other words or phrases. You might say "What **in hot heck** are you doing?" rather than simply "What are you doing?" for added effect. The implicit emphasis from stuffing something in the middle of a word or phrase rivets perception and anchors memory.

Pirates use tmesis a bit more frequently than modern speakers. "Where **in 'ell** is Derrick, that philoserphizin' fuddler?" is always a better option than simply "Where is Derrick, that philoserphizin' fuddler?" as the latter unconscionably squanders opportunities for both emphasis and profanity in a way no pirate could abide.

A few ex-blastin'-amples:

- < "I'm ready for my nightcap." "Abso-**floggin'**-lutely." > (Captain James Hook & Smee, "Hook" 1:04:00)

- "What **a plague** do it matter if it is an English settlement?" (Wolverstone, *Captain Blood: His Odyssey* 310)

- < "Smee, who is this impostor?" "Peter-**floggin'-flyin'**-Pan." > (Captain James Hook & Smee, "Hook" 43:36)

20.5 CLOSING REPETITION

When sentencing pirates to death, judges traditionally ended with an eerily repetitive litany: "To be hanged by the neck till you are dead, dead, dead." (*Villains of All Nations* 161; *Under the Black Flag* 233; *The Pirate Hunter* 2)

It is a bit ironic, therefore, that pirates themselves use repetition at the ends of their own sentences to add emphasis:

- "There's you wi' my ship—**true**, Adam, **true**! But here's me wi' the island **and the treasure**, Adam, **and the treasure**." (Roger Tressady, *Black Bartlemy's Treasure* 315)

- "So get to your shaving and **cheerily**, comrade, **cheerily**." (Adam Penfeather, *Black Bartlemy's Treasure* 329)

- "Ha—rot me! Rot me but you are **afraid** of me—**afraid**, yes!" (Captain Jo, *Martin Conisby's Vengeance* 33)

> Feel free to add a term of address (*e.g.*, "mate," "friend," "sir") or of affirmation ("aye," "yes," "indeed") before the repetition. "The *Katingo*, she were a **speedy craft**, mate, **a speedy craft**." "The sisters Berenguer is beautiful but **cruel**, aye, **cruel**."

CHAPTER 21

Functional Forms

This chapter covers the functional forms of speech used by pirates to accomplish certain purposes—specifically, making assertions (21.1), making negative statements (21.2); asking questions (21.3); and referencing (21.4), characterizing (21.5), and recalling (21.6) things.

21.1 ASSERTION

John Gow should have known from the beginning his piracy career would not go well. On November 3, 1724, Gow and his fellow crew mutinied and attacked their French captain, an old but wiry man named Oliver Ferneau. When they lifted him to throw him overboard, Ferneau grabbed the rope lines above and would not let go. When the mutineers slashed at his throat with a Dutch knife, they missed his windpipe. When they stabbed him in the back, the knife stuck and could not be pulled out for successive blows. When they shot him in the head—twice—Ferneau simply got hold of another rope and started climbing. Only when they cut Ferneau's rope and caused him to plunge

into the sea (that is, not until they attacked something other than Ferneau himself) did the pirates prevail.

The first two vessels sighted by Gow's new pirates carried only herring and salmon. The third they pursued for three days, only to lose sight of it in a patch of haze. After a run-in with a Portuguese vessel, Gow urged that the company leave the Portuguese coast and head to Gow's home in the Orkney Islands, where they could lay low for a while (and where Gow's girlfriend was waiting). Gow's sales pitch was carefully worded: "It is certain that after alarming the coast there will be no staying here, and the shortness of provision and water make voyages dangerous ..." (*General History of the Pyrates* 358–69; *Lives of the Most Remarkable Criminals* 572–603)

Gow did not say "I don't think we can stay here" or "I believe we cannot stay here." Rather, Gow began his statement with the construction "there will be" to downplay his own opinion, to distance himself from what he hoped to depict as freestanding, objective truth: "there will be no staying here."

Pirates use the words "here," "there," and "it" in order to make assertions. For example, a pirate on a long jungle trek might say, "Here's a long walk, and it'll be sound sleep tonight." By using "here" and "it," the speaker gets to his main idea immediately and with conviction. This usage doesn't really exist in modern English; as a result, modern speakers often find themselves forced into longer, clunkier sentences: "This is a long walk we're on, and I'll be sleeping soundly tonight."

Want fewer words, crisper meaning, and an air of objectivity? Open with an assertive "here," "there," or "it."

A last note: Gow's self-distancing use of an assertive "there" was a smart thing, but his company's decision to follow him to the Orkneys was not. After a number of misfortunes and miscalculations, including running the ship aground, they found themselves under arrest and—on June 11, 1725—under the gallows.

21.1.1 HERE

The word "here" is, by far, the most frequently used of the three assertive terms. It is usually used in the form "here's," even when followed by plural nouns ("**Here**'s three liars tellin' me three stories 'bout wharr that treasure be buried") or when used to describe a past event or condition ("**Here**'s a crew wi' nothin' to show fer six months o' voyage, so hung up their cap'n from the yardarm, them did").

- "Well, **here**'s a cap'n with a suspicious turn of mind, and **here**'s Long John handing out firearms to an able-bodied seaman like yourself." (Long John Silver, explaining to Jim Hawkins why he must tell no one of the pistol given him by Silver, "Treasure Island" [1950] 32:29)

- "**Here**'s mighty ill plight you've got yourself into, and **here**'s me a-wondering how I am to get ye out again." (Adam Penfeather, *Black Bartlemy's Treasure* 142)

- "Ned! Ned! Wake up! **Here**'s damned villainy!" (John Sharkey, vainly attempting to wake up his drunk quartermaster on realizing they've been trapped, *The Dealings of Captain Sharkey and Other Tales of Pirates* "How Copley Banks Slew Captain Sharkey" 73)

Particularly popular is the use of "here's" to introduce a noun followed by a participial phrase:

- "Here's Cap'n Flint—I calls my parrot Cap'n Flint, after the famous buccaneer—**here's Cap'n Flint predicting** success to our v'yage." (Long John Silver, *Treasure Island* 54, Chap. 10)

- "They're there ... a day and a half, I reckon, and then next thing I know **here's Press marching** most of his men right back to the ship, and it's up anchor and away." (Henry Nagel, *The Pirate Round* 242)

- "But look'ee now, Marty, **here's me wishing** ye well and you wi' a barker in your fist, 'tis no fashion to greet a shipmate, I'm thinking." (Roger Tressady, *Black Bartlemy's Treasure* 302)

21.1.2 THERE

Use "there" to introduce assertions in the same way as "here." There is no substantive distinction between "there" and "here" determining when one or the other might be used. The choice between them is a matter of taste.

- "And then we fell in wi' the Jamaica fleet and that grey old devil Bishop in command, and **there** was a sure end to Captain Blood and to every mother's son of us all." (Wolverstone, *Captain Blood: His Odyssey* 306)

- "There's you wi' my ship—true, Adam, true! But here's me wi' the island and the treasure, Adam, and the treasure." (Roger Tressady, *Black Bartlemy's Treasure* 315)

Like "here's," "there's" is often used to introduce a noun followed by a participial phrase:

- "There's Providence watching over me this night." (George Fairfax, *The Fortunes of Captain Blood* 151)

21.1.3 IT

Use "it" to introduce assertions in the same way as "here" and "there." Although not as popular as "here," "it" is frequently used to open statements describing events or conditions in either the past ("It were dark treachery when one sailed wi' Flint") or the future ("it'll be gold an' marr gold when we sail wi' Flint").

- "It'll be place and rank for you, messmate, or a chance to swim wi' the sharks." (Long John Silver, *Porto Bello Gold* 51)

- "You'll be back, I'll lay to that! And when ya touch down next time, it'll be me crutch to yer back ..." (Long John Silver, *Dead Man's Chest* 9)

- "'Tis Marty, sure enough, Marty as was bonnet to me aboard the *Faithfull Friend* and since he stood friend to us in regard to Adam Penfeather (with a curse!) it's us shall stand friends t'him." (Roger Tressady, *Martin Conisby's Vengeance* 155)

21.2 NEGATION

Piracy and marriage. Piracy and marriage. Go together like a gun (cannon) and carriage (wheeled cannon base).

Marriage often figures as the cruelest chapter in pirates' lives. Edward Low left Boston and turned to piracy, in part, because of the tragic death of his young wife in 1719; the otherwise barbaric Low was so deeply affected that he made a point of always releasing married prisoners (*Pirates of the New England Coast* 141–42; 160–63; 226–27). Blackbeard apparently did not share the same susceptibility to emotional attachment, collecting thirteen wives in rapid succession. His fourteenth was a sixteen-year-old girl from Bath-Town, North Carolina, and the governor of the colony (whom Blackbeard had befriended) officiated at the wedding. For a few days afterwards, Blackbeard and his bride lived at her family's plantation. The honeymoon ended, however, when Blackbeard invited five or six of his pirate comrades over and repeatedly forced their company on his new wife while he watched. (*General History of the Pyrates* 76; *Pirates and Buccaneers of the Atlantic Coast* 195)

Given the pirate's questionable capacity for wedded bliss, it rings true when, in Jeffery Farnol's novel *Adam Penfeather, Buccaneer*, pirate Absalom Troy promises his love, Antonia Chievely: "[W]hen we're wed I'll go no more adventuring. I'll be done with the sea." (157)

Troy's words ring true also because of his use of predicate negation. Pirates tend to express negative statements not by negating the verbs of their sentences, but their predicates. Thus, while a modern speaker might have said "I won't go adventuring any more," Troy says, "I'll go no more adventuring." Pirates prefer, when possible, to keep the verb as-is and instead negate what comes after. (Bit ironic that Troy happens to swear off piracy in distinctively piratical-sounding terms.)

This section covers distinctive ways in which pirates make negative statements.

21.2.1 PREDICATE NEGATION

When making a negative statement, negate not the verb (as in modern English), but—where possible—the noun or other part of the predicate.

- "But tell **no one** a word of our plans." (Long John Silver, "Long John Silver's Return to Treasure Island" 38:57)

Not: "But don't tell anyone a word of our plans."

- "Now, youngster, listen to me. I've **no time** to waste here." (pirate captain, threatening fifteen-year-old Ralph Rover with a cocked pistol, *The Coral Island* 198)

Not: "I don't have any time to waste here."

- < "Is the poor man their prisoner?" "**Not he**. I watched them come ashore and lay so close I heard them salute him as 'my lord' and saw he went armed." > (Ursula Revell & Japhet Bly, *Winds of Chance* 302)

Not: "No he isn't."

21.2.2 "THERE BE NO" NEGATION

Use phrases like "there's no," "there ain't no," "there was no," and "there'll be no" with gerunds (verb derivatives ending in "-ing" used as nouns, as in "There'll be no **shooting**!") to state negative propositions.

- "[T]here **ain't no** mistakin' a one-legged man." (Long John Silver, *Porto Bello Gold* 21)

- "They're all for a run ashore, and **there'll be no** working them aboardship until they ha' had their fill o' woods and mountains." (John Flint, *Porto Bello Gold* 124)

- "[T]he place on which our habitation was built being an island, **there was no** coming easily at us by land." (Captain Avery, *The King of Pirates* 36)

21.3 INQUIRY

There are two points to remember in forming questions. Both involve using fewer words to ask them.

(1) Don't use "do."

Avoid any form of the helping verb "do," including "does," "did," and "didn't." Thus, "When **do you think** we should sail?" becomes "When **think you** we oughter sail?" or "When **you think** we oughter sail?"

- "I shall also leave it to you, Silver, to lay the powder-train. How much **have you**?" (Andrew Murray, *Porto Bello Gold* 74)

Not: "How much do you have?"

- "**Saw ye** ever a lovelier, sweeter soul?" (Resolution Day, *Martin Conisby's Vengeance* 144)

Not: "Did ye ever see a lovelier, sweeter soul?"

(2) Don't use "have."

When asking questions in the present perfect ("Have you seen a man with one leg?") or the past perfect ("Had you seen a man with one leg before I got here?"), omit the helping verb ("have" or "had") and move the participle before the subject.

Possible pirate equivalents, therefore, include: "Seen you a man with one leg?" "Seed you a man wi' one leg?" "Spied ye a man wi' one stick afore I got 'ere?"

See Chapter 12 for vocabulary used in asking questions and making replies.

21.4 REFERENCE

Pirates had no satellite telephone, no Internet connection, and no fax machine, so news of wars and treaties was hard to come by. Which makes it difficult for one to blame Long John Silver in "The Adventures of Long John Silver" for regretting his failure to attack a French warship. Silver learns for the first time of Anglo-French hostilities from the French officers who board his ship and declare it a war prize. Silver shoots back:

"Why, if I 'ad known this, you'd have 'ad plenty of shot in your hull before you took us." (Long John Silver, "The Adventures of Long John Silver: Turnabout" 6:27)

In one sentence, Silver proves himself an English pirate three times over: He is defiant. He professes hostility toward the French. And he says "if I 'ad known **this**" rather than "if I 'ad known **that**."

Modern English speakers use the terms "that" and "there" to introduce abstract concepts. "**That**'s enough." "**There**'s nothing else I'd like better." But pirates, for whatever reason, tend to use "this" and "here" instead. "**This** be enough." "**Here**'s nothin' else I'd like better."

21.4.1 "THIS" FOR "THAT"

Pirates and modern English speakers both use the term "this" to refer to something nearby, and "that" to refer to something farther away. When speaking abstractly, however, pirates often say "this" when the modern speaker would say "that":

- "I and these my comrades (hale and well) shall be risking death and wounds to win poor wretches from misery to chance o' life—" "And for loot!" "Ay—**this** too!" > (Japhet Bly & Ursula Revell, *Winds of Chance* 69–70)

- "And what, what o' the sacred oath ye swore, the Oath o' Brotherhood, what o' **this**?" (Absalom Troy, *Adam Penfeather, Buccaneer* 42)

- < "Japhet, you rush upon destruction." "**This** is as may be, ma'm, but for the nonce, sweet poppet, be seen and not heard." > (Ursula Revell & Japhet Bly, *Winds of Chance* 334)

21.4.2 "HERE" FOR "THERE"

Pirates use "here" and "there" in the same way as modern speakers with reference to actual places—"here" for places nearby, "there" for places further away. But pirates use "here," not "there," for most abstract purposes.

Thus, where the modern speaker says, "**There** is no good reason for fighting," the

pirate likely would instead say, "**Here** is no good reason fer fight."

- "**Cap'n**, look, **here**'s why they've run! She must have seventy guns aboard." (Patch, pointing out a nearby warship, "The Adventures of Long John Silver: Turnabout" 3:38)

- < "By cock, I dream on't sometimes and wake all of a sweat—" "**Here**'s no time for dreams!" > (Joel Bym & Adam Penfeather, *Black Bartlemy's Treasure* 104)

- "**Here**'s no place, no rest for such outcast dogs as we; 'tis rope or worse an' we be recognized ..." (Barnabas Rokeby, *Winds of Chance* 32)

Of course, pirates do not *always* substitute "here" for "there," but rather do so inconsistently. Note in each of the following excerpts the use of both "here" and "there" for the purpose of reference:

- "Howbeit, I say, 'tis a good song, **here**'s battle in't, murder and sudden death and wha—what more could ye expect of any song—aye, and **there**'s women in't too!" (Abnegation Mings, *Black Bartlemy's Treasure* 32–33)

- "Look'ee, shipmate, in all this crew **there** are no more than twenty men I can count on, nay, less—ten only can I swear by. See now, **here**'s you and Merrilees and Godby, **here**'s Farnaby and Toby Hudd **the** bo'sun, Treliving the carpenter, and McLean his mate, **here**'s Robins and Perks and Taffery the armourer—good mariners all." (Adam Penfeather, *Black Bartlemy's Treasure* 124)

Note also that pirates sometimes use "here" as a substitute for "that" (just as they use "this" in place of the modern speaker's "that"). Thus, "When we took those two Moghul ships—the *Mhari* and *Vij-Tali*—now **that** was a good fight" becomes "When us took they two Moghul ships—the *Mhari* and *Vij-Tali*—now **here** was a good fight."

- < "Look you, Mossoo, this fellow here, this Blood, this doctor, this escaped convict, made believe that he would enter into articles with us so as to get from me the secret of Morgan's treasure. Now that he's got it, he makes difficulties about the articles." "Why, **here**'s paltry invention!" > (Captain Easterling & Peter Blood, *Captain Blood Returns* 32–33)

- "**Here** was scurvy trick, Barnaby, a devilish ill turn, shipmate, to suffer yon hoity-toity, fleering madam to spy me in my weakness, and my phiz all cursed bristles, damme!" (Japhet Bly, *Winds of Chance* 86)

21.5 CHARACTERIZATION

In July 1572, under enemy fire, Francis Drake marched into Nombre de Dios to take the King of Spain's treasure-house. When a Spanish soldier shot him in the thigh, Drake pushed on, blood filling his footprints. When Drake reached the doors of the treasure-house, a thunderstorm broke, driving his men to shelter and rendering their weapons useless. When the rain let up and Drake's men finally burst into the treasure-house—it was empty. The last treasure fleet had sailed six weeks earlier. The attack was an utter disaster.

But Drake tried again. In February 1573, he and his men spied Spanish treasure ships from Peru arrive and unload at Panama. Seeing the treasure packed onto mules, Drake prepared an ambush along an inland trail. But one of Drake's men got drunk and hastily charged a few donkeys carrying little of value, warning away the rest of the mule train.

Strike two.

Drake tried yet again. In March 1573, he learned from French privateers that 190 mules loaded with Spanish treasure were headed for Nombre de Dios. Drake and his men handily defeated the mule-train sentries, then discovered so much gold and silver tied onto the mules' backs that many of the silver bars had to be stuffed into animal burrows and left behind. Drake took a mere fifteen tons of silver with him, returning to England with treasure worth all together about 50,000 pieces of eight. (*Under the Black Flag* 26–31; *The Queen's Pirate* 54–66)

He was the most admired pirate in history. Queen Elizabeth gave him the highest honor she could bestow—a knighthood that made him "Sir" Francis Drake. And his legendary persistence and determination likely earned him high honors from fellow pirates, who might have given genuinely admiring characterization like, "Drake was one to keep standin' on, blow fair, blow foul" or "Drake, he were never the man to strike colors."

Pirates use the phrases "one to," "the one to," "a man to," "the man to," and "a hand to" to characterize others.

- "You always was **one to** give a sick man a chance." (Long John Silver, "The Adventures of Long John Silver: Execution Dock" 12:23)

- "Ah, he was **the man to** have a headpiece, was Flint! Barring rum, his match was never seen. He was afraid of none, not he." (Ben Gunn, *Treasure Island* 100, Chap. 19)

- "You're not to suppose that I'm **the man to** walk into a gin without taking precautions to see that it can't be sprung on me." (Peter Blood, *The Fortunes of Captain Blood* 104)

Pirates use the same phrases—but preceded with negative terms like "ain't," "bain't," "ben't," "hain't," "never," and "not"—in order to form negative characterizations.

- "What I hear tell of Captain Barbossa, he's **not a man to** suffer fools nor strike a bargain with one." (Joshamee Gibbs,

"Pirates of the Caribbean: The Curse of the Black Pearl" 52:56)

- "George here **ain't the one to** lay plans, but if you aims to take this stockade, well, George is a good man in a fight, too good to be rotting down below." (Israel Hands, "Treasure Island" [1950] 55:19)

- "But I'm **not one to** lead a likely lad astray ..." (Long John Silver, *Porto Bello Gold* 29)

Note also the interesting use of "that's," rather than the typical personal pronoun, to introduce a characterization.

"I'm not thinking of Don Ilario, but of that bile-laden curmudgeon Don Clemente. **That's not the man to** let a pledged word thwart his spite." (Wolverstone, *The Fortunes of Captain Blood* 19)

Note three other ways of forming a negative characterization. Just say the subject and verb (like "you be" or "he was") and add:

(1) **no hand at ...**

"I may tell you plainly that I am **no poor hand at** the reading of faces." (Benny Willitts, *The Book of Pirates* "The Ruby of Kishmoor" 237)

(2) **no man for ...**

"I'm **no man for** makin' trouble, but there's them as might say the captain was a mite rash." (Long John Silver, *Porto Bello Gold* 66)

(3) **none of your ...**

"What I gets, I keeps. I'm **none o' your** free spenders, rich today, poor tomorrow." (Long John Silver, *Porto Bello Gold* 65)

21.6 NARRATION

Pirates are masters of the Untellable Tale. William Dampier, in his firsthand account of buccaneering exploits in the late seventeenth century, gives us a good example: He reports that forty French survivors of multiple shipwrecks off the island of Aves in 1678 managed to scramble onto a damaged vessel "where there was a good store of liquor, till the afterpart of her broke away and floated over the reef, and was carried away to sea, with all the men drinking and singing. Being in drink, they did not mind the danger, but were never heard of afterwards." (*A New Voyage Round the World* 35)

How do we know so much pirate history if so many stories end in "and they were never heard from again"? Jack Sparrow makes exactly the same point in conversation with a fellow prisoner in Port Royal's jail: < "The *Black Pearl*? I've heard stories. She's been preying on ships and settlements for near ten years. Never leaves any survivors." "No survivors? Then where do the stories come from, I wonder?" > (*Pirates of the Caribbean: The Curse of the Black Pearl* 29:50)

The beauty of pirate stories is that it's the filigree of the telling that's important, not the pedigree of what's told. This section shows you how pirates do it—how they tell their side of the story (21.6.1), how they liven up stories by shifting tenses (21.6.2), and how they feature themselves in those stories as third-person characters (21.6.3).

21.6.1 SAYS YOU/SAYS I

In conversations, especially heated ones, a modern English speaker will often sum up the other person's side of the argument, or his own, for purposes of clarification or comment. "You say chunky peanut butter has more substance. I say gravel has more substance too, but I don't see you eating gravel."

The terms "you say" and "I say" are quick and easy ways of summarizing viewpoints or positions. Pirates use "says you" or "says I" for the same narrative purpose. "Winter sea's perfeck for fast sailin', **says you**. Perfeck for dyin' in a gale, too, **says I**."

- "What happened to Flint's gold, **says you**. Ben Gunn's cave, **says I**." (Long John Silver, "Treasure Island" [1950] 1:29:22)

- "And yet you ha'n't found the treasure **says you**. If I was a passionate man, Marty, I should call ye liar, **says I**." (Roger Tressady, *Black Bartlemy's Treasure* 304)

- "'She's only a woman,' **says you**. 'True,' **says I**. But in all this here world there ain't her match, woman or man, and you can lay to that, my lad." (Diccon, *Martin Conisby's Vengeance* 69)

Pirates also use "says you" or "says I" to re-count actual conversations—that is, where modern speakers might use "you said" or "I said."

"'With whom?' **says I**, amazed at such idea. 'With your wife,' **says he**. 'That, Barnaby,' **says I**, 'would be notable thought were she any other's wife or I any other's husband.' 'But,' **says Barnaby**, 'but Ursula?' "Lad,' **says I**, 'Ursula is far beyond any buts ...'" (Japhet Bly, relating to Ursula Revell an earlier conversation with Barnabas Rokeby, *Winds of Chance* 152)

Finally, pirates use "says you" not only to summarize another's explicit viewpoint or recount another's statement, but also to suppose or hypothesize what another might be thinking or is likely to believe.

- "And how do you suppose I lost my left stick, eh? Can't say, **says you** ..." (Long John Silver, *Porto Bello Gold* 21)

- "No fear have ye of evil curses, **says you**. Hahh. Properly warned ye be, **says I**." (foreboding pirate voice, "Pirates of the Caribbean" Disney attraction)

- "Well now, what's needed in steerin'? A strong arm, **says you**, and you says true." (Long John Silver, *Porto Bello Gold* 64)

21.6.2 TENSE SHIFT

While recounting past events, shift from the past tense to the present. Do so especially just before and during the climax of the action.

- "But all at once they **seemed** to fall to disputation, Tressady and a small, dark fellow against the four, and thereafter to brawl and fight, though this **was** more butchery than fight, Martin, for Tressady **shoots** down two ere they can rise, and leaping up **falls** on the other two with his hook! So with aid from the small, dark fellow they soon **have made** an end o' their four companions, and leaving them lying, **come** up the beach and sitting below the ledge of rock whereon I lay snug hidden, fell to talk." (Adam Penfeather, *Black Bartlemy's Treasure* 90)

- "When the three ladies **kneeled** down to me, and as soon as I understood what it was for, I let them know I would not hurt the Queen nor let anyone else hurt her, but that she must give me all her jewels and money. Upon this they **acquainted** her that I would save her life, and no sooner had they assured her of that but she **got** up, smiling, and went to a fine Indian cabinet and **opened** a private drawer, from whence she took another little thing full of little square drawers and holes: this she **brings** to me in her hand, and **offered** to kneel down to give it to me." (Captain Avery, *The King of Pirates* 57)

- "When the fire **broke** out, we **sent** word to Marlowe, asking would he help with putting it out. 'No,' **says** he, 'and with the tide making, won't we just be on our merry way.'" (Henry Nagel purporting to quote Thomas Marlowe, *The Pirate Round* 209)

21.6.3 THIRD-PERSONIZATION

Refer to yourself in the third person.

- "Arrgh, black is the day, heavy is my heart, that I should live to see stout Ben Worley turn on ol' **Ned Teach**, what's always trusted him like a brother." (Blackbeard, also known as Edward or "Ned" Teach, "Blackbeard the Pirate" 49:39)

- "Is there a man here that will not obey **Joanna**—no? **Joanna** that could kill any of ye single-handed as **she** killed Cestiforo!" (Captain Jo, *Martin Conisby's Vengeance* 62)

- "When **Captain Sharkey** has a boat **he** can get a smack, when **he** has a smack **he** can get a brig, when **he** has a brig **he** can get a barque, and when **he** has a barque **he'll** soon have a full-rigged ship of **his** own—so make haste into London town, or I may be coming back, after all, for the *Morning Star*." (John Sharkey, *The Dealings of Captain Sharkey and Other Tales of Pirates* "How the Governor of Saint Kitt's Came Home" 24)

A variation is to refer to yourself in the third person *before* making clear that such person is you. The effect is folksy and dramatic.

- < "I'd give a handful o' gold pieces to see him dead and be damned!" "Why, then, **here's a lad to earn 'em, an' that's me**." > (Captain Belvedere & Job, *Martin Conisby's Vengeance* 67)

- "What, messmate, **here cometh one to lay alongside you awhile**, old Resolution Day, friend, mate o' this here noble ship *Happy Despatch*, comrade, **and that same myself**, look'ee!" (Resolution Day, *Martin Conisby's Vengeance* 72)

- "**I know a man as don't forget past benefits and that's Abnegation!**" (Abnegation Mings, *Martin Conisby's Vengeance* 156)

See Section 22.1.5 for a discussion of a particular kind of third-personization: self-naming.

CHAPTER 22

Parts of Speech

In 1721, near the Sierra Leone River, a British official named Plunkett had the audacity to attack Bartholomew Roberts—one of the most successful pirates of all time. Roberts captured Plunkett and, when the two men came face to face, the outraged pirate captain swore blue fire at the prisoner in front of the assembled company. Plunkett, ringed by a throng of jeering cutthroats, silently weathered the abuse. When Roberts finished, however, Plunkett began swearing back at Roberts so much faster and more fluently that the pirates, amused and admiring, let the man live. (*Villains of All Nations* 97)

If a working knowledge of the nuts and bolts of authentic pirate speech can prove a matter of life and death, then this chapter is strong medicine indeed. These pages cover the basic building blocks of the pirate language—the parts of speech: nouns (22.1), pronouns (22.2), verbs (22.3), adjectives (22.4), adverbs (22.5), prepositions (22.6), and articles (22.7).

☠

22.1 NOUNS

In the pirate language, there are distinct rules (to the extent pirates have rules) governing the use of five types of nouns: switched nouns, possessive nouns, non-count nouns, understood nouns, and names.

22.1.1 SWITCHED NOUN

Singularize the plural. Use a singular noun instead of its plural especially:

(1) Where the number of things referenced is specified or emphasized. Thus, instead of "We have nearly five **leagues** more to sail before

we reach Tortuga," a pirate might say, "We've nigh five **league** marr to sail afore us make Tortuga."

"No, he ain't been here this ten **year** or more." (Henry Nagel, *The Pirate Round* 168)

Note the inconsistent application of this usage, even where the number of things referenced in each instance seems extremely significant:

"[Y]ou see afore you Jeremy Jervey, as sailed out o' Falmouth twen**ty odd year** ago as gunner's mate aboard the *Falcon*, with Captain Amos Trevoe and seventy-odd stout **lads** and all of 'em dead." (Jeremy Jervey, *Winds of Chance* 210)

(2) Where the specific number of things referenced is not as important as their sheer numerousness, consistency, or uniformity. Thus, instead of, "I have survived **deserts** and **jungles** in my time, believe me," a pirate might say "I ha' survived **desert** an' **jungle** in me time, be sure o' that."

"Men have sought it vainly, have striven and fought, suffered and died for it, have endured plague, battle, shipwreck, famine, have died screaming 'neath Indian tortures, languished in Spanish **dungeon** and **slaveship**, and all for sake of Bartlemy's Treasure." (Adam Penfeather, *Black Bartlemy's Treasure* 82)

22.1.2 POSSESSIVE NOUN

The possessive form of a noun in modern English typically takes an apostrophe-"s" ('s). The same is true of pirate speech. But pirates also make their nouns possessive in two other ways.

Blank Possessive

Simply use the noun and nothing else. The possessive use is understood. Thus, instead

of "There was blood on the **bosun's** knife," a pirate might say, "Here were blood on t' **bosun** knife."

"It was liker **somebody else'** voice now ..." (George Merry, *Treasure Island* 182, Chap. 32)

Pronoun Possessive

Use the noun immediately followed by a possessive pronoun. Thus, instead of "There was blood on the bosun's knife," a pirate might say, "Here were blood on t' bosun his knife."

- "So the end of it is, we scrapes together what money we have and fit out a ship for to try our luck agin **Black Bartlemy his** treasure." (Joel Bym, *Adam Penfeather, Buccaneer* 285)

22.1.3 NON-COUNT NOUN

Non-count nouns are nouns that are indivisible and do not consist of individual items. They include abstract nouns ("justice," "agony") and cumulative nouns ("food," "carnage"). In modern English, non-count nouns are generally not used with the indefinite articles "a" or "an." In pirate speech, however, non-count nouns are occasionally used with "a" and "an." A pirate might say, for example, "I'll let the p'int o' this 'ere sword work **a sweet justice**" or "I seen **a carnage** abarrd that ship Satan 'imself'd blush at."

- "I got **a great affection** for my neck. I have no wish to hear it cracked by a hangman's knot." (Honesty Nuttall, "Captain Blood" 1:34:43)

- "I gave him an account of all my adventures in the South Seas, and what **a prodigious booty** we got there with Captain Goignet. ..." (Captain Avery, *The King of Pirates* 12)

22.1.4 UNDERSTOOD NOUN

When making reference to a noun used previously, omit it entirely. Do not replace it with a pronoun, as one might in modern English. The omissions in the below excerpts are indicated by an ellipsis [...].

- "You're a good man, doctor. I never seen a better [...]." (Long John Silver, "Treasure Island" [1950] 59:07)
- "'Tis a brave fire I've made and [...] burns well." (Captain Jo, *Martin Conisby's Vengeance* 35)

22.1.5 NAMES

Pirates make three distinctive uses of names: self-naming, full-naming, and "you" naming.

Self-Naming

Refer to yourself by name in conversation. Pirates do so with disproportionate frequency, consistent with a profession rife with aggressive self-assertion.

- "I want Flint's map. And I can risk 'alf my crew to get'n. But that ain't **Cap'n Silver**'s way." (Long John Silver, "Treasure Island" [1950] 58:48)
- "When I broke prison I learnt from my friends—for **Captain Sharkey** has those who love him in every port—that the Governor was starting for Europe under a master who had never seen him." (John Sharkey, *The Dealings of Captain Sharkey and Other Tales of Pirates* "How the Governor of Saint Kitt's Came Home" 22)
- "I've a mind to slit your pimpish ears so that they may see what happens to them as gets pert with **Captain Easterling**." (Captain Easterling, *Captain Blood Returns* 283)

Full-Naming

Address persons—pirates and honest folk alike—by their full names, rather than by their first names, as is typical among modern speakers.

- "Time you learned, **George Merry**, just who is cap'n aboard this here commercial enterprise." (Long John Silver, "Treasure Island" [1950] 33:42)
- "Blowfish, is it? Well, I don't take kindly to insults, **Long John Silver**." (Billy Bones, "Treasure Island" [1998] 3:58)
- < "If you would but sign the articles—" "Enough, **Joshua Hird**! I have risked my soul too often." > (Joshua Hird & Stephen Craddock, *The Dealings of Captain Sharkey and Other Tales of Pirates* "The Dealings of Captain Sharkey with Stephen Craddock" 39)

"You" Naming

Address persons—pirates and honest folk alike—by saying "you," then adding the person's name thereafter.

- "Hear ye, **you Cochlyn and La Boise**, I find, by strengthening you, I have put a rod into your hands to whip myself ..." (Captain Davis, resolving the increasing discord with his two confederate pirate captains by announcing his separation from them, *General History of the Pyrates* 175 & *The Pirates Own Book* 210)

22.2 PRONOUNS

If it's pirate pronouns you're wondering about—switched pronouns, relative pronouns, verb object pronouns, sidekick pronouns, the understood "you"—this section has all the answers.

22.2.1 SWITCHED PRONOUN

Nominative for Objective

Use the nominative form of a pronoun (I, he, she, we, they, who) instead of the objective form (me, him, her, us, them, whom).

- "[A] cheer for Master Penfeather as dare be friend to the likes o' **we** ..." (Martin Frant, *Adam Penfeather, Buccaneer* 92)

- "Although even some o' **they** should know better ..." (Wolverstone, *Captain Blood: His Odyssey* 255)

- "[T]hey thought there was a better than even chance you'd win against **who** you was fighting." (Henry Nagel, *The Pirate Round* 97)

Note the inconsistency with which this usage is observed.

"[F]or look'ee, there is never a ship on the Main will grant quarter or show mercy for **we**; 'tis noose and tar and gibbet for every one on **us**, d'ye see?" (Resolution Day, *Martin Conisby's Vengeance* 111)

Objective for Nominative

Use the objective form of a pronoun (me, him, her, us, them, whom) instead of the nominative form (I, he, she, we, they, who).

- "Now, look here, Jim, you and **me** is goin' to be mates." (Billy Bones, "Treasure Island" [1934] 5:50)

- "You want to have it out with me? **Him** that dares'll see the color of his insides, crutch an' all." (Long John Silver, "Treasure Island" [1972] 1:13:26)

- < "And you will be able to find this place again—in the dark?" "Sure-ly, sir! 'Twas there as Master Perks and **me** took cover the night as **us** 'scaped." > (Adam Penfeather & Joel Bym, *Adam Penfeather, Buccaneer* 318)

Use objective pronouns instead of nominative ones particularly when they are modified by subordinate clauses or participial phrases. Thus, instead of "It was **she** who pulled the trigger," a pirate might say, "It was **her** as pulled the trigger."

- "It was a master surgeon, **him** that ampytated me—out of college and all—Latin by the bucket, and what not ..." (Long John Silver, *Treasure Island* 57)

- "D'ye hear that? **Him** sailing under Hawke?!" (George Merry, "Treasure Island" [1950] 17:54)

Note the inconsistency with which this switch is used.

- "Is **us** to be murdered, look'ee? Doomed men **we** be, lads! Shall **us** wait to be shot, mates? What shall **us** do, Cap'n, what shall **us** do?" (pirates in Roger Tressady's company, *Black Bartlemy's Treasure* 314)

22.2.2 RELATIVE PRONOUN

Relative pronouns are pronouns, like "that," "which," "who," and "whom," that introduce relative clauses: "The *Hispaniola* was the ship **that** sailed yesterday." "We sailed to Flint's island, **which** was hot and bare." "That's the girl **whom** you saw in the tavern." Substitute any traditional relative pronoun with one of these seven alternatives, or with nothing at all:

(1) **as** ("The *Hispaniola* were the ship **as** sailed yesterday.")

"Now, what a ship was christened, so let her stay, I says. So it was with the *Cassandra*, **as** brought us all safe home from Malabar, after England took the *Viceroy of the Indies*; so it was with the old *Walrus*, Flint's old ship, **as** I've seen a-muck with the red blood and fit to sink with gold." (Long John Silver, *Treasure Island* 57, Chap. 11)

(2) **(and) such as** ("The *Hispaniola* were the ship **(and) such as** sailed yesterday.")

"So we went, I say, boldly on shore, and there we began to chaffer with them for some provisions, **such as** we wanted." (Captain Avery, *The King of Pirates* 65)

"[W]e cured 140 barrels of very good beef, **and such as** lasted us a very great while." (Captain Avery, *The King of Pirates* 12)

(3) **what** ("The *Hispaniola* were the ship **what** sailed yesterday.")

"This be a job **what** takes innards." (Blackbeard, "Blackbeard's Ghost" 1:24:04)

(4) **him\her\it\them (that)** ("The *Hispaniola* were the ship **it (that)** sailed yesterday.")

"'Tis said my Lady Brandon and her gallant Sir Rupert Dering—**him** you overthrew, shipmate—do mean to come and take a look at you, anon, though 'tis shame you should be made a raree show—burn me!" (Adam Penfeather, *Black Bartlemy's Treasure* 58) "Martin, there be times when I could joyfully make an end o' you—for her sake—**her that** do love you to her grief and sorrow. ..." (Resolution Day, tapping the butt of his pistol, *Martin Conisby's Vengeance* 144)

(5) **that's** ("The *Hispaniola* were the ship **that's** sailed yesterday.")

"Them of you **that's** dies'll be lucky." (Long John Silver, "Treasure Island" [1934] 1:05:58)

(6) **the which** ("The *Hispaniola* were the ship **the which** sailed yesterday.")

"[I]t was broad day before we got to a certain store-house, situated upon the shore; **the which** we found our men had passed by in the dark of the night, without perceiving it." (Basil Ringrose, describing his company's approach toward Cuidad de la Serena, *Bucaniers of America* Part IV Chap. XIV)

(7) **which same** ("The *Hispaniola* were the ship **which same** sailed yesterday.")

"Pew, he got a thousand pounds, **which same** he blowed in three nights in St. Pierre." (Long John Silver, *Porto Bello Gold* 65)

You can also replace relative pronouns with nothing at all. "The *Hispaniola* were the ship sailed yesterday."

"I want their captain, Peter Pan. 'Twas he [...] cut off my arm." (Captain James Hook, *Peter Pan* 60)

One may use more than one of the above relative pronoun alternatives in the same sentence.

"'Twas he **as** drove their mates out to sea to perish in a leaky boat—ask Abnegation Mings! 'Twas him [...] nigh murdered me more than once, aye me, lad, **as** can't *be* killed according to the prophecy of the poor mad soul aboard the Old *Delight*." (Roger Tressady, *Black Bartlemy's Treasure* 302–03)

Moreover, pirates often use traditional relative pronouns in addition or in combination with the above alternatives.

"To them **what** hunts what I have hid, and to their sons' sons, down through the endless corridors of time, greed **that** spawns murder, hatred **that** corrodes the soul, ambition—the foulest strumpet of all. (Captain William Kidd, "Captain Kidd" 1:19:00)

Note that certain of the above relative pronoun alternatives tend to be used more often with essential clauses—clauses that are necessary to a sentence and are not introduced by commas, such as "He's the man *whom* I once blinded with black powder" or "The ship carries all the treasure *which* we took at Panama." Other relative pronoun alternatives are more typically used with nonessential clauses—clauses that are not necessary to a sentence and begin with commas, such as "He's my brother, *whom* I once blinded with black powder" or "The ship carries all our treasure, ***which*** we took at Panama." Specifically, nothing at all is almost always used with essential clauses, while "and such as" (#2), "the which" (#6), and "which same" (#7) are almost always used with nessential clauses.

22.2.3 VERB OBJECT PRONOUN

The word "that" often serves as a verb object pronoun, introducing clauses that are objects of the preceding verb: "Cap'n Kessler told me **that** you're a fine gunner."

Substitute one of four alternatives listed below for the verb object pronoun "that." The first two alternatives ("as," "as how") can be used in all instances, while the third and fourth ("but," "but what") are used primarily with double-negative verbs—that is, negative verbs like "doubt," "disbelieve," "ignore," "deny," and "dismiss" when modified by negators like "don't," "not," and "never."

(1) **as** ("Cap'n Kessler told me **as** you're a fine gunner.")

"Roger and me don't see **as** you should take a third to share among thirty men, while we share each of us the same among a hundred and fifty." (Captain Easterling, *Captain Blood Returns* 281)

(2) **as how** ("Cap'n Kessler told me **as how** you're a fine gunner.")

"Well, cap'n, that chest been in cabin a longish time. And we all thought **as how** it wouldn't do no harm to open up that chest and make sure that what was in it then, is in it now." (Theodore Blades, "Captain Kidd" 3:37)

(3) **but** ("Cap'n Kessler don't doubt **but** you're a fine gunner.")

"[A]nd I doubt not **but** the post may stand there still." (Captain Avery, *The King of Pirates* 32)

(4) **but what** ("Cap'n Kessler don't doubt **but what** you're a fine gunner.")

"And I'll not deny neither **but what** some of my people was shook—maybe all was shook; maybe I was shook myself; maybe that's why I'm here for terms." (Long John Silver, *Treasure Island* 107, Chap. 20)

Note that pirates, like modern speakers, often use no verb object pronoun at all: "Cap'n Kessler told me [...] you're a fine gunner."

"John was seeing to it [...] the sarvants was all secure, sir." (Billy Bones, *Porto Bello Gold* 44)

22.2.4 SIDEKICK PRONOUN

Use a pronoun immediately after the primary noun subject of a sentence. Thus, "**That one-eyed rascal** killed every crewmember aboard before disappearing into the ocean" becomes "**That one-eyed rascal**, *he* kilt ev'ry man jack abarrd afore disappearin' inter t' ocean." The word "he" in the latter example is a sidekick pronoun.

- "I've bad news for your Excellency. Mendoza, **he** tricked me and sacked your warehouse." (Long John Silver, "Long John Silver's Return to Treasure Island" 30:16)

- "Pew, **he** was rammin' home a charge and leaned out through the port and caught the flash of a carronade." (Long John Silver, *Porto Bello Gold* 64–65)

22.2.5 UNDERSTOOD "YOU"

When using "you" as the subject of a sentence, omit it entirely. It is understood.

- "But when you shall seek me, as seek me ye will, shipmate, [...] shalt hear of me at the Peck-o'-Malt tavern, which is a small, quiet place 'twixt here and Bedgebury Cross." (Adam Penfeather, *Black Bartlemy's Treasure* 63)

- "Didst [...] never want to be a pirate, my hearty?" (Captain James Hook, *Peter Pan* 149)

- "See now, Martin, I have lived here three days and in all this woful weary time [...] hast never asked my name, which is strange ..." (Captain Jo, *Martin Conisby's Vengeance* 28)

Note that "you" is most often omitted as the subject of a sentence when the verb used is a second-person Elizabethan verb—one ending in "t," "st," or "th." The following are the second-person Elizabethan forms of frequently used verbs: "art" (are), "canst" (can), "couldst" (could), "didst" (did), "hast" (have), "shalt" (shall), "wilt" (will), "wouldst" (would).

Note also the inconsistent application of this usage:

"Moreover **you** ha'n't your sealegs yet. [...] Shalt soon find the trick on't." (Absalom Troy, *Adam Penfeather, Buccaneer* 55)

22.3 VERBS

Verbs in the pirate language are beautiful things, as they provide rich and multiple opportunities to talk utterly wrong. Take the following excerpt, for instance:

"Err, **there's** places a friend of Morgan **be** safe and there's places he **ain't**." (Blackbeard, "Blackbeard the Pirate" 12:33)

Note all the instances of bad verb grammar here: "there's" instead of "there are" (noun-verb number disagreement); "be" instead of "is" (noun-verb person disagreement); and "ain't" instead of "isn't" (lack of a real word, which "ain't" ain't).

This section introduces the use of verbs in pirate speech, and the various ways pirates butcher them as colorfully as possible.

22.3.1 SWITCHED VERB

In modern English, a single verb takes different forms. Take the present-tense verb "run," for instance. One says either "run" (I run, you run, we run, they run) or "runs" (he runs, she runs, it runs).

Pirates use the same two forms, but they switch them. That is, they use "run" where a modern speaker would say "runs," and "runs" where a modern speaker would say "run." In switching verbs, pirates use singular verbs with plural subjects ("guns **is** what we got"), use plural verbs with singular subjects ("that gun **were** a big 'un"), use third-person verbs with first-person and second-person subjects ("I **wants** them guns loaded"), and use second-person verbs with third-person subjects ("he **were** the finest gunner about").

Like most usages, the switched verb is an inconsistent phenomenon. Sometimes a pirate will switch his verb, sometimes he won't—and often he'll do both, as in each of the following excerpts:

- "You **come** and **go** as you please, and never a thought or feeling for those you **leaves** behind." (Purity Pinker, "The Adventures of Long John Silver: Miss Purity's Birthday" 10:41)

- "I **were** the one what threw the lead line fer John Flint, I **was**!" (Morley Rowe, *Dead Man's Chest* 250)

22.3.2 PLAIN WRONG VERB

Use an obviously wrong form of any verb, especially an irregular verb (*e.g.*, "knowed"), or a verb that does not exist at all in the English language (*e.g.*, "bain't").

- "[T]here's none on the islands but a lizard or two, and some sich harmless things. But I never **seed** any myself." (Bloody Bill, noting the existence of reptiles on the South Sea Islands, *The Coral Island* 229)

- "An' since we got some time on our side, we can go below and kill this bottle of brandy I **brung** along fer good luck." (Joshua Smoot, *Dead Man's Chest* 224)

- "Lord Yancy will have guns to sell, if you **gots** gold to buy them." (Henry Nagel, *The Pirate Round* 168)

22.3.3 REFLEXIVE VERB

Make active verbs reflexive. Follow any active verb (a verb other than a linking verb like "be" or "seem" and that denotes action or movement) with a corresponding objective pronoun. "We buried the gold on the beach" becomes "We **buried us** the gold on the beach."

One can make reflexive verbs out of both transitive verbs, or verbs that take an object ("I **climbed me** that tree"), and intransitive verbs, or verbs that do not take an object ("I **climbed me** up the tree").

- "As for me, I **kills me** one o' the guards and won free, along o' Surgeon Perks." (Joel Bym, *Adam Penfeather, Buccaneer* 285)

- "I ha'n't fought and hunted with Indians without **learning me** some o' their craft." (Japhet Bly, *Winds of Chance* 300)

- "And sure enough in a while comes the big man Tressady a-stealing furtive-fashion and falls to hunting both in the open grave and round about it but, finding nothing, **steals him** off again." (Adam Penfeather, describing Roger Tressady's attempts to find Black Bartlemy's dagger around Bartlemy's grave, *Black Bartlemy's Treasure* 92)

22.3.4 BE

When using any form of the verb "to be," consider using one of four alternatives instead.

(1) **Dropped "Be":** Omit the verb "be" entirely. ("He cap'n of this here ship.")

"Some of you [...] pretty handy with a handspike-end." (Long John Silver, *Treasure Island* 107, Chap. 20)

(2) **Naked "Be":** Use the word "be" rather than the correct specific form of the verb, especially "am," "is," or "are" ("He **be** cap'n of this here ship") and "were" in the subjunctive. ("I wish I **be** richer.")

"Sorry I **be** for this, mates. I humbly apologize." (Humble Bellows, "The Crimson Pirate" 1:10:34)

(3) **Switched "Be":** As with other verbs, switch forms of "be"—that is, use "is" instead of "are," for example, or "were" instead of "was." ("Olivia and Christian **is** a couple of cutthroats.")

"Then he **aren't** dead, Cap'n?" (Joel Bym, reacting to news that Roger Tressady lives, *Black Bartlemy's Treasure* 103)

(4) **'M:** In sentences in which the subject is a personal pronoun ("you," "he," "she," "we," "they") and the verb is a present-tense form of "be" ("is," "are"), use "'m" instead. (He**'m** cap'n of this here ship.")

- "We**'m** on'y seekin' a bit goold." (mutinying pirate aboard *Royal James*, *Porto Bello Gold* 183)

22.3.5 DO

There are four usages relating to the word "do" and all its forms, including "doesn't," "don't," "did," and "didn't." As always, the only thing consistent about pirate grammar is its inconsistency, so feel free to break these "rules"—the more inconsistent, the better.

(1) **Add "do" for emphasis.** "I know what he thinks." becomes "I **do** know what he thinks." "You have gold." becomes "You **do** have gold."

"Ah, sir, it **do** irk a man's soul and turn his very innards for to see him now ..." (Joel Bym, *Adam Penfeather, Buccaneer* 290)

(2) **Drop "do."** "I do not know what he thinks." becomes "I know not what he thinks." "**Do** you have any gold?" becomes "Have you any gold?"

"What kind of a scurvy dog **you take** me for?" (Long John Silver, "The Adventures of Long John Silver: The Orphans' Christmas" 18:34)

> When asking a question with "do" or "did" ("What do you think of Jamaica?"), either omit "do" without changing anything else ("What you think of Jamaica?") or omit "do" while reversing subject and verb ("What think you of Jamaica?").
>
> When using "don't" or "doesn't" or "didn't" ("It doesn't make sense"), omit that term while adding "no" or "not" after the verb ("It makes no sense" or "It makes not sense").

(3) **Substitute "be" for "do."** "I do not know what he thinks." becomes "I **be** not know what he thinks." "**Do** you have any gold?" becomes "**Be** you have any gold?"

"Here, how many men **be** Morgan got on his ship?" (Blackbeard, "Blackbeard the Pirate" 57:48)

(4) **Switch "do."** "I do not know what he thinks." becomes "I **does** not know what he thinks." "**Do** you have any gold?" becomes "**Does** you have any gold?"

"**Do** it have writing on it? Etchin's o' sort?" (Long John Silver, "Long John Silver's Return to Treasure Island" 25:16)

22.3.6 PRESENT TENSE

When using a present-tense verb, use either (1) the present progressive tense or (2) the future tense instead.

Present Progressive Instead

The present progressive consists of a present-tense form of the verb "be" ("is" or "are") plus a present participle ending in "-ing." The verb in the following sentence is in the present progressive: "He **is leading** the finest company of men on the Main." The present progressive is different from the simple present: "He **leads** the finest company of men on the Main." The present progressive conveys a sense of ongoing-ness and continuity that the simple present does not.

Pirates often use the present progressive when modern speakers would use the simple present. "What is it you **want**?" becomes "What is it you**'re wanting**?"

Below are five circumstances in which pirates are especially likely to use the present progressive instead of the simple present.

(1) **infinitive:** Use the present progressive instead of the present when using an infinitive—that is, the word "to" plus a verb.

"I don't want'**a be tellin'** you yer business, Ben, but if it were me, I'd throw a couple turns about that rail fer the next load ..." (Long John Silver, *Dead Man's Chest* 6)

(2) **subordinate:** Use the present progressive instead of the present in subordinate clauses—that is, groups of related words that include both a subject and a verb but are not the main clause.

"But the *Arabella*'s been at sea these four months, and her bottom's too foul for the speed we**'re needing**." (Captain Peter Blood, *Captain Blood: His Odyssey* 250)

The following excerpt reflects both the subordinate use and the infinitive use of the present progressive:

> < "Darling, you're safe!" "Ha-harr! Safe and sound, he be! And some day when I **be returnin'** to Isla de Oro, I 'opes to **be greetin'** your fine sons and daughters." > (Abbie & Long John Silver, "The

Adventures of Long John Silver: Sword of Vengeance" 25:31)

(3) **desiderative:** Use the present progressive instead of the present where describing or referring to a desire, preference, inclination, or objective of any kind.

"How many men might you **be needin'**, Squire?" (Long John Silver, "Treasure Island" [1934] 27:42)

(4) **supplicative:** Use the present progressive instead of the present when asking for something, or when otherwise phrasing something humbly or graciously in order to convey the sense that it is the addressee's pleasure that governs.

"Excuse the instrusion, Captain Jones, but might I **be interestin'** you in a plate o' me little wife's lamb an' cabbage?" (Long John Silver, *Dead Man's Chest* 27)

(5) **descriptive:** Use the present progressive instead of the present when describing something or conveying one's perception or impression of something.

"You **be lookin'** right pleased, mate, heh-heh, like a ship's cat, sittin' in fish." (pirate at the Cask & Anchor, "The Adventures of Long John Silver: The Necklace" 1:13)

Future Instead

Use the future tense instead of the present tense in the following contexts:

(1) **supposive:** Use the future progressive when engaging in surmise or supposition—that is, when inferring additional information or assuming the likelihood of something happening based on limited but observable facts.

"The fire's slackening. It**'ll mean** the end of Mallard's resistance in the fort." (Captain Peter Blood, *Captain Blood: His Odyssey* 354)

(2) **identificative:** Use the future tense instead of the present when identifying something or someone. (This usage is really a subset of the inference usage above—that is, identifying persons or things based on limited information.)

"And this**'ll be** young master Hawkins, I'll be bound." (Long John Silver, "Treasure Island" [1950] 17:31)

(3) **re-indicative:** Use the future tense instead of the present when commending something to the addressee's attention, especially something he already knows but may have forgotten or otherwise failed to keep in mind.

"And you**'ll remember**, Peter, that boy's threat to you this morning." (Hagthorpe, *Captain Blood: His Odyssey* 141)

(4) **benedictive:** Use the future tense instead of the present when politely declining an offer or otherwise making a gracious, charitable, or generous statement of any kind.

< "John Silver, I owe you an apology." "Ha-harr, there**'ll be** no need for that." > (Governor Strong & Long John Silver, "The Adventures of Long John Silver: The Necklace" 24:36)

22.3.7 PAST TENSE

When speaking in the past tense ("I **saw** three ships late this evening"), consider one of the three following verb usages in place of the past-tense form.

(1) **Use the present-tense form instead.** ("I **see** three ships this evenin' late.")

"Who **hand** out them cutlasses? Who **hand** 'em out?!" (Ben Worley, investigating the circumstances of a deadly sword-fight, "Blackbeard the Pirate" 23:41)

(2) **Use the past participle instead.** ("I **seen** three ships this evenin' late.")

"This is jus' like what the Greeks **done** at Troy. 'Cept they was in a horse, 'stead of dresses." (Ragetti, "Pirates of the Caribbean: The Curse of the Black Pearl" 1:49:07)

(3 **Add "ed" or "d" to the past-tense form of the verb, if possible** (and if it does not already end in "d"). ("I **sawed** three ships this evenin' late.")

"Buckets o' blood spilt in the hold/Flint accused Rip Rap, The treasure ye've **stold**." (song sung by unnamed drunken pirates aboard the *Eagle, Dead Man's Chest* 253)

22.3.8 PRESENT PERFECT TENSE

The present perfect tense in modern English is formed by using the helping verb "has" or "have" together with a past participle. "You **have** already **begun.**"

The present perfect tense in pirate speech, on the other hand, can be formed in any of the following ways.

(1) **has\have + PAST PARTICIPLE** ("You **have** already **begun.**")

Pirates occasionally use the same form of the present perfect as modern speakers use.

"You know I**'ve been** always good to you." (Billy Bones, *Treasure Island* 14, Chap. 3)

(2) **ha'\a' + PAST PARTICIPLE** ("You **ha'** already **begun.**")

This form is similar to the present perfect in modern English, except that "has" and "have" are replaced with the contractions "ha'" and "a'."

"If ye wanted things smooth and easy, ye shouldn't have taken to the sea, and ye should never **ha' sailed** with me, for with me things are never smooth and easy." (Captain Peter Blood, *Captain Blood: His Odyssey* 194)

(3) **switched "has"\"have" + PAST PARTICIPLE** ("You **has** already **begun.**")

"There**'s been** blows, too, and I reckon your friends **has had** the best of it." (Ben Gunn, *Treasure Island* 100, Chap. 19)

(4) **hast + PAST PARTICIPLE** (second person verbs only) ("You **hast** already **begun.**")

"Ha, Ben! How then, lad, how then? **Hast found** what we sought?" (Roger Tressady, confronting Ben after watching him find Black Bartlemy's dagger, *Black Bartlemy's Treasure* 92)

(5) **form of "be" + PAST PARTICIPLE** (intransitive verbs only) ("You **are** already **begun.**")

This usage is available only with intransitive verbs—that is, verbs that do not take an object. ("I **left** after dinner" includes an intransitive verb, while "I **left** the house after dinner" includes a transitive verb, as it takes the object "house.")

"We **are** now **returned** back to our settlement on the north part of the island ..." (Captain Avery, *The King of Pirates* 76)

(6) **do + PAST PARTICIPLE** ("You **do** already **begun.**")

"**Do** you ever **wondered** what it's like not to look at the sand and the sea, always to wear the cloak of night? You're soon to know, boy!" (Israel Hands, "Long John Silver's Return to Treasure Island" 1:30:53)

(7) **been and gone and + PAST PARTICIPLE** ("You **been and gone and** already **begun.**")

"But, Cap'n, blast my eyes, sir, and axing your pardin, but you ... you hain't **been and gone and ... killed** pore Giles, 'ave ye, sir?" (Thomas Ash, *Adam Penfeather, Buccaneer* 204)

(8) **past participle only** ("You already **begun.**")

Use the past participle only, without any helping verbs like "has" or "have."

"We **been** in that wicked, wicked jungle four days now." (Elephiant Yancy, *The Pirate Round* 245)

(9) **has\have** + SIMPLE PAST ("You **have** already **began**.")

"I should **have spoke** much finer than I do now, but that, as your Lordship knows our rum is all out, and how should a man speak good law that **has not drank** a dram." (pirate in Thomas Antsis' company, *General History of the Pyrates* 293)

(10) **form of "be"** + SIMPLE PAST (intransitive verbs only) ("You **are** already **began**.")

This usage is available only with intransitive verbs—that is, verbs that do not take an object. ("I **left** after dinner" includes an intransitive verb, while "I **left** the house after dinner" includes a transitive verb, as it takes the object "house.")

"As soon as I **was got** a little clear of the land, I fired a gun and spread English colours." (Captain Avery, *The King of Pirates* 46)

(11) **simple past** ("You already **began**.")

< "How long we **sailed** together, Nick?" "Six years." > (Ned Lynch & Nick Debrett, "Swashbuckler" 50:38)

22.3.9 PAST PERFECT TENSE

The past perfect tense in modern English is formed by using the helping verb "had" together with a past participle. "We **had gone** to Tortuga by the time Captain Paul arrived." The past perfect is used to indicate a point in time in the past *earlier* than another past event or timeframe.

The past perfect in pirate speech is formed in two additional ways.

(1) **had** + SIMPLE PAST

Thus, "We **had gone** to Tortuga" becomes "We **had went** to Tortuga." "You **had seen** the black-sailed ship" becomes "You'**d saw** the black-sailed ship."

*Bellamy swore he was sorry he could not run out his guns to return the salute, meaning the thunder, that he fancy'd the gods **had got** drunk over their tipple, and were gone together by the ears.* (attribution to Captain Bellamy, *General History of the Pyrates* 586)

(2) **was\were** + PAST PARTICIPLE

Thus, "We **had gone** to Tortuga" becomes "We **were gone** to Tortuga." "You **had seen** the black-sailed ship" becomes "You **were seen** the black-sailed ship."

"We took one Indian prisoner, but could not learn of him what country that was, as not understanding his language: we sought for others, but they **were fled**." (William Dick, *Bucaniers of America* 354)

Note that pirates make inconsistent use of this form. They sometimes use it, they sometimes use the traditional "had"-plus-past participle form instead, and they often use both in the same sentence:

"We **were** now **gotten** into the latitude of 10, 11, and 12 degrees and a half, but, in our overmuch caution, **had kept** out so far to sea that we missed everything which otherwise would have fallen into our hands ..." (Captain Avery, *The King of Pirates* 22)

22.3.10 FUTURE TENSE

Present Instead

When speaking in the future tense ("You'll be sorry when the Portuguese return"), use the present-tense form of a verb ("You **be** sorry when the Portugals return" or "You're sorry when the Portugals return") instead of the future-tense form.

"There's time enough for that, lad, when we're aboard the *Thistle*." (Long John Silver, "Long John Silver's Return to Treasure Island" 48:25)

Future Progressive Instead

When speaking in the future tense ("I **will go**, and you **will stay**"), use the future progressive form of a verb ("I **will be going**, and **you'll be staying**") instead of the future-tense form. The following are four contexts in which pirates make especially frequent use of the future progressive form when speaking in the future tense.

(1) **suggestive:** Use the future progressive when suggesting to the addressee that he say, think, or do (or not say, think, or do) something.

"Ye**'ll not be trusting** overmuch, I hope, to the word of that flabby, blue-faced Governor?" (Wolverstone, *The Fortunes of Captain Blood* 12)

(2) **supposive:** Use the future progressive when engaging in surmise or supposition—that is, when inferring additional information or assuming the likelihood of something happening based on limited but observable facts.

"Now you**'ll be asking** yourself with some impatience, 'Why was this?'" (Blackbeard, "Blackbeard's Ghost" 45:24)

(3) **predictive:** Use the future progressive when making predictions or projections concerning future events.

"If Cap'n Smollet lays 'is 'ands on old Long John, I'll **be swingin'** from that same yard what me goods been hoisted from ..." (Long John Silver, *Dead Man's Chest* 7)

(4) **proclamative:** Use the future progressive when making promises or emphatic assertions of any kind.

"[W]e need not abandon hope, like others of our kind, that one day this outlawry will be lifted. I**'ll not be putting** that in jeopardy by a landing in force on Nevis, not even to save your brother, Nat." (Captain Peter Blood, *The Fortunes of Captain Blood* 85)

Be To

Perhaps the verb form most frequently used by pirates when speaking in the future tense—other than the traditional form featuring the use of the word "will"—is the be-to form. When speaking in the future tense, use a form of the word "be," plus "to" and the verb itself.

"I **will swim** to hell and back." becomes "I**'m to swim** to hell and back."

"You **will stay** here." becomes "You**'re to stay** here."

"He **will die** before he wakes." becomes "He**'s to die** before he wakes."

Note that the "be to" form is a bit more prescriptive than the future tense. That is, it imports some of the same meaning into a sentence as phrases like "supposed to," "be expected to," "ought to," or "should." The sentence "You will stay here" could be either firm command or mere prediction, depending on context; saying "You're to stay here," on the other hand, falls somewhere in between, and brings to the sentence a mild flavor of "You should stay here."

- "We**'re to sail** with the tide tomorrow." (Long John Silver, "Treasure Island" [1998] 34:22)

- "We could steer a course, but who**'s to set** one?" (Long John Silver, "Treasure Island" [1950] 40:48)

- "Do you ever wondered what it's like not to look at the sand and the sea, always to wear the cloak of night? You**'re soon to know**, boy!" (Israel Hands, "Long John Silver's Return to Treasure Island" 1:30:53)

Be Going To

Replace "will" with a form of "be going to" ("is/are/be/'m going/goin'/gonna to"). Thus, "We**'ll board** the ship." becomes "We**'m goin' to board** the ship."

- "We've had council, and according to vote we **be goin' to** draw that tooth for you, Long John." (Patch, "The Adventures of Long John Silver: The Tale of a Tooth" 14:59)

- "You**'m goin' to** be cared for proper." (Long John Silver, "Treasure Island" [1950] 1:17:34)

- < "Guess what, Long John?" "Ha-harr. You **be gonna tell** me it don't hurt anymore." > (Jim Hawkins & Long John Silver, discussing Jim Hawkins' toothache just outside the dentist's office, "The Adventures of Long John Silver: The Tale of a Tooth" 1:35)

Go+Participle

Replace "will" plus verb with "will" plus "go" plus present participle. Thus, "I'll **change** course tomorrow." becomes "I'll **go changing** course tomorrow."

> "I **won't go slittin'** no throats till you have yer lad!" (Alacan the Turk, *Dead Man's Chest* 52)

22.3.11 SUBJUNCTIVE MOOD

The subjunctive mood in modern English is used to convey statements contrary to reality. Modern speakers make frequent use of four words to make subjunctive statements: "if," "wish," "were," and "would."

> "If I **were** rich, I **would** live on my own island."

> "**Were** I rich, I **would** live on my own island."

> "I **wish** I **were** rich."

Pirates also use the subjunctive mood. However, they often use slightly different words when doing so. Specifically, they use:

- **"was" or "be" instead of "were"**

  "No, I would not reckon it too forward, **was** you to help me. ..." (Peleg Dinwid-

die, *The Pirate Round* 210) "An ambitious man, if he **be** bold enough, can carve himself a kingdom." (Captain William Kidd, "Captain Kidd" 22:56)

- **"did" or "an'" instead of "if"**

  < "There's your ship to be cleaned." "I'd ha' mutiny on my hands **did** I call for it!" > (Andrew Murray & John Flint, *Porto Bello Gold* 124) "Ma'm, your selfish grief disturbs my repose, so **an'** you must sob, sob you some other where." (Japhet Bly, *Winds of Chance* 43)

- **"will" instead of "would"**

  "Ye'll be wiser to throw in your lot with me, my lad." (Captain Peter Blood, *The Fortunes of Captain Blood* 166)

- **"were" instead of "would be"**

  "'**Twere** better to take the young 'un ashore. No soldier would dare to fire in the direction of the Governor's little girl." (Long John Silver, "Long John Silver's Return to Treasure Island" 23:13)

22.3.12 CONDITIONAL MOOD

Conditional clauses are clauses that propose something hypothetical. They are typically introduced by the following hypothetical-sounding words: "if," "what if," "how if," "suppose," "whether," "unless," and "until."

- "**If they run**, we'll pursue."
- "**What if they run**? We'll pursue."
- "**How if they run**? We'll pursue."
- "**Suppose they run**. We'll pursue."
- "**Whether they run or not**, we'll pursue."
- "**Unless they turn and fight**, we'll pursue."
- "**Until they decide to fight**, we'll pursue."

Pirates use conditional clauses differently than modern speakers in two ways. Specifically, modern speakers use present-tense verbs in conditional clauses ("If this venture **makes** us rich, I'll buy an island").

Pirates, on the other hand, use either (1) future-tense verbs ("If this venture **will make** us rich, I'll buy an island") or (2) verb infinitives ("If this venture **make** us rich, I'll buy an island").

(1) **future conditional:** Use a future-tense verb (instead of a present-tense verb) with any conditional clause.

"[I]f you have a Mind to make one of us, we will receive you, and if **you'll turn** sober, and mind your Business, perhaps in time I may make you one of my Lieutenants ..." (Captain Avery, *General History of the Pyrates* 51)

Not: "... and if **you turn** sober, and mind your Business, perhaps in time I may make you one of my Lieutenants ..."

(2) **infinitive conditional:** Use the infinitive form of a verb (instead of a present-tense verb) with any conditional clause.

"Well, ma'm, if fortune **prove** kind and my luck **hold**, it meaneth wealth beyond computation, power to sway men's destinies; fleets of ships to sail at my will, armies of men to do my behests ..." (Captain Japhet Bly, explaining to Ursula Revell the significance of the markings on the skull of the Fourth Inca, *Winds of Chance* 144)

Not: "Well, ma'm, if fortune **proves** kind and my luck **holds** ..."

22.3.13 PRESENT PARTICIPLE & GERUND

Present participles and gerunds look alike. Both are formed by adding "-ing" to a verb. However, present participles are used as adjectives ("I'll kill that **lying** rogue.") or in verb phrases ("That rogue be **lying** through his teef."). Gerunds, on the other hand, are nouns: "**Lying** be what that rogue does best."

There are three things pirates do with both present participles and gerunds.

(1) **Add "a-":** Add the syllable "a-" to the beginning of any present participle when used as an adjective following the noun modified ("We buried the treasure all of us, our hands **a-bleeding**.") or as part of a verb phrase ("We was **a-burying** treasure till our hands bled.")—

< "There be dead men **a-laying** forward— dead, look'ee—" "Likely enough, John Ford, and there'll be dead men **a-laying** aft if ye're not back to your gun and lively, d'ye see?" > (John Ford & Resolution Day, *Martin Conisby's Vengeance* 105)

—and to the beginning of any gerund ("We was done with **a-burying** treasure")

"Now look'ee, Martin, what with one thing or another, and this hell-fire ship on our heels in especial, there's stir and disaffection among the crew, **a-whispering** o' corners that I don't like, and which is apt to spread unless looked to." (Adam Penfeather, *Black Bartlemy's Treasure* 124)

Note that "a-" is added to present participles found in verb phrases, but not present participles that precede and modify nouns. Thus, one might say, "That **swashing** Michael Kane be **a-sailin'** the proud *Josephine*," but almost never say, "That **a-swashing** Michael Kane be **a-sailin'** the proud *Josephine*."

(2) **Cut the "g":** Cut the "g" at the end of any present participle, ending it with "-in'" rather than "-ing" ("We was buryin' treasure till our hands bled")—

"There was a small **tradin'** schooner wrecked off one of these islands when we were **lyin'** there in harbour during a storm." (Bloody Bill, *The Coral Island* 220)

—and at the end any gerund as well ("We was done with **buryin'** treasure"):

"And I say there be no **killin'** till I gives the word." (Long John Silver, "Treasure Island" [1950] 40:14)

(3) **Add "of"**: Transitive present participles are present participles that take objects ("You'll be hanged because you were **stealing** money"), while intransitive present participles do not ("You'll be hanged because you were caught **stealing**"). Similarly, transitive gerunds take objects ("I love **stealing** money"), while intransitive gerunds to not ("I love **stealing**").

Add the word "of" after transitive present participles ("We was burying **of** treasure till our hands bled")—

> "If I hadn't took to you like pitch, do you think I'd have been here **a-warning of** you?" (Long John Silver, *Treasure Island* 75, Chap. 14)

—and after transitive gerunds ("Your task is burying **of** treasure"):

> "[Y]ou've rose me above myself by making **of** me Master o' this yere ship Santa ..." (Ned Bowser, *Adam Penfeather, Buccaneer* 210)

Feel free to combine any or all of the above forms with both present participles and gerunds.

- **Add "a-" and cut the "g"**

> "Here we've been **a-workin'** since sunup, **a-shiftin'** cargo and stowin' it aboard ..." (Long John Silver, *Porto Bello Gold* 48) "Here I be, **a-holdin'** the treasure map, and the key as well." (key-brandishing pirate, "Pirates of the Caribbean" Disney attraction [2006])

- **Cut the "g" and add "of"**

> "And what did they do to the beauteous ladies? Why after **courtin' of** their favor, as it were, savin' your presence matey, they slits the veins of their pearly-white arms and uses their blue blood to warm their rum." (Billy Bones, "Treasure Island" [1934] 8:33)

- **Add "a-" and add "of"**

> "Lad, no one's **a-pressing** of you. Take your bearings." (Long John Silver, *Treasure Island* 157, Chap. 28) "And so 'tis Japhet took solemn oath to kill 'em all three and come nigh **a-doing of** it more than once ..." (Jeremy Jervey, *Winds of Chance* 229)

- **Do all three—that is, add "a-" and cut the "g" and add "of"**

> "But he be shorthanded to work the vessel overseas, 'tis **a-seekin' o'** likely lads and prime sailor-men is Penfeather ..." (Sam Spraggons, *Black Bartlemy's Treasure* 311)

22.3.14 PAST PARTICIPLE

Past participles are verb forms that are used with the present perfect ("I have **taken** the gold"), used with the past perfect ("They had **begun** the raid before the defenders could regroup"), and used as freestanding adjectives ("The guns are well **hidden**").

Simple Past Instead

When using past participles ("You're **mistaken**"), use the simple past ("You're **mistook**") instead.

- "Look at his face, mates. You can see it **wrote** on his face!" (George Merry, "Treasure Island" [1950] 1:28:34)

- "Put it away, son. It's not worth you getting **beat** again." (Jack Sparrow, "Pirates of the Caribbean: The Curse of the Black Pearl" 49:28)

- "A remark **spoke** slighting like that could raise a man's blood now, could it not?" (Blackbeard, "Blackbeard's Ghost" 22:46)

Infinitive Instead

When using past participles ("He's **respected** for 'is bloodthirstiness"), use the infinitive form—that is, the basic form of the verb—where the infinitive form ends in "d" or "t" ("He's **respect** fer 'is bloodthirstiness").

- "'Tis like you shall grow **acquaint** with dangers and, seeing pain o' wounds, you shall forget this mighty universe circles but about your puny self and come to know there be something better things than pretty-turned speech, gallantry o' bows and such fripperies." (Captain Japhet Bly, *Winds of Chance* 40)

- "Japhet hath ever **forbid** women aboard— so now—what?" (Lovepeace Farrance, *Winds of Chance* 48)

- < "But surely I heard a woman scream?" "Ay, you did, sir, you did, a poor, **distract** creature we found wandering solitary hereabouts and needeth your healing arts, sir, as do certain o' my poor lads." > (Matthew Swayne & Roger Snaith, *Winds of Chance* 321)

22.3.15 NEGATION

Double Negative

Of all the ways pirates make negative statements, the double negative ("There **ain't nothin'** worse than a thievin' sailor") is—by far—the most important. See Section 18.3 for a discussion of the double negative and various excerpts illustrating its use.

Don't-less "Not"

Avoid using the word "don't." Instead, add "no" or "not" after the verb being negated. Thus, "They **don't fight** like men" becomes "They **fight not** like men."

Do the same with "doesn't" and "didn't." Thus, "It **doesn't make** sense" becomes "It **makes no** sense" or "It **makes not** sense."

- "So ma'm, be warned and **meddle not** again." (Japhet Bly, *Winds of Chance* 114)

- "Ralph, boy, it **matters not** to me which way we go." (Bloody Bill, *The Coral Island* 260)

- "In all this, however, I **had not** the good luck to advance one step towards my own escape ..." (Captain Avery, *The King of Pirates* 73)

Won't-less "Not"

Pirates almost never use the word "won't." They replace "won't" with one of two usages.

(1) **'ll not:** Replace "won't" with "'ll not"— the contraction of "will not."

"You**'ll not** regret it." (Andrew Murray, *Porto Bello Gold* 124)

(2) **stop + PRESENT PARTICIPLE:** Replace "won't" with the word "stop," plus the present participle of the verb being negated.

"Now look here, if you leave this inn right away, we'll **stop bringin'** charges against you for ill behavior." (Long John Silver, "The Adventures of Long John Silver; The Eviction" 6:40)

Lagging "Not"

Say "not" after the verb, not before it.

- "You'd **be not** cap'n of this inn." (Purity Pinker, "Long John Silver's Return to Treasure Island" 34:32)

    Not: "You'd **not be** cap'n of this inn."

- "[Y]ou shall, **troubling not** for the gold or silver, take but the four caskets of jewels ...." (letter from Adam Penfeather to Martin Conisby, *Black Bartlemy's Treasure* 164)

    Not: "You shall, **not troubling** for the gold or silver, take but the four caskets of jewels ...."

Predicate Negation

When making a negative statement, negate not the verb (as in modern English), but— where possible—the noun or other part of the predicate. (See also Section 21.2.1 on predicate negation, and for additional excerpts illustrating the usage.)

- "Those chains will break **no more** bodies, mate." (Nick Debrett, "Swashbuckler" 1:28:56)

  Not: "Those chains **won't** break any more bodies, mate."

- < "Aren't you satisfied with your lot?" "**Not I!**" > (Robert Ormerod & Ben Gunn, *Porto Bello Gold* 144)

  Not: "No, **I'm not.**"

- "You were all for giving me hostages—'twas **no** idea of mine." (John Flint, *Porto Bello Gold* 190)

  Not: "You were all for giving me hostages—'twas **not** my idea."

22.4 ADJECTIVES

Adjective forms distinctive to pirate speech, including those ending in "-like," are better—less rigidly structured, more permissively interpretive—than those of modern English. This section seeks to preserve that verbal tradition by setting out different ways to form adjectives and the use of possessive adjectives.

22.4.1 FORMATION

Adjectives are words that modify nouns: "**blue** blanket," "**speedy** justice."

There are seven distinctive ways that pirates form adjectives. If a modern speaker says "That sick weakling is good as dead," a pirate might say:

(1) **adjective after noun:** "That weakling **sick** is good as dead."

(2) **ADJECTIVE + -like:** "That **sick-like** weakling is good as dead."

(3) **ADJECTIVE + -ish:** "That **sickish** weakling is good as dead."

(4) **a- + ADJECTIVE:** "That **a-sick** weakling is good as dead."

(5) **noun:** "That **sickness** weakling is good as dead."

(6) **all + NOUN:** "That weakling what's all **sickness** is good as dead."

(7) **all of a + NOUN:** "That weakling what's **all of a sickness** is good as dead."

Adjective After Noun

Use an adjective *after*, rather than before, the noun it modifies to make the adjective more emphatic. The usage is appropriate when the adjective is more important to the sentence than the modified noun.

- "Well now, these be predatory tribes very **warlike**, that for the present have cast in their lot with the Spaniards, though—and mark you this—at one time they and these Aztecs were one great race." (Japhet Bly, *Winds of Chance* 197)

- "Indeed! I know it for name of much detested rogue and pirate **notorious**." (Adam Penfeather, on hearing Black Bartlemy introduce himself by name, *Adam Penfeather, Buccaneer* 253)

- "We gave them firearms and ammunition **sufficient**, and left them furnishing themselves with provisions." (Captain Avery, *The King of Pirates* 81)

Adjective + "-Like"

Add the suffix "-like" to any adjective.

- "I guess I'm kinda **sensitive-like**." (Long John Silver, "Treasure Island" [1934] 36:27)

- < "Come! Come!" "Where away, *camarado*? Nay, I'm best here—mayhap she'll be **lonesome-like** at first, so I'll bide here, lad, I'll bide here a while." > (Martin Conisby & Resolution Day, with Martin trying to lead Resolution away from Captain Jo's grave, *Martin Conisby's Vengeance* 175)

- "I know as you meant well, but you freed me agin orders, which don't nowise seem **nat'ral-like** nohow, nor yet right." (Ben, *Winds of Chance* 103)

Adding "-like" does not necessarily change the meaning of the adjective; rather, it simply makes the adjective doubly "adjective-ish" by adding a clearly modifying suffix.

On the other hand, adding "-like" in certain instances can be used or understood to make the adjective less precise and more approximate, in the same way a modern speaker might add "kind of" to an adjective to make clear it is rough and suggestive. Thus, "The boy we saw looked kind of afraid" becomes "The pup we spied showed afeard-like."

More generally, adding "-like" after an adjective can also be used or understood to make the speaker seem less authoritative and more tentative, in the same way a modern English speaker might use "like" before an adjective. Thus, "The boy we saw looked, like, afraid" becomes "The pup we spied showed afeard-like."

Adjective + "-Ish"
Add the suffix "-ish" to any adjective.

- "Us needs a **stiffish** breeze and a smart helm for to weather they galleys, and be cursed to em!" (Ned Bowser, *Adam Penfeather, Buccaneer* 118)

- < "How now, Barnaby, what o' the fight yonder?" "**Sharpish** awhile, Japhet; we've nine good fellows dead, poor Sol Troy among 'em, alas!" > (Japhet Bly & Barnabas Rokeby, *Winds of Chance* 366)

As with its cousin "-like," the suffix "-ish" makes the adjective less precise and more approximate, in the same way a modern speaker might add "kind of" to an adjective to make clear it is rough and suggestive.

"A-" + Adjective
Add the prefix "a-" to any adjective.

"And so good night! I'm **a-weary**!" (Captain Jo, *Martin Conisby's Vengeance* 159)

Noun as Adjective
Use a noun as an adjective. Specifically, use the noun form of the root word of any adjective, rather than the adjective itself.

- "You are a devilish **conscience** rascal, d[am]n ye ..." (Captain Bellamy, using "conscience" to mean "conscientious." *General History of the Pyrates* 587)

- *North told him, deceit was the sign of a mean and **coward** soul ...* (attribution to Nathaniel North, *General History of the Pyrates* 533)

- "A — **fool** agreement, if you broach it now!" (John Flint, *Porto Bello Gold* 84, omission in original)

All + Noun
Add "all" before a noun. Use this "all"-noun combination as an adjective.

- "I fell in with a woman, who I thought was **all virtue**, but she deceived me ..." (Charles Gibbs, *The Pirates Own Book* 100)

- "Here was scurvy trick, Barnaby, a devilish ill turn, shipmate, to suffer yon hoity-toity, fleering madam to spy me in my weakness, and my phiz **all cursed bristles**, damme!" (Japhet Bly, *Winds of Chance* 86)

- "Oh, burn me, here's a soul! 'Tis a wench o' spirit, **all hell-fire spirit and deviltry**, rot me!" (Roger Tressady, *Martin Conisby's Vengeance* 158)

Note that the "all"-noun adjective does not precede the noun modified, as does a conventional adjective ("That was a **bloody and miserable** battle"), but rather forms part of a predicate or modifying phrase ("That there battle were **all blood and misery**").

Note also that the "all"-noun usage has an intensifying effect, such that describing someone as "all violence" is more emphatic than merely calling him "violent."

All of a+Noun

Add "all of a" before a noun as an adjective.

- "I thought Death had her sure last night, she **all of a fever** and crying out for Death to take her." (Resolution Day, *Martin Conisby's Vengeance* 167)

- "Why, smite me stiff in gore if y' aren't **all of a quake** and pallid as a shark's belly!" (Benjamin Trigg, seeing inexplicable anxiety and agitation in Adam Penfeather's face, *Adam Penfeather, Buccaneer* 245)

- "Sometimes I hears him in my sleep and wakes **all of a sweat** I do." (Joel Bym, *Adam Penfeather, Buccaneer* 285)

The "all of a"-noun adjective is often used to refer to a temporary and often acute condition or characteristic: temporary, because the "all of a"-noun's inclusion of the indefinite article "a" makes it ill-suited for reference to permanent or inherent properties, and acute because the "all of" wording is quite emphatic. Thus, a greedy pirate would not be described as "all of a greed"—the usage is awkward in reference to that kind of (generally) permanent characteristic—but a furious pirate certainly could be described as "all of a fury."

Like the "all"-noun, the "all of a"-noun adjective generally does not precede the noun modified, as does a conventional adjective ("A **hungry** crew is a mutinous one"). Instead, it forms part of a predicate or modifying phrase ("A crew what's **all of a hunger** is a mutinous one").

22.4.2 POSSESSIVE

"Of" Possessive

Possessive adjectives are words like "my," "your," "his," "her," "its," "our," and "their." Instead of using a possessive adjective, use "of" plus an objective pronoun.

Thus, instead of "my ship" or "her sword," a pirate might say "the ship of me" or "the sword of herself."

- In place of "**my** ..." use "**the ... of me**" OR "**the ... of myself.**"

- In place of "**your** ..." use "**the ... of you**" OR "**the ... of yourself.**"

- In place of "**his** ..." use "**the ... of him**" OR "**the ... of himself.**"

- In place of "**her** ..." use "**the ... of her**" OR "**the ... of herself.**"

- In place of "**its** ..." use "**the ... of it**" OR "**the ... of itself.**"

- In place of "**our** ..." use "**the ... of us**" OR "**the ... of ourselves.**"

- In place of "**their** ..." use "**the ... of them**" OR "**the ... of themselves**"

"Mind that hole, there. Ol' Bruce stepped into that and broke his leg. Had to shoot him, we did, from **the screamin' of 'im.**" (Israel Hands, "Long John Silver's Return to Treasure Island" 1:24:18)

"A ship as strong as a fort in which to stow a half-million pieces of eight, and this fortress ship in **the hands of ourselves**. A trusting fellow this Easterling for a scoundrel." (Peter Blood, *Captain Blood Returns* 23)

"Doth he appall **the virgin soul o' thee** to the instant slavish obedience so necessary for what is to be?" (Japhet Bly, *Winds of Chance* 14)

Note that the "of"-possessive is typically reserved for instances in which either the thing or the fact of possession referenced is especially significant or intentionally emphasized. Thus, a pirate would likely not say to a dinner companion, "Lend me **the knife of you**," but rather (like the modern speaker) would say simply, "Lend me **your knife**" or (with some added pirate flair) "Lend you me **yarr knife**."

On the other hand, a pirate who finds himself in mortal struggle with a seaman twice his size, then manages to grasp the dagger stuck in his opponent's belt, might say with a steely grimace—just before plunging it into his foe's back—"Lend me **the knife of you**."

"This"\"That" Possessive

Indicative adjectives are adjectives that point to things. They include "this," "that," "these," and "those." When using an indicative adjective plus a possessive adjective, the modern speaker uses the construction "this ... of mine" or "those ... of yours." Pirates, on the other hand, use possessive pronouns like "my" and "your," rather than phrases like "of mine" or "of yours." Thus, instead of "this flask of yours," a pirate might say "this your flask."

- "I mean not to shoot you, and as for Don Federigo, since death is but his due, a bullet were kinder—so charge now **these my** pistols." (Captain Jo, *Martin Conisby's Vengeance* 48–49)

- "Now for **these my** prisoners, seize 'em up, bind 'em fast and heave 'em aboard ship." (Captain Jo, *Martin Conisby's Vengeance* 61)

- "Look, Martino! Yonder is a death kinder than death by the fire and yet I do fear this more than the fire by reason of **this my** hateful woman's body." (Captain Jo, *Martin Conisby's Vengeance* 149)

22.5 ADVERBS

Adverbs are words that modify verbs ("Mo walked **slowly** into the red sunset"), adjectives ("Mo walked slowly into the **deeply** red sunset"), and even other adverbs ("Mo walked **very** slowly into the deeply red sunset").

22.5.1 FORMATION

There are seven ways to form adverbs in pirate speech that are not used in modern

English. These are listed below, along with the resulting pirate equivalents of the example sentence "Mulligan moved stealthily to catch up with the speedily retreating Spaniards":

(1) **adjective as adverb** ("Mulligan moved **stealthy** fer to come up wi' the **speedy** retreating dons.")

"Listen, you swabs, ya live **hard** and ya speak **soft** till I give the word, and you can lay to that, both of you." (Long John Silver, "Treasure Island" [1998] 45:22)

> In addition, use comparative adjectives (...'er) instead of comparative adverbs (more ...'ly). Thus, instead of "He dealt even more **harshly** with the Spaniard," a pirate might say "He dealt e'en **harsher** wi' the Spanisher."

(2) **"all-ADJECTIVE" as adverb** ("Mulligan moved **all-stealthy** fer to come up wi' the **all-speedy** retreating dons.")

"For my part, I don't know and I don't care what the Gospel does to them, but I know that when any o' the islands chance to get it, trade goes **all smooth and easy**; but where they ha'nt got it, Beezelbub himself could hardly desire better company." (pirate, *The Coral Island* 213–14)

(3) **"ADJECTIVE-like" as adverb** ("Mulligan moved **stealthy-like** fer to come up wi' the dons retreating **speedy-like**.")

"Try reas'n'n' first, says I. I never was one to see poor seamen shot down **needless-like**." (Long John Silver, "Treasure Island" [1950] 58:55)

(4) **"a-ADJECTIVE-like" as adverb** ("Mulligan moved **a-stealthy-like** fer to come

up wi' the dons retreating **a-speedy-like**.")

"Now, sit where you are, Bill, **a-gentle-manly-like**." (Pew, "Treasure Island" [1934] 17:16)

(5) **"NOUN-like" as adverb** ("Mulligan moved **stealth-like** fer to come up wi' the dons retreating **speed-like**.")

< "And how say you, Joanna?" "Tush! Here is one that talketh very loud and **fool-like** and flourisheth iron claw to no purpose, since I heed one no more than t'other ..." > (Abnegation Mings & Captain Jo, *Martin Conisby's Vengeance* 157)

(6) **something + ADVERB** ("Mulligan moved **something stealthy** fer to come up wi' the dons retreating **something speedy**.")

"You disappoint me **somethin' fierce**." (Joshua Smoot, *Dead Man's Chest* 197)

(7) **ADVERB- + fashion** ("Mulligan moved **stealthy-fashion** fer to come up wi' the dons retreating **speedy-fashion**.")

"And sure enough in a while comes the big man Tressady a-stealing **furtive-fashion** and falls to hunting both in the open grave and round about it but, finding nothing, steals him off again." (Adam Penfeather, describing Roger Tressady's attempts to find Black Bartlemy's dagger around Bartlemy's grave, *Black Bartlemy's Treasure* 92)

Where two (or more) adverbs are used in a single sentence, one might use either the same adverb form for both/all of them—

"Why, you could have charged him wi' robbery and turned him off the yardarm, all **legal** and **shipshape**." (Orange Povy, using the adjective as adverb form for both adverbs, "Captain Kidd" 41:20)

—or instead use different forms for variety's sake

"But however we do it, it must be done **legal-like** and **honest**." (Captain William Kidd, using both the ADJECTIVE-like as adverb form and the adjective as adverb form, "Captain Kidd" 30:53)

22.5.2 POSITION

Pirates generally use adverbs much earlier in a given phrase or clause than modern speakers. Where a modern speaker uses an adverb in the middle of a phrase or clause (after the subject and before the verb), a pirate might use it *before* both the subject and verb. Where a modern speaker uses an adverb late in a phrase or clause (after the verb), a pirate might use it *before* the verb.

Middle Adverbs Before Subject

Adverbs in modern English often come in the middle of the phrases or clauses in which they appear—specifically, after the subject and before the verb: "I knew Paulie was on this island before I *ever* laid eyes on him." Here, the adverb "ever" comes after the subject "I" and before the verb "laid."

Pirates, on the other hand, typically use such "middle" adverbs earlier in the relevant phrase or clause—specifically, *before* both subject and verb: "I reckoned Paulie, 'ee were on this 'ere spit o' land afore *ever* I lay me deadlights on 'im."

Note this usage applies to abstract adverbs (adverbs referring to concepts, such as "little," "much," "first," "last," "always," "ever," "anytime," "badly"), rather than concrete adverbs (adverbs referring to things one can touch and feel, such as "quietly," "quickly," "strongly," "roughly," "hungrily," "softly"). Concrete adverbs generally take the same position as in modern English.

- "And when you've a mind to do a bit o' explorin', **just you ask** old John, and he'll put up a bit o' grub for 'ee to take along." (Long John Silver, "Treasure Island" [1950] 43:14)

- "One thousand two hundred and three poor souls ha' we freed one way or t'other, since **first we took** and named this ship *Joyful Deliverance* ..." (Ezekiel Penryn, *Winds of Chance* 48)

- "It's the wickedest, prettiest policy **ever I heard** of." (Smee, *Peter Pan* 62)

Late Adverbs Before Verb

Certain adverbs in modern English come late in a phrase or clause—that is, *after* both subject and verb: "**You should think *hard*** about what you're saying." Pirates often move late adverbs to the middle—that is, after the subject, but before the verb or some part of the verb: "**You oughter *hard* think** 'bout what you'm speakin'."

- "The world could **very well do** without Don Serafino de Sotomayor." (George Fairfax, *The Fortunes of Captain Blood* 154)

- "'Deposed.' An' **very pretty wrote**. Your hand o' writin', George?" (Long John Silver, "Treasure Island" [1950] 1:19:44)

- "We've reduced our inflammation but our fever **little abates**, we gain no strength, we languish, for, 'sbud, mem, we refuse t'eat and we must eat t' give Nature a chance, demme." (Crabtree, *Winds of Chance* 89)

22.6 PREPOSITIONS

This section covers added prepositions, dropped prepositions, switched prepositions, and dangling prepositions.

22.6.1 ADDED PREPOSITION

Add the preposition "of" (or "o'" or "on") in two instances: (1) after transitive verbs ("That rope is choking **of** him.") and (2) after

long prepositions ("That rope reaches twice around **of** him.").

After Transitive Verbs

Transitive verbs are verbs that take objects. In the sentence "Mac sailed through the channel," the verb "sailed" is intransitive, as it takes no object. In the sentence "Mac sailed the schooner through the channel," the verb "sailed" is transitive, as it takes the object "schooner."

Pirates often add "of" after transitive verbs:

- "Here I have this confounded son of a Dutchman sitting in my own house, **drinking of** my own rum!" (Long John Silver, *Treasure Island* 45, Chap. 8)

- "The boot's on t'other leg, for hereabouts do lie thirty and eight o' my lads **watching of** ye this moment and wi' finger on trigger." (Roger Tressady, *Black Bartlemy's Treasure* 315)

- "Upon this intelligence they cruised off and on upon the coast for near a month, keeping always to the southward of Lima, because they would not fall in the way of the said flotilla, and so be overpowered and **miss of** their prize." (Captain Avery, *The King of Pirates* 47)

After Long Prepositions

Modern speakers sometimes use the preposition "of" together with the longer prepositions "inside" ("They stayed **inside of** the house during the storm") and "outside" ("He left the ammunition **outside of** the stockade").

Pirates often use the preposition "of" with many other long prepositions, including "aboard," "above," "across," "along," "among," "around," "behind," "below," "beneath," "beside," "between," "beyond," "despite," "except," "throughout," "toward," "under," "underneath," "within," and "without."

- "He's more a man than any pair o' you bilge rats **aboard of** here." (Long John Silver, "Treasure Island" [1990] 1:40:15)

- "Fine flat sand, never a catspaw, trees all **around of** it, and flowers a-blowing like a garding on that old ship." (Israel Hands, *Treasure Island* 142, Chap. 26)

- "So you're blubbering, are you, you obstinate whelp? I don't allow any such weakness **aboard o'** this ship." (pirate captain, *The Coral Island* 201)

For whatever reason, pirates tend not to combine the preposition "of" with one-syllable prepositions like "at," "in," or "to."

22.6.2 DROPPED PREPOSITION

Omit prepositions where, if omitted, their meaning is nevertheless implicit or understood based on the surrounding words. There are no fixed categories of prepositions that are always dropped. Rather, as with most aspects of the pirate language, the speaker has freewheeling discretion. The guiding principle, however, is that the more clearly the other words in a sentence convey the meaning of a preposition therein, the more likely that preposition can and will be omitted.

The preposition "of" (or either of its variants, "o'" and "on") is perhaps dropped more often than any other. This is probably true partly because "of" is used so often that the instances in which it is dropped are correspondingly frequent, and partly because "of" is an almost purely referential term with little freestanding meaning—and accordingly deleted in most cases with little impact on the sense of what remains.

Prepositions that are often omitted are listed below, with the omissions in the accompanying examples indicated by bracketed ellipses [...].

about

"They told us also of another crew of European sailors, which lay as we did on the main of the island, and had lost their ship, and were, as the islanders told them, above a hundred men, but we heard nothing [...] who they were." (Captain Avery, *The King of Pirates* 44)

as

"I shan't trust you aboard my ship, unless I carry you [...] a prisoner ..." (Holford, *General History of the Pyrates* 140)

from

"Saved me [...] cuttin' your throat, you little swab." (George Merry, "Treasure Island" [1950] 1:15:33)

in

"Yesterday at twain [...] the afternoon we weigh'd again, with a breeze at N.E. but at five a gale came up at S.S.W. and blew very strong ..." (Woodes Rogers, *A Cruising Voyage Round the World* 33)

of

"We'm on'y seekin' a bit [...] goold." (unnamed pirate aboard *Royal James*, *Porto Bello Gold* 183)

to

"[H]e told me he lay next [...] the door, with the key fastned to his privy parts, because he had it once stoln out of his pocket ..." (Woodes Rogers, *A Cruising Voyage Round the World* 155)

with

"Mighty pretty. But how are we to get away with it, and us [...] no ship?" (George Merry, *Treasure Island* 166, Chap. 29)

22.6.3 SWITCHED PREPOSITION

Prepositions, especially when used with abstract nouns, are not the most precise words in the world. They usually just connect one word to another. The question "what's the point of that?" conceivably could instead be said "what's the point in that?" or "what's the point with that?" or "what's the point on that?"

Pirates often switch prepositions in this way. That is, they might use a preposition in the same place in a sentence, and for the same purpose, as a modern speaker, but they choose a different preposition from the one commonly used.

The *Primer* provides a sampling of switched prepositions below. It is not meant to be an exhaustive list, but rather as an illustrative sampling to encourage experimentation.

Three additional points to consider:

(1) Note that, as frequently as a given preposition might replace another, the reverse switch might take place just as frequently—with the second preposition replacing the first. That two-way interchangeability is reflected in some of the examples below. (For example, "for" replaces "to" about as often as "to" is used instead of "for.")

(2) Certain preposition switches are idiomatic—that is, they result from the fact that the larger phrases of which they are a part include, as a matter of custom, different prepositions from those used in modern English. For example, modern speakers tend to use the phrase "trust in" ("I only trust **in** myself and my knife"), while pirates instead prefer to use the phrase "trust to" ("I but trust **to** meself and me blade"). Similarly, modern speakers tend to say "along with" ("Take the silver along **with** the gold"), but pirates happen to use the slightly different phrase "along of" ("Take the silver along **o'** the gold").

Thus, be aware as you review the examples below that the switch of one preposition for another is not simply a function of one replacing the other in every context, but often

of one replacing the other only when other terms or phrases are present.

(3) Among the most popular and consistent "switch" of prepositions is the use of "at" rather than "in" (when referring to towns, cities, or regions) or "on" (when referring to ships or islands). "Stout seamen there be **at** Newport, an' ready fer red mischief." "He died **at** Shelter Island, 'ee did, rag-poor and by 'is lone." More examples of the switch use of "at" are provided below.

• **"about" replaces "around"**

< "I've been goin' ashore for thirty years in my shirtsleeves." "Not while I be **about**. Now you'll put your coat on." "Arrgh." > (Long John Silver & Purity Pinker, "The Adventures of Long John Silver: The Eviction" 14:09)

• **"about" replaces "on"**

"Upon deck, you dog, for we shall lose no more time **about** you." (Alexander Mitchel, *General History of the Pyrates* 607)

• **"along" replaces "around"**

"Ever notice a seafaring man **along** this here grog shop?" (Black Dog, "Treasure Island" [1950] 3:01)

• **"among" replaces "from" or "from among"**

"MacMow, an Irishman who was their captain, had five rubies and a diamond, which he got **among** the plunder of the Mogul's ship." (Captain Avery, *The King of Pirates* 73)

• **"at" replaces "in"**

"But I'll tell you I was sober; I was on'y dog tired; and if I'd awoke a second sooner I'd a' caught you **at** the act, I would." (Long John Silver, *Treasure Island* 107, Chap. 20)

• **"at" replaces "on"**

"[N]ow they were a fleet of two barks with several canoes and piraguas, but no guns nor any more ammunition than everyone carried at first at their backs." (Captain Avery, *The King of Pirates* 21)

- **"for" replaces "about"**

< "I care nothing for his threats." "You should. The wise thing'd be to hang him, along o' all the rest." > (Peter Blood & Wolverstone, *Captain Blood: His Odyssey* 142)

- **"for" replaces "as"**

"The sloop was more put to it than we were in the great ship, and being obliged to run afore it a little sooner than we did, she served for a pilot-boat to us which followed." (Captain Avery, *The King of Pirates* 34)

- **"for" replaces "on"**

< "Now if she has chance to luff and bring her broadside to bear ..." "She never shall, John, trust me for this." > (John Fenn, Adam Penfeather, *Buccaneer* 232)

- **"for" replaces "to"**

"I scorn to do any one a mischief, when it is not for my advantage ..." (Captain Bellamy, *General History of the Pyrates* 587)

- **"in" replaces "at"**

"'[T]was not possible for us to travel to the north side at this season; for the rainy season was now in its height, and travelling very bad ..." (Lionel Wafer, *Isthmus of America* 54)

- **"in" replaces "on"**

"I told him it was true, Captain Avery was in the island of Madagascar, and that several other societies of buccaneers and freebooters were joined him from the Spanish West Indies." (Captain Avery, *The King of Pirates* 69)

- **"in" replaces "to"**

"[T]hese Indians of Darien are very fierce withal, and are the same people that killed and tore in pieces that famous Buccaneer L'Ollonais ..." (William Dick, *Bucaniers of America* 337)

- **"of" replaces "for"**

"They understood their business very well, and knew well enough what was the reason of it, though we did not." (Captain Avery, *The King of Pirates* 84)

- **"of" replaces "from"**

"I took no receipt for it of Mr. Gardiner." (William Kidd, explaining under interrogation by Lord Bellomont his failure to obtain a receipt in exchange for hidden treasure entrusted with John Gardiner, *The Pirate Hunter* 254)

- **"of" replaces "in"**

"Now look'ee, Martin, what with one thing or another, and this hell-fire ship on our heels in especial, there's stir and disaffection among the crew, a-whispering o' corners that I don't like, and which is apt to spread unless looked to." (Adam Penfeather, *Black Bartlemy's Treasure* 124)

- **"of" replaces "to"**

"What medicines he left behind were not considerable in comparison of what he carried away ..." (William Dick, *Bucaniers of America* 336)

- **"of" replaces "with"**

"The wise thing'd be to hang him, along o' all the rest." (Wolverstone, *Captain Blood: His Odyssey* 142)

- **"on" replaces "for"**

"We are bound away on the Pirate Round!" (Patrick Quigley, *The Pirate Round* 364)

- **"on" replaces "of"**

"Where's all England's men now? I dunno. Where's Flint's? Why, most on 'em aboard here, and glad to get the duff—been begging before that, some on 'em." (Long John Silver, *Treasure Island* 57, Chap. 11)

● **"to" replaces "at"**

< "Are we safe, sir?" "Ay, ma'm, 'tis blown out sooner than I expected, so I am here to your service." > (Ursula Revell & Japhet Bly, *Winds of Chance* 128)

● **"to" replaces "for"**

"I am bound to Madagascar, with a design of making my own fortune, and that of all the brave fellows joined with me." (Captain Avery, *The General History of the Pyrates* 51 & *The Pirates Own Book* 14)

● **"to" replaces "in"**

"[I]ndeed 'tis to his own interest to keep hidden his part in this affair ..." (Andrew Murray, *Porto Bello Gold* 104)

● **"to" replaces "on"**

"My word of honor to that." (Andrew Murray, *Porto Bello Gold* 46)

● **"with" replaces "by"**

"[W]e assured them they should have fair quarter and good usage upon our honour, but that they must resolve immediately, or else they would be surrounded with 500 men, and we could not answer for what they might do to them." (Captain Avery, describing his encounter with five English sailors and his demand for their surrender, *The King of Pirates* 67)

● **"with" replaces "for"**

"[W]e could not dry our clothes, scarce warm ourselves, and no sort of food for the belly, all of which made it very hard with us." (William Dampier, *A New Voyage Round the World* 16)

● **"with" replaces "of"**

"Here, what's the meaning with all them firelocks?" (pirate on Smith Island, *The Guardship* 94)

22.6.4 DANGLING PREPOSITION

There is a rule in modern English against dangling prepositions. Sentences may not end in a preposition. "This is a bad situation we're in." Your high-school English teacher might urge you to say instead, "This is a bad situation in which we find ourselves" or, simply, "This is a bad situation." There is no such rule in the pirate language. Let your prepositions dangle freely.

● "What manner of craft be this we're cruisin' in?" (Blackbeard, "Blackbeard's Ghost" 31:08)

● "There's too many of them to share the treasure with." (Long John Silver, "Treasure Island" [1934] 1:23:49)

● "When you shipped with the Admiral, you never took scurvy from the salt pork and hardtack. Not with a barrel of apples aboard for the men to chew on." (Long John Silver, "Treasure Island" [1950] 17:59)

22.7 ARTICLES

This section covers the pirate's use (and non-use) of articles—not only the Dropped Article, but also the Switched Article and the "Ye" Article.

22.7.1 DROPPED ARTICLE

Articles are often omitted in pirate speech. There are no hard and fast rules, but be aware of the following seven circumstances in which articles are omitted with greatest frequency. (The omissions in the accompanying examples below are indicated by the symbol [...].)

(1) **Drop articles when starting sentences.** See generally Section 19.1.1: Chopped

Start on the tendency of pirates to dive into the meat of a sentence without much at the beginning.

"[...] Truce be over! Cutlasses, you swabs!" (Long John Silver, "Treasure Island" [1950] 1:00:46) "Aye, through the spine. [...] Bloody mess that'll make." (Burgess, *The Pirate Round* 316)

(2) **Drop articles when listing things**—that is, before any item named in a series of similar items. The repetition makes itemization predictable, so including an article each time becomes pointless.

"They'll be at it again to-morrow or [...] next day, just as if there wasn't a single shark between Feejee and Nova Zembla." (Bloody Bill, describing the island natives' penchant for swimming despite the danger of sharks, *The Coral Island* 240) < "And you are an Englishman?" "I was, but since then I've been [...] slave to be whipped, [...] dog to be kicked, [...] Lutheran dog to be spat upon, and lastly [...] Indian ..." > (Martin Conisby & John, *Martin Conisby's Vengeance* 184)

(3) **Drop articles after transitive verbs**—that is, verbs that take an object.

"So Press beats [...] hell out of Dinwiddie for an hour, and the whole time he's asking, 'Where's Yancy? Where's Yancy?'" (Henry Nagel, *The Pirate Round* 241) "Stand by, lads! Level at the cliff yonder, but let no man pull [...] trigger!" (Roger Tressady, *Black Bartlemy's Treasure* 309)

Note that the omission of articles after transitive verbs is an inconsistent practice. Both examples below were uttered by Adam Penfeather in Jeffrey Farnol's *Black Bartlemy's Treasure*, and even feature the exact same phrase; nevertheless, the article is omitted in the first, but not in the second:

"Since midnight I've waited wi' pistols cocked and never **closed** [...] eye—and yet here was he or ever I was aware ..." (Adam Penfeather, *Black Bartlemy's Treasure* 104) "As for me, shipmate, I shall scarce **close an eye** till we be clear o' the Downs, so 'tis a care-full man I shall be this next two days, heigho!" (Adam Penfeather, *Black Bartlemy's Treasure* 113)

(4) **Drop articles after connective verbs**—that is, verbs that do little else but connect the subject and verb of a sentence. The best example is "be" (in all its forms), but other connective verbs include "seem," "appear," "prove" (as in "the day proved hot"), "constitute," and "amount to."

"Here's no dagger. Here's [...] empty sheath but no steel in't." (Ben, searching the body of Black Bartlemy for a dagger containing the secret to hidden treasure, *Black Bartlemy's Treasure* 91) "Japhet is [...] wily fellow, for see you while he held Ramirez in parley, we were stealing up outboard to take 'em suddenly from above." (Barnabas Rokeby, *Winds of Chance* 57)

Articles are also omitted after present participles of connective verbs:

"I warned you but, being [...] fool, you nothing heeded—no!" (Captain Jo, *Martin Conisby's Vengeance* 21)

Note the following example, reflecting the omission of articles after *both* a connective verb and a transitive verb:

"I was [...] fool not to guess it ere this, but—I have never loved [...] man ere now." (Captain Jo, *Martin Conisby's Vengeance* 37)

Note the inconsistency with which articles are omitted after connective verbs:

< "Yea, indeed I might truly love such a man, Japhet." "And small wonder! For

such man is no man at all but [...] mere thing of your fancy, **a** bodyless vision conjured of your own imagining." > (Ursula Revell & Japhet Bly, *Winds of Chance* 294) "Here's [...] stronghold whence we may command the country round about, **a** place we may defend 'gainst any odds till the crack o' doom—or our food be done." (Japhet Bly, *Winds of Chance* 346)

(5) **Drop articles after prepositions.**

"Sit 'ee down at [...] table t' starboard, if ye kindly will." (Long John Silver, inviting Squire Trelawney, Doctor Livesey, and Jim Hawkins to breakfast, "Treasure Island" [1950] 16:49) "I need no suggestions from [...] scoundrel like you." (El Toro Mendoza, "Long John Silver's Return to Treasure Island" 18:11)

Note the following examples reflecting the omission of articles after *both* a preposition and a connective verb:

"So here's you, Martino, here's you in chains that might have been free, and here's myself very determined you shall learn somewhat of shame and be [...] slave at [...] command of such beasts as yonder." (Captain Jo, *Martin Conisby's Vengeance* 71) "Lookee, Japhet, I'm [...] lonely man, as were we all, with none to care if we perish or no, that live only by [...] might of our swords—well and good!" (Ezekiel Penryn, *Winds of Chance* 110)

Note also that the omission of articles after prepositions is inconsistently observed:

"Hereupon, we o' the Brotherhood fell upon these pirate rogues and fought them by [...] light o' **the** blazing houses (for they had fired the city) ..." (Adam Penfeather, *Black Bartlemy's Treasure* 84–85) "The boot's on t'other leg, for hereabouts do lie thirty and eight o' my lads watching of ye this moment and wi'

[...] finger on trigger." (Roger Tressady, *Black Bartlemy's Treasure* 315)

(6) **Drop articles after the words "like," "as," and "than."**

"There's curst Abner bleeding like [...] stuck pig and yourself untouched ..." (Absalom Troy, *Adam Penfeather, Buccaneer* 17) "But 'tis as [...] woman I judge her best, and as [...] woman she sails along o' me, lad, along o' me!" (Roger Tressady, *Martin Conisby's Vengeance* 157) "And if the reek o' bilge offends thy delicacy, —well, 'tis better than [...] searing bullet or to be crushed 'neath falling spar." (Japhet Bly, *Winds of Chance* 72)

(7) **Drop articles after the word "'tis."** This is really just one example of the general practice of dropping articles after connective verbs—as "'tis" typically means "it is" or "this is" and "is" is a connective verb. However, the omission of articles after "'tis" merits special attention as articles are arguably dropped after "'tis" more frequently than after other connective verbs.

"'Tis [...] trick I learned of the Indians." (Captain Japhet Bly, of his ability to communicate with the natives by smoke signal, *Winds of Chance* 165) "'Tis said my Lady Brandon and her gallant Sir Rupert Dering—him you overthrew, shipmate—do mean to come and take a look at you, anon, though 'tis [...] shame you should be made a raree show—burn me!" (Adam Penfeather, *Black Bartlemy's Treasure* 58)

Note the inconsistent omission of articles after "'tis." Both examples below are from Jeffrey Farnol's *Black Bartlemy's Treasure*, are made by Abnegation Mings in the same conversation with Martin Conisby, and are spoken only moments apart. However, in the first example the article is omitted after "'tis," whereas in the second the article after "'tis" is included.

"'Tis [...] song as was made for dead men, of dead men, by a dead man, and there's for ye now!" (Abnegation Mings, *Black Bartlemy's Treasure* 31) "'Tis a song well bethought on by—by better men nor you, for all your size!" (Abnegation Mings, *Black Bartlemy's Treasure* 31)

22.7.2 SWITCHED ARTICLE

In English, there is one definite article ("the") and two indefinite articles: "a" and "an." In modern English, "a" is used when the following noun begins with a consonant sound ("a vestment"), while "an" is used when the following noun begins with a vowel sound ("an investment").

Pirates, on the other hand, often use "a" even when the following noun begins with a vowel, and when a modern speaker would use "an" instead. Thus, "Yer a thievin' lubber an', what's marr, **a** idiot!"

- "I'll lay you a piece of eight the captain never so much as sarves out **a** extry noggin o' rum." (Long John Silver, *Porto Bello Gold* 48)

- < "Who was yon?" "Pedro the Portingale." "Dead—eh?" "Ay, Cap'n, **a** arrer through the eye!" > (Roger Snaith & Joe, *Winds of Chance* 301)

22.7.3 "YE" ARTICLE

Use "ye" instead of "the."

- "I would not advise any ship to pass betweene it and **ye** maine for the Spaniards have lost severall ships by it ..." (Basil Ringrose, describing the perils of sailing between the island of Lobos and the mainland, *The South Sea Waggoner* Chart 62)

- "I was not upon **ye** deck when **ye** blow was struck." (Joseph Palmer, denying having witnessed Kidd's murder of William Moore, *The Pirate Hunter* 269)

- "Soe soon as you enter the river of Baldivia you will see two branches. The southernmost is **ye** best therfore ships use that and it is to the towne better than 6 leagues." (Basil Ringrose, *The South Sea Waggoner* Chart 100)

Openers, Middlers & Closers

As discussed in Chapter 3: Flourishes, pirates often strengthen their statements of fact with smaller statements of emotion, emphasis, or commentary. Appendix A consists of three lists. First, a list of openers—that is, a list of terms and phrases, including flourishes (Chapter 3), oaths (Chapter 6), and curses (Chapter 7), that are used by one or more pirates quoted in one or more of the *Primer*'s sources at the starts of sentences. Second, a list of middlers: all flourishes, oaths, and curses that are used in the middles of sentences. Third, a list of closers: all flourishes, oaths, and curses that are used at the ends of sentences.

Note that if a term or phrase is listed as an opener, for example, it means only that one or more pirates quoted in one or more of the *Primer*'s sources has used the term or phrase as an opener. While that provides meaningful information about the term's or phrase's typical use, it does not mean, of course, that the term or phrase cannot also be used as a middler or a closer.

Flourishes are marked with an asterik (*). Oaths are marked with a cross (†). Curses are marked with a pound sign (#). See the appropriate chapters for pronunciation, definition, and example.

OPENERS

add to this*
ah*
ah-harr*
airr*
alack (now)*
and more*
and now you see*
and small wonder*
answer I*
arrgh*
as it chances*
as sure as God sees me*†
assure yourself*
aye*
aye faith*
aye verily*
bad cess to you#
balls†
be damned#
bedad†
besides which*
blast my eyes†
blast you#
blast your eyes#
blasted if†
bleed me (but\if)†
bless my guts†
bless your old\rusty heart†
blind me if†
blind you#
blister me†
blood and wounds†
blow me down†
blow my scuttle-butt†

body o' me†
brimstone and gall†
brush my barnacles†
burn and sink me but†
burn me (but\if)†
burn you#
but*
by all that is great and good†
by all what's holy
and unholy†
by cock (but)†
by fire and flame†
by Flint's (body and) bones†
by gad†
by God†
by God's life†
by God's wounds†
by gum†
by heaven(s)†
by hell†
by hook(e)y but†
by my blood†
by my deathless soul†
by my reckoning*
by my soul†
by Satan†
by the blood†
by the blood in my heart†
by the blood of
Henry Morgan†
by the devil's hoof†
by the devil's teeth†
by the devil's twisted tail†
by the eternal holy†
by the eternal Jesus†
by the God above us†

by the gods†
by the holy eternal†
by the horns of Nick†
by the living thunder†
by the powers (but)†
by the saints†
by thunder†
certes*
cherish my guts†
Christ†
come (NAME)*
come now*
confound it†
confound you#
content you*
crikey†
curse it†
curse me (if)†
curse me for a canting
mugger if†
curse me for a lubber but\if†
curse me with everlast-
ing torments but†
curse you#
cursed if†
damme (but\if ...)†
damn me (if)†
damn me for EPITHET†
damn my blood†
damn my buttons†
damn my eyes (if)†
damn my gizzard(s)
for a EPITHET but†
damn my lights and
gizzard if†
damn my soul (if)†

damn you#

damn you for EPITHET#

damn your __#

damn your blood#

damn your eyes#

damnation†

damnation seize my soul if†

darr*

dash my buttons†

dear heart but†

death and damnation†

death and wounds†

demme†

depend (up)on it*

the devil†

devil a doubt but*

devil burn me (but)†

devil burn you#

devil doubt it but*

devil take you if#

dog bite me†

drownd (and sink) me if†

d'ye see*

ecod†

egad†

err*

faith (now)*

favor*

fetch me up daft if†

fire and death†

fire and thunder†

first and last*

for my part*

for sure*

'fore God†

from hence*

gadso; gad so†

give me leave to say*

glory be†

God damn you (__)#

God love you†

God rot your bones#

God sink me but†

God's blood and wounds†

God's body†

God's death†

God's my life†

a God's name†

God's wounds†

good lack*

great guns (but)†

gut me (but\if)†

ha*

ha-harr*

hang it†

hang me for lewd cur if†

h(e)ark you*

h(e)arkee*

h(e)arkee in your ear*

h(e)arkee me*

h(e)arkee now*

harr*

hear me*

hear you*

hear you me*

hell†

hell and corruption†

hell and furies†

hell and the devil†

hell-fire†

hell's fury\furies†

here (now\you)*

hillo*

holy poker†

huzza*

I am much mistaken if*

I cannot question but*

I dare prophesy*

I dare say*

I dare swear†

I do protest*

I doubt not*

I fancy*

I fear*

I give you my bible oath*†

I have pleasure in saying*

I hold that*

I judge*

I lay*

I may tell you plainly*

I protest*

I reckon*

I say(s)*

I swear to Christ†

I tell you*

I tell you true*

I tell you what it is*

I think it but reason*

I verily believe*

I will not omit to tell you*

I won't say as+NEGATIVE*

I would wager a
handsome venture*

I'd wager*

if I may make so bold*

if I mistake not*

I'll be bound[†]

I'll be hanged if[†]

I'll gamble*

I'll lay my head*

I'll lay you a ___*

I'll swear to it[†]

I'll take my (affi)davy[†]

I'll tell you plain*

I'll wager*

I'll warrant (me)*

I'm a dog if*[†]

I'm a lewdly yapping cur if[†]

I'm bound[†]

I'm free to say*

I'm telling you*

in faith*

in fine*

in the fiend's name[†]

in the meanwhile*

it is plain beyond disputing*

it's in my mind*

it's odds*

I've taken a notion into my old numbskull*

Jesus[†]

Jesus and Mary[†]

lay me bleeding if[†]

let me burn if[†]

let me die but\if[†]

let me perish but\if[†]

let me rot and perish if[†]

like enough*

listen here*

little wonder*

look here (now)*

look now*

look you (here)*

lookee*

lookee here (now)*

lookee now*

Lord[†]

Lord love me (but)[†]

Lord love my eyes[†]

Lord love us[†]

Lord love you (now)[†]

love me[†]

love my eyes[†]

love my innards[†]

love my lights[†]

love my limbs[†]

malediction[†#]

(you) mark*

(you) mark me*

(you) mark my word*

mark this*

mark well my words*

mark you (here)*

may God strike me dead if[†]

may I be damned eyes and liver if*[†]

may I drink a bowl of brimstone and fire with the devil if*[†]

may the devil seize me if[†]

maybe*

mercy of God[†]

methinks*

mind (this\you)*

Mother of Heaven[†]

mother's love[†]

name of God[†]

not but what*

now*

now I tell you*

now look here*

now lookee*

now then*

o(h)*

od rot me[†]

od rot you[#]

od's blood[†]

od's bobs, hammer, and tongs[†]

od's body[†]

od's fish[†]

od's (my) life (but)[†]

od's wounds[†]

odso[†]

oho*

on my faith[†]

on my soul[†]

on my soul's salvation[†]

perceive me now*

perish and plague me but[†]

plague on it[†]

plague seize you[#]

regard now*

rip my jib if[†]

rot me (but\if)[†]

rot my bones[†]

rot you[#]

's fish[†]

's heart[†]

saint's blood[†]

say now*

'sblood; 's blood[†]

'sblood and death[†]

'sblood and 'ounds[†]

'sbud[†]

scupper, sink, and burn me if[†]

'sdeath[†]

'sdeath and blood[†]

see here*

see now*

see you*

shiver my soul[†]

shiver my timbers (if)[†]

sink and burn me but[†]

sink and drownd me[†]

sink me (but\if)[†]

sink me in blood if[†]

sink me now if[†]

smite me blind and speechless but[†]

smite me deaf, blind and dumb if[†]

smite me dumb[†]

smite me stiff in gore if[†]

snake sting me[†]

snoggers[†]

so d'ye see*

so it is that*

so so*

split me (but)[†]

split my sides[†]

stab me but[†]

stand by to go about*

stap me (but)[†]

stap/step my vitals[†]

strike me[†]

strike me blind[†]

strike me deaf, blind, and bleeding if[†]

suffering catfish[†]

sure*

sure enough*

sure now*

surely*

sweet merciful heaven[†]

'swounds and blood[†]

there is this much to say, and of that you may believe me*

thing of it is*

thunder[†]

'tis in my mind*

to be sure*

to own the truth*

to speak it all in a word*

truly*

unless I am mistook*

upon my life[†]

upon my soul[†]

verily*

well and good*

well now*

well so*

what*

what I say(s) is*

what I says to you is*

what would you say but*

(and) what's better*

(and) what's more*

(and) what's worse*

while this was doing*

why (now\then)*

without doubt*

word is*

yea*

you can choke and let me rot if[†]

you (can) lay to it*

you look here*

you mark (me)*

you mark my words*

you may be sure*

you may depend upon it*

you may take it*

you must believe*

you see*

you'll allow*

you'll not deny*

(')zounds (but)[†]

MIDDLERS

and be damned[†#]

and mark you this*

as I judge*

as I say*

as I (do) think*

as like as not*

aye*

be sure*

bedad[†]

by cock[†]

by God[†]

by heaven(s)[†]

by thunder[†]

curse you[#]

damme[†]

d'ye see*

faith*

for sure*

forsooth*

a God's name[†]

I dare swear[†]
I dare to think*
I doubt not*
I must needs say*
I reckon*
I say(s)*
in a manner of speaking*
in fine*
incredible fact*
lookee*
mark my words*
mark you*
may I perish*[†]
no doubt*
now*
plague on it[†]
(od) rot you[#]
says I*
shiver my sides[†]
shiver my timbers[†]
sure enough*
sure now*
think ye*
what's better*
(and) what's more*
what's more to me*
which is better*
which is worse*
why*
with a curse*[†#]
with a wannion*[†]
ye gods[†]
yea*
you lay to it*

CLOSERS

aha*

ain't it?*
alack*
alas*
all right*
all right?*
all told*
amen, so be it*
and a pity it is*
and all*
and (so) be done*
and be done with it*
and bloody end to them
as shall gainsay me*
and damn all*
and fair enough*
and glad of it*
and I know it*
and nothing more*
and quite right*
and small blame either*
and small wonder*
and such*
and that*
and that's fair*
and that's true*
and the like*
and there's for you (now)*
and this I swear[†]
and welcome*
and what not*
and willing*
and you know it*
arrgh*
as ever (was)*
as I do know*
as I guess*

as I hear*
as I (do) think*
as I'm a soul[†]
as it were*
as I've reason to know*
as like as not*
as the case were*
as you might say*
as you'll agree*
aye (so\verily)*
aye?*
bad cess to you[#]
(and) be cursed to you[#]
(and) be damned[#]
(and) be damned to it[†#]
(and) be damned to you
(with all my heart)[#]
be sure of that*
(and) belike*
beyond doubt*
b'gad; b'ged[†]
bible oath[†]
blast you[#]
blast your deadlights[#]
blast your eyes[#]
bless your (old) heart[†]
(and) bone-rot you[#]
the bones[†]
burn and blast your bones[#]
burn me (but)[†]
else[†]
burn you[#]
by all accounts*
by Christ[†]
by cock[†]
by cock's body[†]

by God[†]

by hook(e)y[†]

by Satan[†]

by the holy poker[†]

by the looks of it*

by the powers[†]

by thunder[†]

Caesar's ghost[†]

confound you[#]

(a) curse on you[#]

curse you[#]

damme[†]

dammem[#]

damn my blood[†]

damn you[#]

damn your blood[#]

damn your eyes[#]

the devil[†]

devil a doubt*

devil burn you[#]

devil damn me if I don't[†]

do you hear?*

do you see*

dog bite me[†]

(you) don't make
no doubt of that*

d'ye hear?*

d'ye see*

d'ye think?*

d'ye understand?*

every one*

first and last*

for all love*

for all o' me*

for all the world*

for certain*

for sure*

for the love of God[†]

forsooth*

glory be[†]

God damn me (if I don't)[†]

God damn my soul[†]

God damn you[#]

God's blood[†]

God's light[†]

gut me if[†]

ha*

ha-harr*

ha-hurr*

hear me?*

heigho*

here and now*

I can tell you*

I dare swear[†]

I don't reckon*

I doubt*

I grant it*

I judge*

I lay*

I lay my oath+
SUBJECT+VERB[†]

I reckon*

I say(s)*

I say again*

I should say so*

I shouldn't doubt*

(and) I shouldn't wonder*

I swear (to Jesus God)[†]

I take it*

I tell you*

I vow+SUBJECT+VERB[†]

I vow and protest[†]

I wager*

I warrant me\you*

I will so*

I won't say no*

I wouldn't doubt*

if ADJECTIVE'er can
be said by mortal
seaman+OATH\CURSE[†#]

if I recollect*

if my name's NAME[†]

if the God of my good
mother sits aloft indeed[†]

if what I hear be right*

if you asks me*

if you kindly will*

if you please*

I'll be blown[†]

I'll be bound[†]

I'll be sworn[†]

I'll lay (to that)*

I'll wager*

I'll warrant (me)*

I'm sure*

I'm thinking*

in faith*

in the devil's name[†]

in very truth*

is my notion*

it seems*

let me perish[†]

let that rest there*

like (as not)*

look you*

lookee*

looks like*

Lord love me\you[†]

love my eyes[†]

mark me\you*

mark that*

maybe*

(a) mercy's sake[†]

(you) mind*

(and) more's the pity*

my backside*

my privy parts*

my rear*

my socks[†]

neither*

never a doubt*

never doubt it*

never you fear*

(and) no bones about it*

no less* [*no'oo lass*]

(and) no mistake*

none denying*

not a doubt*

not if my name's NAME*

now*

o(h)*

on my soul[†]

or burn me[†]

or call me dogsbody[†]

or curse me for pa-
pistical Spaniard[†]

or damme/demme[†]

or I be not NAME[†]

or I'm a buttered parsnip[†]

or I'm a cur-dog[†]

or I'm a dog[†]

or I'm a flounder[†]

or I'm a fool else[†]

or I'm a forked radish[†]

or I'm a lubberly Dutchman[†]

or I'm a mere forked radish[†]

or I'm a pickled mackerel[†]

or I'm a radish[†]

or I'm a salted codfish[†]

or I'm a shark[†]

or I'm a shotten herring[†]

or I'm a soused gurnet[†]

or I'm a stockfish[†]

or I'm mistook*

or I've got a dead
man's dinghy[†]

or let me drownd[†]

or may I burn, choke,
and perish[†]

or may I rot[†]

or may I sink and per-
ish in blood[†]

or so*

or souse me for a gurnet[†]

or strike me dumb[†]

or ye may gut me
for a preacher[†]

right enough*

rot me\you[†]

savvy?*

say(s) I*

says you*

see*

see you*

shiver my sides[†]

shiver my timbers[†]

sink and scuttle me[†]

sink me (if ...)[†]

sink you[#]

split me[†]

sure (and certain)*

sure enough*

surely*

that's a true word*

(and) that's all there is of it*

that's clear*

(and) that's flat*

then*

(and) there's an end on\to it*

'tis beyond doubt*

to be sure*

to my sorrow*

to the devil with
your black soul[#]

true as true*

true enough*

truly*

'twould seem*

upon my honour*

well and good*

when all is said*

(the) which God for-
bid\forfend*

with a curse[†#]

with a wannion*

without a doubt*

you can have my balls
for breakfast if[†]

(and) you can\may
lay to it\that*

you don't make no
doubt of that*

you may be sure*

you see*

you'll allow*

you'll be a bold man\
one to say no to that*

APPENDIX B

Sound List

On March 20, 1724, in the Bay of Honduras, Francis Farrington Spriggs boarded a sloop out of Newport, Rhode Island. Short on men, Spriggs informed the vessel's crew that they were now the newest members of his pirate company. The captain's mate, however, proved resistant. Dixey Gross was a "grave, sober man," and no matter how politely he was asked or how savagely he was threatened, he steadfastly declined to join.

Seeing his efforts were pointless, Spriggs finally decided Gross would not have to join the company and instead would receive a formal discharge—written on his back. Gross was sentenced to receive ten lashes of the whip from every man on board. (*Pirates of the New England Coast* 279–80)

Pirate words involve strange sounds. Nothing, however, like the dry crack of those being written on the back of a dead man.

Appendix B provides an alphabetical list of modern English sounds—consonants, vowels, sound combinations—that frequently take on a different pronunciation when spoken in the pirate language. Each entry sound specifies a pirate counterpart and then provides an excerpt reflecting the use of that sound. Note that more than one pirate counterpart is sometimes listed for a given modern English sound.

☠

"a" ("happen") = "ar" ("harpen")
Avarrst [avast]!" (Long John Silver, as Purity leads him into the kitchen to sober him up, "Long John Silver's Return to Treasure Island' 41:28)

"a" ("happen") = "ay" ("haypen")
"So if 'tis all the same to ee, ma'm, I'd rayther be tied up again all reg'lar and shipshape and take my half-dozen according to orders, thanking you kindly, ma'm, I'm sure." (Ben, *Winds of Chance* 103)

"a" ("happen") = "eh" ("heppen")
"Say, have ya set your eyes on the bewitched maiden in your trevels?" (libidinous pirate, "Pirates

of the Caribbean" Disney attraction [2000])

"a" at the end ("soda") = "er" ("soder")

"You told Squire Trelawney and all of us he was done in aboard the *Hispanioler* [*Hispaniola*]." (Long John Silver, "Long John Silver's Return to Treasure Island' 1:15:40)

"ah" ("pocket") = "arr" ("parrket")

"He'll be comin' face-to-face with ol' Flint himself, he will, and be made to give proper accountin' for his evil ways. **Arrmen**." (Long John Silver, "Long John Silver's Return to Treasure Island" 6:18)

"ah" ("pocket") = "aah" ("packet")

"Who beat your **faahther's** manservant? Why did your **faahther** say there are no pearls?" (Long John Silver, "The Adventures of Long John Silver: The Pink Pearl" 15:40)

"ah" ("spot") = "uh" ("sput")

"Would it be too much to ask for a small **nuggin [noggin]** o' rum?" (Long John Silver, "Long John Silver's Return to Treasure Island" 34:57)

"air" ("scare") = "eer" ("sceer")

"I'll have fourteen cannon up **theer** on the 'eadland." (Blackbeard, "Blackbeard the Pirate" 43:54)

"air" ("scare") = "ayerr" ("scayerr")

"'Aul away **thayerr [there]**!" (Long John Silver, "The Adventures of Long John Silver: Ship o' the Dead" 20:07)

"al" ("salt") = "arr" ("sarrt")

"Why, there's a full cargo of my ol' shipmates that sailed with Hawke **becarrmed [becalmed]** right here, in Bristol." (Long John Silver, "Treasure Island" [1950] 18:42)

"al" ("salt") = "awrl" ("sawrlt")

"Now, we'd all best get some sleep. We'll need **awrl [all]** our strength to strike." (Long John Silver, "The Adventures of Long John Silver: Pieces of Eight" 6:15)

"ar" ("chart") = "ah" ("chaht")

"Hard to **lahberrd [larboard]**!" (Long John Silver, "The Adventures of Long John Silver: Sword of Vengeance" 2:33)

"ar" ("chart") = "ahrr" ("chahrrt")

"Fer **stahrrters [starters]**, just a glass o' rum for an ol' sea-farin' man on a cold, wet day." (Billy Bones, "Treasure Island" [1998] 5:57)

"ay" ("paper") = "aah" ("papper")

"She was at the boarding of the Viceroy of the Indies out of Goa, she was; and to look at her you would think she was a **babby**." (Long John Silver, recounting the exotic travels of his aging parrot Cap'n Flint, *Treasure Island* 55)

"ay" ("paper") = "eh" ("pepper")

< "Oh, this is vile, cruel country!" "Well, **mebbe** so, now and then, ma'm, here and there. ..." > (Ursula Revell & Jeremy Jervey, *Winds of Chance* 213)

"ay" ("paper") = "i" ("piper")

"What d'ye **s'y [say]** to a dash o' rum, matey?" (Jemmy, *Porto Bello Gold* 139)

"ay" ("paper") = "ah" or "ahrr" ("pahper" or "pahrrper")

"Here, we've no time for **belahhborin' [belaborin']**. (Long John Silver, "Long John Silver's Return to Treasure Island" 55:00)

"aw" ("long") = "aah" ("lang")

< "And who scuttled our plans?" "Governor **Strahng [Strong]** himself." > (Purity Pinker & Long John Silver, "Long John Silver's Return to Treasure Island" 36:47)

"aw" ("long") = "arr" ("larrng")

"I've taken a fancy to the lad here. I **tharrt [thought]** maybe you'd put him into my care." (Long John Silver, "Long John Silver's Return to Treasure Island" 31:02)

"aw" ("long") = "or" ("lorng")

"It would've warmed your 'eart to see 'im standin' there in **nort [naught]** but his underwear, prayin' for his life." (Long John Silver, "The Adventures of Long John Silver: The Eviction" 25:51)

"d" ("ladies") in middle = "j" ("lajies")
"[T]his is a strange port to me, as plies usual to the West **Injies**." (Long John Silver, *Porto Bello Gold* 23)

"d" ("crawled") at end of words = "t" ("crawlt")
"**Tolt** ya I were famous!" (Henry Morgan, *Dead Man's Chest* 128)

"ee" ("preacher") = "oo" ("proocher")
"Somewheers off the Abrollos Shoal, I'd say, your honour. Wi' Brazil to **looard [leeward]** and the Main right afore us." (Ned Bowser, *Adam Penfeather, Buccaneer* 166–67)

"eh" ("special") = "aah" ("spaahshul")
"But now I **rackon** the dons has their bellyful, see how thick they lie afore our rampire!" (Ned Bowser, *Adam Penfeather, Buccaneer* 340)

"eh" ("special") = "er" ("spershul")
< "I promise you, Long John Silver, should you ever venture beyond the breakwater, I will peel your skin like a mango." "You make it sound real **appertizing**." > (El Toro Mendoza & Long John Silver, "Long John Silver's Return to Treasure Island" 28:26)

"eh" ("special") = "ay" ("spayshul")
"Morgan's sittin' on all the loot of Panama. Hang him and it all goes back to the King in England, where I can never lay my hands on it **agayn**." (Blackbeard, "Blackbeard the Pirate" 31:20)

"eh" ("special") = "i" or "ai" ("spyshul")
"I recall taking a prize ship off **Pyru [Peru]** once." (Long John Silver, "Treasure Island" [1934] 1:24:04)

"en" ("sadden") = "ing" ("sadding")
"[R]ight here in the **garding** under the blessed apple-trees." (Long John Silver, *Porto Bello Gold* 44)

"er" = "ar"
"Why should I **consarn** myself as am no more'n quartermaster o' the old *Walrus*?" (Long John Silver, *Porto Bello Gold* 49)

"er" = "uh"
< "Who are you?" "**Faahthuh [Father]** Christmas." > (Long John Silver, "The Adventures of Long John Silver: The Orphans' Christmas" 15:12)

"h" at the start of words is silent
"I have a son of my own, as like you as two blocks, and he's all the pride of my '**art**." (Black Dog, *Treasure Island* 10)

"i" ("mighty") = "arr" ("marrty")
< "Can it be entered at low time?" "**Arrgh [aye]**. There's a kind of a passage being dug there, in a manner of speakin', by nature." > (Captain Smollett & Long John Silver, "Treasure Island" [1950] 43:47)

"i" ("mighty") = "ah" ("mah-ty")
"Easy, **ma** hearties!" (member of cheating gambler's pirate company, "The Adventures of Long John Silver: Devil's Stew" 2:06)

"i" ("mighty") = "aw" or "ough" ("moughty")
"An' what 'ave we got that they **mought** want?" (George Merry, "Treasure Island" [1998] 1:09:48)

"i" ("mighty") = "oi" or "oy" ("moyty")
< "Where's Finney!" "**Woy**, 'iz lordship's aft, Admiral." > (Alan Lewrie & pirate aboard the *Caroline*, *The Gun Ketch* 311)

"i" ("pillow") = "eh" ("pellow")
"Howsomever, **sperrits** don't reckon for much, by what I've seen. I'll chance it with the **sperrits**, Jim." (Israel Hands, *Treasure Island* 139)

"i" ("pillow") = "ee" ("peelow")
< "Who is this Black Pirate?" "A sound enough lad, but he seems to be suffering from an **affleection** of the heart." > (lady prisoner & MacTavish, "The Black Pirate" 56:08)

"ing" ("sailing") = "in" ("sailin'")

"Gunners! They be unarmed, mates, so take yer time **strippin'** off her **plankin'**!" (Ezra Pritchard, *Dead Man's Chest* 182)

"iar" or "ire" ("liar" or "fire") = "iyee'err" ("liyee'err" or "fiyee'err")

"'Twere better to take the young 'un ashore. No soldier would dare to **fyerr** in the direction of the Governor's little girl." (Long John Silver, "Long John Silver's Return to Treasure Island" 23:13)

"oh" = "er"

"Out of **Barbaders**, I am, in the brig *Constant*." (Long John Silver, *Porto Bello Gold*)

"oi" or "oy" ("toy") = "i" or "y" ("tie")

"Milk! I've been **p'isoned**." (Long John Silver, "Long John Silver's Return to Treasure Island" 35:23)

"oh" ("blow") = "oh-oo" ("blowoo")

< "He'll do it, Captain—walk the plank rather than give in. He's terribly stubborn." "**I knowoo**." > (Ross & Long John Silver, "The Adventures of Long John Silver: The Tale of a Tooth" 22:34)

"oh" ("stow") = "ooh" ("stoo")

"We'm on'y seekin' a bit **goold**." (unnamed pirate aboard *Royal James*, *Porto Bello Gold* 183)

"oh" = "uh"

"Long John don't know it, but Miss Purity's important errand is for me to pass the word in **Portuh Belluh [Porto Bello]** so he can't get a loan from any of his usual sources for raisin' the wind." (Ironhand, "The Adventures of Long John Silver: Devil's Stew" 8:04)

"oo" ("foolish") = "er" ("ferlish")

"I mean **ter** say as you'm going by the river ...." (Jeremy Jervey, *Winds of Chance* 248)

"oo" ("foolish") = "oy" ("foylish")

"Not one doubloon, not one **joyell [jewel]**, leaves this island till that lad be found."

(Long John Silver, "Long John Silver's Return to Treasure Island" 1:35:06)

"oo" ("foolish") = "uh" ("fuhlish")

< "I would join your Company." "**Wud** ye, now? An' what are your qualeefeecations?" > (Michel & MacTavish, "The Black Pirate" 20:45)

"oor" ("pour") = "ar" ("parr")

"Why, keep you no cabin boy, a cap'n of **yarr [your]** position?" (Long John Silver, "Long John Silver's Return to Treasure Island" 19:45)

"or" ("borrow") = "ah" ("bahrow")

"The Governor, he was tellin' me that Sir Percival Harwood be sendin' his son Algy there **tomahrohoo [tomorrow]**, on the inter-island packet." ("Long John Silver, The Adventures of Long John Silver: Dead Reckoning" 5:03)

"or" ("morning") = "ar" ("marning")

"How one small sack of coins can blind a man to real **farrtunes asharr** be beyond me." (Long John Silver, "Long John Silver's Return to Treasure Island" 18:27)

"or" ("morning") = "er" ("merning")

< "I may need him yet." "What **fer**?" > (Ben Worley & Blackbeard, debating the fate of Edward Maynard, "Blackbeard the Pirate" 43:08)

"or" ("morning") = "oor" ("moorning")

"I stepped out before the rest, seemin' to be awful anxious to be at the savages, tripped my foot on a fallen tree, plunged head foremost into a bush, an ov **coorse**, my carbine exploded!" (Bloody Bill, *The Coral Island* 259)

"or" ("morning") = "uh" ("muhning")

"Now, uh, don't **fuhget [forget]** to lay it into the lads an' stuff their heads full o' learnin'. (Long John Silver, "The Adventures of Long John Silver: Dead Reckoning" 9:49) "ow" ("powder") = "arr" ("parrder")

"**Narr [now]**. And when you're doing sentry-go, just ease off a p'int on the rum." (Long John Silver, "Treasure Island" [1950] 56:06)

"ow" ("powder") = "uh" ("puhder")

"I will then land you four, with sufficient provisions, and bear away in the *James* to the **so'th'ard [southward]**. ..." (Andrew Murray, *Porto Bello Gold* 184)

"ow" ("powder") = "owoo" ("powooder")

"Patch! Come 'ere! Lively **nowoo!**" (Long John Silver, "The Adventures of Long John Silver: The Tale of a Tooth" 16:05)

"r" = "rr"

"Here, uh, uh, have ya, have ya a nice **starr** for the top?" (Long John Silver, decorating the Christmas tree at the Cask & Anchor, "The Adventures of Long John Silver: The Orphans' Christmas" 2:51)

"s" = "sh"

"Look 'ee, Master Ormerod, I went to sea for to be a swearin', cutlass-lashin' pirate, and they put me in a livery-**shuit!**" (Ben Gunn, *Porto Bello Gold* 145)

"s" = "x"

"It is soe windy but **expetially** from September till Aprill, w[hi]ch are times for the north winde." (Basil Ringrose, *The South Sea Waggoner* Chart 28)

"s" = "z"

< "Where's the dog in charge of you?" "'E's dead, **zur**." "... And the mates?" "Oh, they be dead, too, **zur**." > (Arthur Ballard & John Laidlaw, *The Gun Ketch* 278)

"t" = "tt," not "d"

< "Them that live'll have a tale to tell." "If anyone does live." It's that or stay here and be **slaughttered**." > (Long John Silver & Old Stingley, discussing a proposed trek through the Panamanian jungle, "The Adventures of Long John Silver: Pieces of Eight" 8:09)

"th" = "f"

"She wants to be taken to the Captain. And she'll go **wiffout** a fuss." (Pintel, "Pirates of the Caribbean" 34:43)

"th" = "t"

"I never seed a boy **wit** a kinder face." (Long John Silver, *Porto Bello Gold* 23)

"uh" ("blood") = "ah" ("blahd")

"We carries the longboat through the jungle, fighting slimy ground and a million hungry **mahsquitoes** all the way. (Long John Silver, "The Adventures of Long John Silver: Pieces of Eight" 5:11)

"uh" ("wonder") = "aw" ("wawnder")

"All that canister an' grape-shot a'splangin' an' whirrin' about in here ... oh, 'tis a terror **wot** ye'd inflict on these poor lasses!" (Billy Doyle, assuring Alan Lewrie that attacking his cave will mean death for Doyle's women prisoners, *The Gun Ketch* 160)

"uh" ("punish") = "er" ("pernish")

"The last time I 'eard of you they was fixin' for you to dance at the end of a rope in **Tartuger [Tortuga]**." (Long John Silver, "The Adventures of Long John Silver: Devil's Stew" 5:28)

"uh" ("stud") = "ooh" ("stood")

"Can't you reach any further, you **stoohmp [stump]**-winged bilge rat?!" (pirate prisoner, frustrated with his comrade's inability to secure jailhouse keys from a nearby dog, "Pirates of the Caribbean" Disney attraction)

"y" at the end of a word = "eee" (drawn out and pronounced keenly)

"And shows most unaccountable understanding and **humanitee**, so it do. ..." (Long John Silver, *Porto Bello Gold* 20)

Pirate Company Articles

Articles, or ship's articles, are like a country's constitution. They are the rules and principles by which the members of a pirate company agree to conduct themselves. Below are the articles of various pirate companies in history, literature, and film, listed by captain in alphabetical order.

☠

Banks, Copley

Food should be the same for all, and no man should interfere with another man's drink! The Captain should have a cabin, but all hands should be welcome to enter it when they chose. All should share and share like, save only the captain, quartermaster, boatswain, carpenter, and master-gunner, who had from a quarter to a whole share extra. He who saw a prize first should have the best weapon taken out of her. He who boarded her first should have the richest suit of clothes aboard of her. Every man might treat his own prisoner, be it man or woman, after his own fashion. If a man flinched from his gun, the quartermaster should pistol him. (*The Dealings of Captain Sharkey and Other Tales of Pirates* "How Copley Banks Slew Captain Sharkey" 68)

Blood, Peter

We, the undersigned, are men without a country, outlaws in our own land and homeless outcasts in any other. Desperate men, we go to seek a desperate fortune. Therefore, we do here and now band ourselves into a brotherhood of buccaneers, to practice the trade of piracy on the high seas. We, the hunted, will now hunt. Therefore, to that end, we enter into the following articles of agreement:

First, we pledge ourselves to be bound together as brothers, in a life-and-death friendship, sharing alike in fortune and in trouble.

Second article: All monies and valuables which may come into our possession shall be lumped together in a common fund. And from this fund shall first be taken the money to fit, rig, and provision the ship. After that, the recompense each shall receive who is wounded is as follows: for the loss of a right arm, six hundred pieces of eight; left arm, five hundred; for the loss of a right leg, five hundred; left leg, four hundred.

If a man conceal any treasure captured, or fail to place it in the general fund, he shall be marooned, sent ashore on a deserted isle and there left with a bottle of water, a loaf of bread, and a pistol with one load.

If a man shall be drunk on duty, he shall receive the same fate. And if a man shall molest a woman captive against her will, he too shall receive the same punishment.

These articles entered into this twentieth day of June, in the year 1687. ("Captain Blood" 1:02:48)

Kidd, William

The man who shall first see a sail, if she be a prize, shall receive one hundred pieces of eight.

That if any man shall lose an eye, leg or arm or the use thereof ... shall receive ... six hundred pieces of eight, or six able slaves.

That whosoever shall disobey command shall lose his share or receive such corporal punishment as the Capt. and major part of the company shall deem fit.

That man is proved a coward in time of engagement shall lose his share.

That man that shall be drunk in time of engagement before the prisoners then taken be secured, shall lose his share.

That man that shall breed a mutiny riot on board the ship or prize taken shall lose his shares and receive such corporal punishment as the Capt. and major part of the company shall deem fit.

That if any man shall defraud the Capt. or company of any treasure, as money, goods, ware, merchandizes or any other thing whatsoever to the value of one piece of eight ... shall lose his share and be put on shore upon the first inhabited island or other place that the said ship shall touch at.

That what money or treasure shall be taken by the said ship and company shall be put on board of the man of war and there be shared immediately, and all wares and merchandizes when legally condemned to be legally divided amongst the ships company according to articles. (*The Pirate Hunter* 19–20)

Low, Edward
Formal Articles

1. The Captain is to have two full Shares; the Master is to have one Share and one Half; The Doctor, Mate, Gunner and Boatswain, one Share and one Quarter.

2. He that shall be found guilty of taking up any Unlawfull Weapon on Board the Privateer or any other prize by us taken, so as to Strike or Abuse one another in any regard, shall suffer what Punishment the Captain and Majority of the Company shall think fit.

3. He that shall be found Guilty of Cowardice in the Time of Engagements, shall suffer what Punishment the Captain and Majority shall think fit.

4. If any Gold, Jewels, Silver, &c. be found on Board of any Prize or Prizes to the value of a Piece of Eight, & the finder do not deliver it to the Quarter Master in the space of 24 hours he shall suffer what Punishment the Captain and Majority of the Company shall think fit.

5. He that is found Guilty of Gaming, or Defrauding one another to the Value of a

Ryal of Plate, shall suffer what Punishment the Captain and Majority of the Company shall think fit.

6. He that shall have the Misfortune to loose [sic] a Limb in time of Engagement, shall have the Sum of Six hundred pieces of Eight, and remain aboard as long as he shall think fit.

7. Good Quarters to be given when Craved.

8. He that sees a Sail first, shall have the best Pistol or Small Arm aboard of her.

9. He that shall be guilty of Drunkenness in time of Engagement shall suffer what Punishment the Captain and Majority of the Company shall think fit.

10. No Snaping of Guns in the Hould. (*Pirates of the New England Coast* 146–47)

Other Articles

[Author's note: These are additional articles reported in the accounts of George Roberts and Philip Ashton, prisoners captured and held by Low and his company on separate occasions. Roberts and Ashton reported learning of these articles during conversations with Low's men.]

"You must know that we have an article which we are sworn to, which is, not to force any married man, against his will, to serve us ..." (members of Low's company, encouraging their prisoner George Roberts to claim he is married in order to secure his own release, *Pirates of the New England Coast* 162)

"[It] was against one of their articles, it being punishable by death, to hold any secret correspondence with a prisoner ..." (George Roberts, reporting a conversation with members of Low's company, *Pirates of the New England Coast* 169)

"[I]f any of the company shall advise, or speak any thing tending to the separating or breaking of the company, or shall by any means offer or endeavour to desert or quit the company, that person shall be shot to death by the quarter-master's order, without the sentence of a court-martial." (article quoted by members of Low's company to

George Roberts, *Pirates of the New England Coast* 170)

"I learned from some of them, that it was one of their articles, not to draw blood, or take away the life of any man, after they had given him quarter, unless he was to be punished as a criminal ..." (Philip Ashton, recounting how he finally realized why his life was being spared despite repeated refusals to join Low's company, *Pirates of the New England Coast* 232)

"He [one of Edward Low's gunners] put him [Edward Low's quartermaster] in mind of the penalty, which was death, to any one who should infringe their laws ..." (George Roberts, recounting a description of the understood penalty for the violation of Low's articles, *Pirates of the New England Coast* 180)

Lowther, George

[Author's note: The similarity between Low's articles and those of George Lowther is no coincidence. Shortly after his start in the piracy business, Low became Lowther's second-in-command (in late 1721) and struck out on his own with forty-four other members of Lowther's company in May 1722.]

1. The Captain is to have two full Shares; the Master is to have one Share and a half; the Doctor, Mate, Gunner, and Boatswain, one Share and a quarter.

2. He that shall be found guilty of taking up any unlawful Weapon on board the Privateer, or any Prize, by us taken, so as to strike or abuse one another, in any regard, shall suffer what Punishment the Captain and Majority of the Company shall think fit.

3. He that shall be found Guilty of Cowardice, in the Time of Engagement, shall suffer what Punishment the Captain and Majority shall think fit.

4. If any Gold, Jewels, Silver, &c. be found on board of any Prize or Prizes, to the Value of a Piece of Eight, and the Finder do not deliver it to the Quarter-Master, in the Space of

24 Hours, [he] shall suffer what Punishment the Captain and Majority shall think fit.

5. He that is found Guilty of Gaming, or Defrauding another to the Value of a Shilling, shall suffer what Punishment the Captain and Majority of the Company shall think fit.

6. He that shall have the Misfortune to lose a Limb, in Time of Engagement, shall have the Sum of one hundred and fifty Pounds Sterling, and remain with the Company as long as he shall think fit.

7. Good Quarters to be given when call'd for.

8. He that sees a Sail first, shall have the best Pistol, or Small-Arm, on board her. (*General History of the Pyrates* 307–8)

Morgan, Henry
General Articles

Providing they capture a prize, first of all these amounts would be deducted from the whole capital. The hunter's pay would generally be 200 pieces of eight. The carpenter, for his work in repairing and fitting out the ship, would be paid 100 or 150 pieces of eight. The surgeon would receive 200 or 250 for his medical supplies, according to the size of the ship.

Then came the agreed awards for the wounded, who might have lost a limb or suffered other injuries. They would be compensated as follows: for the loss of a right arm, 600 pieces of eight or six slaves; for a left arm, 500 pieces of eight or five slaves. The loss of a right leg also brought 500 pieces of eight or five slaves in compensation; a left leg, 400 or four slaves; an eye, 100 or one slave, and the same award was made for the loss of a finger. If a man lost the use of an arm, he would get as much as if it had been cut off, and a severe internal injury which meant the victim had to have a pipe inserted in his body would earn 500 pieces of eight or five slaves in recompense.

These amounts having first been withdrawn from the capital, the rest of the prize would be divided into as many portions as men on the ship. The captain draws four or five men's portions for the use of his ship, perhaps even more, and two portions for himself. The rest of the men share uniformly, and the boys get half a man's share.

When a ship has been captured, the men decide whether the captain should keep it or not: if the prize is better than their own vessel, they take it and set fire to the other. When a ship is robbed, nobody must plunder and keep his loot to himself. Everything taken—money, jewels, precious stones and goods—must be shared among them all, without any man enjoying a penny more than his fair share. To prevent deceit, before the booty is distributed everyone has to swear an oath on the Bible that he has not kept for himself so much as the value of a sixpence, whether in silk, linen, wool, gold, silver, jewels, clothes or shot, from all the capture. And should any man be found to have made a false oath, he would be banished from the rovers, and never more be allowed in their company.

... If anyone has a quarrel and kills his opponent treacherously, he is set against a tree and shot dead by the one whom he chooses. But if he has killed his opponent like an honourable man—that is, giving him time to load his musket, and not shooting him in the back—his comrades let him go free. The duel is their way of settling disputes. (*The Buccaneers of America* 71–72)

Articles Drawn Up Before
Venture Against Panama in 1670

All the officers assembled, and voted that Morgan should receive a share of one-hundredth of the proceeds. This proposal was then made known to the crews, who also gave it their vote. Then a general agreement was drawn up as to what the captains should receive for their ships. The other officers—the lieutenants and bos'ns—assembled and voted that the captains should be given the value of eight men's portions for their ship, as well as their own personal share. The surgeons would receive 200 pieces of eight for furnishing their medicine chests, in addition to their personal share like every man on board. The carpenters would get an extra 100 pieces of eight.

Then the rewards were stated for those who behaved with extraordinary gallantry—such as being the first to tear down the flag on a fort and run up the English colours. This would earn an extra fifty pieces of eight, while a man who brought in a prisoner when intelligence was needed would have an extra 200. As for the grenadiers, they were to receive five pieces of eight extra for every grenade they threw into a fort.

Compensations were also laid down for those mutilated in battle. A man who lost both legs would receive 1,500 pieces of eight over and above his ordinary share, or he could choose fifteen slaves instead. A man who lost both hands was to have 1,800 pieces of eight, or eighteen slaves, whichever he preferred.

For the loss of one leg, either right or left, a man was to be awarded 600 pieces of eight or six slaves. For the loss of either hand, the same compensation was offered. If a man lost an eye or a finger, he would receive 100 pieces of eight, or one slave. As recompense for the pain of a body wound which necessitated the insertion of a pipe, the amount was 500 pieces of eight, or five slaves. For a stiff limb, be it arm, leg or finger, a man received the same compensation as if he had lost it entirely.

All these rewards and compensations were to be taken out of the common booty, before this was divided up. ...

A special article was also drawn up: Ships taken at sea or in port would form part of the general share-out, but there would be a prize of 1,000 pieces of eight for the buccaneers who first boarded an enemy vessel. If the captured ship proved to be worth more than 10,000 pieces of eight, the reward would be one-tenth of the value.

Boarding any ship other than an enemy was forbidden on pain of death, so that news of their raid should not spread. (*The Buccaneers of America* 171–73)

Phillips, John

1. Every Man shall obey civil Command; the Captain shall have one full Share and a half in all Prizes; the Master, Carpenter, Boatswain and Gunner shall have one Share and quarter.

2. If any Man shall offer to run away, or keep any Secret from the Company, he shall be maroon'd, with one Bottle of Powder, one Bottle of Water, one small Arm and Shot.

3. If any Man shall steal any Thing in the Company, or game to the Value of a Piece of Eight, he shall be maroon'd or shot.

4. If at any Time we should meet another Marooner [pirate], that Man that shall sign his Articles without the Consent of our Company, shall suffer such Punishment as the Captain and Company shall think fit.

5. That Man that shall strike another whilst these Articles are in force, shall receive Moses's Law [39 lashes of a whip] on the bare Back.

6. That Man that shall snap his Arms, or smoak Tobacco in the Hold, without a Cap to his Pipe, or carry a Candle lighted without a Lanthorn, shall suffer the same Punishment as in the former Article.

7. That Man that shall not keep his Arms clean, fit for an Engagement, or neglect his Business, shall be cut off from his Share, and suffer such other Punishment as the Captain and the Company shall think fit.

8. If any Man shall lose a Joint in Time of an Engagement, he shall have 400 pieces of Eight, if a Limb, 800.

9. If at any Time we meet with a prudent Woman, that Man that offers to meddle with

her, without her Consent, shall suffer present death. (*General History of the Pyrates* 342, *Pirates of the New England Coast* 315–16)

Roberts, Bartholomew

I. Every Man has a Vote in Affairs of Moment; has equal Title to the fresh provisions, or strong Liquors, at any Time seized, and may use them at Pleasure, unless a Scarcity make it necessary, for the Good of all, to vote a Retrenchment.

II. Every Man to be called fairly in Turn, by List, on board of Prizes, because, (over and above their proper Share) they were on these Occasions allowed a Shift of Cloaths: But if they defrauded the Company to the Value of a Dollar, in Plate, Jewels, or Money, MAROONING was their Punishment. If the Robbery was only betwixt one another, they contented themselves with slitting the Ears and Nose of him that was Guilty, and set him on Shore, not in an uninhabited Place, but somewhere, where he was sure to encounter Hardships.

III. No Person to Game at Cards or Dice for Money.

IV. The Lights and Candles to be put out at eight a-Clock at Night: If any of the Crew, after that Hour, still remained enclined for Drinking, they were to do it on the open Deck.

V. To keep their Piece, Pistols, and Cutlash clean, and fit for Service.

VI. No Boy or Woman to be allowed amongst them. If any Man were found seducing any of the latter Sex, and carry'd her to Sea, disguised, he was to suffer Death.

VII. To Desert the Ship, or their Quarters in Battle, was punished with Death or Marooning.

VIII. No striking one another on board, but every Man's Quarrels to be ended on Shore, at Sword and Pistol, thus: The Quarter-Master of the Ship, when the Parties will not come to any Reconciliation, accompanies them on Shore with what Assistance he thinks proper, and turns the Disputants Back to Back, at so many Paces Distance: At the Word of Command, they turn and fire immediately, (or else the Piece is knock'd out of their Hands). If both miss, they come to their Cutlashes, and then he is declared Victor who draws the first Blood.

IX. No Man to talk of breaking up their Way of Living, till each had shared a 1000 l. If in order to this, any Man should lose a Limb, or become a Cripple in their Service, he was to have 800 Dollars, out of the publick Stock, and for lesser Hurts, proportionably.

X. The Captain and Quarter-Master to receive two Shares of a Prize; the Master, Boatswain, and Gunner, one Share and a half, and other Officers one and a Quarter.

XI. The Musicians to have Rest on the Sabbath Day, but the other six Days and Nights, none without special Favour. (*General History of the Pyrates* 211–12)

Rogers, Woodes
First Articles

I. THAT all Plunder on board each Prize we take by either ship, shall be equally divided between the Company of both Ships, according to each Man's respective whole Share, as ship'd by the Owners or their Orders.

2. That what is Plunder shall be adjudg'd by the superior Officers and Agents in each Ship.

3. That if any Person on board either Ship do conceal any Plunder exceeding one Piece of Eight in value, 24 hours after the Capture of any Prize, he shall be severely punish'd, and lose his Shares of the Plunder. The same Penalty to be inflicted for being drunk in time [of] Action, or disobeying his superior Officer's Commands, or concealing himself, or deserting his Post in Sea or Land-Service; except when any Prize is taken by storm in Boarding, then whatsoever is taken shall be his own, as followed: A sailor or Landman 10l. Any Officer below the Carpenter 20l.

A Mate, Gunner, Boatswain, and Carpenter 401, a Lieutenant or Master 801. And the Captains 1001. [O]ver and above the Gratuity promis'd by the Owners to such as shall signalize themselves.

4. That publick Books of Plunder are to be kept in each Ship attested by the Officers, and the Plunder to be apprais'd by Officers chosen, and divided as soon as possible after the Capture. Also every Person to be sworn and search'd so soon as they shall come aboard, by such Persons as shall be appointed for that purpose: The Person or Persons refusing, shall forfeit their shares of the Plunder as above.

5. In consideration that Capt. Rogers and Capt. Courtney, to make both ships Companies easy, have given the whole Cabin-Plunder (which in all probability is the major part) to be divided as aforesaid; we do voluntarily agree, that they shall have 5 per Cent, each of 'em, over and above their respective Shares, as a Consideration for what is their Due of the Plunder aforesaid.

6. That a Reward of twenty Pieces of Eight shall be given to him that first sees a Prize of good Value, or exceeding 50 Tuns in Burden.

7. That such of us who have not sign'd already to the Articles of Agreement indented with the Owners, do hereby oblige our selves to the same Terms and Conditions as the rest of the Ships Company have done; half Shares and half Wages, &c. (*A Cruising Voyage Round the World* 23)

Supplemental Articles
Concerning Plunder

We the officers, seamen and landmen belong to the ship *Duke*, having made several former agreements concerning the equal sharing of plunder, do now desire and agree, that each man give an exact account of all clothes, goods of value, or necessaries of any kind he has over and above his dividend deliver'd him at Gorgona, or has purchased

of others since, to be rightly charged to him in his account of plunder, by the agents appointed; and to restore whatever he has taken without the agents['] knowledge, and to prevent any persons detaining and concealing any goods or riches of any kind, now or for the future, more than their respective shares, in order to aright distribution of plunder, except arms, chests, knives, Roman relickts[,] scizzars, tobacco, loose books, pictures, and worthless tools and toys, and bedding in use, which are not included in this agreement; and those that ha[ve] already only things of this kind, are not liable to a penalty: We do voluntarily sign this, and offer our selves to be obliged firmly by these presents, to be under the penalty of 20 shillings for every shilling value taken hid or conceal'd by any of us, or removed out of any prize without written orders from the commanders publickly; and that none but the agents already named, or to be named here after, shall detain in possession any plunder; but whatever is found conceal'd shall be valued, and the persons that hid it to be fin[e]d as aforesaid, which penalty we acknowledge to be laid on us by [o]ur own desire, consent, and approbation, over and above the former penalty agreed on, that any person shall lose his share of every prize or purchase taken, whether cargo or plunder, that conceals of either the value of half a piece of 8. And this to remain in force, to the end of the voyage.

And to encourage discoveries of such concealments, whatever person discovers the fraud of any, who shall be so imprudent as to detain more than his due, in any goods that has not been shar'd before as plunder, or purchas'd of the owners['] agent or commanders; the informer of such fraud shall ha[ve] one half given him gratis, cut of the offender['] shares and wages; the other half for the use of the ship['] company as plunder; which information shall be encouraged by the commanders of each ship, in order to